1 MONTH OF
FREE
READING

at
www.ForgottenBooks.com

By purchasing this book you are eligible for one month membership to ForgottenBooks.com, giving you unlimited access to our entire collection of over 1,000,000 titles via our web site and mobile apps.

To claim your free month visit:
www.forgottenbooks.com/free873840

ISBN 978-0-266-60133-3
PIBN 10873840

Wildlife IN NORTH CAROLINA

BIENNIAL REPORT ISSUE
FOR THE BIENNIUM
JULY 1, 1966 · JUNE 30, 1968

25 CENTS / JANUARY 1969

State of North Carolina
Wildlife Resources Commission
RALEIGH, N. C. 27602

T. N. MASSIE, SYLVA
CHAIRMAN
DR JOE M ANDERSON, JR., NEW BERN
JAMES A. BRIDGER, BLADENBORO
HUGH G. CHATHAM, ELKIN
JAMES A. CONNELLY, MORGANTON

CLYDE P. PATTON, RALEIGH
EXECUTIVE DIRECTOR
J. HOLT EVANS, ENFIELD
ROBERT G. SANDERS, CHARLOTTE
JAY WAGGONER, GRAHAM
G. L. WOODHOUSE, GRANDY

His Excellency, The Governor of North Carolina
The Honorable Members of the General Assembly
Raleigh, North Carolina

Dear Sirs:

     This 11th biennial report for the period July 1, 1966 to June 30, 1968 is submitted with our special gratitude for the generous help and encouragement given by the Governor and members of the General Assembly on wildlife conservation and boating safety work.

     It has been a period of dynamic, satisfying progress made possible by team effort among governmental agencies, private organizations, and individual citizens to whom we are indebted and grateful.

     In looking to the future with new hope for further improvements, we invite suggestions, criticism, and advice. These will help us to render a service to the people of North Carolina that is no less than the best.

              Sincerely,

              T. N. Massie, Chairman
              Wildlife Resources Commission

IN NORTH CAROLINA ■

The official publication of the NORTH CAROLINA WILDLIFE RESOURCES COMMISSION, Raleigh 27602. A monthly magazine devoted to the protection and restoration of our wildlife resources and to the improvement of hunting and fishing in North Carolina.

VOL. XXXIII, NO. 1   JANUARY, 1969

WILDLIFE IN NORTH CAROLINA recognizes the need for close cooperation between State and Federal conservation agencies and the people who hunt and fish—to bring about a restoration of our renewable resources. The Editor gratefully receives for publication news items, articles, and photographs dealing with the North Carolina out-of-doors, but reserves the right to reject material submitted. Full credit is given for all materials published.

WILDLIFE IN NORTH CAROLINA is published at the Wildlife Resources Commission offices, Motor Vehicles Building, 1100 New Bern Ave., Raleigh, N. C. 27601.

Second class postage paid at Raleigh, North Carolina 27602.

SUBSCRIPTIONS—Fifty cents per year, one dollar for two years. Make remittances payable to WILDLIFE RESOURCES COMMISSION. Any employee of the Wildlife Resources Commission may accept subscriptions, or they may be forwarded to Post Office Box 2919, Raleigh, N. C. 27602. Stamps cannot be accepted.

Wildlife circulation this issue, 122,690.

BIENNIAL REPORT ISSUE

EDITORIAL STAFF

ROD AMUNDSON _____ EDITOR
DUANE RAVER _____ MANAGING EDITOR
LUTHER PARTIN __ WRITER-PHOTOGRAPHER
JOHN PARKER _____ OUTDOOR SAFETY
TOM JACKSON ___ WRITER-PHOTOGRAPHER

Administration

THE biennium was a period of increased activity in outdoor recreation and an ever greater effort on the part of the Wildlife Resources Commission was necessary to keep abreast of the demand. The Commission completed its purchase of a 14,290-acre tract of land in Caswell County, providing additional public hunting grounds in north-central North Carolina. Five new game restoration areas were established comprising, in all, more than 43,000 acres. These areas were obtained by cooperative agreement or lease from the Federal Government and private landowners. An additional 23,000 acres were leased on a short-term basis for hunting purposes and made available to sportsmen. A

Dr. Joe Anderson, Commissioner from District 2, makes a point about Lake Mattamuskeet during a Commission meeting held in Raleigh.

new trout hatchery site was acquired in Wilkes County. Five new boat access areas were acquired, developed, and opened for public use.

The General Assembly enacted into law several measures designed to strengthen the effectiveness of the Commission's wildlife and boating program. Added protection was given bear and deer, additional funds were provided for waterfowl management by an increase in the non-resident hunting license, and the penalty was increased for violation of the Commission's regulations applying to the taking of wild turkey. A very important step was taken when the General Assembly allocated a small portion of the gasoline tax revenue to the Wildlife Resources Commission to help the Commission expand its boating safety program. However, unless extended, these funds will not be available beyond this biennium.

The divisions of game and protection continued their vigorous enforcement of the game, fish, and boating safety laws and regulations. The Commission's authority to administer fish, game, and boat laws, and to make regulations pertaining thereto is set forth in Chapters 75A and 113, and in Article 24

of Chapter 143, of the General Statutes of North Carolina.

The policy-making body of the Commission is composed of nine citizens, selected by the Governor, one from each of the nine geographic wildlife districts established by the Wildlife Resources Law. The Commission determines its own organization and methods of procedure and selects and appoints an executive director, who is charged with the supervision of all activities under the jurisdiction of the Commission. The terms of the members overlap so that those of three members expire every two years. This arrangement provides for continuity of program with a resultant stability of policy. The general principles guiding the Commission in its management of the fish and wildlife resources of the State is succinctly stated in its motto "More Sport for More People— Equal Opportunity for All." During the biennium, the Commission approved funds for new office headquarters and a warehouse and storage depot for Commission equipment.

The Commission adopts budgetary plans for the proper use of the Wildlife Resources Fund; holds public hearings; considers and adopts regulations governing

This is one of the several Commission meetings held annually. Often these meetings are held near some field activity of the Wildlife Commission in order to examine problems first hand. Commission Chairman T. N. Massie is shown in foreground, conducting this meeting.

4

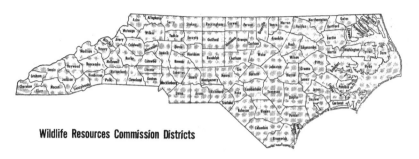

Wildlife Resources Commission Districts

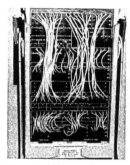

The development and enhancement of the data processing capabilities of the Commission was a function of the data processing section attached to Administration. Section Manager Charles Overton is shown here developing a flow chart for a group of programs which will become a segment of the data processing system. Above is a plugboard which was used in the processing of the Commission's hunting and fishing licenses. A new procedure has been developed and is now in operation.

open seasons, bag and creel limits on game and inland fishes; registers motorboats and promotes boating safety; enters into cooperative agreements with other agencies and individuals; and handles matters pertaining to personnel. The Commission's Statewide program is based on five fundamental functions: regulation, enforcement, management, research, and education. These functions are accomplished through the operation of six divisions; namely, Protection,

Game, Fish, Education, Engineering, and Finance and Personnel.

As of June 30, 1968, the Commission had 322 employees. While assignment of responsibility for primary work has been specific, each employee has been encouraged to assist in the implementation of the Commission's five-point program wherever circumstances permit.

The action programs of each division for the biennium are related in the following pages.

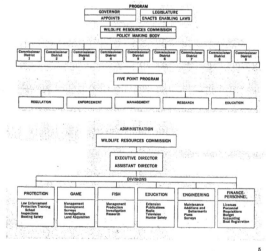

NORTH Carolina's outstanding wildlife and boating safety programs derive much of their success from the diligent work of a proud group of officers who enforce the laws and regulations which insure the future of hunting and fishing and the safety of our waterway users. To give real meaning to the Commission's motto, this group of officers continued to pursue a vigorous program of law enforcement aimed at the relatively small number of people who violate the rules of fair play and sportsmanship.

The long-established policy of firmness, fairness and impartiality was strictly followed, and the work done by the enforcement staff contributed in a major way to both the control of unlawful activities and the good public relations enjoyed by the Wildlife Resources Commission. Much progress was made in apprehending those persons who wilfully

The public is urged to aid the Protection Division staff by notifying the local protector of any wildlife regulation infraction. Right, equipment of the S.B.I. and other law enforcement agencies is utilized frequently.

stole game and fish resources from the public, or who intentionally disregarded the safety of others while using our public waters. In recognition of the importance of a sound law enforcement program, and being aware of the continuing expansion of outdoor activities, the Commission strengthened the Division of Protection during this biennium by adding personnel.

Organization

In January of 1968 the Division was reorganized by adding nine wildlife patrolmen to its staff, bringing the number of wildlife patrolmen to thirty-six. Each of these men was made responsible for an area which included the territories patrolled by several wildlife protectors. The patrolmen and protectors in each of these patrol areas constituted a co-ordinated team capable of handling most problems which arose in any area. The total number of wildlife protectors remained at 102, and each district also had a district super-

Teams of men in each district were trained to conduct boating safety demonstrations. Right, the use of radiological monitoring equipment such as this, was taught all division field personnel.

visor and an assistant supervisor. One airplane patrol pilot was also added to the Division staff. The Division now has a supervisory pilot and an airplane stationed in Raleigh, with other patrol planes and pilots stationed at Kinston and Hickory.

The nine new wildlife patrolmen positions were added as a result of legislation enacted by the 1967 General Assembly, which allocated to the Commission for boating safety work a small portion of the gasoline tax paid by boaters into the Highway Fund. This allocation was for a two-year period only, and additional legislation will be required during the current General As-

sembly to continue or increase this allocation.

During the two-year period several officers retired or resigned, and these were replaced by younger men who were carefully screened, selected, and trained in the recruit training school.

Training

In recent years the emphasis in enforcement has been on professionalism. Modern law enforcement r e q u i r e s thorough knowledge of laws and regulations and their application, plus training in many related fields. The Division continued to emphasize careful selection and

thorough training of all of its personnel. Recruit and In-service training was handled largely by the Institute of Government at the University of North Carolina at Chapel Hill. Due to the emphasis placed on teamwork, thorough training and supervision was necessary for supervisors and wildlife patrolmen, and special schools in these subjects were conducted for these personnel. District-level training in less formal subjects was conducted quarterly by the staff in each district.

Special training was also given in a number of subjects not directly concerned with wildlife law enforcement. In co-operation with the State Civil Defense Agency, all Division field personnel were trained in radiological monitoring, and one officer in each district was trained to become an instructor in this subject. Also, one man in each district was trained as an instructor in first aid techniques.

Of particular interest during the spring of 1968 was the training of teams of men in each district to conduct boating safety demonstrations and courtesy boat examinations. This was done with some of the gasoline tax money allocated for the boating safety program. These teams of three or four men each were specially trained and equipped to conduct waterside demonstrations of safe boat handling and rescue work. Although it was impossible to maintain accurate records, it is safe to say that tens of thousands of boaters and prospective boaters were contacted in this way.

Equipment

New and better equipment to accomplish the assigned duties was obtained during the biennium. Approximately one-half of the patrol cars assigned to the Division were replaced each year. Many water patrol units were replaced. Both outboard and inboard-outboard rigs were used, depending on the nature of the body of water where they were to be used. In addition, the nine new men were fully equipped with cars, boats, motors, radios

The enforcement of wildlife and boating laws occupied 90 percent of the officers' field time. Here, a routine fishing license check is made.

The conviction rate in wildlife law cases runs over 96 percent, indicating well-prepared cases and effective courts. Below, three major items of equipment which enable wildlife protectors to move swiftly on land, water, and in the air.

Table I	
	Biennium 1966-1968
Number hunters and fishermen checked	751,371
Number violations	18,664
violation rate	2.48%
Number convictions	18,102
conviction rate	96.99%

Table II	
	Biennium 1966-1968
Number boats checked	141,089
Number violations	4,921
violation rate	3.49%
Number convictions	4,756
conviction rate	96.65%

Radio communications are maintained with headquarters and base stations as well as between all field vehicles. This network makes possible rapid relay of messages to all Division personnel.

Courtesy boat inspections were held at many strategic locations throughout the state. Below, Division personnel worked closely with U. S. Fish and Wildlife Service field personnel.

and all other necessary equipment.

Administration

The Division continued to function through a well-established chain of command. Continued attention was given to streamlining the administrative work of the Division, including the application of machine data processing methods to many of the forms and reports used by the Division.

Field Operations

The Division's primary function of law enforcement occupied most of its men's time during the past two years. Officers averaged about 90% of their time on enforcement activities involving hunting, fishing, and boating. The number of hunters and fishermen checked, as indicated in Table I, increased slightly over the previous biennium, and the number of boats checked as indicated in Table II, increased tremendously. Violation rates continued to be low. Fewer than 3% of the hunters and fishermen checked were in violation and only 3½% of the boat operators checked were found to have some discrepancy. The conviction rate for all hunting, fishing and boating law violations continued to be in excess of 96%, indicating that the officers were taking sound, well-prepared cases to court.

Air patrol became an even more important part of law enforcement activity. Each of the three patrol craft was flown approximately 600 hours each year and was used for all phases of law enforcement work. All were particularly effective on boating safety patrols and in the apprehension of night deer hunters. During the biennium, the air craft were responsible for the detection and apprehension of 914 violators, most of whom would have gone undetected

without the use of the aircraft. During periods of heavy workload, an additional aircraft was sometimes rented to supplement the air patrol program.

The Commission's modern, flexible communications system played a vital part in the activities of the Division. Better use of the system, and more frequent reports of violations by the public, aided in apprehending many violators in the act of breaking the law.

Education and public relations activities continued to be an important part of field operations. Officers presented many programs concerning various phases of wildlife and boating safety work to many educational and outdoor groups. The work of the boating safety teams was particularly impressive, and attracted much public attention.

In addition, field officers supervised maintenance on fishing and boating access areas, assisted with reporting and evaluating fish kills, worked with many field trial groups, conducted surveys for other divisions of the Commission, and aided with the establishment of the Uniform Waterway Marking System on certain bodies of water. The Division worked closely with the management and enforcement agents of the U. S. Fish and Wildlife Service in management and enforcement activities involving migratory game.

Summary

The work of the Division of Protection continued to be the foundation for the success of the wildlife and boating safety programs. Both the Commisson and the public continued to recognize this during the past two years, as indicated by the respect shown by individual enforcement officers and the fact that relatively few sportsmen in North Carolina became involved in violations of the laws and regulations. ♦

Division of Inland Fisheries

THE Division of Inland Fisheries carries out a program of research, management, production, regulation, and education to improve the fresh-water fisheries resources of the State. Information obtained from these five phases of the program during the biennium was used to formulate and execute sound fishery management practices.

Biological research conducted throughout the State during the biennium provided the basic framework for applied management of the public inland fishing resources of North Carolina

Anadromous-Fish Study

Anadromous fishes are those which spend their normal life cycle in salt water but move well into fresh water to spawn. During the biennium, information was obtained concerning the time and place of anadromous fish migrations. In addition, the exploitation of these migrations by both commercial and sport fishermen, as well as the time and location of spawning by striped bass and American shad within the Inland Fishing waters, was studied.

The first phase of the study was a questionnaire mailed to special - device fishing license holders. The resulting data, not yet completely analyzed, will indicate the harvest of anadromous fishes by gear used, by species, and by watershed.

Wildlife protectors cooperated in the second phase of the study, which concerned the sports fishery for anadromous fishes. They did this by interviewing all anglers they encountered and who were attempting to catch these fishes. This survey ended with the biennium. Hence data analyses are incomplete.

The third phase of the study involved an identification of the spawning areas of anadromous fishes in the streams of coastal North Carolina during the spring spawning periods, and to collect

The striped bass offers Tarheel anglers some prime fishing in many coastal areas. This is one of the game fishes that was under study during the biennium.

eggs of spawning fishes. The anadromous fish study confirmed the existence of spawning activity by anadromous species in several areas where heretofore it was unknown or merely suspected.

An egg sampling device was designed and constructed to minimize difficulties encountered with egg nets during the study. This apparatus should prove to be of considerable value in future studies involving the collection of the suspended eggs of anadromous fishes.

American Shad

Operation of the three navigational locks on the Cape Fear River for passage of American shad continued each year of the biennium. The passage of American shad through these locks during their annual April-June spawning run was started in 1962 as a cooperative project of the Division of Inland Fisheries, the U. S. Bureau of Commercial Fisheries, and the U. S. Army Corps of Engineers. The aims were to re-open about 60 miles of the Cape Fear to shad spawning, and thereby restore the shad population to its size prior to 1915 when the first dam was built on the river. In the six years of locking operations, the shad fishery has again approached the magnitude of the early 1900's.

The three-year-old fish whose parents had been locked upstream in 1963 returned to the Cape Fear River in 1966. During 1966, approximately 4,100 American shad were passed through the locks and the sport catch was 862 fish. By 1968, from 20,000-30,000 shad were passed through Lock Number 1, and sport fishing was exceptional.

Fishermen referred to the 1968 spawning run as the largest since the locks were built some half-century ago.

Restoration of the American shad fishery in the Cape Fear River was one of the major accomplishments of the Division of Inland Fisheries.

Striped Bass

North Carolina possesses a

race of striped bass indigenous to Albemarle Sound, of sufficient size to maintain both an extensive commercial fishery and a considerable sport fishery. In addition, the voracious nature of the striped bass makes it appear to be an ideal answer to providing additional predation in large fresh - water reservoirs where existing predatory game fishes are unable to hold rough fish and stunted pan-fish populations in check. It would, at the same time, provide excellent sport fishing.

The Division of Inland Fisheries has developed techniques whereby: eggs can be taken from striped bass ripened naturally or artificially by hormone injection; hatch these eggs in jars with a success rate averaging about 50 percent; rear the resulting fry in hatchery ponds with a success level of approximately 20 percent; and transport fingerlings with negligible mortality. There are still refinements to be made in the techniques, but the relocation of the species through fingerling releases is now feasible for testing.

R e s e a r c h involving water quality that affects this species at various stages of development has been of particular significance in solving problems related to hatching, holding, and rearing fingerlings in ponds.

During the biennium, the Weldon striped bass hatchery concluded its most successful year in the numbers of eggs and fry

processed. The major factor contributing to this success was the experimental purchase from commercial fishermen of sexually immature female fish for physiological maturation by hormone injection. By this method, the spawning of striped bass could be programmed.

Roanoke Bass

The Roanoke bass, *Ambloplitis cavifrons,* was described by Cope in 1867 from a single three-inch specimen recovered from the Roanoke River in Montgomery County, Virginia. The species remained unrecognized in North Carolina until it was encountered in Fishing Creek during the survey and inventory of the Tar River basin during 1963. Inquiry of local anglers revealed that this fish is taken seasonally in small numbers from several headwater streams of the Tar River basin. Locally called "red eye," the Roanoke bass is very popular among the few who fish for it because it appears to outgrow any of its associated species. The few specimens that have been recovered for study indicate that this comparatively rare species might prove an extremely valuable warm - water sport fish if more were known of its effective management. To this end, the Division of Inland Fisheries sought the following objectives: (1) determining the more efficient types of gear for capturing Roanoke bass; (2) obtaining brood stock for artificial propa-

gation experiments to test the feasibility of hatchery rearing; (3) identifying the preferred habitat of this species; (4) delimiting the distribution within North Carolina; and (5) determining characteristics that will distinguish the Roanoke bass from the rock bass.

Wire traps, fyke nets, and angling seem to be the most effective methods for capturing Roanoke bass. The preferred habitat seems to be associated with pool-riffle complexes in unpolluted streams near the fall-line. The complete distribution of the species is still undetermined. All specimens collected to date have been taken from the Tar and Neuse river watersheds.

Brood fish stocked in hatchery ponds at Fayetteville produced several hatches of young in the spring of 1968. These young fish will be used in further studies aimed at determining the potential of this species as a game fish.

Threadfin Shad

One of the principal factors in maintaining a harvestable population of game fish is a continuous supply of available forage species. The threadfin shad was successfully introduced i n t o North Carolina waters in 1961 and has proved to be one of the more important forage species in several of our reservoirs. These waters, however, are beyond the normal temperature range of this species and the threadfin usually winter-kills. Most of the reservoirs concerned must be restocked each spring to maintain a supply of young shad during the summer growing season.

Studies are being made of the basic biology, ecological requirements, and the role of the threadfin shad as a forage fish, particularly in small lakes that are under intensive fish management. Division biologists have been successful in determining the age, size, and sex composition of threadfin populations. Spawning habits, fecundity, and various factors contributing to mortality from handling and hauling are being investigated.

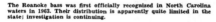

The Roanoke bass was first officially recognized in North Carolina waters in 1963. Their distribution is apparently quite limited in the state; investigation is continuing.

All efforts to transport this fish failed. Once Waccamaw silversides were handled in any way they went into shock followed by fatal paralysis.

Transporting the coastal shiner has been successful. This species can be introduced as forage for game fishes in the relatively unproductive natural black-water lakes of coastal North Carolina.

At the higher elevations of western North Carolina, fish population studies in cool-water reservoirs have revealed an acute need for additional forage species with a high reproductive potential. Neither the gizzard shad nor threadfin shad do well in this habitat, and the kokanee, introduced into Natahala Reservoir over a five-year period, apparently failed to become established.

Recent success of the alewife in New York reservoirs suggested a potential for the success of this species in North Carolina. The Division of Inland Fisheries collected 815 adult alewives from commercial pound nets in the Chowan River on March 13, 1968, and transported them to Lake Lure and Lake Adger. Hauling mortality for this delicate fish was 42 percent. To date it has not been determined whether the species has become adapted to these lakes. A further attempt to relocate alewives to Lake Adger will be made in March, 1969.

Another potential forage species for the cold mountain lakes was investigated when an attempt was made to introduce smelt into Glenville Reservoir. Eggs were obtained from New Hampshire in May, 1968. It was planned to hold the eggs in the Marion Fish Hatchery until they developed to the eyed-stage. This attempt failed, probably due to water temperature shock. Further attempts to introduce smelt into Lake Glenville will be made in the spring of 1969.

Management of Municipal And State-Owned Lakes

Many small lakes of North Carolina offer an excellent situation in which to develop and maintian superior sport fishing. A small-lakes management program was initiated during the 1964-66 biennium and has made rather significant progress to date. The lakes concerned are small enough to permit intensive management of sport-fish species, and yet large enough to support significant fishing pressure. Each of these lakes displays many unique qualities. The best use of each requires the identification of its species characteristics, followed by the development and application of fish-management techniques appropriate to the fish species best adapted to these particular lakes.

The small-lakes program includes both research and management. In the research category, new management procedures are being tested at Lakes Concord and Fisher in Cabarrus County and at the Sandhills lakes in Richmond and Scotland counties. In the management category, installation of additional cover, introduction of forage, and introduction of game species are practices being applied to lakes throughout the State.

A development of particular interest is in the use of old automobile tires as "fish-hides" to replace the old "brush shelters" used by many for years to concentrate fishes for sport harvest. About a dozen tires are perforated to let air escape, tied together with a decay-resistant line, and tossed into a pile at the bottom of water 5 to 12 feet deep. A buoy is used to mark the spot. Experiments in Lake Concord revealed a considerably higher harvest of fishes from tire hides than from brush shelters in the same area. This simple and inexpensive method of concentrating fish for harvest is now being used in many Commission - managed lakes throughout the State.

The Sandhills Wildlife Management Area lakes are being utilized to test the feasibility of supplementally feeding fish to produce a harvestable crop in waters of low productivity, and which normally do not support much fishing pressure. The tests have shown that good-quality catfishing can be maintained for about 20 cents per pound of catfish harvested.

Small lakes, municipally and state-owned, were studied during the biennium to determine the best fish management programs for these waters. Fish shelters made of old tires (above) were installed in experimental areas and marked so that fishermen could find them.

During the biennium, all state-owned lakes and many municipally-owned lakes under contract for management were studied to determine the management procedures which would produce the greatest possible sport fish harvest under the particular circumstances prevailing at each lake.

W. Kerr Scott Reservoir

Since both cold- and warm-water, large reservoirs support much of the sport fishing in the Piedmont and Mountains of North Carolina, additional information was needed to increase their carrying capacity and harvest. W. Kerr Scott Reservoir, a 1,470 acre impoundment, was chosen for study because it is one of North Carolina's newer reservoirs having a high recreation potential but which has not produced even fair sport fishing. Data and techniques to be ob-

tained from the reservoir study should be applicable to similar impoundments at comparable elevations.

Information obtained from this research project will support a detailed chemical and physical analysis of the reservoir; help to determine the effects of the habitat upon the fish population; and provide data on relative abundance, food habits, growth rates, reproduction, and seasonal distribution of fishes. Information is also being collected on fishing pressure, fishing success, and the degree of utilization, by fishermen, of fishes available in this type reservoir.

Some tentative conclusions reached to date are:

- Fourteen species of fishes representing six families, inhabit W. Kerr Scott Reservoir.
- Carp is the dominant species in the reservoir, comprising 59 percent of the weight of the total fish population.
- The basic productivity of W. Kerr Scott Reservoir is low.
- Thermal stratification is well defined by June.
- The catch-per-hour on the reservoir is 0.5 fish weighing 0.2 pounds, and the average length of a fishing trip is 3¼ hours.

Effects Of Water Temperature Increases On Fishes

A study on the effects of thermal pollution on the fish population in Lake Norman was begun during the biennium. This study was designed to determine the effects that heated waters have on the spawning, migration, movement, food habits, growth, disease, parasitism, catchability, and physical condition of fishes within the reservoir.

Cooling water for the Marshall Steam Plant condensers is drawn from the reservoir's lower layer under a skimmer wier in one arm of Lake Norman and, following passage through the condensers, is discharged into an adjacent arm of the reservoir. Currently, the maximum volume of discharge approaches 750 cubic feet per second with a maximum temperature gain of 9°F. The volume

of discharge, and perhaps the temperature gain, will increase with each addition to the plant's generating capacity.

The condenser discharge from the Marshall Steam Plant exerts three major influences upon Lake Norman fishes: A temperature increase; the creation of a current, and seasonally substandard dissolved oxygen concentrations. How these influences, singly or in combination, affect the fishes in the reservoir is not known. It is estimated that three years will be required to appraise the effects of thermal pollution on Lake Norman.

Currituck Sound

For many years Currituck Sound has been one of the more famous largemouth bass fishing spots in North America. A factor influencing fishing success in Currituck is the moderate salinity of the water. For this reason, a scheduled monitoring of salinities within the Sound has been maintained to detect any change resulting from storm breakthroughs or from pumping of sea-water into Back Bay by the City of Virginia Beach, Virginia either of which could have a disastrous effect on the fresh water sport fishery.

Currituck Sound is also threatened by a major ecological change by the invasion of Eurasian watermilfoil. This exotic plant has spread very rapidly since it was first detected in the Sound in 1965. It is now found throughout the Sound and is entering other Albemarle Sound tributaries, particularly those along the Outer Banks. Many acres of Currituck Sound are now impassable to boat travel due to heavy infestations of milfoil.

Technical assistance was rendered the U. S. Army Corps of Engineers in recent tests to determine the feasibility of chemical control of milfoil. Final results are not yet available, but preliminary observations point toward selective control with 20% granular 2, 4-D butoxyethanol ester at 100 pounds per acre. Chemical treatment of the entire Currituck Sound is not economically feasible but the growths in

12

A 1966-67 study included chemical, thermal and hydraulic regimens of the main stem, and of such tributaries as were required to determine its suitability as trout habitat. Additional studies determined fish populations, bottom organism populations, and fishing pressure.

The finding that the Tuckaseigee River between Dillsboro and the town of Tuckaseigee had water quality suitable for a put-and-take trout program led to a decision to stock brook and brown trout in the river during 1967 and 1968.

Prior to this stocking, an estimated 70 anglers fished this segment of the river during 1966. After the program was initiated, well over 2,000 fishermen-trips have been made to the Tuckaseigee River and its tributaries.

Extreme low flows were found to be a limiting factor for trout in the main stem of the Tuckaseigee River. These flows undergo extreme fluctuations, depending upon power generation at the Cedar Cliff and Little Glenville power plants. In this connection, a request was made to the Tennessee Valley Authority to consider constructing a low-head reregulating dam on the main stem near the junction of the East and West Forks to provide a minimum instantaneous flow of 40 second-feet.

Cold-Water Stream Studies

During the biennium, data from a complete creel census of eleven Wildlife Management Areas were tabulated and analyzed to determine the trends of the Management Area fishery, characteristics of the trout fishery, returns from stocking, and the value of trout stream renovation. This long-range study covered the period from 1950 to 1966.

Some of the conclusions reached are:

- There has been a steady increase of fishing pressure on these Areas from 1938 to 1963.
- When the permit cost was increased by 50 cents in 1965, the number of fisherman-trips declined 21.6 percent.

- The average catch per hour on the Management Area streams ranged from 0.8-0.9 trout and a catch per trip range of 3.8 to 4.5 trout.
- The heaviest fishing pressure (28 percent of the season total) occurred during the month of April. A progressive decline of pressure occurred each month thereafter.
- Fishing pressure increases immediately following stocking.
- Each Management Area stream in western North Carolina primarily serves anglers from within a 25 mile radius.
- The high percentage of hatchery trout harvested immediately following stocking serves to provide a buffer for the wild trout population, and a more efficient harvest of hatchery trout.
- A more uniform rate of catch could be obtained by reducing the number of trout stocked per trip by more frequent stocking.
- A highest rate of return from catchable-size hatchery trout occurs from in-season stocking. The lowest rate of return comes from fall releases.
- The increase in fish available to anglers which can be achieved by stocking fingerlings is negligible if a wild-trout population is already present in the stream.
- Beyond a certain minimum intensity of fishing pressure, the number of hatchery fish stocked determines the total catch irrespective of the number of wild trout present.
- Total catch can be increased by stocking of additional trout.
- Fishing pressure increases following stream renovation primarily because of high catch rates resulting from the large number of yearling fish included in post-renovation stocking.

The Reliability of Partial Creel Checks As Indicators of Seasonal Totals

A study of the reliability of partial creel checks on Management Areas, as indicators of season totals, was made to assess the accuracy of sub-sampling techniques which are more economical than complete creel studies.

The data for these determinations were obtained from three Wildlife Management Area trout streams on which a complete creel census had been maintained for several years: Davidson River, North Fork French Broad River, and Lost Cove Creek. Daily and seasonal catch data for each stream were tabulated, including fisherman-trips, fishing pressure, total catch, and hourly catch rate. The data covered three consecutive fishing seasons except for Lost Cove Creek where only two years of data were comparable.

The comprehensive analyses of these data indicated that the percent of error associated with the techniques tested was too great to manage the North Carolina trout program on an economical and efficient basis.

Supplementary Feeding in a "Native Trout" Stream

Because North Carolina has many relatively unproductive trout streams, a preliminary study was undertaken to determine the extent that supplementally fed trout in a natural stream would increase the total catch and "take home" harvest under North Carolina's "native trout" restrictions. These restrictions permit only the use of artificial lures having one single hook and impose a creel limit of four trout per trip and a minimum size of 10 inches for rainbow and brown trout and 6 inches for brook trout. The economical and biological feasibility of feeding pelletized trout food to the standing crop of trout in a natural stream becomes an important aspect of supplemental feeding and were considered in the study.

Curtis Creek was chosen as the study stream and Newberry Creek the control stream because both had been renovated in 1963, were about the same size, and both were located in the same general area of the Mt. Mitchell Wildlife Management Area.

The conclusion reached from the preliminary study was that supplemental feeding of a "native trout" stream apparently increases the carrying capacity, provides a better growth rate, and may benefit the macrobenthos population which provides more food for trout. To make the operation economically sound, some type of automatic, non-electric feeder will have to be developed which can operate under all weather conditions.

At the present time, a similar study is being carried out on Armstrong Creek where more variables can be controlled.

"Native Trout" Stream Research

The "native trout" concept is high-catch-low-kill fishing and at this time appears the ultimate answer that trout management can provide to meet the mounting fishing pressure for trout fishing. This imposes a creel limit of four fish per day, a minimum size limit of 10 inches; the prohibition of all baits other than one single-hook artificial lure, and all stream stocking restricted to fingerling trout releases made only when investigation has revealed a shortage of naturally-propagated fish.

The "native trout" stream project ended during the biennium with the two following conclusions being drawn:

● "Native trout" streams provide a greater catch per acre because the trout can be caught and released several times before they reach the minimum size limit, thus providing greater sport.

● The trout populations in "native trout" streams are more stable in number and weight per acre than are those of regular trout streams.

Trout Stream Improvement

The South Toe River on the Mt. Mitchell Wildlife Management Area appeared to fall short of its trout recreational potential so it was deemed advisable to correct its habitat limitations by the addition of stream improvement devices. South Toe River had many riffles but few pools

Several aspects of "native trout" streams aimed at better fishing were under study during the biennium.

so a study was undertaken in 1967 to locate those areas wherein pools could be created by stream improvement devices without significantly increasing the downstream water temperatures.

The study showed that thirteen major stream improvement devices would create a better pool-riffle ratio and would have negligible effects on the downstream water temperatures. Of these, nine were low-head dams which could be created by moving large boulders. The other four structures would be built with gabions—or cubical wire retainers filled with 8 to 14-inch rocks and wired together. The four gabion structures were needed in the wider areas to serve as either deflectors or low head dams.

The nine boulder placement dams were installed during the biennium in cooperation with the U. S. Forest Service. The gabion structures will be installed next fiscal year.

Small-Boat Navigation Improvement

Many lowland streams, particularly in eastern North Carolina, are littered with snags, log jams, and fallen trees. This situation tends to improve fish habitat in certain respects, but it also precludes boat travel—with the consequence that many miles of excellent fishing water are inaccessible, or hazardously so, to the fishermen and particularly so where the terrain is too swampy for travel along the stream

complex of liquid wastes. In most cases, nothing is known of the biological effects of the waste components, either individually or in combination.

The Water Quality Section of the Division of Inland Fisheries is concerned both with the acute and chronic toxicity of waste substances which affect fish or fish-food organisms through alteration of water quality in the receiving waters. Studies are made of these wastes to determine their effects on fish upon request for assistance by the Department of Water and Air Resources, in which agency the entire responsibility for water pollution control in North Carolina is vested.

A major function of the water quality section, in cooperation with district fishery biologists and wildlife protectors, is to evaluate the fish kills that occur in the inland waters when so requested by the Department of Water and Air Resources. During the biennium, Commission personnel investigated 34 fish kills in the public waters of North Carolina. Evaluation reports on these fish kills were prepared and submitted to the Water and Air Resources Agency.

These cooperative investigations resulted in collection of the first fines assessed in North Carolina for pollution-caused fish kills. Total collections during the

Progress in fish production included the selective breeding of trout brood stock (left) and the study of optimum hatching temperatures for striped bass eggs at the Weldon hatchery.

bienium were $12,612.52.

Trout Catch Surveillance

A system of wildlife protector interviews for determining catch rate data in time to influence subsequent stocking was developed for North Carolina trout streams. This system produced the first catch data ever recorded from some 1,600 plus miles of "Designated Public Mountain Trout Waters" in North Carolina.

The number of fisherman-contacts made during the opening month of April was 9,685; May, 4,364; and June, 3,315—bringing the accumulative total of interviews to 17,364 during the biennium.

Fish Production

In the past two years, a number of improvements to the hatchery system was effected. At Weldon, the old wooden building which provided storage space and living quarters was torn down and replaced by a cinderblock building similar in appearance to the hatchery building.

At Fayetteville Hatchery, a new brick residence was constructed for the superintendent. The two assistants' residences were renovated.

At Armstrong Hatchery, 10 new 100' x 8' raceways were completed. This unit completes the construction of Armstrong.

Seven and one-half acres of land were purchased on Basin Creek adjoining Doughton Park in Wilkes County as a site for a new hatchery ultimately to replace Roaring Gap where a rapidly failing water supply is becoming critical. A site has been surveyed on Basin Creek within the confines of the park for a dam and pipeline to provide a water supply for the hatchery. Funds have been allocated for this construction and work will begin in the summer of 1969.

At Waynesville, a new highway is taking some land adjoining the present road which requires the removal of the residence, aerator, and three ponds. Work is now underway to relocate the pipelines and to rebuild the aerator. Some curtailment of production is necessary while this change-over is being carried out.

Following some experimentation, a new trout feeding program was initiated in 1966 utilizing pellets instead of meat. Production costs since the change have been reduced considerably.

The selective breeding of trout brood stock has progressed to the point that superior strains of brown and brook trout are available. The rainbow strain is gradually improving and should soon meet our required criteria.

Other Activities

During the biennium, planning-level personnel of the U. S. Soil Conservation Service and the U. S. Army Corps of Engineers have worked closely with the Bureau of Sport Fisheries and Wildlife and Wildlife Commission personnel in all stages of flood control and watershed development project planning so that any detrimental effects of such projects could be recognized early in the planning. This procedure eventually will result in considerable reductions in fishery losses. Meanwhile, the ever increasing number of these projects is endangering the future of stream fisheries in North Carolina due to the effects of impoundment, dredging, clearing, and snagging on stream habitat.

The Division of Inland Fisheries reviews all flood control project plans and makes recommendations designed to minimize fishery losses. Where losses are unavoidable, they are evaluated and mitigation is requested.

Considerable effort was expended during the biennium on farm pond consultation, dispensing fishing information and setting up fishing regulations. In addition, public relation functions such as preparing articles for "WILDLIFE in North Carolina" and other publications, assisting with television and movie productions for the Division of Education, and presenting programs for civic and sportsmen organizations were carried out. ♣

The final phase of the Armstrong Hatchery was completed with the construction of these 10 raceways.

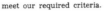

All flood control project plans of other agencies were reviewed by the Division and recommendations made.

THE Division of Game is responsible for providing technical guidance for the Commission's game management program. It employs 22 professionally trained biologists with field assignments from the mountains to the coast. It employs 32 area managers and assistants whose primary function is production of game on wildlife management areas that aggregate over 600,000 acres. The rest of the 64-member staff consists of equipment operators and utility men, two stenographers, and one bookkeeper. In addition, 376 part time laborers were employed in various capacities in all parts of the state.

Recognizing that our limited staff is inadequate, by itself, to provide wildlife services throughout the length and breadth of our state, cooperative wildlife programs were conducted with many other agencies at the federal, state, and local levels. Major cooperators were the U. S. Fish and Wildlife Service, the U. S. Forest Service, the U. S. Soil Conservation Service, the U. S. Park Service, the U. S. Corps of Engineers, the local Soil and Water Conservation Districts, the North Carolina Wildlife Federation, and many of its local wildlife clubs. To each of these, and many others, the Wildlife Commission owes a debt of gratitude for continuing assistance with game management in North Carolina.

Game Lands Program

Development of 31 game lands under the care of refuge managers and assistants continued to be a major Division of Game activity during the biennium. Basic areas of effort included maintenance of boundary line markers, deer pastures and other wildlife food plantings, and improvement of roads and foot trails. In addition, area managers supervised scheduled hunting and fishing.

For administrative purposes, the 31 areas were divided into

This is an aerial view of the northeast corner of the waterfowl food production project impoundment at Lake Mattamuskeet. The water level control pump is in the center of the photo. The insert shows equipment used to chop woody vegetation for conversion into waterfowl food plants.

four groups each under the direction of a refuge supervisor. A brief summary of activities and accomplishments on each group of areas follows:

Eastern areas with managers-in-residence are Lake Mattamuskeet, Holly Shelter, and Croatan. Other un-manned areas under the care of this segment include Gull Rock, Northwest River Marsh, Goose Creek (including the Pamlico Point waterfowl hunting area), Angola Bay, and Orton Plantation Waterfowl Refuge.

At Lake Mattamuskeet two impoundments aggregating about 1,100 acres were brought near to completion at the close of the biennium. Water levels will be controlled by low-head pumps to provide for production of waterfowl foods. It is expected that this will improve substantially the area's attractiveness to waterfowl.

The Holly Shelter peripheral drainage program was continued with about 12 miles of canal being dug. The purpose of this project is to increase production of timber and wildlife food plants near the edge of a bay where the mineral soil is within four feet of the surface. On the Croatan area a drawdown structure was installed at the outlet of Great Lake to provide for lowering the water level a maximum of three feet. Early summer draw-down was followed by airplane seeding of the exposed shoreline to browntop millet, this to be followed by re-flooding in early fall to provide several hundred acres of prime waterfowl feeding area.

In addition to this, 345 acres of upland food plantings were maintained on eastern areas, as well as 82 miles of roads, 54 miles of hunting lanes, and 283 miles of boundary lines.

Central areas with managers-in-residence include Caswell, Uwharrie and Sandhills. The Cowan's Ford Waterfowl Refuge and the Morris Mountain Game Restoration Area are also maintained by this project segment.

A major accomplishment was the completion of payment for the 14,290-acre Caswell area, which was purchased from the U. S. Forest Service. On this area 209 acres of cropland were leased to local farmers who were required to leave a small portion of their crops unharvested for the benefit of wildlife. An additional 573 acres of Commission-planted food and cover on this and the other central areas, sustained substantial populations of small game that provided hunting for sportsmen who live in metropolitan areas in the central part of the state.

The major effort on the Uwharrie Wildlife Management Area was devoted to maintenance of pastures for the benefit of the resident deer herd and the conducting of deer hunts. Personnel assigned to this area se-

Hunter access trails have greatly increased hunter success rates on Holly Shelter. Rotary mower and crawler tractor (insert) do this work.

Refuge Supervisor Grady Barnes and Manager Sam Moore inspect germinating millet seeded on exposed shoreline of Great Lake, Croatan Wildlife Management Area. Insert shows drainage structure used to control water level at outlet of lake.

Portions of the Sandhills Wildlife Management Area have been leased to commercial peach growers with stipulations that vegetative cover beneficial to wildlife be maintained.

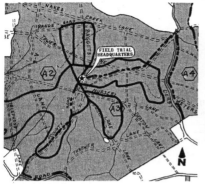

Bird dog field trials are an important part of the Sandhills area public use program. Shown at left is a map of the FIELD TRIAL AREA, Sandhills Wildlife Management Area near Hoffman.

cured leases necessary to the establishment of the Morris Mountain area, and followed through with boundary marking and improvement of access facilities.

The Sandhills area continued to serve as a major dove hunting area as well as to provide deer and quail hunting. A long-range plan for completing development of the 32-mile field trial course was initiated, as was a new program of wildlife habitat improvement through leasing lands for peach production by private growers.

Waterfowl food plantings were maintained on the Cowan's Ford area to provide food for wintering waterfowl on Lake Norman.

Northern areas with managers-in-residence include Thurmond Chatham, Daniel B o o n e, Mt. Mitchell, South Mountains, Flat Top, Rich Laurel, and Harmon Den. Western areas with manag-

ers-in-residence include Pisgah, Sherwood, Wayah Bald, Standing Indian, Fires Creek, and Santeetlah. Also five un-manned game restoration areas are maintained by the western segment—Green River, Beaverdam, T o x a w a y, Blue Valley and Caney Fork. The work done on these areas is combined into a single summary because the individual areas are so similar. All are in the mountain section of the state, and provide the bulk of big game hunting opportunity in this section. About one-third of the big game harvested in the mountains was taken on these areas, and much of the remainder was taken on bordering lands.

The primary activity of personnel assigned to these areas was protection of the game from poaching and stray dogs, and enforcement of use-restrictions which spell the difference be-

tween game and no game in this section of the state.

The importance of these restrictive use regulations was brought into sharp focus during the biennium. A special study revealed that less restrictive hunting regulations off the wildlife management areas has been the primary reason for failure of deer to reach potential population levels. On a major portion of the lands between these areas, the deer population is only a small fraction of what it could be if the hunting pattern were modified by changing statewide hunting regulations.

Operations of these wildlife management areas i n v o l v e d maintenance painting and posting of 746 miles of boundary lines, keeping 1038 miles of foot

Over 40,000 hunters checked in on management area deer hunts each year. Some brought their camps with them!

HARVEST OF GAME ON GAME LANDS WITH CHECK STATIONS — 1966-67 AND 1967-68

AREA	BEAR	BOAR	DEER	SQUIRREL	GROUSE	RACCOON	RABBIT	QUAIL	DOVE	DUCKS	GEESE	TURKEY
Santeetlah	8-9	81-65	71-87	223-465	2-3	38-47						
Fires Creek	1-0		96-94	240-243	43-16	16-19						
Standing Indian			93-94	281-122	59-27	44-59						1-2
Wayah Bald			105-74	223-323	18-14	18-25						
Sherwood	6-3		199-103	73-99	29-11	25-39	51-7	0-1				
Pisgah	19-3		571-350	4838-7831	29-19	325-242	6-12	1-0				
Harmon Den	1-0		62-35	174-165	22-6	4-0						
Rich Laurel	2-2		93-59	286-418	40-7							
Flat Top			182-94	400-221	35-9	4-7		1-0				
Mt Mitchell			198-128	146-172	3-0	51-13						
Daniel Boone			375-219	706-1363	1-1	70-40						
Thurmond Chatham			107-49	62-0	4-0		1-0	7-0				
South Mountains			78-51	117-289	0-1	14-28						
Uwharrie			124-209	759-304			0-42					
Sandhills			82-93	8-33			18-0	1087-1112	10771-16248			
Holly Shelter	10-4		63-79									
Croatan			17-28									
Lake Mattamuskeet										1605-942	895-843	
Annual Totals	47-21	81-65	2486-1846	8536-12048	285-114	609-519	78-61	1096-1113	10771-16248	1605-942	895-843	1-2
Biennial Totals	68	146	4332	20584	399	1128	137	2209	27019	2547	1738	3

trails open for use by hunters and fishermen, and maintenance of 394 acres of pasture plantings (by planting, top-dressing and mowing) as a supplement to native foods. In addition, several hundred apple trees were kept pruned and several hundred fruit - producing shrubs were planted.

In a further effort to spread deer herds throughout the mountain section, two of the new game restoration a r e a s mentioned above were stocked with 32 deer that were caught by box traps and tranquilizer dart guns. A deer track count study conducted on these new areas showed that the new populations are not only surviving, they are increasing.

The most significant feature of these areas is that they represent a middle-ground between the intensive use restrictions on the manned wildlife management areas and the less intensively regulated territories o u t s i d e these areas. As such, they constitute an experiment in low-cost game restoration which, if successful, may point the way for more extensive big game restoration in the future.

Small game public hunting areas, seven in number, were established by lease agreement during the biennium. This also was an innovation, the purpose of which was to provide hunting opportunity for our increasingly urbanized hunter population.

While these were mostly wooded areas they included operating farms and, in order to hold the nuisance factor to a minimum to protect farming operations, hunting was restricted to three days per week. A season permit was required in addition to the hunting license and a substantial increase in use was observed in the second year of the biennium. These areas were managed by personnel of the upland game program and enforcement of regulations was by the local wildlife protectors. In addition to posting of boundary lines, development included planting of food patches for the game and preparation and distribution of maps to expedite hunter use.

The public dove hunting area program was continued through the biennium with operation of 15 areas each year. (In addition, some of the small game public hunting areas also doubled as dove hunting areas.) Substantial public use was observed on these areas which in most cases were operating farms on which dove hunting rights were leased by the Commission and landowners were paid to provide dove-attractant food plantings through normal agricultural practices.

Upland Game Restoration

A primary function of this program is to provide, free of charge, planting materials beneficial to upland game for use on farms throughout the state, together with advice on where and how the plantings should be made. These services were provided by the district game biologists and the materials were produced by the plant nursery crew on the Sandhills and Caswell Wildlife Management Areas.

Planting materials were distributed to nearly 10,000 cooperators during the biennium. Materials distributed included 37,-815 five-pound units of annual seed mixture, 9,712 three-pound units of perennial seed units, 7,658 two-pound units of sericea seed, 3,432,000 shrub lespedeza seedlings and 313,260 multiflora rose seedlings.

To satisfy federal aid requirements, surveys were conducted to determine utilization of planting materials distributed. These surveys indicated that more than 80 percent of the seeds and seedlings distributed produced plantings helpful to wildlife in every county of the state.

In addition to advice on how and where to plant these materials, district game biologists answered over 500 requests for on-the-ground assistance in planning wildlife development on privately-owned lands. Also, as a result of biologist contacts, several utility companies have substantially expanded their programs of wildlife plantings along their rights-of-way. These were designed to hold down the cost of maintaining cover that would not interfere with power lines and that would prevent soil erosion, while at the same time provide additional public hunting lands.

District biologists also supervised establishment and operation of controlled shooting preserves during the biennium. Emphasis was placed on modification of regulations so as to expand hunting opportunity in a manner that would be commercially profitable to the operator but at the same time prevent commercial exploitation of native game birds. An improved record keeping system during the second year of the biennium showed that 3663 man-days of hunting were provided by the 32 preserves in operation.

The cooperative raccoon trapping and restocking program was also conducted by this segment of the Division of Game. During the biennium a total of 2,308 raccoons was trapped in the eastern part of the State and distributed through 25 hunt clubs in the west. In this program the Commission acted as broker and reimbursed the clubs for one-half of the cost of the raccoons.

Wild Turkey Restoration

Wild turkey restoration was under the supervision of a biologist who worked with other Commission personel, sportsmen and cooperating agencies. During the biennium, the initial phase of an experimental habitat improvement program on the Standing Indian Wildlife Management Area was completed. Twelve new fields were cleared and seeded to various grasses and clover, and 36 forest opening sites were treated with herbicides. This experimental program is designed to determine the reaction of a small, remnant population of wild turkeys to intensive habitat improvement on a large, well-protected management area.

Surveys and studies conducted

Commission Turkey Biologist, Thad Cherry holds a tom turkey trapped on Camp Lejeune. Many of the wild turkeys used for restocking by the Commission have come from Camp Lejeune.

Shrub lespedeza seedlings are lifted out of the nursery bed with a potato digger for shipment to landowners, statewide. Right, James Odum inspects a planting of Egyptian wheat which is under observation as a wildlife food.

included track - count - in - snow censuses, spring gobbler counts, investigation of reproductive success, and studies of internal parasites and food habits. Survey data and random field observations indicated very poor wild turkey reproduction throughout most of the turkey range in 1967 and only fair in 1968.

A number of areas were inspected and evaluated in an effort to locate an area which the Commission could develop and manage primarily for wild turkeys. Most of the areas were either too small, had inferior habitat or were otherwise unsuitable. This search is being continued, as such a wild turkey management area would be most valuable in providing managed turkey hunting as well as trapping stock for future restoration efforts.

Toward the end of the biennium, the Commission adopted what is no doubt the most realistic turkey hunting seasons ever established in North Carolina. For 1968-69, a shorter, more restricted winter season and our state's first general spring turkey season will be more consistent with biological principles, and will be similar to the turkey hunting seasons in all other states through the southeast. This type of biologically oriented regulation has proven elsewhere to be one of the essential keys to successful wild turkey restoration and we look for this action to be the turning point in wild turkey restoration in North Carolina.

Waterfowl Surveys and Management

Waterfowl populations during the biennium were the highest recorded in the past several years. With the increasing size of the wintering flocks, the duck kill has begun to improve following several years of record low kills. In addition to the several ground and aerial waterfowl population surveys, banding efforts were coordinated with the U. S. Fish and Wildlife Service as part of the continuing study of migrations, annual survival, differential vulnerability and many other factors relating to waterfowl management.

An impoundment program for marshes bordering the mainland portion of the Goose Creek Wildlife Management Area was formulated and a working agreement was signed with the Beaufort County Mosquito Control Commission. Work was begun on the first impoundment which is located on Smith Creek. This impoundment was scheduled for completion by late summer 1968.

The destruction of prime waterfowl habitat, especially the wooded swamps in the eastern part of the state, through federally sponsored programs, continued to be a major problem. Several projects were surveyed and

Left to right, Commission Biologist George Burdick, Protector T. H. Robbins, and Federal Refuge Manager John Davis check pump removing water from an impoundment in the southwest section of Lake Mattamuskeet. Insert shows spike rush, wild millet, three-square and wild millet beginning to shatter. These waterfowl foods have seeded naturally here.

Management area food trails, constructed to provide access to remote areas, help spread hunting pressure and in-

Unauthorized stocking with domestically-reared "wild boar" threatens to become a serious problem in western North Carolina due to conflict with other interests in the area.

a wildlife damage assessment report was prepared for each. Some mitigation for habitat losses was thereby realized.

Game Lands Forest Management

Of the 176,557 acres of state-owned game lands managed by the Wildlife Resources Commission, about 70 percent is in forest cover. The forest lands are under the management of three professional foresters and four sub-professional assistants. Timber inventory has been a continuing activity and was brought to near completion on the third major wildlife management area during the biennium.

Forest management has been wildlife oriented. Timber sales have been so located as to maximize game food and cover. Controlled burning has helped to maintain seed-producing legumes for the benefit of wildlife and at the same time prevent the build-up of fuel that would result in timber-killing wildfires.

There were 32 timber sales during the biennium on four wildlife management areas, with a gross income of $317,095.57. This is an increase of about 11.5 percent over the 1964-66 biennium and represents a cost to income ratio of one to three. Under G. S. 105-296.1, 15 percent of the gross receipts in the amount of $47,564.33 was paid in lieu of taxes to counties in which the wildlife management areas are located.

Concrete fords were constructed on several wildlife management area roads to provide long-lasting stream crossings cheaply.

Game Surveys and Investigations

A major achievement during the biennium was conduct of the periodic statewide game kill survey to estimate the number of hunters, trips and kill of the various game species. A summary of the 1967-68 statewide game kill survey and comparable data for 1964-65 are presented in the table at the bottom of the page.

The crops of approximately 4,000 quail harvested by hunters on the Sandhills management area were examined and the food items identified. A complete analysis of the data is currently underway. A preliminary analysis of the data from this study is of particular interest. Quail on this area show a decided preference for long leaf pine seed, when

Electronic data processing equipment was utilized in many divisional studies.

it is available. While feeding on long leaf pine seed, found primarily on open ridges, the quail are more available to the hunter. Pine seeds are generally not available to quail after mid-December due to seed sprouting. At this time the quail move to the densely vegetated swamp areas to feed upon fruit of sweet red bay, and thus the birds are more difficult to find.

Continued studies in the population dynamics of various game species appear ready to bear fruit in the form of techniques that have direct management application. Among these techniques are methods for estimating annual productivity, survival and mortality in our deer herds.

Electronic data processing services in the Commission's Division of Finance and Personnel were most helpful in conduct of these studies. A modest expansion of these facilities, including computer service, would greatly increase our capacity to conduct studies that would increase efficiency of field operations and expand our capacity to increase production of wildlife and hunting opportunity.

In addition to research activities the project leader coordinated the Commission's hosting the 20th annual Meeting of Southeastern Association of Game and Fish Commissioners duing October of the first year of the biennium. The meeting, which was held in Asheville, attracted approximately 750 participants from twenty-three states and two territories. ◆

	TOTAL KILL		TOTAL NUMBER TRIPS		TOTAL NUMBER HUNTERS	
Species	1964-65	1967-68	1964-65	1967-68	1964-65	1967-68
Deer	39,793	38,688	894,035	953,844	125,083	174,033
Bear	628	1,654	37,938	57,193	10,899	12,833
Boar	*	797	*	27,280	*	6,110
Squirrel	3,544,319	2,995,229	2,504,823	2,236,665	270,938	317,602
Rabbit	3,078,019	2,078,719	2,384,947	1,886,581	257,153	289,240
Fox	*	35,262	*	156,161	*	19,284
Raccoon	*	186,447	*	356,660	*	44,004
Quail	2,826,640	2,159,718	1,626,897	1,220,808	174,314	182,043
Dove	3,002,220	2,977,288	968,667	866,837	152,507	168,894
Grouse	63,043	*	88,873	*	23,070	*
Ducks	142,375	*	185,337	*	29,485	*
Geese	27,938	*	74,661	*	13,300	*

*This species not included in survey this year.

Division of Education

MORE than 20 years ago, a speaker at the North America Wildlife Conference said, "An uninformed, and often misinformed, public is the greatest bottleneck in the field of conservation today."

This statement still holds true, although great strides have been made in getting general information on conservation of natural resources across to the public.

In its program of informing the people of North Carolina of the need for conserving our wildlife resources, and in obtaining active cooperation in wildlife

"Wildlife" copy is set in type, ready for printing by The Graphic Press. Below, a news release is being placed in envelopes for mailing to over 500 outlets. Right, a film is edited for a TV program.

management, the Wildlife Resources Commission engaged in these major educational activities: publications, audio-visual aids, news communications, and extension.

Publications

WILDLIFE IN NORTH CAROLINA, the official monthly magazine of the Wildlife Resources Commission, is by far the major project among the division's various publications. From under 100,000 copies per month, two years ago, circulation of the magazine grew to 113,500 at the end of the biennium, averaging 110,500 per month during the two-year period. Since the magazine goes to all libraries, public schools, barber shops, and the waiting rooms of doctors, dentists, and hospitals, the monthly readership can be conservatively estimated at 650,000 people.

Although intended primarily for sportsmen and conservationists, WILDLIFE has become a family magazine, and is as popular with the youngsters who will be tomorrow's sportsmen, as it is with the hunters, fishermen and boaters of today.

After maintaining the same annual subscription fee of 50 cents for the 20 years WILDLIFE IN NORTH CAROLINA has been published, rising production costs and an ever-increasing volume will, during the next biennium, necessitate an increase in this fee.

In addition to the magazine, the Division of Education produced and distributed pamphlets and bulletins to thousands of people, especially elementary school teachers and students, on request. The division also completed a comprehensive study of the Commission's boating access areas and produced, from information collected during this study, a boater's guide, *North Carolina Wildlife Boating Access Areas*, which is being sold to the boating public at production cost, 75 cents per copy. The division also produced and began distribution of several new free pamphlets as well as reissuing the more popular ones already available. The list of publications currently available from the Wildlife Commission includes 46 titles.

Audio-Visual Aids

The Commission's audio-visual program has expanded considerably during the past biennium. In addition to maintaining a comprehensive library of 16mm motion picture sound films for free distribution to a wide variety of audiences, the division's photographers exposed thousands of feet of motion picture film for future use in motion picture and television production.

Moving from the planning stages with a pilot film, the division began regular production of a 13-week television program.

Television Production

The division took a significant step forward in conservation education during the biennium with the initiation of the television series, "Wildlife in North Carolina." The series, consisting of 13, one-half hour programs, was produced at WUNC-TV in Raleigh, the State's educational television facility.

The "Wildlife" series was first aired in October of 1967 by the ETV network. By early summer of 1968, the series had been aired by commercial stations in New Bern, Greensboro, Raleigh, Durham and Wilmington. The series was offered free of charge to any television station in the state that would air it at a reasonably popular time.

At the studios of WUNC-TV, "Wildlife in North Carolina" host John R. Parker, Jr., interviews guest Talmadge Wiggins. The series is video taped for weekly release over educational network and other stations.

The Commission's weekly radio program continued to be aired by some twenty stations over the State, free of charge.

Division personnel believe that the program reached tens of thousands of Tarheel citizens who otherwise might not have access to the outdoor conservation message. Due to the Commission's involvement in three highly important outdoor areas, hunting, fishing and boating, the series justifiably treated a variety of associated subjects. But whatever the theme of a particular program, each was designed to carry a conservation message or a boating or hunter safety message.

As the bienium neared an end, division personnel were already working on a new series for the following two years. As well as starting production of the new series, planning was underway for producing, technically speaking, a more professional type of s e r i e s. Color production and sound production, as opposed to straight studio narration, are definitely needed to effectively deliver the conservation message and to make the outdoor type of program truly appealing to all citizens. This type of production requires equipment more refined than presently available in the division.

Of course, the very best in production is of limited value unless the series is aired throughout the state by the vast commercial network. All concerned were greatly appreciative of the public service time allotted by those stations which aired the series. It is hopeful that coverage in the western half of the state can be arranged during the next biennium.

Still Photography

The Commission's still photographers exposed and printed hundreds of rolls of black and white and color film, producing photographs for use in the Commission's own publications and for distribution to the mass media. In addition to photographs published by the Commission, the division's photo files were heavily utilized by newspapers, magazines, textbooks publishers, encyclopedia editors and many other educational and mass media publishers.

The division's still photography program also included color slide program production, film strip planning and production and photo documentation of the activities of other divisions.

Radio

Division personnel produced a weekly radio program throughout the biennium. The program was recorded on magnetic tape and distributed to 20 to 30 cooperating stations. The service is offered free of charge to any station wishing to use it, the only cost to the station being the five cent postage fee for returning the tapes for re - use. This amounted to giving the Commission's wildlife conservation activities about $300 per week worth of air time free. The cost to the Commission per station for production and mailing was about 15 cents per week.

News Communication

During the biennium the Commission enjoyed excellent relations with newspapers, radio and television stations. As news occurred pertaining to Commission activities, news releases on the subject were prepared and sent to all news media, surprisingly to a number of out-of-state news media who requested them. In addidtion, a weekly outdoor feature column entitled, "Rod And Gun," was sent to about 75 newspapers and radio stations, and a weekly outdoor feature entitled, "Carolina Outdoors" was written for use by the Associated Press.

A measure of the results of t h i s activity was obtained through the use of a press clipping service.

Extension

Personnel of the Division of Education, and other divisions, made hundreds of appearances before such organizations as women's clubs, civic clubs, wildlife clubs, garden clubs, scouts and in classrooms, giving talks and lectures illustrated with colored slides. During both years of the biennium personnel worked closely with youth camps involving several thousand youngsters. The contact varied from lecture-demonstrations at camporees to seminars for teachers and youth leaders.

Commission personnel also cooperated closely with the various conservation groups in the state, from the small, local groups to the state-wide organization of the Wildlife Federation, in encouraging and coordinating the conservation efforts of laymen and professionals alike to help insure the wise use of North Carolina's wildlife resources.

Boating Safety

The division's boating safety effort was primarily through the WILDLIFE magazine, television, radio, the film library, free literature, technical correspondence and various administrative activities presented shared with other divisions.

The Division of Education is the Commission's smallest, having only six professional employees, so by necessity personal contact in the area of boating safety was limited during the biennium. Logically, it was more efficient to allot time and effort to high coverage methods.

Division personnel consulted with citizens, clubs and wildlife protectors hundreds of times during the biennium on boating safety activities. A boating safety slide series was produced during the biennium and was used primarily by wildlife protectors but was also available to the public. The WILDLIFE magazine carried a monthly boating column throughout the period.

Division personnel spent considerable time collecting and recording boating accident statistics. The program, however, is not an education function and may be reassigned as the boating program grows.

Hunting Safety

In the field of hunter safety, the division continued, during the biennium, the joint program with the National Rifle Association whereby volunteers were certified as hunter safety instructors. Also as a part of the joint program, Division personnel with the help of the wildlife protectors, collected and maintained hunting accident records. Copies of the reports were forwarded to NRA.

As was true in boating safety education, the division's efforts were directed so as to reach the most people. Hunter safety films from the Commission's free library received heavy use. Thousands of pieces of literature were distributed. The literature consisted of reports from the WILDLIFE magazine and specially prepared material.

It should be pointed out that the Commission has no legal responsibility in hunter safety education. However, the need is recognized. The work of the Commission as well as individual citizens quite likely prevented an increase in hunting accidents during the biennium.

Displays and Exhibits

The demand for seasonal displays and exhibits, particularly for local fairs and boat shows, far exceeded the supply during the biennium. Assistance was given to wildlife protectors and field biologists in securing or planning such displays, and in many cases, photographs, charts, etc., were mounted and distributed for exhibit use. The numerous requests for such display material pointed up the great need for consideration of some type of permanent, portable wildlife display.

A new and different approach to the State Fair exhibit was successfully tried both years of the biennium. Under the guidance and supervision of personnel of the Division of Inland Fisheries, an exhibit of live animals was set up in cooperation with State Fair officials. The exhibit was housed in a large circus type tent supplied by the State Fair, and consisted of many large cages constructed to Wildlife Commission specifications by State Fair carpenters. Animals such as deer, alligators, skunks, snakes, etc., were obtained from authorized animal exhibitors, or brought from wildlife management areas.

The only expense to the Commission was for the food consumed by the animals, and the cost of incidental items such as padlocks, etc. Tens of thousands of people crowded the tent all during the Fair, showing the interest that this sort of exhibit can create. It is hoped that this type of exhibit can be continued at the State Fair each year. ♦

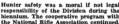

Hunter safety was a moral if not legal responsibility of the Division during the biennium. The cooperative program with the National Rifle Association continued.

Many youth groups were instructed in basic conservation (left). The State Fair exhibit drew thousands of visitors.

Division of Engineering

DURING the major portion of the biennium Division of Engineering personnel consisted of the Division Chief, two Engineering Technicians, three Equipment Foremen, and the Division Secretary. Near the end of the biennium an Assistant Division Chief was employed.

The Assistant Chief of the Division was employed primarily for work with boating and fishing access areas, although his duties were not confined to this category. Assisting him in the access area work were the Division Chief, two Engineering Technicians and, from time to time, the three Equipment Foremen. This phase of the work consisted of location of suitable sites, getting surveys made, optioning the property, and negotiating for purchase.

Access area work by the Chief, Assistant Chief, and Engineering Technicians was not confined to locating, surveying, and optioning of sites. They were also charged with maintenance of existing areas. This was accomplished either by formal contract, informal contract or force account, using Commission-owned heavy equipment and Commission personnel. Jobs in the latter category were performed by the equipment foremen and temporary operators under the direct supervision of the division chief, assistant chief and/or one of the engineering technicians. Some project plans were drawn by division personnel in the Raleigh office. When the work load did not permit this, consulting engineers or architects were employed. Such outside engineers or architects were supervised by the Division Chief or Assistant Chief.

The Division was assisted by the Division of Protection in minor maintenance and policing of the access areas. Each wildlife patrolman was authorized to spend a limited amount on each area for removal of refuse, mowing grass, filling holes, grading, etc. However, no maintenance of a major nature was undertaken on any of the areas without express prior approval of, and usually under direct Division of Engineering supervision.

Six new boating access areas were completed during the biennium, bringing the total of areas in operation on June 30, 1968, to 88.

Primary duties of the three equipment foremen were refuge and hatchery road construction and maintenance, and similar work. In order to make full use of the equipment owned by the Division, each of the foremen hired temporary heavy equipment operators as they were needed. In almost all operations, additional laborers were employed for brush cutting, pipe laying, drill operating, root and rock removal and a myriad of other tasks associated with earthwork construction.

A majority of the equipment foremen's work consisted of refuge and hatchery road work, building of dams and bridges, clearing of fields for pasture plantings, and draining swampy lands for increased timber pro-

Commission construction projects often call for the use of heavy equipment operated by Division personnel. Construction and maintenance of Commission roads included the building of low-water bridges such as this (below) which will withstand sudden water rises without damage.

duction and improved wildlife habitat. In addition, the foremen and heavy equipment were used on construction and maintenance of access areas.

The foremen were charged with the use of: 4 heavy bulldozers, 1 light bulldozer, 1 front-end loader, 3 draglines, 2 compressor-drills, 3 tractor-trailers, 5 dump trucks, 3 stake body trucks, 3 arc welders, 3 oxyacetylene welders, 1 concrete mixer, and an assortment of light power tools. In addition, the foremen took care of ordinary maintenance of the equipment in the field. In the case of major breakdowns where the equipment was movable, it was hauled to a shop of the distributor for the particular piece of equipment. For non-movable break - downs, specialized mechanics were called in to work on the equipment in the field.

Minor repairs at fish hatcheries and wildlife management area residences were carried out by hatchery superintendents or refuge managers under the direction of the Chief or Assistant Chief of the Division of Engineering. This work consisted of re-roofing several of the buildings, replacement of windows, repair of porches, plumbing, etc.

New fishing and boating access areas developed by the Division during the biennium were:

Big Swamp Creek — Lennon's Bridge — Robeson County

Chowan River—Cannon's Ferry — Chowan County

Chowan River — Tunis — Hertford County

Hancock Creek — Craven County

Tillery Lake — Norwood — Stanly County

Yadkin River — Concord Church — Davie County

Other projects completed by the Division were: new residences at Mattamuskeet Wildlife Management Area, Holly Shelter Wildlife Management Area, and the Fayetteville Fish Hatchery. Plans were initiated for a new duplex residence at the Waynesville Fish Hatchery, but these were incomplete at the end of the biennium. A new office and sleeping quarters were added to

the striped bass hatchery at Weldon. Additional raceways were added at the Armstrong Trout Hatchery. A contract was awarded for construction of a new residence at the Sandhills Wildlife Management Area, but this project was just being started at the end of the biennium.

At the end of the biennium the following fishing and boating access areas were in operation.

Alligator River — Gum Neck Landing — Tyrrell County

Apalachia Reservoir — Cherokee County

Badin Reservoir — Lakemont — Montgomery County

Bear Lake — Jackson County

Big Flatty Creek — Pasquotank County

Big Swamp Creek — Lennon's Bridge — Robeson County

Black River — Hunt's Bluff — Bladen County

Careful project planning and cost estimation preceded actual field work. Many management area roads were reconstructed during the biennium, and maintenance continued to require considerable time of the Division.

Black River — Ivanhoe — Sampson County

Blewett Falls Reservoir — Pee Dee — Anson County

Cape Fear River — Elwell's Ferry — Bladen County

Cape Fear River — Avent's Ferry Bridge — Chatham County

Cape Fear River — Fayetteville — Cumberland County

Cape Fear River — Lillington — Harnett County

Cedar Cliff Reservoir — Jackson County

Chatuge Reservoir — Jackrabbit — Clay County

Chatuge Reservoir—Ledford's Chapel — Clay County

Cheoah Reservoir — Graham County

Chowan River — Cannon's Ferry — Chowan County

Chowan River — Edenhouse Bridge — Chowan County

Chowan River — Tunis — Hertford County

Contentnea Creek — Snow Hill — Greene County

Dan River — Leaksville — Rockingham County

Dan River — Milton — Caswell County

Dawson Creek — Oriental — Pamlico County

Deep River — Carbonton — Moore County

Deep River — Sandy Creek — Randolph County

East Lake — Mashoes — Dare County

Fontana Reservoir — Tsali — Swain County

Gaston Lake — Henrico — Northampton County

Gaston Lake — Stonehouse Creek — Warren County

Gaston Lake — Summit — Halifax County

Hancock Creek — Craven County

Hickory Lake — Steel Bridge — Alexander County

Hickory Lake — Oxford — Catawba County

High Rock Lake — Southmont — Davidson County

High Rock Lake — Dutch 2nd Creek — Rowan County

Hiwassee River — Grape Creek — Cherokee County

Hiwassee Reservoir — Hanging Dog — Cherokee County

Inland Waterway — Coinjock — Currituck County

James Lake — Canal Bridge — Burke County

James Lake — Linville Arm — Burke County

James Lake — North Fork — McDowell County

James Lake — McDowell — McDowell County

Kerr Reservoir — Nutbush Creek — Vance County

Kitty Hawk Bay — Avalon Beach— Dare County

Lake Rim — Cumberland County

Lake Wylie — Withers Bridge — Mecklenburg County

Little River — Hall's Creek — Pasquotank County

Lookout Shoals Lake — Catawba County

Lumber River — McNeil's Bridge — Robeson County

Meherrin River — Murfreesboro — Hertford County

Mountain Island Lake — Davidson — Mecklenburg County

Mountain Island Lake — River Bend

— Gaston County

Nantahala Reservoir — Choga Creek — Macon County

Nantahala Reservoir — Rocky Branch — Macon County

Neuse River — Bridgeton — Craven County

Neuse River — Goldsboro — Wayne County

Neuse River — Richardson's Bridge — Johnston County

Northeast Cape Fear River — Holly Shelter — Pender County

Northeast Cape Fear River — Kenansville — Duplin County

Pamlico Sound — Englehard — Hyde County

Pasquotank River — Elizabeth City — Camden County

Pee Dee River — Red Hill — Anson County

Rhodhiss Lake — Castle Bridge — Caldwell County

Rhodhiss Lake — Dry Pond — Caldwell County

Rhodhiss Lake — John's River — Burke County

Roanoke Rapids Reservoir — Thelma — Halifax County

Roanoke River — Hamilton — Martin County

Roanoke River — Gaston — Northampton County

Roanoke River — Weldon — Halifax County

Santeetlah Lake — Ranger — Graham County

Scuppernong River — Columbia — Tyrrell County

Shelter Creek — Pender County

South River — Ennis' Bridge — Bladen County

South River — Sloan's Bridge — Bladen County

South Yadkin River — Cooleemee— Davie County

Tar River — Bell's Bridge — Edgecombe County

Tar River — Falkland — Pitt County

Tar River — Greenville — Pitt County

Tar River — Old Sparta — Edgecombe County

Tar River — Rocky Mount — Nash County

Tillery Lake — Lilly's Bridge — Montgomery County

Tillery Lake — Norwood — Stanly County

Tillery Lake — Swift Island —Montgomery County

Tuckertown Reservoir — Flat Creek —Rowan County

Waccamaw Lake — Columbus County

White Oak River — Haywood's Landing — Jones County

Yadkin River — Concord Church — Davie County

Boating access areas planning and construction consumed much Division time during the biennium. This is the Thelma area on Roanoke Rapids Reservoir in Halifax County.

THE Commission expanded its service to sportsmen during this biennium as wildlife revenue increased from $7,270,478 for the biennium ending June 30, 1966 to $8,364,595 for the biennium ending June 30, 1968.

The Division of Finance and Personnel began the biennium with a staff of seventeen employees consisting of the Division Chief, twelve accounting clerks, two stenographers and two stock clerks.

In order to facilitate the handling of the duties of this division, the work is separated into seven work units.

Administrative Unit

The primary duties of this unit consisted of the following:

Performing stenographic duties, doing research on all applicants for license agencies, bonding license agents, handling all division correspondence, handling collection of bad checks, operation of microfilm machine, checking all magazine subscriptions and preparing work orders for IBM Unit, writing all requisitions, coding all purchase orders, preauditing monthly oil company credit card statements and preparing deposits of all Commission receipts, and also processing Workmen's Compensation claims for payment.

Payroll and Bookkeeping Unit

The primary duties of this unit consisted of the following:

Keeping the Commission's books covering expenditures, receipts and encumbrances; preparing all budgetary reports, preparing payrolls, preparing all personnel forms, maintaining personnel records, collecting rent on Commission-owned houses, handling all insurance, and retirement papers and claims, and preparation of annual salary increment schedule.

Auditing Unit

Requisitions, purchase orders, and all invoices were audited and coded. Invoices and Workmen's Compensation claims were prepared for payment. Claims for reimbursement of State road tax on non-highway use of gasoline were also handled in this section.

This section administered the Capital Improvement fund which consists of the following: preparing allotments, auditing invoices, writing vouchers, and preparing monthly and annual reports.

Federal Aid Unit

This unit kept the books and all financial records pertaining to projects which were jointly financed by the U. S. Fish and Wildlife Service and the Commission. Other duties consisted of auditing invoices and requisitions pertaining to federal aid projects, maintaining an inventory of all equipment and motor vehicles purchased jointly by the Commission and the Federal Government, preparing vouchers for recovery of funds from the U. S. Fish and Wildlife Service.

Hunting and Fishing License Unit

The primary duties of the Li-

Accurate records of all licenses dispersed to agents are essential to the Commission's financial system.

cense Unit were as follows:
- Consigning all hunting and fishing licenses to bonded agents.
- Consigning permits and licenses to all refuge personnel for special management area hunting and fishing.
- Collection of monies from the sale of all licenses and permits.
- Auditing all reports covering license sales from protectors and license agents.
- Keeping individual records and books covering all license sales by agents.
- Issuing duplicate licenses.
- Preparing reports pertaining to license sales.

During the biennium the revenue from hunting and fishing license sales increased from $5,-417,676 for the biennium ending June 30, 1966 to $6,022,769 for the biennium ending June 30, 1968.

Motorboat Registration Unit

The functions of this unit were as follows:
- Providing the public with applications for boat numbers and certificates.
- Receiving applications and fees for boat certificates.
- Assigning boat numbers.
- Issuing temporary and permanent certificates.
- Issuing duplicates and transfers of ownership.
- Auditing all applications and depositing all registration fees in the special fund required by law.
- Maintaining permanent records of all boats registered,

both by number and by name of owner.
- Preparing quarterly reports to the U. S. Coast Guard in accordance with federal requirements.

As of December 31, 1967, this section had registered 59,098 boats of over 10 horsepower and issued the certificates of number covering them.

Stockroom Unit

This unit maintained a stockroom of office supplies and publications as well as maintaining a stock of tires, batteries, and other items for the Commission's fleet of over two hundred cars and trucks and over one hundred boats. Stock record cards and a perpetual inventory were kept covering the receipt and issue of these items.

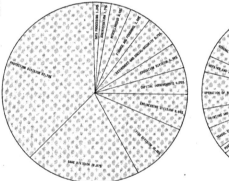

WHERE THE LICENSE DOLLAR WAS SPENT

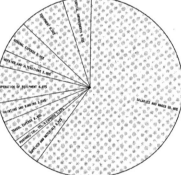

WHAT THE LICENSE DOLLAR BOUGHT

CODE 26741 — WILDLIFE BUDGET — JULY 1, 1966 - JUNE 30, 1968

	1966-67	1967-68
I. ADMINISTRATION		
Salary — Director	$ 15,499.98	$ 15,996.96
Salaries and Wages—Staff	33,284.48	36,666.95
Postage, Tel., Tel., and Exp.	1,200.00	1,200.00
Travel Expense	2,039.30	2,380.01
General Expense	4,940.42	4,985.63
Commission Expense	8,457.25	11,416.95
TOTAL	$ 65,421.43	$ 72,649.50
II. FINANCE AND PERSONNEL		
Salaries and Wages—Permanent	$ 69,338.61	$ 76,576.90
Salaries and Wages—Temporary	1,432.40	3,000.45
Supplies and Materials	11,651.12	9,740.28
Postage, Tel., and Exp.	18,000.00	22,000.00
Travel Expense	94.82	427.94
Printing and Binding	29,537.16	30,720.00
Operation of Equipment	789.26	741.81
Repairs and Alterations	2,138.88	2,468.07
General Expense	2,727.36	3,147.40
Equipment	3,442.44	2,868.04
TOTAL	$ 139,152.05	$ 151,690.89
III. WILDLIFE PROTECTION		
Salaries and Wages—Permanent	$ 949,911.13	$1,093,501.98
Salaries and Wages—Temporary	5,757.26	7,047.28
Supplies and Materials	2,488.53	3,094.05
Postage, Tel., Tel., and Exp.	8,734.00	8,824.00
Travel Expense	77,635.57	82,135.15
Operation of Equipment	157,725.16	167,207.01
Motor Vehicle Exchange	80,000.00	142,809.45
Equipment	43,231.81	60,944.95
Uniforms	11,581.59	23,638.57
TOTAL	$1,337,065.05	$1,589,202.44
IV. EDUCATION		
Salaries and Wages—Permanent	$ 49,764.21	$ 51,679.79
Salaries and Wages—Temporary	590.00	878.25
Supplies and Materials	5,664.66	5,850.61
Postage, Tel., Tel., and Exp.	3,000.00	4,000.00
Travel Expense	4,557.29	4,569.61
Printing and Binding	44,843.64	48,250.00
Operation of Equipment	339.07	442.01
Repairs and Alterations	531.39	724.48
General Expense	4,255.30	3,876.17
Motor Vehicle Exchange	1,500.00	—
Equipment	792.04	1,015.10
Motion Pictures	2,249.45	2,082.91
TOTAL	$ 118,087.05	$ 123,398.93
V. FISH MANAGEMENT ADMINISTRATION		
Salaries and Wages—Permanent	$ 27,054.00	$ 29,214.00
Salaries and Wages—Temporary	405.63	1,247.00
Supplies and Materials	318.42-CR	2,667.56
Postage, Tel., Tel., and Exp.	900.00	900.00
Travel Expense	1,830.98	2,546.89
Printing and Binding	—	208.00
Operation of Equipment	614.25	1,022.29
Repairs and Alterations	63.87	137.50
General Expense	552.50	1,560.85
Motor Vehicle Exchange	—	1,373.00
Equipment	159.59	355.35
TOTAL	$ 31,262.40	$ 41,232.44
VI. WAYNESVILLE HATCHERY		
Salaries and Wages—Permanent	$ 16,500.00	$ 19,515.00
Salaries and Wages—Temporary	500.00	273.13
Supplies and Materials	8,893.44	7,052.54
Postage, Tel., Tel., and Exp.	150.00	150.00
Travel Expense	709.18	772.94
Operation of Equipment	700.00	892.68
Power and Lights	222.21	159.15
Repairs and Alterations	2,300.25	221.45
General Expense	2.80	50.00
Motor Vehicle Exchange	977.94	
Equipment	51.00	299.57
TOTAL	$ 31,006.82	$ 29,386.46
VII. MARION HATCHERY		
Salaries and Wages—Permanent	$ 22,989.61	$ 25,320.00
Salaries and Wages—Temporary	—	488.00
Supplies and Materials	11,085.65	9,282.56
Postage, Tel., Tel., and Exp.	350.00	350.00
Travel Expense	835.40	540.77
Operation of Equipment	993.33	1,099.22
Power and Lights	275.15	296.47
Repairs and Alterations	2,633.67	4,174.92
Motor Vehicle Exchange		2,681.00
Equipment	152.46	316.23
TOTAL	$ 39,315.27	$ 44,549.17
VIII. FAYETTEVILLE HATCHERY		
Salaries and Wages—Permanent	$ 15,096.00	$ 15,541.02
Supplies and Materials	9,052.07	4,226.24
Postage, Tel., Tel., and Exp.	350.00	349.22
Travel Expense	712.26	704.29
Operation of Equipment	932.31	915.71

	1966-67	1967-68

XXVI. COOPERATIVE RESEARCH

General Expense	$ 5,696.36	$ 10,133.85

XXVII. STATEWIDE WATERFOWL MANAGEMENT

	1966-67	1967-68
Salaries and Wages—Permanent	$ 8,424.00	$ 8,058.37
Salaries and Wages—Temporary	5,971.60	3,598.80
Supplies and Materials	2,904.37	1,182.30
Postage, Tel., Tel., and Exp.	200.00	200.00
Travel Expense	1,144.89	1,347.41
Operation of Equipment	1,148.60	977.24
Repairs and Alterations	421.73	—
General Expense	414.07	816.06
Motor Vehicle Exchange	1,528.03	
Equipment	3,881.22	4,828.49
TOTAL	$ 26,038.51	$ 21,008.67

XXVIII. DATA PROCESSING UNIT

Salaries and Wages—Permanent	$ 30,999.11	$ 35,677.09
Supplies and Materials	2,396.68	1,604.87
General Expense	15,484.52	19,445.46
Equipment	115.00	1,159.97
TOTAL	$ 48,995.31	$ 57,887.39

XXX. FISHERIES MANAGEMENT COORDINATION

Salaries and Wages—Permanent	$ 15,060.00	$ 16,305.81
Salaries and Wages—Temporary	132.00	188.80
Supplies and Materials	156.31	159.16
Postage, Tel., Tel., and Exp.	275.00	275.00
Travel Expense	386.38	342.40
Repairs and Alterations	29.92	52.94
General Expense	—	355.10
Equipment	203.66	20.71
TOTAL	$ 16,243.27	$ 17,699.92

XXXI. FISHERIES SURVEY AND MANAGEMENT

Salaries and Wages—Permanent	$ 90,676.50	$ 97,096.97
Salaries and Wages—Temporary	24,850.42	24,931.21
Supplies and Materials	6,329.56	5,627.22
Postage, Tel., Tel., and Exp.	1,360.00	4,060.00
Travel Expense	6,875.51	6,714.41
Printing and Binding	29.36	2,760.00
Operation of Equipment	8,009.09	8,234.53
Power and Lights	59.10	50.60
Repairs and Alterations	100.26	175.83
General Expense	1,455.00	1,560.00
Motor Vehicle Exchange	4,119.00	4,119.00
Equipment	5,758.29	5,463.53
TOTAL	$ 148,622.09	$ 160,793.30

XXXII. LAKE MANAGEMENT STUDY

Salaries and Wages—Temporary	$ 2,115.35	$ 1,204.22
Supplies and Materials	392.79	40.20
Postage, Tel., Tel., and Exp.	75.00	75.00
Operation of Equipment	3.63	
Power and Lights	52.65	50.14
Repairs and Alterations	32.96	—
Equipment	303.14	
TOTAL	$ 2,975.52	$ 1,369.56

XXXIII. POWER RESERVOIR MANAGEMENT

Salaries and Wages—Permanent	$ 2,970.15	$ 5,814.00
Salaries and Wages—Temporary	1,145.00	1,480.15
Supplies and Materials	272.30	289.65
Postage. Tel., Tel., and Exp.	100.00	100.00
Travel Expense	344.60	146.47
Operation of Equipment	422.02	401.32
Power and Lights	56.00	—
General Expense	87.00	105.00
Motor Vehicle Exchange	1,375.00	
Equipment	478.83	524.99
TOTAL	$ 7,250.90	$ 8,861.58

XXXIV. RIVERS AND STREAMS PROJECT

Salaries and Wages—Permanent	$ 15,378.00	$ 12,595.33
Salaries and Wages—Temporary	987.50	937.00
Supplies and Materials	1,309.18	1,352.39
Postage, Tel., Tel., and Exp.	200.00	200.00
Travel Expense	743.47	1,003.04
Operation of Equipment	1,049.95	666.13
Power and Lights	1.30	6.00
Repairs and Alterations	7.50	138.60
Motor Vehicle Exchange	1,373.00	1,373.00
Equipment	767.18	790.26
TOTAL	$ 21,817.08	$ 19,061.75

CODE 26741 — WILDLIFE BUDGET (Continued)

	1966-67	1967-68
XXXV. ENGINEERING		
Salaries and Wages—Permanent	$ 44,453.00	$ 48,930.00
Salaries and Wages—Temporary	14,459.00	14,355.50
Supplies and Materials	918.25	947.82
Postage, Tel., Tel., and Exp.	950.00	950.00
Travel Expense	12,552.25	10,516.17
Operation of Equipment	14,566.38	16,733.27
General Expense	434.52	564.32
Motor Vehicle Exchange	22,162.78	20,661.96
Equipment	33,792.20	46,030.53
TOTAL	$ 144,288.38	$ 159,689.57
XXXVI. ACQUISITION AND DEVELOPMENT OF		
LANDS AND WATERS—ENGINEERING		
Salaries and Wages—Temporary	$ 12,979.50	$ 11,485.81
Supplies and Materials	3,304.98	2,395.93
Operation of Equipment	19,766.48	15,776.05
Repairs and Alterations	69,990.58	70,260.03
General Expense	1,078.38	770.98
WILDLIFE PROTECTION		
Repairs and Alterations	$ 19,107.95	$ 19,326.00
General Expense	16,888.38	16,865.54
EDUCATION		
Printing and Binding	$ 57,474.00	$ 57,474.00
TOTAL	$ 200,590.25	$ 194,354.34
XXXVII. MISCELLANEOUS RECEIPTS		
Workmen's Compensation	$ 10,291.20	$ 7,272.73
State Retirement	139,702.31	144,035.96
Insurance and Bonding	11,255.92	11,386.26
Counties Share Timber Receipts	22,584.37	23,582.72
General Expense	6,109.79	11,287.00
Bus Transportation	600.00	549.60
Social Security	81,569.30	91,920.86
Radio Communications	10,720.22	10,938.90
TOTAL	$ 282,833.11	$ 300,974.03
XL. U. S. FOREST SERVICE		
Payment of U. S. Forest Service		
Part of Receipts	$ 75,000.00	$ 75,000.00
XLII. WELDON HATCHERY		
Salaries and Wages—Temporary	$ —	$ 40.00
Supplies and Materials	2,706.12	660.29
Postage, Tel., Tel. and Exp.	100.00	100.00
Travel Expense	108.65	233.05
Power and Lights	90.65	90.30
Repairs and Alterations	245.77	114.84
Equipment	—	28.00
TOTAL	$ 3,251.19	$ 1,266.48
XLIII. CAPITAL IMPROVEMENT FUND		
Transfer to Capital		
Improvement Fund	—	$ 376,126.20
REFUND OF RECEIPTS AND		
EXPENSES	$ 168,414.83	$ 98,863.75
TOTAL EXPENDITURES	$3,759,571.05	$4,459,677.90

RECEIPTS

	1966-67	1967-68
Hunting and Fishing Licenses	$2,982,580.55	$3,040,189.96
Management Area Receipts	125,156.80	158,904.66
Federal Cooperation	521,941.50	526,634.54
Miscellaneous Receipts	13,163.01	5,336.48
Sale of Surplus Property	36,150.76	33,683.94
Sale of Publications	44,103.95	49,529.33
Rent of State Property	9,223.30	9,035.30
Caswell Area Receipts	7,827.50	27,994.98
Reimbursement from		
Motorboat Fund	91,434.00	175,194.00
Federal Reimbursement from		
Capital Improvement	39,233.25	—
Receipts from Department of		
Motor Vehicles for 4th Floor of		
Motor Vehicles Building	—	200,000.00
Refund of Receipts and Expenses	168,414.83	98,863.75
TOTAL	$4,039,229.45	$4,325,366.94

SUMMARY OF COMMISSION RECEIPTS
FOR TEN YEAR PERIOD 1958-59 - 1967-68

The following table gives a picture of the growth in Wildlife Revenue during the past ten years.

Fiscal Year	Receipts
1958-59	$2,510,835.93
1959-60	2,567,586.85
1960-61	2,707,684.24
1961-62	2,977,927.24
1962-63	3,145,216.21
1963-64	3,213,184.84
1964-65	3,446,620.80
1965-66	3,823,857.59
1966-67	4,039,229.00
1967-68	4,325,366.00

HUNTING LICENSES AND PERMITS

	1966-67		1967-68	
	Number	Value	Number	Value
Resident Combination Hunting and Fishing Licenses	171,606	$1,029,636.00	180,030	$1,080,180.00
Resident County Hunting Licenses	138,711	208,066.50	128,857	193,285.50
Resident State Hunting Licenses	119,683	478,732.00	123,943	495,772.00
Nonresident State Hunting Licenses	5,204	101,478.00	5,408	105,417.00
Nonresident 6-Day Hunting Licenses	2,582	40,021.00	2,550	39,525.00
Resident State Trapping Licenses	1,318	3,954.00	910	2,730.00
Hunting Guide's Licenses	262	1,310.00	255	1,275.00
Resident County Trapping Licenses	1,379	2,758.00	1,004	2,008.00
Controlled Shooting Preserve Licenses	105	525.00	111	555.00
Management Area Hunting Permits	55,756	232,310.50	48,870	203,052.50
Fur Dealer's Licenses	87	1,361.00	67	1,046.00
Nonresident Landowner's Licenses	1	5.00	8	40.00
Nonresident Trapping Licenses	3	75.00	3	75.00
Lake Mattamuskeet Hunting Permits	2,900	5,800.00	2,067	4,134.00
Bush Blind Licenses	275	343.75	279	348.75
Waterfowl Blind Licenses	388	388.00	424	424.00
Shooting Point Licenses	224	2,016.00	232	2,088.00
TOTAL	500,484	$2,108,779.75	495,016	$2,131,955.75

Hunting Licenses are sold for fiscal year, and fishing licenses are sold for the calendar year. Since combination hunting and fishing licenses are on a fiscal year basis, the total income derived is included in the hunting license table.

The comparative figures shown above are for the license years and cannot be added together to obtain a total revenue figure for any fiscal year. The correct revenue figures for the fiscal years 1966-67 and 1967-68 are shown in the budget.

FISHING LICENSES AND PERMITS

	1966		1967	
	Number	Value	Number	Value
Resident State Daily Fishing Licenses	108,013	$ 81,009.75	108,853	$ 81,639.75
Resident County Fishing Licenses	32,310	48,465.00	32,919	49,378.50
Resident State Fishing Licenses	102,570	410,280.00	115,372	461,488.00
Nonresident State Daily Fishing Licenses	29,194	43,791.00	28,217	42,325.50
Nonresident State 5-Day Fishing Licenses	9,748	34,118.00	9,888	34,608.00
Nonresident State Fishing Licenses	5,439	43,512.00	5,998	47,984.00
Resident Special Trout Fishing Licenses	64,883	64,883.00	59,601	59,601.00
Nonresident Special Trout Fishing Licenses	3,042	9,126.00	2,886	8,658.00
Resident Special Rough Fish Licenses	5,994	8,991.00	6,058	9,087.00
Resident Special Shad-Herring-Mullet Licenses	8,341	12,511.50	7,796	11,694.00
Nonresident Special Rough Fish Licenses	31	93.00	16	48.00
Nonresident Special Shad-Herring-Mullet Licenses	60	180.00	41	123.00
Lake Rim Daily Permit	761	761.00	839	839.00
Lake Rim Special Permit	20	300.00	28	420.00
Management Area Special Daily Permits	26,966	40,449.00	25,220	37,830.00
Resident State Bow and Arrow Fishing Licenses	499	748.50	643	964.50
Nonresident Bow and Arrow Fishing Licenses	1	3.00	1	3.00
Game Fish Propagation Licenses	15	75.00	15	75.00
Non-Game Fish Propagation Licenses	14	7.00	14	7.00
TOTAL	397,901	$799,303.75	404,405	$846,773.25

Wildlife Program

REGULATION

EDUCATION

ENFORCEMENT

RESEARCH

MANAGEMENT

LITHO BY THE GRAPHIC PRESS, INC., RALEIGH, N. C.

Wildlife

IN NORTH CAROLINA

25 CENTS / FEBRUARY 1969

February's Cloak

February's light, transparent cloak
Donned within the night
Clings tightly, shines brightly
Then crumples in the sun.

Nell Lewis

STATE OF NORTH CAROLINA
ROBERT W. SCOTT
GOVERNOR

NORTH CAROLINA
WILDLIFE RESOURCES COMMISSION

ORVILLE E. WOODHOUSE, CHM. _ _ GRANDY
JAY WAGGONER, V. CHM. _ _ _ _ GRAHAM
DR. JOE M. ANDERSON, SEC'Y _ _ NEW BERN
JAMES A. BRIDGER _ _ _ _ _ BLADENBORO
HUGH G. CHATHAM _ _ _ _ _ _ ELKIN
JAMES A. CONNELLY _ _ _ _ MORGANTON
J. HOLT EVANS _ _ _ _ _ _ _ ENFIELD
T. N. MASSIE _ _ _ _ _ _ _ _ SYLVA
ROBERT G. SANDERS _ _ _ _ CHARLOTTE

CLYDE P. PATTON
EXECUTIVE DIRECTOR

EUGENE E. SCHWALL
ASSISTANT DIRECTOR

DIVISION CHIEFS
ROD AMUNDSON _ _ _ _ _ _ EDUCATION
FRANK B. BARICK _ _ _ _ _ _ _ GAME
J. HARRY CORNELL _ _ _ INLAND FISHERIES
ROBERT B. HAZEL _ _ _ _ _ PROTECTION
J. THOMAS WILLIAMS _ FINANCE-PERSONNEL
C. FLOYD WILLIAMSON _ _ _ ENGINEERING

WILDLIFE IN NORTH CAROLINA recognizes the need for close cooperation between State and Federal conservation agencies and the people who hunt and fish—to bring about a restoration of our renewable resources. The Editor gratefully receives for publication news items, articles, and photographs dealing with the North Carolina out-of-doors, but reserves the right to reject materials submitted. Full credit is given for all materials published.

WILDLIFE IN NORTH CAROLINA is published at the Wildlife Resources Commission offices, Motor Vehicles Building, 1100 New Bern Ave., Raleigh, N. C. 27601.

Second class postage paid at Raleigh, North Carolina 27602.

SUBSCRIPTIONS—Fifty cents per year, one dollar for two years. Make remittances payable to WILDLIFE RESOURCES COMMISSION. Any employee of the Wildlife Resources Commission may accept subscriptions, or they may be forwarded to Post Office Box 2919, Raleigh, N. C. 27602. Stamps cannot be accepted.

Wildlife circulation this issue, 122,840.

IN NORTH CAROLINA

The official publication of the NORTH CAROLINA WILDLIFE RESOURCES COMMISSION, Raleigh 27602. A monthly magazine devoted to the protection and restoration of our wildlife resources and to the improvement of hunting and fishing in North Carolina.

VOL. XXXIII, NO. 2   FEBRUARY, 1969

IN THIS ISSUE

EDITORIAL STAFF

ROD AMUNDSON _ _ _ _ _ _ _ _ _ EDITOR
DUANE RAVER _ _ _ _ MANAGING EDITOR
LUTHER PARTIN _ _ _ WRITER-PHOTOGRAPHER
JOHN PARKER _ _ _ _ _ OUTDOOR SAFETY
TOM JACKSON _ _ _ WRITER-PHOTOGRAPHER

The canvasback holds a place of considerable honor among waterfowl hunters. They are handsome birds although many ducks outshine them in coloration. Soon this regal bird will be heading back to the nesting grounds of west-central Canada and the border states of the U. S. west of Minnesota. The key to numbers returning next fall will be water conditions during the nesting season this spring.

PHOTO BY TOM JACKSON

PHOTO BY MIKE GADDIS

Here are two old, top quality double-barrelled shotguns. Top,
Parker Brother's "V" grade; bottom, Lefever "E" grade.

Seasoned with Time

by Mike Gaddis

TO be as young in years as I am, I suppose I'm really quite antiquated in tastes when it comes to hunting and fishing. At least this has been suggested to me on occasion.

For example, I shoot a side-by-side double of early American vintage, hunt an English setter, am a bait-caster by preference, and maintain a tackle collection which includes several hundred wooden casting plugs, long dropped from manufacturers' catalogs.

Most will agree that this is rare in these days when automatics and over-and-unders are in vogue, when pointers are the overwhelming champions of the bird hunting set, when spinning dominates the angling field, and when tenite mini-lures and ultraspinners set the tackle pace.

I do not prefer the older tools of the trade because their use increases the amount of game I take or the number of fish I catch, although their performance can probably be equated to most of the gear being manufactured today. Rather, equipment and schools of thought seasoned with time carry a quality and quiet dignity which seems to have been shelved in recent years.

One afternoon last fall I was sitting against a tree picking a limit of doves when a casual acquaintance walked up. Expressing some interest in the shotgun across my lap, he asked what it was. With noticeable pride I replied, "Parker."

"What?" he asked. The puzzled look on his face reflected his bewilderment.

I then took great pains in explaining that Parker Brothers was one of the finest makers of the vintage American double-gun, and that its guns, although no longer being produced, were noted for quality and handwork.

His next question concerned cost, and I suggested that this would probably compare favorably with the purchase price of a brace of started pointer pups from a good bloodline.

Grunting disdain he eyed his contemporary automatic, stroked its stamped, impressed checkering and said, "Hummph! Bet I can kill just as many birds with this as you can with that old thing!"

His reaction was not uncommon. Rather it was quite typical. And he was probably right.

But herein lies the tragic loss of dignity both hunting and fishing have suffered. Too many contemporary sportsmen ask only how-to, where-to, how-quick, and how-much. In short, they have only a passing acquaintance, not familiarity with their sport.

If meat is the only concern of either hunter or fisherman, he will profit more from a visit to the butcher shop or the fish market. It will save a lot of frustration. Any serious sportsman who has been afield enough to be worthy of the name, knows that the number of unproductive trips outweigh productive ones. However, we remember what we wish to remember, so the good trips stand out. Yet, preservation of quality in hunting and fishing requires more than passing acquaintance in order to sustain the fortitude necessary to produce successful trips.

To me nothing more engenders this type of fortitude during slump periods than studying, owning, using and appreciating vintage hunting gear and fishing tackle.

It is quite satisfying to occasionally turn back a few pages and examine the fruits of an earlier day when the word "sportsman" defined a code of ethics and not merely a participant, when quality was

The author examines one of his prized shotguns, a Parker which exemplifies pride of workmanship. Right, fishing tackle out of the past, an early-day casting reel, and a Heddon "Dowagiac" five-hooked plug.

a byword and when labor costs allowed the craftsmanship necessary to sustain it. Nowhere is this quality better exemplified than in the guns and tackle of yesteryear.

In sporting guns, the period of time between the late 1870's and the depression years was the era of the side-by-side double. Interest in wingshooting as a sport rather than for the market was increasing toward the end of the nineteenth century, the war was over, and gunsmiths and hardware firms rallied to produce the required arms. Advanced thinking and technology had allowed the development of a major breakthrough, the breech-loader. The next 50 years saw the rise and ebb of the ultimate in the American shotgun.

The prominent names during this period were Parker Brothers, A. H. Fox, Ithaca, Lefever, Baker, and L. C. Smith. These six firms represented the best and provided a firearm heritage which will probably never be matched again.

Each firm, in an attempt to please its customers and to provide quality arms for sportsmen within a wide economic range, offered a number of grades, or different qualities, in its particular line of guns. Grades were in some cases designated by name such as Trojan and Sterlingworth, but usually by alphabetical or numerical means such as the Lefever E, D, C, B, A, and AA grades in ascending sequence. The quality of the gun and thus the grade were determined by such factors as the composition and quality of the steel used in its production, the quality of the wood used in its stock, the fineness and design of the checkering pattern, and the extent and artistry of the engraving.

The time required to produce the higher grade guns was measured in months. Even the less expensive field grades required several weeks of handwork. Notable examples of the latter are the Parker Trojan, the Fox Sterlingworth and the Lefever Durston Special.

Although they have become prominent in recent years, it was during this earlier period that refinements such as the ventilated rib, single-selective trigger, beavertail forearm, selective automatic ejectors and skeletal steel buttplace came into being.

From the early 1800's on, developments and refinements were also occuring at a rapid rate in fishing tackle.

Around 1850, George Snyder, a Kentucky watchmaker and silversmith, developed the first bait casting reel—so named because it was first used to cast live bait. Later, when the wooden minnow arrived on the scene, it was initially called a "bait," and later a "plug," and sometimes "lure."

Early reels of reputable make to follow Snyder's included the Meek, the Milam, and the Talbot. The Talbot reel probably best set forth the standard of excellence for the times. It was made of German silver with a balance crank, boasted a spool of aluminum, and ends which turned in corundum jewels.

Only a few of the reels were commercially available at that time and in their early years the makers built reels mostly for their friends. Some of these reels were quite individualized. Dr. James Henshall in his "Book of the Black Bass" describes a reel made by B. F. Meek in 1846 for a New Orleans artist which included in its mechanism a bell-click (drag). The bell was tuned in thirds and this produced chime-like tones when line was being pulled from the reel with the click-drag engaged. This allowed the owner to truly listen to the "music of the reel" while playing a fish.

Terminal tackle was also in a transitory state at this time. When treble-hooked lures first came into being, their use was outlawed by some states as "unsportsmanlike," because it was feared that too many fish would be killed. In addition to signifying mortality, the word "kill" was somewhat synonymous with "catch" in fishermen's vernacular.

When it was later shown that the use of treble hooks was, after all, sporting, and made no appreciable difference in the number of fish caught or in the mortality rate, several companies apparently infatuated with the idea brought out wooden min-

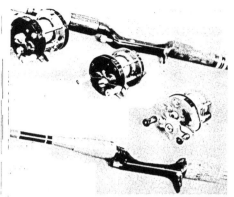

Casting reels like these three modern, free-spool models, are helping return bait casting to popularity. When matched with suitable rods, they will handle very light lures. Right, a portion of the author's old lure and tackle collection.

nows richly endowed with trebles. Examples were the Heddon "Dowagiac" minnow and the Pfleuger "Neverfail." Each of these plugs were bespangled with a total of five trebles!

As spinning tackle became popular, bait casting fell by the wayside somewhat. However, it is now making a good comeback, probably due to reels such as the Ambassadeur 5000 and 5000C, and Pfleuger's new Supreme. These are free spool reels with greatly reduced backlash potential which allows an angler efficient casting flexibility over approximately the same range of lure weights as does spinning tackle.

But during the time bait casting was backsliding and spinning was the watchword, casting lures naturally followed suit. A great many favorites of seasoned fishermen were dropped by manufacturers during this period. They were too large and too heavy, by spinning standards, to make the change.

With spinning came the craze for ultra-light and manufacturers switched from large wood to small plastic lures. This sounded the death knell for more old casting favorites and discriminating anglers bemoaned their passing.

Three things are readily outstanding about these "obsolete" lures: they were beautifully balanced, their hardware was made to hold fish (unlike many contemporary successors), and they were made of wood. The arguments for wood over plastic, and vice-versa, go on and on, but to any man who still takes time to admire a lure before asking it to go to work for him, and who has experimented with the two, I would venture that wood takes top place.

This seems substantiated, in part, by the fact that two of the largest most reputable manufacturers of fishing tackle still offer wooden plugs. The Creek Chub Bait Company of Garrett, Indiana, offers their famous Pikie series of lures in wood on option and Heddon of Dowagiac, Michigan, has brought back some of their most famous plugs in wood in their "Classics" series, such as the Zarragossa, Joint-Vamp, and Basser.

Old books as well as the older tools of the trade can be a lasting source of enjoyment. You will find the writing style quite refreshing in books by Henshall, Havilah Babcock, Hart Stilwell, Archibald Rutledge, Robert Ruark, and others of the same school. These men have achieved immortality by their ability to weave a wealth of hunting and fishing advice into enjoyable stories. They can be read and re-read with lasting appreciation. As with anything of quality, age only improves its value. I do not find this quality in today's "how-to" articles.

A. J. McClane, fishing editor of *Field and Stream* magazine, and I were sitting in his home one day admiring some of my old plug collection. After some discussion he remarked that there was nothing really new in hunting and fishing, speaking of present day "innovations." The veracity of this statement is brought home when one studies their past history. The only things which seem to have changed are quality and atmosphere.

At any rate, the next time you hit a slump take a little time to learn more about your hunting and fishing heritage. Drop back a few years; it fills the void very nicely, and rounds out the whole in which the acts of hunting and fishing are really only a part. ◆

During fall and winter, trawlers catch flounder in shoal areas mainly off Oregon and Ocracoke Inlets. Trawls are fished continuously, 24 hours a day and hauled to the surface every 1½ to 3 hours to empty the catch. Flounder boats usually remain at sea for 3 to 6 days depending on weather and how good the catch is.

An average trawl net has a mouth spread of 60 feet. When a vessel uses two nets, the trawls are smaller. Flounder trawls, unlike shrimp trawls, are usually made of 5-inch stretch mesh in the tail or cod end. The larger mesh size is more selective in catching mostly flounder and other large fish and allowing smaller fish to escape.

A pound net is another good flounder catcher. It consists of a leader and a pound. The leader is stretched out from shore and supported upright in the water by wooden stakes. The leader ends at an opening into the pound or trap. Fish swim along the leader, enter the funnel-like entrance of the pound, and thus are trapped. Several pound nets are sometimes set in a continuous row so the entire distance covered by a series of leads and pounds

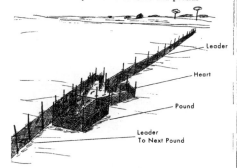

Leader

Heart

Pound

Leader
To Next Pound

The pound net is a type of commercial fish trap used for many types of salt-water fishes. The fish follow the leader nets into the heart or funnel, and thus into the pound. The result is a basket of flounder like this. Note the white undersides of these fish ready for processing.

These commercial fishermen sort a catch from a trawl. At least one of the fish is of bragging size. Sports fishermen, too, (right) enjoy the flounder in sounds, estuaries, and inlets. It is a hard fighter and is excellent eating.

may be nearly a mile. Actual setting and arrangement of the gear varies among fishermen. Pound nets are used mainly during fall when chilled sound waters initiate fish movement toward inlets.

Commercial fishermen find money, and sport fishermen sport while gigging or spearing flounder at night under the brightness of underwater spot lights attached to small boats. During the dark hours, flounder move near shore and lie motionless on the bottom, well camouflaged, waiting for food. Often, when the bottom is soft, flounder will be partially buried or "bedded down." Fishermen detect bedded flounder by the barely visible outline and partially exposed head and eyes. Rising tide is considered the best time for gigging. Flounder seem to go offshore to deeper water on falling tide.

From 1960 to 1964 the yearly commercial flounder harvest ranged from 1,236,000 to 2,450,000 pounds. In 1965 the catch jumped to 4,721,000 pounds, the largest from 1957 to 1967, and had a dockside value of $951,000. The 1967 catch was 4,330,000 pounds.

Catching Flounder for Fun

Substantial numbers of flounder are taken by sportsmen with hook and-line and with spears fishing at night. In New Jersey a large number of flounder were tagged and released back into the water. Forty percent of those released were later recaptured by sportsmen. Sportsmen and summer vacationists contribute heavily to the overall harvest, but precise North Carolina sport fishing records are not available for comparison with commercial catches.

Flounder Research

What lies ahead for the North Carolina flounder? Assuming history repeats itself, future demands for flounder will continue to be high. To evaluate and maintain this resource, much more research is necessary. Present information is useful in describ-

Of the many facets of the flounder that need further study, migration is of great importance. This eight-incher has been tagged and when it is released, it is hoped that the tag return will shed light on its movements.

ing the fishery, but more information on movements and development of the young, migration patterns, mortality estimates, and accurate fishery statistics on individual species must be obtained.

Wide range research is important because flounder know no state lines. Perhaps a flounder caught in New Jersey is actually a North Carolina migrant. Facts learned by biologists along the Atlantic seaboard are important, therefore, in managing the flat ones in North Carolina.

An important phase of the research is a tagging program. Flounder as small as three inches long have been tagged by attaching small plastic tags to their backs with steel wire. Commercial and sport fishermen can help by promptly returning any tag they find. Only with the cooperation of fishermen can biologists succeed in their tagging program. A reward will be paid for each tag returned to the U..S. Bureau of Commercial Fisheries, Woods Hole, Massachusetts. Fishermen finding tags should send them immediately.

Easy to Identify

Although there are several species of flatfish, in North Carolina only three species of flounder are abundant and taken by fishermen—the summer flounder, the southern flounder, and the gulf flounder. Summer and southern flounder are the most abundant.

The top side of a flounder can be brown, gray, or olive and have varying patterns of pale or dark spots, depending on the species. The bottom side is always white or pale. They can change their topside body coloration to match different colored bottoms on which they lie as a method of camouflage for protection from their enemies. The body is pan-shaped and they have both eyes on one side of their head.

Normal Baby Flounder Changes

Spawning occurs offshore during late fall, winter, and early spring, depending on locality and species. Females are capable of producing several thousand eggs in a single season. The eggs are buoyant and are fertilized externally. Both eggs and very young fish are at the mercy of ocean currents. Young flounder migrate inshore and use the estuaries as nursery grounds.

When a young flounder first hatches, it has an eye on each side of its head and swims in a normal fashion, like a gold fish. But as it grows, one eye *migrates* over the top of the head and situates itself close to the other eye by the time the fish is one inch long. The young fish has then turned completely on its side and now has both eyes on the "top" side. In this flat position it changes swimming style and adapts an undulating swimming motion (forming a continuous series of "s" shapes with its body as it swims).

Flounder feed on a variety of small sealife including shrimp, small fish, and crabs. Being strong and active swimmers, they are effective predators.

Flounder Move About

Flounder are found in North Carolina coastal shallows in the spring and summer, and mostly in deeper offshore waters during fall and winter. Tagging studies, both inshore and offshore, have shown seasonal patterns of migration from shallow inshore waters to deeper offshore waters. Summer flounder stay in estuaries for about the first year of life, and the southern flounder remains there for the first two to three years of life. ✦

This is the first of a series of articles about salt water fish of our coast that are of interest to both the commercial and sports fisherman. This article is available in booklet form from the Research and Development Section, Division of Commercial and Sports Fisheries, Morehead City, N. C. 28557.

The Day The Tree Fell

by Grace S. Draper

It wasn't a very large hickory tree, but it had stood in our yard — it had belonged to us, we thought. But the wind during that August storm twisted it and tortured it until it could endure no longer; and so it crashed to the ground. Luckily, for us, it fell across our yard, not toward the house.

Not until it fell did we know forces were at work inside its trunk that had caused deterioration in a large part of it. This was the home of a busy family of carpenter ants, who hastily removed themselves and all their belongings after the tree fell! The next morning after the storm, a pair of Carolina wrens was observed busily working through the tree's branches, occasionally stopping to perch astride a twig and jauntily sing a wren duet; we noted these wrens quickly found a family of worms, also busily engaged in their own work (and Nature's way) of breaking down an old, deserted squirrel's nest, also in the tree. The squirrels will miss the many nuts usually collected and cached away each year from the tree. Just as the birds will miss sitting in its branches each spring and summer morning, and welcoming the sun with their songs; we will miss their songs from the tree, too.

So our tree really did not belong to us alone. When it lived, it was a haven for birds and squirrels, and ants and other insects; it furnished shade in the summer, and a golden symphony of color in the fall when the leaves turned; its nuts were food for little animals, such as the squirrels and chipmunks. If our tree had fallen in the forest, many of Nature's helpers (such as bacteria and various types of fungi) would have set to work decomposing the broken trunk until it became reduced to rich soil, beneath fallen leaves to nurture other seeds that might grow into trees and other plants from the woodland floor, as well as to furnish homes and haven for assorted small members of the animal kingdom. And a marvelous cycle of Nature would have begun all over again.

As we built a crackling, fragrant, hickory-smoke fire in our fireplace that February night, with logs from our fallen tree, we remembered these things.

9

Ownership of Wildlife

This statement by Assistant Director Schwall was presented before the U. S. Senate Committee on Commerce, December 13, 1968, on behalf of the Wildlife Resources Commission.

MR. Chairman and members of the Committee, my name is Eugene Schwall. I am Assistant Director of the North Carolina Wildlife Resources Commission. I am appearing on behalf of Executive Director Clyde Patton, the Wildlife Resources Commission, and more than one and one-half million North Carolina sportsmen.

The North Carolina Wildlife Resources Commission is the lawfully constituted a g e n c y charged with the responsibility for the management, protection, and regulation of the State's wildlife resources. In accomplishing these responsibilities, the Commission responds to the public interest on the State level. It functions in a democratic manner, holds public hearings on wildlife matters throughout the State, and represents and protects the interests of sportsmen and conservationists.

We are firmly convinced that historically, legally, and morally the State of North Carolina has the right and the responsibility to conserve, manage, and regulate the taking of fish and resident wildlife on public and private lands and waters within the territorial boundaries of the State. We believe that this right and responsibility supersedes and transcends that of the Federal Government.

The basic concept accepted in this country since colonial times holds that ownership of wildlife is separate and distinct from ownership of land. This concept has been judicially recognized, and it now appears only proper that it be legislatively recognized as well. North Carolina, being one of the thirteen original sovereign States, at no time ceded any of its lands to the Continental Congress. Federal lands in the State have been acquired by purchase or gift from private landowners and traditionally have been subject to State wildlife laws. We contend that the Federal Government occupies a position in the State no different from that of any other landowner and therefore is entitled to no wider privileges respecting ownership of wildlife living upon its holdings. For many years, State and Federal agencies have worked hand in hand in accordance with this accepted concept. Basically, we wish to continue that practice.

The United States Constitution reserves to the States and the people therein all rights not specifically granted to the Federal Government. There is nothing in that document, nor in its amendments, that would convey responsibility for ownership, conservation, or management of wildlife to the Federal Government. The United States Supreme Court has upheld the concept divorcing wildlife ownership from land ownership in rulings that all species of resident wildlife are held in trust by the individual States for the people. This long-time State responsibility has been challenged recently by action of the Department of the Interior on the premise that, because the Federal Government owns land, it also owns the wildlife on this land. This challenge has caused the States to seek clarification and confirmation of the States' historic and legal rights to manage their wildlife in order to accomplish a firm and complete resolution of the present dispute between the States and the Federal Government in this matter.

Morally, there is no acceptable alternative to State ownership of resident wildlife. If its management and regulation were the sole perogative of the landowner, extermination of the wildlife resource in many places would be inevitable. Each l a n d o w n e r would hasten to harvest *his* crop before it moved across the property boundary line and was taken by his neighbor. The non-landowner, comprising an increasing percentage of the population, would have no place to hunt and the State would be without jurisdiction to license or otherwise control hunters and fishermen. Ultimately, this could result in the virtual extermination of resident wildlife in many areas. It could also render State wildlife agencies legally, financially, and physically incapable of protecting, managing, and restoring wildlife so decimated to its natural productivity.

Recent action of the Department of the Interior, stemming from a solicitor's Opinion (71 I.D. 469), points up the need for clarification and reaffirmation of the historic right and responsibility of the States to manage and regulate fish and resident wildlife on public lands and waters within their boundaries. Subsequent modification of this action by the Secretary of the Interior is commendable. However, it does not cover all the issues involved on all Federal lands, nor is it a permanent solution. Any solution administratively dictated, no matter how satisfactory it might appear today, is subject to change tomorrow.

Congressional action is needed, and needed now, if State programs to conserve and protect wildlife are to be preserved. Unless something is done immediately, the revolutionary opinion released by the U. S. Department of the Interior could quickly lead the nation's landowners to follow this same concept and claim ownership of wildlife on their land. As we have already pointed out, this would pave the way for the eventual destruction of this valuable public resource.

We support the basic intent and purpose of the proposed legislation as embodied in S. 2951 and S. 3212 and strongly urge this Committee to act favorably on this legislation.

We are grateful for the opportunity you have given us to appear before you and express our views. ♦

NEW FISHING WATER!

This is another of the stories of fish management in action. This time it takes a rather different tack in opening up already-existing fishing water rather than improving them otherwise. Result: better fishing.

PHOTOS BY TOM JACKSON

by Mike Bowling
Fishery Biologist

THE Wildlife Resources Commission's Division of Inland Fisheries in cooperation with the Division of Engineering, has launched a navigation project that embodies a new concept in fisheries management. The "boat navigation improvement" project will complement an existing statewide project of providing fishermen with boating access areas and boat launching ramps.

Surveys by Commission personnel showed that many excellent fishing areas in eastern North Carolina streams were inaccessible to the boat fishermen, including some streams which h a v e Commission - provided launching ramps. Over the years, trees have died from old age, lightning, and disease and have fallen into and across the streams, thereby completely blocking boat passage. Hurricanes, wind, and ice storms, as well as the usual ravages of time, have added to the process, further choking the streams. All of this has been good for the fish by providing them with cover and a source of food, since food organisms often attach to and grow on the trunks and limbs

under the water. However, it is frustrating to the fishermen who cannot get to the better fishing areas or drift from one boat landing to another seeking productive fishing.

The purpose of the boat navigation improvement project is to open a channel to provide for the passage of small boats while maintaining maximum cover which is so valuable to the fish population. The year-round fish populations in smaller streams are almost directly related to the amount of food and cover present. Studies in the southeast have shown that complete stream clearance will nearly eliminate the normal fish populations. Cover is more valuable in Coastal Plain streams than in other geographic regions because many of these streams are quite acid, and this condition inhibits spawning to some extent. Therefore, in order to insure recruitment into the population, it is vital that most of the young survive and escape predation. The small fish must have cover to accomplish this.

The boat navigation improvement project is being accom-

plished by a three-man crew equipped with a specially designed boat, chain and bow saws, and a small, but powerful portable winch. Trees which block the stream are cut, if necessary, and pulled over to the side of the stream so that the main channel is cleared. Whenever possible, the fallen trees are placed so that they will also protect the stream banks. The logs help keep the banks from being undercut by the water which would also cause the banks to slough off and drop other trees into the stream. This usually occurs in bends of the stream, and the fallen trees are placed on the outside of the bend and against the bank.

Within three years time it is estimated that over 900 miles of presently inaccessible waters in some of our better Coastal Plain streams will be opened to boat fishermen. Additional benefits from this project include stream bank stabilization in bends, some flood protection by enhancing stream runoff, prevention of sand bar build-up in the main channel, and providing shelters for waterfowl and fur bearers between the stream bank and the main channel. ◆

12

This stream is almost completely choked with brush and trees. The problem is to open it up. The wide work boat brings specialized equipment to the spot and the task begins.

There is no alternative to getting in where the problem is! Here, Biologist Bowling and crew chief Charlie Brown, fish for a connection on an underwater log. Sometimes a power saw is helpful (below) in cutting the obstruction before removal.

The drag attached to the cable is reeled off and carried to the log or tree. Many obstructions removed have blocked the stream for years. The result is "new" fishing water.

A small, powerful portable winch is put into action, slowly hauling the obstacle from the stream. It takes a mighty big log or tree to stop this crew.

NO GOOSE HUNTING HERE!

by Steve Price

Yes, Virginia, there is a real Mother Goose.

Her name is Mrs. Hazel Ross Gaddy, and for nearly half of her 73 years she has been playing the role of Mother Goose on her Ansonville farm, better known as Lockhart Gaddy's Wild Goose Refuge.

The refuge isn't big—only 300 acres of farmland and a 10-acre pond—but the geese don't mind; for each year some 12,000 to 15,000 Canada geese and wild ducks come to the refuge to spend the winter. This is perhaps the only place in the United States where visitors can observe Canada geese at really close range, for the birds become so tame they will even eat out of a person's hand.

It all started in 1926, when Lockhart Gaddy, a long-time hunter and fisherman, bought five wild geeses, clipped their wings so they could not fly, and used them as hunting decoys. Live decoy hunting was prohibited a few years later, so the geese were allowed to use the Gaddy fish pond and roam over the farm.

In October, 1934, the pets called nine wild geese down to the water, and Gaddy started to feed them, a task he would perform every succeeding winter until his death 19 years later. The nine wild visitors stayed at the little pond until March, then left for their summer nesting grounds in northern Canada, near Hudson Bay.

The following fall, 14 wild geese came to the farm, and the next year the number increased again. Each winter the Gaddys patiently fed their wild visitors and cared for them, and after five years, the number of Canada geese wintering on their pond had increased to a hundred.

More years passed, and the number of birds grew. By now not only Canada geese were stopping over, but also snow, white-fronted and blue geese as well. Some stopped only for a short rest, but many remained for the winter, and friends and visitors to the farm soon began to call it Lockhart Gaddy's Wild Goose Refuge. Both the Federal and state wildlife agencies provided game wardens for the refuge during the hunting season. The agencies still provide wardens, but more are needed.

In the three-year period of 1944-46, U. S. Fish and Wildlife Service bands were put on many of the birds at the Gaddy refuge, while others were banded at the Jack Miner refuge in Kingsville, Ontario. Later identification proved many of the same birds were wintering at the Gaddy sanctuary each year.

Mrs. Gaddy is certain the geese recognize her, and she has given some of the birds names. They will run to her when feeding time comes, and she patiently gives handouts to all her feathered pets.

But in March the geese become restless and anxious to return to their northern homes. For several days before they actually leave the refuge, they fly nerv-

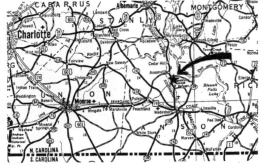

The Anson County goose refuge rates a spot on each North Carolina highway map. It is pinpointed here for easy location on your next visit.

ously over the little pond, as if testing the weather, or just getting directions. Then, about the 15th of the month, they begin the long journey back. Only the wounded or sick spend the summer at the refuge, and they usually nest near the pond. Wild Canada geese mate for life, and from four to nine eggs are laid each spring.

Feeding the winter visitors is a problem, and Lockhart Gaddy spent all summer preparing for it. Corn was planted and then harvested, so as to be ready for the earliest arrivals in October. Then in September, much of the farm was seeded in barley and oats to furnish browsing ground for the geese.

On February 19, 1953, Lockhart Gaddy died, as he was feeding the geese he had protected for so long. Today his grave lies in a little wooded knoll overlooking his pond and wild pets. Mrs. Gaddy has carried on the refuge work with the help of Robert Bennett, who loves the wild birds as much as she does.

The number of visitors coming to the now world-famous refuge increases each year. In 1967-68, some 20,000 persons came, and the guest book has signatures from residents of all 50 states as well as from several foreign countries. The refuge has been featured in dozens of newspapers and in numerous magazines, including *Life*.

To help defray the cost of hiring extra wardens during the winter, 25¢ admission is charged, and for an additional 10¢ the visitor may purchase a can of corn and feed the birds. The refuge is open daily from 8 a.m. to 5 p.m., October 1 to April 1, and is located just off highway U. S. 52 in Ansonville, N. C., 10 miles north of Wadesboro and 50 miles east of Charlotte.

Mrs. Gaddy lives in a small hilltop home overlooking the refuge and the pond. She waits eagerly for each October and the coming of her wild pets, and she welcomes them as if they were close friends, which they are.

So you see, Virginia, there really is a Mother Goose. ◆

Suitable food is available so that visitors may feed the waterfowl. Although Canada geese are the prime attraction, many species of ducks drop in also. Mrs. Gaddy is shown below with many of her friends at feeding time.

SKIPPER'S CORNER
by John R. Parker Jr.

SALES figures for recreational boating are released at the end of each year by the National Association of Engine and Boat Manufacturers' (NAEBM to those of you who care for boating jargon), and the Boating Industry Association (BIA). These figures, as you would expect, most always show sales growth. Figures released jointly by NAEBM and BIA in December show retail sales increased by five percent in 1968 hitting a new high of $3,150,000,000. Friends, that's a lot of row boats. And we might add it includes a few air-conditioned cruisers, marine power plants of all kinds, safety equipment, boat hooks, fishing chairs and everything right down to the 13-cent number you put on the bow of your registered boat.

You say, what has all this to do with me, a 15.4 foot (average length of outboard boat purchased in 1968) trihedral operator from Lake James? Well, if you purchased that average boat last year, you contributed to that huge figure just mentioned. That's right, part of all that took place here in the Old North State where boating is a big business as it is wherever there is suitable "habitat" (to borrow a game management expression); that is to say, wherever there is suitable boating water.

Since we are dropping figures, here is another one for you to stow away. The Outboard Boating Club of America estimates that over $57,000,000 marine fuel tax dollars are potentially available for boating programs across the nation annually. As you will recall, the upcoming legislature will decide whether or not tax monies paid on fuel used in boats will again be used for boating

safety in North Carolina. Continued financial aid by marine fuel funds is the hope of many.

If we can agree that boating is in fact pretty big, what has caused it? The following list of ideas is presented by the boating industry. See if you agree with their assessment as to why boating has grown from the keel laying stage of the early fifties to what it is today.

Factors Affecting the Growth of Boating

1. The creation of navigable water in landlocked areas by power and conservation projects.
2. Availability of quality stock boats and motors in quantity, in a wide variety of types and price ranges.
3. The family acceptance of boating as a sport for all members to participate in together. Women take to boating quite readily and enjoy a holiday afloat with the family. Boating also permits the family to enjoy allied sports together, such as water-skiing, swimming, fishing, skin diving, SCUBA diving and exploring out-of-the-way places. No other participation sport is so broad.
4. A boat can be financed as easily as an automobile. Most of the large financing corporations have programs which extend credit to dealers. Many local banks now make consumer loans to boat purchasers.
5. There is freedom, solitude and relaxation on the waterways.
6. The adventure and romance associated with boats and the sea. When a man gets in his boat, he is master and lord of her from stem to stern. Depending on the individual this can be one of the strongest attractions boating has for a prospective skipper.
7. The high standards of living enjoyed by Americans and the relatively great amount of leisure time they have.
8. The growing ease with which beginners can learn boating, thanks in great measure to instruction provided by the

American National Red Cross, Boy Scouts of America, U. S. Coast Guard Auxiliary, U. S. Power Squadrons, the YMCA, marinas, boating dealers, special schools and some public schools in waterfront communities.

Safety Formula For Boating

The U. S. Coast Guard has devised a safety formula known as the 4-A's: Approved, Assigned, Acquainted, and Available. Approved means that every piece of lifesaving equipment carries the Coast Guard approval stamp. Assigned is to remind the skipper that every person aboard should be assigned an approved device. Acquainted means that everyone aboard should know how to use the device, and Available indicates that the skipper store the device so that it is immediately accessible in the event of need. Children and non-swimmers wear life-saving devices at all times.

Staying With The Boat

It is common knowledge among boaters that when the old ship rolls over or in some other way puts you in the water, your best bet is to stick with her. Stay with the boat *except* when water temperature is such that your survival chances are nil. Cold water kills. And with much of the Carolina surface water running from the mid-thirties to mid-forties in February, you must get out of it as quickly as possible. Can you make the swim to shore? Can you pole or row the flooded craft to shore? Such a situation may present you with the biggest decision of your life. Minutes count. Retain body heat in any way possible once on shore. Walk, build a fire, seek shelter and keep telling yourself that you can make it. ♦

The Winston-Salem Squadron of the U. S. Power Squadrons will start a free, safe boating class on February 27 at 7:30 p.m. Classes will be held in the St. Pauls Episcopal Church on Summit Street. For more information contact C. N. Siewers, 2580 Warewick Rd., Winston-Salem, N. C.

RESOURCE-O-GRAM
A ROUNDUP OF THE LATEST WILDLIFE NEWS

Mark Your Calendar

If you are sincerely interested in conservation of wildlife and other natural resources, mark your calendar for the dates February 20, 21, and 22. These mark the annual meeting of the N. C. Wildlife Federation at the Sheraton-Sir Walter Hotel in Raleigh. Delegates from wildlife clubs throughout North Carolina will attend the three-day meeting, but the general public is invited to attend any and all of the various meetings on the agenda.

Hunting Season Draws To End

By the end of February hunting seasons on most game species will have closed. An exception is the raccoon-opossum season in many counties, which ends March 1.

In general the 1968-1969 hunting season is considered by many hunters as being from good to excellent. There were, as usual, localities where hunting was poor, and weather conditions, especially during the earlier part of the season were not favorable.

More Hunting to Come

Turkey hunters are looking forward to a spring gobbler season this spring. In Eastern N. C. the season will be from April 14 to May 3, and in the lower Piedmont the season will be from April 14 to April 19. The official regulations regarding the spring gobbler hunting seasons, by necessity, are somewhat complicated, and the Wildlife Commission urges turkey hunters to study the regulations carefully before engaging in springtime turkey hunting. Spring gobbler hunts are scheduled on several wildlife management areas, and dates and rules on these are published in the current hunting and trapping regulations.

Attention Shad Fishermen

Due to an error the 1969 fishing regulations booklet has conflicting rules on shad fishing. Page 11 indicates a creel limit of 25 American and hickory shad, and page 14 indicates no creel limit on nongame fish. Shad are not game fish and the Wildlife Resources Commission has amended the regulations to remove the shad creel limit.

How Fish Develop

by J. H. Cornell

PHOTO BY JACK DERMID

THE development of a fish, like any other vertebrate animal, follows the fertilization of an egg by a sperm. Nature provides three basic methods for the development of eggs into new animals, and all three are followed by fish.

The first method, internal fertilization and internal development, is that followed by the mammals, such as a cow, for example. The egg is extremely small, and when it is fertilized it develops within the body of the female. The new individual receives its nourishment from the blood stream of the parent, through the walls of the blood vessels into the blood stream of the embryo. The new individual is highly developed before it ever sees the light of day.

The second method, internal fertilization and external development, is the method used by the reptiles and birds. Fertilization of the egg takes place internally just as it did in the first method. However, the egg is released from the ovary, fertilized, and begins development within the female's body. In this method, however, there is no source of nourishment for the new individual except from that stored in the egg itself. The food materials are stored in the yolk of the egg. When this method of development is followed by an animal, it is obvious that the egg must be much larger to provide the new individual with an adequate food supply during the early period of development. The development of a baby chick is a common example of this method.

The third method is external fertilization and external development. In this case the eggs are released by the female parent without previous fertilization. The sperms are released by the male parent at the same time. Since the egg is incapable of movement, but since the sperm is equipped with a tail for swimming, this method can be followed by animals that live in the water. It is by far the most common method among the fishes. In this case, the new individual receives no nourishment except that contained in the egg, and consequently the eggs are relatively large.

Actually, there are examples of all three methods of fertilization and early development among the fishes. The first method is followed by some of the fishes. The second method, somewhat modified, is followed by many of the so-called "livebearers," as the mosquito fish or Gambusia, for example. Although the young of the Gambusia are actually born alive, this is a modification of the second method which consisted of internal fertilization and external development. There is no connection between the new individuals developing in the eggs and the body of the female parent. The development is actually external to her tissues, and the eggs are simply retained within the body cavity during the early period of development. It is very similar to the situation of a hen sitting on a nest of eggs to keep them warm during the incubation period. Nearly all of the fish, however, follow the third method. Among some species there is an actual pairing of the fish, wherein one male and one female produce a family of youngsters. In other cases there are large groups of a species gathered together, wherein the reproductive products are released simultaneously and the fertilization of any egg is purely a matter of chance. Some of the fishes build elaborate nests and provide considerable parental care during the development period, while others simply broadcast the eggs free in the water at the time of fertilization, and leave them to the whims of nature.

Let's take a look at the newly laid and fertilized egg of a smallmouth bass and see how the individual develops. The egg is about one-tenth of an inch in diameter, and is adhesive so that it will stick to the gravel of the bass nest. The nuclear material of the sperm and egg fuse to form a single cell. Most of the space within the egg, though, is the yolk material. This is surrounded by a membrane called the vitelline membrane, then by a layer of water which has been absorbed through the chorion of the egg capsule. This single cell divides into two, then into four, eight, sixteen, and so on, until a mass of tissue is formed. In each egg there is a yellow oil droplet that is lighter than the rest of the egg and lies near the uppermost yolk. The embryonic bass develops from this tissue of cells on the upper side of the yolk above the oil globule. As the cells continue to divide, the tissue becomes differentiated so that the eyes, heart, brain, body cavity and spinal cord can be recognized. This new individual is still within the egg capsule, and is very much smaller than the yolk sac. As the embryo develops, the food material in the yolk sac is slowly absorbed, and the developing fish becomes larger as the yolk becomes smaller.

After some three or four days the bass has reached a size of about one-fifth of an inch and is curled inside the shell around the yolk sac. At that stage it hatches out of the egg membrane and straightens out into a fish form, still with the yolk sac attached, but free from the egg capsule. At this stage of development the fins are a continuous fold of skin. The dorsal fin, anal fin, and tail fin are all connected until the fin rays develop and assume the form in which the fisherman recognizes them. Of the paired fins, the pectorals first develop as small folds of skin just behind the head region. The pelvic fins are not formed until the yolk sac has been nearly absorbed. The rays in these fins develop soon after. Within a day after hatching, the eye becomes dark as the pigment is formed, and soon afterward dark spots form on the body itself.

As the young fish develop and absorb the food supply, they make better and better efforts at swimming, although the weight of the yolk sac continues to take them back downward to the nest. Depending on the temperature of the water, which governs the speed of development, the young smallmouth will rise from the nest in one to two weeks after the eggs are deposited. At that time they are entirely black, and unlike the largemouth fry which are nearly transparent at that stage of life. As soon as the yolk sac is absorbed, the fry begin to feed on the microscopically small animals in the water and grow rapidly. The body soon assumes the shape of the adult, and the fins become entirely separated from each other. Scales begin to develop on the young fish before they are an inch long.

In addition to the color, there is another major difference between the largemouth and smallmouth bass at this stage in their existence. When the young smallmouth bass are sufficiently developed to begin swimming and can leave the nest, they scatter to all parts of the water and there is little evidence of schooling or parental care beyond that point. The largemouth fry, on the other hand, leave the nest in a group and remain in a school for several days afterward. The male parent guards this school and apparently makes some attempt to keep them herded together so that he can protect them better.

Actually, the greatest hazards to the survival of a bass occur during the embryonic period. Water fluctuations may expose the nest to air and cause the death of all the eggs. A temperature change of as much as 11 or 12 degrees can kill every embryo before it has a chance to hatch. In spite of the best efforts of the male bass to guard the eggs, some predators succeed in raiding the nest and eating the eggs. A sudden storm on the watershed may wash quantities of silt into the water and deposit a layer of mud over the eggs. This will promptly suffocate them. Pollution at this time is especially serious. Fingerlings and adults can withstand considerable temperature changes and some amounts of pollution, but the embryos are particularly susceptible to any toxic substance in the water.

Among the cold water fishes, such as trout, the eggs develop over a much longer period of time. Since those eggs are characteristically buried in gravel in extremely cold spring water, the development period of the embryos is much more extensive. However, the same general method of development exists, and the young individuals are supplied with food by the attached yolk sac. As it disappears by absorption, they must learn to feed on the materials and organisms in the water near them. They can swim in pursuit of food at that stage of development, but many are lost because they failed to learn to use their mouths in feeding themselves after the absorption of the yolk sac.

The free-spawning fish, such as the striped bass, develop as the eggs drift along in the current of some turbulent river. They receive their oxygen supply, and are kept from being covered with silt, by the fact that during the embryonic period the egg is not in a nest but is rolling along the river bottom in the current. Depending upon the speed of the current, a new individual may be many miles from the point where the egg was laid when he finally hatches and begins to swim and feed.

It is at this stage in life that there is found the

Fish at this stage of their development are called sac fry since they are still dependent on the yolk sac for nourishment. The critical stage comes when they must find food for themselves.

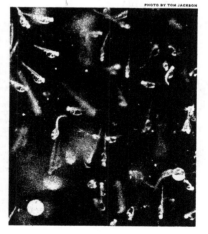

greatest competition for food among all the fishes which may inhabit a body of water. The young of all species feed on the plankton materials, either animal or vegetable, which may be in the habitat. After a short period of development, though, the characteristic food preferences of the various species begin to assert themselves. For example, when the largemouth bass reaches a size of about 2 to 2½ inches he ceases being an insect feeder to some extent, and begins feeding on very small fish if they are available. This characteristic makes it possible for the young bass to feed extensively on young sunfish which spawn slighter later than the bass.

The striped bass is much more voracious. Even at a length of less than an inch the young fish will attempt to eat each other. In an aquarium it is not unusual to see chains of four or five striped bass fry each attempting to swallow another one

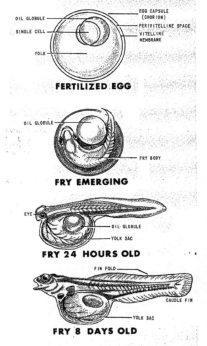

FERTILIZED EGG

OIL GLOBULE
SINGLE CELL
YOLK
EGG CAPSULE (CHORION)
PERIVITELLINE SPACE
VITELLINE MEMBRANE

FRY EMERGING

OIL GLOBULE
FRY BODY

FRY 24 HOURS OLD

EYE
OIL GLOBULE
YOLK SAC

FRY 8 DAYS OLD

FIN FOLD
CAUDLE FIN
YOLK SAC

tail first. In these cases the first fish may be caught by the tail but may be too large to be swallowed, and while the second fish is attempting to swallow the first, still a third may attempt to swallow the second one. Chains of several fish are not at all unusual in situations where adequate food is not available for them at a very early age.

The rate of development among fishes depends on the food supply. Warm-blooded animals, such as the mammals, start out in life with their ultimate size predetermined by their inherited genetic structure. If they do not have enough food to reach this size, they die of starvation. When they reach their predetermined size, no further growth takes place, except, possibly, additional weight. Among the cold-blooded animals, however, growth goes on all during the life of the individual so long as the food supply is adequate On the other hand, at any stage in its life a fish can stop growing because the food supply is insufficient, and can maintain itself with a minimum supply of food without having enough for further development in size.

This accounts for the tremendous number of small fish in some waters, where the number of fish is too great for any one individual to grow up. The most rapid growth rates take place in new bodies of water, such as new impoundments, where the fish stocked, either from a hatchery or from natural sources, have an almost unlimited supply of food. Here there is little loss through predation or starvation, and extremely rapid growth results.

Another limiting factor on the growth and development rate among fishes is the water temperature. Each fish has a critical temperature below which it does not have the ability to digest and assimilate food regardless of its abundance. This means that in northern waters, the growth rate of fishes is generally slower than for smaller species farther south.

In the largemouth bass, for example, the critical metabolism temperature is in the vicinity of 55 degrees. During all that part of the year when a body of water is below that temperature, the bass will not grow. Development ceases during the winter months. The extent of seasonal differences determines the speed of development in different waters, even when the food supply is similar. It is this interruption of growth in winter that is shown in fish scales. It permits the age of a fish to be determined by scale inspection. The material of which the scales are composed shows a break in the growth rings during the period when no growth is taking place. It is on this basis that the age, and consequently the rate of growth, of individual fish can be determined.

All these factors affect the development of fish: those which may be lethal in the embryonic stage, those which may prevent development in the fingerling stages, and those which may prevent normal development later in life. It is fortunate, indeed, that the reproductive potential of fish is so great. Otherwise, the large fish, which the fisherman considers a prize, would be scarce indeed. ◆

Sassafras

by Grace S. Draper
Pleasant Garden, N. C.

When you were small and a bit "under the weather," did *your* mother ever prepare for you a cup of "sassafras tea" from the bark of sassafras roots? This was certainly not as "brisk," perhaps, as our imported teas of today, but an old-fashioned remedy, nevertheless.

The twigs, bark, and roots of the sassafras are spicy and aromatic, and formerly were believed to have medicinal qualities. Among the required items for shipment from the New World by the early settlers were sassafras root and bark, and the tree was cultivated and grown in European gardens and nurseries. Today the aromatic oil of sassafras is used to some extent for flavoring candies and root beer, as perfume in soaps and disinfectants, as a mild stimulant, and as flavoring for bad-tasting medicines. And, as an indication that sassafras tea is still used as a "spring tonic," packaged sassafras root chips from Tennessee may be purchased at the local supermarkets for brewing hot tea! The young leaves and twigs are quite mucilaginous, and children love to chew them for their refreshing flavor. At one time a preparation for soothing eye inflammation was made from "mucilage" of sassafras.

Representatives of the sassafras (a member of the laurel family) are found in Asia and on the Island of Formosa (Taiwan). It is believed that a sassafras once grew in Europe, but it became extinct during the last Great Ice Age. The lone species of American sassafras, which is native to the eastern United States, is common throughout our state in dry, well-drained soil. It seems to like particularly fence-rows, roadsides, and neglected fields, where seeds are probably dropped by birds. The genus name *sassafras* was derived from the word *salsafras*, which refers to its medicinal properties, and was given to it by early French settlers; the species name *albidum* refers to its light-colored wood.

The tree is unusual because of the variety of leaf shapes found on a single plant—some are shaped like a regular one-thumb child's mitten, another will have two lobes, and a third will be a simple oval leaf with no lobes. It ranges in size from a shrub to a large tree, and many grow to over 40 feet in height, although most of us know it as only a small and slender tree. The largest known specimen is in Madison, N. J., and it was called "Green Stick" by the Indians because of the bright yellow-green twigs, a color which persists in the twigs throughout the tree's life.

The dark blue berried fruit, which ripens in August and September, is eaten by 25 species of birds, including the catbird, kingbird, red-eyed vireo, flycatcher, robin, quail, and wild turkey; leaves are browsed by woodchuck, white-tailed deer, and black bear.

Its wood is too weak and brittle to be of much commercial value, but it is used for cabinets and interior finishing, in boxmaking, in boat building, and in cooperage (repair of barrels, tubs, casks).

This tree has few insect enemies and is an interesting tree in many ways for transplanting. Small wild trees should be cut from the parent root system a year or two previous to moving.

White sand and sunshine, the eternal pounding of the sea. Across the litter of shells washed up on the beach, the shadow of a seagull skimming and sweeping in flight, alerting the timid sandcrab, who backs swiftly into the safety of his sandy home.

Up and down the beach, tiny sandpipers, hopping, skipping on stilted legs, peck at icy wavelets, in search of silvery minnows, scratching frothy patterns left upon the sand — to find their daily bread.

Here and there, a shell collector roams the strand, searching for mysterious treasures washed up by the restless sea.

Down the beach, a large fisherman braves icy waters to cast hook and line into the foaming surf, and the faint echo of a child's laughter drifts in the tangy air.

Here, ghosts of summer laughter linger, like forgotten footprints in the sand, long erased by time and tide.

This is winter — on the beach.

Now and then a lone figure, lost in thought, is silhouetted against the shimmer of the sea. Here, by the sea, problems and heartaches seem smaller, when matched against the vastness of the deep.

Every season has its reason. Winter, on the beach, is a time of stillness, a time of waiting — a brief, restful interlude when the sea reclaims its own.

Now, winter winds beat at craggy jetties, a boat creaking in a sunny lagoon. Sometimes winter brings snow, painting the beach with a glistening purity, matching its still white beauty against the wilder beauty of the sea. And winter brings bleak northeasters, when whitecaps flash angrily and roar to shore.

There are winter days when mist and rain steal in from the ocean, and the beach jealously shuts out all but its own. Then the seagull sits wearily on his pilings, a sandcrab ambles boldly among the

by Louise Lamica

Winter on the Beach

seaoats, and tiny sandpipers seek happier hunting grounds.

Winter on the beach is an Eden for nature's glory, for pink and white sunrises, blue and gold days, and dark, mysterious nights. Winter is a time for blazing sunsets, that send long shadows stealing across the strand — and pale winter moonlight that seeks out the seagull, nodding on his roost.

Winter is a resting time for the sturdy seaoat, long a foe of lashing wind and wave. Listen closely and you hear the seaoat's rustle, as it settles more securely in the shifting sands. "Patience," seems the whisper, "there is a time for all things."

Once in a while, an errant breeze from the Gulf Stream visits the beach, pushing back the cold north winds, as if playfully reminding winter her hold is not complete. Then, from cottages along the shore comes the song of saw and hammer, and smoke drifts in the air. And the promise of spring rides on each balmy breeze.

Soon, winter will give way to March winds and April laughter. And May will hurry into summer. When once again laughter will fill the air, and balmy nights perfumed with moonlight will haunt the strand.

But for now, winter winds moan around the jetties, and ice crystals form on the silken green moss on craggy rocks. The seagull's shadow skims over the sandpiper, and the seaoat rustles faintly in the shifting sands.

This is winter — on the beach.

A Pond In Winter

by Ralph Mears

THIS winter as you are out riding in the country with your parents, stop by that frozen pond you see across the field near the woods; it is not as deserted as it may seem. If you could hide and observe what was going on around that seemingly deserted pond, you would be in for a big surprise.

A hawk drifts high and lazily over the pond. As he dips down and back up again, he's not just cruising around up there. His sharp eyes are seeking prey for his next meal and he knows there is life down there around the pond. One thing he sees is a cottontail somewhere in the undergrowth just a few feet from the pond.

The rabbit knows there is danger lurking everywhere and his natural instinct tells him to crouch low in the undergrowth.

Mr. Hawk's extraordinary eyesight catches and recognizes every paw print in the snow, every slight movement and perhaps his ears catch the rustling sound coming from the dry grass.

Stalking through the nearby wooded thicket is a fox. He is looking for his next meal too. Our grey bunny, sitting on the cold ground, his breath fogging the air, knows of these prevailing dangers, too. All he can do now is wait and watch until he thinks the coast is clear.

Meanwhile, our hawk has also seen the fox. Two on one, and one for one. This is one of the maddening triangles in the life, survival, and death in the animal kingdom.

As yet the fox has not smelled out Mr. Cottontail. As he turns in another direction to seek food, the rabbit spots an opportunity to escape. Trembling, he stands up, sniffs the air, and makes for the safety of a dead log some 50 feet away where he has his winter home. Will he make it? Mr. Fox has

seen him and is getting closer and closer in his quest of rabbit for supper. If only our bunny can make it safely to the dead log. Whew! Just in time and safe once again in the comfort of home. Even if his winter supply of food is a bit restricted, he feels safe.

Mr. Fox noses around trying to find a way into the log to get his supper. Reluctantly he heads back to the pond in hopes of finding something else. Rabbit is safe; Mr. Hawk glides off.

But this is not the end.

A small head appears out of a tiny hole. It's a muskrat and he's hungry too. He slowly looks one way and then another. The coast seems to be clear and he emerges from his hole.

A muskrat slides into the water of the pond through a broken place in the ice along the water's edge. Old vegetation clings to the banks of the pond. And along the shoreline is a cluster of water beetles gathered around a bubble of water under the ice. Two fish doze in a heap of leaves on the bottom of a cove. Life for the fish is slow with the water temperature hovering near freezing.

The rotting vegetation on the bottom of the pond saps the oxygen of the pond and thousands of creatures may suffocate. If deep snow shuts out sunlight plants won't help make oxygen and some pond dwellers may die. But where is Mr. Muskrat? He's gliding through the reeds into a hole, and up through a tunnel. In a twinkling he's inside a large den lined with leaves. This is where he shakes off droplets of water from his thick fur and settles down to sleep.

So our pond isn't so deserted and idle as it may seem. Life scampers on almost as if it were summertime. Nature seldom sleeps, even in winter. ✦

Scenes From The Past
by Fred Kelly

DR. Thomas J. Henchey and I are transplanted North Carolinians, now living in the Palm Beaches, so it is natural for us to reminisce when we get together. Recently he was telling me about the time he played professional baseball in 1909, for the Edenton, North Carolina team; but I was more interested in his visit to Nags Head. He tells it so well, suppose we listen to what he has to say:

"An old friend of mine by the name of Frank Bond invited me, at the end of the baseball season, to take a trip with him down to Nags Head, as he was going to build a cottage down there. We started out in Frank's boat for Columbia, where he was going to pick up a schooner-load of lumber. A few days later we left Columbia and finally landed at Nags Head. Nobody bought any land there in those days. They just built a house anywhere they pleased. Frank Bond picked out a nice spot near a friend of his and built his summer home there.

The population there was composed mostly of Elizabeth City folks and Edentonians. The only way to get there was by boat since there were no roads or bridges within miles of the place. The Mail Boat went down the Sounds once or twice a week. Looking at the shore from the Sound, the white sands of Kill Devil Hill looked like an enormous snow bank. The Nags Head folks got their fresh meat from Manteo, where they butchered a cow once a week. The Nags Head folks knew which day the cow was to be butchered and we all went over to Manteo by boat. This was a special occasion.

While my friend Frank Bond was building his house, I hunted most of the time. There were wild hogs, wild cattle and wild horses in abundance. One day I was hunting about two miles south of Nags Head on the Sound side, when I saw a big herd of wild cattle coming up the shore towards me. There were three or four vicious looking bulls heading the bunch. The leader was an ugly looking brute, so I took to the water and stood waist deep as they approached. Every eye in the herd never left me. As they got opposite me, the old lead bull would take a few steps and stop. All of the others did the same, all eyes fastened on me. They finally passed on and I returned to the shore.

There were quite a few wild ponies around and I became interested in their method of getting drinking water. The ponies would dig holes with their hoofs, like a dog, and let the water seep in through the sand.

About this time an old eagle began soaring around me. I stood steady as an Indian cigar stand and just watched his shadow, hoping he would come over me, but he was always just out of gun shot. I finally gave up. Looking toward the ocean there were what looked like a million birds of all kinds. I decided to try them. I laid my gun down at my feet and filled up my pipe and lit it and waited, but they never came close enough.

I finally ran across a beautiful mound of freshly cut grass, which looked like a little hay cock. As I came up to it I saw a little bit of a hog's ham about the size of my hand exposed. I figured that someone at Nags Head had killed the hog and had covered him up until they could return with a cart. As I started away, I gently kicked the hog on the little exposed spot and an explosion took place. With a roar the hog broke out from under the grass pile and my heart stopped beating. He bolted just like a rabbit from his bed and ran about 75 yards and then turned to look at me and started to bark at me like a scared dog. He then bolted and ran.

Old North Carolina has some wonderful memories for me, as I have hunted in the Roaring Gap section fifty years ago and for the next twenty-five years, I have had a log cabin in the mountains about fifty miles north of Asheville. Electricity and radio and TV have made a wonderful change in the State, in the past fifty years, but I am glad I saw it before all these improvements came along." ◆

"Here for Sure"

Dear Sirs:

I am a subscriber to *Wildlife* and read it from cover to cover every month and thoroughly enjoy it. I read about the cougar in Wildlife and I thought that I would write and tell about the one my mother and I saw. We live about the center of Randolph County, about 8 miles northeast of Asheboro, N. C. on Deep River. My mother looked out of the door one Sunday morning and saw this big, long cat standing in the road, about 100 yards from the house. It was about six or seven feet long and a charcoal color. It was larger than a hound dog with a very long tail.

One day I was in a field, a short distance from my house, looking for crows. I blew my predator call and waited about twenty minutes. There about 50 yards from me was this big cat which was like the cougar in the picture on page 10 of June Wildlife. He was sitting, watching

Walter Don Augustine

Mr. Walter Don Augustine is stationed at Pittsboro, Chatham County. He was born in Pender County in 1941, and is the son of Mr. and Mrs. W. F. Augustine. In 1958, he graduated from Burgaw High School. He was previously employed as Supervisor at Carlisle Poultry and Egg Company in Burgaw.

Walter attended Pre-service School for wildlife protectors at the Institute of Government at Chapel Hill in June 1964. In October 1965, he was employed as a Wildlife Protector Trainee in District Four, and was promoted to Wildlife Protector and transferred to Pittsboro in February 1966.

Mr. Augustine has attended five In-service Training Schools. He is a member of the District Five Wildlife Water Safety Team, the Southeastern Association of Game and Fish Commissioners, Law Enforcement Section, and the State Employees Association.

Mr. Augustine is married to the former Mary Lee Rivenbark of Burgaw. They have one child, Walter Lee, age nine. They are members of Pittsboro Baptist Church.

DIVISION ENFORCEMENT RECORD FOR DEC. 1968

HUNTING & FISHING

Persons checked	20,571
Total prosecutions	916
Total convictions	873
Total cases not guilty	21
Total cases nol prossed	17
Total cases dismissed	5
Total fines collected	$16,999.30
Total costs collected	$ 9,363.82

BOATING

Persons checked	177
Total prosecutions	44
Total convictions	40
Total cases not guilty	3
Total cases nol prossed	0
Total cases dismissed	1
Total fines collected	$ 30.00
Total costs collected	$ 432.00

All fines and any arrest or witness fees are paid into the school funds of the counties in which the violation occurred, and no part of the fines or costs collected are paid to the North Carolina Wildlife Resources Commission or its personnel.

---

every move I made. Suddenly he just ran off. This cougar was a gray and charcoal color. There are four or five people around here that have seen these cats. I say cats because there are three or more around here.

My father has a farm pond between my house and his. These cats make tracks in the red mud. He has cut some of the tracks out of the mud. I showed one that just about filled up a gallon can to the Wildlife protector of Randolph County. He said it must be a large cat. Also this cat or another one got in a farmer's pigs one morning and killed two pigs about 100 to 125 pounds each. The farmer got one glance at it but it got away. This one was yellow.

These cats follow the deer herds that have spread out from Uwharrie Forest. These cats have been bayed two times that I know of. Once he killed several dogs and ran several fellows into their car. I am trying for a real good picture of one of these cats. When and if I do get one I will send *Wildlife* one. The big cats are here for sure. This cat could be the plain Old Painter. I have heard three hollowing at one time to each other.

Yours very truly,
Gilbert Haithcock
Franklinville

Wild Ponies

DEAR SIR:

I would like to know if the state of North Carolina has any plans to protect the wild ponies on the Outer Banks.

These ponies have been in North Carolina for decades running wild on the Outer Banks and should be protected as are the wild ponies in Chincoteague, Virginia, in the Assateague Island National Seashore in Maryland and Virginia.

The National Park Service should protect and preserve the wild ponies in the Cape Lookout National Seashore, and should not remove them as is now planned. I would like to ask that you do everyting possible to get the North Carolina Wildlife Resources Commission to protect and preserve these wild ponies in the wild state.

TOMMY LIPREY, JONESVILLE, SOUTH CAROLINA

Please see "The Wild Ponies of Ocracoke Island" in July, 1968 WILDLIFE.—Editor

Hog Wild

DEAR SIRS:

My brother, grandfather and I recently had an experience while fishing at Mr. Curtis Fulp's lake in rural Ellerbe which we could hardly believe ourselves and everyone we tell it to say they have never heard of it either—but we actually saw it.

We saw a sow hog get in the water at the edge of the dam and walk along the side in the water and stick its snout in the water and came out with a good-size *live* bass and ate it. We saw the fish, wriggling—so we *know* it was alive. Have any of you readers ever heard of this before? Please let us know about this.

DAVID STEWART JR.,
ELLERBE, NORTH CAROLINA

Last fall, Ulmont Ives of Raleigh found this yellow-poplar leaf. It had a width of 11", circumference of 36". Next?

The fulvous tree duck is a rare visitor to North Carolina at best, and apparently this one strayed from its normal path and ended up on a Wake County farm pond. It was found dead with one foot damaged in some way.

Protector Walton B. Chason, (left) displays two awards he received for meritorious service during 1968. The plaque was awarded as Outstanding Officer of the Year by the Southeastern Association of Game and Fish Commissioners. The citation was presented by the Shikar-Safari Club International in recognition of Protector Chason's achievements in his field. Wildlife Protection Chief Bob Hazel is at right.

★ ★ ★ ★ ★ ★ ★   ★ ★ ★ ★ ★ ★ ★

Steve Tilson of Brevard sends this 1964 photo of his father and brother with a brown of 8¾ pounds, and a rainbow of 7½ pounds, respectively, from the Davidson River. A pleasant day, but a sad ending. The brother lost his life in Vietnam December 21, 1967.

ARACHNIDS

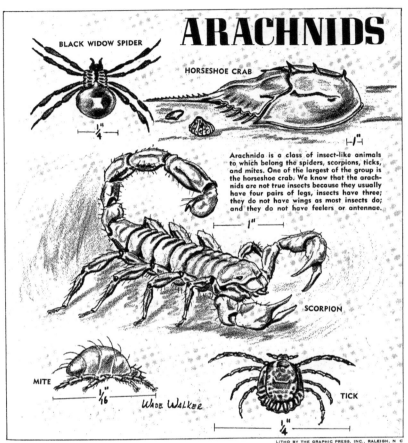

BLACK WIDOW SPIDER

HORSESHOE CRAB

Arachnida is a class of insect-like animals to which belong the spiders, scorpions, ticks, and mites. One of the largest of the group is the horseshoe crab. We know that the arachnids are not true insects because they usually have four pairs of legs, insects have three; they do not have wings as most insects do; and they do not have feelers or antennae.

SCORPION

MITE

TICK

WADE WALKER

LITHO BY THE GRAPHIC PRESS, INC., RALEIGH, N C

Wildlife IN NORTH CAROLINA

25 CENTS / MARCH 1969

WILDLIFE IN NORTH CAROLINA recognizes the need for close cooperation between State and Federal conservation agencies and the people who hunt and fish—to bring about a restoration of our renewable resources. The Editor gratefully receives for publication news items, articles, and photographs dealing with the North Carolina out-of-doors, but reserves the right to reject materials submitted. Full credit is given for all materials published.

* * *

WILDLIFE IN NORTH CAROLINA is published at the Wildlife Resources Commission offices, Motor Vehicles Building, 1100 New Bern Ave., Raleigh, N. C. 27601.

* * *

Second class postage paid at Raleigh, North Carolina 27602.

* * *

SUBSCRIPTIONS—Fifty cents per year, one dollar for two years. Make remittances payable to WILDLIFE RESOURCES COMMISSION. Any employee of the Wildlife Resources Commission may accept subscriptions, or they may be forwarded to Post Office Box 2919, Raleigh, N. C. 27602. Stamps cannot be accepted.

Wildlife circulation this issue, 119,075.

Wildlife
IN NORTH CAROLINA ■

The official publication of the NORTH CAROLINA WILDLIFE RESOURCES COMMISSION, Raleigh 27602. A monthly magazine devoted to the protection and restoration of our wildlife resources and to the improvement of hunting and fishing in North Carolina.

VOL. XXXIII, NO 3   MARCH, 1969

IN THIS ISSUE

EDITORIAL STAFF

ROD AMUNDSON _ _ _ _ _ _ _ EDITOR
DUANE RAVER _ _ _ _ MANAGING EDITOR
LUTHER PARTIN _ _ WRITER-PHOTOGRAPHER
JOHN PARKER _ _ _ _ _ OUTDOOR SAFETY
TOM JACKSON _ _ _ WRITER-PHOTOGRAPHER

Considerable confusion surrounds the identification of ocean-going shad of our coastal rivers. And this cover painting may not be of a whole lot of help. It shows the hickory shad at top, and the American or white shad. Both hit artificial lures in the spring and you can see that they are similar in appearance. The American is much the larger, reaching four pounds and better. Painting by Duane Raver.

LATE SNOW

Whatever has attracted the attention of this red fox, is likely to end up as a light lunch. The late snow has only served to whet the appetite of the fox as he searches the grassy hummocks for field mice or a dozing rabbit.

PHOTO BY KARL H. MASLOWSKI

The Teaspoon

by Dwight L. Peterson,
Clinton, N. C.

Illustrated by Chuck Sauber

What the little net lacked in size was more than made up by the boy's enthusiasm. But would it be enough?

T HE old wood box sat behind the kitchen stove and Pete was keeping it filled to the brim regularly. He wasn't taking any chances at having his father remind him of his responsibility. Even the cows and hogs stood close attention. Their only problem was indigestion from being over fed! "Well, they got their problem," he thought. "I've got mine." Maybe he was over doing his chores and being a little extra smart, but he dreaded the thought of waiting another year. After all, he'd be ten in another month.

Sitting around the pot bellied wood stove in his uncle's store and listening to his father and the other men folk spin fishing tales made his desires soar. He would sit wide eyed, afraid he'd miss one word, until his father called it a night and said they'd best be getting on home, there was corn to plow or tobacco to hoe at first sun.

But just to sit and listen was one thing; to have voice was another. And to have voice you had to have something to voice about. Pete was a sitter. He guessed this was one of the main reasons he wanted to catch a shad so badly. Shad weren't just ordinary, every-day fish like a bass or bream, they were ocean

fish! Pete often thought of the shad exploring the ocean depths and then, as if by magic, every spring, entering the fresh water streams for spawning. Shad had been places and seen things that Pete could only visualize in his imagination.

It was Saturday morning at breakfast when his father looked at him and said, "Soon be time for the shad to start running, made any plans?" Pete almost choked on a mouthful of grits.

He glanced at his mother, she winked, then smiled. They had been talking about it a lot lately. "Be patient, just be patient," she had said. "Don't nag your Pa. He'll mention it in his own time. Your chances will be much better if you don't pester him."

"Yes—yes sir," he squeaked in a forced, high pitched voice after the lump of grits went down.

"We'll be needin' new poles for the dip nets; care to come along and help cut them?"

His father got his answer when Pete turned his glass of milk over on his mother's new table cloth. His father gave him that hard look, which was usually more effective than a good tanning, got up and stalked over to where his coat and hat hung on the wall peg. Pete held his breath. Somewhere between the

wall peg and back door his father began humming. It was a good sign so he felt better. At the door his father turned, looked at him and smiled. "Get your coat and hat while I crank the truck," he said.

He was in a dazed dream as the truck bounced along the bumpy dirt road toward Frank Wiliford's place. Mr. Wiliford had a nice stand of juniper in a swampy area on his farm and his father had asked permission to cut poles for the nets. As the truck wheeled down a cart path, Pete could see the swamp at the distant 'end. Anticipation was bubbling out his ears and he could hardly sit still, but he tried to remain calm and mature. The truck squealed to a halt and he was out before his father cut off the engine.

"Get the axe out of the back," his father said.

Eagerness was shining through Pete's falsified calmness but it didn't bother his father, who never seemed to hurry anything. Walking slowly, his father looked over each sapling carefully. Picking one, he motioned for Pete to start hacking. Five long minutes later Pete dropped the axe, wiped sweat and felt sorry for the tree. It stood strong, badly hacked from ground level to about a foot above. A cross eyed beaver could have done better, he thought. His father took the axe and neatly finished the job.

With four nice juniper poles cut and loaded, Pete sat silent, watching the passing wintry scenes as the old truck bounced toward home. "Soon the ice will disappear from the sloughs and the trees will begin to bud," he thought and felt good inside.

It took all afternoon to prepare the poles. They had to be sawed the right length, trimmed and staked down in an egg-shaped position. The large ends were crossed and nailed, two extra pieces were added above and below the cross to serve as handles. The bows would remain in this position until the sap dried out then they would hold their shape without force. Bamboo briars had been cut to serve as ribs in the nets and the thorns had to be stripped before they could be attached to the bows. It was at this point of construction that Pete, quite by accident, neatly wrapped a long, gangly bamboo briar around his father's neck—with the thorns still on. He quickly dropped his hammer and nails, grabbed his neck and went into the house. Pete stood petrified. Moments later he came from the house with large blotches of iodine decorating the wounds. Pete's mother came to the back door and looked out. His father was humming, but this time through tight teeth.

In the twilight they stood back and admired their work. All was complete except for the chicken wire. His father put his arm around him and squeezed a little. At first he felt so proud and good inside, then a little sick. His net looked terribly small beside his father's. It reminded him of the strong man and the midget at the county fair. Then he began to visualize a two or three pound shad flopping around inside the net and he felt better again.

When Pete's mother called them to supper, they went toward the house together, arms around each, talking shad. The hard part was ahead. The waiting for spring.

It was on a Sunday afternoon when Jeff Wilson drove into the front yard. Sunday school and church were over and Pete and his mother and father had just finished the usual big Sunday dinner. As they sat on the front porch enjoying the first warmth of spring, Mr. Wilson grunted his way from under the steering wheel of the big car and stood outside patting his round jelly-type stomach. He lived somewhere far off, at least twenty or thirty miles, and Pete had him figured for a money man. Charlie Hayes, who lived down the road apiece, was making a net measuring up to Mr. Wilson's request, so Pete knew he had come to talk shad.

After the usual "howdy do's," "how are you's" and "how things been," the subject of shad finally bobbed up in the conversation. Mr. Wilson said shad were being caught down the coast and they would be up Willow River in a few more days. Pete stood breathless, waiting for the part of the conversation he was sure to come. Finally, his father mentioned the dip nets, and right off Mr. Wilson said, "First shad net, son?"

Pete smiled meekly and nodded. He was glad they had finished the nets a few days before. His looked better with the chicken fence wire. But doubt was beginning to rise as he watched Mr. Wilson standing there, sort of in shock.

"What's the boy going to catch? Minnows?" he said, then roared with laughter.

"Not minnows. Shad," said Pete's father. He had been smiling, but he wasn't smiling anymore. "It's a shad net, Wilson, or don't you know one when you see it?"

"But it ain't no bigger'n a teaspoon," Mr. Wilson said with a humble tone.

Pete wasn't feeling so good when Mr. Wilson left. His stomach had a tumbling feeling—like things were jumping around inside him. His father saw his lip begin to quiver so they sat down on the back steps and had a talk. His father told how f o l k s

laughed at him when he first used chicken wire in his dip net instead of the regular netting. But it made sense when he explained the advantages, not tearing on snags, briars and things like that. And the first season he used it he caught more shad than anyone in the community. Of course, most everyone changed over to chicken wire then. It didn't make much difference that the wire was a lot cheaper than the netting.

Pete's father sat silent for awhile, rubbing the back of his neck and looking out across the fields. "Pete," he said. There was sympathy in his voice.

"Sir?"

"What would you do if one of those sandy curves out on the road pitched you and your bicycle?"

Pete pondered the question thoughtfully a few seconds then answered. "I'd just get up and start again."

"What would you do if the sand was real bad and you couldn't get started?"

"I'd push it through."

His father looked at him and smiled. "See what I mean?"

Pete nodded.

The next few days, between farm chores, Pete spent his spare time out behind the barn dipping air with his teaspoon. "Bump," he'd say and dip. "Bump" and dip like crazy. Then his father would help by tieing a string to the net, stand back, and when Pete would least expect, jerk the string. "Bump," he'd say, and Pete would dip like crazy. Pete felt a little silly but it was serious business to his father. "It's no different than practicing with your rod and reel," he'd say. "Reflex, that's the key, reflex. When a shad strikes that net you got to dip then, not later."

The shad arrived on schedule, as they always did, and by this time, with all that practice, Pete figured he had become about the fastest dip net dipper in the community. He would soon know just how good he really was.

The nights were crispy cool, the days warm to hot, birds carried bits of straw and grass in their beaks, bees buzzed around the wisteria, it was spring in top form. The long awaited moment had arrived. A fading sun found Pete, his father and his Uncle Luke hauling their dip nets down to Willow River. From dark until around nine o'clock was the time to catch shad. They ran better and the nets were difficult to see in the darkness. As they neared the river, Pete could see cars and pick up trucks parked here and there, the men milling around, unloading and preparing their nets. The old truck squealed to a halt and everyone looked in their direction. Pete felt sick, his stomach had that tumbling feeling again. His father nudged him gently with his elbow, winked and smiled. Pete crawled out into the lion's den.

Mr. Wilson was there, fat and all, but he never spoke a word. Fred Stokes was the first. "Hey, Pete," he said. "You got the spoon, but where's the soup bowl?" Carl Wilkes was the next. "Dip nets are going out of style, Pete. They're catching shad with rod and reel, and on artificials. Why don't you tie a yellow buck tail on that spoon and do a little casting?" Then everyone laughed.

Pete smiled dryly at the jabber and remembered the things his father had said.

Grabbing the teaspoon he headed for Uncle Luke's fishing boat. Everyone in the group stopped and watched. The teaspoon was awkward at balancing so he carefully placed each step in the slippery mud along the river bank. The over-sized knee boots of his father's he had borrowed didn't help matters. But he made it. Turning, he grinned victoriously at the gaping silent group.

He had one foot in the boat, the other on the river bank, calculating how to balance the teaspoon and get his foot off the river bank and all of him and the teaspoon into the boat. Slowly and very gracefully the boat moved away from the bank and into the river current. He was doing the split. The silent, gap-

ing watchers broke the silence. His father grabbed his arm and Uncle Luke the boat. He was saved from the ducking but not from the tears.

The tears soon dried and Pete realized he was exactly where he had wanted to be for a long time. They had the boat tied at both ends, parallel and flush against the river bank. His father sat in the bow fishing for shad moving upstream and Uncle Luke in the sterm for those moving downstream. Pete figured his chances at a shad would be very slim; he was wedged in between.

Finally the evening light faded to darkness and the frogs and crickets began to chirp and croak a swamp melody. Great horned owls perched high on cypress limbs and added their part to the melody. Pete shivered in the darkness but not from the strange sounds that broke the silence of the swamp. He shivered from excitement and anticipation.

Suddenly, from downstream, there was the sound of a heavy, rolling splash. Someone from downstream yelled, "SHAD IN THE HOLE."

Pete shook with excitement. "Was that somebody catching a shad, Pa?" he said.

His father answered in a whisper. "No, that's the shad playing around. A buck will chase a roe and a roe will chase a buck, and they'll wallow, splash and play

until they get tired, then they'll settle down in some deep hole until they decide to move and play again."

There was another splash from upstream, then again downstream, and then across the river from Pete. He closed his eyes tight, whispered a small prayer and gripped his teaspoon so tight his knuckles were whitie. Then came the solid "bump" of the shad as he stuck the net. He dipped like crazy. Opening his eyes he could see the shad boiling and splashing the water inside the net.

"I got him! I got him" he yelled.

His father dropped his net and came to the rescue. Uncle Luke did the same. The boat paddle was knocked into the river, a few gallons of water dipped in the boat, Uncle Luke lost his hat and Pete's father cut his finger, but other than that every thing went fine. Soon the shad was safe in the boat, and Pete had realized why his father had made his net so small. If it had been any larger he would never have been able to handle it.

Uncle Luke's store was as quiet as an Egyptian tomb. The group watched as Uncle Luke eyed the store scales through spectacles dropped down on his nose.

"Four pounds, two ounces," he announced.

The fishermen began pound-

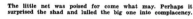
The little net was poised for come what may. Perhaps it surprised the shad and lulled the big one into complacency.

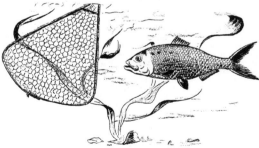

ing Pete on the back and shaking his hand.

"Want to sell that teaspoon, son?" asked Mr. Wilson.

Pete shook his head and grinned. "No sir," he said.

"Since you caught the one and only shad tonight, and with a teaspoon, maybe you better give us the details," said Carl Wilkes.

Fred Stokes brought Pete a chair and he sat down. The group was silent and listened.

"Well, it was like this—" Pete began. ✦

Perhaps the best part was the telling of the adventure. Now, at last, Pete had something to "give voice" to.

Mulberry

by Grace S. Draper

WHEN we think of the mulberry tree, we immediately associate it in our minds with the glamorous and magical word "silk" and the rearing of silk worms, known as "sericulture." But our familiar native southern mulberry tree, the red mulberry (*Morus rubra L.*), is only a relative of the oriental white mulberry tree, which is the silk producing tree, courtesy of the silk worm and its cocoons. The white mulberry was introduced into this country in an unsuccessful attempt to develop a silk-producing industry, and it is occasionally found in the wild, having escaped from cultivation.

History records that in 1619, James I ordered the Virginia colonists to devote attention to the rearing of silk worms, and encouraged sericulture by bounties and rewards. The colonists found that the silk worms would not feed on the red mulberry leaves, only on the imported white mulberry leaves. It is said that Mrs. Charles Pinckney in 1755 raised silk worms and spun sufficient silk for three dresses; and that on a visit to England, she presented silk for one dress to the Dowager Princess of Wales, and for another to Lord Chesterfield, keeping the third dress length for herself. At another time, eight pounds of raw silk from the colonies was sent to England to be woven into material for a gown for Queen Charlotte, wife of George III, for whom the city of Charlotte was named. However, probably due to the climate and partly due to the inexperience of the colonists, the industry failed to flourish.

In 1830 another attempt at sericulture was made in this country, with many valuable crops and orchards being plowed under to allow for the cultivation of white mulberry trees. This attempt also proved to be a failure, and so have subsequent large-scale trials since that time.

The red mulberry is found throughout our state. It is a small tree—it may grow up to 50 feet in height—often to be found growing in the shade of larger trees. Its rough and hairy leaves may have various shapes on the same tree (as does the sassafras), some heart-shaped, some mitten lobed, others rounded and pointed, with serrated edges. These leaf shapes are pictured above.

The hanging, purple-berried fruit of the red mulberry is eaten by many songbirds, as well as animals, when it ripens in mid-summer. It is very sweet and slightly elongated in comparison to blackberries, with a hard stem that goes all the way through the center. In line with their resourcefulness, old-timers made mulberry pies from this fruit!

If the white man was not successful in building a fabric-producing industry around our red mulberry tree, the Choctaw Indians of Florida did succeed in making a coarse hemp-like cloth, and ropes, from the tree's fibrous bark. Isn't it strange that Indians in our part of the world would have discovered a type of cloth could be made from this particular tree's bark, when peoples of China had discovered in far earlier times (and kept secret for 2,000 years) that silk worms, who fed on another kind of mulberry tree, could spin cocoons from which a very beautiful and expensive cloth could be made? ✦

CRAZY QUAIL

by Luther Partin

THE two pointers up ahead were sure acting funny—moving in circles with heads up and tails wagging furiously. Occasionally they would flash point in a half-hearted way, tails never stopping, as if to say, "Watch your step, there's birds around here somewhere, but I can't pin 'em down."

They were in a stand of small saplings about 30 yards from the edge of a cornfield. The field had been harvested, leaving a good cover of stalks, leaves and shucks on the ground with grains of corn visible here and there. Since it was getting late in the afternoon, it seemed logical that a covey might have fed in the cornfield and gone in the woods to loaf a while before roosting.

When we caught up with the dogs, we found very little ground cover for quail, only a few vines of honeysuckle on a carpet of leaves. Most of the honeysuckle growth was in the crowns of the young saplings. Some of them had such a thick mass of honey-

suckle it was hard to see how they got enough sunlight to stay alive.

The dogs began to make wider circles now, going maybe 50 yards out, but always returning to the same spot to go through the same routine. Occasionally one would freeze momentarily, tail rigid, foot up and head down, then resume his confusing pattern.

We finally decided that a covey might have been here, but flew out just ahead of the dogs. They might have been bunched up to roost early; this would explain the hot scent the dogs seemed to smell for a few seconds, but couldn't pinpoint.

While we were speculating as to where the birds might have gone, I leaned against a persimmon sapling that had an unusually heavy mat of honeysuckle in the top. Included in the thick mat was an accumulation of pine needles. The whole thing looked so strong it was almost tempting to climb up and take a nap on

it. We found very shortly that the quail had already yielded to the temptation.

About the second time I jostled the tree it sounded as if the woods had exploded. The others were shooting before I could understand what was happening. Roughly a dozen quail had been sitting in that clump of honeysuckle and pine needles. It took a little shaking to make them move. I've shaken out quite a few squirrels and possums in my time and even a coon or two, but quail—never before.

None of us had ever seen such a crazy thing and, quite frankly, before this I would have had to know a fellow pretty well to believe him when he said he had seen it. (This doesn't apply to pear trees on the first day of Christmas.)

That was several hunting seasons back. During the time in between, quail have done a lot of things they're not supposed to do. Some of the bird hunting stories told around the store don't sound quite so unbelievable now.

A veteran quail hunter from the Sandhills section told of some unusual quail behavior about ten years ago that sounded strange at the time, but not so much so now. His dogs were working a typical scrub oak-wire grass ridge with a few small longleaf pines scattered here and there, but plenty open for shooting. The dogs picked up a scent, trailed a little way, then pointed. But before he could get close, they began to move again, pointed for a few seconds, then moved a little further and pointed again.

This kept on for several hundred yards until our hunter decided the dogs were after "something besides quail." He knew that a little ahead of the dogs the ridge ended in a narrow finger of turkey oak and wire grass surrounded by open fields on three sides. He figured that whatever it was would have to cross the field to get to the nearest patch of woods on the other side. Hoping to at least see what the dogs were trailing, he cut sharply to his right and ran to the edge of the field. From here he ran almost parallel to the dogs and headed for the end of the wooded area.

While he was still out of gun range his mysterious quarry ran out of the wire grass and headed across the open field "like the devil was after them." It was a covey of quail and they weren't about to wait around for the dogs, much less fly for a hunter. He fell in behind them, hoping to cut the distance and make them fly but they went into road gear and left him "like he was toting a millstone." Just before reaching the other side, they took to the air and were last seen headed for Barbecue Swamp.

We observed for the first time three years ago an occurrence that is apparently a quite frequent thing with many hunters these days. A large covey of birds flushed wild before the dogs with a lot of clucking and a few whistles thrown in. They headed straight into the woods and down an incline toward the creek about a quarter of a mile away. The thoughts of fighting briars and brush in the bottom didn't stop us; but, as it turned out, there were worse things than that waiting for us.

It seems that every one of these birds perched in holly trees. Beginning about a hundred yards in the woods, we began to hear them fly out behind us. We never got a shot, in fact, we didn't even see most of them. They let us walk under or by them and then headed out in the other direction.

Most any quail hunter who goes more than once a year has experienced one or more of these things and he is usually quite vocal about it. Occasionally, someone wants to know what the Wildlife Commission is going to do about making quail "act like they ought to." Unfortunately, wildlife agencies don't have much more control over the whims of wild creatures than appropriate agencies have over the actions of people.

There are some who hold that quail have always acted erratically in front of inexperienced dogs or hunters, and during dry,

wet, hot or cold spells. (It seems that you would have to deal with one of these every time you go.)

We have a growing number of new quail hunters each year and many of the older hunters are not hunting as much as they once did. This all averages out to less experience on the hunter's part, but where it really shows up is in the dogs. Young dogs can't be expected to perform like veterans and old dogs that are hunted one day a week have a tendency to behave like young dogs. They may be more interested in burning the wind than sniffing it. Most hunters will agree that slowing down or stopping them at the right time is less likely to scare up birds. This applies to hunting quail or selling insurance.

Quail obviously assume that anything flying overhead is a potential enemy; and take evasive action. If they make this same assumption with two and four-legged animals prowling nearby, they're bound to be mighty nervous all the time. And we do have rapidly growing numbers of people and domestic pets invading the habitat of the bobwhite quail.

One acquaintance who hunts in various parts of the state says that quail are unpredictable in areas that have deer hunting with dogs. Deer season opens a month ahead of quail in the Coastal Plains and several adjoining Piedmont counties. In counties that don't have a deer season, he says the woods are full of dogs dumped out by people trying to get rid of them. So his theory is that quail are in a constant state of excitement these days (sounds a lot like people).

There's no doubt that quail respond to hunting pressure. The sight of dog and man, the booming of a gun and maybe the sting of pellets are not lost on them—they catch on pretty quick.

It's often told as a joke that quail change from a field bird to a woods bird on opening day. We can't buy the idea that quail can read hunting regulations, but it's pretty obvious that they can quickly learn that people, dogs

and the sound of guns mean trouble. And it's to their credit that they can find ways of avoiding some of that trouble. Passenger pigeons either couldn't figure that well or couldn't do anything about it, and we know what happened to them. ❧

Count On Crappies

by Duane Raver
Photos by the Author

Tree-tops, brush, most anything protruding from the water, brings joy to the heart of the crappie fisherman. The water here is perhaps four feet deep.

IF there is such a thing as a "reliable" fish, it very likely is the crappie. We're speaking of early spring when thse bright little panfish are on their spawning grounds, because this is far and away the best time to make consistent catches. When this will start is a bit hard to say, since the water temperature has to be "just right" and water conditions may affect the event greatly. But it can be anywhere from March to June, so be ready.

Now, neither the white or black crappie will win many prizes when it comes to the underwater fighting department. They aren't the scrappers that their cousins the bluegills are, and we might as well start from there. One of their greatest virtues is their vast numbers and willingness to tangle with an artificial lure. Of course, they are a fine fish for the minnow fisherman too, in the spring, but there's usually no need for live bait.

The crappie is most frequently thought of as a "big water" fish—reservoirs, large lakes, and in the Coastal Plain, big rivers. Most farm ponds with the speckled pan fish get overpopulated within a couple of years, and the result is a bunch of barely-usable, stunted crappies. This will happen in big water, too, but not as frequently.

Gaston Reservoir, in north Warren and Halifax counties is the site of the story presented here, but you can select any one of a dozen similar impoundments this spring. Unless you've been told specifically where to fish, first check with local fishermen. If this proves to be a little less than red hot, watch for boat concentrations and head for the crowd. You may not find this much help, since many of our waters aren't fished to this extent. So, striking out on your own, head for the nearest cove which has water of around four to eight feet deep. The key to locating spawning crappies very likely is "brush" . . . tree tops, inundated bushes, and the like. Crappies almost demand this brush for egg-laying, although they generally do not deposit the eggs directly on the branches, etc. The nests, if they can be called that, are hastily fanned out spots in among the stickups, as the brush is often called. Hundreds of fish may be cruising a cove of a few acres with more waiting to move in.

If you can see the twigs and branches sticking out of the water, always try a few casts. Now needless to say, lure snagging is frequent, and lost tackle is one of the prices you must pay for this type of fishing. This isn't helped any by the fact that tackle should be fairly light in crappie fishing. For example, for maximum sport, ultralight gear is best. A five-foot spinning rod, teamed with a small, open-faced reel and four-pound test line is fine. Lures boil down quickly to two or three basic types. The old reliable is the jig. You can fashion your own for a few pennies apiece, or watch the sales and pick up a supply for 20 or 30 cents each.

One of the best types is tied with maribou feathers. These fluffy feathers give the jig a "live" look in the water and often produce better than standard bucktail or other hair jigs. Color isn't critical, but white and yellow turn the trick most often.

Tiny spinners may fill in well at times, but run the cost up when the light line snaps on a snag. Small spoons and plugs, or in fact, just about anything that resembles a small minnow, will take fish. If the crappies are there and in a striking mood, almost anything that you put in front of them will be gobbled up. But remember, crappies don't go far for the lure, nor are they in a hurry. The slower a lure can be fished, the better.

It takes a bit of courage to pitch a lure (particularly a fast-sinking jig) into a grove of trees. But unless you are experiencing some snags, you aren't reaching the most fish. A reel-and-twitch retrieve, trying several speeds and twitches will reveal the best method. Generally the fish are plentiful enough that you don't mind losing a few after they're hooked. But if many are freeing themselves before being hoisted aboard, try setting the

10

Pictured here beside this ultra-light spinning outfit are four variations of the jig; all will take crappies. The fish taken on this particular trip were almost all white crappies and ran fairly small. Let's hope your fish are bigger!

hook a bit more decisively and playing them a little more carefully. Crappies have very tender mouths which tear easily and they can be lost at any time. Landing a fish is sometimes a problem too. The accepted method, at least with the small ones, is to grab the line and lift them in. But a landing net assures a few more flopping in the boat. And then there's always that big bass that sneaks in among the crappies and makes off with the lure! If the crappies are hitting like they should be, there won't be time to string each one. A waiting cooler full of ice helps save time, and generally makes the fish better table fare too. Most folks scale the crappies, cut off heads and fins, remove entrails and fry. For almost bone-free eating, try filleting and skinning the fish. The fillets won't be large unless you've found some real lunkers, but the eating will be less tedious. ◆

Generally the fish will be numerous when a crappie spawning area is located. A cooler of ice makes it easier to quickly place unhooked fish in safe keeping. Consistent catches are common for several weeks, but you have days when activity is mighty slow. Check your spots often.

Reflections

IS there anyone among us who has never watched an old and gentle woman laying out the silver on Sunday afternoon? With infinite care she takes the heavy oiled cherry chest from its accustomed place on the high shelf and lowers it heavily to the dining room sideboard. Then turning the tiny brass or silver key, slowly, carefully and with all the ceremony of a priestess, she raises the wooden lid.

One at a time she brings out the faded maroon velvet bundles, places them side by side, in a row, and unties their velvet ribbons. Then, fold by fold, along the time-worn creases, she unwraps the dull glowing silver, turning each piece in her hands, examining it carefully before selecting the next. She finds pleasure in each familiar piece: each nick and scratch is a fond memory, each bent prong or chipped blade a remembrance from the past. After the meal, the ceremony is reversed. Each piece is cleaned and polished and folded away, a treasure to be taken out on special occasions.

Hunters are like this. Each folding away in the velvet of his own memory, with infinite care, that fat canvasback drake that swooped past the blind so fast in the wind it scared him, and then, unbelievingly, turned, circled again, set its wings and dropped right into the decoys; folding away that canvasback and laying it alongside his first squirrel, alongside the triple he made on quail once, alongside each of the other treasured memories he has acquired in a lifetime of hunting.

With the hunting season gone, many of us are already looking back over the year, picking our best shots, our best mornings, our best hunts; selecting and turning each carefully in our minds, checking and polishing before folding it away.

Perhaps then, when we have paused to examine our treasures, we realize more than at any other time just which experiences are valuable enough to fold away in velvet with the other silver, and which ones are the cheap, nickel-plated stuff that we are not always so proud to show. Perhaps, too, more of us should spend more time separating the silver from the nickel-plate. A more conscious and deliberate examination of our outdoor experiences might lead us to seek quality rather than quantity; might lead us to realize that one finely wrought piece of silver is worth more than a fist full of stamped, nickel-plate.

According to one nationally famous fisherman, a man grows into a fisherman through three stages. At first, he is eager to catch a lot of fish. Then as he begins to tire of quantity, he stalks only large fish. Finally, however, he no longer concerns himself with the size of the fish, but moves into the third stage of his development and seeks only those fish which are hardest to catch. At this point, he has come to realize that the pursuit is as important as the prey; that sport is not measured in pounds and inches or numbers. He learns, rather, that the quality of his experience is infinitely more important than the quantity. This is true of both hunters and fishermen.

As we review the past season, then, selecting those "pieces of silver" which we will treasure and take out later, proudly among friends, let each of us consider what he could have done to make each trip better. Did any of us spoil an entire day by shooting a duck on the water? Does any of us have, among his experiences of the season, an illegally slaughtered doe? Did any of us, in greed, tarnish the season by shooting out an entire covey?

In short, let us examine our outdoor experiences for the past year and weigh the silver against the nickel. Have we increased our talents? ◆ Tom Jackson

12

The Woodcock

by F. Eugene Hester

PHOTOS BY THE AUTHOR

THE woodcock is an unusual game bird with short legs, a pot belly, large eyes and a bill twice as long as a woodpecker's. He actually is a shorebird, closely related to snipes and sandpipers but, unlike his relatives, he chooses to live in wet woodland rather than along exposed mud flats or the seashore. His coloration is a combination of several shades of brown, cinnamon, black and gray, providing excellent protective coloration.

This interesting bird eats earthworms and other animal life which he finds mainly by probing in the soft earth with his long bill. This 2.5 to 3.0 inch bill is especially equipped for detecting and capturing food and can be opened and closed with-

The Woodcock

out moving the rest of the bill. In addition, his nose openings are near the base of his bill, making it possible for him to breathe when his bill is sunk a couple of inches into the mud. His feeding habits have earned for him the nickname of "timberdoodle" and "bogsucker."

The woodcock's home is mainly the eastern half of the United States and extending into the edge of Canada. The northern half of this range is the main nesting area, but some nests are found throughout its entire range. The nest is a simple cup-shaped depression in open, well-drained woodland. Four cinnamon-colored eggs with dark spots are laid and are incubated for 21 days. The nest is generally unconcealed, but the coloration of the female blends perfectly with the leaves and twigs of the forest floor, providing adequate camouflage.

Only a few hours after they hatch, the young are ready to leave the nest and follow their mother. By the time the young birds are three weeks old they are beginning to fly and by four weeks they are almost full grown. During the hunting season woodcocks usually weigh 6 to 8 ounces.

In autumn, woodcocks migrate southward to spend the winter in the southeastern United States. Although most woodcock spend the winter in the lower Mississippi Valley, many of them winter in North Carolina and other southern states. Many of them are killed incidental to quail or rabbit hunting, but some hunters enjoy specifically hunting for woodcock, and even train dogs to hunt for these birds. Their colors provide such wonderful camouflage that it is difficult to see woodcocks before they flush. Often, however, their presence can be detetcted by the probe holes they make with their bills and by characteristic chalk-colored droppings about one-inch in diameter.

Woodcocks are interesting and puzzling birds. An area that has many of them one day may be completely barren the next day or next week. Probably these erratic fluctuations are caused by temporary stop-overs by groups of migrating birds.

The best places to look for woodcock are young forest areas on poorly drained land. Alder thickets are ideal. Moisture content is a very important consideration; the right combination of cover and moist soil with earthworms for food seems to be the winning combination for woodcock hunting. Look for them in alder thickets along small streams and the borders of swamps. ◆

The woodcock has wonderful protective coloration which provides very effective camouflage for his incubating female. The nest (below) is typically a shallow depression on the ground in open woodland. A clutch of four eggs is common.

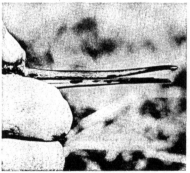

The woodcock can open the tip of his bill to capture food underground without opening his entire bill. Also note the position of the nostrils near the base of the slender bill; the bird breathes while probing for earthworms.

14

This ten or twelve-day old chick has found a tasty (?) earth-worm for lunch. In less than three weeks, he will be almost full grown and will be flying fairly well. Hunting woodcock with a good dog can be an interesting and exciting sport. The results of a hunt are these 6- to 8-ounce birds. They are ex-cellent eating when properly prepared.

by Diane Dean

Photo by Jim Dean

"LET me get this straight," said the seafood market clerk with a look of disbelief. "You want a dozen and a half blue channel crabs, but you want them alive. That right?"

"Yes, if you have them," was the reply.

"George!" hollered the clerk through the back door. "We got any live crabs out there? Yeah, have you got 18?"

A faint affirmative answer came back, and the clerk turned back to his customer. "You sure you don't want me to dress them?" he asked.

"Positive," was the answer.

Shortly, the crabs were brought out and placed in a cooler with some ice to keep them inactive.

"I guess it's none of my business, but what are you going to do with live crabs," asked the clerk, "keep 'em for pets?"

"No," laughed the buyer. "I'm going to steam them alive, and then eat them."

With that, she left the seafood clerk shaking his head slowly. Not many people buy crabs alive.

The strange thing about this true story is that it happened in a seafood market on the coast of North Carolina, where crabs are common. The point is that this clerk, like many other Tar Heels, apparently didn't know that hardshell crabs, steamed alive in vinegar and heavily caked with rock salt, coarse black pepper and seafood seasoning, constitute some of the finest eating known.

As far as I know, and I have eaten in many seafood eateries all over the state, steamed hardshells are almost completely missing from Tar Heel menus. In fact, you have to go to Maryland—or maybe Virginia—to find them offered in restaurants, and they're so popular there that restaurants specialize in them.

Not only are steamed crabs a rarity in this state, so are several other excellent crab dishes such as crab soup and good crab cakes. You can usually get a crab cake, deviled crab, crab meat panned in butter or softshells—in season —in the Tar Heel state, but that's about it.

To be sure, the crab meat panned in butter and the soft-shells are two dishes that aren't neglected in this state, and you can usually count on a feast when you find them. But in many places, you're likely to be disappointed with the crab cakes or crab Imperial, and you can't even find steamed crabs. The crab cakes, especially, are often mediocre; nothing more than greasy, hard cakes of shredded crab meat heavily mixed with bread filling.

It is unfortunate because blue channel crabs can be superb fixed in any of a dozen ways. The meat is tender, sweet and flaky, flavored somewhat like lobster, but with none of the toughness of lobster meat.

The only problem with crab dishes is that crab meat is often expensive unless you catch the critters yourself. Of course, you can do that by using a fish head weighted on a string and a long-handled net. By standing on a pier or wharf, you can often catch quite a few. Even if you can't catch them, you can sometimes buy them alive. The price for live crabs varies, but generally they are cheaper than fresh crab meat. If you buy it already dressed, it is quite expensive. If you do prefer it dressed, by all means get fresh backfin lump meat. It's more expensive, but it's free of all the shell fragments which make even the finest prepared dish a chore to consume.

If you don't like crab it probably isn't your fault. The chances are that you've never had crab fixed the way it should be fixed. Before you pass up crab as a culinary catastrophe, try these recipes.

Crab Cakes

Good crab cakes are easy to make, and once you've tried one of these, you'll never be content with one of those commercial jobs with all the flavor of a soggy birdnest.

Here's what you'll need:

1 lb. fresh crab meat (backfin lump)
1½ teaspoons Worchestershire Sauce
1 egg
1 tablespoon prepared mustard
½ tablespoon salt
dash of pepper
2 tablespoons mayonnaise
1 slice bread, trim crusts

To prepare, soak the bread in beaten egg, then tear it into small pieces and add the remaining ingredients, including the crab meat. Try not to break up the lumps of meat. Toss and carefully form into cakes about the size of hamburgers, then brown in hot oil. This recipe will make six large cakes or eight medium ones. The result is a crab cake that has only enough breading and seasoning to hold the crab meat together and flavor it. Better double that recipe. Nobody ever eats just one crab cake.

Softshell Crabs

This is an easy dish to prepare, and one of the most rewarding. You can buy the softshells dressed during the crab molting season. Season with salt and pepper, then fry in a mixture of half shortening and half butter until crisp. The flippers and legs will be like french fries, and you can eat the whole works. Serve on two slices of toast with sliced tomato and a dip of mayonnaise.

Crab Soup

Thick crab soup is a delight, especially served on a cold, raw day following a successful surf fishing or duck hunting trip. Basically, it is a vegetable soup with crab meat added.

Simmer one ham bone until you have a good ham stock, then add two cups of peeled tomatoes, two large chopped onions, two and a half cups of potatoes, two and a half cups of fresh corn, two cups of lima beans, one long red pepper, one-half teaspoon of cracked coarse pepper, one cup of carrots, one cup of okra, one tablespoon of sugar and tablespoon of salt. Simmer several hours, adding water if necessary. Then add one and a half pounds

of fresh backfin lump crab meat and cook another half hour.

Serve with crackers, hot coffee and wait for the applause.

Crab Imperial

If you want something fancy for a special occasion, try this dish.

Assemble the following:
½ fresh green pepper, finely diced
1 medium - sized piece of canned pimento, finely diced
1 teaspoon dry mustard
¾ teaspoon salt
¼ teaspoon white pepper
1 raw egg
⅓ cup mayonnaise
2 tablespoons melted butter
1 pound fresh crab meat (backfin lump)

Mix crab meat with other ingredients, taking care not to break up lumps of meat, then toss lightly. Divide mixture into four portions, then place in separate casseroles (large sea shells make attractive serving dishes, and will withstand the cooking heat). Coat each serving with a light topping of mayonnaise and sprinkle with paprika. Bake at 300 degrees for approximately 20 minutes.

Serve with tomato slices, cole slaw and french fries.

Steamed Hardshell Crabs

At last. This is the one that separates the men from the boys, one you won't forget no matter what happens.

Buy, beg or catch one dozen live blue channel crabs, selecting on the basis of weight, not size. To keep them inactive, that is, from crawling all over the kitchen, keep them iced down in a cooler.

Here are the ingredients. The amounts are not given because they vary with tastes.
Vinegar
Water
Seafood seasoning
Rock or flake salt
Coarse ground black pepper

Pour equal amounts of vinegar and water into a large pot until the mixture is about an inch deep, perhaps a little more. Place a rack in the pot to keep the crabs out of the liquid. If you don't have a rack, pile old silver-

ware (not sterling) or rocks in the bottom to keep the crabs dry. Put in a layer of live crabs, then sprinkle generously with rock or flake salt, pepper and seafood seasoning (Old Bay, Sauers or McCormicks). Make sure each crab is coated. The more seasoning you use, the hotter the crabs will be, but true afficionados prefer them hot. Some experimentation may be necessary with the first batch to get the recipe seasoned to your preference.

Cover the pot so that the crabs will not crawl out when the heat begins to cook them, then steam until they are red. It usually takes about 45 minutes. While the crabs are steaming, it is a good idea to cover the table (or floor) with newspapers and get into some old clothes. A bathing suit is ideal. Provide each guest with a wooden mallet or a table knife. (Either will crack the crabs. Use the knife's handle as a mallet).

Place the crabs on the table, then dig in. Be sure to provide plenty of cold beer or iced tea with iced water held in reserve for those whose tongues suddenly sprout flames from the hot seasoning.

To eat, break off each claw, then crack the claws open and suck out the meat. Then turn the body of the crab over on its back and pull off the tab. Crack the belly of the crab by placing the blade of the knife in the groove that you find on the underside and hitting it with the heel of your hand. Then pull off the lumps of shell and meat on each side where the legs are connected. What you have is two large pieces of backfin lump. Scrape the gills off each lump and anything else you don't want to put in your mouth. Pull the paper-thin shell away from the backfin lump meat, then eat it like a popsickle, holding the legs.

You've never eaten better in your life.

One word of warning. This dish is not for the squeamish, but if you like seafood, you'll love this, even if it does take about a gallon of tea (or something) to keep the fire down in your mouth. ♦

NORTH CAROLINA WILDLIFE

RESOURCE-O-GRAM
A ROUNDUP OF THE LATEST WILDLIFE NEWS

Public Hearings on Hunt Regulations Scheduled

As they have for the past 20 years, Tarheel hunters and trappers will be given an opportunity to speak their views on establishing the 1969-1970 regulations for taking fur bearers and nonmigratory game birds and mammals. (See also special article in May issue). Following are dates, times, and places, subject to minor change:

May 13, 1969	District 9	Sylva	Courthouse	7:30 p.m.
May 14, 1969	District 8	Morganton	Western Piedmont Community College	7:30 p.m.
May 15, 1969	District 7	Yadkinville	Courthouse	7:30 p.m.
May 16, 1969	District 6	Albemarle	Courthouse	7:30 p.m.
May 19, 1969	District 5	Graham	Courthouse	7:30 p.m.
May 20, 1969	District 4	Whiteville	N. C. Highway Com. Shop	11:00 a.m.
May 20, 1969	District 4	Fayetteville	N. C. Highway Patrol Barracks	4:00 p.m.
May 21, 1969	District 3	Rocky Mount	City Court Room	7:30 p.m.
May 22, 1969	District 2	Jacksonville	Courthouse	7:30 p.m.
May 23, 1969	District 1	Edenton	Courthouse	7:30 p.m.

Mountain Trout Season Opens April 5

The big day for mountain trout fishermen this year is April 5 when thousands of anglers will toss assorted baits and lures into nearly 2,000 miles of designated mountain trout fishing streams. In addition to having a valid state or county fishing license, all trout anglers 16 years old or older must have in their possession a valid trout fishing license costing $1.25 ($3.25 for non-residents), and on game lands where trout fishing is permitted, a daily trout fishing permit costing $1.65, or a season permit costing $15.25. The season permit will be valid for fishing on game lands anywhere in the state. Game lands fishing permits for central and eastern game lands, costing $3.25, will not be valid on game lands where trout fishing is available. NOTE: AS WAS THE CASE LAST YEAR, NO LICENSES OR PERMITS WILL BE AVAILABLE AT CHECKING STATIONS OR FROM GAME LANDS PERSONNEL. THEY MAY BE PURCHASED FROM LOCAL, AUTHORIZED LICENSE DEALERS.

Ready For Fishing? Boating?

With spring comes the advent of the boating and fishing seasons, and the Wildlife Resources Commission advises fishermen to be properly licensed, and boat owners to have their boats properly registered, numbered, and required safety and lifesaving equipment aboard. Combination hunting-fishing licenses are valid through July 31. Fishing licenses expired last December 31.

WILD AREAS

by Duane Raver

"**C**ONSERVATION of natural resources — their wise use — is universally approved. Yet vigorous disagreement often exists as to what constitutes wise use of a particular resource at a particular time. Different people react differently to the wide variety of physical, biological, economic, social, esthetic, and spiritual factors involved. Wilderness preservation, for example, has long been accepted as a desirable objective; but it took years to get the basic concept embodied in law, with the details of establishment and administration still to be worked out, and with no assurance that the primitive character of a wilderness area can be permanently preserved in the face of increasing hordes of visitors."

So begins Samuel T. David, Dean Emeritus, School of Natural Resources at the University of Michigan in his Foreword to the book, "Guidelines to Conservation Education Action*." Actually only a relatively small group of Americans will read these words, and even fewer will be motivated to any sort of positive action. Yet our irreplaceable wild areas are indeed dwindling.

Many of our natural resources, including the bulk of the harvestable wildlife in our State and Nation, should be used, but used wisely, rather than strictly "preserved." This concept is often unacceptable, or at best questioned, by those who would place all natural resources off limits except to observe or possibly to stroll through and not disturb in any way.

Yet the preservationist, that vastly out-numbered voice literally crying out in (and for) the wilderness, should be heard and heeded at least to the extent that some wild or untampered areas are permitted to be just that, maintained as Nature intended. Such locations, away from most influence of man, are

* Published by the Izaac Walton League of America, 1326 Waukegan Road, Glenview, Illinois.

difficult to find. And once discovered, often are ear-marked for immediate change in one way or another; "progress" we usually label it, and we certainly are for progress . . . aren't we? Thus they dwindle, these bits of Nature, study areas for y o u n g minds, "Islands of Green" as the National Audubon Society calls them.

To the person who now sees very little if any importance in these plots ranging from a few square yards of sandy beach to several square miles of misty mountain forest, except as potential development sites for housing, industrial complexes, and other dollar-dominant uses, to this person, any other use or argument aimed at saving the areas "as is," is well nigh futile. To this person, we ask only rational thought and consideration in the direction of setting aside unique green acres as inviolate sanctuaries for future generations to have and to hold.

TO speak of urgency in this matter could be likened to a debate as to whether to call the fire department while your house slowly burns down around you . . . it may be too late already; and most surely is for thousands of acres which never should have been touched by anything but the careful foot of a hiker. But you say, I don't know of these places until the auctioneer's gavel pounds the sale closed. Seek them out, have local organizations such as garden clubs, civic organizations, park commissions and so on, constantly on the lookout for them.

One group to watch for and to listen to is the band of dedicated conservationists whose organization grew out of an early December meeting held at the Betsy-Jeff Penn 4-H Camp near Reidsville, N. C. Dr. Arthur Cooper of the N. C. State University Botany Department served as chairman. The weekend meeting entitled, "Wilderness Workshop" was jointly sponsored by the North Carolina Academy of Science and the Wilderness Society, Head-

quartered in Washington, D. C. The theme of the meeting was the urgent action needed for natural area preservation in North Carolina.

A local need points this out and concerns a 55-acre tract a dozen miles f r o m Raleigh. Known locally as "the bluffs," or more properly, Hemlock Bluffs, it is thought to be a remnant of the ice age that descended on mid-America and brought a chilling climate to North Carolina and then retreated some 15 to 20,000 years ago. Several interesting things come together on this bit of Wake County. For one thing it has several large hemlock trees clinging to its steep-sided bluffs. These trees, perhaps the easternmost in the State, should have died out thousands of years ago; but still seedlings persist under at least one of the parent trees.

And to further this mountain-like setting, galax abounds under much of the shrubby vegetation. The bluffs in the area are some 60 feet high and drop suddenly to a creek bed, Swift Creek, which under normal rains, carries a meandering stream over the rocky bed. All along the face of this bluff, the temperature is always a few degrees below that of any of the surrounding area, perhaps offering one reason why the hemlocks have persisted.

BUT what next for this patch of Nature? At the first auction, a local insurance man bid some $60,000 for the tract only to see his bid raised on the last day set for the closing of the deal. At this writing, the issue is still somewhat in doubt, but the land most certainly will be in private ownership, whatever the outcome.

The impetus and often the final action on such areas must come from the state's people. Governmental agencies can lend some support and advice, but without the desire of the citizenry, land acquisition for such purposes is at best slow, and usually much too fragmentary. This places the bulk of the burden squarely in your lap. What is your next move on wilderness areas? ◆

19

SKIPPER'S CORNER
by
John R. Parker Jr.

WHEN I suggest that it is time for spring maintenance, time to pull boat and trailer from beneath their winter cover, some of you will say that I'm at least a few weeks behind. That is, some of you have by now lifted aboard a string of bass or shad or checked out your rig on a warm weekend cruise. I say, there ought to be more skippers like you.

Most members of the boating fraternity, however, are just beginning to have n a u t i c a l thoughts. Spring maintenance is a little hazy still. It's mixed up with memories of that last covey of quail, flock of greenheads or a fast basketball game. But nevertheless, it must be done. Don't you agree?

Proper storage last fall means less work now. As we occasionally comment, most of the Carolina small craft fleet does go into storage except for the hardiest of fishermen and, of course, hunters such as waterfowlers.

If your rig is one that was in proper storage, there remains only to check essentials like steering, lights, trailer bearings, tire inflation, put the safety equipment and other miscellaneous equipment on board, refuel, check the water pump and cast off.

What lies ahead if you just rolled the rig in the corner of the yard or just took an extra turn on the line down at the dock? Anything from shoveling out the pine straw to scraping the barnacles may welcome you and help devour your spare time.

Rather than belabor our introduction to spring with too many words, let's suggest a few items to help kick off the new season. We will leave out standards like: battery charging, waxing the fiberglass hull and motor tune-up so don't overlook them.

Life saving devices: Have you ever tried one on? When the water warms, why not have the entire crew go over the side, each in his own life vest?

Lights: Check out the trouble in that flickering navigational light now. It might flicker at a critical time.

Keel: This part of your boat takes a lot of knocks. Is it properly supported on the trailer? If wood, perhaps a metal strip is due for protection. Fiberglass may need repair, too.

Bilge exhaust: Does that electric blower actually come on when the switch is thrown? Remember gasoline fumes belong in the gas tank.

Compass: Is it truthful?

Anchor line: Still trying to anchor in 15 feet of water with 20 feet of line? Try at least 50 feet.

Shoes: (for you and your boat) Good boat shoes with non-skid soles are worth the investment.

Charts: How much do you really know about the waters you visit? Another good investment.

Safety: (in general) As a group, tens of thousands of us

interested in boating, we were more careless last year than in 1967. We, in fact, upset a three-year downward trend in boating fatalities. For the year ahead, let me suggest that we all resolve to learn more about boating safety, the boat law and also get to know the fellow in your area who enforces the law, Wildlife Proctector or Coast Guardsman.

New Access Areas in '68

The Wildlife Resources Commission's Division of Engineering completed seven fishing and boating access areas in 1968 bringing the total to 93. The seven new areas are: Tarheel Access Area on the Cape Fear River in Bladen County; High Hill Access Area on the Lumber River in Robeson C o u n t y; Lennon's Bridge on Big Swamp Creek in Robeson County; Snow's Cut on the Intracoastal Waterway in New Hanover County; Brice's Creek (near New Bern) in Craven County; Concord Church on the Yadkin River in Davie County and Troy on the Little River in Montgomery County.

Fiberglass can sustain many abuses, but a chunk of Piedmont granite or an eastern cypress knee can cause real problems. A fiberglass patch kit, sharp chisel, sandpaper and a little time can put the boat's hull back in good shape.

In case of real motor malfunction, your powerplant needs a qualified outboard mechanic. This is good preventive maintenance and a good time for close inspection. Right, the inexpensive scissors jack comes in handy in many trailer rig operations. Here, wheel bearings are inspected. Semi-annual inspection is advisable.

Don't forget the air horn. Better check that pressure can. Remember, a sound-producing device (horn or whistle) is required on craft 16 feet in length or over. Right, the tool kit may need some attention too. Socket and handle at right fit trailer wheel lugs.

This original equipment trailer winch was replaced with an easy-loading, 4 to 1 ratio winch filled with wire cable. All lights (above) should be placed in working order. Perhaps the problem is simply a loose base on the bulb. Lights are required between sunset and sunrise.

Plenty of line and two anchors are fine, but don't forget to have shorter dock lines, even for smaller craft. Note too, the numbers on the author's MFG "duck boat" have been re-varnished to add to their longevity.

North Carolina's Real

Big
Game

by Steve Price
Illustrations by Wade Walker

Wooly Mammoth

TODAY a sportsman would have to look long and hard to find truly "big game" in North Carolina. In fact, anything larger than a deer or bear is non-existent.

But it wasn't always that way. With the extinction of the dinosaurs at the end of the Mesozoic era some 65 million years ago, the age of mammals began, and the geographical area that is now North Carolina contained some mighty big game indeed.

One of the largest mammals was the mammoth, a close relative of today's existing Asian elephant. Mammoths were not common in North Carolina, although they certainly ranged this far south.

They were better adapted to live further north where their wool coat kept them warm, and where they could eat the branches of birch and hemlock trees. They grew to a height of nine or 10 feet, and had tusks that grew to nearly the same length.

Nearly-whole mammoths have been found frozen in Alaskan and Siberian quicksand, and paleontologists believe they came into Alaska via the Bering Strait, in company with the ancestors of the mountain sheep and Alaskan brown bear and the forerunners of the bison. From Alaska, the mammoth migrated across the country.

A second or third cousin of the mammoth once found in this state was the mastodon—another elephant-like creature that differed mainly in the structure of its teeth—those of the mastodon

limited it to eating light foliage.

MASTODONS were quite common, judging from the abundance of bones and teeth found. It probably looked very similar to today's elephants, except that it had shorter legs, a heavier body that was covered with hair, and tusks that occasionally curved upward to form a half circle. The mastodons, like the mammoths, also came into the New World from Asia and migrated into New York and southward after the recession of the last great ice sheet. Some of the bones appear so fresh that Thomas Jefferson thought in his day that the creature might still be living in the more remote parts of North America.

Scattered remains of teeth and bones of the mastodons have been located in several North Carolina counties, including Pamlico, Carteret, Pitt and Edgecombe; some of the finds are on display in the State Museum in Raleigh.

The mammoth and mastodon appeared relatively recently in the geologic time table—around a million years ago during a period known as the Pleistocene Epoch. Long before these two

animals migrated into the New World, however, North Carolina had other forms of "big game."

This was the age of mammals that began around 65 million years ago and which was brought about by two major factors: the development of modern types of vegetation that assured abundant food supplies; and the disappearance of the great predatory reptiles, the dinosaurs. These two conditions gave the mammals a free hand for development and the extraordinary manner in which the mammals took advantage of it is, according to one scientist, one of the greatest marvels of scientific history.

Some of the other "big game" that developed during this period to range over North Carolina

Sabre-toothed Tiger

22

Mastodon

included the giant beaver, the sabre-tooth cats and the glyptodonts.

THE glyptodonts were perhaps the most bizarre mammals ever to inhabit North America. Sometimes as much as 12 feet long, they migrated northward into this country from South America. They were armadillo-like creatures, encased in a solid carapace, with thick immovable plates joined at their edges, and rings of bony armor sheathing their long tails. With such a heavy covering the glyptodont was through necessity an open country animal, although it ranged from California to the North Carolina coast.

Another animal found primarily in the north but one that made it this far south was the giant beaver, who bore some resemblance to the beaver of today. They were as large as small bears, with incisor teeth averaging about nine inches in length. Where they originated, we don't know, but quite possibly they were indigenous to North America. North Carolina has yielded only a few teeth of these creatures, but larger remains have been uncovered in South Carolina.

Some of the most ferocious of the early mammals present in Pleistocene times included the great cats, or sabre tooth tigers. These animals were similar to today's African lion and leopard, differing mainly in the size of the upper canines which formed great, curving sabres six to eight inches long. The lower canines were much reduced, but when used with the upper molars formed a formidable weapon for both offense and defense.

These are by no means all the species of "big game" to be found in North Carolina during the Pleistocene Epoch, for the fauna of that period was remarkably rich and varied. In addition to the animals already described, there were also peccaries, bears, wolves, horses and giant sloths.

Why some became extinct and others did not is still an unanswered question, although theories abound. Some attribute the end of the mammoths to a lack of oil glands, so that there was no oily secretion to repel water when the animal was exposed to rain or melting snow. The wool became water-logged or perhaps frozen, so the mammoth perished from the cold.

Others believe the sabre tooth cats may have hastened the end of the mammoth and mastodons, for the two certainly ranked high on the cats' menu, judging from the frequent finds of both sets of bones intermixed in tar pits and peat bogs. Why the cats disappeared is another question—perhaps the coming of man hastened their demise, as he possibly did that of some other mammals.

Still others suggest changes of climate, the onset of new diseases, enemies, and a survival of the fittest, as causes for extinction. Probably all of these, as well as others, were factors in the process, something we may never know. So while a hunter today may have to look long and hard for a chance at "big game" he certainly wouldn't have a million years ago! ♦

Glyptodont

Lunchtime – For Fish

by Duane Raver

MOST everybody likes to catch big fish, or at least know that there are some big ones to be caught! And most farm pond owners want these big ones just as quickly as Nature can grow them. But fish, like any other animals, must have adequate food in order to grow, and the right kinds of food at the right times. Until recently, the concept of artificially feeding warm water fish in their natural habitats had been considered impractical if not unnecessary.

Over the last few years, however, many fishery biologists and fish culturists have come to look on this type of feeding in a new light. Although it should be thought of as still in the experimental, trial stage, perhaps this providing of extra food for warm water fish (bluegills and their close kin, particularly) holds the key to larger fish at a faster rate. Each piece of water must be judged by itself—size of pond, natural food, water quality, species of fish present, annual harvest desired, etc.

Since not all species respond to artificial feeding (bass, for example, rarely benefit directly from dry food) don't expect the entire fish population to sprout up overnight. But if you have a pond with a moderate water flow through it, one that has a high population of bluegills which you feel are not finding enough natural food, an automatic fish food dispenser may be your answer.

One such device that we recently saw demonstrated is called "E-Z Feed," a model designed and built by L. Edward Gallup of Cary, N. C. Ed has a picturesque pond right at his front door and has tried all sorts of fish combinations and management procedures for many years, the latest being the fish feeding experiment.

Although the idea of a fish feeder was easy to come by, the device itself took considerable figuring and thought even before the first pilot model could be constructed. And even then, at least one working model was tested and abandoned after a few weeks in favor of a better, more sophisticated type. One thing was for sure right from the beginning: the bluegills would eat the food, it was simply a matter of getting it to them in the right amounts at prescribed times and for the correct duration, automatically.

The present model, (which has a patent pending on it), ready for sale, uses a large capacity, weather-tight food storage bin, a precision auger to convey the food through a release opening, a low RPM motor to drive the auger, and timing device for completely automatic operation. The entire unit is self-contained except for the timer, which can be installed nearby. For areas away from A. C. power sources, a battery operated model is under development.

The food used in the feeder is a pelletized material specially formulated for fish. It has been a standard item in trout culture for years and is available in various sizes, both floating or sinking types.

The feeder, although originally designed for use on ponds where maximum yields of sport fish are desired, is also effective in fish hatchery operations and eliminates much hand work and manpower. It is even adaptable to other automatic feeding operations such as chickens, livestock and pets.

The designer and builder, Ed Gallup, makes no claims for better fishing in the waters in which the feeder is used, but one thing is for sure, fish gobble up the pellets, and the bluegills which respond to the dinner bell in his pond are growing every day. ♦

CRACKSHOTS and BACKLASHES by Rod Amundson

Provide Habitat PLACES WHERE WILDLIFE LIVE

NATIONAL WILDLIFE WEEK 1969 | NATIONAL WILDLIFE FEDERATION
March 16-22 | and State affiliates

It is rather interesting to note that the theme for this year's National Wildlife Week is "Provide Habitat — Places Where Wildlife Live." About 15 or 16 years ago the "Week" was established around such themes as "Save the Whooping Crane" or "Save the Prairie Chicken." While these were worthwhile thoughts, they lacked national scope, interest, and application. Very few Tar Heels or Californians got very much worked up about saving prairie chickens or whooping cranes or Florida's key deer.

But everyone, everywhere, can do something about restoring wildlife habitat. Over the past 20-odd years the Wildlife Resources Commission has distributed free of charge hundreds of tons of wildlife habitat seeds, millions of s h r u b lespedeza seedlings— enough to make a strip 15 feet wide stretching from Cape Hatteras to a point in the Pacific somewhere beyond Hawaii.

This, of course, has helped produce game to keep pace with a growing number of hunters. But the people of our state and nation must realize that every stretch of superhighway, every new factory site, every new housing development, and expanded airport destroys more and more wildlife habitat each year. There is no tapering off of this encroachment in sight.

Among the danger spots in habitat destruction are our wetlands, the vast stretches of salt marshes along the coast, swamps being drained to lower the water table in order to add a few more acres of crop land, and so on.

In the northern plains states we have a situation wherein one agency of federal government pays farmers to drain marshes to produce more grain, while another is trying to buy up these same marshlands for waterfowl production. To mix a couple of metaphors, this amounts to a paradox tossed on the horns of the well-known dilemma.

If you are much over 50, you can with reasonable resignation say to heck with it—let somebody else worry about it. If you are 30 or younger, you are a one-digit statistic in half of the population of the United States and a member of a generation that must face a choice between correcting the environmentally destructive mistakes made by your elders or succumbing to them.

If you are in the in-between group, you ought to be old enough, making enough money, and influential enough, to be concerned not only about restoring and improving wildlife habitat, but the air people breathe, the water people drink, and the food people eat—all, hopefully, uncontaminated by the poisonous effects of progress being made by the most affluent culture and society the world has ever known.

Joseph D. Moore

Joseph D. Moore is stationed at Lexington, Davidson County. He was born in Marietta, Georgia, March 2, 1944. His parents, Mr. and Mrs. Wayne D. Moore of Route 4, Hayesville, North Carolina, moved to Clay County when he was two years old. Dan is a

graduate of Hayesville High School. He served four years active duty in the U. S. Air Force and received his discharge in July 1967. He served one year of his duty in Thailand.

Dan completed the Pre-service School for wildlife protectors at the Institute of Government at Chapel Hill in December of 1967. He was employed by the Commission on May 1, 1968 as a Wildlife Protector Trainee, and was stationed at Albemarle, Stanly County. On July 1, 1968, he was appointed wildlife protector and was transferred to Lexington. Dan attended Defensive Tactics and Pursuit Driving Schools at the Institute of Government July 1968.

Mr. Moore is a member of the Southeastern Association of Game and Fish Commissioners, Law Enforcement Section. He is a member of the First Methodist Church of Hayesville.

Mr. Moore is married to the

All fines and any arrest or witness fees are paid into the school funds of the counties in which the violation occurred, and no part of the funds or costs collected are paid to the North Carolina Wildlife Resources Commission or its personnel.

former Della Mae Woods of Hayesville.

The theme: "Provide Habitat —Places Where Wildlife Live" is excellent. It has depth, soundness; it makes sense; more sense, perhaps, than many of us realize. Wildlife and people for uncountable years have occupied this earthly globe, more or less harmoniously. No one has yet successfully shown that any species of wildlife has ever consciously or unconsciously destroyed its own habitat and, ergo, itself. Only humans have this capacity.

For thousands of years people have been destroying each other by means ranging from fist fights to organized warfare. Now, through the findings of nuclear physicists, we have the capacity of destroying not only ourselves, but our total environment in one single, blinding, senseless flash.

The prospect of such a catastrophic end is beyond comprehension. Such a calamity will in all probability never occur. Instead, we humans, the highest form of intelligent life, seem to be doomed to go on gradually, by attrition, destroying our habitat, and ultimately, ourselves.

Let's provide habitat—places where wildlife live. Perhaps

while doing so we can provide habitat in which people may live! ✦

Clean Waters?

DEAR SIR:

Much emphasis has been on keeping North Carolina beautiful, cleaning out and making sparkling waters by getting rid of foreign objects in these waters.

Returning to my home state, I have found the rivers and streams in worse shape than when I left. In many places old cars have been put on the river banks right to the edge of the river to supposedly help hold up the riverbanks. What happens when these cars rust and become washed away along with the glass, etc., leaving nothing to uphold the riverbanks and filling the rivers with waste? This is not only taking away the beauty of the waters, but it is quite dangerous, too. There has been much comment made about this dumping of old cars into the rivers and most of the people feel that this should not continue to be done.

Surely something can be done about such a thing. Why have these old cars been allowed to obscure the beauty of the rivers and add to the foreign objects placed in the rivers daily?

Thank you for your time. I sincerely hope that something can be

done to help beautify our rivers and streams.

Sincerely,
WOODROW ROGERS
WHITTIER

Dear Mr. Rogers:

This will acknowledge receipt of a letter written by you to Mr. Rod Amundson, Chief, Division of Education, Wildlife Resources Commission, relative to the above subject.

The receipt of complaints by this Department relative to these practices is not unusual. In fact, investigation of a complaint similar to yours was made by personnel of this Department several years ago in your community. The investigation revealed that there was considerable evidence of the dumping of items, such as bottles, cans, paper, boxes, abandoned household furniture, automobiles, washing machines, stoves, refrigerators, etc. along the banks and in the streams. In addition to the above named items, there was evidence of the dumping of household garbage along the banks and in the streams in the area. All of these items are defined as solid waste and may or may not influence the quality of the waters. These practices are prevalent throughout western North Carolina and throughout the State for that matter.

While we agree that this practice is undesirable and certainly does not enhance the quality of the waters, the Statutes do not provide the Department of Water and Air Resources with the authority to deal with matters relative to the disposal of solid waste, such as heretofore described.

It is suggested that you report your complaint to your local health department and/or to your Board of Commissioners. There is a possibility that your County has ordinances which are provided for the control of such practices; if not, they may be encouraged to adopt such ordinances.

By copy of this letter, we are informing Mr. Amundson and Mr. J. M. Jarrett, Director, Sanitary Engineering Division, North Carolina State Board of Health, of your complaint and our position in the matter.

If we can be of further service to you, please so advise.

D. L. Coburn, Chief
Water Pollution
Control Division

Transplanted Access Area

DEAR SIR:

Concerning your January issue the picture on page 29 is not Thelma or Roanoke Rapids Reservoir. It is Gaston just across the Roanoke River from Roanoke Rapids: Note Federal Paper Board Inc. in center of picture and bridge in right—this is on Roanoke River just below tail-race. Incidentally Mr. R. C. Brown, resident

New officers elected by the Wildlife Resources Commission at its January meeting are Chairman, Orville L. Woodhouse, Grandy (center); Vice-chairman, Jay Waggoner, Graham (left); Secretary, Dr. Joe M. Anderson, New Bern. Election is held annually.

manager of Federal Paper Board Inc. is my fishing partner and I know he would not appreciate your moving him to Thelma.

In regard to the Roanoke bass, page 10, I have caught what we call Red Eye Chub in Little Fishing Creek a tributary of Fishing Creek. These weigh about a pound to a pound and a half. I have caught them spin casting on a jitter bug. Do you think we are talking about the same species?

W. GRAHAM LYNCH
ROANOKE RAPIDS

Mr. Lynch and quite a few other readers are correct, of course; we did transplant this access area because of a last-minute photo change, and failure to change the cutlines. Thanks to all of you that set us straight. Since the Roanoke bass and the rock bass (redeye) are very similar in appearance, there's really no telling at this distance which fish is being taken from Little Fishing Creek. Anyone who thinks that he has caught a Roanoke bass, should relay this information to Fishery

Biologist, William B. Smith, Route 3, Box 131, Rocky Mount, N. C. 27801.

Fish Book

The second edition of the popular booklet, "Some North Carolina Fresh-Water Fishes", is now available from the State Museum of Natural History. A total of thirty-nine fishes are treated in the book, with thirty-six of these illustrated in full color. For your copy, send 40 cents in coin, to Fish Book, State Museum, Box 2281, Raleigh, N. C. 27602.

SUMMARY OF 1969 TROUT REGULATIONS ON WESTERN GAME LANDS
WHERE A SPECIAL FISHING PERMIT IS REQUIRED 1/& 2/

Rainbow

Brown

CLASSES OF REGULATIONS

NATIVE TROUT REGULATIONS
a. Creel limit - 4 trout
b. Size limit - brook trout 6", rainbow trout 10", brown trout 10"
c. Lures - artificial lures having one single hook (may be restricted to "flies only")

TROPHY TROUT REGULATIONS
a. Creel limit - 1 trout
b. Size limit - brook trout 12", rainbow trout 16", brown trout 16"
c. Lures - artificial flies having one single hook

GENERAL TROUT REGULATIONS
a. Creel limit - 7 trout
b. Size limit - none
c. Lures - bait or artificial lure having one single hook

GAME LAND	STREAM (INCLUDING UNLISTED TRIBUTARIES)	MILES	COUNTY	REGULATION
BEAVERDAM	Beaverdam Creek	5	Buncombe	General Trout
BLUE VALLEY	East Overflow Creek	9	Macon	General Trout
	West Overflow Creek	6	Macon	General Trout
CANEY FORK	Caney Fork	20	Jackson	Closed to fishing
	Wilson Creek	3	Avery	NATIVE TROUT
	Upper Creek	9	Burke	NATIVE TROUT
	North Harper Creek	5	Avery	NATIVE TROUT
	South Harper Creek	3	Avery	NATIVE TROUT
	Harper Creek	2	Avery	NATIVE TROUT
DANIEL BOONE	Steels Creek	8	Burke	NATIVE TROUT
	Lost Cove Creek	5	Avery	TROPHY TROUT
	Gragg Prong	2	Avery	General Trout
	Rockhouse Creek	4	Avery	General Trout
	Craig Creek	2	Avery	General Trout
FIRES CREEK	Fires Creek	17	Clay	General Trout (except fish as bait is prohibited)
FLAT TOP	Big Creek	8	Yancey	General Trout
HARMON DEN	Cold Spring Creek	6	Haywood	General Trout
	South Toe River	25	McDowell	NATIVE TROUT
MT. MITCHELL	Curtis Creek	4	McDowell	General Trout
	Newberry Creek	3	McDowell	General Trout
	South Mills River headwaters to Wolf Ford	6	Transylvania	NATIVE TROUT
	South Mills River Wolf Ford to Turkey Pen Station	8	Henderson & Transylvania	TROPHY TROUT
	South Mills River Turkey Pen Station to Refuge boundary	4	Henderson	NATIVE TROUT
	North Mills River	4	Henderson	General Trout (artificial lures only)
PISGAH	North Fork French Broad	20	Transylvania	General Trout (artificial lures only)
	Avery Creek	5	Transylvania	General Trout (artificial lures only)
	Looking Glass Creek	4	Transylvania	General Trout (artificial lures only)
	Davidson River (above Looking Glass Creek)	8	Transylvania	General Trout (artificial lures only)
	Davidson River (Looking Glass Creek to Management Area boundary)	4	Transylvania	General Trout
	Bent Creek	6	Buncombe	General Trout

GAME LAND	STREAM (INCLUDING UNLISTED TRIBUTARIES)	MILES	COUNTY	REGULATION
RICH LAUREL	Big Creek	1	Madison	General Trout
	Hickey Fork	3.5	Madison	General Trout
	Big Santeetlah Creek	13	Graham	General Trout (except fish as bait is prohibited)
	Little Santeetlah Creek	5	Graham	General Trout (except fish as bait is prohibited)
SANTEETLAH	Deep Creek	6	Graham	General Trout
	Bear Creek	5	Graham	General Trout
	Slick Rock Creek (above Tenn. State line)	8	Graham	NATIVE TROUT
	Slick Rock Creek (on Tenn. State line)	3	Graham	General Trout
	Big East Fork Pigeon River	10	Haywood	General Trout
SHERWOOD	Left Prong West Fork Pigeon River	8	Haywood	General Trout
	Middle Prong West Fork Pigeon River	5	Haywood	General Trout (artificial lures only)
	Right Prong West Fork Pigeon River	3	Haywood	General Trout
SOUTH MOUNTAINS	Jacob Fork	5	Burke	General Trout
	Whiteoak Creek	5	Burke	General Trout
	Shinney Mountain Creek	4	Burke	General Trout
	Long Branch	2	Macon	General Trout
	Kinsey Creek	4	Macon	General Trout
STANDING INDIAN	Nantahala River (above concrete bridge)	10	Macon	General Trout
	Nantahala River (concrete bridge to Management Area boundary)	2	Macon	General Trout (artificial flies only)
	Dungeon (Dungear) Creek	2	Wilkes	General Trout
THURMOND CHATHAM	Joshua Creek	4	Wilkes	General Trout
	Pike Creek	4	Wilkes	General Trout
	Toxaway River	12	Transylvania	General Trout
TOXAWAY	Horsepasture River	6	Transylvania	General Trout
	Thompson River	4	Transylvania	General Trout
WAYAH BALD	Wayah Creek	6	Macon	General Trout

1/ Trout season - One-half hour before sunrise on April 5, 1969 to one-half hour after sunset September 1, 1969.

2/ Management Area streams open on all Wednesdays, Saturdays, Sundays, and legal holidays

NOTE: For further details see "1969 North Carolina Inland Fishing Regulations."

Brook

LITHO BY THE GRAPHIC PRESS, INC., RALEIGH, N. C.

Wildlife

IN NORTH CAROLINA

25 CENTS / APRIL 1969

Wildlife

IN NORTH CAROLINA ■

The official publication of the NORTH CAROLINA WILDLIFE
RESOURCES COMMISSION, Raleigh 27602. A monthly magazine
devoted to the protection and restoration of our wildlife resources
and to the improvement of hunting and fishing in North Carolina.

VOL. XXXIII, NO 4   APRIL, 1969

STATE OF NORTH CAROLINA

ROBERT W. SCOTT
GOVERNOR

NORTH CAROLINA
WILDLIFE RESOURCES COMMISSION

ORVILLE L. WOODHOUSE, CHM. _ _ GRANDY
JAY WAGGONER, V. CHM. _ _ _ _ _ GRAHAM
DR. JOE M. ANDERSON, SEC'Y _ _ NEW BERN
JAMES A. BRIDGER _ _ _ _ _ BLADENBORO
HUGH G. CHATHAM _ _ _ _ _ _ _ _ ELKIN
JAMES A. CONNELLY _ _ _ _ _ MORGANTON
J. HOLT EVANS _ _ _ _ _ _ _ _ _ ENFIELD
T. N. MASSIE _ _ _ _ _ _ _ _ _ _ SYLVA
ROBERT G. SANDERS _ _ _ _ _ CHARLOTTE

CLYDE P. PATTON
EXECUTIVE DIRECTOR

EUGENE E. SCHWALL
ASSISTANT DIRECTOR

DIVISION CHIEFS

ROD AMUNDSON _ _ _ _ _ _ _ EDUCATION
FRANK B. BARICK _ _ _ _ _ _ _ _ GAME
J. HARRY CORNELL _ _ _ INLAND FISHERIES
ROBERT B. HAZEL _ _ _ _ _ _ PROTECTION
J. THOMAS WILLIAMS _ FINANCE-PERSONNEL
C. FLOYD WILLIAMSON _ _ _ ENGINEERING

Wildlife in North Carolina recognizes the need
for close cooperation between State and Federal
conservation agencies and the people who hunt
and fish—to bring about a restoration of our renewable resources. The Editor gratefully receives
for publication news items, articles, and photographs dealing with the North Carolina out-of-
doors, but reserves the right to reject materials
submitted. Full credit is given for all materials
published.

* * *

Wildlife in North Carolina is published at the
Wildlife Resources Commission offices, Motor
Vehicles Building, 1100 New Bern Ave., Raleigh,
N. C. 27601.

* * *

Second class postage paid at Raleigh, North
Carolina 27602.

* * *

SUBSCRIPTIONS—Fifty cents per year, one dollar for two years. Make remittances payable to
WILDLIFE RESOURCES COMMISSION. Any
employee of the Wildlife Resources Commission
may accept subscriptions, or they may be forwarded to Post Office Box 2919, Raleigh, N. C.
27602. Stamps cannot be accepted.

Wildlife circulation this issue, 116,386.

IN THIS ISSUE

EDITORIAL STAFF

ROD AMUNDSON _ _ _ _ _ _ _ _ _ EDITOR
DUANE RAVER _ _ _ _ MANAGING EDITOR
LUTHER PARTIN _ _ _ WRITER-PHOTOGRAPHER
JOHN PARKER _ _ _ _ _ BOATING EDITOR
TOM JACKSON _ _ _ WRITER-PHOTOGRAPHER

The brown trout is not always
brown. As a matter of fact,
there are times when this largest of our mountain trout displays shades of blues and burnt
oranges. This bright colored
male seems to be trying to rad-
iate the hues of its rocky stream
home. He serves here to introduce an issue that is oriented
toward the mountains of the
Tarheel State.
Painting by Duane Raver.

PHOTO BY JACK DERMID

Excitement of Discovery

There's something about the finding of
a bird's nest that is fascinating. But it
is also a bit tempting to tamper with it
too. This cardinal's nest has been hidden
in a winged elm in some s e c l u d e d
thicket. Leave them alone.

On Trout and
Trout Fishing

by Chester Davis
Winston-Salem Journal-Sentinel

IF North Carolina is to provide the best trout fishing the streams of this state are capable of providing then we, as trout fishermen, must turn away from the old practice of catch-and-kill and, in its place, adopt a philosophy of catch-and-release.

That conviction is not based on a purist's distaste for so-called meat fishing. It is, instead, an inescapable conclusion resulting from some hard facts that confront us.

The first of these is the economic fact that the Wildlife Resources Commission cannot afford to continue to enlarge its put-and-take trout stocking program in an effort to match the mounting demands for more fish from an ever-growing army of trout fishermen.

The rather recent reduction in the state's creel limit recognizes this fact. The regulations on management area streams reflect the same recognition. Here the trend is toward reduced creel limits, larger size limits and to flies-only or one-hook artificial lures.

The Commission will, of course, continue to stock public waters. But that stocking is likely to remain at something like present levels rather than, as has been the case in the past, attempt to keep pace with an ever-growing, almost insatiable demand.

As this occurs—that is, as we hold stocking at about present levels in the face of a steadily enlarging number of anglers—there will be enormously increased rod pressure on our native trout population.

THERE are a number of reasons why our native trout, the fish that are the real basis of our trout fishery, cannot hold up under any substantial increase in rod pressure if that rod pressure is on a catch-and-kill basis.

We must recognize that our trout fishery is marginal or, as Nelson Bryant, outdoor writer for the New York Times recently said, "Trout fishing in North Carolina is good but it is also fragile."

It is fragile for these reasons: *Temperature.* We are located at the extreme southern end of the trout's range on the Atlantic seaboard. Our water temperatures in the summer tend to get up about as high as a trout can tolerate. Let this delicate balance be tipped—as it can readily be tipped by cutting away stream cover—and what was once trout water becomes smallmouth bass water. *Food.* Our free stone streams, utterly lacking any limestone, are very marginal in terms of producing insect life. They don't begin to produce the nymphal life or the fly hatches found on typical limestone streams. This, again, is a limiting factor in terms of population. *Scouring.* Our southern mountains quite frequently catch the whip lash of hurricanes. The incredible rains that are typical of such great storms literally take out the bottom of our streams. This scouring aggravates the already marginal problem of adequate food.

CONFRONTED by these facts we have no choice but to seek means through which we can protect our native trout population from the impact of even heavier rod pressure. At this moment, the most effective tools for doing this are those associated with the so-called fishing-for-fun philosophy; reduced creel limits, larger size limits, restrictions on the use of live bait and treble hooks and the acceptance of a fishing philosophy which emphasizes catch-and-release rather than catch-and-kill.

To the extent we do this we can continue to provide good—even very good in some instances —trout fishing in North Carolina.

Sooner or later most experienced trout fishermen adopt the catch-and-release philosophy even in the absence of regulations. They no longer feel that they must bring in a basket full of glassy eyed, very dead fish to prove their prowess as anglers. That's for the beginners and for that most unfortunate of men, the competitive angler.

The charm of trout fishing does not lie in killing fish nor does it lie in eating fish. It lies, instead, in the *sport itself*.

Trout fishing is, to begin with, the most solitary of all types of fishing. You can, of course, fish in teams or even in coveys if you like. But to experience trout fishing at its magnificent best you fish alone, setting your own pace and always learning as you go alone.

Properly selected, the tools of trout fishing are the most delicate, best balanced of all fishing tools. A well matched fly rod, line and tapered leader is a pleasure to use in itself: a pleasure that deepens as your skill ripens.

THEN there are the endlessly varied challenges of the sport itself. The challenge of correctly approaching the water you intend to fish, the challenge of "reading" that water wisely, the challenge of properly presenting your fly and maintaining a dragless float with that fly. On occasion, there are the puzzles of selecting just the right fly for the moment and, as often as not, this may be as much a matter of fly sizes as it is of pattern.

There are, of course, expert fly fishermen. But there is no man who has mastered the sport. The very best have days when they can't even "buy" a fish and even the very best of them know that there is always something more to be learned, something new to be mastered.

Add to these things the fact that trout fishing ordinarily is done in the most beautiful of all fishing settings. A gin-clear stream with its succession of pools, riffles, slides and half-seen pockets is a pleasure just to sit beside and study even when you have no rod in your hand with which to implement your study.

Because it is a demanding sport, trout fishing sweeps your mind clear of all cares except those happy ones related to the fishing itself.

And then there is the trout. Brook, brown, rainbow there is no more beautiful, no more wary, no more challenging fresh water fish. Alive they are beauty. Dead they are meat. As someone—I think it was Lee Wulff—once said, "A trout is altogether too beautiful a fish to be caught only one time." ♣

There's got to be more to trout fishing than catching and killing trout. The success of any trout management program depends on your cooperation.

Backpacking On the Appalachian Trail

by Steve Price

ERHAPS no other modern wilderness trail has gained as much fame as has the Appalachian Trail, the 2,000-mile "footpath through the wilderness" leading from Springer Mountain, Georgia, to Mt. Katahdin, Maine.

Conceived in 1921 as a path to follow the backbone of the Appalachian Mountains, the Trail is now world famous, and is enjoyed by thousands each year who come to hike, camp or simply enjoy the scenery of the Appalachians. As one writer has expressed it, the Trail is "remote for detachment, narrow for chosen company, winding for leisure, lonely for contemplation . . . it beckons not merely north and south but upward to the body, mind and soul of man."

Winding its way around the headwaters of the Chattahoochee River in the Blue Ridge of northern Georgia, the Trail enters North Carolina in the rugged Nantahala National Forest near Shooting Creek. From here it continues northward to Fontana Dam.

Fontana marks the second phase of the Appalachian Trail in North Carolina, for here begin the Great Smokies and Great Smoky Mountains National Park. For the next 70 miles the Trail leads through the center of the Park, following the crest of the Great Smokies along the North Carolina-Tennessee line and often passing through virgin spruce, fir and balsam forests reminiscent of the North Woods.

From Davenport Gap, the northern boundary of the Park, the Trail enters Pisgah National Forest,

Sweet-smelling fir and balsam stretch skyward along much of the Trail. A camper makes one last check of his pack in a clearing before going on.

another rugged, beautiful wilderness area characterized by steep gorges and high peaks.

The Great Smokies portion of the Appalachian Trail is the most popular among North Carolina campers, and indeed it is one of the best traveled sections of the entire 2,000-mile path.

Here wildlife, including black bear and white-tailed deer, abound; sleeping shelters and camp sites are larger and more comfortable; the Trail is well-kept and well-marked; and the scenery is spectacular.

From Fontana Dam, on the Little Tennessee River, the Trail ascends, sometimes steeply, for seven miles until it reaches Doe Knob (elev. 4,520) ft.). This is the crest of the Great Smokies, and the Trail follows this crest for the next 30 miles to Newfound Gap.

Newfound Gap (left)—halway between Fontana Dam and Davenport Gap. Here, equipment is stored prior to an outgoing expedition. Below, Fontana Lake forms the starting point for many Trail hikes.

Wildlife of some sort is frequently popping into view. Much of it is of the smaller variety—song birds, squirrels, grouse—but the bear isn't far away. Generally, they are not dangerous.

Slightly over 14 miles from Fontana the Trail reaches one of the steepest but most spectacular climbs of the Park, the ascent of Thunderhead. There are actually three peaks of the Thunderhead Ridge, and the Trail follows open crest during the mile and a half climb. Jagged boulders and open rocks lie along the Trail here, and on overcast, misty days, climbers are often lost to view from each other as they disappear in and out of the clouds.

Continuing from Thunderhead, the Trail alternately descends and ascends steeply to Clingmans Dome, following along a knife-like ridge over the summit of 6,582-foot Mt. Buckley. Clingman's Dome, at 6,643 feet the highest point on the entire Appalachian Trail, may be reached by automobile

Large shelters have been placed about one day's travel apart on the trail, but it's first-come, first-served, so be prepared with an alternate shelter. They're limited to one night use.

from Newfound Gap, and Trail users are often joined at the Dome by dozens of sightseers from nearby areas.

At Newfound Gap, seven and a half miles further, the Trail crosses highway U. S. 441 and a large parking lot overlook. From here it is 16 miles to Gatlinburg, Tenn., and 20 miles to Cherokee, N. C. This is approximately halfway between Fontana Dam and Davenport Gap, and is a favorite starting and ending place for short Trail trips. There are no public accommodations here, although a bus does stop in the parking lot during its run into Cherokee and Gatlinburg.

Four miles north of Newfound Gap, the Trail passes around the precipitous peak of Charlies Bunion, where hikers climb along a sheer cliff with a rock wall on one side and nothing but space on the other. Here, to the east, the jagged peaks of the Sawtooth Range ripple in the distance and to the northwest Mt. LeConte (elev. 6,593 ft.) sends its challenge to the world below.

The vegetation now is largely spruce and fir, much of it virgin forest similar to that found in central Canada. The crest line is particularly sharp in this portion, with a hiker being able to stand with one foot in North Carolina and the other in Tennessee. This portion of the Trail was cleared in 1933-35 by the National Park Service, and is easily identifiable by its worn condition.

The 70-mile hike from Fontana Dam to Davenport Gap may be made easily in eight days with frequent stops for rest and photography. The first half of the trip, to Newfound Gap, is steep and hard, but from the gap to Davenport the Trail drops some 3,070 feet in altitude.

Campers should be in good physical condition and versed in outdoor lore before undertaking an Appalachian Trail trip. Youngsters, families and coeds are frequently encountered on the Trail, but each knows his own limitations and travels accordingly. More than one party has found the Trail too steep and has had to turn back for lack of preparation.

Camping facilities along the Trail are in the form of three-sided, open front rock shelters, with wire-covered bunks accommodating 12 to 14 persons. Camping is restricted to one night's use and is on a first come, first served basis.

The shelters are placed about one day's journey apart, or about every five to eight miles, and there are 15 of them between Fontana and Davenport Gap. Shelters in the Nantahala and Pisgah sections have room for only five or six campers, and hikers traveling here are advised to carry tents.

Water is provided at each shelter in piped springs. Numerous additional springs cross the Trail at various points and are unmistakable and sometimes marked.

Garbage pits and latrines are also located at each shelter. Trail users are asked to pack all garbage out with them, rather than burying it, as bears often find the shallow cans and leave them strewn about the campsite.

Campfire permits are required of anyone camp-

ing on the Trail, and these may be obtained free of charge by writing to Park Headquarters, Great Smoky Mountains National Park, Gatlinburg, Tenn. Wilderness permits are also available, and do not confine campers to Trail shelters as do campfire permits.

Wildlife to be seen along the Trail includes, deer, ruffed grouse, squirrels, chipmunks, and black bear. The bears are most often found near the Trail shelters, and indeed, occasionally enter into the shelters in search of food.

Campers are strongly urged to put their packs on the wall pegs provided in the shelters, but even this is no guarantee they will be safe. One camper on the Trail recently strung his pack 12 feet off the ground, between two trees. During the night Mr. Bruin climbed one of the trees and leaped for the pack, which he promptly ripped to shreds.

Some campers have found a burning campfire will discourage the hungry bears, while others have discovered a long-burning candle will do the job. Both, however, have a habit of going out in the wee hours of the night, when the bears seem to prowl the most.

Bugs are not a problem on the Trail until hot weather begins in earnest around mid-summer. Small black flies, called "no see-ums," can make life miserable for campers unless an insect repellent is taken along. Mosquitoes and larger flies will also be encountered.

Perhaps one of the most interesting aspects of traveling along the Trail is watching the changing trees. At the lower altitudes, beech, maple and oak predominate, while a little higher yellow birch takes over, and still higher the fir, spruce and balsam are found. Then, as one descends again, the order is reversed. Closer to the ground, clover and

ferns abound, and in early June rhododendron breaks out in all shades of pink and purple.

Outfitting for a trip on the Trail should be done with care. Sturdy, well broken-in hiking boots are a must, as is a rain coat or poncho. Warm clothing should be taken, for temperatures often range 15 to 20 degrees cooler at the higher altitudes. Packs should ride comfortably and firm and should be padded to prevent chafing. Canteens, snakebite kits, hand axes and flashlights are also on the list of essentials.

For food, most backpackers prefer the light, freeze-dried foods, available from many national sporting goods firms. These foods, relatively inexpensive, are light and need only water and heat when being prepared. Practically any food is available freeze-dried, from spaghetti dinners to scrambled eggs, and they may be obtained in individual or family-size servings.

One item campers will find a tremendous help in their trips is the "Guide to the Appalachian Trail in Tennessee and North Carolina," publication No. 24 of the Appalachian Trail Conference, 1718 N. Street N. W., Washington, D. C. This $3.75 book gives very detailed information of the Trail in the Great Smokies and also in the Pisgah, and includes detailed maps of the routes.

So get your hiking boots on and load up your pack. There's fun and adventure waiting for you when you give the Appalachian Trail a try. And after you've hiked part of it, you may just decide to go the entire 2,000-miles! ✥

by
John R. Parker
Jr.

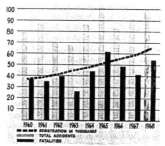

BOATING ACCIDENTS 1960-68

APRIL is the month that sess boating activity really getting underway and, unfortunately, the accompanying tragedy. Without a great deal to say about the unhappy side of boating in North Carolina, we would call your attention to the accident chart below; it gives you the annual picture. However, in looking back at a more detailed chart, for 1968, I find that there were two fatal (three fatalities) and six non-fatal boating accidents in April. This is slightly better than the record for April, 1967. Let's try to make this April, that month of crappie, shad, and restless bass even safer.

Motor Fuel

We claim no similarity to an outboard engineer. And perhaps some of these thoughts are a bit less than original; however, when we cruise across a good bit of information, we simply like to pass it along with credits, of course. We recommend to your reading, "Fuel For Your Outboard," by Willard Cloud, in the February, 1969 issue of *Popular Science*. If you don't get the opportunity, here's some of what the article included.

First, as you may know, the old standby, marine white gas is almost a thing of the past. This fine outboard fuel, free of additives, is getting more difficult to find. There is still a very popular brand on the market, however. Secondly, Mr. Cloud points out that many of the "marine" gasolines sold at marinas are simply regular grade automotive gasolines. They have additives to reduce gum formation during storage. The question Mr. Cloud raises is "What, if anything, is automotive gasoline doing to your outboard?" Also, what about the new oils and associated mixture ratios?

Well, it seems that the gasoline question is rather simple to answer. Use unleaded white gasoline if available; motor manufacturers still recommend it. However, according to Cloud the petroleum companies say it doesn't matter. Regardless, if you have read your motor manual, you know to use regular auto gas (if the better, more expensive white is not available) rather than premium. The premiums have additives, "unhealthy" for two-stroke outboards, which combat spark plug fouling, etc. in four-stroke automobile engines.

The author also warns against buying the low quality white gasoline, that is sometimes advertised as appliance, lamp, or stove fuel. The experts say it's better to use regular automotive fuel than these. Low-lead light aircraft fuel is also regarded as a good outboard fuel, says *Popular Science*.

The new outboard oils are reportedly designed to modify some of the detrimental effects of leaded gasoline. The major outboard manufacturers recommend there relatively new 50-1 ratio oils as opposed to petroleum company outboard oil. (The outboard company made oils are generally a little more expensive.) And all concerned agree that pure automotive oils are taboo. Here again it contains the wrong additive. And as Mr. Cloud says about pure automotive oils,

they are designed for a long life, while outboard oils are designed for a short but happy life. Out board companies say their special designed oils are, in lay terms, simply better for the motor.

The "new oil" mixes better, motors are better and require less of the new oil. Some companies even recommend 100-1 with their special oils. But some of the older motors still require more oil or the older, safer 24-1 ratio which is o.k. to use if you are uncertain of your engine requirements. But then, why be uncertain? Read that motor manual, or better still, check with a reputable dealer.

Which oil? Which gas? You don't have to be an engineer to understand that you want top performance and long life from your investment. The choice is yours.

And How We Burn Gasoline

Thousands upon thousands of gallons are burned each year by North Carolina pleasure boaters. By the time you read this, North Carolina may or may not have a new marine fuel tax law. Most of you will remember that the 1967 version, SB 601, was a two-year appropriation bill, leaving future funding in doubt. If, as you read this, a new bill has been introduced and its outcome is in question, you may wish to have a part in that outcome. Wouldn't you like to see your unclaimed marine fuel tax dollars go into a progressive statewide boating program?

A flash of red streaked around a corner of my Chapel Hill cottage, then I heard a thump against one of my living room windows. Fluttering against the outside glass, a brilliantly red cardinal, or redbird, attacked the window furiously with his stout reddish bill, strongly rounded wings, and claws. Apparently he had seen his own reflection in the window and thought it was a rival bird. He was fighting to drive it out of my garden which he claims for his own.

After awhile, the cardinal, slightly smaller than a robin, alighted on my window sill. Through the glass I saw him excitedly raise the sharp crest of red feathers on top of his head. The small area of jet-black feathers around his bill and under his chin showed in sharp contrast to the otherwise complete red of his head and body. He panted for breath and his brown eyes flashed anger.

For two April days, this male of the pair of cardinals that nest in my garden had fought his reflected image in the window. Had it been a live cardinal facing him he would have driven it away, but when he looked at the glass, his reflected image was always there to challenge him. Like each pair of robins, catbirds, and mockingbirds, that nested in my yard each spring and summer, the cardinal was fierce in the defense of his nesting territory. From it he drove away *any bird of his own kind*

*John K. Terres, field naturalist and free lance writer, is the author of SONGBIRDS IN YOUR GARDEN, a book about bird attracting, and the recent book, FLASHING WINGS: The Drama of Bird Flight. He frequently writes nature articles for magazines, and is the author or editor of some thirty books of natural history. Mr. Terres now makes his home in Chapel Hill. (See "A Walk with a Naturalist," December, 1968 *Wildlife*).

though he tolerated *other* kinds of birds, just as my catbirds, robins, and mockingbirds tolerated him. Seemingly, this is nature's way of assuring each pair of nesting birds sufficient food and freedom from competition, from their own kind, to raise the broods of youngsters they produce each summer.

To prevent the male cardinal from injuring or exhausting himself I put a screen over the outside of the living room window. He could no longer see his image in the glass and this ended his futile and dangerous battle with the window.

Frank M. Chapman, formerly the head of the bird department of the American Museum of Natural History, New York City, once found out the limits of a male cardinal's territory by using a mirror. He started by placing the mirror upright in the middle of the bird's territory near the bush in which its mate was nesting. Immediately, when the male cardinal saw its reflected image in the glass, it began to dash at it and to spar with it just as though it were facing another male.

Gradually, Chapman moved the mirror away from the nesting tree, 25 feet at a time, and each time the cardinal came back to fight its reflected image. When Chapman had moved the mirror about 110 feet away from the nest, the cardinal no longer fought its own image. It lost interest because the supposed rival it had seen in the glass was outside of its own territory, and therefore it was no longer a "threat" to be chased away.

Of the approximately 650 kinds of native North American birds, the cardinal is one of the most brilliantly-colored, and has a variety of rich, whistled songs to match the glory of his red feathers.

Aretas A. Saunders, a well-known student of the songs of American birds, studied the cardinal over its wide range from Canada south to the Gulf States, west through Texas, Arizona, and New Mexico. In Delaware, he listened to a male cardinal that sang 28 different songs in three days. The cardinal is one of the earliest birds to sing in the morning, often while it is still dark, and it sings in every month of the year. It is not usually a migratory bird and is generally a year-round resident wherever it lives.

In the South, where it is called Kentucky cardinal, Virginia redbird, crested redbird, and other names, it reaches its greatest numbers. It is the official State Bird of North Carolina, Virginia, Ohio, West Virginia, Illinois, Kentucky and Indiana. Equally at home in dark remote swamps, field borders, thickets, hedgerows, and in town and city gardens, it is one of the best loved birds in America. Besides those who love it in the South, people in the North admire the cardinal for the same reason, and are getting to know the bird better as it has gradually extended its range there during the last 20 years.

WHEN I was Editor of Audubon Magazine for the National Audubon Society in New York, my office window on Fifth Avenue overlooked Central Park. Each year at least half-a-dozen cardinals that I knew nested in the 800-acre park, along with robins, grackles, and other wild birds. Sometimes, in spring, I saw a peregrine falcon that nested on the stone ledges of a building overlooking the Park, swoop down and pluck a park pigeon or starling out of the air, but I never saw one of them attack a cardinal. The cardinals nested in the densest thickets and rarely flew high enough above the trees to tempt a peregrine.

When the male cardinal had finished his "battle of the window" in my Chapel Hill garden this spring, he followed the female everywhere. The male's courtship of the female is very devoted and I had often seen him catch some of the early green spanworms on my elm tree and then feed them to the female. While he did so, she fluttered her wings and whined piteously, like a baby bird. This is the courtship feeding, indulged in by cardinals, blue jays, and other songbirds. Apparently it strengthens the bond between the birds through the nesting days ahead.

THE female cardinal is yellowish-brown, with bright red feathers only on her wings, tail, and in the crest of feathers on top of her head. She sings, too, which is unusual in female birds, and sometimes I have heard her singing softly on the nest. Our female usually lays three white eggs, splotched with reddish brown (cardinals lay two to four eggs in a set and do not start to incubate them until the last egg in the set is laid.) In twelve days the eggs hatched. Nine days later, when the three pink-feathered youngsters left the nest, the male took over their care while his mate built another nest and laid another set of eggs for her second brood.

To attract cardinals the year round, I put whole or cracked corn in my bird feeders, along with the sunflower seeds in the wild birdseed mixtures that one can buy at grocery or feed stores. In spring and summer my pair of cardinals and their young eat many of my garden insects—Japanese beetles, plant lice, grasshoppers, cicadas, bark beetles, woodborers, and others. In late summer and in fall, they eat the seeds of wild grapes (a favorite), blackberries, dogwood berries and other wild fruits. They are especially fond of the seeds of smart-weeds, bindweeds, and foxtail grasses.

One of the most fascinating experiments I have ever heard of concerned what may have been the first introduction of the cardinal into a northern state. It happened near Boston, Massachusetts in 1897, about 70 years ago. Cardinals were very rare in Massachusetts at that time, and were not known to nest there. One day a wild cardinal appeared in a backyard of a quiet country house near Brookline. The housewife put out food for it, and the cardinal came to her porch everyday that winter to be fed. In the spring, the cardinal became restless and sang a great deal.

The housewife thought that the cardinal was looking for a mate. At her suggestion, a neighbor brought over a female cardinal in a cage to see what the wild male cardinal would do. At that time cardinals could be kept as cagebirds, which is no longer permitted in this country where almost all songbirds are protected by state and federal laws.

The male cardinal eagerly courted the female from outside her cage for 17 days. Each day he brought her food which he fed her through the bars of the cage. One day in April the owners of the caged bird opened the door and gave the bird her freedom. Within a week she had built her nest in a shrub in the garden and by May, four young cardinals had left the nest. This was the first known record of a cardinal ever receiving young in Massachusetts. Perhaps some of the cardinals that one sees in Massachusetts today may be descendents of the 1897 pair of the Brookline garden.

HOW long will a cardinal, or redbird, live? Dr. C. Hart Merriam, a brilliant American naturalist of two generations ago, head of a federal organization that preceded the present Fish and Wildlife Service, wrote that his grandmother had one in captivity for 21 years. Alexander Wilson, a Scot who came to America in the early 1800's and became the "father of ornithology," wrote that in Peale's Museum in Philadelphia, there was a stuffed skin of a cardinal that was more than 21 years old when it died.

I know of a wild cardinal that lived for more than seven years in a garden at Glenholden, Pennsylvania; another in Arizona lived to the same age; and at La Crosse, Wisconsin, one lived for nine years before it was shot and killed. The "champ" or the oldest cardinal I know of in the wild, lived in a garden at Nashville, Tennessee. He was almost fourteen years when he died, apparently of old age. ♦

PHOTOS BY JOEL ARRINGTON

Exploring Linville Gorge

by Steve Price

DURING my years of camping, I have pitched a tent in some of the wildest, most inhospitable places in the United States, including snow-covered mountain summits, alligator-infested swamps and wind-blown ocean islands. Few trips, however, have been as hard or as thrilling as a trip I made one summer down Linville Gorge.

Linville Gorge, scoured out by the turbulent churning action of the Linville River, is a tremendous 12-mile canyon located in the western part of North Carolina, just off the Blue Ridge Parkway near the towns of Marion and Morganton. The river, tumbling for over 2,000 feet in its chaotic rush down the gorge, is cradled in a wild, untamed land, known as the Linville Gorge Wilderness.

Named for explorer William Linville, who along with his son was scalped by Indians here in 1766, this 7,600-acre tract of land was set aside in the 1964 Wilderness Act of Congress. It is one of the most rugged areas in the eastern United States, and has been called the "Grand Canyon of the East" by many.

It offers a challenge to outdoorsmen everywhere, and because it has received little publicity, few travelers have invaded the rugged beauty of its boundaries.

Many tourists driving along the scenic Blue Ridge Parkway near Marion, about 50 miles north of Asheville, stop to see famous Linville Falls, the actual beginning of the gorge. These upper and lower cataracts may be reached by an easy 15-minute walk along well-worn paths, but few who view them realize that even more spectacular scenery may be seen further down the gorge itself.

GEOLOGISTS believe the falls were once 12 miles to the south, on the edge of the broad Catawba Valley. The constant eroding action of the river wore away the soft layer of underlying rock, causing the falls to "walk" up the mountain. After millions of years the falls reached their present location—after creating a miniature Grand Canyon along the way. Future movement of the falls will probably be much slower, due to a layer of hard quartzite that now underlays the falls.

There are several entrances into Linville Gorge,

12

all of them Indian-like foot trails that lead through a dense forest of oak, ash, pine and sourwood. These paths, named Bynums Bluff, Cabin, Babel Tower, Sandy Flats, Conley Cove and Pinchin Trails, are marked at their starting points along state road 105.

This single lane gravel road follows the western ridge of the gorge, from the town of Linville Falls to state highway 181 north of Morganton.

Once inside the gorge at the river's edge, the traveler is greeted by an awe-inspiring spectacle. As far as the eye can follow, the river is white rushing water, and gargantuan boulders that have washed loose during flood water or fallen from the steep cliffs above. The rocky cliffs rise nearly perpendicularly for hundreds of feet in places, and only then do they give way to a heavy forest undergrowth of mountain laurel, rhododendron and chokeberry.

To the west is Jonas Ridge, rising nearly 1,400 feet from the floor of the gorge. Further down one sees the fantastic rocky Pinnacle of Hawksbill Peak, its weird summit shaped by countless ages of wind, rain and storms. Still further are Table Rock Mountain, suggesting some ancient fortress; and the Chimneys, a jumble of overhanging cliffs. All are covered with virgin timber.

HUNTING and fishing are permitted in the gorge during season. Bear, deer, ruffed grouse, squirrel and raccoon may be found in the area, and brown and rainbow trout lie at the foot of the many fast rapids, waiting for an angler's fly. Other wildlife in the gorge includes rattlesnakes and copperheads.

Camping and hiking are also permitted in the gorge, and all those doing so are strongly advised to notify the Pisgah National Forest Ranger in Marion of their plans. More than one party has had to be rescued from the gorge in recent years. A hiking trail just above the river follows the gorge for about five miles, leading out of the canyon at Conley Cove, just beyond Wiseman's View.

For those not planning to enter the gorge, the U. S. Forest Service has constructed a special vantage point at Wiseman's View. Located approximately four miles from Linville Falls along state road 105, this overlook provides a breathtaking view of the entire eastern rim of the gorge and several miles of the winding river below. Picnic tables, drinking water, trash disposal cans and comfort stations are also located here. This is not a campground, however, and overnight camping is prohibited.

This then, is Linville Gorge—a mighty, savage canyon that only Nature could create. It is one of the few remaining spots that has not felt the impact of civilization, and because of its near inaccessibility, it has truly remained a natural paradise. ♦

A group of Boy Scouts, hiking the gorge, stops to make camp and cook their supper. "Be Prepared" should be your motto here, too!

Linville Falls is only the beginning of the gorge, and the river tumbles and seethes its way down many miles of spectacular scenery.

Wildlife Management Area Personnel- Their Job

by A. E. Ammons
Wildlife Area Manager
Staff Photos

There are always "just a few more things" to be done by wildlife management area personnel, no matter what season of the year. Lee Boone checks hunt permits during a busy time.

"MORE sport for more people, equal opportunity for all." This is the motto of the Wildlife Resources Commission. In its effort to continually improve North Carolina's wildlife program in keeping with this motto, the Wildlife Resources Commission now manages 52 public hunting areas across the state. Of these areas, 19 are under the direct assignment to one or more specially trained wildlife managers. These areas are developed to offer prime hunting to the sportsmen of North Carolina. As a result of intensive management and protection, some of them provide good deer, bear, and waterfowl hunting, and small game has prospered on all of them.

The primary responsibility of the personnel assigned to these areas is to produce a harvestable surplus of the wildlife species which occur and to protect this game from illegal hunting and predation. This protection effort never ceases, while the many other management and developmental practices are carried out seasonally during the course of the year.

Some of the jobs accomplished by the area managers include the following: pasture plantings, which benefit most all wild creatures, are maintained on all areas occupied by deer, although they are limited on some areas due to the rugged terrain. These pastures are periodically fertilized according to soil test recommendations and are replanted as the need arises.

Existing fruit trees on the areas are pruned and properly fertilized for maximum yield for the benefit of the game, and new trees and fruit producing shrubs are planted where possible.

Browse cuttings or openings are established at selected spots over an area to provide new sprout growth within easy reach of the deer. This is done by selecting a site where the forest has matured beyond a browsing stage and by simply cutting everything on the site which is usually from one to two acres in size. This not only starts new sprout growth from stumps of fallen timber, but opens the forest to permit small seedlings to grow. The fallen brush and trees offer excellent cover for small game.

Salt stands are maintained on the areas to supplement the wild animals' natural requirement for salt and other trace materials.

When new areas are established, they are sometimes stocked with deer from other areas which have an established herd. Box traps have been used to catch these deer for many years and more recently the capture gun which fires a dart-like projectile containing a tranquilizing drug has been used very effectively. The capture gun has also been used for immobilizing deer to be ear tagged with colored streamer tags for the purpose of tracing the movements and migration habits of deer on a given range.

Road maintenance and the clearing of hunter access trails are important prerequisites 'in' effecting an even distribution of hunters over an area. All roads and trails are clearly marked with appropriate signs. In addition the major trails 'on some areas have been marked with paint to assist hunters in finding their way in strange country.

The boundaries around the management areas are kept properly painted and posted with signs in order to distinguish these areas as special places where special rules and regulations apply.

The result of most of the year's work in development and management culminates with the game harvest during the open hunting season. Management area personnel conduct the scheduled hunts on their respective areas. In addition to patrolling the area, checking hunters for proper permits, enforcement of safety requirements and bag lim-

14

its, the area manager is also responsible on deer hunts for proper collection of deer jawbones and other specimen material. This material is used by the game biologists for study to determine different deer age classes and population levels. This information is necessary in order to set seasons for proper harvest.

Most of the management areas have public fishing waters which must be stocked periodically. These waters must then be patrolled regularly to insure proper compliance by the fishermen with license and permit requirements.

As previously stated, the job of wildlife protection is always primary in each man's mind as he goes about the many other duties which are essential to the operation of a wildlife management area. While pruning an apple tree, he might hear a pack of stray dogs chasing deer on the area. He must pursue these predators until they are captured and removed from the area, or next year's deer crop will surely suffer.

He may be driving a farm tractor and hear a gunshot on a distant ridge. The farm work must be halted temporarily and every effort must be expended to apprehend the apparent trespasser. Or he might be in his truck headed toward a distant corner of the area to replace boundary signs which have been torn down by a wind storm, or more probably by vandals, when he receives a call from the local county wildlife protector for assistance on a report of pre-season hunting in another part of the county. These examples are not fictitious; actually they are quite commonplace in the daily routine of management area personnel.

The reader might conclude from this that a wildlife area manager must be a jack-of-all-trades. This is certainly true to a great degree. But to make sure that they are well-qualified and well-trained, the Commission screens all applicants for physical fitness, aptitude, interests, and general knowledge; and then sends job candidates to a special three-week basic training school conducted by the Institute of Government at Chapel Hill. After graduation and employment, area managers attend periodic special training schools. This special training, plus natural interest and intense dedication to a career in wildlife management, makes these men very special jacks-of-all trades who are qualified, trained and capable of conducting the great variety of tasks required to insure that a wildlife management area serves its intended purpose — production of sustained crops of harvestable wildlife for the benefit and well-being of the sportsmen of North Carolina. ◆

The management of people often takes as much time as looking after the wildlife! Forestry Aid John Tucker helps with checking in hunters and affixes a sticker to the pickup windshield. Many areas. have trout streams which need stocking (lower), and this often means back-packing the fish to headwater areas.

Holly Shelter Area Manager C. A. Manning, Jr., cuts a lane for improved hunter access (above), while Caswell Area Manager Earl Sanders checks a wildlife food planting of sorghums.

Meeting The Demands For Southern Hardwoods

by J. S. McKnight

Southern Forest Experiment Station
Forest Service, U. S. Department of Agriculture
Stonville, Mississippi

ANYONE who buys high-quality southern hardwood logs, or the products made from them, knows that there is a supply problem. Costs are rising rapidly, largely because supplies are dwindling. The latest statistics indicate that native hardwood timber of standard lumber and veneer size and grade is being cut 50 percent faster than it is growing. Meanwhile, demands for hardwoods for pulpwood in the South have increased eightfold in the last ten years, and some of the most productive sites for timber growing are being cleared for other uses.

Having spent many years in hardwood research, I look upon these developments with less alarm than most wood buyers. I believe that sufficient volumes of southern hardwood can be grown, that forest productivity will be greatly increased, and that economic forces now at work will speed the necessary changes in log and wood marketing, and in resource management.

Satisfying demands for southern hardwoods will be an imposing, but not impossible challenge. Neither men, nor industries, nor nations do things much sooner than they have to. Thus, it is not surprising that forestry is only beginning to make progress with southern hardwoods. In the past,

saw logs from old-growth timber in the South readily filled half of the Nation's needs for hardwood lumber and veneer.

Now, of course, the needs of the traditional industries, along with those of a rapidly growing pulp industry, must be met in second-growth stands —stands that occupy a steadily shrinking land area.

The best southern hardwoods grow on broad bottom lands, but competition for such sites is increasing. Farming, damming, and drainage have taken many of the best sites out of timber production. In the lower Mississippi Valley, over a million acres have been cleared in the last few years. Elsewhere, some satisfactory hardwood sites have been converted to pine, and most stands have been cut with little thought of regeneration or future timber potential. There has been too little, if any, coordination of harvests to assure that round products reach their highest use. Thus, landowners often have not received maximum returns, and have not been encouraged to grow hardwoods.

I think, however, that these negative aspects of the southern hardwood supply problem will be more than offset by positive ones. In spite of land clearing, 100 million acres in the South are occupied principally by hardwoods. At least two-thirds

---

This is the first of a series of five articles on hardwood management by Mr. J. S. McKnight of the Southern Forest Experiment Station of the U. S. Forest Service. The author has been engaged in hardwood forest management research in the South for the past 20 years and is considered to be the outstanding expert in this field. We are reprinting these articles, which first appeared in the **National Hardwood Magazine** because of the importance of hardwoods to wildlife. Many of Mr. McKnight's findings and recommendations in regard to hardwood management are applicable in North Carolina. We invite the attention of landowners to profit from these articles since more emphasis on hardwood production in North Carolina would be highly beneficial to wildlife.

of these acres are now economically amenable to forest management for hardwood production. About 40 million acres could be managed for southern hardwoods; the remainder are in the Appalachian hardwood territory.

What are these southern hardwood lands like? With some important exceptions, such as the deep brown loam bluffs east of the Mississippi Valley, they occupy fertile stream and river bottoms and swamps. The length of the growing season and the rainfall distribution are the envy of foresters in the rest of the Nation.

To realize the tremendous productive potential of these lands, we must manage them. The trees must be protected, because their enemies also thrive in the warm, moist climate. Landowners must learn to look upon well-formed young hardwoods as valuable property. They must learn to release and nurture such trees. With the prices lumber and veneer logs are bringing today, these need not be painful lessons. The value of wood produced in unmanaged hardwood stands averages about $2 per acre per year. Through management, this average figure could probably be multiplied by five in a reasonably short time.

A log buyer tends to think of pulpwood buyers as competitive, but he is not necessarily correct. By supplying a market for small, suppressed, and/or poorly formed trees, pulp companies can substantially increase the net profits that are possible from hardwood management. Stumpage prices for logs and veneer bolts are 3 to 47 times as large as those for southern hardwood pulpwood. The many high-quality logs that find their way to pulp mills are mainly the result of poor marketing rather than real competition.

Many other things can and must be done to increase the supply of high-quality southern hardwoods. Some will be discussed in articles in subsequent issues. Most important, probably, is that landowners must be supplied with technical advice, and convinced that they need it. Since profits from managed stands are much larger than those from unmanaged stands, hardwood forestry should not be too difficult to sell.

Researchers, timbermen, foresters, and manufacturers—we must all become salesmen for hardwood forestry. First, of course, we must believe we can succeed. One need only look to the South's pine forests to learn what can be done. Research at the Southern Hardwoods Laboratory is showing that forestry can do for hardwoods what it has done for pine. The technical resources for a progressive program are becoming available. With a positive and cooperative approach, we can gather the human and economic resources needed for success. ♦

Standard lumber and veneer logs still make up 80 percent of the harvest in hardwood forests. Pulp makers (right) are rapidly adding hardwoods to their mixes, and the volume of hardwood cut for pulpwood may soon equal or exceed that cut for other uses.

Nature's Daily Mystery

by Charlotte Hilton Green

NATURE'S *Daily Mystery!* I have found it an unfailing source of interest in school work, in camp with 4-H boys and girls, with scouts, with student-teachers, even in the home or as a game at parties. Back in my school teaching days I had used it, in somewhat different form, and later found a similar (and cleverer device) at the Audubon Nature Camp in Maine. (It is their title I have borrowed.)

Briefly, the device is a wall chart with this title printed on it, said chart can be attractively decorated with black and white sketches, or colored cutouts. (In the schoolroom I found it well to have the decorations seasonal, at least changed often, as the chart becomes worn in time and too, children like "new faces.") On this chart the "mystery" is thumb-tacked, or put on with stickup tape. It can be either the object itself, a picture, statement or query, bit of descriptive verse, or even a conundrum. It can take numerous forms.

Near by, on shelf or table, is the "Mystery Box" (shoe box does fine) the top fastened down and slit in it. Near at hand are small slips of paper for the answers and the child's name, and pencil, hanging on string, so it will not be mislaid.

At the end of each day or session the teacher or leader takes down the mystery and checks names and answers in the box. The following morning a new "mystery" is put up, the correct answer to the old one, and the names of all who answered it correctly. (I found it easiest to list the names alphabetically, with a check after them for each day for those who gave the right answer. In this way children take pride in making a good score.)

(One year, in school, we tried placing a green star by the names of all who had made a week's score, a blue star for the 2nd week, a silver one for the 3rd, and a gold one for the 4th. The next month we began all over again, and there was great pride and friendly rivalry for the gold stars.)

At our annual 4-H Wildlife Conference, where a group of outstanding boys and girls from all parts of the State have won this camp period as a reward for successfully carrying out wildlife projects, and where for years I had charge of Nature

Below are the words "Lift the flap and take a peep then name me." (The flap should be over the yellow band on the tip of the tail, which helps identify the bird as "cedar waxwing."

No. 5. Still another bird mystery. Again have picture of bird completely covered. At right top, small flap cut in paper, which raised, shows head of bird. On top left a large question mark, and below the following: "My crest, my beak and my dinner really give me away." If you need more help, turn up flap and read. (On under side of flap is printed: "Not a belted earl, but a belted . . . ?) It is the belted kingfisher.

Another mystery might be "Heavenly Arithmetic." With our Apollo 8 and our astronauts, and the Morehead Planetarium in the State, "sky mysteries, space, et al" should be popular, and may be worked out in various ways, by giving a few facts and figures. Thus, light travels at the rate of 186,270 miles a second (one of the latest figures, though 186,000 miles is usually given as easier to remember)—so "How far would it travel in ten minutes?"

Another might be entitled "Heavenly Designs."

"What is my name and what part of the heavens and at what time of the year am I found?" For this one, outline in dots any of the more common and better known and easily identified constellations, as the Big and Little Dippers, Orion, Cassiopeia, the Northern Cross. Of course, there should be a star map available somewhere, either in a Nature Corner, on wall, in books of astronomy, or monthly star maps.

Right here it should be pointed out that there must be "keys" to all these "mysteries" somewhere in the room, as stated just above. Books, magazines, pamphlets, charts, bird pictures, other devices, where students or those participating, can run down the answers.

When I went to the 4-H Camp I always took as much material as I could pack in the car, maps, charts for completion, books on birds, trees, stars, ferns, wild flowers, animals, fossils, insects, stars. By taking up the "mysteries" with things seen on our early morning Nature hikes, with questions and activities, with the lectures of other members of the staff and their field trips, we covered a wide range, there was much for the youngsters to "run down" and they became familiar with some of the best in Nature literature. My Nature Library is a bit more worn and thumbed than if it had remained on my Study shelves, but throughout the length and breadth of the State the children who came to those camps in those years have a better idea of good Nature literature—to say nothing of having good practice in using an index!

Often children enjoy sharing the responsibility of providing some of the "mysteries" and once the thing is underway, they will bring ideas, suggestions, and materials for it, actually faster than they can be used. Too, the teacher or leader can have materials at hand a sort of "Mystery Bank" for days when she has been to busy to "garner" any herself, or nothing has been brought in.

Do children tire of them? Never, in my own experience. And in teaching I found it one of the best means of getting children to school on time. Here let me quote from one of my student-teachers. (Some years ago I had a class of teachers in an eastern town—requested by the principal. We met once a week, in the room of the biology teacher in the high school, an excellent teacher, yet with not enough natural history background. She literally "lapped up" the nature study and became one of the best nature study teachers in the State, as she combined it with her biology courses.)

When I first introduced the "Nature's Daily Mystery" to this class of teachers,, she—and the others—were delighted, but her comment, "How in the world could I find a new mystery—that is usable—for every school day in the month, much less for a year?

Three years later she wrote me: "We are still using the "Mysteries" and they are more popular than ever. We haven't missed a single school day. There's a rush each day for the children to get into class to see the day's mystery and to be one of the first to solve it. And usually the whole high school drifts in sometime during off periods of the day, to see what we have, and we rate a write-up in the school paper several times a year. My chief regret is looking back to the boys and girls who passed through my classes in the years before, without any of this nature work."

In case there is any space left, here are a few more mysteries.

"Wanted—a name. I am *not* a moss but a flowering plant, related to the pineapple family. You will find me on many of the trees along our coastal rivers and swamps, or in many parts of the Deep South. I am not a parasite, not a lazy thief. I do not steal my food from the tree, but garner my own from air and dust and moisture. Sometimes a certain warbler likes to build her nest in me—I make a nice swaying cradle for her babies."

The answer—Spanish moss.

One mystery that caused a great searching through charts, bird pictures on walls, and books was the picture of a young bird. Under it was the legend "Some folks say only a mother could love anything that looks like me. But to her I am probably beautiful. One of my parents is on the chart, so name me. I look a little like my parent, if that will help you."

It was a picture of a young turkey vulture. On the wall was a chart of "The Hawks of Carolina."

Another that is important for children to know and that we always use, is a photograph of two native plants—one with three leaflets, the other with five. Underneath is the legend:

"Leaflets three, quickly flee
Leaflets five, let it thrive.
Berries white, quick, take flight
Berries red, show no dread." What are they?

The first, poison ivy; the other the harmless and beautiful Virginia creeper.

And so they go—the possibilities are endless—as is usually the interest shown. ♦

The Human Race In a Mad Race To Erase Itself From The Face of This Place in Space Called Earth

by Richard Carlton Ward*

THE most nearly universal attribute of living organisms is their capacity to behave as if they were guided by intelligence. Of course, the "intelligence" is more apparent than real, as most living creatures do not reason things out as a wise man would do but act upon instincts and reflexes in the case of animals and tropisms, periodisms, and nasties in the case of plants. We speak of stimulus and response in living organisms, and the differences between a biotic response and a purely physical or chemical response are two: Firstly, in a purely physical response, as the flight of a batted ball, the energy comes from the stimulus (the bat), while in a biotic response, such as the leap of a frog, the energy comes not from the stimulus (perhaps a fly) but from the frog itself. Secondly, a purely physical response is not related to the preservation of the individual or its kind, is not adaptive, while a biotic response is adaptive. This means that a biotic response is

*The author is Assistant Professor of Biology at Guilford College. This article is reprinted from the "Biophile Bulletin" published by Guilford College.

such as will under the ordinary circumstances to which the species usually is subjected insure the survival of the individual or its perpetuation through its progeny. We consider behavior which gets the best results in the long run intelligent behavior when we are talking about human beings, and so, since living organisms ordinarily behave in this manner they appear to us to be guided by intelligence. Creatures that fail to adapt to their environment perish.

The one living creature that seems no longer to share this nearly universal attribute with his fellow creatures is the human. The human race no longer acts as if it were guided by intelligence, as it is no longer behaving in such a way as to insure its own survival and perpetuation. Like little boys playing with matches in a hay-loft, he is likely to suffer a hot but short future. Some experts estimate that the U.S.S.R. already has enough atom bombs to exterminate all life on this earth, but we need not fear that they will get ahead of us in the arms race, as we already have ten times

that many. John F. Kennedy said, "Either man will bring an end to war, or war will bring an end to man."

The waste of resources in warfare and war-preparations is not the only matter in which man is endangering his chances of survival. The population-bomb is a greater peril than the hydrogen bomb, and the wretched conditions of poverty being caused by the explosive increase in population are just such as might lead to a war in which nuclear bombs might be used. It is particularly distressing to note now that already five nations have joined the nuclear brotherhood of destruction. Over half of the world's population is perpetually hungry with the present population of 3.3 billion, and at the present rate of increase, world population will reach 7.3 billion by the end of this century. Even if this does not result in a major war, the strain upon the world's resources in prospect can scarcely be overestimated.

Industrialization is often regarded as a solution to the world's economic problems. This is just a modern way of saying, "Let them eat cake." In the first place industrialization does not make food. We cannot feed people on gadgets. In the second place, industrialization is filling the whole world with poisons in the air, in the ground, and in the waters. The wastes from our factories, etc. are filling our airs with noxious fumes. Some experts claim that air-pollution does more damage to lungs than smoking does. Much cropland has been ruined by air-pollution by fluorides and other industrial waters just when a world-wide food shortage is threatening. Agricultural chemicals, especially insecticides and herbicides, are leaching into our underground water-supplies and our rivers and from there being washed into the oceans of the world. The oceans seem to be the dumping ground for all our wastes, and just at a time when many scientists are predicting that the sea is going to have to be the principal source of man's future food supply, other scientists are predicting that some day soon there may be a massive dying-out of plankton in the seas as a result of the ubiquitous D.D.T., etc. It used to be that people were advised to go out of doors for fresh air. Now the situation is getting so bad that frequently people have been advised to stay indoors. Some students of air-pollution have predicted that it will not be long before nobody will dare go out of doors without a gas mask.

Forests are rapidly being cut down and turned into cropland in many parts of the world. The resulting damage to watersheds is aggravated by the pollution of what water remains. Further damage to food and water supply is being done by "suburban sprawl," as arable land is turned into parking-lots and hard-packed lawns.

Albert Schweitzer said, "Man has lost the power to foresee and forestall. He will end by destroying the Earth." Man, alone among living creatures, is acting more like a cosmic force bent on destruction of himself and all around him than like a living organism with a system of response to stimuli that will insure his own preservation.

What can man do then to save himself and preserve life on this Earth? An increasing number of scientists are saying that nothing can be done, that it is already too late. Those who are more optimistic will almost without exception, point to Conservation with population limitation as the sine qua non of survival.

Any increases in the food supply will continue to be useless as long as the population continues to increase at the present rate. We cannot end poverty for an unlimited population. We can not end war as long as most of the people of the world are dissatisfied with their lot. Unless the educational systems of the world wake up soon and alert the people to the peril of their predicament, the chances that the Earth will continue to be a habitable place are very slight. ◆

Third Annual
"Wildlife in
North Carolina"
Photo Contest

RULES

1. Photographs taken in North Carolina, by North Carolina residents, which show any native North Carolina wildlife species will be eligible.

2. Eligible photographs must:
   (a) Be taken in North Carolina between August 1, 1968 and July 31, 1969.
   (b) Be taken and submitted by residents of North Carolina.
   (c) Show native North Carolina wildlife species (any animal, fish, bird, insect, etc.) General outdoor or landscape photographs should not be submitted.

3. Only black and white prints should be submitted. Do not send negatives. However, negatives of the 10 winning photographs must be submitted on request.

4. DO NOT SUBMIT: (a) Prints or enlargements more than 8 x 10 inches in size; (b) Prints with retouching or art work, or prints made from negatives with retouching or art work; (c) composite pictures, multiple printing or montages; (d) framed pictures.

5. Entrants should submit no more than three photographs each. Each photograph should be submitted as a separate entry and each entry should include with the submitted photographs, the following information printed on the back of each photograph: (a) Name of entrant; (b) Complete address and zip code of entrant; (c) Date photograph was taken; (d) Place photograph was taken; (e) Type of camera used; (f) Type of film used; (g) Shutter speed and f stop settings used (except for photographs taken with box cameras); (h) Type of flash equipment used if photographs were not taken with available light.

6. Contest is open only to amateur photographers. No photographer who earns more than $100 per year from photographic pursuits will be considered an amateur.

7. All entries must be received no later than midnight July 31, 1969. Mail entries to: WILDLIFE PHOTOGRAPHY CONTEST, Wildlife Magazine, Box 2919, Raleigh, North Carolina 27602.

8. All photographs submitted become the property of Wildlife Magazine and may not be returned.

9. First prize is $25.00; second prize is $10.00; third prize is $5.00; seven honorable mention prizes of a subscription to Wildlife magazine. The winning photographs and honorable mentions will be printed in Wildlife magazine.

10. Photographs will be judged by Wildlife magazine on the basis of photographic excellence, and the general appeal and interest of the subject. The decisions of the judges will be final.

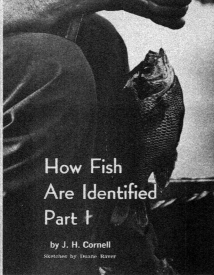

How Fish Are Identified Part I

by J. H. Cornell

Sketches by Duane Raver

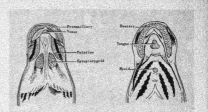

THE fisherman can identify the species of fish he is most interested in by observing their external characteristics. The structure of the fins and the numbers of supporting rays in the fins are characteristics which provide for identification in most cases. The number of rows of scales, and the number of scales in each row, are also important characteristics of each species.

Color is generally an undesirable identification characteristic because its intensity is so greatly affected by different types of water, by the age of the fish, and by the occurrence of spawning seasons. Also, colors tend to fade quickly after a fish dies.

An exception to this in the identification of trout is that the brook trout always has a white margin on the leading edge of the pectoral, pelvic, and anal fins. The rainbow trout may have a bright red streak on its side, especially when caught in limestone waters. In soft waters, however, the red streak may be almost entirely lacking except in breeding season. A better mark of identification is the fact that the dark spots on the dorsal fin are arranged almost in rows.

The brown trout has fewer and larger spots than the rainbow, and on the posterior part of his body the spots are restricted to the upper half. He has only a few spots on his tail.

When we consider that there are more than 3,300 species of fish north of Panama to be identified, and that North Carolina has approximately 350 species, the identification of each one is a complicated task, at least. Actually, the average fisherman is not interested in the identification of all these species, but only those which are of most interest and importance to him.

Upon being asked what they have caught, fishermen have been known to reply, "a couple of bream and some perch." But when the stringer was lifted from the water, it was observed to contain two bluegills, four crappies, one small black bass, and a golden shiner minnow. In order to be able to observe regulations on game fish, the fishermen should be able to recognize at least the game fish species.

Instead of valuing the catch entirely on the basis of numbers or on size of individuals, the fishermen who can recognize the various kinds he has caught obtains a much greater satisfaction and sense of accomplishment. The more he knows about each fish on his stringer, the more he appreciates the complexities of nature which have made it possible for him to catch a representative of that particular species.

Since most of our fish are covered with scales, one of the primary points of distinction among the species is what is known as the "scale formula." When a fisherman catches a specimen which he does not recognize, and when he wishes to obtain information for later identification, his first step should be to determine the scale formula. First he should count the number of rows of scales from the forward edge of the dorsal fin down to, but not including, the lateral line. Next he should count the number of scales in the lateral line itself, beginning at the edge of the operculum and counting each scale in the line to the tail. The third step is to begin at the forward edge of the anal fin and count the number of rows of scales up to, but not including, the lateral line. A typical scale formula, then, might be 11-74-17 as might be found in the smallmouth bass. The number of rows of scales on the cheeks is another characteristic which helps identification in some cases. A smallmouth bass has seventeen or eighteen rows, while the largemouth has nine or ten. It is a much more dependable characteristic than trying to distinguish them by the length of the maxillary bone.

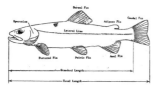

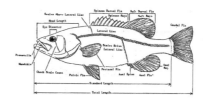

This same characteristic is used to distinguish between the pickerel or jack and the muskellunge, for example. The cheek of the pickerel is entirely scaled, while the muskellunge cheek is without scales.

The dorsal fins are most important in the identification of fishes. In one large group of fishes, the dorsal fin is single and contains only soft supporting rays. Such a dorsal fin is characteristic of the trout, the shad, and the minnows. Another large group has two dorsal fins which may be either slightly attached or completely separate. Among these species, the first dorsal is supported by stiff spines, while the second dorsal is supported by the soft rays. There may be one or two spines at the beginning of the soft dorsal.

In indicating the structure of the dorsal fins, Roman numerals are used to indicate the spines and Arabic numbers are used to indicate the soft rays. In the smallmouth bass, for example, the dorsal fin is indicated as "X, 13 to 15," and the largemouth is indicated as "X, 12 or 13." In these examples, the comma between the numerals indicates that the two dorsal fins are joined. If they were entirely separate, as in the case of the yellow perch, the numbers would be separated by a dash instead of a comma.

The yellow perch has thirteen spines in the first dorsal, which is entirely separated from the second dorsal. The second dorsal is supported by one spine and fourteen soft rays. Consequently, the dorsal fin formula for the yellow perch is "XIII-I,14."

The structure of the anal fin is similarly indicated. The formula for the anal fin of a largemouth bass would be "III, 10 or 11." The anal fin of most of the sunfishes contains three spines and a varying number of soft rays. Both the largemouth and smallmouth bass have three spines in the anal fin, but the rock has six spines. The crappies also have six anal spines, and must be differentiated by some other characteristic.

In addition to the actual structure of the fins, their location is often an identifying characteristic. In differentiating between the black crappie and white crappie, for example, color is useless as an identifying characteristic in spite of their names. The anal fin of both is "VI, 17 or 18." The dorsal fin of the white crappie has five or six spines, however, while the black crappie has seven or eight. One of the easiest means of identification is that the front edge, or "insertion," of the dorsal fin is farther back on the white crappie than it is on the black crappie. The distance from the eye to the insertion of the dorsal fin in the white crappie is much greater than the length of the fin itself. In the black crappie, the length of the fin almost exactly equals the distance from its insertion to the eye. Since the fins are of comparable size, this shows how far back the fin is located and differentiates between the species.

The shape of the tail or caudal fin is important in the identification of some species. For example, the blue catfish and channel catfish have deeply forked tails, but the various bullheads all have tails that are nearly square. The various species of bullheads are most easily separated by the number of rays in the anal fins.

Among the sunfish the shape and structure of the operculum or gill flap is an identifying characteristic. In the bluegill sunfish, for example, the gill flap is blue-black, nearly square, and has a soft edge. In the robin, or yellow belly sunfish, the ear flap is the same color, but it is long and narrow. Because the ear flap is so long, it frequently is incorrectly called the "long-eared sunfish." The long-eared sunfsh is not known to exist in North Carolina waters.

The arrangement of teeth and the types of teeth are important characteristics in some species. For example, the Kentucky bass or spotted bass looks very much like a largemouth bass to the average fisherman. It has a similar dark stripe down its side, and the fin formulae and scale counts are intermediate between those of the largemouth and smallmouth. The internal structure of the spotted bass is similar to the smallmouth, in that it has straight pyloric cecae rather than forked as they are in the largemouth. The one easily identifying characteristic is that the Kentucky or spotted bass has teeth on its tongue, and these teeth are lacking in both the largemouth and smallmouth.

The inclination of the average fisherman may be to say "So what?" It just means this! If you catch a 5-pound largemouth, you have a nice fish. If you catch a 5-pound smallmouth, you have one worthy of mounting as a most unusually large specimen of the species. If you catch a 5-pound Kentucky or spotted bass, you probably have a world record. Identifying your fish makes fishing more fun. ♦

April Beginning of Fishing, Boating Seasons

Mountain trout fishing gets under way half an hour before sunrise on April 5, with nearly 2,000 miles of designated mountain trout waters stocked with keeping-size fish. State and federal hatcheries have produced over 600,000 trout for pre-season and in-season stocking. Regardless of weather, about 20 per cent of all trout caught will be taken on opening days.

Meanwhile, April will see the beginning of the main run of shad and herring upstream to spawning areas, and it can be safely predicted that sport fishing for shad will involve more anglers than ever before. Later in the month, depending on water temperatures, the annual spawning run of striped bass will begin, and continue through May. Striped bass fishermen will again be paid $20.00 per million for ripe striped bass eggs at the Weldon striped bass hatchery.

Don't Forget To Mark Your Calendar!

This is a reminder that as they have for the past 20 years, Tarheel hunters and trappers will be given an opportunity to speak their views on establishing the 1969-1970 regulations for taking fur bearers and nonmigratory game birds and mammals. (See also special article in May issue). Following are dates, times, and places:

Date	District	Place	Location	Time
May 13, 1969	District 9	Sylva	Courthouse	7:30 p.m.
May 14, 1969	District 8	Morganton	Western Piedmont Community College	7:30 p.m.
May 15, 1969	District 7	Yadkinville	Courthouse	7:30 p.m.
May 16, 1969	District 6	Albemarle	Courthouse	7:30 p.m.
May 19, 1969	District 5	Graham	Courthouse	7:30 p.m.
May 20, 1969	District 4	Whiteville	N. C. Highway Com. Shop	11:00 a.m.
May 20, 1969	District 4	Fayetteville	N. C. Highway Patrol Barracks	4:00 p.m.
May 21, 1969	District 3	Rocky Mount	City Court Room	7:30 p.m.
May 22, 1969	District 2	Jacksonville	Courthouse	7:30 p.m.
May 23, 1969	District 1	Edenton	Courthouse	7:30 p.m.

Southeastern Crow Shoot & Calling Contest

April 18-19 are the dates for this annual event sponsored by the Junior Chamber of Commerce of Henderson, N. C. This regional get-together of the best crow callers and hunters has grown to national importance over the years. For details, contact D. Gene Hatley, Chairman, 1417 Sunset Ave., Henderson, N. C., 27536.

CRACKSHOTS and BACKLASHES
by Rod Amundson

Use and Abuse Of The Estuary

DEAR SIR:

As a member of "Wetlands and Estuaries for Tomorrow" and a graduate student in Natural Resources at Oregon State University, I was quite interested in the statement, entitled, "Where To Now For Wetlands?" prepared by H. E. Harrison, Jr., in the December, 1968 issue of WILDLIFE IN NORTH CAROLINA.

The estuary is a "natural" for being one of the most productive areas in the world. Nutrients are carried in suspension from as far as the headwaters of the drainage basin. The current from the river and the tide keeps the nutrients available for the plants which grow stratified in suspension and on the shallow bottom, within the plant producing rays from the sun. According to the June-July issue of *National Wildlife*, the estuaries produce twenty times the food of the open sea, seven times the food of an alfalfa field, and twice as much as a corn field. The May, 1968, issue of the *Commercial Fisheries Review* states that the estuaries support seven out of the ten top commercial fisheries and, in fact, six of the nine commercial canning groups depend on estuaries.

The vulnerability of the estuaries to both reclamation projects and population is alarming. In an industrial state like California, only 33 percent of the estuarine area remains (National Wildlife, 6-7, 1968). San Francisco Bay, one of the most scenic and publicized in the world, was once home port for a large commercial fishing fleet. Today there are zero fishing boats. From a harvest of 15,000,000 pounds of oysters and 300,000 pounds of clams, it now produces neither in commercial amounts. The bay has not been fished out; it has become a cess pool with 257 square miles (1/3 of the total) reclaimed. The bay has 80 sewage outfalls and receives 60 tons of oil and grease *daily!*

The bay is reviving, however, since the creation of the San Francisco Bay Conservation and Development Commission by the California State Legislature in 1965. Not only is the bay being slowly cleaned up but, equally important, reclamation projects are at a standstill.

Elsewhere in the nation the problem is certainly not less severe. New York City was drying up in the summer of 1965 while the Hudson River, large enough to supply the city's domestic use, flowed by so polluted it was unusable. The long awaited, judicious look at the use and abuse of our most precious resource, water, is slowly coming into focus as abuses become the concern of everyone who fills a glass from the tap. *McCall's* (November, 1968) states, "One out of every two Americans is drinking water of unknown quality or water that may not measure up to federal standards." Since many of the large urban areas are located within close proximity to our estuaries, this is another indication of the degree of estuary abuse.

Urban sprawl is slowly swallowing up our open countryside at an alarming steady rate. The large urban areas located on estuaries are using the "wasted" swamp and marsh for reclamation projects. The sprawl will have to stop at the ocean's edge; why can it not be stopped at the edge of the marshes, now that we know their dominant biological role in the marine ecosystem? Marine biologists tell us that an oyster pumps eight gallons of water through its system every hour. This water must be clean. Industry uses many more gallons. The paradox is thus: Industry must also have clean water. Why then does industry pollute its water source? Why can't the industries treat water after they use it? A lot of us would benefit . . . including the oyster.

JOHN MACDIARMID
SOMES BAR, CALIFORNIA

APRIL
(A Schoolboy's Lament)

The sights and sounds of April
Are good to see and hear,
I reckon it is just about
The best time of the year.

All outdoors is calling me
But I must go to school,
'Cause for all girls and boys
It, sadly, is the rule.

I see my little girl-friend
Stopping for me at our gate,
I grab my books and we rush off,
It won't do to be late!

But when, in 'rithmetic, I look
At problems eight or nine,
I think how high's a crows nest,
Way up in a tall pine.

When on our maps, in geography,
We study 'bout the States,
I think of how the red birds call
Their shy and pretty mates.

Then in our English sentences,
When diagrams we make,
I dream of outdoor picnics,
And hot-dogs, cokes and cake.

I enjoy April's blooms and showers
But it 'minds me, don't you know,
Of flowers I'll be planting,
And of grass, and grass, to mow.

So, sights and sounds of April
Are good to hear and see,
Tho it's a time of mixtures
Of good, and bad, for me!

Maj. Carlos U. Lowrance

Just Plain Cuckoo

DEAR SIR:

Consider the sad plight of the rain crow: a one-time highly respected weather prophet, now a nobody, ignored and forgotten, his whole life disrupted by our weather bureau, aided and abetted by radio announcers who give forth at frequent intervals about barometric pressure, relative humidity, probability of precipitation, and so on.

The poor rain crow is so confused he has gone completely cuckoo. He flies around laying eggs in other birds' nests and even eats hairy caterpillars.

It all adds up to one thing: he is now just a cuckoo. Well, on second thought, what's so bad about that?

KNOW YOUR PROTECTOR

Clarence L. Beaver

Wildlife Protector Clarence L. Beaver, stationed at Dobson, Surry County, was born July 25, 1939, in Cherokee County. He is the son of Mrs. Elizabeth Fleming Beaver of Murphy, North Carolina, and the late Mr. Avery Beaver.

Clarence received his high school education at Murphy High School, Murphy, North Carolina. Prior to his employment with the North Carolina Wildlife Resources Commission, he spent three years as a Military Policeman in the U. S. Army, and was later employed by Lay and Company as assistant manager of a chain store.

Clarence completed the Basic Recruit School for Wildlife Protectors at the Institute of Government in Chapel Hill in July 1966. He was employed as a Wildlife Protector Trainee in October 1966 and assigned to Henderson County. In May 1967, he was transferred to Surry County as Wildlife Protector. Since his initial employment, Clarence has completed four in-service training schools.

Mr. Beaver is a member of the Southeastern Association of Game and Fish Commissioners, Law Enforcement Section, and a member of the N. C. Association of Wildlife Law Enforcement Officers.

Mr. Beaver is married to the former Vena Robertson of Murphy, North Carolina, and they have one son, Trent, age 3. The Beavers are members of the Salem Baptist Church in Dobson.

The crow is just a crow, the jaybird is a jaybird, and the starling is a starling. Each a part of Nature's over-all design, each fulfilling his destiny, each in his own way serving some useful purpose for mankind.

Some of these birds we may not like, but after all there is more to Nature than just bluebirds and butterflies.

Personally, I love the call of the cuckoo and wish I could hear it more often.

WILLIAM W. WILLIAMS, RALEIGH

Only a Hunter Understands

DEAR SIR:

It's fun, but only a hunter would understand. You can't hunt for years without learning something about the sport, the people who participate in the sport, the game which makes the sport, and the weather which spoils the sport.

You even learn things about dogs and wives and soon recognize that both need plenty of training. Both need a preseason obedience course well in advance of the first day. Then there's that matter of equipment. But why don't I start from the beginning and list some of the things I've learned about people, dogs, game, equipment, weather, and other things.

A hunting partner usually oversleeps.

A wife never sleeps sounder than when her duck hunter husband wants his breakfast at 4:00 A.M.

Hunters who use shot larger than size 2 on waterfowl are rank amateurs.

A deer hunter's sure-footedness can be measured by the amount of mud on the seat of his pants.

Worthless bird dogs outnumber good dogs about 10 to one.

A long-haired setter can change from a bird dog to a burr dog long before the day is over.

Squirrels can't stay hidden longer than 20 minutes, and I can't sit still longer than 19 minutes.

Bucks are not so dumb. They let the ladies step out of the clearing first.

Bear hunters who dress in black are not likely to come back.

Every year the hills get steeper, the brush thicker, the barbed wire fences higher, and the hour of rising just a little later.

FLOYD SPROUSE
MARSHALL

"Shad Comeback"

The April, 1969 issue of *Field And Stream* magazine has an article by Jim Dean, Burlington *Times-News* outdoor writer, entitled "Carolina Shad Comeback." This coverage looks good and should enlighten sportsmen everywhere about the Tarheel shad story in the Cape Fear River.

Wetlands

DEAR SIRS:

The last issue of WILDLIFE IN NORTH CAROLINA (November, 1968) containing the article on estuaries and coastal marshes was excellent. Surely a great deal of education on the unique place they hold in the ecology of the coastal regions is necessary before the general public gets "fighting mad" enough to guarantee their protection. The dollar spent now on their preservation will be returned manyfold tomorrow, but their story must be told over and over to your readers.

Sincerely yours,
JAMES R. HARLAN
Conservation Consultant
Federal Water Pollution Control Administration

26

The Wonder of April

The soft green grass of springtime pushes up through the brown earth of the hillside on which I stand.

All around, as far as eye can see, other green mist is stealing softly over winter's silhouette, splashing its bright colors gaily against the starkness of bare limbs reaching up to a gentle April sky.

New life is stirring furiously—birds are building nests among the branches, and the willow in proud new leaf sways gracefully with every breeze.

On the floor of the forest nearby, myriad species of insect and plant life awaken, changing the stillness of the woods into a frenzy of activity.

On the small, sandy beaches of a creek near the hillside, paw prints lead to the water's edge. Prints of the fox or the 'possum, emerging from their winter beds to stretch in the warming sun, in search of food to break the long winter's fast.

Many of nature's creatures have not survived the winter. Even now, buried among the sodden, brown leaves of the woods may be the carcass of a fox or muskrat, or other hapless creatures of the woods.

Near the hillside, fast blending with the earth, lies a small heap of feathers and bristle, all the mortal remains of a large bird that fell in majestic flight.

And sadness for the end of any life, like a chill wind, steals over the beauty of the April day.

Yet, as soft as April sunshine, come the words of long ago . . . "Not a sparrow falls without My Father's notice."

But what of man, highest of creation, yet most vulnerable to the pangs of sadness of life's coming to an end.

The same assurance, come down through the ages, blends with the soft spring day and the brightness of its sunshine.

"I am the Resurrection and the Life," this Man said once for all times and ages. "He that believeth on Me, though he were dead, yet shall he live."

Nearby, in full leaf, stand monarchs of the forest—a lone pine and a gaunt swamp cypress—their life span greater far than man's or nature's creatures.

And it makes no sense at all that life in any form—short at best—should end and cease to be.

The assurance of His words is written indelibly in new life stirring all around me—in the red-tipped fronds of maples, the birds of springtime, and a sycamore in full growth near the creek or a verdant forest glen.

Because with approaching spring comes Easter, and among His many promises was another. "Fear not," He said. "Ye are of more value than many sparrows."

The message is borne on every wafted breeze, the trails of wild jasmine flinging its yellow beauty against the palette colors of the trees, in the heady fragrance of the deep swamp riding on every gentle wind, and the tiny paw prints on the creek bank leading to the water's edge.

This is the magic and beauty of April.

This is the promise and wonder of Easter. ◆

LOUISE LAMICA

SMOKEY SAYS . . .

keep

North Carolina

GREEN

FISHERMEN

CAMPERS

HUNTERS

MOTORISTS

Put Out That FIRE!

LITHO BY THE GRAPHIC PRESS, INC., RALEIGH, N. C.

Wildlife IN NORTH CAROLINA

25 CENTS / MAY 1969

WILDLIFE IN NORTH CAROLINA recognizes the need for close cooperation between State and Federal conservation agencies and the people who hunt and fish—to bring about a restoration of our renewable resources. The Editor gratefully receives for publication news items, articles, and photographs dealing with the North Carolina out-of-doors, but reserves the right to reject materials submitted. Full credit is given for all materials published.

* * *

WILDLIFE IN NORTH CAROLINA is published at the Wildlife Resources Commission offices, Motor Vehicles Building, 1100 New Bern Ave., Raleigh, N. C. 27601.

* * *

Second class postage paid at Raleigh, North Carolina 27602.

* * *

SUBSCRIPTIONS—Fifty cents per year, one dollar for two years. Make remittances payable to WILDLIFE RESOURCES COMMISSION. Any employee of the Wildlife Resources Commission may accept subscriptions, or they may be forwarded to Post Office Box 2919, Raleigh, N. C. 27602. Stamps cannot be accepted.

Wildlife circulation this issue, 117,500.

IN NORTH CAROLINA ■

The official publication of the NORTH CAROLINA WILDLIFE RESOURCES COMMISSION, Raleigh 27602. A monthly magazine devoted to the protection and restoration of our wildlife resources and to the improvement of hunting and fishing in North Carolina.

VOL. XXXIII, NO. 5   MAY, 1969

IN THIS ISSUE

EDITORIAL STAFF

ROD AMUNDSON _ _ _ _ _ _ _ _ _ EDITOR
DUANE RAVER _ _ _ _ _ MANAGING EDITOR
LUTHER PARTIN _ _ WRITER-PHOTOGRAPHER
JOHN PARKER _ _ _ _ _ _ BOATING EDITOR
TOM JACKSON _ _ _ WRITER-PHOTOGRAPHER

The mockingbird isn't very selective about its nesting site, using everything from sweet gum trees to honeysuckle. It rarely nests more than 12 feet from the ground, however. The mocker is a possessive bird, often driving all other birds from "its territory." Its ability to imitate other birds is fantastic. Photo by Luther Partin.

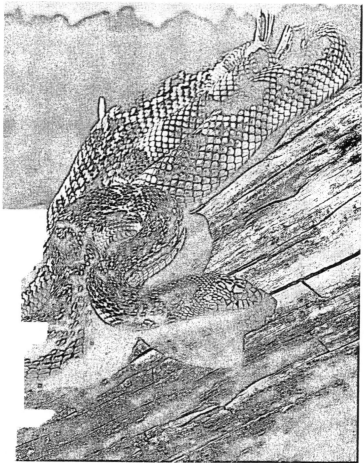

PHOTO BY JOEL ARRINGTON

PINE SNAKE

A five-foot northern pine snake isn't an exceptionally large one, the U. S. record is 83 inches. This powerful constrictor feeds on small mammals and birds and is a beneficial controller of rodents. The pine snake prefers the sandy pine barrens and dry mountain ridges west of a line from Wilmington to Leaksville.

Fishing Western North Carolina

by Chester Davis
Winston-Salem Journal-Sentinel

FISHING in the Piedmont and Coastal Plains sections of North Carolina is typical of the fishing to be found throughout the mid-South. In North Carolina's 25 mountain counties, the fishing more nearly resembles that found at the higher altitudes in such states as New York and Pennsylvania.

In geographic terms Western North Carolina can be described as a mountainous stepladder. On the west there is the Unaka Range which terminates in the Great Smokies. On the east there is the front range of the Blue Ridge chain which rises abruptly and towers over the rolling hills of the Piedmont.

The Great Valley of Virginia runs south into North Carolina between the Unakas and the Blue Ridge. But as you follow the valley south you encounter transverse ranges which provide the ladder's rungs.

With altitudes ranging from roughly 2,500 feet (lower in the valleys) to more than 6,000 feet, these are the highest mountains in Eastern America. They are also among the best watered. There are few areas in Western North Carolina where the annual rainfall doesn't average substantially more than 50 inches a year.

The differences in fishing techniques and fish species encountered here result from the effect altitude and heavy forest cover have on air and water temperatures, water quality and, through these, on fish species.

There are two general types of fishing in this area: stream and lake. Farm pond fishing, while it is gaining in popularity, is by no means as important a recreational outlet as it is in the Piedmont and Coastal Plain regions.

The farm pond fishing found in the mountains differs from its lowland counterpart primarily in the fact that a growing number of the mountain ponds are stocked with trout, primarily rainbows.

Stream Fishing

Stream fishing begins at the lower elevations where one finds the largest of the western rivers.

These large streams include the upper French Broad, Hiwassee, Little Tennessee, Watauga and New Rivers. A number of other major and potentially great fishing streams—the Pigeon, the Toe and Tuckaseigee, for example—are too badly polluted to be of interest to anglers. This is true, also of the lower French Broad.

In their lower stretches these large streams are transitional waters in which warm water species such as the largemouth bass give way to colder water fish like the smallmouth and rock bass. Higher up, as is the case on the French Broad above Brevard and on up to Rosman, the smallmouth gives way to trout, both rainbow and brown.

The large mountain streams are fished from the bank, from boats and by wading. This is the case, for example, of the New River in Ashe and Alleghany counties. Quite often shallow riffles rule out boats of the type customarily used on lakes. Here rubber rafts, flat bottom skiffs and canoes work better.

As you move higher up these streams and up their tributaries, the angler leaves his boat behind and fishes from the banks or he wades.

Equipment

Like all North Carolina streams these are free stone rather than limestone waters. They are not difficult to wade if you are properly equipped. Proper equipment means felt-bottomed wading shoes or boots, and in the spring and fall and

during summer days chilled by rain, chest high waders or, on smaller streams, hip boots.

Rain gear is imperative since showers are common and, at the higher altitudes, chilly. On trout water, insect repellant is a must and it is advisable to have a can of repellant in your jacket.

The same is true of a snake bite kit. These mountains are no more infested with biting insects or snakes than similar areas in other states. But on a damp still day the the tiny no-see-ums can eat you alive and the copperhead and rattlesnake are found throughout the mountains.

On the larger, lower waters of the state's major streams anglers use bait, spinning, and fly rods as well as the cane pole. They use both live bait and artificials.

In these waters the species sought include the large and smallmouth bass, rock bass, a variety of the sunfish and on some streams (and, frequently, at some seasons such as the spring spawning period) walleyed pike and white bass. In the Tennessee drainage of southwestern North Carolina the muskellunge is a native, albeit a none too common one.

On these large streams the fly fishermen favor bass weight rods and weight-forward tapered lines.

A seven-to-nine-foot leader tapered from about 30 pounds down to six is a good choice. Streamer flies of reddish hue are favorites. Fly-spinner combinations also are productive.

Spin and bait casters use a variety of spinners, small spoons and plugs. If there is any one favorite, it probably is the Mepps spinner, sizes zero to three, silver blade and bucktailed treble hook.

A good rule of thumb to bear in mind in fishing these predominantly bass waters is to stick with the lure you have found to be most productive of bass in other streams you have fished. Your confidence in the lure you use—and your acquired ability in its use—is half the battle. But in fishing water that is new to you, it is advisable to check on the locally favored lures.

It is the same with live bait. Worms, spring lizards, crayfish and hellgrammites are the favorites of the natives.

Trout Waters

As you move up the streams into trout water, brown and rainbow first and then the brook trout —"speckled trout" to the mountaineer—in the highest and coldest headwaters, your tackle should be more refined.

Lighter, shorter rods—down to six feet but with seven foot rods being more nearly the usual choice —are in order, as are longer leaders and lighter tippets. Here, as elsewhere, far-and-fine is the rule for the trout fisherman working a North Carolina stream in times of low, incredibly clear water.

On these streams your approach to the water you intend to fish should be as stealthy as a stalking cat. This and the care and delicacy with which you present your fly are more important than fly size or pattern. Fish slowly and fish with short casts that you progressively lengthen as you carefully work over the water ahead of you that is within delicate presentation range. Don't let the promise of great pools blind you to the productivity of riffles, runs and hard-to-reach pockets.

North Carolina trout fishermen tend to use standard patterns in the standard (10 to 16 ordinarily) hook sizes. A list of the favorite dry flies would include the Wulff Royal, Lady Beaverkill, Irresistible, Cahill, Light and Dark, Hendrickson, Mosquito and the like. The Deer Hopper frequently is a good late summer choice.

The favored nymphs and terrestrials include the Tellico, black ant and a variety of stone fly, caddis and may fly nymph imitations. Some very productive native anglers tie on a bushy dry—a heavily tied Wulff Royal, for example, and then tie a 12- to 16-inch tippett to that fly and put a sinking pattern—often a black ant—on it. The dry fly serves as a bobber signaling a strike and will take fish as well. While the technique is far from easy, nymphs are most effective when fished in the upstream cast—down stream float manner of dry flies.

Don't let a sharp shower with accompanying rising, dingy water send you scampering for home.

On the good trout water of this state the water clears rapidly and some of the finest trout fishing occurs as the water begins to fall and clear.

At this time large nymphs and streamers are most effective. The Muddler Minnow, Mickey Finn, Black-Nosed Dace and Gray Ghost are all good bets as streamers.

Now let's turn to the lake fishing to be found in Western North Carolina.

Reservoirs

There are no natural lakes in the area. There are, however, a rather large number of man-made impoundments. These range from great power reservoirs like Fontana (10,670 acres) on down to trout ponds only a few acres in size.

The reservoirs ordinarily are fished from boats. They are water filled mountain valleys and, as such, offer very little shelf for the wader to work.

The species found in lakes like Fontana, Nantahala, Santeetlah, Cheoah, Calderwood and the like, include large- and smallmouth bass, walleyed pike, white bass, crappie, a number of the sunfish, rainbow and brown trout as well as cats and some other rough fish. (Not all species are found in all the lakes named.)

Tackle used on these species is the same as used elsewhere with a few local exceptions in tools and techniques. On Nantahala, for example, a silver and brass spoon trolled deep is favored for summer trout fishing. On Cheoah some of the best anglers stalk fish in canoes. Once they spot a cruising trout they guess his probable course and place a small dry fly ahead of him.

Fishing in the reservoir is best in May and June and from mid-September on to cold weather, ordinarily early in November. During hot weather fishing is slow for all anglers except the most experienced local men who know intimately the water depths, oxygen distribution and spring holes of the reservoirs.

Lacking that, fish very early and very late and keep your eye peeled for a native who is willing to share his accumulated know-how with you on either a fun or fee basis.

In the spring and fall work the shoreline and the shallows. Popping bugs and lures are a good choice in this fishing. In mid-summer, except at dawn and dusk, hunt your fish in deep water with deep running lures. Fish the points carefully bumping the bottom on your retrieve. This last is done best with plastic worms with weedless hooks or with plugs that retrieve on a nose down, tail up manner.

Dedicated winter anglers have surprisingly good luck on North Carolina's mountain lakes. Some work the deep water of the points of land with plastic worms for bass and walleyes. Others fish the mouths of streams for trout entering on or returning from spawning runs. (Trout fishing in the reservoirs is permitted year around. This is not true on the streams.)

Salmon eggs (often encased in a bit of sheer

Pollution, Politics and the Present

by Bill Gulley
N. C. State University

AT the present time, on the present agricultural scene, the United States is faced with "example-setting" unlike any other demonstrated by her since her infant, almost embryonic, days at a certain bay in Boston.

Robins, research and regulation during the past 20, 25 years have not settled a grave issue in the minds of the public. Shaped by attitude, when thoughts of dead robins and "pollution" were klaxoned to heavy headline impact in newspapers, over journalistically yellow radio stations and some TV outlets, a terrible word came to replace terrible thoughts in many persons' minds.

Pesticides! They will be the death of more than bugs, some said. Robins first, then Man. All because of pesticides. Senate investigations. Formulation of investigating committees. Reports. Then, further investigations, legislation, rules, regulations and finally compliance.

Now, the death knell is being sounded for one of the first chemicals to come on the scene, developed and formulated before World War II, but available in quantities at a time of crisis where the argument between nations numbered more than two and centered over larger areas of Earth than one bay in Boston.

DDT is coming a c r o p p e r after many years of hard work, providing health and plenty for billions. Economic advantages were enjoyed through its control of insects and diseases that threatened to cut into production of food, fiber and shelter materials, and where human and animal health was concerned, Man himself did not have to face wartime plagues and disease epidemics.

The bell is tolling for DDT. Conservationists, chemists, and control officials are cooperating in many senses of the word to see that agriculture, forestry and other users of chemicals similar to DDT—chlorinated hydrocarbon pesticides—will receive suitable materials to prevent insects from increasing to dangerous levels. Prices of food and other products of the soil should not increase at the producer level. Replacement chemicals and new controls for pests previously curbed by DDT and its friends should handle the production problems of various commodities formerly made more efficient by such pesticides.

One friend of the farmer is being put to rest. A friend of public health is being sent back to the shelf. The forester is looking to other aids to control pests ravaging his plantings. DDT is crawling back into the test tube, pulling the stopper in tight behind. Much evidence indicates it does not leave the scene after doing its job; it hangs around longer than most other chemicals used in pest control.

The search is continuing for other rapidly—or timed—decaying pesticide chemicals which can do as well as DDT in certain instances. New methods are being pressured to m e e t the challenge of insect and disease organisms that pose a threat to our comfort, health and food and fiber production.

DDT is becoming a milestone on the road to newer chemicals, knowledge and methods to aid man in his struggle to control the detriments in his environment. ◆

A Museum Comes of Age

by Lois Peithman

THE Charlotte Nature Museum is celebrating its twenty-first birthday this year, having grown from an idea of an interested group of citizens who were concerned because city children were deprived of much contact with nature. But today Charlotte children and adults have a far greater understanding of wildlife and the natural sciences because of the group who cared.

On current exhibit are dinosaurs and fossils, which have been a tremendous success. Kids and parents cluster around the Tyrannosaurus attacking a Tricerotops while listening to a blow-by-blow account of the fight through a telephone hook-up. The prehistoric animals were made of papier mache by museum staff members, volunteers who had a g r a n d time making them as authentic and frightening as they must have been. Because of space limitations, however, the animals had to be made to one-fourth scale. But even at this size, the dimension of Tyrannosaurus Rex's feet is something to behold. Around the room are dioramas of dinosaurs, and even in the small cases, the size of them compared to the trees makes one shudder at the sound of thunder their feet hitting the ground must have generated!

The fossil of a prehistoric Coelopsis (an early bird-like dinosaur) mounted on the wall brings much comment, as the illustration of how a fossil became a fossil brings exclamation from more adults than children.

The majority of fossils on exhibit have been found in North Carolina. There are fossil fragments of a Phytosaur of the Pekin Formation from the Triassic Period which were found in a clay pit 1½ miles from Gulf, North Carolina, by the Pipe Products Company. Also found there (and included in the exhibit) are fossil remains of a Dicynodont, a mammal-like reptile which continued from the Permian through Triassic periods and became extinct in the early Jurassic time. This find is a first for North Carolina as these fossils are usually found no farther east than Arizona.

From the newly-completed live animal room come noises of the various animals housed there. The flying squirrels' cage has been ringed with low-level red lighting so they are frisky while the museum is open and sleep at night in their nests under a bright light. The owls stare unblinkingly and delight the children who wonder why THEIR necks "don't turn all the way around, too." The entire animal room is devoted mostly to species found in North Carolina. Since the state has mountains on one side and the Atlantic on the other, the animal room is indeed varied. The sea aquarium has sea anemones, starfish, urchins, which few people would be fortunate enough to see even if they went to the beach. The fresh-water pond has alligators from the Cape Fear River area and a variety of turtles such as the "pancake," soft-shell and red-eared slider.

In the outdoor animal enclosure there are two does and a young buck. The buck is growing his first antlers which brings everyone back constantly to check on his "growth." In a nearby cage is Holly, the red fox, who was brought to the museum as a small pup. When she was young she had the run of the museum, but after teething on the telephone cables, a home was built for her outdoors. She is still taken for walks on a leash, thoroughly enjoying the 29-acre wooded forest surrounding the Museum. It is on these walks that she greets old friends with a cat-like cry and a wag of her tail.

At left, "Spotty" the fawn gets some personal attention from the Museum Director's daughter, Lynn Peithman, and friend. Large enclosures and clean surroundings assure the well-being of the animals. The Paw Paw Nature Trail, above, beckons visitors the year 'round. "How-to" workshops are conducted as part of the instructional program of the museum. Below, Jack Crouch and Will Webb participate in a Fish Taxidermy session.

Charlotte's Nature Museum recorded 280,-000 visitors in 1968; all of them came away with a better understanding of how to live in harmony with Nature. They explored the past in exhibits like "Fossils and Dinosaur" shown at left. Come with us on a short trip.

This Museum has a lovely nature trail entirely in its natural state except for paths which keep people from tromping over the plants. A printed nature trail guide is provided to those who are interested, and numbered redwood posts along the trail are keyed to the guide. The trail has been named the Paw-Paw Nature Trail since there are so many paw-paw trees in the area. Not much fruit from the tree is found, however, due to the squirrels who know a good food when they see it.

Workshops at the museum are many and varied. There are introductory workshops for four and five year olds in making animals of clay and handling live animals from the animal room. The older children are introduced to North Carolina rocks and minerals, plants and even their medicinal purposes. Fifth and sixth grade students can choose from such subjects as taxidermy, classifying and studying birds, reptiles and mammals in vertebrate taxonomy, and conservation of plants and animals.

North Carolina's Charlotte Nature Museum is finding a painless and fun way to help children learn about nature. If just to open the door a small bit to a child or adult to the why's and ways of nature; this is their prime purpose for being. ◆

Hardwood Log Marketing Should Be Improved[*]

by J. S. McKnight

Southern Forest Experiment Station
Forest Service
U. S. Department of Agriculture
Stoneville, Mississippi

STAND on a corner near a pulpwood yard and watch the trucks hauling hardwoods. Invariably, you will see bolts that would yield veneer or furniture dimension stock. With high-quality hardwood logs in short supply, we obviously can no longer afford such under-utilization. We must channel forest products into their highest uses, both to reward the landowner for good management and to satisfy industrial needs for veneer, saw logs, and pulpwood.

An example of a helpful approach to the marketing problem can be found in a tax-paying cooperative, Forest Owners, Inc., of Yazoo City, Mississippi, which for 8 years has furnished a group of landowners with a marketing service. The cooperative was described in an American Pulpwood Association Technical Paper by J. A. Altman. Nearly 200,000 acres of forest land are served by the cooperative. Attempts are made to consolidate small sales into large ones, and thereby make logging for multiple products practical. These large sales attract efficient operators who would not be interested in small sales if they were offered separately. The cooperative also has a dependable logger available. He is trained to handle all products from the forest, and since he knows the markets supplied by forest owners, he is able to consolidate the products from several sales to gain the highest return. Forest management and marketing are carefully coordinated to assure maximum earnings to both logger and landowner.

An example of what an individual can do is found on the Spanish Forts Estate near Daphne, Alabama. There, Charles O. Oswell is harvesting three classes of pulpwood and two classes of logs. Close planning and supervision are paying off in good silviculture and in profits. Oswell has a variety of markets, and he is taking full advantage of them.

Some large hardwood companies are getting maximum value from logs and bolts by careful channeling, starting at the stump and ending in the mill yard. For example, Chicago Mill and Lumber Company of Green-

[*]Reprinted from NATIONAL HARDWOOD MAGAZINE, volume 42, number 3, pages 40-41. March 1968.

This is the second of a series of five articles on hardwood management by Mr. J. S. McKnight. We are reprinting these articles which first appeared in the **National Hardwood Magazine**, because of the importance of hardwoods to wildlife. Many of Mr. McKnight's findings and recommendations in regard to hardwood management are applicable in North Carolina. We invite the attention of landowners to profit from these articles since more emphasis on hardwood production in North Carolina would be highly beneficial to wildlife.

Mountain Hiking

by Bethany Strong

H AS the "madding crowd's ignoble strife" pursued you even to your favorite Smoky Mountain campground, where the blare of your neighbor's transistor radio drowns out the peaceful splashing of water over rocks, and rows of camper wagons obstruct your view of trees and mountains? Try off-season camping, or better yet, back-packing. A combination of the two methods practically guarantees utter solitude in the mountains.

June through August are understandably popular months for camping. The weather is warm, but not hot in the mountains, and the mountain laurel, purple and white rhododendron, flame azalea and other showy flowers are blooming. Yet the charm of early spring in the mountains rivals e v e n that of summer.

Ferns uncurl from the forest floor, trees sprout an apple-green haze of new leaves, and by April the tiny sweet white violets are visible among their broad leaves, redbud trees are blossoming dark pink, and you can find the graceful yellow trout lily nodding on its stalk beside woodland paths.

And who can dispute the beauty of October's c o l o r s in the mountains? The rich scarlet of sourwood and sumac leaves contrasts sharply with the dark green of spruce-fir forests, and every shade of orange and yellow can be found in the turning leaves of various deciduous trees. When you spread your sleeping bag on a pallet of rusty-red dogwood leaves under a bright October moon or climb your way to a panoramic view atop a lookout tower on a crisp autumn morning, you somehow make these beauties particularly your own.

With a bit of initiative and the proper equipment, you can enjoy the delights of mountain camping almost any season of the year.

I N spring and fall, the mountain camper should be equipped with warm clothing, including gloves and headgear; long underwear isn't a bad idea, either. The best type of sleeping bag is the well-insulated, mummy-style bag for cold weather. If you plan to camp at a campground accessible to automobiles, you can take any amount of blankets and tents, but if you decide to back-pack into more remote areas, you'll want to be sure that every ounce that you put on your probably over-burdened back is absolutely necessary.

Back-packing enables you to avoid crowds in the mountains, even in mid-summer, because most people won't go anywhere that they can't take their cars. To plan a back-packing trip, you will find most useful a topographic map, which indicates paths, altitude changes, a n d water sources. Such a map of the Great Smokies National Park can be obtained from a Visitors' Center in the Park or from the U. S. Geological Survey in Washington, D. C. Or you can simply plan to back-pack on the Appalachian Trail through the Smokies, which has frequent water sources and three-sided shelters every few miles for overnights. Cars can be left at Davenport Gap, Newfound Gap, or Fontana Village, where the Trail crosses roads.

A pair of sturdy, comfortable boots is the most important item of equipment for back-packing, for your poor feet have to bear not only your own weight, but also that of your sleeping bag and food. In addition, you may have to negotiate rocky terrain and ford small streams. Many people find that two pairs of socks, thin cotton or rayon ones next to the feet, and thicker wool ones on the outside, prevent blisters. Extra clean, dry socks wrapped in plastic bags are worth their weight to carry, though you may find you can do without other extra items of clothing. Even in midsummer, long-sleeved shirts, sweaters or jackets are necessary at night.

The type of pack chosen determines the comfort of the hiker. The cheapest ones are suspended from the shoulders by straps, but these cause sore shoulder and back muscles in a very short time. Packs with frames that rest at least a part of the weight on the hips are most comfortable. The weight of the pack itself is also important; modern light-weight frames and fabrics are available.

The army poncho, available in many army surplus stores, is an

Light-weight, comfortable pack frames (above) help carry loads over long distances. This is a typical trail through Nature's wonderland.

The best spice for camp food is a hiker's appetite and a nip in the spring air. Left, the mountains have many little-traveled byways criss-crossing the trail. Below, is a "sophisticated shelter" of the U. S. Forest Service.

incredibly useful item for the hiker. Large, square and hooded, it can be worn over the pack while hiking during a rainstorm or fashioned into a make-shift lean-to. It has snaps around the edges, so it can be wrapped around a sleeping bag and snapped snugly, serving as both ground-cloth and sky-cover. A large square of light-weight plastic sheeting is also useful for lean-to purposes and for protecting packs at night, and it's much lighter to carry than even the lightest-weight tents.

Dead wood for building fires is plentiful in most mountain areas (be sure to get a *campfire permit* from a ranger before building fires in the Smokies Park), but you may have the problem of wet wood, so it's worth carrying little blocks of commercial fire starter, available in hardware stores. In addition, you may find useful the tiny, light-weight Sterno stove (really no more than a frame to hold a can of Sterno fuel, with a small pan that fits on the frame) for quick heating of coffee water or simple cooking.

Spring and fall outings particularly, call for warm clothing even when the going is vigorous. Note the stout hiking shoes and boots. Although many mountain streams present inviting scenes, it's best to rely on springs for drinking water; they are plentiful.

A group of hungry hikers will eat with great gusto almost any food cooked over a campfire after a mountain hike.

However, careful food planning is important if the backpacker is to avoid either carrying extra weight or suffering hunger pangs. Freeze-dried foods are available, but you can easily outfit a hiking expedition for several days with items found in every grocery store. Dried soup, instant mashed potato flakes and envelopes of instant breakfast are useful because they offer a lot of nourishment with very little weight. Powdered milk can be used as a drink and mixed with the instant potatoes and instant breakfast. Powdered lemonade and iced tea, mixed with cold spring water, make refreshing summertime drinks. Dried fruit is another valuable item. It provides quick energy on the trail and can be stewed for meals; it can also be combined with fresh wild strawberries or blueberries

in such delicacies as Cornstarch Blancmange. By all means, take advantage of what the forest itself has to offer. If you're a skilled fisherman, you can provide your group with fresh fish suppers, if fishing regulations permit.

Air-dried sausage needs no refrigeration and is handy for summer hikes. In cooler seasons, other kinds of packaged meats may be included in the menu. Avoid canned goods, which weight packs down unnecessarily.

Mountain hikers need water canteens, but filling them is seldom a problem, since there is an abundance of clear, pure springs and streams.

A word about bears: unless you plan to use the shelters on the Appalachian Trail, which provide bear-proof metal food

barrels or tall poles on which to hang food packs, you should arrange to protect your food supply from the night marauders. This can be done by tying a rope between two trees, clothesline fashion except much higher (yes, that entails climbing the trees first!), throwing another rope over that one and tying the food pack on it, safely above reach from the ground and from either tree. Remember, bears are expert tree climbers. And *never* sleep in the open with food on your person or in your sleeping bag.

The rewards of back-packing and of exploring the beauties of the mountains in various seasons are many, but until more people are convinced of this, you aren't likely to find the trails crowded when you yourself take to the mountains with your supplies on your back. ♦

What a Mess!

by Marshall Staton, P.E.

Assistant Director,
Sanitary Engineering Division
North Carolina State Board of Health

NORTH CAROLINA, the land of variety vacation, has always been known as a beautiful state. From the mountains, through the Piedmont, to the ocean, it has been admired and enjoyed by many who have used its resources for business, industry, and recreation.

We are fortunate to be blessed with abundant water resources. Many large reservoirs, rivers, sounds, together with miles of sandy beaches along the Atlantic Ocean, provide many opportunities for water-oriented sports. With this resource readily available and with tourism as the state's third largest business, aquatic recreation has increased rapidly in recent years. Recreation authorities predict that the trend of increasing aquatic recreation will continue. I am informed that where land and water meet, there is going to be recreation.

Our excellent water resources are the basis for much of the vacation activity in the state. It is enjoyable and beneficial to one's health to get away from the daily work routine and participate in aquatic sports directly or indirectly. The term "aquatic recreation" in a broad context includes many areas of activity such as fishing, boating, swimming, diving, skiing, hunting for waterfowl, sight-seeing, picnicking, camping, and many others.

Recreation must be enjoyable if it is to thrive and the surroundings or environment must be clean and pleasing for it to be enjoyable. Within the past few years, there have been an increasing number of articles written concerning the detrimental impact that man is making on his environment. Some of what has been written is true and can be substantiated. Some is thought to be true, but is more difficult to prove. The purpose of this article is to describe to you what is actually developing into a serious threat to the aquatic recreation potential of many areas in North Carolina, and to bring to your attention pictorial evidence that I hope will stimulate action to abate this rapidly increasing problem.

This article is specifically directed toward the degradation of our aquatic recreational areas caused by littering. The thoughtless disposal of articles of solid waste and garbage along the shoreline and in the waters of the state is cause for considerable alarm among persons working in health, recreation, wildlife, and other conservation agencies. Also, there is justifiable reason for much concern by the owners of the property on which the littering is occurring.

As much energy is used by those who participate in water sports and as many outings last from several hours to a week or more, food, drink, and accessories are usually carried along. Most of these items are packaged in containers of materials that are practically indestructible by natural processes. Some of these are various types of plastic materials including milk cartons, sandwich containers, bottles, eating utensils, aluminum cans, paper, etc. If these are discarded on the ground after use or thrown into the water, they will remain there indefinitely unless someone removes them.

Some years ago, it was probably not too significant if a fisherman left an empty bean or sardine can and a paper sack at an isolated lake or river side fishing site. This should not have been done. However, at that time we were not making the demands on water recreation areas that we are today.

The demand has increased many fold within recent years. A rapidly increasing population and an economy that is becoming more industrialized is contributing to expansion and crowding of urban areas. This in itself tends to produce stress and creates a greater desire to get away for periods of relaxation. Other important reasons for this increase are more leisure time, better salaries, and a much improved highway system which permits an ever increasing number of boats to be transported long distances within a short time. The Wildlife Resources Commission, recognizing a need for access areas has contributed to the recreation boom by constructing 94 boating access areas throughout North Carolina. The isolated fishing, swimming, or boating sites of a few years ago that were seldom visited, or visited by only a few,

14

This ideal campsite on private property was turned into a stinking mess of decaying garbage, flies and rats by public use. Campers will look for another spot, while the landowners will have to clean this up.

Public use does not have to mean misuse and thoughtlessness. These campers have kept their surroundings clean and will leave the spot ready for others to enjoy. How are your outdoor manners these days?

are no longer isolated and today the visitors are many—tomorrow there will be more.

I observed one dramatic example of an individual seeking to get away from his daily routine and to find privacy. This person owned a house boat and anchored it in a cove on a large reservoir owned by the Federal Government. The boat owner placed a rope supported on floats across the cove in an effort to demonstrate to all that this was his domain instead of public water to be enjoyed by all. He arrived there first and staked out his claim by closing off the cove for his own use. This reminded one of the homesteading laws of the West.

The pictures accompanying this article demonstrate that we are rapidly destroying excellent areas that have been used for aquatic recreation. This degradation is not local or sectional, but is statewide and this entire magazine could be filled with similar pictures obtained from practically all areas of our state. It is my opinion that one major reason for these conditions is due to a lack of awareness by those who are contributing to the problem. For some reason, it is the easiest, most thoughtless, and a seemingly harmless act to throw an empty can or bottle out of a boat. This should never be done as it is detrimental to the reservoir and may cause an injury to the people using the water. As may be seen from one of the pictures,

the cans and bottles that were thrown into the water did not sink, but washed up on the shoreline and are a hazard to the people desiring to use this beach. Also it is unacceptable aesthetically as a suitable area for recreation.

I am sure you are thinking that if this is such a problem, why do the law enforcement officials not police these areas. This is being done. A considerable number of citations were issued and arrests were made by protectors of the Wildlife Resources Commission last year. Under their regulation, they arrest persons for littering on any of the 94 public boating access areas that they have constructed. Also under Chapter 75-A of the General Statutes known as the Boating Safety Act, they arrest persons for littering on the water.

Several difficult problems are encountered through the law enforcement process. These are (1) The person littering generally must be caught in the act or witnesses provided to testify as to the act being committed. However, arrests have been made and convictions obtained in some instances on circumstantial evidence. (2) The enforcement action, if carried out by the protectors of the Wildlife Resources Commission, is made only at public access areas or on the water. Much littering is on private, undeveloped property of reservoir shorelines. In some instances where conditions have become

intolerable, the local health department has had to require the owners of such property to clean up the litter deposited by people who have used it without permission—actually trespassers. Such littering has occurred frequently and in significant amounts along the shoreline of the large reservoirs of the electric power corporations and those owned by the Federal Government. While visiting one reservoir owned by the Federal Government during the late autumn of 1968, I noticed huge quantities of solid waste that appeared as windrows along the shoreline. This material was floating until the water was rapidly drawn down about sixty feet in the reservoir for emergency power production.

I would think it possible but hardly feasible for the power companies and Federal Government to restrict shorelines from use by the public and thus control a portion of the problem. This would be an almost impossible task to perform. It is my belief that in an effort to be good neighbors, the power companies have not restricted their shorelines which would thus prohibit recreation. They have, instead, periodically attempted to clean up much of the mess caused by others.

Another approach to the problem is regimentation. That is, permitting access only at certain points. Camping, fishing from the shoreline, swimming and other

● continued on page 31

Your Hunting Regulations
HOW THEY ARE FORMULATED

The 1947 General Assembly of North Carolina created the Wildlife Resources Commission with authority to set the seasons and bag limits on nonmigratory game and fur bearing animals, and to regulate the areas in which they may be taken. The Commission can adjust seasons and bag limits according to the relative abundance or scarcity of individual species, or other significant factors.

After all relevant information has been recorded, field personnel meet in Raleigh with administrative personnel to assimilate and evaluate Wildlife conditions, examining regulations of the previous year, species by species, evaluating and discussing the status of each in the various sections of the state. The staff then recommends proposed regulation changes to the nine-member Commission for further study.

Through post-hunting season observations and surveys, Wildlife Resources Commission field men estimate wildlife populations throughout the state to provide information on the carry-over of each species as an indication of the production potential for the reproductive period.

The Wildlife Resources Commission meets to examine the information obtained by field surveys and the staff recommendations. By virtue of their locations in various parts of the state, the nine Commissioners are in a position to hear the sportsman's voice, in each area, as well as the recommendations of the Commission's technical staff. After considering the available biological data, the staff recommendations and the sportsmen's suggestions, the Commission formulates proposed regulations for the coming year.

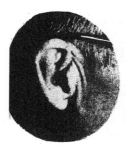

May 13, 1969	District 9	Sylva	Courthouse	7:30 p.m.
May 14, 1969	District 8	Morganton	Western Piedmont Community College	7:30 p.m.
May 15, 1969	District 7	Yadkinville	Courthouse	7:30 p.m.
May 16, 1969	District 6	Albemarle	Courthouse	7:30 p.m.
May 19, 1969	District 5	Graham	Courthouse	7:30 p.m.
May 20, 1969	District 4	Whiteville	N. C. Highway Com. Shop	11:00 a.m.
May 20, 1969	District 4	Fayetteville	N. C. Highway Patrol Barracks	4:00 p.m.
May 21, 1969	District 3	Rocky Mount	City Court Room	7:30 p.m.
May 22, 1969	District 2	Jacksonville	Courthouse	7:30 p.m.
May 23, 1969	District 1	Edenton	Courthouse	7:30 p.m.

Dates, times and places of a series of public hearings are announced through the news media and in WILDLIFE magazine, and the proposed regulations are presented to the sportsmen at hearings in each of the Commission's nine districts. The proposals are explained in detail and sportsmen are invited to express their views and opinions. Records are kept of the dialogue at public hearings so that the Commissioners may study these suggestions along with letters from those sportsmen who are unable to be present.

Following the public hearings, the nine Commissioners meet again in Raleigh and adopt the official regulations for the coming season, after weighing all of the factors involved.

Once adopted by the Wildlife Commission, these regulations have the effect of law, the violation of which constitutes a crime. They are published by the Commission and shipped to license dealers throughout the state to be distributed to sportsmen when they purchase their hunting, fishing and trapping licenses.

North Carolina Field Trials

by William F. Brown

Editor, "The American Field"
Reprinted from "The American Field"

HARD on the heels of the inaugural North Carolina Open Quail Championship, the North Carolina Field Trial Association sponsored an Open Derby and Open All-Age Stake over the Sandhills Wildlife Management Area at Hoffman, N. C. Competition began on Wednesday afternoon, March 12, and was concluded late Saturday afternoon, March, 15. The program was an interesting follow-up to the initial Championship and the dedicated North Carolina field trialers who made both these programs possible have good reason to feel proud of the results.

There were obstacles to be overcome. An unprecedently severe ice storm had felled majestic long-leafed pines on the field trial grounds and the debris kept the courses from the tidy appearance that had been achieved previously. But 'tis an ill wind that blows no good, and perchance the storm may result in improvement later, though it is hard to estimate how long it may take.

The grounds and even the weather was much the same as obtained during the Championship running. The courses yielded a sufficient amount of game—bevies being moved a bit spottily at times —and the sun shone in a bright blue sky. The spring warmth expected in these latitudes at this season was not up to expectations, although temperatures were higher the final day of running.

The North Carolina Field Trial Association is a complete organization, the parent club of fourteen member groups that sponsor recognized trials. It has been blessed with splendid leadership, but never more so than now with the talented James W. Tufts of Pinehurst, N. C., president and enterprising W. Dwight Smith of Norwood, N. C., secretary-treasurer. With true executive talent, Jimmy Tufts delegates authority and responsibility to various committees, entrusted with the details of Association activities, and these committees function efficiently. President Tufts and Secretary Dwight Smith were present at the drawing, which was handled by Carl T. Lippard of Charlotte, N. C., chairman, and the expert handling of this presaged the smoothness with which the two-stake program would be run, following completion of the inaugural North Carolina Open Quail Championship.

There are those who have complained of the tightness of the Sandhills Wildlife Management Area courses. As mentioned, the devastating ice storm ravaged the pine woods—estimates ranged to a 40% loss—and the territory will be more open when all of this is cleared, though that will take considerable time. But even of greater significance is the work that has been accomplished during recent years. Right now, for a dog that wants to run but will handle, a wide, classy exhibition can be rendered. A dog that orients himself quickly to cover and topography, and is conscious of his handler, may show unbelievably well though ambitious in his running. Handlers and judges learn quickly where to seek or look for a dog whose pattern is consistent, and a dog's progress through a course is charted with sufficient visibility at critical junctures.

North Carolina has a progressive Wildlife Resources Commission, made up of T. N. Massie, chairman, of Sylva; Dr. Joe M. Anderson, vice-chairman, of New Bern; J. Holt Evans, secretary, of Enfield; James A. Bridger of Bladenboro, Hugh G. Chatham of Elkin; James A. Connelly of Morganton, Robert G. Sanders of Charlotte, Jay T. Waggoner of Graham and Orville L. Woodhouse of Grandy. Clyde P. Patton is executive director and Frank B. Barick is chief of the Division of Game.

Members of the Commission make up what is known as the Field Trial Committee, and this is headed by James A. Connelly as chairman, Holt Evans, Bob Sanders and Jay Waggoner.

Jim Connelly was in attendance throughout the Championship running and several of his associates also witnessed much of the trial. Clyde Patton had graced the drawing with his presence and there is no doubt that a spirit of close and cordial cooperation exists between the Wildlife Resources Commission and the field trialers of the Tar Heel State.

Aware of what has been transpiring in other states, on both federal and state-owned lands, the North Carolina group intends that the development of the Sandhills tract will make it one of the finest field trial complexes in the country. Strong encouragement is given by the bird dog fans, particularly those in Rockingham, Charlotte, Greensboro, Winston-Salem, for all realize what the development of this immense tract will mean for the future, for posterity.

Fortunate, indeed, that R. Lyle Morgan is manager of the Sandhills WMA. A dedicated member of the Division of Game, he knows the requirements, has assisted in the formulation of a program that has brought steady improvement and which promises much in the years ahead. One is reminded of what Anthony Imbesi has accomplished on his Briardale Farms grounds at Estell Manor, N. J. The planning is sound and if the execution is carried through, both areas will one day astound all witnesses.

The reader is referred to the report of the North Carolina Open Quail Championship for details—such as headquarters at Lonnie McCaskill's Village Motel in Rockingham, C. H. Burgess furnishing the horses and serving luncheons in the clubhouse on the grounds, and Lyle Morgan as marshal. He also provided details of the running.

Part of the contingent stayed at the Holly Inn in Pinehurst, and the grounds are easily accessible from the world-famous resort. Many enjoyed the color telecast of Quail Hunting at Pinehurst, N. C., a segment of the American Sportsman program, which was T-V'd the Sunday before the start of the trials. Bing Crosby and Gaylord Perry were featured with Frank Swaim. Fred Wood supplied dogs and horses. Jimmy Tufts told of the eventful days when the program was being filmed. ♦

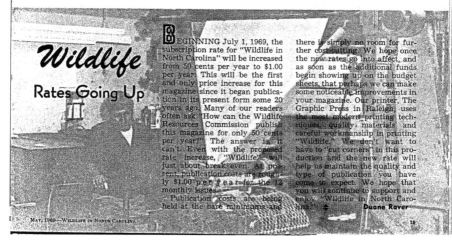

Wildlife Rates Going Up

BEGINNING July 1, 1969, the subscription rate for "Wildlife in North Carolina" will be increased from 50 cents per year to $1.00 per year. This will be the first and only price increase for this magazine since it began publication in its present form some 20 years ago. Many of our readers often ask "How can the Wildlife Resources Commission publish this magazine for only 50 cents per year?" The answer is, it can't. Even with the proposed rate increase, "Wildlife" will just about break even. At present, publication costs are roughly $1.00 per year for the 12 monthly issues.

Publication costs are being held at the bare minimums and there is simply no room for further cost-cutting. We hope once the new rates go into affect, and as soon as the additional funds begin showing up on the budget sheets, that perhaps we can make some noticeable improvements in your magazine. Our printer, The Graphic Press in Raleigh, uses the most modern printing techniques, quality materials and careful workmanship in printing "Wildlife." We don't want to have to "cut corners" in this production and the new rate will help us maintain the quality and type of publication you have come to expect. We hope that you will continue to support and enjoy "Wildlife in North Carolina." ♦ **Duane Raver**

by
John R. Parker
Jr.

PHOTOS BY JOHN R. PARKER, JR.

Early morning on the lake. A beautiful scene, but does the flooded skiff indicate past trouble? Enjoy Nature's beauty, but don't forget safety. Inlets like the one below beckon to the small craft skipper. Be careful in these tricky waters. Use the buddy system.

PATROL boats of the Wildlife Resources Commission are now designated as Marine Emergency First Aid Units. Each will carry a Red Cross emblem. Patrol boat operators, at special training sessions, were awarded Advanced First Aid Certificates early this year. Protection Chief Bob Hazel said that this joint program with the Red Cross' Southeastern Area Office is one of the first of its type in the nation.

Incidentally, twelve of the Commission's protectors are First Aid Instructors.

Demonstration Teams

Last boating season approximately 24,000 people observed boating safety demonstrations given by the Commission's Safety Teams. Persons interested in having a team perform before school groups, camps, and at civic gatherings, should send a request to R. B. Hazel, Chief, Division of Protection, Box 2919, Raleigh, N. C. 27602.

Polyethylene Containers For Gasoline

There is no Federal or state regulation prohibiting the use of polyethylene containers for gasoline on uninspected motorboats. Some small manufacturers are advertising using them for storage of flammable liquids. Persons using such containers for gasoline should be warned that at temperatures as low as 140° F., gasoline will permeate polyethylene with ease, especially in thin sections. Temperatures in the trunk of a car or in a covered space in an outboard runabout can easily reach this figure on hot summer days, and start a fire.

Unconventional Craft

According to the U. S. Coast Guard, increasing numbers of unconventional watercraft are appearing on United States' waters. These craft fall into two main groups—amphibious automobiles, and "thrill craft." The latter includes power swimmers, jet powered surfboards, one-seat inboards, inflatable runabouts, and one-man water scooters. Most of these craft are considered as Class A, closed construction, and if over ten horsepower, they must be numbered. Amphibious automobiles may retain the automobile registration attached to the vehicle along with the motorboat number. The requirements for lifesaving devices, lights, ventilation, fire extinguishers, flame arrestors, etc., are valid requirements for these craft, and it is somewhat doubtful if they can meet these requirements from a space basis alone.

Communications

The U. S. Coast Guard will have new radio facilities this season enabling its boarding teams to communicate on the same frequency as the Wildlife Commission. This will be a plus for patrol coordination, search and rescue, etc.

Testers Merge

Anyone who has looked closely at a Christmas toaster or electric drill has no doubt noticed the letters UL. The Underwriters Laboratories, of course, test many things giving the buyer a feeling of security. In boating, it's the Yatch Safety Bureau. This does not mean that a boating item must carry the Bureau's label to be safe and serviceable. However, many boat equipment manufacturers do use this service. The Bureau and Underwriters Laboratory recently merged and the National Safety Council calls it a major step to further boating safety. A safety tip from this bit of incidental information might be to buy equipment from reputable manufacturers. And remember, items such as life preservers and fire extinguishers need Coast Guard approved markings. ◆

RESOURCE-O-GRAM
A ROUNDUP OF THE LATEST WILDLIFE NEWS

Don't Say You Didn't Know !

Your attention is directed to an article on pages 16 and 17, this issue. It tells how North Carolina's nonmigratory game regulations are established, and lists the dates on which public hearings will be held.

Daylight Saving Won't Save Confusion

Daylight saving went into effect at 2:00 a.m. Sunday, April 27. Although clocks will be set an hour ahead, this doesn't change the time for trout fishing. The sun will continue to rise on schedule, and trout fishing, daily, will continue to begin half an hour before sunrise and end at sunset on designated mountain trout waters.

But if you live close enough to a trout stream to do some after-work angling, you will get off work an hour earlier and hence get in an extra hour of fishing.

Caution — Dry Weather Ahead

May is usually a dry month in North Carolina, and dry weather brings on the usual forest fire hazard. Wildlife and Forestry officials warn fishermen and other outdoorsmen to be particularly careful with smokes, matches, etc. If you use a campfire, be certain all the embers are completely drowned before you leave it.

Leave Those Woods Babies Alone !

If you chance upon an "abandoned" fawn out in the woods, take a good look at it, then move along. Odds are more than 100 to one that it is not abandoned, and taking such an animal home with you out of misguided kindness is a serious violation of state law.

Deer and other wild creatures make cute, lovable pets—for a while, but almost invariably they die or become nuisances, if not downright dangerous.

Special Trout Fishing Regulations

For special regulations on trout fishing in Great Smoky Mountain Park, write to National Park Headquarters, Gatlinburg, Tenn. 37738.

Birding and Birders in the Carolinas

by Merilyn D. Hatheway,
Secretary, Carolina Bird Club

"CHAT" BY H. DOUGLAS PRATT

A common interest in birds and a mutual understanding of the need for their protection unite the members of the Carolina Bird Club. This enlightened concern is shared by members of all ages and backgrounds: from backyard birders, high-school hikers, and amateur naturalists to graduate students, professors of ornithology, and museum specialists. No organization has matured more graciously than the Carolina Bird Club. Having grown from a group of 75 three decades ago to our present status of over 1500, our program has expanded in scope, and our activities have made an impression upon the Carolinas.

Mr. Harry T. Davis, Director Emeritus of the North Carolina Museum of Natural History, provided us with a wealth of material relative to the formation and early history of the CBC. He informs us that for years the Raleigh Natural History Club met and held programs on nature and the out-of-doors. And in 1936 a group in this club whose primary interest was in birds met to form the Raleigh Bird Club. This expanding interest in bird study throughout the state prompted the RBC to join with other groups to form the North Carolina Bird Club in March 1937. Invitations were sent out and 74 persons from all over the state attended the organizational meeting in Raleigh under the leadership of Mrs. Charlotte Hilton Green. The first officers of the NCBC were headed by C. S. Brimley, co-author of *Birds of North Carolina*. In 1948, the NCBC was reorganized to include the natural history groups in South Carolina and this resulted in the present organization.

What kinds of people contribute to the programs of the Carolina Bird Club. What kinds of contributions do they make? To answer these questions we interviewed four active members who we feel are representative of the kinds of people who make the club tick. We wish we could have interviewed many more, because there are scores of other members whose contributions to the club would well illustrate the activities of this exciting organization.

It is always so rewarding to call on that wonderful lady of nature, Mrs. Charlotte Hilton Green! Those of you who read her columns in the Raleigh *News & Observer*, "Out-of-Doors in Carolina," follow her comings and goings not only in the Carolina Bird Club but in the whole world of Nature itself. (See "Nature's Daily Mystery," April *Wildlife*.) Whether it be following her up the high tower stairway at Lake Mattamuskeet before dawn to see those marshlands awaken to the honking of geese or walking briefly up a rather steep dirt road behind the Green Park Hotel at Blowing Rock to see a fall sunset and hear the twittering of red crossbills, you know that Charlotte Hilton Green lives in harmony with her environment.

Mrs. Green has lived and worked in North Carolina since 1920 when she moved to Raleigh with her late husband. They came from New York State, where in her early days she had played a strong part in introducing nature study courses to elementary teachers and pupils. Devoted and alert, she makes nature come alive to all who read her writings.

Early in the 1920's the Greens built a house on a winding dirt road in the woodlands. Today, although in another house, she lives on the same White Oak Road, where her library overlooks old trees and large shrubs. It is a real working library, nothing fancy by any means, but with valuable old books and articles on birding and natural history. There are maps on the walls, and things are stashed in boxes, along book shelves, and on tables beside her desk, which is in front of a large window. On top of all the notes and papers lie her binoculars, ready to watch for a woodpecker or nuthatch that may have landed on a tree behind the house. She has a window feeder directly behind her desk, and during my last winter visit there were purple finches, titmice, chickadees, and kinglets at close range. And it was there that we sat down to talk about how she came to write about birding in the Carolinas.

She told me that in the early days of the Raleigh Garden Club a bird study group asked to meet at her home, where they could observe the birds at her feeding stations, birdbaths and birdhouses. This enthusiastic group encouraged her to contribute articles to the *News & Observer* of general interest to farmers and housewives. Out of this series of articles grew her first book, *Birds of the South*, and later on another series on trees evolved into her *Trees of the South*. Her present column, *Out-of-Doors in Carolina*, has continued for 35 years her vital interest in conservation, nature, and their relation to people. Mrs. Green also serves as a reviewer for leading publishing houses, and the new books that come in are stacked beside her reading chair or on top of end tables. She is at her typewriter every morning at 9 A.M.

I noticed that a recent *Audubon* magazine was opened to a page describing a trip coming up this spring to the Galapagos Islands. Mrs. Green told me that she and her sister were going up to Washington to attend an illustrated lecture on the Galapagos, and she wondered if she might not try to make the trip to the Islands herself! For her activities extend far beyond her working library. She is a regular counter in our local Christmas and spring bird censuses and always covers her area by driving with a friend up and down the streets and walking the roadside areas where she can record the birds. In fact, she is a great one for walking. She never misses, rain or shine, snow or ice, a long walk around the neighborhood she loves so much, observing the birds and other things of nature, and keeping in shape.

Mrs. Green is also an active member of the N. C. Shell Club, and belongs to a book club, and is involved in church and civic groups, as well as Delta Kappa Gamma, an educational sorority. Basic to all her interests is her feeling for Nature, and what Nature has to offer, and what contribution she may make to the world around us. As we sat in her living room she asked to read something written years ago by a very famous botanist, Liberty Hyde Bailey, whom she met at Cornell. "Nature is ever our companion, whether we will or no. Even though we shut ourselves in an office, Nature sends her messengers. The light, the dark, the moon, the cloud, the rain, the wind, the falling leaf, the fly, the bouquet, the bird, the cockroach—they are all ours. If one is to be happy he must be in sympathy with common things. He must live in harmony with his environment. One cannot be happy yesterday or tomorrow, he is happy here and now, or never."

Mrs. Edna Lanier Appleberry, Wilmington, wrote a letter full of interesting highlights of her long and varied career which involved so many young people! Mrs. Appleberry writes, "Wildlife has always interested me from the time I was a very small girl when I picked up a 'pretty worm' as a gift for my Mother. It must have been a scarlet kingsnake and was definitely not appreciated by her. The gift brought a drastic punishment and the stern command to never again pick up any crawling thing. It didn't stop me from collecting but it did teach me never to take my finds to my Mother or any other grownup.

"When I grew older my first absorbing interest was in marine life. I was more or less precipitated into bird study by fortunately learning about habitats, bird songs, and bird identification by studying with Mr. Gregor Rohwer of the USDA. And as early as 1945 we tried our first bird census, which created interest as we counted 61 species. Then along came some younger birders, among them Robert P. Holmes III of Mt. Olive, John Trott, Jr., Sandy McCullock, John Carr and Bill Craft. That was in 1946 and together with others in our area we accounted for 97 species. As this sparked interest of some out-of-state boys, and the number of observers grew, so did the count numbers until we reached 164.

"Perhaps it was a bit late for me to become an expert but that I could help the cause by encouraging young people had the support and interest of my late husband and of many friends in Wilmington.

"Through almost daily talks in the schools, and as a Nature Counselor for Boy Scouts and Girl Scouts, it was possible for me to plant in the minds of hundreds of young people an awareness of wildlife and the need for conservaton. That some of it took root I know because of many incidents such as the following. One night I attended a lecture on snakes at the college. Afterwards I spoke to the young man who had collected the live specimens and asked how he became interested in herpetology. He laughed and said, 'You ought to know, Mrs. A, since you got me interested when I was 16 and a swimming counselor at a scout day camp and I just went on from there.'

"Many of the fifty or more out-of-town boys who came to see me while they were in school are either in teaching some form of natural history in colleges or are in some type of work such as Audubon, forestry, marine life, etc., and I like to think they learned from me accuracy and integrity in reporting and respect for the wishes of property owners on any land on which they might work.

"In addition to these young people, many photographers, botanists, and birders and other scientists from at least 24 states and many Canadian provinces have come here to work with me. Thus birding has brought me many friends of all ages, a wide range of interests and a great joy in life which is only known to those who become aware of the natural history of the world around them."

Dale Lewis, of Raleigh, one of the many teenagers who has found an interest in birds leads to a better understanding of conservation, is but one of many young people who spend their Christmas holidays counting birds. This past year Dale participated in Audubon bird censuses in Norfolk, Cape Charles, and Back Bay, Virginia, as well as at Bodie-Pea Islands and in Raleigh.

For young people who are interested in learning about animals, particularly birds, and have a desire to help conserve them, Dale finds that the Carolina Bird Club provides many educational and enjoyable opportunities. Because the three meetings held each year occur during weekends, high school and college students are able to attend without missing classes. He finds that when qualified ornithologists share with less experienced club members their knowledge of the birds, these trips are more meaningful. Visiting heron rookeries, photographing an active bald eagle's nest, and seeing countless numbers of ducks and geese are but a few of the prized experiences I've had over my past three years of membership in this organization, says Dale.

Dale, an Honor Society senior at Broughton High School in Raleigh, has plans for continuing his interest in birds. His summers have been spent as head of nature lore at Camp Sea Gull, where he has captured rattlesnakes and studied waterfowl. This year he hopes to use his spare time in closer study of birds in the Pamlico County area, not only identifying birds but studying their habits, and when he goes off to college in the fall he plans to work with outstanding ornithologists towards a degree in this field.

"Meeting interesting people seems to go along with birding," Dale remarks. Last summer he traveled up the Atlantic coast, visiting national wildlife refuges along the way. On Mount Desert Island he met birder William Russell, who is studying the woodcock as a game bird. "We were camping out in his back yard," Dale added, "and you never really appreciate the out-of-doors and the fascinating diversity of nature until you camp out." An avid quail hunter, too, Dale finds no conflict with his bird-watching. He and Venus, his English setter, spend many a weekend following quail and grouse.

Doug Pratt follows the activity of the CBC for a different reason. The sketch of the chat is but one expression of birding through art. The picture was recently published in the CBC publication THE CHAT, a quarterly which carries feature articles on birds as well as field notes and special topics under the headings of back-yard birding, conservation, and Carolina bird-watchers. All members receive this publication as well as a *Newsletter,* which gives additional information about upcoming events and special items about local bird chapters affiliated with CBC.

H. Douglas Pratt, Charlotte, is presently teaching advanced biology at Ashley High School in Gastonia and has exhibited his drawings and paintings in the Charlotte area. Although Doug has never studied art, he began sketching birds while only a sixth grader. An active member of the local club in Charlotte as well as the CBC, Doug has pursued his interest in observing and studying birds in the wild as far away as Ecuador and Mexico, as well as in other parts of the United States. "I never draw or paint a species unless I've observed it in nature," he said, "but I use books, drawings, photographs, and bird skins to find the correct color patterns, structure, and details." He remarks that from very early in his bird-watching

days, even before actively joining CBC, he has read THE CHAT. He finds that the field notes and scientific papers make interesting reading and are valuable reference material for his illustrations.

Promoting bird study and conservation throughout the Carolinas is a major activity of the Carolina Bird Club. Responsible citizens should endeavor to protect the total environment from needless destruction and exploitation. In direct proportion to the Carolina Bird Club's success in attracting members from all parts of the two states, it has been able to speak out effectively on behalf of the protection of wildlife and the conservation of natural resources. It is not enough to feed birds and admire their beauty; we must assure a wholesome environment for all living creatures.

Each spring, fall, and mid-winter, CBC members gather for an exciting weekend of field trips, informative programs, and lively discussions with fellow birders in a friendly, informal atmosphere. Often families attend, with the quick eyes of young birders spotting the unusual bird, while wildflowers or seashells may enthuse their elders who find birding from the mountains to the sea a truly stimulating experience.

The Carolina Bird Club welcomes as members all who are interested in bird study or conservation. It is not necessary to be a resident of the Carolinas; indeed, many members are from other states. For more information you may write:

Carolina Bird Club, Inc.
Headquarters, P. O. Box 1220
Tryon, N. C. 28782

All living things must live together in harmony. We can learn much from Nature—including the birds—if only we would take the time.

PHOTO BY JACK DERMID

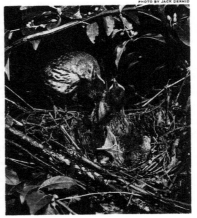

How Fish Are Identified

Part II

by Duane Raver

FISH, like most living things, are classified in orderly groups, and they all fit nicely into their special categories. Each fish has a scientific name and often several common names, and each fish can be identified and named precisely by using a rather technical device called a "key." First of all, do not be dismayed at this rather complicated appearing puzzle. By using a fish that you already know and following it through the key, you will see how the placement unfolds from item to item and soon falls into the right place. The use of technical terms is almost unavoidable in scientific keys. When such terms appear, it may be necessary to refer to the first part of "How Fish Are Identified" in *Wildlife In North Carolina* for April. A short list of words and their meanings is available for reference.

The "Family Key" is used to find the family to which the species in question belongs. For example, the trout family, SALMONIDAE, or the catfish family, ICTALURIDAE. Once we n a r r o w the question of identity to this grouping, we are ready to pick out the precise fish from a selection of two or several fish in the family. In the case of the gars and bowfins, we have only one fish listed under each of these families, making selection simple; however, in the case of the sunfish, thirteen species are included.

Selection of one individual from a family group can usually be done using either a description or a picture showing a distinctive characteristic. Thus, you will find many (not all) of the species found in North Carolina listed under their respective families, along with one or several distinguishing characteristics. Where possible, a sketch of a classifying feature also is shown. By reading the descriptions of the fish listed and comparing the sketches with the fish in question, you will arrive at the correct identification.

A final check on the correctness of your findings may be obtained from a text on fishes by reading their complete descriptions or by asking a more experienced fisherman. Use the location where the catch was made, size, and even the method of capture in your identification. You may find fish identification very interesting and worth further study.

A Key to the Families of North Carolina Fishes

1A. Tail rounded or unsymmetrical _____ 2
1B. Tail forked or slightly so; symmetrical ___ 3
2A. Body covered with diamond-shaped plate-like scales; nose beak-like: LEPISOSTE-IDAE, the Gars.

2B. Body with cycloid scales; head rounded: AMIIDAE, the Bowfins.
3A. Dorsal fin with more than one spine; pelvic fin without a spine _____ 4
3B. Dorsal fin with more than one spine; pelvic fin with a spine _____10
4A. Chin with barbels; body scaleless: ICTAL-URIDAE, the Catfish.
4B. Chin without barbels; body with scales __ 5
5A. Gill-slits extended far forward below; gill-membranes free from isthmus _____ 6
5B. Gill-slits not extended far forward below; gill-membranes united to isthmus _____ 9
6A. No adipose fin developed _____ 7
6B. Adipose fin developed: SALMONIDAE, the Trout.
7A. Belly with strong scales forming a sharp keel: CLUPEIDAE, the Shad and Herring.
7B. Belly without a sharp keel _____ 8
8A. Front of head shaped like a duck's bill; head scaled: ESOCIDAE, the Pickerel.
8B. Front of head not shaped like a duck's bill; no scales on head: HIODONTIDAE, the Mooneyes.
9A. Mouth fitted for sucking; pharyngeal teeth numerous: CATOSTOMIDAE, the Suckers.
9B. Mouth not fitted for sucking (may be inferior); pharyngeal teeth fewer than nine on each side: CYPRINIDAE, the Minnows.
10A. Dorsal fin single (almost separated in large-mouth b a s s): CENTRARCHIDAE, the Sunfish and Black Bass.
10B. Dorsal fins—2, separated or but slightly joined _____11
11A. Anal spines—3: SERRANIDAE, the Sea Bass.
11B. Anal spines—1 or 2; PERCIDAE, the Perches.

See Next Page for Guide to the Species.

Terms and Their Meanings

Anterior	Forward, toward the head end.
Barbel	A flexible feeler-like organ on the head of certain fish, containing sensory organs.
Isthmus	That portion in the throat region of a fish directly behind the chin area.
Keel	The mid-line of the belly of a fish. May be sharp, formed by scales like the peak of a roof.
Posterior	Behind, toward the tail end.
Ray	Rods or fibers supporting the membranous portion of a fin, may be either bony (spinous rays) or cartilaginous (soft rays).

A GUIDE TO FISH IDENTIFICATION

Use the family key on page 25 to determine in which family your fish belongs. Then with the help of these descriptions and sketches, it will be easy to find the correct name of the species in question.

FAMILY CLUPEIDAE: Shad and Herrings

ALEWIFE (Pomolobus pseudoharengus)
Mouth small with lower jaw not greatly longer than upper. Upper jaw **not** notched. Scales in lateral series: 50.

AMERICAN SHAD (Alosa sapidissima)
Upper jaw notched. Scales in lateral series: 60-65.

HICKORY SHAD (Alosa mediocris)
Lower jaw much longer than upper.

GIZZARD SHAD (Dorosoma cepedianum)
Posterior extension of dorsal fin greatly elongated. Fresh water only.

FAMILY SALMONIDAE: Trout and Salmon

BROOK TROUT (Salvelinus fontinalis)
Dorsal fin and back mottled with olive, worm-like marks. Ventral fins edged in white.

RAINBOW TROUT (Salmo gairdneri)
Dorsal fin and back spotted. Tail heavily spotted. Side pink or red.

BROWN TROUT (Salmo trutta)
Body chocolate brown to olive-yellow. Tail with few spots. Body spots with light "halo."

FAMILY ICTALURIDAE: Catfishes

CHANNEL CATFISH (Ictalurus punctatus)
Tail deeply forked. Body of specimens under 2 pounds, steel gray with dark spots. Rays in anal fin: 25-29.

WHITE CATFISH (Ictalurus catus)
Tail forked. No spots on body. Rays in anal fin: 19-21.

YELLOW BULLHEAD (Ictalurus natalis)
Tail square—not forked. Color—olive yellow. Chin barbels—white or cream. Anal rays: 24-27.

BROWN BULLHEAD (Ictalurus nebulosus)
Tail not forked. Anal rays: 17-22. Chin barbels gray or brown.

FAMILY ESOCIDAE: Pickerels

CHAIN PICKEREL (Esox niger)
Cheek and opercle scaled. Rays in dorsal fin—usually 14. Chain-like markings on body. Size—up to 8 pounds.

REDFIN PICKEREL (Esox americanus)
Cheek and opercle scaled. Rays in dorsal fin—11-12. Body with vertical bars. Size—rarely over 11 or 12 inches.

MUSKELLUNGE (Esox masquinongy ohioensis)
Lower half of cheek and opercle without scales. Size from 10 to 20 pounds. Not common.

* * * *

FAMILY SERRANIDAE: Sea Basses

STRIPED BASS (Roccus saxatilis)
Spinous and soft dorsal fins separate. Base of tongue with teeth. Body with rows of spots forming stripes. Size—up to 50 pounds.

WHITE BASS (Roccus chrysops)
Spinous and soft dorsal fins separate. Base of tongue with teeth. Body striped. Inland waters. Size—up to 4¾ pounds.

WHITE PERCH (Roccus americanus)
Spinous and soft dorsal fins connected. Tongue without teeth. Body only faintly striped. Mostly coastal. Size—up to 2½ pounds.

* * * *

FAMILY PERCIDAE: Perches

YELLOW PERCH (Perca flavescens)
Spinous dorsal fin sooty, without posterior spot. Teeth weak, not canine. Body with dark, broad vertical bands.

WALLEYED PIKE (Stizostedion vitreum)
Spinous dorsal with dark spot at posterior base. Teeth strongly developed. Body with faint blotches. Ventral lobe of tail with white spot.

* * * *

FAMILY CENTRACHIDAE: Sunfish and Black Bass

SMALLMOUTH BASS (Micropterus dolomieui)
Dorsal fin without deep notch between spinous and soft portions. Scales small, with cheek scales in 14 to 18 rows. Upper jaw extending only to posterior edge of eye pupil.

LARGEMOUTH BASS (Micropterus salmoides)
Spinous and soft dorsal fins almost completely disconnected. S c a l e s large, with cheek scales in 9 to 12 rows. Upper jaw extending beyond posterior margin of eye.

WARMOUTH (Chaenobryttus gulosus)
Mouth large, tongue with teeth. Body mottled with yellow-olive and purples. Opercular flap poorly developed. 3 anal spines.

REDBREAST (Lepomis auritus)
Mouth large, no teeth on tongue. Body with faint vertical bars. Breast orange. Opercular flap long, narrow.

GREEN SUNFISH (Lepomis cyanellus)
Mouth large, no opercular flap. Blue lines on cheek Dark spot at posterior base of anal and soft dorsal fins.

COMMON BLUEGILL (Lepomis macrochirus macrochirus)
Mouth small. Dark spot at base of posterior portion of soft dorsal fin. Opercular flap rounded and dark blue or black. Body with vertical bars.

REDEAR SUNFISH (Lepomis microlophus)
Opercular flap firm with posterior border pink or buff. Pectoral fin long, pointed. Coloration not bright.

PUMPKINSEED (Lepomis gibbosus)
Opercular flap firm with red or orange spot. Cheeks with bluish streaks. Coloration bright, with golden underparts.

ROCK BASS (Ambloplites rupestris)
Dorsal spines 11 or 12. Anal spines 6. Mottled, with bronze spots forming lateral rows below lateral line. Western N. C.

FLIER (Centrarchus macropterus)
Dorsal spines 11 to 13. Anal spines 7 or 8. Bronze-green color with spots forming lateral rows. Body shape rounding. Eastern N. C.

WHITE CRAPPIE (Pomoxis annularis)
Dorsal spines 5 or 6. Body more elongate with dark markings forming vertical bars. May be light or dark in general color.

BLACK CRAPPIE (Promoxis nigro-maculatus)
Dorsal spines 7 or 8. Body robust with dark markings forming no pattern.

FAMILY LEPISOSTEIDAE: Gars
LONG-NOSED GAR (Lepisosteus osseus)
Diamond-shaped, plate-like scales. Nose beak-like, narrow, with many small teeth.

* * * *

FAMILY AMIIDAE: Bowfins
BOWFIN (Amia calva)
Head rounded, body elongate. Continuous dorsal fin along two-thirds of back. Tail rounded. Gular plate under lower jaw.

* * * *

FAMILY CASTOSTOMIDAE: Suckers

LAKE QUILLBACK (Carpiodes cyprinus)
Mouth sucker-like. Dorsal fin very high and sail-like in front, tapering to narrow posteriorly. Scales large. High "shouldered."

LAKE CHUBSUCKER (Erimyzon sucetta)
Mouth inferior, semi-sucker-like. Soft dorsal fin, narrow at base. Scales large. Body of sub-adults with distinct black stripe mid-laterally. Robust body.

REDHORSE SUCKERS (Moxostoma sp.)
Sucker-like mouth, elongate body with small head. Medium large scales. Fins orange or reddish. Body golden or silver. Anal fin pointed.

WHITE SUCKER (Catostomus commersoni)
Sucker-like mouth, Elongate body with small scales: more than 50 in lateral line. Color, entirely silver or dusky above, silver below.

HOG SUCKER (Hypentelium nigricans)
Large sucker mouth, large head with tapering body. Large pectoral fins. Body, mottled with olive.

SPOTTED SUCKER (Minytrema melanops)
Body distinctly spotted, with each scale bearing spot. Body moderately robust. Color, dusky.

* * * *

FAMILY CYPRINIDAE: Minnows
CARP (Cyprinus carpio)
Mouth inferior with barbels at corners. Large scales. Body with high shoulder, mostly olive to orange. Size—large, up to 30 pounds.

GOLDEN SHINER (Notemigonus crysoleucas)
Small mouth and rapidly tapering head. Lateral line decurved toward ventral area. Anal fin falcate. Size— up to 12 inches.

PHOTO BY JACK DERMID

I Made a Bluebird Cry

by Carlton Morris

ACCORDING to the poets, birds always sing, though recently someone has come up with the opinion that they don't sing at all. Instead they're angry and quarrelling and making noises to keep predators and other birds away from their nests. This is what the experts say, but if you would settle such an insignificant matter, ask a born and bred country boy before he reaches courting age. After he reaches that age, the birds usually have more sense than he does. Sometimes they cry.

Did you ever hear a bluebird cry? I did. I made one cry.

Nowadays they tell us all bluebirds are gone. Some people say our civilization overtook them and they couldn't survive our pollution and pesticides. A few years back some experts came up with the theory that some strange disease took them all away and not a one could be found in all the land.

I pray they're all wrong and they'll come back again.

There are people who spend all their lives looking at and studying birds of all species. I'm not that involved, but as a youngster I knew the names and habits of every bird I had ever seen from the lowly and contemptible English sparrow to the great bald eagle that nested in a giant cypress a few miles up river from our farm.

We always had a family of bluebirds around our home in those years, and when by chance I pass that way, especially in spring and summer, I remember them as though it was yesterday when I made the bluebird cry.

In those years all farms had a big gate for the farmyard and a little gate in front of the house. Our bluebirds nested in a fence post near our front gate. I was always on friendly terms with them, but my father forbade me going near that post during their nesting season. He said a mother bird would desert her young if a human blew his breath in her nest. But our bluebirds seemed so tame and friendly I couldn't resist the temptation. They were the years before mass production on the farms when a mule and 40 acres were supposed to support a family. There was no weed or grass killer and almost all crops had to be chopped by hand. So it was that many a day I left my hoe buried in the cornrow with the handle upright while I went to the house for the midday meal and an hour of rest. And many a time I would return to find one of our bluebirds perched daintily atop my hoe handle.

One bright morning I remember how a mocker sang on the top of our chimney. She mimicked all the birds along our coastland and then she simply lay back her head and sang as though her heart would burst. From a pine thicket in front of our house, a turtle dove mourned her sad-sweet song. Three crows flew high overhead, arguing back and forth, never missing anything below for they're the smartest birds alive. I saw the bluebird return from a quick breakfast and dive into her post home.

Barefoot, I tip toed up and placed a hand over the fence post. Moving my hand a fraction, I peeped inside. There she sat, still as a mouse looking up at me with bright, beady eyes. Somehow I felt I had done her a terrible wrong. Quickly I moved my hand and stepped back. She popped out of the post hole in an instant and perched on the fence only a few feet way. I looked once again into her nest at four beautiful, blue eggs and then I heard her tiny, plaintive voice, and I could swear she was crying. I left a running, feeling guiltier than sin and I never went there again.

In other years I had seen the young birds when they first hatched out as they tried to hang to the wire fence or post. The parents stayed there right on up to hatching time, but I never saw the youngsters. They never used the post again.

I left there a long time ago while the bluebirds were still with us. I remember they didn't sing like the mockers and didn't come down on the ground and destroy crops like redbirds, quail or sparrows. They were just there, part and parcel of the world and prettying up God's countryside.

They were gentle and more friendly than any of the other birds.

Now they're all gone and it makes me sad to remember how I once made one cry.

Sometimes you almost get the feeling that about all man is good for is to make something cry. ◆

How To Catch Fish

The educated sportsman is the happy sportsman—he knows how to hook the big ones.

North Carolina State University this year will conduct its 18th annual short course in sport fishing at Hatteras on the scenic Outer Banks, June 15-20. Designed to interest both the veteran fisherman and the novice, male or female, classes combine education and sport fishing with the majestic beauty of Hatteras Island.

Classes will meet to study marine biology, lures and tackles, casting, salt water fly fishing and characteristics of the Gulf Stream. Three major fishing excursions will include an all-day trip to the Gulf Stream and the two half-day trips inshore and in the sound. (Last summer, students in the sport fishing class caught nearly 900 fish of all kinds, shapes and sizes.)

Conducted by the North Carolina State University Division of Continuing Education and the Department of Zoology, the course is taught by University Staff members, tackle manufacturers and guest lecturers.

Additional information on the course may be obtained from Gene Starnes, NCSU, Division of Continuing Education, Box 5125, Raleigh, N. C. 27607.

A thrashing dolphin reluctantly comes aboard during a sunny off-shore trip. Ready to go?

PHOTO BY TOM JACKSON

British Friend

DEAR SIRS:

I have for the last three months received a copy of "WILDLIFE IN NORTH CAROLINA" from some unknown source in North Carolina. If it is my friend's desire to remain unknown it is all right with me.

I can assure you and my unknown friend that I enjoy reading the interesting accounts of your wildlife, and the efforts your organization take to preserve it.

I would respectfully suggest the possibility of your finding a small space in your magazine to print a short appreciation note to my unknown friend for the pleasure I obtain and knowledge gained through his generosity.

SAM AGER,
94 CRESSING ROAD, BRAINTREE, ESSEX, ENGLAND.

Predator Value

DEAR SIR:

While I agree in part with Mr. G. O. Kelver's comments in the November 1968 issue of *Wildlife in North Carolina* concerning preservationists (and I assume he is referring to those who oppose hunting and not to those who support the preservation of wilderness areas, wild rivers or marshlands) there is another facet to consider.

We kill the coyote, timber wolf and other predators and wonder why we have the problems associated with the population explosions of such animals as elk, deer and many rodents. Often man kills the predator with the excuse that the predator is hurting game but ecologically speaking, the predator helps the game by insuring its vitality. While a natural predator kills the weak and the sick, the "sportsman" prefers the strong and the healthy.

Perhaps many of the preservationists remember that in this country the passenger pigeon and the Carolina parakeet were hunted to extinction. Other animals such as the Eskimo curlew (may already be extinct), the grizzly and the whooping crane (one was accidentally shot this year) are still threatened with extinction because in the past there were inadequate protection laws. Animals such as the cougar and the black-footed ferret are still being hunted to extinction.

I agree, however that the greatest threat of all to wildlife is the improper use of the land. No species, including man, can long survive the destruction of its environment.

Sincerely yours,
THOMAS C. SOUTHERLAND, JR.
PRINCETION, NEW JERSEY

James R. Modlin

Wildlife Protector James R. Modlin, stationed at Waynesville in Haywood County, was born October 10, 1936 in Ahoskie, North Carolina. Mr. Modlin grad-uated from Ahoskie High School and attended East Carolina University before entering the Air Force where he served four years.

Mr. Modlin completed the Pre-service Training School for Wildlife Protectors at the Institute of Government at Chapel Hill in July of 1967, and in October of that year was assigned as Wildlife Protector Trainee in Mountain Home, North Carolina. In November 1967, he was appointed Wildlife Protector and transferred to Waynesville.

Mr. Modlin is a member of the Southeastern Association of Game and Fish Commissioners, Law Enforcement Section, and the National Rifle Association. He is married to the former Mary Pritchard of Las Vegas, Nevada, and they have one son, John Russell, age eight months.

DIVISION ENFORCEMENT RECORD FOR MARCH 1969

HUNTING & FISHING

Persons checked	19,573
Total prosecutions	299
Total convictions	285
Total cases not guilty	9
Total cases nol prossed ..	3
Total cases dismissed	2
Total fines collected	$4,620.00
Total costs collected	$3,419.40

BOATING

Persons checked	3,757
Total prosecutions	43
Total convictions	43
Total cases not guilty	0
Total cases nol prossed	0
Total cases dismissed	0
Total fines collected	$ 75.00
Total costs collected	$560.25

All fines and any arrest or witness fees are paid into the school funds of the counties in which the violation occurred, and no part of the fines or costs collected are paid to the North Carolina Wildlife Resources Commission or its personnel.

Preparing Woodchuck

Cleaning: Open stomach, remove entrails as soon as killed and keep covered. This is to keep flies off the meat until hunter gets home. Then skin woodchuck, removing a brown fatty substance from the pit of the forelegs (if not removed, the meat is very bitter). Slit the hind legs and remove the white sinews. The meat is now ready to be washed and cooked.

Cooking: Boil in water to which salt, black pepper, a little red pepper, a medium-sized onion, and a tablespoon of vinegar has been added. Cook until meat is about done or tender.

Remove meat from water and put in a baking pan or dish. Spread barbecue sauce over meat and bake in oven slowly (300°) for 30 minutes. Baste meat during this time. Do not burn and dry meat.

Remove from oven and serve hot with baked sweet potatoes, your favorite vegetables and corn muffins.

Regular barbecue sauce from the store may be used or your own.

Barbecue Sauce

¼ c. chopped onion
2 c. catsup
¼ c. Worcestershire sauce
1 T. prepared horseradish mustard
¼ tsp. each of garlic salt, red hot pepper, black pepper, (thyme, oregano, savory—crushed)
2 drops Tabasco sauce

Cook onions in hot oil until tender—not brown. Add remaining ingredients. Simmer uncovered 10 to 15 minutes. Yields 2¾ cups.

MRS. E. BRENT
EAST ORANGE, NEW JERSEY

Deterioration Stemmed?

DEAR SIR:

For sometime your magazine seemed to be deteriorating into a hunting, boating, and fishing publication. I am happy to see more real wildlife pieces such as, "We, the People," September; "Night Bird of Mystery," "Summer Birds in Your Backyard" of August; "The Voyage of the Diamond City," October and "The Marshlands—Wetlands" in November.

There were four in December that I enjoyed, "A Walk With A Naturalist," "Wildlife in Wood," "Our Priceless Heritage," and "Not A Sparrow Falls." As to February, there were "No Goose Hunting Here," "Sassafrass," "Winter On the Beach," "A Pond in Winter." These are the types of things I like and one would expect to find in *Wildlife*. As Manley Hopkins wrote, "What would the world be, once bereft of wet and wildness? Let them be left. Oh, let them be left, wildness and wet; Long live the weeds and wilderness yet!"

And I echo, "without them, we would be indeed bereft . . . ."

THELMA W. GUNTHORPE
SHELBY

Frustrated

I went out turkey hunting,
Took my little dog along,
It was a lovely morning,
And I was feeling strong.
Old Trixie took to barking,
Not far in front of me,
Flushed a big turkey gobbler
It was a sight to see!
He flew 'way above us,
Lit in a big pine tree,
And Trixie kept on barking,
Excited as could be.
I raised my little gun up,
And took, I thought, dead aim,
But when I pulled the trigger,
No gobbler downward came.
Instead o' that, he sailed away,
And left me weak and sore,
And now my lovely morning
Wasn't lovely anymore.

Major Carlos U. Lowrance

● continued from page 15
activities would be permitted only at designated areas operated as concessions. As a general principle, most people are opposed to regimented activities and would hope the problem could be corrected through a different approach. However, if the problem continues to increase, this approach may become mandatory. I have seen many miles of clean areas where shoreline property had been leased for homesites and/or organized camping areas. This may be the most logical long range approach to the problem.

Looking at the problem from another viewpoint, it would appear that if people can bring full containers of food, drink, and other consumable accessories to an area, they could carry the empty containers back to their homes or to a designated place where the waste could be deposited for later disposal. This would require the use of a litter bag, empty picnic basket, or box, and should cause no great inconvenience. However, before we can expect people to do this, they must first be made aware of the problem that is being created by the recreation masses. Litter bags for automobiles have been in general use for some time. Why not for boats and individual

camp sites? A clean camp can be maintained and should be left clean for those who will use the site later. Plastic litter bags may be obtained from Outboard Boating Club of America, 333 N. Michigan Avenue, Chicago, Illinois, 60601.

There may be better ways to prevent littering. If you have ideas, we at the State Board of Health, and I am sure the Wildlife Resources Commission, would appreciate hearing from you. I would expect that much improvement could be realized if those who subscribe to *Wildlife* would refrain from littering. If you happen to be one who is partially responsible, why not try a litter bag next time. I am sure that the wildlife clubs, other conservation organizations and the members of the United States Power Squadrons could have a tremendous impact for good in promoting the idea of proper disposal of solid waste and garbage.

The accumulation of this material affords excellent breeding areas for flies, mosquitoes, rats, and other undesirable pests that can ruin a person's well deserved rest from his daily activities. This is not intended, however, as a scare article. It is a fact. The solid waste problem is serious; it is increasing rapidly, and will impair our recreation areas if corrective action is not forthcoming. It is within the power of those who use the waters of the state and the shoreline of these waters to prevent it. I believe we all agree this great resource is worth protecting and requires attention. ◆

Part of the litter thrown overboard ends up on the beach. It is unsightly any place, and this young skipper knows that it is an illegal and irresponsible act to litter the waters of the state.

LITHO BY THE GRAPHIC PRESS, INC., RALEIGH, N

Wildlife IN NORTH CAROLINA

25 CENTS / JUNE 1969

STATE OF NORTH CAROLINA

ROBERT W. SCOTT

GOVERNOR

NORTH CAROLINA
WILDLIFE RESOURCES COMMISSION

ORVILLE L. WOODHOUSE, CHM. _ _ GRANDY
JAY WAGGONER, V. CHM. _ _ _ _ _ GRAHAM
DR. JOE M. ANDERSON, SEC'Y _ _ NEW BERN
JAMES A. BRIDGER _ _ _ _ _ BLADENBORO
HUGH G. CHATHAM _ _ _ _ _ _ _ ELKIN
JAMES A. CONNELLY _ _ _ _ _ MORGANTON
J. HOLT EVANS _ _ _ _ _ _ _ _ ENFIELD
T. N. MASSIE _ _ _ _ _ _ _ _ _ SYLVA
ROBERT G. SANDERS _ _ _ _ _ CHARLOTTE

CLYDE P. PATTON
EXECUTIVE DIRECTOR

EUGENE E. SCHWALL
ASSISTANT DIRECTOR

DIVISION CHIEFS

ROD AMUNDSON _ _ _ _ _ _ _ EDUCATION
FRANK B. BARICK _ _ _ _ _ _ _ _ GAME
J. HARRY CORNELL _ _ _ INLAND FISHERIES
ROBERT B. HAZEL _ _ _ _ _ _ PROTECTION
J. THOMAS WILLIAMS _ FINANCE-PERSONNEL
C. FLOYD WILLIAMSON _ _ _ ENGINEERING

WILDLIFE IN NORTH CAROLINA recognizes the need
for close cooperation between State and Federal
conservation agencies and the people who hunt
and fish—to bring about a restoration of our renewable resources. The Editor gratefully receives
for publication news items, articles, and photographs dealing with the North Carolina out-of-
doors, but reserves the right to reject materials
submitted. Full credit is given for all materials
published.

• • •

WILDLIFE IN NORTH CAROLINA is published at the
Wildlife Resources Commission offices, Motor
Vehicles Building, 1100 New Bern Ave., Raleigh,
N. C. 27601.

• • •

Second class postage paid at Raleigh, North
Carolina 27602.

• • •

SUBSCRIPTIONS—Fifty cents per year, one dollar for two years. Make remittances payable to
WILDLIFE RESOURCES COMMISSION. Any
employee of the Wildlife Resources Commission
may accept subscriptions, or they may be forwarded to Post Office Box 2919, Raleigh, N. C.
27602. Stamps cannot be accepted.

Wildlife circulation this issue, 116,230.

IN NORTH CAROLINA ■

The official publication of the NORTH CAROLINA WILDLIFE
RESOURCES COMMISSION, Raleigh 27602. A monthly magazine
devoted to the protection and restoration of our wildlife resources
and to the improvement of hunting and fishing in North Carolina.

VOL. XXXIII, NO. 6   JUNE, 1969

IN THIS ISSUE

EDITORIAL STAFF

ROD AMUNDSON _ _ _ _ _ _ _ _ EDITOR
DUANE RAVER _ _ _ _ _ MANAGING EDITOR
LUTHER PARTIN _ _ WRITER-PHOTOGRAPHER
JOHN PARKER _ _ _ _ _ _ BOATING EDITOR
TOM JACKSON _ _ _ WRITER-PHOTOGRAPHER

The brown pelican is a bit of a
clown, but he's all business
when it comes to lunch time.
Diving from as much as sixty
feet, the pelican seldom misses
his quarry of menhaden. An
adult bird weighs around 8 or
9 pounds and has a wing spread
of some 6½ feet. Scattered
North Carolina nesting records
include Royal Shoal and Shell
Castle Island. Photograph by
Jack Dermid.

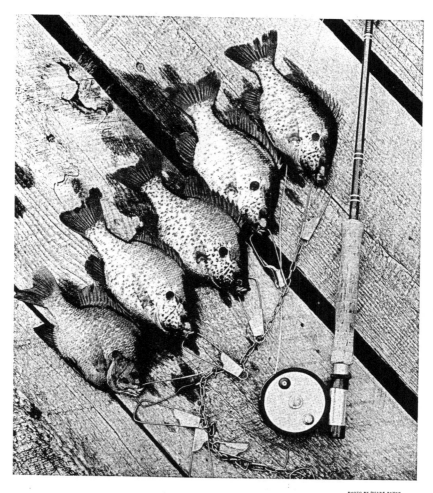

Reel Sport

The shellcracker or redear sunfish isn't generally considered a ready customer for the fly fisherman, but these four along with the lone bluegill, fell to a tiny white streamer. If you can find some late spawners, you may be in for some good fun.

Fishing
Piedmont
North Carolina

by Jim Dean

TOP-NOTCH fishing at your doorstep.

That's the best way to describe the Piedmont section of the Tarheel State. Despite what some fishermen think, you don't have to travel to the coastal regions or to the mountains to find some of the best fishing in the state. The area from roughly Raleigh to Gastonia holds the majority of the state's population. It also offers some of the state's finest fishing.

Perhaps the best part about it is that you can find this excellent fishing close to home. Within this region are countless lakes, ponds, rivers and streams that yield lunker largemouth bass, whopping landlocked striped bass, strings of big panfish and a variety of other popular species such as pickerel, catfish and carp.

Think of it this way. Within a few miles of your home—and it really makes little difference where you live in the Piedmont—you can fish waters that hold largemouth bass over 10 pounds, bluegills as big as dinner plates and catfish that are too big to land with a net.

"So how come I don't catch fish like that?" might be your reaction. One reason may be that you're spending too much time looking for greener pastures elsewhere. The biggest secret to catching fish —any fish—is persistence.

The pond or lake down the road from your house is more likely to yield a bragging-size fish than some heralded hot spot several hundred miles from home, because you can fish the nearby spots more frequently, and the more you fish the better fisherman you become. There are exceptions, of course, but the rule is generally sound.

FOR instance, Alamance County is a Piedmont representative that is fairly typical. It is certainly not noted for any outstanding fishing spots. And yet, over the past few years, anglers have caught so many big bass in its ponds and lakes that a local paper was forced to limit the running of pictures to bass that weighed over seven pounds. Even so, hardly a week would pass that some happy, sunburned angler would not appear at the door with a bass exceeding that limit. In the period of two years, several bass over 12 pounds were caught, and a great many more in the eight- to 10-pound range. Not only were anglers catching big bass, they were also bringing in bluegills and shellcrackers that weighed up to 56 ounces and carp that had to be brought in a pickup truck.

This same situation exists in most of the Piedmont region, although in some areas, other species are prevalent.

If you know the Piedmont's myriad lakes and streams are capable of producing such fish, and you're willing to take enough time to give them a fair chance, there is no reason why you shouldn't be hiking to your local paper in the near future with a fish that will bug the outdoor editor's eyes.

Once you've cancelled that long fishing trip and vowed not to let something as trivial as work get in the way of some serious fishing, what do you do? If you're not already a knowledgeable fisherman, and even if you are, you might pick up a few tips. Such information might even be valuable to anglers who live in the Coastal Plains or the mountains. After all, they are also looking for greener pastures, and guess where they go?

For the sake of simplicity, let's divide the Piedmont's top fishing into species.

LARGEMOUTH BASS

Although it's no doubt true that panfish are the Piedmont's bread and butter fish, the largemouth bass grabs most of the glory. He probably deserves it. He's big, brawny and often difficult to catch.

The best way to catch a mounting-size largemouth is probably the result of a fairly recent invention. (Live minnows are often standard, but since surviving minnows can choke a farm pond, let's stick to artificial baits). Less than a decade ago, various types of rubber and plastic lures appeared on the market. Most fishermen laughed at them. They aren't laughing anymore. The fact is that more big bass are caught on wiggly plastic worms than any other bait in the Piedmont—maybe even in the entire South. If you had to be content with only one lure for big bass, you could do much worse than a plastic worm. Many anglers who fish exclusively for big bass use nothing else, and although individual techniques vary, there are a number of tips which are generally accepted as essential.

The most popular colors for these eel-like lures are purple, black, blue, green and red—probably in that order. Your choice might depend on what's producing best in your area, however. Most good fishermen buy them unrigged and rig them themselves with a single weedless hook ranging in size from 2/0 to 4/0 depending on the length of the worm. Worms range from very small to well over 10 inches, but the best all 'round size is about six inches. Make sure the worm you select is "soft" and "flexible." Some fishermen don't use weedless hooks, but you'll find that grass and stumps are annoying beyond belief if you decide to use a hook without a weed guard.

One of the mainstays of Piedmont fishing is the largemouth bass. This 14 incher was fooled by a plastic worm. Dinnerplate bluegills like the one below, are waiting in lots of ponds. Crappies (below, right) are very popular also.

SOME anglers like to use worms without any added weight, but if you use weight, never pinch a split shot on the line ahead of the worm. That's inviting trouble, especially if you hook a nice fish. The split shot weakens the line, just as an overhand knot would. A better method is to buy weedless hooks that have a weight already molded onto the hook shank. The worm slides easily over the weight and hides it. Egg sinkers are also good, and don't pinch the line. You can also buy ready-rigged worms with more than one hook, but they hang up more frequently and lack a good wiggly action.

The technique is to cast out and let the worm sink to the bottom. Don't neglect deep water, especially in hot weather. Then retrieve slowly in jerks and twitches. When you feel a strike, or what you think might be a strike, let the bass "run" with the worm until you think he's swallowed it. You've got to make sure the bass feels little or no resistance when he strikes, or he'll drop it. When you think he's swallowed it, slowly tighten your line and let him have it hard.

Spinning tackle is the choice of most worm fishermen, and they like to use line testing at least eight-pounds because of the likelihood of hooking a big bass.

You should also equip yourself with several other types of lures. You'll need a couple of surface lures for use when the bass are hitting on top of the water. A good choice would be a floating lure with props on each end like the Smithwick Warhorse. You might also want to try an old favorite such as the Jitterbug or Hula Popper. You'll find that generally the best surface fishing is in early morning or late evening. Also select a couple of floating-diving lures such as the Rebel or L & S Bassmaster, and be sure to add at least one or two deep-diving lures such as the Hellbender, Waterdog or Bomber.

PANFISH

Panfish, and that means almost anything that fits in a frying pan, are fished for in the Piedmont with a zeal that approaches fanaticism, and with good reason. If anybody finds a better way to spend an afternoon than fishing for fat bluegills, shellcrackers or crappie, please let the rest of the angling world in on it. It is sport supreme.

The cane pole, cork and worm (real, slimy type) constitute the basic and most popular method. It's cheap, simple and needs no elaboration here. Never was born a Tarheel lad that didn't understand from birth the rudiments of cane pole fishing.

There are variations, however. By using spinning tackle, you can increase your range and perhaps your catch. Use a snap-on cork, and fish as you would with a cane pole. The only difference is that you can cast farther and cover more good spots.

THE best bait for most panfishing is probably either a red worm, a cricket, a grub or a catalpa worm. If you're fishing for crappie, insist on small minnows about an inch and a half long.

You may prefer to use artificials. A fly rod and floating popping bug is classic tackle for bluegills (bream) in the spring when they are spawning in shallow water. A small, white or yellow popper or a rubber spider—even a black ant—will work wonders.

If you want to try artificials with spinning tackle, use light line testing about four-pounds on an ultra-light rod and equip yourself with such proven lures as the Meatgetter, tiny Mepps and small Doll Flys. You'll find other local favorites, but keep your choices small. Almost any fish that inhabits the Piedmont will take such lures, and the sport they provide is superior. It isn't rare to come in with an assortment that includes large bream, crappie, bass and even pickerel. It's grab-bag fishing at it's best, and don't neglect the small streams.

ROCKFISH AND WHITE BASS

For no other reason than that they are cousins, the rockfish (striped bass) and white bass are lumped together in their discussion.

Rockfish are not widespread in the Piedmont,

The white bass is an elusive critter except during its spring spawning run, and you may have a bit of difficulty locating him. It is a fine, hard-fighting fish, though.

but that doesn't diminish their popularity. In Kerr Reservoir, and in the spring (usually April) on the Dan River above the lake, rockfish of true bragging size are caught in abundance. In the lake, most are caught trolling deep running lures such as Bombers, Waterdogs, Hellbenders and big Rebels. Occasionally, schools of rock will thrash the surface to a froth feeding on schools of threadfin shad, and that's the signal to switch to something that runs shallow or floats. The best advice concerning rockfish in Kerr Reservoir is to go with someone who is familiar with the fishing or hire a guide, especially the first time out. It will be money well spent, and you'll agree when you try to lift a catch of eight to 20-pound rockfish out of the boat.

WHITE bass are found in many larger lakes in the western part of the Piedmont. Some efforts have even been made to establish populations of these fish in lakes in the middle of the Piedmont. White bass, which range up to about five pounds, are avidly sought after. They are school fish, and where you catch one, you're likely to catch more. The technique is similar to striper fishing. Using small spoons and other local favorites, many anglers troll until they locate a school then cast for the fish. Like rockfish, white bass sometimes feed on the surface and provide fast action. Some anglers even fish for whites at night.

For both rock and white bass, a fast boat is a help. Sometimes it's necessary to cover a lot of ground to find the fish, especially if you're fishing the "breaks" when fish are on the surface.

ROUGH FISH

No one knows exactly why such fish as carp and catfish are called "rough" fish unless it's because they are such rough customers on the end of a fishing line.

Both species are found in most Piedmont waters, though catfish may be somewhat more widespread. It's a good idea to check the spot you plan to fish and find out whether these species are available before going.

Both catfish and carp like muddy water, and tend to feed almost exclusively on the bottom. Of course, you can catch them in clear water, but you'll still find them smack-dab on the mud. Most anglers use spinning and casting rods with one or two hooks strung in front of a round bottom sinker. Corks are rarely used.

For catfish, you'll find a variety of "stink" baits running the gamut from chicken entrails to blood-soaked dough. Minnows and worms are also often good. Shrimp—the kind you buy in a fish market—can be excellent.

For carp, doughballs of various types are perhaps best, although many swear by canned corn. Dough-ball recipes are legion, but they usually include some bizarre substance like anise oil or strawberry jello (honest)!

Both species are usually cautious biters, and knowing when to set the hook is not an art learned from books—only trial and error will teach you this.

Spanish Treasure of Topsail Island

CLOUDS had been building up over the land masses all afternoon. The fishing on the piers on Topsail Island had been slow all day. A few bluefish had been caught by bottom fishermen and fewer by a small band of the dedicated "jiggers" or plug fishermen. Unfortunately, because the heat had seemingly put the fish down, the only rewards most of the fishermen had received were burnt legs and peeling noses.

Most of the anglers on the pier were using light rods in the six to seven foot category. Preferences for this type of angling seem to run toward a rod with a light tip, but one that is heavy enough in the butt section to handle a strong fish. A rod is too light if it does not have the "beef" to bring in a lively fish. The larger or "surf" spinning rods become difficult to handle all day long because of their weight. Though most anglers tend to use spinning outfits, the pier was sprinkled with fishermen using casting and spincasting reels. The spincasting reels were those of larger size with greater line capacity than most fresh-water, push-button reels.

Most of the lures being pitched into the surf resembled a chrome metal tube with a slanted lead head. The first step to using these is to lean over the pier railing (watch yourself!) and hold your rod so that the rod tip points toward the water. Common sense will tell you how far to lean over the edge! As the lures were reeled in, the rods were pumped in a lure-jerking manner. The flattened head of the lure causes a darting action. Thus comes the action!

Other favorite lures used included "SeaHawks." These are used in the same manner as the before discussed "JurkJiggers" and "Nickeys." The Hopkins spoon is also found in most of the anglers' tackle boxes. Used in pairs, leadhead jigs are also fish producers.

As the sun began to sink behind the clouds that billowed in the west, anglers that lined the pier began to shout as they saw fish make passes at their lures. Soon these flashes came more frequently as larger predator fish discovered the schools of baitfish that had been around the pier all day. Baitfish began to dance on the surface as the slender shapes of silvery fish charged through the baitfish schools. Several of the anglers let out yells as fish nailed their lures. The fish were quickly identified: the barracuda shaped head and sleek forked tail showed that these fish were mackerel. The golden spots on their sides, much the same as Spanish doubloons, marked them as Spanish mackerel.

Lures flashed against the oncoming dusk as they were cast far out into the green waves. Arched rods and sizzling drags testified to the ability of these fish as fighters. An hour's furious fishing produced a number of Spanish mackerel and a fair pile of bluefish. Most of the blues were small, going about ½ to 1½ pounds. Although there were a few small Spanish taken, most were in the two- to three-pound class. A fighting fish this size taken on light salt-water tackle is real sport.

Topsail Island piers don't have a monopoly on this wonderful type of fishing; almost any pier on the Carolina coast has runs of Spanish mackerel and bluefish. This is the main ingredient of a fine day's fishing. One tip, fish toward the deep end of the pier or at least away from the muddy water of the breakers. Clear water can, at times, be a great boon to the plug fisherman.

Though this brand of fishing isn't new, it hasn't really gained too much popularity until the last few years. Try casting your lure into the briny deep and maybe you will come up with a "Spanish treasure" of memories for yourself.

Jerold F. Mayes

It's Their Business, Too

Studying a map of Company lands to determine the best sites for wildlife food planting are (l. to r.) Wildlife Commission District Game Biologist Jack Donnley; Alan Carlson, Assistant Manager of North Carolina Woodlands; George Henderson, WESTVACO'S District Forester; Quentin Bell, Manager of N. C. Woodlands; Grady Barnes, Supv. Eastern Wildlife Management Areas. Signs like the one above, set aside 17,000 acres on which the company has established game refuges. To insure safe working conditions and safe hunting, WESTVACO closes small sections of its property while company employees are working there.

by Tom Jackson

CONSERVATIONISTS and nature lovers who flinch at the sound of a chain saw and scowl at the sight of a log truck should take a closer look in eastern North Carolina where a large timber and pulpwood company is demonstrating that conservation is their business too.

In cooperation with the North Carolina Wildlife Resources Commission, WESTVACO—for West Virginia Pulp and Paper Company—has initiated a company resources management program to insure that the company's timberland and farming operations take into account the local wildlife resources and habitat.

Under the direction of Quentin Bell, manager of the North Carolina Woodlands division of WESTVACO Timberlands, the company's wildlife program in Dare, Tyrrell, Hyde and Washington counties provides excellent hunting for hundreds of Tar-

heel sportsmen while conserving habitat for future game populations.

WESTVACO has built and erected wood duck nesting boxes on company property, is providing game food plantings on its loblolly pine plantation, has planted brown top millet in Tyrrell County to improve dove hunting, has established a 17,-000-acre refuge for the hard-pressed black bear, and hopes that a developing 5,000-acre farm project will provide much additional food for quail, dove and waterfowl in the area.

In addition, the company has co-operated with Wetlands and Estuaries for Tomorrow, the Wildlife Resources Commission, the U. S. Fish and Wildlife Service and the North Carolina Forest Service to construct a 100 acre experimental waterfowl impoundment in Dare County. The impoundment, constructed at the company's expense, has been turn-

ed over to Wetlands and Estuaries for Tomorrow for three years. The conservation group will manage the improvement for waterfowl while research projects are underway there. If the impoundment is successful, the company may then consider constructing additional impoundments.

WESTVACO has also opened nearly 300,000 acres of company property to public hunting. For a nominal charge—to cover road maintainence and related expenses—Tarheel sportsmen can enjoy excellent hunting for bear, deer, squirrel, rabbit, quail, dove and waterfowl. A brochure, "Happy Hunting," which outlines the WESTVACO hunting, is available from the company's office in Manteo.

Hopefully more large companies in North Carolina will follow the WESTVACO lead and make conservation their business too. ⬧

To help train future sportsmen, the company has established this park and nature trail in Dare County. Above, WESTVACO has placed wood duck nesting boxes on many creeks and canals on company property in eastern North Carolina.

Wildlife Protector Larry Barnes and WESTVACO'S District Forester George Henderson, check on some of the browntop millet which the company strip plants on newly cleared farmlands. Above, a harvested corn field on company land provides this hunter with some dove hunting.

Barnes, (right) and Henderson look for deer sign in one of the game food plots planted between rows of pine seedlings in areas where timber has recently been harvested. Below, Quentin Bell, Manager of North Carolina Woodlands, Norman Spell, Public Relations Director for WESTVACO'S Timberlands Division, and E. A. Thorne, Secretary of Wetlands and Estuaries for Tomorrow, examine a flood-kill area on WESTVACO'S property and plan an experimental impoundment to make the area more attractive to waterfowl.

A Boy, His Dad, and A Fish

by Roy Martin

"Do you think we'll catch any?"

The boy was about four. Sitting on a small, up-ended wooden box he grasped the cane pole tightly. He watched the floating cork.

"Maybe," said the man squatting next to him, "if you don't scare 'em off talking."

The man pulled up sharply on his pole.

"Got it again," he said, shaking his head. He drew in the line and took the hook in his fingers.

The boy watched as his father rummaged around in the moist dirt of the worm can. He speared a red wiggler, squirming and elusive, onto the hook.

The young one grimaced.

"Do you reckon that hurt?"

The father glanced over at the boy, wiping his hands on soiled khaki trousers.

"I read someplace once where they ain't got no nerves in the middle," he said, angling the pole upward and dropping the cork back onto the water. "It probably just tickles."

"You don't hear 'em hollar, do you?"

The boy looked up. The pair sort of grinned together.

They were silent for a time, watching the ripples in the water cut by flitting insects and low swooping birds, watching corks react to curious fish.

"You want a drink?"

The boy nodded and stood up, putting a foot on his grounded fishing pole. His father reached back to a styrofoam cooler and, stirring around in the ice, came up with a can.

"I want to open it," the boy said, voice rising, hands nervously batting the air.

He took the can, pulled the tab and jerked away the top.

He swallowed noisily, then paused, uttering an "ah."

The fellow patted the boy lightly on the back and stood up, pushing a tattered hat down over his eyes against the ebbing sunlight.

Suddenly, he said in a half-shout, pulling the small, wiggling bream up from the water. "We got one."

"That's good, that's good," said the child, jumping around excitedly."

The man pried out the hook, keeping firm hold on the fish. He picked up a nearby bucket, moved quickly to the bank and scooped up water.

"That'll hold him," he said, dropping the fish into the bucket.

The boy watched the fish swirl around in the water, then went back to his place. Hook rebaited, the father was watching the corks.

"Did it hurt his mouth when you took the hook out?" The expression was inquisitive.

"I don't know," answered the man, shifting gaze from corks to boy.

"Why?"

"You mean why don't I know?"

"Un-huh."

"Well," he said, arching his fishing pole upward and dropping the cork in a new spot, "I'm not a fish. Never have been."

"Oh," responded the boy, "oh." ◆

Hunting, Trapping Rules to be Established June 10

On June 10 the Wildlife Resources Commission will meet in Raleigh to establish the 1969-1970 regulations for taking furbearing animals and non-migratory game. Regulations established by the Commission will be based primarily on the species concerned; their relative abundance, and their ability to progenate their kind for future hunters and trappers.

In establishing these regulations, the Commission will give due consideration to the ideas and opinions expressed by hundreds of outdoorsmen who attended a series of 10 public hearings between May 13 and May 23, but may be expected to follow conservation principles to the ultimate benefit of the people and wildlife concerned.

Wait For Migratory Game Bird Regulations

Although seasons and bag limits on nonmigratory game and furbearing species will be set June 10, there will be a time lapse before seasons on doves, ducks, geese, and other migratory game birds will become official. Seasons and bag limits on migratory game are established by the U. S. Fish and Wildlife Service, and probably won't be announced until late summer. While doves, rails, woodcock, snipe, and sora are likely to be fairly plentiful again this fall, the waterfowl count will be determined largely by the availability of moisture this spring and summer in the northern nesting grounds.

June is a Critical Month For Game Species

During June much of next fall's harvestable supply of game is being hatched or born. This is the critical period, one during which people are urged to keep their canine and feline pets confined or at least curtailed. Stray or feral dogs and cats, plus household pets, are an important limiting influence on the supply of game for fall hunting.

Subscription Rate Goes Up July 1

Effective July 1, 1969 the subscription rate for Wildlife in North Carolina will be increased from 50 cents per year to $1.00 per year. There still will be a 20% discount for club subscriptions in blocks of 25 or more.

BOAT				MOTOR		TRAILER
Length	Plywood	Fiberglass	Aluminum	HP	PRICE	PRICE
	PRICE					
12	125-200	190-255	170-330	5 - 9.8	$295. - $435.	$100. - $150.
14	145-260	210-325	235-390	9 - 20	$360. - $495.	$125. - $180.
16	185-400	340-500	320-500	18 - 35	$455. - $595.	$160. - $260.

+   +   =

EQUIPMENT

ITEM	PRICE	Sub Total
Life Saving Device (vest)	$ 3.00 - 10.00	
Life Saving Device (cushion)	$ 3.00 - 6.00	
Boat Seat	$ 5.00 - 15.00	
Paddle	$ 3.00 - 5.00	
Oars (pair)	$ 9.00 - 15.00	
Oar Lock Set	$ 4.00 - 6.00	
Anchor (8-10 lb. mushroom)	$ 3.00 - 6.00	
Line ¼ inch (100 feet)	$ 3.00 - 6.00	
Light Set (Bow & Stern)	$ 6.00 - 9.00	
Spare Tire Kit	$15.00 - 25.00	
Trailer Dolly	$15.00 - 20.00	
Trailer Jack	$ 6.00 - 12.00	
First Aid Kit	$ 3.00 - 8.00	
Hand Lantern	$ 4.00 - 10.00	
Fire Extinguisher (2½ lb. dry chemical)	$ 6.00 - 12.00	
Transom Pad	$ 3.00 - 5.00	
Bilge Pump (manual)	$ 4.00 - 8.00	
Electric Trolling Motor	$50.00 -210.00	
Battery for above	$25.00 +	
Battery Box	$ 4.00 - 7.00	
Tool Kit	$ 5.00 - 8.00	
		Total

Note: Motor listing does not include less expensive air cooled engines which start as low as $130.00 for five horsepower. Also, electric starting and generator equipped motors were generally not considered. However, the price range does cover one company's electric starting nine horsepower. Consider weight of boat, motor and equipment as well as boat length in selecting a trailer. One rule of thumb, if all of above comes to within 100 lbs. of trailer capacity, buy next largest size.

IT has been a year since commenting on that very popular subject—boat purchase. In the June, 1968, article, I did not discuss a most important subject, price. "Nice rig; how much?" is a question often heard at boat ramps and boat dealer showrooms. So let us price what may very well be, even in this day of futuristic designing, the most useful and practical of the line, the open, trailer weight, fishing utility craft.

Figures for this simplified cost schedule were gathered from major outboard motor manufacturers, several leading boat and trailer manufacturers, including those in North Carolina and two major mail order concerns. The boats included in the price schedule have, for the most part, conventional hulls. The smaller ones could be car-topped so you would wish to leave off trailer price. Boats selected are open, have no steering wheel or windshield or other fancies. In drawing the line at $500 for the boat, some of the slick-looking fiberglass open construction boats were omitted. Cost variation in a particular line, especially noticeable in aluminum, is usually due to type of construction, thickness or gauge of the aluminum, or dimensions may vary by a few inches. Plywood thickness will also affect price. In fiberglass, the tri-hull will cost more.

Even though a motor range is suggested, remember there is no blanket rule for matching. This holds true for the entire rig but is especially important regarding motor selection. A 9- or 10-horsepower motor, normally considered ideal for fishing may in fact be too much power for a light 12 footer. Check the capacity and motor requirement plate on the transom. An overpowered boat can indeed spell trouble but an underpowered boat can mean poor performance and dissatisfaction.

Decide on boat usage, check your finances, get dealer help (ask for a demonstration), and don't buy until you are sure. Good luck.

Where The Boats Are

We can't actually be sure where the boats of which we are about to speak are physically located. However, Mecklenburg County, upon which sprawls the metropolis of Charlotte, has over twice as many boats registered as has the coastal plain county of highest registration, New Hanover. The figure is about 3000 to 6000. To say the least, 30,000-acre Lake Norman has had an influence on the Mecklenburg figure.

Overloading Can Be Fatal

Overloading is one of the most common and potentially fatal mistakes a boat owner can make. Many serious accidents are the results of overloading.

A small boat may have a seating capacity for several passengers, but this doesn't mean that the boat can safely carry that number. Don't count the seats. Know the boat's passenger and weight capacity.

Most reputable boat builders give this information on capacity plates affixed to the gunwale. When figuring total weight, remember to include any gear.

If your boat doesn't have a capacity plate, check with your marine dealer or write the manufacturer. Don't take chances by guessing.

And remember, any recommendations are for fair weather and do not relieve the operator's responsibility for good judgement. If weather and water conditions are adverse, the load should be reduced accordingly (if you must go out). An overloaded boat will easily swamp or capsize because it cannot react to waves and other actions properly.

Boating Information

The National Association of Engines and Boat Manufacturers offers a free literature and film loan service. I recommend that you be fairly specific as to subject when requesting information. The address: 537 Steamboat Road, Greenwich, Connecticut 06830.

No Wake

It has been mentioned before in this column, but this thing of No Wake Speed in congested areas is certainly worthy of continued consideration. The open water may be churned to a froth but the area in and about marinas, ramps, anchorages, etc., should never feel the high speed thrust of the propeller. Many boaters are quite willing to slow down, but not quite to the point where the wake of their craft flattens out. The busiest of boating areas will take on a safe and tranquil appearance if that last 100 or so yards to the dock is run at idling speed.

Chart Booklet

A new edition of a booklet containing symbols and abbreviations used on all nautical charts issued by the U. S. Government is now available. The booklet also contains changes to the aids to navigation system and illustrations depicting new technological advances in the construction of aids. Send 50 cents to Coast and Geodetic Survey (C.44), Rockville, Maryland 20852.

This boat is well within the boundaries of a marked No Wake zone at a popular Tarheel boating area. The operator has slowed his craft, but not to idling speed. Wake is actually heaviest for most craft when operated just below planing speed or just above idling speed.

Ski boats too often figure in boating accidents. Yet they do not have to crop up that frequently. The scene here looks safe enough: an alert operator, an observer, and a skier wearing a ski belt. These elements should spell fun not tragedy. Note too, the boat remains a safe distance from shoreline obstacles.

Shelby's Junior Hunter's Club

Wildlife Patrolman Lewis N. Baris discusses gun handling with attentive members of the Junior Hunters' Club.

THE program is an unique one, and its value will be measured in the lives it may save in the future. The Junior Hunters' Club, originating in Shelby some months ago, has brought its first session to a close. Young hunters, ages 11-14, have gained invaluable information, knowledge, and experience that may serve to protect the lives of their fellow hunters as well as those of private citizens later.

The program, sponsored by the Shelby Parks and Recreation Department, began on January 13, and came to completion on March 8. At the opening session, 37 boys reported for enrollment, a n d most all these were around when the session was completed.

According to Bob Clark, the Superintendent of the City Parks and Recreation Department and a member of the 15-man board of directors, there were six prime motives for getting the program started. The first and foremost was safety —all phases of safety from firearms care and usage, to the safest way to cross a fence with a gun.

Other phases of the club program included the teaching of proper hunting techniques and the appreciation of using priv-

ate lands and farm areas for the hunt. The boys w e r e taught not to abuse property, and to respect the rights of others.

They were taught wildlife species, breeding habits, proper hunting seasons, types of foods eaten by wildlife, and where each species is likely to be found. In general, the club members were taught an over-all appreciation of hunting as a recreational outlet.

Under the gun safety phase, they learned the care, cleaning and handling of the firearm.

The program was set up in such a way that boys would come together for 12 sessions —the first, of course, was a full session devoted entirely to safety. The boys were instructed on loading, carrying and shooting of firearms, and then viewed a movie on the subject.

Even though one session was set aside entirely for safety, every session revolved around this topic. In the second class-session, the care and cleaning of firearms was covered. Henry Weathers, Jr. and

C. D. Coates were the instructors.

When the group met for the third time, the hunting phases of the program were brought into view, the first hunting instruction coming in the fields of coon and fox hunting. The session involved safety factors, the number of hunters involved, and the types of clothing to wear. The following Friday, the club members had their first taste of the real thing as the "Big Coon Hunt" was launched. Leo Green, Hoyt Craft, and Ben Clary were the leaders of the hunt. During the hunt, two coons were caught, and the hunters came home around midnight—one youngster was minus a pair of shoes —his were lost in the chase. Of course, there's some question if he was doing the chasing or being chased!

The fifth session, directed by Jim Hearn, Roy Dedmon, and Bill Ivey, covered the various techniques of deer and rabbit hunting. In that session, the type of guns and shells, the distance of dogs, and the hunter's position, were the primary topics—the group also viewed a movie to illustrate the topics covered.

From then to the end of the session, the group was well versed in the other varieties of hunting such as quail, dove and fox. The program also covered a session on taxidermy in which the group learned various techniques of preparing mounted animals.

They were also given even a broader range of actual hunting with a rabbit hunt headed up by Carl Martin, Clary, Hearn, Dedmon and Weathers. The agenda also called for a quail hunt and a fox hunt.

Up to this point, the schedule called for no guns, just dogs. The final session was to cover range firing techniques in which the boys were to learn range rules, range safety, and receive instruction on the scoring system of range firing.

At the conclusion, all boys who wished to take the test, were given a written examination. The testing was not mandatory; but those who passed the course exam were awarded the privilege of wearing the Junior Hunters' Club emblem on their hunting jackets.

Of the 37 boys who enrolled, 26 elected to take the exam and 21 passed it. For the most outstanding member of the Club during the 12-session period, a gun cleaning kit was given—furnished by Tillman's Firestone. Ernie Holland of Route 7, Shelby, was the recipient of the award.

Lewis Barts, the local wildlife patrolman, presided over the sessions, as well as serving on the Board of Directors, informing the club not only on the rules of safety, but explaining at length that his job is to be a "friend to the hunter as well as a wildlife protector."

On the final sesson of the Junior Hunters' Club, the boys were taken on a fox hunt and treated to a weiner roast by Roy Dedmon.

This type of program is probably the only one of its kind anywhere that exposes the boy to these particular types of activities.

Even though the first session is completed, the program is not over; similar training courses will be considered for next year and perhaps other communities will follow the example set by Shelby. ◆

A Bird a Week . . .

by Charlotte Hilton Green

L ONG ago, in my early teaching days, we tried it. We had little to work with and had to use our own ingenuity . . . and provide our own supplies. But anything new, or unusual, appealed to the children.

At first it had been "Learn a Bird a Week." Most of the children liked the idea, but when I grew more experienced and wiser, and changed it to "Let's Learn a Bird a Week," they liked it a lot better! The first had been more of a command; the second became more a contest, a challenge! And was much more popular.

The plan used: Each week we would have a good picture of the bird, in color, on the wall. Close by a 4x6 filing card stating all the salient facts about the bird: name, family, size, coloring, pattern, shape, plumage, voice, foods, (the bird's value) nest, eggs, young, range, habitat, etc.

Before the end of the week the children were expected to know all these details, then to find out all else they could about that particular bird, from books, magazines, papers, leaflets, others—and especially from their own observation. At the end of the week that bird and card were taken down, put in the "Bird Frieze" on another wall, and a new "Bird of the Week" put up.

That got them started, and interested, and most of them became intrigued and learned many more birds.

CARDINAL — OUR STATE BIRD

Family FRINGILLIDAE: Grosbeaks, Finches, Sparrows, Buntings.

Male: Red Crest, Black face. Female, brownish-red, reddish Crest & Tail. Same shape & size as male. 8-9 inches.

CARDINAL Only Red Bird With Crest! Similar species: Summer Tanager NO CREST; Scarlet Tanager, Black Wings. Belong different families.

VOICE: Series slurred whistles, several variations: what-cheer-cheer-cheery; pretty, pretty, pretty. Note, a thin, short clip.

FOOD: Wild fruits, seeds, grasses & weeds; beetles, crickets, insects. Easily attracted feeding-stations.

NEST: Weed stems, leaves, lined with grass; in bushes, vines, thickets, trees, often close to houses. EGGS: 2-4, whitish, heavily splotched. Often 3 broods. Incubation, 12.

RANGE: U. S. pretty much eastern half country, south Great Lakes & New Eng. Range been extending northward recent years. Non-migratory. N. C. Whole State all seasons.

TUFTED TITMOUSE Family: PARIDAE
(Titmice & Chickadees)

(Small gray birds, smaller than most sparrows, with proportionately longer tails & small stubby bills; extremely active, hanging upside down, if need be, to feed.)

TITMOUSE, both sexes similar: gray back, tufted head rusty flanks. (No other small gray bird has tufted crest.) 6-6½ inches. Young resemble adults.

VOICE: Clear, whistled "peto-peto-peto." Noisy. Joyous.

FOOD: Insects, wasps, bees, caterpillars, larvae, berries.

NESTS: In cavities hollow trees: often take over Bluebird houses, or old Woodpecker holes. Nest lined with moss, leaves, fine grass. 5-7 eggs, white, or cream, speckled, more than one brood.

RANGE: Pretty much eastern U. S. IN N. C. whole State at all seasons.

Excitable and inquisitive birds, easy to entice to feeding-stations, where their antics can be enjoyed.

Algae: "Grass of Many Waters"

by Alton H. Gustafson
Chairman, Department of Biology
Bowdoin College

MAN, his domestic animals, and many populations of terrestrial animals a r e l a r g e l y dependent on members of the grass family for their food, either directly or indirectly. Similarly, the animal life of aquatic environments is dependent for food on several groups of photosynthetic plants collectively known as the *algae*. Although 25,000 species of algae have been described and given scientific names, relatively few have common names. One may refer to such conspicuous examples as rockweeds, kelps, Irish moss, pond scums, mermaid's tresses, and a few others, but the remainder have not been called sharply to the attention of laymen. Their important place in the natural world has not been generally recognized. These numerous, abundant, diverse, ubiquitous, and fascinating organisms are well worth study for many reasons. Perhaps the recent concern with problems of pollution will serve to direct proper attention to them.

Terrestrial plants p o s s e s s roots, leaves, stems, and reproductive structures such as cones and flowers; and we utilize these as recognition marks for the various groups included among the 350,000 species known the world around. The algae do *not* possess any of these organs. Although they carry on the same fundamental processes as the terrestrial vegetation, they are organized in a wholly different manner. Their forms range from simple, single cells, to colonial aggregates, to simple and branched filaments, to structures resembling higher plants, and some are very complex. They include some of the tiniest plants as well as some of the largest such as the giant kelps. Their sexual organs are unicellular in contrast to those of the terrestrial types which are always multi-cellular. They lack

the vascular systems by which land plants transport materials from one part of the plant to another. Finally, they do not have embryos, although all land plants do.

The cells making up the bodies of both land plants and the algae are very similar in general features, but they differ from one another in a number of distinct ways. The major differences lie in the nature of the photosynthetic pigments, the cell walls, and the food reserves which they produce. These features are useful in distinguishing the eight recognized groups of algae.

ALGAE are essentially aquatic organisms, growing in all our natural bodies of water from the smallest to the largest, the coldest to the warmest supporting any kind of life, the freshest to the supersaline, and from the surface to hundreds of feet in depth. A large number of kinds grow on moist surfaces such as the soil. Others grow on or in other types of plants and animals. Some species grow in close association with certain fungi to form those numerous, varied, and widespread growths known as *lichens*.

Many single-celled and some colonial representatives of green algae, yellow-green algae, eugle-

Spirogyra

Anabaena

Euglena

Meridon

Surirella

Cyclotella

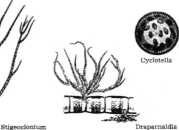

Stigeoclonium

Draparnaldia

16

noids, and dinoflagellates are motile: they can move about by means of hair-like structures called *flagellae* which are normal cellular features. The reproductive cells of many algae are also motile.

Most species of algae are not motile, and thousands of kinds spend most of their lives attached to solid objects of great variety. Intertidal algae such as the rockweeds are excellent examples. Some of the larger algae, such as the gulf weed *Sargassum*, float about and pass most of their lives in this state. Indeed, the Sargasso Sea, an area as large as Texas, is named for and characterized by the presence of great floating masses of gulfweeds.

Of special interest are the thousands of small species whose members float about at the mercy of winds, waves, tides, and currents. Collectively known as the phytoplankton, they are extremely important as primary producers. In oceanic waters, two groups of unicellular algae, the diatoms and the dinoflagellates, carry on most of the photosynthesis essential to all nongreen organisms. The products of this process serve to feed small herbivorus animals, these in turn are consumed by larger animals and these in turn furnish food for still larger forms. The algae are the starting points for many of the food chains and food webs which have been recognized. When one considers the vastness of the oceans as compared to the land surfaces of the earth, the idea that these tiny algae carry on more photosynthesis than does the terrestrial flora is not unreasonable.

In addition to their extremely critical role as primary producers, the algae are important to animal life in other ways. As a by-product of photosynthesis, they release oxygen and, thus, aerate the waters to the benefit of the animal life which requires it in its respiratory activities. The plants provide protection and shelter for the many small animals which live among them. They provide breeding grounds in which eggs may be laid, the

young produced, and the juvenile stages developed until they seek wider horizons for their activities. In light of these considerations, the necessity for obtaining knowledge about the place of the algae in aquatic life becomes very apparent.

ASEXUAL reproduction takes several forms in the various groups of algae. A common method is by *fragmentation*. A portion of a plant simply separates from its parent and becomes a new plant which may grow to normal size. *Cell division* is characteristic of most algae. Here an original cell produces another, identical to itself, by a rather complicated division of the cellular components. Both cells grow back to normal size, and the process may be repeated several times in the course of a day.

Most algae produce one or more types of *asexual spores*. Here a cell may divide its contents into several or many parts. Each one becomes a spore capable of growing into an entire new plant. Spores may be motile or non-motile, produced in vegetation cells or in cells specialized for the purpose. In any event, the process may lead to the production of very large numbers of new individuals.

Some spores are *resting stages*. They are resistant to adverse environmental circumstances, and they tide the organism over until more favorable conditions prevail, at which time they germinate to produce a new plant. Many algae winter over by means of resistant resting spores.

Sexual reproduction occurs in most groups of the algae. Indeed, this form of reproduction may have originated among primitive algae. The ramifications of the phenomena associated with sexual reproduction in the algae are beyond the scope of this short article, and we touch upon the subject lightly. Suffice it to say that, in general principles, the fundamentals of the process are the same as in animals. Special cells called *gametes* or sex cells unite with one another, as is the

case with the sperm and the egg in higher animals. The product of the union, the *zygote*, may grow into a new plant or it may divide first and give rise to several new individuals. Sometimes special sex organs and highly differentiated gametes are produced. In some cases, male and female plants occur, and in others, both male and female structures appear on the same plant. Further, since many sex organs may occur on one plant, the opportunities for increasing the number of organisms is very great.

In summary, reproductive devices in the algae have the potential for yielding very large numbers of offspring and account for some of the phenomena to be mentioned later.

ALGAE may spread rapidly from one region to another, and if the proper conditions prevail in the newly invaded territory, the distribution may be increased. They may be carried by water movement to every portion of the body of water in which they grow. They may be transported inadvertently by many other agencies. Birds, water-inhabiting animals, m a n, boats, and winds are prime agents for carrying entire plants or spores to new regions.

Under certain combinations of environmental circumstances such as high temperatures, adequate light, and favorable concentrations of mineral substances, some types of algae reproduce at a rapid rate causing *algal blooms*. Diatoms, dinoflagellates, blue-green algae, euglenoids, and some types of green algae are notorious b l o o m producers. Whole ponds, lakes, streams, and even hundreds of square miles of oceanic waters have been recorded in bloom states over a long period of time. The widely publicized "red tides" are blooms of certain dinoflagellates.

The release of huge quantities of the wastes of civilization into streams, rivers, ponds, lakes, and even arms of the ocean have stimulated the development of such blooms. This phenomenon has become more noticeable in recent years as our population has increased and more and more pollutants have been poured into our waters f r o m industrial plants, paper pulp mills, sewage outlets, etc. The condition of some of the Great Lakes has been called to our attention dramatically in the last few years.

These wastes contain materials ideally suited for algal growth, and they flourish. The growths become so thick they prevent light from reaching deeper waters. The algae in this lower region cannot carry on photosynthesis, and thus they and the animal life suffer from depletion of oxygen. Bacteria and fungi attack the vegetation, but they, too, utilize oxygen, and the bodies of water become stinking masses of half-decayed vegetation and dead animals. Thus, under the circumstances described, the algae which normally tend to purify the waters simply add to the unwholesome condition.

Civilization is in serious trouble, which will increase unless man takes the necessary steps to adjust the balance which once prevailed.

ALGAE are almost ideal organisms for many kinds of research and have long been used to simplify study of fundamental problems in biology. This use has accelerataed in the last few decades coincidentally with our increasing ability to grow many kinds in pure culture. Upwards of a thousand species of algae are now being grown in this manner and may be obtained from depositories in several countries.

Studies of productivity—both in natural waters and under controlled experimental conditions —occupy many algologists, for, as basic members of the food chains and food webs occurring in aquatic surroundings, their contribution is of fundamental significance. We have become more conscious of this as the problems associated with water pollution have come to the fore.

Lichens, those curious mixed growths of algae and fungi, have attracted the attention of naturalists for more than two centuries. Only recently have they been grown in pure culture, and attempts to ascertain the relative roles of the two components show some hope of realization.

A number of kinds of algae have been used directly as a source of food by man. Oriental peoples have been more appreciative of their value in this respect than have people of the western world, although there is now world-wide interest in the potentialities. Japanese people cultivate a number of species as food sources. Certain red algae are sources of agar, a gelatinous substance used as a basis for making the culture media used in growing microorganisms for study in medicine and in commercial applications. The Irish moss, *Chondrus crispus,* is widely used as a basis for blanc-mange and other confections. Colloids extracted from this species have come into prominence in making ice cream, puddings, and chocolate milk. Alginic acid derived from the cell walls of certain brown algae is used in foods and in various capacities in the textile industry.

Coastal dwellers in various parts of the world have made fairly extensive use of algal material as a vegetative manure, which adds humus to the soil as well as such important scarce elements as·potassium, phosphorus, and nitrogen that are released as they rot away in the soil.

The *diatoms* so useful to aquatic animals as food have some direct economic benefits for man. Their silicon walls are very durable. When a diatom dies, its shell sinks to the bottom of the body of water in which it grows. Over long periods of time, vast quantities may accumulate as fossils on ocean bottoms. Great deposits of "diatomaceous earth" laid down in various earth geological strata have become exposed in later times. Found in many places on our globe, such deposits may be hundreds of feet thick and run for many miles, thus testifying to the enormous numbers which inhabited ancient seas as they now inhabit modern waters. They are mined and used in many ways in industry.

Many algae, especially green and red algae, precipitate large quantities of calcium carbonate in carrying out their metabolic activities, and this becomes converted to limestone rock in the course of time. Prominent ancient deposits are known from many parts of the world, and the same activity is being carried on currently. This may be observed in the great coral reefs of the tropical and semi-tropical seas of the world. Coral animals and the algae seem to contribute about equally to the making of coral reefs. Some members of the blue-green algae also precipitate limestone now as they did in ancient times. They also form travertine rocks in hot springs where they live at temperatures as high as 85 degrees centigrade as shown so colorfully in the springs in Yellowstone National Park.

Interestingly enough, the blue-green algae have long been known from ancient fossil-bearing rocks in North America and recognized as some of the oldest fossils with an estimated age of at least 500 million years. A few years ago in the Lake Superior region, additional beds of fossiliferous blue-greens were found whose age has been put at approximately 1.5 billion years; and even more recently, beds discovered in Australia have been estimated to be about 3.5 billion years old. These relatively primitive plants have been in existence for a longer period of time than any other known organisms.

Scientists believe that the early atmosphere of the earth did not contain free oxygen as it now does. When photosynthetic algae evolved, they released free oxygen into the atmosphere as a byproduct of the chemical reactions involved in the manufacture of carbohydrates. The earth's atmosphere contained oxygen from this remote period on, until now about 20 per cent of the atmosphere is oxygen. This great event made it possible for many oxy-
● **continued on page 31**

18

Valuable Wetlands are Fast Disappearing

Public awakening to the value of wetlands has been painfully slow, and the initiation of action to reverse the destruction of these areas will perhaps be even slower. Will it be too late?

By Anthony S. Taormina

Regional Supervisor, Fish and Game, New York State Conservation Department

CONSERVATION is generally defined as the wise use of natural resources. It may also be defined, in the words of Aldo Leopold, as a state of harmony between man and the land. Among our most important, but still unappreciated, natural resources are the coastal salt-water marshes with their associated shallow water areas and tidal mud flats — known collectively as marine wetlands. Much has been written about these rapidly disappearing, irreplaceable wetlands in the past few years. Nevertheless they are still being converted to housing projects, marinas, airports, dumps and other man-made structures.

Just how often such uses of this particular resources can be rationalized as "wise use" is a perplexing problem as the value of something is dependent on the needs and interests of the people involved. Those who desire fill for housing projects or deep water for marinas or space for dumps declare that such projects are more necessary to the people than the existing "expendable" wetland areas which must then be sacrificed.

Conversely, many conservation - minded individuals and groups state that in most cases salt marshes and mud flats are more important to them and to the community than are more houses, garbage dumps or parking lots for boats. Public officials who try to be responsive to the wishes of the majority of their constituents oftentimes find it very difficult to weigh the judgements of one group against another. After all, they want their decisions to be reckoned as monuments to their good judgement and not as tombstones to their poor judgement.

It is with this problem in mind, then, that the following presentation of some of the complex values of marine wetlands is offered.

Plants, in the presence of sunlight, minerals and water, manufacture the basic ingredients for sustaining life. The productivity of marine wetlands surpasses, unbelievably, some of the most fertile farm lands in the country.

Of course, the food production is not of ready value to man. Rather, man harvests the indirect by-products in the form of fish, shellfish, crustaceans, waterfowl, etc.

The production of food in a wetlands area involves an intricate interaction of the basic components of marine "estuaries," the islands of salt grass "meadows" or *Spartina* marsh, the mud algae which thrive on the bottom and bank edges or mud flats of the wetlands, the microscopic plant life (phytoplankton) in the open water and the mixing of fresh with salt water to form the unique brackish environment.

As salt grass dies and falls into the water—a never-ending process as long as there are salt meadows—the microscopic life (bacteria, fungi, etc.) convert the plant tissues into particles circulating in the rich sea waters, which are high in proteins, minerals, carbohydrates and vitamins. Picture this process as a marine food factory wherein the foods thus prepared are made available to the teeming populations of hungry creatures by way of the excellent distribution system performed by rhythmic tidal action of the water. The patrons of this manufacturing and distribution plant are varied indeed and in number: Clams, oysters, mussels and scallops, as well as all the small fishes, crustaceans and other marine animals which feed on the microscopic life and in turn are fed upon by larger fishes, birds, mammals and man, himself.

In summary, the process of food production demands an efficient nutrient exchange, moving water, accessibility to light and year 'round primary production.

Furthermore, a fifth factor deserves recognition—time. Rich estuarine areas have achieved an inner harmony only through thousands of years of evolution and development. Ironically, very little time is needed to upset nature's monuments. Once

Waterfowl, such as this wood duck, depend on swamps and marshes for sanctuary and survival.

Properly managed, wetlands can afford good hunting for many wildlife species including the marsh hen which these hunters are stalking. Careful planning is the key.

destroyed they are lost and cannot be readily replaced through man's efforts.

The value of *Spartina* marshes then as basic food-producing areas can be considered greater than the value of the finest wheat or rice-producing areas in the world. As such, they are worth at least $1,000 an acre.

Marine Life Habitats

Because of their productivity, harbors and bays, with their associated wetlands, are nursery areas for many forms of marine life and living areas for many others. The teeming populations of bait fish such as killifish, silversides, anchovies and mullet, which thrive in the shallow bay areas, are most vital to the nourishment of larger fishes of significant commercial and recreational value such as the striped bass, bluefish, eels, weaks and flounder.

Furthermore, the small fishes are essential to the nourishment of many birds including terns and herons in the summer and grebes, loons and mergansers in the winter. The abundance of food and the natural protection afforded by marshy bay areas is essenial to the survival of the young of many important food and sport fishes such as the flounder, stripers, bluefish and blackfish. Furthermore, there are many other marine creatures including crustaceans (crabs), mollusks (shell-

fish) and terrapins which are dependent on the specialized nature of shallow bays for their optimum growth and survival. The value of such bay bottom for the production of commercial shellfish alone is phenomenal. For example, vast areas of shallow bay bottom (2' to 12' depth) produce at least 30 bushels of clams per acre per year. This amounts to one bushel from an area 48' x 30'. Considering an average price of clams to the digger of $7 per bushel, the value of such flats in annual yield is $210 an acre. However, this is a naturally renewable resource—a perpetual source of food as well as some recreation which costs *nothing* to produce. Therefore, the actual worth of such a resource is its capitalized value. At an acceptable net return of 5 per cent, an acre of bay bottom is worth $4,200 just for shellfish production. There are many areas that produce many times this amount—and are worth correspondingly more. Yet, dredges have been steadily chewing away at these valuable habitats. Thus, we may have shell-producing tidal flats worth at least $4,200 an acre being sold as "cheap fill" to be dumped on marshes worth at l e a s t $1,000 per in acre in order to develop housing sites or other "improvements." The wisdom of such use becomes even more questionable when it is recognized that such housing projects

invariably require additional expenditure of public funds.

Furthermore, nutrient - rich cesspool effluents from houses along the shore usually seep into the adjoining waters and add to the pollution load.

Wildlife Habitat

The specialized nature of wetlands makes them critically important to much wildlife, especially waterfowl (ducks, swans, geese, brant), the multitudes of shorebirds (sandpipers, turnstones, plovers, rails) and such wading birds as egrets and herons. Also, in some cases, they provide habitat for such fur-bearers as muskrats, raccoons and mink. All in all, they are essential to the continued existence of many creatures with whom we share and enjoy the bountiful earth.

In the case of shorebirds and wading birds, wetlands are most important during the spring, summer and fall. However, for many species of waterfowl, especially brant, swans and many ducks, the shallow bay areas, which are rich in plant and animal food, are most important as overwintering areas. Furthermore, the extensive vegetated shoreline along undeveloped estuarine streams provides excellent habitat for a wide variety of song birds as well as small mammals which add substantially to the overall wildlife populations.

Just what is an acre of bay bottom worth with its snails,

20

duck clams, eel grass and sand worms? To man, snails, marine worms and various algae are worth very little, but to wintering black ducks and other creatures, they are the key to survival. This value of the bay bottom then, is a further magnification of its worth which some ecologists would justify at $500 an acre or more.

Unfortunately, it has been the fate of wetlands to be labeled nuisance areas by some people. For this reason any destruction of such areas has been considered "progress." Of course, there are certain species of nuisance insects such as the salt marsh mosquito and some midges and flies that flourish in these habitats. Some control of nuisance insects is unquestionably desirable. As our knowledge of control techniques increases, controls will be not only less destructive to habitat but also more selective to the particular species to be destroyed. Furthermore, we must recognize with great concern that while pesticides do kill mosquito larvae, these chemicals also destroy countless other creatures, especially the larvae of shellfish and crustaceans.

Biologists are becoming especially concerned a b o u t the amount of persistent chlorinated hydrocarbons such as DDT currently being detected throughout our environment. In fact, there is a surprisingly high amount of chlorinated hydrocarbons in the marine water of some estuaries. Since such pesticides remain as destructive agents within the intricate food chains for many years, their presence in high concentrations must be viewed with alarm by all those people responsible for maintaining the quality of our priceless marine environment. We need studies to determine their origins as a prerequisite to use regulations.

Value in Erosion Control

Salt-water marshes have proven to be invaluable buffer zones, lessening the violent effects from hurricane-swept waves on an otherwise unprotected shoreline. Salt-water marshes are in effect natural breakwaters, with the resiliency of the millions of stalks of cord grass serving to mitigate the shock of pounding waves. The nearly indestructible peaty salt meadows absorb the charging waters where much of its violence is spent before it can be expended on man-made structures or vulnerable shorelines.

Each dredging operation which removes the stable peaty salt marsh with the adjoining shallow bottom increases the vulnerability of adjoining channels, shorelines, and man-made structures to damage from the storms as well as from accelerated tidal flow. The nearly indestructible peaty salt marsh barriers are worth more than the most expensive bulkheading at a minimum of $100 per foot of edge.

When correlated with the development of desired marinas or channels necessary for the economic growth and recreational enjoyment of the community, the sale of fill is a favorite way to reduce the cost of such operations. But public officials have a responsibility not to sell fill, unless, as mentioned earlier, a desirable project will be fulfilled which will stand as a monument to their good judgment rather than a serious liability to future citizens and taxpayers. The value of any developed project must be weighed against the attendant physical and biological losses, which also are economic losses. Most wetlands and their associated bay bottoms are serving a greater good to the townspeople in their present form than in the modest income they might bring as saleable fill.

Furthermore, dredging operations for gravel or sand which cut deep holes behind existing barrier beaches (or steep slopes along creek banks) can seriously decrease the stability of the existing slopes. Barrier beaches are generally composed of unstable s a n d s which cannot be expected to maintain slopes much steeper than those established over a long period of time through natural processes prior to dredging. Years ago, engineers recommended that a minimal grade of one on seven is necessary to hold sandy slope. Yet, in some cases, publicly sponsored dredging operations are currently leaving vast holes behind beaches with grades less than three on one!

Value as Education Areas

Wetland areas provide ideal opportunities for the study of biological processes. They serve as invaluable natural laboratories for students of all ages. They provide demonstrations of many life processes upon which elemental food chains are based. Moreover, they are immediately adjacent to a rapidly expanding population of millions of people whose interests in the natural wonders of the world are awakening.

Who knows what proportion of future generations will become avid bird watchers, naturalists or photographers, thrilling to the sight of a snowy egret or plummeting osprey? Certainly, it will become greater than it is today, especially as many of our birds and other wildlife become less abundant. Who can foretell what inspirations the sound of cackling geese winging over the bay edges on a still November evening will instill in the future armies of harassed commuters? The value of wetlands for the enjoyment of such pleasure must be classified in the same realm as listening to a fine symphony or watching a classical ballet or viewing a Renaissance painting. These values are infinite according to the individual.

Psychological Values

In the past decade, our estuarine areas have experienced vast changes which appear quite minute when compared with future projections. As the miles of blacktop and concrete stretch over the horizon, will there be corresponding areas of quiet relief to calm the senses and refresh our minds? Or will urbanism completely dominate the environment and consume men's basic natural heritage?

The answer to these questions must be almost immediate, for once the natural areas have been
• continued on page 31

Of Tales
and Tomes
by Jim Wood

FOR a long time, I've been tramping after ducks, hunting them when I could, standing slack j a w e d in awe when I couldn't, watching until the fast travelling f l o c k s were swallowed by the horizon. Days of some jubilance, and days that have not b o r n e much fruit. Blue bird days some call them. And even they were not all lost. It's only that you get skunked. Days of bitterness in w i n t e r along Maine's rock strewn coasts. Soggy mornings in Panama's rainy season with the little teal, fat from the wild rice popping into the decoys like b e e s after a blossom. Saucy little waterfowl. What a delight!! All along the coasts, places like Back Bay, Mattamuskeet, Brigantine, Merry-meeting Bay, come back so strong in memory.

But the best durn duck hunt I ever made I didn't shoot a time, and every year when the dog days have about got me down I make this hunt again, the wind quickens along the edges of the marsh grasses, the old greenheads are going down wind at a hundred miles an hour, the smell of powder is hardly more than you can stand. You might guess along about this time that this hunt

is not an actual one, and it isn't, but it's a real one, and its fascination diminishes not one whit with the passing of years.

Nash Buckingham wrote it years ago. Some f o r t y odd years, and he c a l l e d it "De Shootinest Gent'man". It will live forever in the lore of water-fowling. Buckingham still lives in Memphis nearing ninety, just as zealous of the outdoor world he knows and loves so well as he has always been, has written much rousing good outdoor r e a d i n g, and "De Shootinest Gent'man" has become a classic in his time. No man who loves ducks should grow up and be gone without knowing its magic.

A whole long string of books on waterfowl have pushed off the presses in recent months. Some good additions to the tales of ducks and geese. The **Living World** series of books e d i t e d by John Terres has covered a long list of the birds and beasts and working on m o r e. Lippincott publishes these and they have been a spendid contribution thus far. "The World Of The Canada Goose" is one of the last additions, written by Oregon's Joe Van Wormer, q u i t e prolific

among **Living World** writers.

This book has some of the finest pictures I have seen on the Canada goose. I enjoyed a real chuckle over the several that recorded the old gander at his morning bath. Joe worked long, hard, imaginatively capturing t h e s e magnificaent birds on film. Most Carolinians would at least recognize a wild Canada, such is his f a m e among our folks, and this is the sort of book that advances one from amateur standing to semi authority. The **L i v i n g World** books, all of them, follow a format that is unbending, but it is clean cut, readable, authoritative i n f o r m a t i o n. "The World Of The Canada Goose" is most surely a good one.

John Brickell's book "The Natural History of North Carolina", originally an Irish publication of 1737, offers some wonderful asides on the fish and fauna of Carolina in days when it was so rich as to be almost unfathomable. Now in reprint by the Johnson Publishing Co. of Murfreesboro, Brickell's observations of his days along the coast makes fascinating reading, and since Brickell was a doctor, his professionalism crept in and he offers a prescription for almost all of the aches and pains that beset man, using Nature's bounties for prescriptions.

On swans along the coast. "They were in such vast numbers on each side of the fresh water creeks and rivers that at a distance it seems to be land c o v e r e d with snow. About Christmas they are frequently so fat that some of them are scarce able to fly." I like a roast goose about as well as anything but Brickell may have discouraged me from trying one had I had occasion to talk to him. "They are plenty here in winter, eat well, being nourishing, though hard of digesting and are apt to breed agues in cold weakly constitutions. The grease cures baldness, helps deafness, good for palsy, lameness, and cramps. The dung is used with success in jaundice, scurvy, gout".

Mallards were just thick according to Brickell, but coarse eating, not much esteemed. And what with great flocks of old bull necked canvasbacks, wood ducks, and teal readily available it is understandable enough to call a m a l l a r d "coarse".

On seeing the a d v a n c e notices on Paul Johnsgard's

"Waterfowl" I could scarcely wait to get a copy in hand. The magnificent color portraits of several species was a sampling that promised much more in a book that covers all the world's waterfowl. I was no less enthused when I at last got hold of it. In waterfowl literature it will not reach Nobel status being largely just the facts but what a string of wildfowl photographs! And this is enough to make it a prize among those who love waterfowl. No place else can you find this between just two covers. Johnsgard, a professor of zoology in Nebraska at present, has likely seen more ducks and geese and swans than any other man and has photographed almost

all of them.

Some of the birds are captive fowl but this in no manner that I can see detracts from the total of the book. All of the birds are healthy, in full feather. One real shortcoming of this book is that part of the pictures are not in color. The black and white is good enough in competence, but m u c h subtle coloring is lost. A regal portrait of the king eider pair for instance, with the rich creamy greys of the male's head, would have been just one more picture. There is much in this book that will cause its pages to develop dogearedness in the years to come I'm certain. It is going to be a pleasure owning this one.

FLASHING WINGS: The Drama of Bird Flight, by John K. Terres. Doubleday and Co., N.Y. N.Y. 1968. $4.95. Indexed and with Appendix. Illus. with drawings by Bob Hines.

How does a bird fly? For centures man was baffled by the mysteries and miracles of birds in flight. Today scientists know the answers in a general way and now a noted nature writer has put these answers into an interesting book.

John Terres has built his book around his famous peregrine falcon, The Princess, a bird he trained and flew before World War II. He explains how he trained his bird to fly at crows and other wild game, and the steps involved in training a falcon to obey its owner's wishes. From The Princess, Terres, who was the editor of Audubon Magazine for many years, soars into the mysteries of bird flight.

From his book the reader will learn that mallard ducks sometimes fly 20,000 feet above the earth, and the lammergeyer, or bearded vulture, 25,000 feet; that the spine-tailed swift and peregrine falcon may fly at more than 200 miles an hour; that the common loon can dive through the air in excess of 100 miles an hour. He will learn that some birds can fly underwater; how birds use their muscles and wings in flight; how body and wing shape influence flight; how a hummingbird flies like a helicopter and builds a tremendous reserve "fuel" for its long over-the-water migration flights.

The book is more than a scientific exploration of the dynamics of bird flight, told in simple, easy to understand language. It is a sensitive work by a sensitive man who has never apparently lost his sense of wonder at the living world around him.

PHOTO BY TOM JACKSON

Thrifty pole-size trees will produce the high-quality logs of tomorrow. They can be helped by eliminating useless competitors like the hollow cedar elm shown at right.

Getting the Most From Southern Hardwood Stands*

by J. S. McKnight
Southern Forest Experiment Station
Forest Service
U. S. Department of Agriculture
Stoneville, Mississippi

ONE of the ultimate solutions to shortages of high-quality hardwood logs may well be extensive, carefully tended plantations of genetically superior trees, and this possibility will be discussed in a subsequent issue. It must be recognized, however, that good logs take a long time to develop, even in plantations. For at least 20 to 30 years, therefore, the sole source of quality lumber and veneer timber will be the pole and small-sawtimber trees of today. We must get the most from our existing trees by concentrating our management efforts on them.

This is the third of a series of five articles on hardwood management by Mr. J. S. Mc-Knight. We are reprinting these articles which first appeared in the **National Hardwood Magazine**, because of the importance of hardwoods to wildlife. Many of Mr. McKnight's findings and recommendations in regard to hardwood management are applicable in North Carolina. We invite the attention of landowners to profit from these articles since more emphasis on hardwood production in North Carolina would be highly beneficial to wildlife.

Young trees that have the potential to produce high-quality logs must be identified, protected, and nurtured if our hardwood stands are to meet the severe demands that will be made on them over the next few decades. Even the pulpwood supply for the next 25 years will depend largely upon that proportion of today's saplings and poles which can be spared from growing stock.

Beginning Management

To manage a forest, one must first find out what there is to work with, then plan a course of action. A simple reconnaissance is all that is needed to obtain the necessary information for beginning management. An appropriate procedure for taking inventory is described in *Agricultural Handbook 181*, which is available from the U. S. Department of Agriculture.

Concentrations of valuable, or potentially valuable, timber must be located, along with open or nonproductive areas. Damage to growing stock by fire, storms, insects, and livestock, together with relative densities of cull or weed trees, should be noted. For stands regarded as operable, a clear picture of logging and marketing conditions should be obtained.

First priority must then be given to protection, especially from fire. The danger of fire is often overlooked, with disastrous results, in bottom land stands, which are wet much of the year. During droughts, hot fires often kill young trees and wound large ones in river bottoms. These wounds provide entry for rots, which advance up the main trunk at a rate of 1 to 2 feet per decade. A stand that has been burned over may be riddled with heart rot and still appear healthy to the casual observer.

Hardwood lands are heavily used by hunters, who may accidentally or carelessly start wildfires. Leasing to hunting clubs or requiring permission to hunt has been found advisable.

Protection of hardwood forests from diseases and insects is, so far, largely a matter of prevention. Elimination of fire greatly reduces losses to heart rots, the most costly diseases. Usually it is also beneficial to harvest or deaden trees that are infested with trunk-boring insects, and trees of such low vigor that attack is likely.

Hardwood seedlings can be destroyed by grazing and browsing animals. Large concentrations of cattle or hogs may retard growth of large trees by

*Reprinted from NATIONAL HARDWOOD MAGAZINE, volume 42, number 4, pages 44-45. April 1968.

compacting the soil and reducing water percolation. It is necessary, therefore, to control grazing, and sometimes to prevent it entirely by fencing.

Improving Abused Stands

In most unmanaged stands, fire, high-grading, liquidation cuts, and other destructive influences have created a forest with a high proportion of undesirable trees. Usually, however, there is a nucleus of good growing-stock trees in groups or patches. Stunted, cull, and weed trees should be removed so that the good trees have room to develop. Pulpmills provide a market for much small and low-grade material, making many cleanup operations profitable.

No cutting at all, however, is better than premature harvest of a significant amount of desirable or effective growing stock, just to make a sale. In any case, all undesirable trees that are unmerchantable should be killed to provide openings for reproduction and/or growing space for desirable trees. Injections of 2,4,5-T and 2,4-D have proved effective in such work.

Improvement cuts ultimately mold a hardwood stand into patches of even-aged trees. Such groups should be thinned and cleaned of weak and inferior trees periodically to provide adequate growing space for the best individuals. The first commercial thinning in an even-aged stand is normally required when the dominant trees are 8 to 10 inches in diameter. At this time, a large number of weakling 6- to 8-inch trees, which are of minimum size for pulpwood, can be harvested.

A second thinning may be made when the dominants average 14 to 16 inches in diameter, and a third when they average 20 to 22 inches. Openings large enough for development of reproduction should not be created unnecessarily, since the purpose of thinning is to speed growth of selected crop trees. Reproduction can be provided for at the final harvest, when trees are from 28 to 34 inches in diameter.

Ages and densities for thinning stands vary greatly by site and species. For example, cottonwood requires 5 to 10 years to reach pulpwood size, whereas green ash normally requires 20 to 30 years. Much of the necessary scientific information for managing hardwood forests has been and is being learned at the U. S. Forest Service Southern Hardwood Laboratory in Stoneville, Mississippi. This information is made readily available to foresters and landowners.

The techniques I have outlined are simple and might be greatly refined, but, as presented, their continuous application in a majority of southern hardwood stands would probably assure a sufficient, sustained supply of high-quality logs for the next few decades. Cleanup and intermediate cuttings would satisfy most of the hardwood needs of the pulp industry, because such cuttings include more than half of the total volume of wood in most management systems, and an even larger proportion of the material removed in the first managed cut in abused stands. ♣

"The Long House"

by

HIGH on a sandy hill covered with long leaf pine, where the migrant Indians of North Carolina might have d w e l t, stands the unique home of The Moore County Wildlife and Conservation Club. Known as the "Long House" since it was designed after the Indian long houses of this same region, it is the pride and joy of each of the 200 or so members of this active and enthusiastic group.

Construction began in 1962 as a result of need, primarily, to increase membership and unite the "old faithfuls" under our very *own* roof. No special building program was started but like Topsy it grew! Mr. J. T. Overton and Mr. Albert Tufts' gifts of two adjoining tracts of land amounting to about ten acres "put us in business." First came the lake, which lies under the hill below the building. It is the product, as is the whole endeavor, of the engineering minds and active work of several members. A small lake fed by springs, stocked, where members can fish, and young ones can learn to cast and begin early to appreciate the angler's joys is the result. It is also a watering place for wildlife and on an early morning you might see the opossum waddle down to the water's edge. Damp earth carries the imprint of birds and other wildlife that have been to drink and sniff and munch. Many years ago these same hills were stocked with wild turkey. Groups within the club interested in planting, plan water life and plant cultivation along the dam and where the water flows into the lake.

The building itself is pole construction—the ridge beam being about 36 feet high with poles on 5 foot centers. Roof and side wall support is entirely of creo-soted poles and the roof poles are 50 feet long. This was made possible by help from Gulf Creosoting Company and Mr. Howard Butler's eagle eye for length and straightness. Mr. Butler designed and engineered the project. There is no way the club could have obtained or paid for the professional engineering, knowledge, construction advice and design ability that went into this "one of a kind" project. The generosity of members provided the know-how, the materials, and a great deal of the labor. Within the club's diversified membership, half of which is female, is professional ability in engineering, design, construction, folklore, art and horticulture. From this pool of ability and interest has come The Moore County Wildlife Long House.

RESEARCH was widespread and acquired from the University of North Carolina at Chapel Hill, the Town Creek Indian Mound at Mt. Gilead and various parts of Central America. The floor composition is similar to that used by the Mayan Indians composed of clay, sand and cement puddled to form a durable hard finish.

Dr. George Heinitsh, Bill Davis and Howard Butler devised the process after several hunting trips to the Yucatan Peninsula.

Besides being beautiful with its natural dark tones of brown and flashes of primitive color in the roof, the structure is adaptable to the club needs. At a regular monthly supper meeting it is not unusual to arrive and find Ralph Mills, Hardy Barber or Horace Mullinix busily cooking for all in large iron pots hung over the round central fire place. It is made of carefully collected

26

Here is the story of an unique base of operations and home for an active wildlife club of the Sandhills region. The long house is pictured in color on the back cover.

brownstone and sandstone from old chimneys and is covered by a huge round metal hood that vents through the roof at the center beam. The hood and fireplace were designed by members as were the cast iron "Bow and Arrow" and "War-Hammer" finials atop the iron supports which swing the pots away from the fire for serving.

The aluminum roof reflects the heat from the fireplace back into the room and is adequate warmth except for the very cold winter months, when the club visits for meetings in the four corners of Moore County. Creative art in wood, metal and oil reflect the Indian motif.

At Christmas the club party is always at the Long House and such fun! It is usually early in the month and begins the Christmas feeling! For days before the party members begin to decorate with the natural greens of the Sandhills. The tree is expected to be at least a 24-foot native cedar and is lavishly decorated with popcorn balls, hand-made ornaments, cranberry strings, papermache figures, decorated cookies, candy canes, and such lovely things fashioned by hand. Holly, pine and running cedar garland the walls and adorn the tables. On party night after a fine dinner and a Christmas program of carols, music and stories around the fire, Santa comes! In his bag is a gift for everyone which he personally distributes. The bag is filled by members, each brings a gift and puts it in the bag for some one else. The friendliness and enjoyment is truly Christmas in the old Moore County manner. After the party the decorated building is offered to other or-

ganizations for their Christmas parties.

SUMMER brings outdoor picnics for supper meetings with brimming baskets filled by the famous cooks of Carthage, West End, Aberdeen and over the county. The delicious home-cooked food is shared on David McCallum's long tables usually out-of-doors overlooking the lake as the summer moon rises. We sit and listen to programs on varied subjects as the membership includes a cross-section of our county: farmers, retired service personnel, craftsmen, professional men and women, retired business executives, working men and women, sportsmen, law enforcement personnel, gardeners, horsemen, peach growers, tree farmers, and just plain nice folks!

Programs cover water and soil improvement, game preservation, animal and bird life, forest and tree conservation, hunting and fishing, water safety, youth and conservation and numerous local subjects.

Committees are kept busy by our President, "Red" Overton and Past President, Lee Buchan with on-going projects such as the Long House's nature trails. These trails were laid out by Mr. Rassie Wicker of Pinehurst and supervised by Mrs. Albert Tufts. Plants are to be collected throughout North Carolina's woods and swamps and replanted along the trails with appropriate identification markers.

Gun and hunting safety is another planned project and it is hoped that a target area may be constructed for training new and young sportsmen.

It is the club's wish that related organizations use the Long House and its facilities. The Girl Scouts do primitive camping on the hill side; the Moore County Hunt stops there for lunch and rest on their annual Fifty Mile Trail Ride; The Order of the Eagle meets here and dances again the tribal dances of early Indians against an appropriate background.

At the end of the long main room attached to the cross poles is a ceremonial thunder-bird with a 30-foot wing spread. It is most special in that it was designed by Mr. Don Moore and his art classes of Southern Pines High School as a project and then was made and meticulously painted by Mr. Francis Clarke.

Its striking design is authentic and dominates the room. A small replica was also made to be used outside. Both figures are of intricate workmanship and were a labor of love made by the late Mr. Clarke, a retired banker, who has left his quiet influence on the club.

As time goes on the kitchen will be completed to extend under the A frame from the front to back along the left side of the structure. Rest rooms and storage area balance on the opposite or right side. Facilities for cooking and serving will be ample, modern, convenient and attractive.

For this building no particular financial plan was set up or pursued. A questionnaire to the membership indicated that almost 90 percent favored building our own Wildlife Club home. The original budget was based on $4,-500.00, much has been donated and with several benefits and membership assessment of $7.00 per member the present outstanding debt is a $1,500.00 bank loan. The money-making events of bazaars, raffles, concessions for horse shows, turkey shoots and a planned square dance are all so enjoyable that we consider them as fun rather than work and are an asset to club life. All our finances are watched over and we have been guided for the life of the club by our indispensible Treasurer, Mrs. Estelle Wicker. She is the last word and the law! Right beside Estelle is Mrs. Cornelia Vann, Secretary to the club since its beginning and the pillar of the organization. These two ladies are "All American Moore County Wildlifers."

Any second Tuesday evening at 6:30, if you are in the Sandhills, the "Latch is always out at the Long House."

The Osprey

Few people have had the opportunity to observe a pair of ospreys nesting. I had the chance, however, last spring when a pair chose a dead tree at the edge of a marsh behind my house.

Ospreys belong to the order Falconiforms, (which includes eagles, falcons, and other hawks) but are separated into their own family, Pandionidae, because, among other reasons, their outer toe is reversed and all of their t a l o n s are approximately the same length.

Ospreys, with a body length of 21 to 24 inches, have white underparts, neck, and head, while the back and the wings, with a spread of 4½ to 6 feet, are dark brown. In most subspecies there is a dark eye streak.

The female osprey lays her two to four eggs, which are usually heavily spotted with dark brown, on a bulky nest of driftwood and other material found along the beach. The flat-topped nest is usually used many years, each year more material being added so that they often obtain a diameter of five feet.

The mainstay of the ospreys' diet is fish. He catches it by circling above the water until, sighting a fish, he dives down and picks the fish out of the water.

Many hawks and eagles repeatedly steal the ospreys' meal b e c a u s e they aren't as skillful at fishing as he is.

The eggs never hatched in the nest I was watching. Before they could, a very high wind snapped the tree and sent the nest, with the eggs in it, crashing fifty feet to the ground.

— Tom H. Saunders Jr.

CRACKSHOTS and BACKLASHES
by Rod Amundson

Warning Given to Farmers on Liability

Whenever any person . . . has negligently, or unlawfully, caused pollution of the waters or air . . . in such quantity, concentration, or manner that fish or wildlife are killed as a result thereof, the Board (of Water and Air Resources) may recover, in th name of the State, damages fom such person.—From G. S. 143-215.3 (7).

ON September 14, 1968, a farm employee was operating an insecticide spray machine on lands along a small stream in eastern North Carolina.

When the spray tank ran dry, he stopped at a bridge across the stream to refill it. In the process, he accidentally allowed the tank to overflow slightly. Into the water below fell some of the insecticide.

On September 21, 1968, personnel of the North Carolina Wildlife Resources Commission reported a fish kill in the vicinity of the bridge. Personnel of the Department of Water and Air Resources immediately joined the Wildlife Commission in an investigation of the kill.

In the stream, the investigators counted 561 dead fish. They also found concentrations of chemicals sufficient to have caused the kill. On the stream bank they found two empty insecticide containers labeled with the chemicals found in the water. They found two witnesses who reported having seen the farm employee filling the spray tank at the bridge on September 14.

The result was a bill to the farm owner of $572.41. This included the value of the fish killed, the cost of replacing them, and the expenses of the investigation by the two agencies.

When a report of the investigation of the kill was given recently to the Board of Water and Air Resources, several members had a question.

How much of an effort, they wondered, had been made to inform the farmers of the financial liability they might incur from similar occurrences? It was generally agreed that no matter what effort in this direction had been made, perhaps it had been insufficient.

As a result, the Department of Water and Air Resources, the State Department of Agriculture, the Agricultural Extension Service, and others are cooperating in efforts designed to alert farmers as to their potential liability under the statutes.

Information regarding the law has been and is being distributed among agricultural officials and individuals throughout the State by mailings, through the news and broadcast media, and through agricultural and other publications. Among those alerted are the Extension Chairman and the Pesticide Coordinator in each county, who are receiving, among other material, copies of this newsletter.

Wild Dog Problem

DEAR SIR:

As a future game conservationist, I have posed myself with the problem of free-roaming dogs in the forests of North Carolina. In my own native Burke County, wild dogs have greeted me with a showing of teeth while deer hunting and trout fishing, even in the Daniel Boone Refuge. I understand that hunters were actually attacked in Georgia where there is a worse problem of this than in North Carolina.

I believe that approximately fifty to sixty per cent of Western N. C. deer are killed or harmed permanently in some way from the fawn to the adult stage during dog-deer assaults. It is not a pretty scene to see an exhausted, shocked whitetail burst from the brush with a seventy pound mongrel closing in. If my own dog were involved, I would think twice about NOT killing it.

These dogs are strays from homes, lost hunters' companions, and unwanted pups which have gone back to their inherent killing of game and livestock in order to stay alive.

Could not a group of biologists or individuals propose a program to shoot and dispose of unidentified dogs in a humane manner? Can collarless dogs be killed upon encountering in a vicious situation or threatening of wildlife?

One must also remember that these free-roaming canines are usually the first to contract and spread rabies.

With proper disposal of these strays, a fivefold increase could be expected in the western counties' deer herd.

Sincerely,
WILLIAM B. CASH
MORGANTON

Another Woodchuck Fan

Dear Sir:

A friend of mine gave me the February issue of *Wildlife* in which is

James M. Lewis

Wildlife Protector James M. Lewis, stationed at Beaufort in Carteret County, was born April 28, 1937, in Brunswick County. He is the son of Mr. and Mrs. John P. Lewis of Winnabow, North Carolina. James graduated from Bolivia High School, Bolivia, North Carolina. Prior to em-

ployment with the North Carolina Wildlife Resources Commission, he was employed by the North Carolina State Highway Commission.

James completed the Basic Recruit School for Wildlife Protectors at the Institute of Government in Chapel Hill, North Carolina in 1961. He was employed as a Wildlife Protector Trainee in February 1962 and stationed in Beaufort. In September 1962, he was appointed Wildlife Protector and assigned to Carteret County. Since his initial employment, James has completed f o u r In-service Training Schools.

Mr. Lewis is a National Rifle Association Hunter Safety Instructor; member of the Southeastern Association of Game and Fish Commissioners, Law Enforcement Section; and Carteret County Law Enforcement Officer's Association.

Mr. Lewis is married to the former Joan Ramseur of Winnabow, North Carolina, and they

DIVISION ENFORCEMENT RECORD FOR APRIL, 1969

HUNTING & FISHING

Persons checked	60,351
Total prosecutions	1,032
Total convictions	999
Total cases not guilty ..	14
Total cases nol prossed .	17
Total cases dismissed ...	2
Total fines collected	$ 6,381.25
Total costs collected	$12,853.75

BOATING

Persons checked	10,352
Total prosecutions	277
Total convictions	270
Total cases not guilty	1
Total cases nol prossed ...	5
Total cases dismissed ...	1
Total fines collected	$ 405.75
Total costs collected	$3,799.42

All fines and any arrest or witness fees are paid into the school funds of the counties in which the violation occurred, and no part of the fines or costs collected are paid to the North Carolina Wildlife Resources Commission or its personnel.

have two children; Cheryl Ann, age 9 and Stuart Alan, age 2. The Lewis family attends the First Baptist Church in Beaufort, North Carolina.

---

an article on the woodchuck in Ashe County and that they are a worthless pest; well, to me they are far from that. Enclosed is a trout fly which I make and use as my #1 trout producer. In 1968 I caught over 300 trout and a good many of them were taken on a woodchuck winged fly.

Body of flies are made different colors and the chuck tails vary in color from buff to black so can have several combinations of colors of the flies. I use the tails only and the hair is very shiny and durable the wing—chuck tail—will always outlast the body.

I get most of the tails from chucks that have been killed with cars along the roads and at present have about 20 tails on hand.

To process tail—take out bone, wash thoroughly, remove all fat. Let dry until fur is dry then put 20 Mule Team Borax on flesh side and let dry out thoroughly. Rewash if you wish. Split tail open to remove the bone, then wash. There is no place you can buy these tails that I know of and think some boy could make a few dollars selling tails to fly tiers. Believe me, the tails make wonderful flies. They are my *secret weapon* on trout both as a stream fly and for trolling in the lakes. Have

some of your friends try them out, but they will not catch trout where there aren't any.

I use to hunt quail around New Bern and Oriental and have spent many happy hours in your wonderful state. Just thought you might be interested. Tell your friends to get busy on some darn good flies.

Roy S. Munson
499 Frost Rd.
Waterbury, Connecticut 06705

Trout Weed?

Dear Sir:

Help—we need information—our Boy Scout troop has been trying for a year to get an answer to this question.

Last year some of our troop were on vacation in the Smokies and while fishing for trout met Indian fishermen. The Indians were using a bait which was some sort of vegetation, green in color and had a definite aroma. They said it grew locally but would not say what it was. Also, they crushed it before putting it on the hook so it could not be visually identified by our scouts.

They were fishing in the Fontana Dam area. The Indians really caught trout while the catch of our boys was not as good using lures and bait.

I know it is not a policy to give a written reply to inquires; however, can an exception be made in this case. If not, perhaps a reply can be put in Crackshots and Backlashes in your *Wildlife* magazine.

I have been a subscriber for a good many years and have just renewed my subscription. My magazine really makes the rounds among our boys.

Thanking you in advance.

Joseph C. Sliwinski
53 Centre Street
Freeport, New York 11520

Dear Mr. Sliwinski:

Without having the plant you described in hand it would be impossible to identify the one the Indians used for taking fish. It is possible, however, that they were using the leaves of wild ginger which have a very pungent aroma and are common to the North Carolina mountains.

If we publish your letter perhaps some of our good readers can help with this.

Yours very truly,
Rod Amundson, Chief
Division of Education

30

Fishing Waters

The Graphic Press, Inc., of Raleigh has compiled and published a book that will prove of immense value to every fisherman who fishes or wants to fish North Carolina's bountiful supply of inland fishing waters. The 240 page, 8½ x 11 inch volume entitled, "A Catalog Of The Inland Fishing Waters of North Carolina," contains over 7,000 individual pieces of fishing water, carefully indexed for reference. The name of the body of water, exact location, boat access, type of fish present, and even a measure of fishing success expected is at the angler's finger tips.

The book also contains two-color maps of the entire state, paintings of 36 important freshwater fish in color, and has a tough, water-resistant mylar coated cover. It's designed for use, and is based on authoritative information originally collected and compiled by Dr. Fred Fish of the North Carolina Wildlife Commission's Division of Inland Fisheries. It has been termed the finest guide for fishermen ever published. It is available now from the Graphic Press, Inc., Post Office Box 9118, Raleigh, N. C. 27603. Cost is $4.85 (North Carolina residents add 15 cents sales tax) postpaid.

ALGAE

● continued from page 18

gen-utilizing animals to evolve.

Algae, along with many other plants, are known to release chemicals into their surroundings which are antagonistic, irritating, antibiotic, deleterious, or poisonous to other organisms. By this means, the distribution of some organisms is controlled, thus providing an explanation for the observed fact that certain organisms are not compatible and cannot occupy the same territory. An outstanding and much studied case of this kind is the famous "red tide" brought about by the prodigious growths of some types of dinoflagellates. We are only beginning to sense the extent to which such phenomena may be involved in the ecological picture. Further, there is good evidence pointing to the possibility of deriving chemical substances useful in medicine from these versatile plants.

A N algologist might argue that much of what has been outlined here necessitates an understanding of the varied life cycles which the algae manifest. To a degree this is true, but perhaps enough has been written to indicate their importance in the natural world. ◆

Early last spring the Avery County Agricultural Stabilization and Conservation Service personnel designed and erected this display centering around the importance of conserving wildlife. It became a national award winner as ASCS County Display of the Month. Congratulations to the Avery County folks.

WETLANDS

● continued from page 21

devoured in the name of "progress" there are no reprieves. Wetland and harbors offer needed retreats from the advancing tides of development. To the ever-increasing flotillas of recreational boaters, uncluttered salt meadows provide vistas of peaceful landscapes in much the same fashion that uncluttered parkways please the touring motorist. Their value cannot be measured directly, for one cannot weigh directly the benefit of an harmonious environment.

Certainly, the opportunity for future generations to enjoy these rich experiences in the heart of an otherwise intensive suburban environment has immeasurable value and must be preserved at all costs. ◆

THE LONG HOUSE, Home of the Moore County Wildlife and Conservation Club.

LITHO BY THE GRAPHIC PRESS, INC., RALEIGH, N. C.

Wildlife

IN NORTH CAROLINA

25 CENTS / JULY 1969

STATE OF NORTH CAROLINA

ROBERT W. SCOTT
GOVERNOR

NORTH CAROLINA
WILDLIFE RESOURCES COMMISSION

ORVILLE L. WOODHOUSE, CHM. — — GRANDY
JAY WAGGONER, V. CHM. — — — — GRAHAM
DR. JOE M. ANDERSON, SEC'Y — NEW BERN
JAMES A. BRIDGER — — — — BLADENBORO
HUGH G. CHATHAM — — — — — ELKIN
JAMES A. CONNELLY — — — MORGANTON
J. HOLT EVANS — — — — — ENFIELD
T. N. MASSIE — — — — — — SYLVA
ROBERT G. SANDERS — — — CHARLOTTE

CLYDE P. PATTON
EXECUTIVE DIRECTOR

EUGENE E. SCHWALL
ASSISTANT DIRECTOR

DIVISION CHIEFS

ROD AMUNDSON — — — — EDUCATION
FRANK B. BARICK — — — — GAME
J. HARRY CORNELL — — INLAND FISHERIES
ROBERT B. HAZEL — — — PROTECTION
J. THOMAS WILLIAMS — FINANCE-PERSONNEL
C. FLOYD WILLIAMSON — — ENGINEERING

WILDLIFE IN NORTH CAROLINA recognizes the need for close cooperation between State and Federal conservation agencies and the people who hunt and fish—to bring about a restoration of our renewable resources. The Editor gratefully receives for publication news items, articles, and photographs dealing with the North Carolina out-of-doors, but reserves the right to reject materials submitted. Full credit is given for all materials published.

• • • •

WILDLIFE IN NORTH CAROLINA is published at the Wildlife Resources Commission offices, Motor Vehicles Building, 1100 New Bern Ave., Raleigh, N. C. 27601.

• • • •

Second class postage paid at Raleigh, North Carolina 27602.

• • • •

SUBSCRIPTION—One dollar per year, two dollars for two years. Make remittance payable to WILDLIFE RESOURCES COMMISSION. Any employee of the Wildlife Resources Commission may accept subscriptions, or they may be forwarded to Post Office Box 2919, Raleigh, N. C. 27602. Stamps cannot be accepted.

• • • •

Wildlife circulation this issue, 117,928.

IN THIS ISSUE

EDITORIAL STAFF

ROD AMUNDSON — — — — — — — — EDITOR
DUANE RAVER — — — — — MANAGING EDITOR
LUTHER PARTIN — — WRITER-PHOTOGRAPHER
JOHN PARKER — — — — — BOATING EDITOR
TOM JACKSON — — — WRITER-PHOTOGRAPHER

Not many of us will ever see a full-grown blue marlin charge out of the Gulf Stream, hooked or otherwise. This one is trying to make a meal of the scattering flying fish and not a boat in sight. This one is a relatively small marlin, around 300 lbs. The North Carolina record is a hefty 810 pounder caught on 130-lb. test line off Cape Hatteras, a World Record for this line strength.
Painting by Duane Raver.

PHOTOGRAPH BY HUGH MORTON

Flow Gently

One of the most beautiful sections of western North Carolina forests is located on the slopes of Grandfather Mountain. This stream is a tributary of Wilson Creek, which runs through the Daniel Boone Wildlife Management Area.

By Bob Simpson

Boating the Inland Waters of North Carolina

THERE are literally thousands of miles of streams, rivers, lakes and impoundments in North Carolina, plus a 300-mile (as the goose flies) coastline of bays, sounds and miscellaneous puddles. Almost every type of boating is available, from the whitewater rapids of the upper Piedmont and mountains to the sluggish tidal flats, of the coast. One could spend most of a lifetime just exploring the vast waterways of this state.

Early Years

At one time these waterways were the life arteries of North Carolina. Great rivers like the Chowan, Tar, Neuse, Cape Fear and Pee Dee opened up the interior. Sounds like the Albemarle, Pamlico, Currituck and Bogue, along with lesser small sounds, made coastal settlement possible and were the major lines of communication.

Specialized means of transportation were developed for these waters: the spritsail skiff, a small, shallow-draft sail-boat for cruising shoal waters, the dugout for coastal rivers, each evolving into new breeds. There was the coasting schooner that hauled the heavy freight, and the stern-wheel steamer that used to chug up rivers and through sounds. The dugout evolved into a plantation boat, the john boat and the barge, and boating reached a zenith in North Carolina in the 1850's, when river navigation was highly developed, made more efficient by many canals, like the early Club Foot Canal in Carteret County, dug in the 1790's.

Then, with the War between the States, came the decline. It was not until nearly a century later, in the 1950's, that a new boating boom developed. New boats of fiberglass, aluminum and plastics entered the picture, and new designs: the various hard-chined planers, patterned after the World War II PT boats were followed by the multi-hulled vessels, as catamarans and trimarans, evolved into everyman's boat, the Boston whaler type. A blue

billion sailboat styles developed, from the Moth that had originated in Elizabeth City in the late twenties, to Lightning, Sunfish, Sailfish and all manner of fish and insect boats, from mere plastic floats with a sail to the most elaborate rigs.

Scores of Choices

Today there are scores of choices for the North Carolina boatman. To select the best boat, one must first decide its intended use: fishing, exploring, cruising? And where? Obviously a 25-foot inboard isn't suited to the upper Yadkin, and a john boat isn't ideal for Pamlico Sound.

Let's start on the salt water sounds. There are several major considerations: speed, for sounds are large; stability, for sounds can be rough; and use, are you planning to haul water skiiers, skin dive, picnic aboard or fish?

All boats are a compromise. Some are worse. If you are going to fish, an anchor easy to get at is wonderful—have you ever tried to crawl over a flimsy windshied onto a slippery deck to anchor in rough water? Do you need shelter from the sun and wind? Are you going to be cruising the channels, or cutting across the sand bars? Perhaps the Boston whaler is for you, or the Simmons sea skiff. If water skiing is your game, who cares about the ease of anchoring, or how much the boat draws? You want a conventional hard-chined V-hull that carries lots of pull power, and maybe a shelter from sun and wind. It won't interfere with a fishing rod either. Perhaps you are a loafer; try a sailboat. For a few hours take a day sailer, but for sound and river cruises you'll need a heavier vessel. Another choice might be the pontoon-rigged house-boat, ideal for a comfortable few nights on Kerr Reservoir. Whether water is fresh or salt, lake, river, or sound, these factors apply.

In selecting a boat, the three major considerations are price, design and portability. All are in-

Perhaps the backbone of the Tarheel boat armada is the open runabout with a 35- to 65-horsepower outboard. This scene is the Avent's Ferry Bridge area on the Cape Fear.

terrelated. While price is an obvious factor, design hinges on use, as does portability. Portability could mean lugging a boat over shoals, off sandbars or across a field, or it may mean trailing it.

A good, well-balanced trailer and boat combination will not interfere seriously with operation of an automobile. The heavier the boat, the slower the acceleration and the longer the required braking time. A 20-foot boat and a 20-foot car become little different from a 50-foot truck.

But suppose you are a wilderness advocate who fly fishes or plugs for bass. Then portability means something else. A rubber raft is ideally portable and stowable and will float the roughest rapids. It's a little hard to paddle, though. Now a canoe is still one of the most favored means of water travel in America. It is fast, quiet and, despite some opinions, remarkably stable, even in white water. It is light and will carry quite a cargo. Then there are folding boats, and the old favorite, the flat-bottomed, square-ended, slab-sided john boat. The john boat is not so light, and it won't take rough water, but it is very stable, and a small motor hooks on easily. It is perfect for standing up in, if stand you must.

The Southport Harbor operated by the State Ports Authority has expanded considerably since this photo and represents a fine harbor for small craft in this area.

Of course, there is the pram, a preshrunk cross between a rowboat and a john boat. The standard rental boat is a flat-bottomed skiff, more seaworthy than a john boat, with higher freeboard.

Probably the most overrated and oversold boat is the baby cabin cruiser that carries a 90 h.p. motor, sleeps 8 and cruises at 30 mph. This is the boat that most people look at first and soon find most unsuitable. Its design is for going from dock to dock fast; it pounds unbearably; it has too much freeboard for easy swimming, is too heavy for easy portability. It is expensive, consuming prodigious amounts of fuel and draws too much water. Even if 8 people could sleep on it, as the neat little diagram shows, no one could turn over or blow his nose. Too many people in too small a boat is unsafe, unsanitary and ruinous to friendship. Still, it may be the boat for you.

Boating Pleasure

But boating can be leisurely. It may be drifting down a slow river, where great oaks, leaning over the banks, hang gray beards of moss into the deep waters. A blue-green dragon fly rides the tip of a fishing rod, and a kingfisher flashes from his high perch to snatch at a minnow, returns to sit and watch. Golden glints of sunlight sneak among the leaves to glitter on the water. A lazy turtle slides off a rotten log and disappears beneath the surface. There is only the sound of a gentle wind high in the tree tops.

Towards evening a snadbar ahead juts out into the river's elbow. The boat slowly grinds to a stop. A few branches are assembled for an evening campfire. The sky is clear, so there is no need of a tent. The day's catch of bass sizzles in the pan, with hot biscuits on the side, and coffee steaming in a mug. Stars appear from the dying sky, and a crescent moon follows the long-gone sun.

Lonely strains come from a harmonica, the fire flickers and snaps, the distant barking of a dog is answered by the sleepy hooting of an owl. The canoe is pulled higher for security, camp surveyed and out come air mattress and sleeping bag. Suddenly, it's pink in the east, and there's another day to be savored, of gentle sights, of varied greens and brilliant blues, of jumping fish and quiet thoughts. This is floating a river; this is escape.

Perhaps you prefer excitement—white water, icy cold, spine tingling, spray flying, roller coaster action in a rubber raft that bounces off rocks, tosses and twists. If you're shooting rapids in a canoe or kayak, the secret is to be running just a bit faster than the water, to keep you in control. But don't be too daring—wear a life jacket.

Speaking of safety, life jackets are the most important single piece of equipment you can have. Get good ones, get enough and learn how to put 'em on in a hurry. Keep them available; in case of capsizing or fire, they're worthless stowed in the forward locker.

Other equipment vital to safety includes an oar or paddle big enough for effective use, a bailer big enough to throw a gallon or more at a scoop, an anchor with plenty of line (have you ever seen a boat go over a spillway because of no anchor and an inadequate paddle?). A spare, small (under 10 h.p.) outboard motor will bring you home if the big one fails. Learn how to rescue someone overboard; it's harder than you realize if you don't know how.

Learn a couple of good knots, including the bowline. Read your weather, and just don't take stupid chances. Boating is one of the safest sports there is, even to shooting the rapids, in the right craft, to be sure. Exploring remote wildernesses, water skiing and racing are all safe sports, for those who learn the right way and don't skip the basic safety rules.

As for boat operation, high speed boating, with or without attached water skiers, is fun, exciting and spectacular, but it has the greatest potential for danger and bad manners of any form of boating. Hitting a wake can flip rail-sitters overboard; leaving a wake at a landing can cause a lawsuit. A careless lookout can lose a skier, or run down a swimmer.

Where to Go

In North Carolina there are 25 major watersheds. A state road map will show dozens of lakes, rivers and impoundments ranging from beautiful Hiwassee, Santeetlah, Fontana or Nantahala in the mountains to the Piedmont and lakes like Norman and High Rock to the coastal plain and Bladen Lakes, Waccamaw and remote Lake Phelps. Then there are a dozen or so major and minor rivers that lead to the salt and the vast waters of the sounds that lie between the mainland and the Outer Banks, from big Pamlico to little Masonboro. These sounds and rivers are worth days of wandering. Among the deeper rivers of the west, a friend recommends the French Broad, adding, "Do it in warm weather; after we upset 18 times, we quit counting."

Sail

Sailboats are coming back in style in North Carolina, too. Sailboat regattas fill the summer, on Kerr Reservoir, on the Neuse River out of the romantic fishing village of Oriental, on Elizabeth City's Pasquotank River, on the sounds near Morehead City and Wrightsville Beach, at new Cape Lookout National Seashore. Interest is growing in ocean racing, coastwise.

And why not? Is there more romance in dream and in reality than to be sailing on a warm summer evening, the only sound the ripple of water and the occasional flutter of sails? The breeze is your servant, and chances are a moon will be sending a shaft of light across the blue-black waters. There may be the cry of a skimmer winging by, or the haunting moan of some buoy. A lighthouse beam may sweep the sky, and channel markers may wink at you or appear suddenly, ghostlike, alongside. The soft summer air is damp with dew, and the phosphorescence of the wake is a color from outer space. There are the canted deck, the whisper of wind, then the clatter of blocks, the squeaking of lines and slap of canvas as you call, "Ready about!" and start off on a new tack.

The secret of happy memories is to choose the right waters, have the proper equipment and use good manners. Fishing and water skiing don't mix. Alcohol is a poor mixer, too. No veteran boatman will allow himself or his crew an alcoholic drink until the anchor is down, the sails furled and the ship secure.

Don't try to fish, or anchor for the night, in a channel. It's a highway, not a parking lot. Know the waters, and the weather, for any open body of water can get rough in a hurry. You may picture yourself as a salty, bearded mariner round the Cape, but others will look on you as a fool, while the mortician rubs his hands in anticipation. The greatest hazard is fire, which can result from as simple a mishap as kicking over a gas can.

Boating can be, should be, a safe, active sport without the need for a rule book ever at hand. It tops them all, whether boating takes the form of fishing, sailing, camping, water skiing, shell collecting, exploring, or just sitting with your feet on the cockpit coaming, the sun, breeze and water your only companions. ⧫

PHOTO BY DEPT. OF CONSERVATION & DEVELOPMENT

Deer Predation in North Carolina

and other Southeastern States

Part 1

by Frank B. Barick
Chief, Division of Game
North Carolina Wildlife Resources Commission
Presented at Southeastern Deer Symposium, Nacogdoches, Texas,
March 25, 1969.

PHOTOS COURTESY GEORGIA STATE GAME & FISH COMM.
Deer killed by dogs or other predators are often difficult to confirm unless considerable physical evidence is found.

THE primary objectives of this study were to identify the principal predators of deer in the southeastern United States and to determine their impact on deer herds and deer management. In doing this we have attempted to also identify other forms of deer mortality and assign numerical values to each, in relation to total population and annual drain.

Study Procedure

In conducting a study such as this, two general approaches might be considered. One would be to study intensively a single or small number of areas over a long period of years. Another method would be to study less intensively a larger number of areas over a shorter period of time. Since we were assigned this subject only a few months ago, we chose the latter course.

The individual study units were manned wildlife management areas rather than counties or states since it was felt that personnel on such areas could provide the most nearly accurate information due to their close personal observation of limited land areas. While predation is usually "controlled" on such areas, the magnitude of loss in spite of control, as well as extent of control exerted, provide valuable insight into the magnitude of the predation problem in localities not subject to intensive protection.

To secure information on these areas, a questionnaire was devised for completion by resident wildlife area managers throughout the southeast. The questionnaire was filled out by all area managers in North Carolina that have any responsibility for deer management—28 in all. Each man was sent a copy of the questionnaire and instructed to study it but *not* fill it out. They were filled out in the course of a series of meetings attended by the author so as to insure clear understanding of the meaning and intent of each question.

Five copies of the questionnaire were sent to the director of each southeastern state with the request that they be completed by managers of five rep-resentative areas. Completed questionnaires were returned by ten states (Arkansas, Florida, Georgia, Kentucky, Louisiana, Mississippi, Missouri, Oklahoma, South Carolina, Tennessee). Some states enclosed supplementary information with their replies and one state (Virginia) sent relevant information in place of the completed questionnaires.

Thus, the study is a compendium of replies to a questionnaire completed by resident managers of wildlife areas, and an evaluation of these replies.

It is obvious, of course, that our evaluation of data from other states is more tenuous than that of North Carolina data. Thus, our report is based primarily on North Carolina data, with somewhat gross checks for corroboration and comparison in other states.

Study Units

Manned wildlife management areas in North Carolina range from 6,000 acres to over 86,000 acres in size. The larger ones have several managers assigned and the average assignment per manager is about 15,000 acres. However, some are assigned as few as 6,000 acres while others have over 28,000 acres.

Managed hunts are conducted on all but one of the North Carolina areas included in this study. The deer harvested are brought through check stations. Resident area managers spend a substantial portion of their time through the year patrolling for illegal hunting and they are authorized by law to kill dogs running deer as well as to control other predators.

A limited amount of food planting and browse cutting is done but in most cases this provides only a very minor portion of the total food supply. In most cases basic productivity of the land is lower than that of surrounding privately-owned land.

Deer populations are considered to be at or above an estimated capacity of one per 50 acres since annual harvest averages less than 200 acres per kill.

Wildlife management areas in states other than North Carolina included in this study are similar in some respects and different in others. Some areas are much larger and some are much smaller. Some do not have resident managers and some have professionally trained biologists as managers. Most provide public hunting but some are recently established areas that have not yet been hunted and at least one is a refuge area closed to all hunting.

Quality of Data

While this does not pretend to be a "scientific" study in which basic data are compiled by trained biologists, it does, in our opinion, contain the best information available within the specified limitations of time. The North Carolina data may be characterized as having four degrees of reliability:

1) Numbers of deer killed and checked out on managed hunts may be considered to be as near accurate as field data can be.

2) Mortalities classed as "known" or "observed" are, in about one-third of the North Carolina data, based on records kept by the area manager. In other cases it was purely memory, or a combination of some records, and memory.

3) "Estimates" of mortality were based on the assumption that it would be impossible to observe all mortalities and therefore "estimated" mortalities are greater than "known" mortalities. It was also assumed that values for "estimated" mortality more closely approximated actual mortality than did values for "known" mortality.

4) "Estimates of potential mortality" might also be called "educated guesses" and would, of course, have the lowest level of reliability.

Examination of replies showed some "estimates" as being extremely low and others as extremely high. However, there was throughout a fairly close grouping about the means. There might have been some reluctance to divulge information on extent of dog control in spite of legal authority for same but we believe this was, to a substantial extent, overcome by assuring anonymity.

Analysis of Data

North Carolina data indicate that predation of deer reaches significant levels only in the western mountain section of the state. It also appears that predation is least significant in the eastern coastal plain section which is characterized by vast wetland areas. Accordingly, the data are grouped so as to derive average values for 23 mountain areas, three coastal plain areas and two mid-state piedmont areas. While no attempt was made to similarly regionalize the data from other southeastern states, it was obvious that the predation problem is considered to be much more serious on some areas than others.

The questionnaire specified that all data be in reference to one single calendar year—January 1 through December 31, 1968—so that averages derived could be considered as *annual* values. Also, since much of the study is concerned with western North Carolina areas where dog predation is a significant problem, and since these areas average about 15,000 acres in size, average figures in regard to them may be considered as annual values for 15,000-acre units.

Data in regard to individual area size and numbers of dogs controlled were omitted from tabulations to assure anonymity and to preclude controversy irrelevant to the purpose of this study.

Respondees were asked to indicate whether their replies in regard to dog predation were based on records, memory or both so as to provide insight in regard to reliability. Of 23 western North Carolina area managers, nine indicated that their replies were based on records, seven on memory and seven on some of each. In comparing the number of dogs reported controlled by those in each group, both the range in values and average values were quite similar. The observed number of deer killed by dogs, however, varied substantially. Those basing replies on records averaged 0.7 observed deer killed per year per 15,000 acres while those basing replies on memory averaged 1.6 and those basing replies on both records and memory averaged 2.9. In spite of this divergence, the average of estimated deer kills per area was almost identical—11, 9 and 10, respectively. While these observations may not be a reflection of reliability, they do indicate a considerable consistency and the probability that this element of consistency characterizes all estimates.

In the case of both dog predation and bobcat predation, questions were asked in regard to control so as to verify the presence of these predators on the areas. Similarly, a question called for the number of poachers apprehended to determine the level of concern with illegal hunting and illegal kills.

In computation of total drain and total population, values for *estimated* losses rather than *known* losses were used. This approach was used because *known* losses are obviously minimal and it is obvious that many unobserved losses occur. Hence we assumed that *estimated* losses would more nearly approximate the actual. The term "total drain" is defined as all removals of deer from the population, whether by death or live transfers.

Total deer populations were computed in the same manner on each area, in accordance with an obviously arbitrary procedure. It was assumed that the populations were stable on all areas, i.e., that reproduction added 25 percent to the spring population and that annual drain removed this number by the following spring.

Since these computations were based on the assumption of a 25 percent increase through reproduction, the "total population" was considered to be five times the annual reproduction which was

These photos should convince any skeptics that dogs can in
fact catch and seriously injure and kill full-grown deer. It is
a problem in many states that must be dealt with.

considered to be the same as the annual drain.
Hence "total population" was computed as five
times the annual drain.

While these assumptions are rather gross, they
are nevertheless reasonable and well within the "ball
park." Since there was no evidence of starvation
or disease during the survey year, no allowance
was made for it. Also there was no attempt to include consideration of prenatal mortality or immediately postnatal mortality.

Predation by Dogs

There are some skeptics who question the ability
of dogs to kill deer. Some claim that they are capable of killing only fawns or pregnant does or deer
that have been wounded by hunters or incapacitat-
ed by disease or parasites. While there may be
reason, in some cases, to question reports even of
"known" kills by dogs, we have too many reliable
reports of observed kills of healthy deer to discount
dogs as predators. In addition, many deaths by car,
train, fence, drowning and cold water shock may be
attributed to chasing by dogs.

Most dog kills occur in the mountain region of
North Carolina where swamps and lakes are not
available as means of escape. However, each year
we received reliable reports of a few deer being
run down and killed by dogs on eastern wetland
wildlife management area hunts where the use of
dogs is allowed. (Use of dogs in hunting deer is not
allowed in the central and western parts of North
Carolina.)

None of the several hundred dogs controlled on
western North Carolina areas was accompanied
by its owner, but 62 percent of them showed sign
of being owned and even the "strays" showed signs
of domesticity. In questioning area managers about
this point we attempted to determine whether any
of the "strays" could be considered as true wild
dogs that had been born and reared in the wild and
had developed into a special breed completely in-
dependent of civilization. None of the area man-

agers could certify to this development. On the
contrary, most "strays" were described as appearing to be recently separated from human ownership.

Dog ownership was even more evident on eastern
areas where most dog control activity occurred
during the hunting season. (Use of dogs is allowed
in deer hunting in this section.) Only about five
percent of the dogs were strays and 89 percent of
the dogs were picked up during the hunting season.
Thus, dog predation is not a year-round threat in
eastern swamplands. In strong contrast, however,
dog activity, as evidenced by season of control, was
practically uniform throughout the year on western areas: 32 percent in the fall, 26 percent in the
winter, 25 percent in the spring and 17 percent in
the summer.

On eastern areas most dogs controlled were deer
hounds (85 percent) with the remainder about
equally divided between beagles, bird dogs and
"mixed" breeds. On western areas 54 percent were
"mixed curs" and 28 percent were hounds. Most of
the remainder were beagles, shepherds and collies.
Eighty-three percent were in the act of chasing
deer when they were controlled and nine percent
had actually cornered their quarry and were in the
act of killing or feeding on them. In most of these
cases the deer were saved and only 37 "known"
deer kills were listed. They included 10 fawns, 17
does and 10 bucks. The number of "known" dog
kills per area varied from zero to nine and averaged
1.6 on western areas.

On intensively protected wildlife management
areas in western North Carolina, the average annual loss of deer to dogs per 15,000 acres is 1.6
"known," 10 "estimated," and 37 "potential" (without dog control). Before attempting to consider the
impact of stray dogs on deer herds in unprotected
localities, let us consider further the credibility of
these values.

First, is it reasonable to estimate that actual kills
are six times more numerous than known kills, i.e.,

10 versus 1.6? Since many of the known kills were the end result of intercepted dog races, what is the possibility of the area manager hearing and intercepting all dog races? In order to do this he would have to be on the area full time (24 hours per day) and able to hear all races. Assuming he were centrally located in a 15,000-acre area, and this seldom is the case, he would have to hear all races in a radius of 2.7 miles. Since dog races occur at all hours of night and day, sleep alone could reduce the area manager's exposure to dog races by at least one-third, and travel away from the area could easily reduce it by another one-third. Thus, the normal routine of existence would prevent him from hearing more than one-third of the races. However, all those occurring during his time on the area do not occur within hearing distance for this would require hearing all races within a 2.7 mile radius. If we can reasonably assume that he is unable to hear more than half the races that occur while he is on duty, it immediately becomes obvious that he cannot attempt to intercept more than one-sixth of the races. Thus, an "estimated" dog kill six times the "known" kill is not at all unreasonable (—unless he can "train" his deer to lead the races to the refuge headquarters and there is some indication that this can be done to a limited extent).

While it is not so difficult to rationalize an average annual loss of ten deer per year per 15,000 acres of protected area, it is more difficult to rationalize a "potential" loss of 37 deer without protection. It is of course obvious that more deer would be killed by the dogs if the dogs were not controlled, but is an average of 37 per year reasonable? Perhaps we can best answer this question with a series of other questions: Since stray dog control averaged three dogs per month per area, how much damage would the average of 36 dogs (per year) brought under control do if they were not all on the area for the full year but accumulated at the rate of three per month? We believe that each of these questions could be reasonably answered in the affirmative and that the average potential loss of 37 deer per year per 15,000 acres is not unreasonable.

To further explore the impact of this' level of predation, let us consider two hypothetical examples. Consider first a 15,000-acre area with a deer population of one per 50 acres or a total population of 300 deer and, at a 35 percent reproduction rate, an annual increment of 75 deer per year. In this case a dog predation rate of 37 deer per year would remove 50 percent of the annual increment. Next consider another 15,000-acre area, less remotely located, closer to human habitation, more heavily infested with free-running dogs, that has been stocked with 50 deer. It is immediately obvious that unless dog control is initiated prior to stocking, the deer herd will have little, if any, chance to exist, much less multiply and expand.

It is also obvious that under such circumstances, control of free-running dogs is the most important

A potential deer killer? Many abandoned dogs follow their natural instincts in chasing and killing game such as deer.

single function of the wildlife area manager. These considerations also underline the importance of his being headquartered *on* the area rather than in town several miles away. And it also demonstrates the importance of having legal authority to exercise control.

One further aspect of dog predation should be considered, namely that of ownership, for herein lies the crux of the problem. If dogs were wild animals rather than personal property it would be a relatively easy matter to bring them under control. Man has successfully extirpated much more secretive and crafty animals—such as wildcats, panthers, wild turkeys and others. But the fact that dogs are personal property precludes some very effective control procedures. And the fact that they are mass produced by people on a "sustained yield" basis, and not only allowed but actually encouraged to roam uncontrolled, magnifies tremendously the problem of deer restoration.

However, these circumstances also identify the solution to the problem, i.e., cooperation of dog owners by keeping their dogs confined. Thus, the best tools for control of this problem include magazine and newspaper articles, radio and personal communication. Also helpful is court prosecution of people who allow their dogs to run deer where prohibited by law. Since actual control of dogs by wildlife protectors is limited to designated wildlife management areas, establishment of deer herds by overflow into the surrounding areas is virtually impossible if the local people are not sufficiently concerned to control their dogs.

While most of this section on Predation by Dogs is based on data from western North Carolina wildlife management areas, data from other states indicate that the problem is not peculiar to North Carolina. Replies to questionnaires indicate that this is also a serious problem in parts of Georgia, Virginia, Tennessee, Oklahoma, South Carolina and Mississippi. ♦　**(Continued next month)**

Boating Safety Week Proclaimed

Governor Robert Scott has proclaimed the week of June 29 - July 5 as Safe Boating Week in North Carolina. This year the Fourth of July falls on a Friday, which means another long holiday weekend for Tarheels and their visitors from other states. In his proclamation Governor Scott urged boaters to observe the laws and regulations pertaining to boating safety, and the rules of common sense and courtesy.

Check Your License, Please?

Please check the hunting or fishing license you carry in your billfold. If you have a hunting license, it expires July 31. This applies also to a combination hunting-fishing license. Your resident state fishing license or resident county licenses are valid until midnight December 31. When a wildlife protector approaches you and says, "May I check your license, please?" be sure you have the proper one with you.

Hunting, Trapping Regulations Ready

By the 1st of August, when you will need to replace your hunting or combination hunting-fishing license, license dealers will be equipped to supply you with a copy of the official 1969-1970 regulations. The booklets will contain special regulations for hunting on game lands.

Regulations for taking migratory game birds are established by the U. S. Government, and will be announced at a later date

Banner Year At Striped Bass Hatchery

Sport and commercial striped bass anglers on the Roanoke River brought in 89,135,000 striped bass eggs to the hatchery at Weldon. Of these, 55,000,000 were water-hardened at the hatchery and released in the river to hatch in a natural manner. Of the remaining 34,135,000 eggs 25,512,000 hatched (68%) for stocking purposes.

PHOTO BY TOM JACKSON

Umstead State Park: for Your Health

By
Charlotte Hilton Green

THE greatest *health* asset a state can have is a "green oasis" where people can go to tramp (or even "jog") study nature, picnic, camp, do research. Where children, in particular, can have nature trail hikes under competent leadership. And where a bit of God's green earth is kept inviolate for generations to come.

Such a place is our Umstead State Park, situated strategically within reach of several growing cities. About 11 miles from Raleigh, 13 from Durham, a little more from Chapel Hill, it is an area of 5,200 acres deeded to the State of North Carolina by the United States of America. "The State shall use the property exclusively for a public park, recreation, conservation, and educational purposes. Otherwise it reverts to the federal government."

It is as plain as that.

Umstead is a place for those without large estates to find a "green oasis" for walking about, for en-joying the out-of-doors, to note the trees, shrubs, wild flowers, birds, small animals; for camping and study, for research—for all the vast masses who need a quiet place to view and study God's handi-work—to meditate—and to breathe fresh air. -

Umstead is unique—an unusual tract of land that could not be duplicated elsewhere in this section and that, for its original purposes, ecological natur-al history, research projects and such to schools, universities, students, *health* and recreation, is of vast importance.

Mr. Eugene Upchurch, former park naturalist, explains "Ecologically Umstead includes sections typical of three different habitats: one high area juts into a region typical of the higher Piedmont and lower mountains (here rhododendron grows naturally); the low eastern part is somewhat typical of higher coastal areas, and yet another section has some conditions similar to the Sandhills." A "three in one"—thus all in all this park has some species of birds, animals, plant and insect life typical of these three different habitats.

Need? As William Hamnett, Director of the N. C. Museum of Natural History, points out: "With the 'population explosion' and the rapid growth of this area, within the next 10-15 years Raleigh, Durham and Chapel Hill will almost reach the boundaries of Umstead State Park. How necessary then, to have a 'breathing place'—a *healthy* outlet—limited to what it was given to the State for!"

Uses? Education—and *Health?* Quoting Dr. Fred Barkalow, professor of zoology and forestry, North Carolina State University: "Five colleges—University of North Carolina State University, Duke, Shaw, St. Augustine—several smaller colleges and junior colleges, and scores of high schools, conduct an assortment of activities, including research projects, classes, field excursions there. Furthermore, each year untold thousands of high school and grade children, scouts, 4-H and FFA youngsters assemble there for natural history and *health* ac-

William B. Umstead State Park has several camps designed for organized group use. They are in constant demand and are a source of learning experiences as well as recreation.

PHOTO BY LUTHER PARTIN

tivities by park naturalists, school teachers, college personnel, scout, religious, and other civic leaders.

For *17 years* Greensboro schools have sent several 5th grades for a week's outdoors school held in this park. Why Umstead instead of some place nearer home, to transplant several 5th grades, teachers, extra equipment and such? Because there is nothing nearer Greensboro that has suitable accommodations and a variety of environment—as already pointed out.

Do the children like it? Let's stay throughout with one of the 5th grades, as I have done. "Classes held beside a running stream, while climbing about rocks, in woodland or open fields, during stops on a nature trail, on, the steps of a rustic cabin. Perhaps a 'cook-out' for supper, followed by a campfire and informal talks learning first-hand something about the voices of the night and of the stars overhead."

(Such was the opening paragraph of an article on Greensboro's Camp School at Umstead State Park that I was asked to do (a few years ago) for a national magazine which had heard good accounts of those outdoor classes.)

As preparation, in the Greensboro schools much preliminary work is done in previous months. Under guidance the children assist in the planning, of all phases of it being integrated with their school work. They discuss menus, studying what foods are best to build bone, good blood, protect

Healthful fishing and boating are popular on this picturesque lake in Umstead State Park. Swimming is available as a group activity at the day camps on another Park lake.

PHOTO BY LUTHER PARTIN

teeth. They study costs of foods and other supplies, as well as transportation, number of cars needed, and such. "Now I see some sense in arithmetic," was the comment of one child who had disliked the subject."

The children were encouraged to earn all or part of the cost—by yard work, paper routes, babysitting, home help. (Too, interested individuals, civic groups, or both often share the costs of such camps, especially in the underprivileged areas.)

At camp the children share in the work, different groups taking their turn at K.P. They keep their own cabins and grounds neat; each group has its captain, elected by the children. At start of all trips there is roll call; teachers keep records; it is known where each child is at any given time. *Health* is rigidly guarded; a nurse is always at camp. No child is allowed to fish or swim without a parent's signed permission—and lifeguards keep close watch during such activities.

There is no risk to *health*, or exposure. For occasional rainy days when classes must be held indoors, alternate programs and materials are arranged in advance, including slides, wildlife movies and shorts, *health* projects, maps, an adequate nature library.

Classes are held in two-hour sessions with field trips including all phases of wildlife, nature trails, soil conservation, contour ploughing, terracing, wise planting, ground cover, forestry.

In forestry children learn how to identify trees, how they grow, their uses, how "weed trees" can crowd out good trees; how pines are important timber and pulpwood trees for the South; how to plant them; what ones are valuable for wildlife. How carbon dioxide is absorbed from the air by trees and plants by photosynthesis. They learn that photosynthesis is one of the most important processes in the whole world, for it is the source of all the food of both plants and animals. It is the only process by which large amounts of oxygen are turned back into the air. Without photosynthesis we should soon have no food to eat or o x y g e n to breathe.

But children, important as they are, are not the only ones using the park. As Park Superintendent Myers Braxton informs me, "This year's attendance records (through Oct. 31st) were 321,000. Breaking down these figures in that period there have been 105,000 picnickers, 22,000 Sunday afternoon conducted nature hikes—and 34,000 hikers on their own.

"Churches, too, have held camps for retreats, study sessions, meditation."

All this the park has to offer—education, recreation, inspiration, spiritual retreats—and it is free. (A small fee is charged for fishing and boating.) The park is integrated, and there have been no problems. (That alone makes it outstanding.)

Perhaps, totaling it all up, Umstead's greatest asset is to *Health*—physical, mental, spiritual.

How shall we use Umstead Park—or any of our parks, both state and national? It's up to us. ◆

13

This Place May Die

by Dwight L. Peterson
Clinton, N. C.

I know a place where the wild wind blows and a man feels free . . .

SPRING had vanished and the hot summer sun bore down hot and dry. Heat waves struck the already drought stricken land and bounced back toward the sky in a dancing haze. The light pack on my back was no burden but beads of sweat trickled down my face and off the end of my nose. Thoughts of the ham sandwiches in my pack made my mouth water and I had happy and impatient thoughts of lunch time.

Nestled snugly beneath hovering oaks, cypress, pine and black gum, was the creek. I paused a moment, took a deep breath of fresh clean air, felt the tingle of satisfaction and waded in up to my knees. The water was cold and sent a sensation through my body like an electric shock. I cupped some water in my palm and splashed my sweaty face. My day had begun.

Six Runs Creek. A legend of memories for some, a thin marked line on a map for others. Six small tributaries at its head gave it its name. Narrow at the beginning but much wider at its destination and union with Great Coharie Creek; thus, forming Black River and on to the Atlantic.

I refuse to argue which is my favorite way to fish this small creek, but I think the way I fished that day holds the spot-light. But, of course, this method of fishing can only be accomplished when the creek

is not in freshet stage. I wore clothes I did not mind getting wet or soiled, and tennis shoes with holes cut in the sides and toes to protect my feet. The pack on my back carried essential items.

The spinning rod felt good in my hand and I swished it back and forth a couple of times to limber up. I pulled line from the reel, threaded it through the eyelets and tied on a lure. A few practice casts in shallow water and I was ready for the six hour fishing journey to the next bridge downstream. A light breeze had risen from somewhere and whispered softly t h r o u g h the pines. My thoughts were free and pleasant.

I moved very slowly so as not to create too many waves and ripples in the water ahead of me. First action came near a log jam. Standing waist deep in the cold water I dropped the lure as delicately as possible into a deep pocket near the logs and creek bank. The lure had moved about three feet when a bright flash bolted from the dark waters and struck the lure with lightning speed. The rod tip zipped into an arc when I struck back.

Snags and long fingery limbs jutted out here and there throughout the deep hole. I had to horse the fish and maneuver him amidst the obstacles. Much of the pleasure of play was lost in the frantic battle against tangle. Carefully I backed toward a sandbar and seconds later had the largemouth safe on land. I slipped him on my stringer and tied the stringer to my belt.

With a smile and a thought that today was going to be a good one I waded out into the water and again started downstream. It was then I really noticed the log jam and the tangle of brush and debris stretching completely across the creek. At first, I had just glanced at it, not really noticing it, but now it was a complete barrier and I knew I would have to walk the bank around.

The bank was slippery and I used bushes and roots as hand holds to reach the crest of the bank. As I pulled myself to the crest, my eyes fell upon a stake driven in the ground and a few feet out from the creek. It was flat and triangular shaped, with numbers marked on one side. There were other stakes, and there were blazed trees, some had bottle caps nailed on the blaze like it could have been a bench mark or something of that sort. A narrow trimmed path, like surveyors would cut, trailed through the woods, and trees along each side were painted with orange circles around them. Then, I remembered the newspapers and the talk and the plans of the canal. My heart sank.

I detoured the log jam and began fishing again. My day of pleasant fishing was beginning to change in atmosphere and attitude. Each time I detoured a log jam which was often, there would be the little stakes with numbers, the surveyors path, and the orange circles painted on the trees.

By noon I had caught several fish but had released them all except one large bream, a jack, and a few largemouths. I put the fish in the water, tied the stringer to a small birch near the water edge, and fell in on the ham sandwiches.

14

Perhaps the consequences of some channelization projects won't be this dire, but the contrast is rather stark. Many small streams have already felt the body blows.

My lunch wasn't as enjoyable as I had anticipated and I was disappointed. Each mouthful seemed to grow in my mouth. But, after a time, I got it down and lay back on the clean smelling pine needles to rest. A red-tailed hawk circled high overhead and I could hear his high-pitched cry. The wind in the pines still moaned softly but the music had changed and sounded depressive. It's strange how the sounds of nature can be heard in so many different tones. The sounds fit the mood of the person, I suppose. They were fitting mine now, and my thoughts drifted when I closed my eyes and listened; and thought . . .

● The creek was gone and I could see the canal with its tapered banks and wide brims, with no trees within several feet. And it was long and straight, like drainage canals around a field, with only slight turns at intervals. And there were no fish, maybe a few minnows darting here and there amidst the aquatic grasses bending and swaying to the current. The water was shallow, probably ankle deep, until it rained, and then, a rushing, threshing turmoil of water gushing toward the Atlantic. Deep, notched, ugly gashes were cut in the banks from erosion. There were no shad in the springtime and everything was desolate and barren.

Then, the creek came back to mind and it was beautiful and natural as it had always been. And I thought of my boyhood and the happy care-free years. The camping trips, the hikes, the old swimming hole on a summer afternoon, and the happy laughter of children splashing and playing in the cold water; always cold water. And the races to the creek on a hot summer day when a barn of tobacco had been put in. "Last one in is a rotten egg," we would shout . . .

● Where will man and his progress draw the line, I thought? Or will man, through his "progress," finally destroy the things that are vital to his very existence? The idea of the canal is only a drop of water in the ocean compared to the world, but the idea is there. And there are other projects, many more. Drainage is needed, that's for sure; the creek should be cleaned out—most everyone will agree to that. The log jams create dams and back water onto the fields all too frequently. But why not clear the stream by some other means, like snagging? (See "New Fishing Water", Feb., 1969 *Wildlife*.) All that's necessary is to free the water, and the natural beauty of the stream can remain. It can probably be done at a fraction of the cost it would take to dig a canal. And at this point in time, can man put a dollar sign on nature??

When man has pushed nature into the background and sits down to a lunch of little pills and gulps them down with distilled, chemically-treated water, what will he pay to hear the wind in the pines, the high-pitched cry of a hawk over-head, the feel of a fish on a line, the mellow sounding voices of coon hounds on a cold moonlight night? Will man in the future go to a book and flip through the pages, and look at the pictures, and say to himself, "I wish I could see a *real* tree; I wish I could hear the whispering of wind through the trees; I wish I could hear the bubbling, pleasant sounds of a clean stream; I wish my forefathers had thought of these things, and protected them and conserved them way back in 1969 . . ."

My pick-up companion was waiting at the bridge when I arrived. His eyes widened when he saw my catch, and then he smiled. "Man! You had a good day. You must have had a ball."

I didn't answer, just lay my fish on a newspaper in the foot of the car and got in.

He stared at me with a strange look, as if he didn't understand my attitude, and said, "You act like something's on your mind."

"There is," I said . . .

I know a place where the wild wind blows and a man feels free . . . but this place may die. ◆

THIS Corner of WILDLIFE, especially during the month that includes National Safe Boating Week, is primarily reserved for safety rules, regulations, boating tips, and the like—things to reduce accidents. To consider what happens in the event of an accident may be deemed negative thinking. However, when boat insurance is considered, insurance representatives and their countless satisfied customers would say that this (insurance) is definitely positive thinking.

Have you ever stopped to think just what would happen to your (uninsured) pleasure boating if: a SCUBA-equipped thief surfaced at the stern of your 25-foot sportfisherman, changed the name and eased her out of the slip. Or if that trailer hitch and safety chain failed and your prized ski boat took off down the bypass on its own; or if you misjudged the ol' stump location and instead of fishing near it, you ended up impaled on it. And if all that doesn't concern you, then perhaps a small law suit from the fellow who sat down on your fish gaff might start you thinking—insurance.

What's it all about? Is it necessary? Let's briefly introduce the idea, then you be the judge. First, that 25 footer mentioned above was quite likely insured against theft; the investment would be too large to think otherwise. It is usually the smaller craft that is not adequately covered. But your fishing skiff is your yacht and worthy of at least some protection. Marine insurance dates way back with 1547 reportedly the first date of issuance in England. In general, marine insurance has its roots in those early insurance underwriters who formed Lloyd's of Lon-

don. The marine insurance business still utilizes some archaic terminology. And marine insurance can be difficult for the untrained reader to comprehend. However, when it comes to coverage, it all boils down to a situation similar to your auto policy—property damage, liability and medical coverage, are all available and desirable. If you can afford only limited coverage, then liability may be the most important.

Probably the most convenient and most economical method for the small craft operator to obtain protection is by adding his boat, trailer and equipment to his homeowner's policy.

Generally, small boats and motors, within certain horsepower limits, (25 horsepower for outboard, 50 horsepower for inboard and 26 feet for sailboats according to one major company), are automatically covered in a comprehensive homeowner's or tenant homeowner's policy. Liability insurance which covers you if you cause injury to someone else is significant, usually running to $25,000.00 at no extra cost. Physical damage limits are relatively much less with $500.00 as a standard limit. And this nominal coverage usually does not apply to the many perils that face the skipper and his craft.

Most automobile policies also automatically give you liability coverage in the event of a boat or trailer highway mishap. However, if you flip that fiberglass beauty off the trailer at 60 mph, you pick up most of the tab unless you have insurance other than already mentioned.

Does the idea of wiping out your uninsured pleasure craft frighten you? What then is the next step? First, get the advice of your insurance representative. Ask about extended coverage on your homeowner's policy (additional premium, of course). But be certain that type of policy extension will give you all the marine coverage desired. Consider those unusual hazards to which your craft may be exposed.

Adding coverage via your

homeowner's policy may g you all the coverage desired smaller small craft. Some co panies require something otl than a rider on your homeov er's policy for larger boats.

The next step is the true b policy. There are companies tl specialize in marine insuran there are those that can "fix y up with something." And y family insurance man may be prince of a fellow but may kn nothing about boats or boat surance. So, this may be a ti to pick and choose or get furtl advice.

One source of insurance through boating clubs or asso ated organizations. They offer risk boat policies at "club rate All such plans are relativ easy to understand and invo filling in the blanks and sign the block of desired covera signing the document and sei ing the check. We have rea to believe that most of these p icies are a sound investment. I you may wish to investigate pr to investing.

The exact title of the separ boat policy may vary from co pany to company, as well coverage, but many use a sta ard breakdown.

The breakdown refers to cov age and is often described follows: 1. Limited-named pe (perils must be named in or for insured to recover loss) Broad-named perils, adds lision, and other traditional pe of the sea such as groundi sinking, etc. 3. All risk and co prehensive insurance against most every occurrence usually a $25-$100 deductible basis cheaper rates. Another metho often used to describe boat ins ance; that is (1) the outbo policy and (2) the yacht pol The outboard policy, of cou covers outboard craft and outboard engine, trailer, trai ing and equipment are usu considered. The yacht policy called, is applied to "traditio craft" such as the inboard cr er, sailboats and the inboard-drive is usually covered un this category.

Liability and medical cover

would come usually in another section of the policy regardless of above mentioned terminology.

Coverage under either type of policies is usually similar. Of course, large cruisers, charter boats, etc., bring about the need for more extensive coverage and the various workings of the big world of marine insurance.

Outboard policies are usually recommended in the all-risk form and there is evidence that pleasure craft insurance in general is moving toward same. However, you may wish to look into limited insurance to reduce premiums.

What are you insured against? Well, almost anything, if you wish to pay. All risk includes such items as fire, explosion, lightning, theft, collision, trailer, liability for damage to other boats, loss of motor overboard, hitting submerged objects, sinking, capsizing, storms, damage in transit, and protection at anchor or underway.

There are limits to coverage. Some are: ordinary wear and tear or gradual deterioration, latent defect (in an engine block for example), ice damage, or items common to most insurance such as war. And remember most companies will not insure just any old tub. The company may elect to survey the craft at their expense if there are questions about its soundness.

The big question is, what's it going to cost me? One rule of thumb for small boat coverage, figures out at about $4.00 per hundred dollar value of the boat, motor, equipment and $2.00 per hundred dollar value for the trailer. One leading company quotes $149.00 for all risk, $50.00 deductible coverage on $4500.00 inboard-outdrive. Incidentally, this price was for seven months coverage, 12 months coverage cost $179.00.

Factors affecting the annual premium vary from company to company. For example, diesel engines are less expensive to insure than gasoline engines, faster boats often cost more to insure and anything that indicates hazardous use may affect the cost.

Quite often a base price such as mentioned above can be reduced by certain insurance credits depending on the company. One such credit, called a proficiency discount by one company, offers a five percent discount for being an active member of the U. S. Power Squadron or the U. S. Coast Guard Auxiliary. Built-in fire extinguisher equipment is considered for credit by many companies. And a company may issue a rebate if your boat is not used for a long period of time.

There are hundreds of incidental facts that we might mention, but for hundreds of facts, you had better check with your insurance representative. However, let's examine a few: water skiing may affect premium; renting your pleasure boat or hiring out without such coverage could affect your recovery in case of loss; it is recommended that you notify your insurance company if you sell or trade; remember the company expects you to salvage what you can in an accident, so don't set your accident up for unusual survey; your coverage may be jeopardized if willful misconduct is proven; most insurance companies do not insure racing boats but racing associations will; evidence of breaking and entering may be required before loss by theft is covered; and many policies are figured on using the craft for six or seven months and

storing her for the remainder, you may want coverage for year-around activities.

Now, of course, it is not for me to use this space to sell you on insurance. But one thing for certain, I don't even want to think about replacing at my complete expense, that is, the craft at dry dock in the Parker's garage.

One final thought—if an accident occurs—play it straight and as one author suggests, recover what is due you but don't try to make a profit on your misfortune; it will only make the rates go up for all of us.

Literature Display Rack

Marine dealers and marina operators will be interested to know that the Fifth Coast Guard District (that district which includes North Carolina, Maryland, and Virginia) is offering a free literature display rack. The idea originated in and is being tested by this district. The attractive rack, complete with numerous safety pamphlets will enable the boaters to leave your place of business better informed. It will also enable you to keep various literature neatly arranged and displayed. If you feel you can put a literature rack to good use, then write: B. L. Stabile, Commander, U. S. Coast Guard, Chief Boating Safety Branch, Fifth Coast Guard District Headquarters, Portsmouth, Virginia 23705.

It is the duty of every skipper to chart a safe course for his crew, and those with whom he shares the waterways. Safe Boating Week is simply a time set aside to remind us of that responsibility. Let us not forget at the Week's end this slogan: The Golden Rule of Boating—Safety First—Insures Happy Days Afloat.

PHOTO BY JOHN R. PARKER, JR.

New Homes for Fish
"Fish Hides"

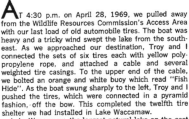

by James R. Davis
Fishery Biologist

PHOTOS BY LUTHER PARTIN

AT 4:30 p.m. on April 28, 1969, we pulled away from the Wildlife Resources Commission's Access Area with our last load of old automobile tires. The boat was heavy and a tricky wind swept the lake from the southeast. As we approached our destination, Troy and I connected the sets of six tires each with yellow polypropylene rope, and attached a cable and several weighted tire casings. To the upper end of the cable, we bolted an orange and white buoy which read "Fish Hide". As the boat swung sharply to the left, Troy and I pushed the tires, which were connected in a pyramid fashion, off the bow. This completed the twelfth tire shelter we had installed in Lake Waccamaw.

Lake Waccamaw, the largest natural lake on the east coast of North Carolina is a black-water lake comprising 8,936 acres with a maximum width of 5.3 miles. It has a maximum depth of 10.8 feet and an average depth of 7.6 feet. The shoreline length is approximately 14.2 miles. The perimeter two-thirds of the lake bottom is composed chiefly of sand with the center third being of pulp and fibrous peat. At present, the lake supports a good palagic fish population and fair fishing. The most important fish species harvested from Lake Waccamaw are white perch, largemouth bass, pumpkinseed, and bluegill. Past fishery management on the lake has been confined to stocking largemouth bass, bluegill, redear sunfish, and threadfin shad as well as closing certain sections of the lake to fishing during the spawning period.

In an effort to improve fishing in Lake Waccamaw, Mr. James A. Bridger, District IV Wildlife Commissioner from Bladenboro, suggested that old tires be used to construct "fish hides" with the areas marked so that fishermen can locate them.

Lake Waccamaw with its sandy bottom is an ideal testing site for freshwater fish hides. Previous Commission experimentation in North Carolina with such devices was conducted during the summer of 1968 in two small Piedmont lakes. Initial data indicate that sunfish concentrated near the shelters and that fishermen caught more and larger sunfish for the amount of effort exerted than they did in areas where there were no fish hides.

Permission for the installation of tire shelters in the two lakes was obtained from Mr. Thomas Ellis, Division of State Parks, Department of Conservation and Development, with an agreement that they be marked and anchored according to State and Federal regulations. Styrofoam buoys and old tires were obtained and transported to Lake Waccamaw in February. During April, they were assembled into sets of six each. The installation took place during April. The fish shelters were located so as to form an east-west line across the lake at intervals of approximately 2,000 feet. Approximately 30 tires were used for each fish hide and final assembly was in a pyramid-shaped matrix on the bottom. The

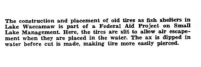

The construction and placement of old tires as fish shelters in Lake Waccamaw is part of a Federal Aid Project on Small Lake Management. Here, the tires are slit to allow air escapement when they are placed in the water. The ax is dipped in water before cut is made, making tire more easily pierced.

twelve "hides" were assembled by connecting the tires with ¼ inch polypropylene rope to which was attached three cement-filled tires which would serve as an anchor. Prior to being assembled, each tire was sliced with an axe on top and bottom so that trapped air would escape when the tires were placed in the water. We found that the easiest method to cut the tires was to lay each tire on a solid board or log and cut it with an axe. By dipping the axe in water prior to making the cut the axe blade easily passed through the thick rubber of the tire, a trick we learned from an old fisherman. If the tire shelters prove successful, more may be installed in the future.

If you, as a pond owner or fisherman, are interested in constructing fish hides from old tires, I suggest you use them in ponds with generally clean bottoms. Ponds with old stumps and fallen trees usually have sufficient cover. If you decide on building fish hides, I would recommend one such device per two acres of water with the suggestion that they be located in water in excess of six feet. Remember, cut the old tire casings top and bottom so that air can be released when they are placed in your pond and construct the hides to provide the greatest amount of hiding space for fishes. This can be done by assembling the tires on land so they will stand upright when placed on the bottom of the pond. Anchors would not be needed in ponds of less than ten acres. ✦

At upper left, Fishery Biologist James R. Davis and Wildlife Patrolman Troy Sigmon, display one section of tires ready for the pile. Above, James A. Bridger, District 4 Wildlife Commissioner, and Biologist Davis ready one of the marking buoys. Lower left, the tires are placed in the water and the marker anchored. Better fishing should result.

Swamp Drainage:

A Non-Ecological Approach to Resource Management

by Randy Perry
STAFF PHOTOS

IT is past time that all natural resource managers and planners, whether they be foresters, landscape architects, wildlife biologists, city planners, or soil conservationists, realized the demand for an ecological approach to resource management. It is no longer feasible or sensible to completely sacrifice one natural resource for the sake of better management of another. All resource managers must now be ecologically conscious, and realize that all of our natural resources must be managed in a unified manner if we are to conserve them for future generations. Understanding should not be canceled by expertness.

Natural swamps are one of North Carolina's more valuable natural resources, both economically and aesthetically. However, our natural swamps are continually being threatened by drainage, and little consideration is given to the ecological consequences involved for land, timber, wildlife, water, or even man.

Through research, it has been determined that the practice of overdrainage in the coastal plain threatens the destruction of an estimated 1½ million acres of organic soils through oxidation. According to the January 1969 issue of *Mechanix Illustrated*, Dr. Rainer Berger of the University of Colorado claims that the earth is now in one of the driest periods it has had in the last 40,000 years! He also points out that the last major dry period was some 5000 years ago, but was not as severe as the one at present. In 1968 alone, drought losses in North Carolina have been estimated by reliable sources at about $146 million. One can easily see the threat posed by drainage.

MANY of our natural swamps in the Southeastern United States have already been irreversibly destroyed by the practice of channelization and drainage, and the physical effects of these drainage projects on the watershed are more than a mere removal of water from existing croplands. Channelization can cause the water to be drained from adjacent farmlands too fast. The right of way clearing through the heart of the swamp removes much of the standing vegetation that retards the quick removal of water from the land. As a result of this clearing and increased channelization, the surface water drains from the land at such an accelerated rate, that much topsoil is also taken by erosion. The farmer's land is literally drained; drained of important soil nutrient elements, fertilizers, and other farm chemicals. The farmer receives no benefit from these substances when they float down a ditch and eventually cause stream pollution.

Farm drainage in North Dakota has actually been accused of causing floods—simply by removing surface water too quickly. By eliminating natural land basins, potholes, depressions, and flora which catch, store, and cause ground penetration, runoff waters are shed from the uplands more quickly. This increased runoff f l o o d s into the streams above their natural capacity to transport it—thus creating locally flooded conditions. Some means must be left to retard water if floods are going to be controlled. Complete swamp drainage is not the cure for flooding that is alleged.

The effects of natural swamp drainage on fish and wildlife populations are far-reaching, and in

Drainage ditches lace eastern North Carolina, often carrying the life blood of the area, water, from the valuable wetlands.

The value of a swamp in terms of timber, water supply, wildlife sanctuary, and fishery resources, is tremendous.

most cases irreversible. Natural swamps support populations of largemouth bass, warmouth, redbreast sunfish, yellow perch, fliers, redfin pickerel, and chain pickerel. Some of the best fishing of Eastern North Carolina is provided by these fish species in swamp areas. When a drainage project converts a natural swamp into a drainage canal, these important fish species are replaced by less desirable rough fish that can withstand the altered environment.

Stream siltation is a major national problem, especially in drained swamps. The farmer needs the valuable topsoil that erodes into drained swamps; fish and wildlife do not, and the effects of stream siltation on their existence is often lethal.

First, siltation causes a lowering of the productivity level of the swamp. Silt causes decreased light penetration in the water, thus many important "producer" aquatic plants and phytoplankton cannot survive. As the phytoplankton is eliminated, the zooplankton will also decrease in total amount of biomass present. With valuable oxygen and food producing plant life eliminated or sharply reduced, fish face serious shortages of clean water, food, and oxygen.

Stream siltation also causes a reproductive problem for fish. Once fish eggs are spawned, silt deposition often completely covers the eggs and suffocates them.

During the spring and summer months channelized streams usually contain the least amount of water. This is also the period of maximum breeding for fish. Oftentimes in drained creeks the water is too low during this period for egg deposits to be made. Many fish eggs that are spawned eventually end up desiccated or devoured by predators.

IN an effort to gain some insight into the detrimental effects of swamp drainage on the existing fishery resources, the North Carolina Wildlife Resources Commission conducted a study. Fisheries Biologists Jack Bayless and William B. Smith of the North Carolina Wildlife Resources Commission reported on these effects in "The Effects of Channelization Upon the Fish Populations of Lotic Waters in Eastern North Carolina." In this study 23 channeled streams and 36 proximate natural streams were compared. The following is quoted directly from the report abstract:

"These comparisons indicated that reductions in the magnitude of 90 percent occurred both in weight of game fish per acre, and in number of game fish exceeding six inches total length per acre, following channelization.

The data further revealed that no significant return towards the natural stream populations occurred within a 40-year period following channelization."

Fish have very little choice in a drainage canal. Either they remain and reproduce at a lower level, providing physiological conditions permit, or migrate in search of better aquatic habitat. The fish that can remain face many hardships in their search for food, clean water, and a spawning and rearing grounds. Predation, starvation, and disease are usually more prevalent within such a population living under such physiological and ecological stresses. Population reduction is the end result.

Fish species that cannot physiologically withstand heavy stream siltation or low water levels must migrate or perish. The fish that do leave in search of better habitat suffer great losses from starvation, predation, and competition from other fish species. The complete fishery resources will be severely altered in an apparently irreversible manner.

Wildlife populations are faced with a similar problem. Ducks cannot effectively reproduce and rear their young on open canals of flowing dirty water. The open habitat allows increased predation from hawks, dogs, foxes, turtles, and man. Ducks must move out. But how much is a duck worth? It is impossible to accurately answer such a question. Wildlife has a value that cannot be measured in dollars and cents.

The wood duck is found in great numbers in many natural swamps of North Carolina. This duck is North Carolina's own in a sense. It is one of the most hunted duck species in North Carolina. Also, in North Carolina, more woodies are killed than any other species. Other ducks using swamps in significant numbers include blacks and mallards.

NATURAL swamps offer seclusion and isolation unlike any other form of habitat. Deer and bear make extensive use of bottomlands and swamps as escape routes from dogs and man. Mast production in natural swamps helps maintain populations of squirrels, turkeys, and many bird species other than waterfowl. Raccoons, rabbits, otter, and mink also flourish in natural swamps and bottomlands. The carrying capacity of a swamp in its natural state is extremely high, but is sharply curtailed by drainage.

What happens to existing wildlife when drainage occurs? Since prime habitat for many species is destroyed, they must abandon their home territories or cease to exist. Man often invades these drained areas.

When wildlife populations are forced to abandon an area in an effort to search for better habitat, losses occur. Populations moving into new areas face increased competition from species already present. Increased predation may occur since the abandoning individuals are not totally familiar with their "new" surroundings. Starvation and disease may also increase. As a result of swampland destruction, the total wildlife resource is seriously jeopardized.

Little does man realize that he is also an animal species. Sure man is more advanced than animal species such as ducks and deer, but how much more advanced? Man is the only animal that has ever waged an all-out war on his own species. Man requires the same 20 amino acids for protein synthesis as wildlife species. Man is like other wildlife species in that he requires food, water, air, and shelter as the basic necessities of life. Swamp drainage virtually eliminates most of these four essentials, not only for wildlife, but also for man. Sure wildlife is affected more severely and more quickly than man, but man will eventually be affected—probably to a greater degree than wildlife.

With water pollution a major problem in the United States, clean water becomes an even more valuable resource. Swamp drainage l o w e r s the water table drastically. Many farmers complain about having to deepen their wells. During drought periods farmlands suffer tremendous water shortages, but new drainage projects are continually being planned and put into operation. In many areas creeks are being used as a water source for municipalities. More of these creeks will be needed for use as a water source in the future—yet drainage projects continue to multiply and flourish.

Many health officials promote swamp drainage projects in the name of mosquito control. Swamp drainage projects could only cause a potential increase in existing mosquito populations. By draining bottomlands, extremely small potholes a few inches deep will almost always remain in some locations. These small areas are not large enough for significant duck usage, but exactly suit the mosquitoes' needs for egg laying and larval development of their y o u n g. Mosquito populations thrive in such stagnant pools in supposedly drained areas. Increased mosquito populations mean more localized DDT spraying, thus adding to the tremendous problem of air and water pollution.

The *Aedes aegypti* mosquito, the one that carries yellow fever, prefers to breed in old water-containing tires and empty cans near wellings, and does not breed in significant numbers in n a t u r a l swamps. In most cases swamp drainage projects accelerate mosquito breeding rather than control it.

NATURAL swamps contain extremely valuable tupelo and cypress timber stands. Hardwood bottomlands, characterized by surface water only in the winter, contain other important tree species such as ashes, blackgum, sweetgum, and several species of oak. Besides the sanctuary provided in these areas, wildlife food production is also high. Berries, gum mast, and acorns are produced in enormous quantities in natural, unaltered swamps and bottomlands.

The timber value of these tree species is tremendous. Two-thirds of all hardwoods produced in the United States come from the swamps and bottomlands of the Southeastern states.

The rot-resistant qualities of cypress wood are well known. Cypress timber is used extensively where exposure to weather is an important factor.

Tupelo root wood is often used as floats on fishing nets. Veneer of tupelo gum is often stained and used as paneling or furniture.

Hardwood veneer is a main source of income in Eastern North Carolina. High quality hardwood products are in great demand, and natural swamps and bottomlands play the important role of providing the necessary conditions for proper growth and development of these valuable trees.

North Carolina is a national leader in the production of hardwood plywood, much of which is produced from tupelo gum. This state is also a national leader in wood furniture production. Why import these important tree species when they can be grown right here in the swamps and bottomlands of North Carolina?

Tupelo and cypress require surface water for long periods each year to maintain maximum growth. Both seed dispersal and germination depend upon a watery atmosphere. Tupelo and cypress improve the quality of water in swamps by slowing runoff and causing silt deposition.

In Agricultural Handbook Number 181, November 1960, *Management and Inventory of Southern Hardwoods*, U.S. Department of Agriculture, the following statement is made concerning tupelo-swamp blackgum stands: "Artificial drainage will decelerate growth or kill older trees if it permanently lowers the water table. Prolonged droughts cause mortality and induce insect attack."

No longer is it considered economically feasible to convert hardwood bottomlands and swamps into pine stands. Softwood production is now more approximately in line with the demand. Under swamp conditions, blackgum, tupelo, and cypress can develop tremendous volumes of timber. These species can actually out produce southern pines. Good hardwood wetlands containing ample water can produce growth rates sometimes exceeding 1000 board feet per acre per year. Wildlife popula-

Once destroyed, a swamp is usually gone forever, in its place a piece of soggy ground often abandoned as useless. It makes better sense to leave it like this scene.

tions can most always be expected to decline whenever pines replace a good hardwood stand.

WHAT does the future hold for our natural swamps in North Carolina? From the North Carolina Soil and Water Conservation Needs Inventory of 1962 the future looks dim, unless corrective actions are enforced upon swamp drainage. Of the total 211 watersheds in North Carolina, 208 of them were found in need of "improvement." According to the "Watershed Box Score" made available by the North Carolina Soil and Water Conservation Committee, in 1968 North Carolina had submitted 83 applications for watershed improvement. Also, 115 watersheds were in the "priority for planning," "approved for operations," or "under construction" category. Nine watersheds had already undergone works of "improvement." In 1968, North Carolina ranked fourth in the nation in the number of watersheds approved for operations.

Recommendations to ameliorate the threat swamp drainage poses to our natural resources might include the following: (1) Prevention of complete swamp drainage when only better field drainage is needed. (2) Stronger mitigation measures for destroyed fish and wildlife populations. (3) More accurate education of farmers and the general public as to the detrimental and long term effects of swamp drainage projects. (4) Greater consideration given to the professional opinions of foresters and wildlife biologists. (5) The establishment of water banks. (6) More research be conducted on the effects of swamp drainage on all natural resources.

Steps must be taken to ensure that our swamps will be managed in an ecological manner. No longer can the soil conservationist consider only soil, the wildlife biologist consider only wildlife, and the forester consider only trees. All resource managers must unify their knowledge and consider all resources in a plan that will provide for future generations. Short-term, quick dollar projects must be viewed with caution. ✦

"So what? It's none of my business; let 'em chew up the swamps. And besides, I can't do anything about it. I've got problems of my own without sticking my neck out for a bunch of stagnant swamps." O.K., but don't say we didn't try to tell you.

PHOTO BY TOM JACKSON

OUTWARD BOUND

By Steve Price

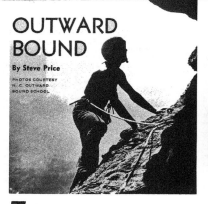

When a knot is the link between you and a tumble, you learn to tie one correctly. This rope bridge was a student project, and its maker is the first to cross; successfully, we might add.

THE school term is 26 days, and the courses include rock climbing, camping, fire-fighting, river-rafting and mountain rescue training.

The campus is the rugged Linville Gorge Wilderness area near Morganton, North Carolina, but activities may take place as much as 50 or 100 miles away—reached by cross-country hiking.

The students are high schoolers, college fraternity men, or even young executives. The average age is 19, but some may be in their 40's.

Sound challenging? Something to try this summer?

The name of the school is Outward Bound, and for the past 28 years it has been helping young men throughout the world discover greater self-awareness. more compassion and a deeper sense of responsibility through demanding wilderness experiences.

OUTWARD Bound came to North Carolina in 1967, and today it is one of but five such schools in the United States. The history of the program, however, actually dates to 1941, when famed European educator Dr. Kurt Hahn founded the first Outward Bound school in Aberdovey, Wales. Its purpose was to help train young merchant marine seamen to gain greater self-confidence and to better cope with the adverse conditions they often faced.

The idea spread rapidly and successfully, for today there are 26 Outward Bound schools in 13 free countries, including New Zealand, Australia, Germany, Malaya and Kenya. The American schools, located in Oregon, Colorado, Minnesota, Maine and North Carolina, are private, non-profit institutions each governed by an autonomous board of trustees. National headquarters is Outward Bound, Inc., of Andover, Massachusetts.

There are 35 members of the board of trustees for the North Carolina school. They include Rufus M. Dalton of Templon Spinning Mills, Inc,. chairman; Dr. Frederick S. Barkalow Jr., zoology professor at North Carolina State University; former governor Luther Hodges; and present Governor Bob Scott.

Director of the North Carolina school is 39-year old. Murray E. Durst, a graduate of San Jose State College and a long-time educator. He is assisted by a permanent staff of six other men, each well qualified for outdoor instruction and especially skilled in rock climbing and mountain rescue work, for these are two of the major training activities of the North Carolina school.

While Durst and his fellow adult leaders run the school, the responsibilities of the course are placed on the students. The instructors gradually place more and more duties on the students so that each one has the opportunity to discover his own potential in challenging situations.

And what situations they are!

"We start our day about 6 a.m.," Durst explains, "with a two or three mile run along mountain trails, followed by a cold water dip.

"From the very first day we begin teaching skills to help the student during the latter part of the course. This includes instruction in map and compass use, fire-fighting, woodsmanship, first-aid, unit organization and expedition planning.

"We have to work fast," Durst says, "because the students soon apply each new skill they have learned. They'll learn rope work in the morning and be climbing on rocks that afternoon."

Students occasionally have a chance to practice their fire-fighting and rescue training in real-life situations while the course is in progress. During the summer of 1968, Durst says, the students helped rescue a party stranded in Linville Gorge and also aided in fighting four forest fires, one of which nearly reached the Outward Bound headquarters.

Students plan and take two training expeditions with instructors and near the end of the 26-day course they make a final trek without the adult leaders. The students have three or four days to complete these hikes,

After practicing rope work in base camp, students move to the mountains to test what they have learned. Right, mountain rescue work by helmeted students. Falling rocks are often a hazard.

What is beyond for students of this rugged school? Whatever it is, chances are they will be better prepared for it. Even the Linville River is no match for the determined students.

which may range up to a hundred miles in length. Along the way they'll follow their own map routes and backpack all their supplies.

WHILE as many as 60 students may attend an Outward Bound course at once, they do not all work together. Upon arrival in base camp they are divided into nine to 12-man crews. A senior instructor and assistant are assigned to each crew, and work closely with them throughout the course. Each crew is generally a great cross-section of youth, coming from all walks of life. Some have traveled from as far away as California and Canada to attend the North Carolina school.

Sometime during the course the students are sent into the wilderness on what Durst believes is the high point of Outward Bound training. This is the "solo," during which each student experiences three full days living alone in the mountains. He carries with him a bare minimum of equipment that may include only a dozen matches, a knife, a plastic groundcloth and one day's rations. He will either live off the land or fast, but most of his time will be spent in deep meditation and self-examination. Here he will be alone from the de-

mands of society and able to set his own private goals.

Many students also believe the solo to be the highlight of their Outward Bound experience. As one North Carolina youth expresses it, "Outward Bound school was one of the greatest learning experiences of my life. Now I look at my problems as if they were mountains, and I know that I can ascend them."

Anyone may apply to Outward Bound. The minimum age is 16 but there is no maximum age. Good health and the desire to complete the course are the only other qualifications.

There will be six Outward Bound courses offered this year at the North Carolina school, running from June 7 through September 5. Cost of the course is $400, and this includes all necessary camping and mountaineering. equipment except boots, which Durst explains, "should be personally chosen by each student."

Limited and full scholarships are available from various organizations, including Outward Bound, Inc., in Andover. For additional information and applications to the North Carolina school, contact the North Carolina Outward Bound School, P. O. Box 817, Morganton, N. C. 28655. ✦

Island Camping

By Bodie McDowell

Left, Danny Gentry handles boat launching duty. Above, Ronald Yates takes a sleeping bag from son Eddie as another camp is made.

FAMILY camping means different things to different families.

To some, it is camping in a luxury type vehicle in an improved camping area that offers electricity and water on every site, to others it is simply pitching a tent and setting up in some remote area.

The Ronald Yates family of Lexington has camped in both of these type areas, and they prefer the latter. Their favorite out-of-the-way camping spot is any one of several islands in High Rock Lake, just a few miles from their home.

The island camping is primitive, and this is the way the Yates clan likes it. All camping gear and plenty of fishing tackle is taken across the lake by boat to an island that Ronald picks out in advance.

When the family of Ronald, Mrs. Yates and their son and two daughters make this trip, a large high powered outboard rig is used in order that everything that they need can be taken across in one trip.

But sometimes Mom and the girls stay home, and it is this type trip that young Eddie enjoys most. For then, he and his dad will take along one other adult male, and all the time is devoted to fishing.

Ronald takes a lot of short cuts when he is off on one of these fishing weekends with Eddie. Such luxuries as silverware and plates that call for a lot of dish washing are left behind, and the anglers use paper plates to eliminate some of the work.

Ronald and Eddie do their own cooking on these trips, and they don't carry along nearly so much cooking equipment as when Mrs. Yates and the girls camp with them. They just take along a big frying pan, a couple of pans and a coffee pot.

"We don't even bring a gas stove when the wife and girls don't come with us," Ronald said. "We just dig us a pit and cook over an open fire. We enjoy the cooking part of the trip, but not the cleaning up. We usually wait until we get back home and then give everything a good scrubbing."

Of course, he didn't say that he and Eddie did the actual cleaning of the cooking equipment when they return home, but hinted that Mrs. Yates and the girls did this chore.

As said before, fishing becomes the prime purpose of the trip for Ronald and Eddie, and they usually manage to catch enough white bass, largemouth bass, crappie and bream to have at least one meal of fresh meat during the trip. To the delight of Eddie, his dad usually takes along a few steaks for one meal.

Spinning tackle—both closed faced and open faced—is the favorite fishing equipment for Ronald and Eddie. Their lures vary from deep running lures for trolling to top water plugs for casting in the spring and fall. And they also use plastic worms in the heat of summer, fishing them deep for largemouth bass.

Their camping equipment on a father-son trip is very simple.

26

Camp appetites are always keen, and Ronald Yates prepares for hungry fishermen to come ashore for lunch. But too soon the tent must come down, the campsite cleaned, fire pit covered and then the trip home.

Just the basics with no frills. It consists of a tent, a sleeping bag for each person, the pots and pans, paper plates, an axe and one cooler for the perishable foods.

"We make out O.K. with just these items," Ronald said. "When the girls come along, it is quite different. Eddie and I can use the small fishing boat and bring everything we need in one trip, but when they come, we have to bring the bigger boat."

They always strive to bring everything t h e y n e e d, and enough of it so they don't have to head out to a store.

"We even bring along cookies and crackers and soft drinks for between meal snacks, so we are usually pretty well set," Ronald said. "Sometimes, though, we'll forget something, but this isn't a problem. We just hop into the boat and head up to the store. This usually is about a 20-minute run, but can be longer, depending on where we are camping."

These runs to the store are few and far between for this family, whether everyone is a-long or just Eddie and his dad. They learned long ago that meal planning is the one most important phase of getting ready for an island camping weekend, so they aren't often caught short.

"The way we do this is to plan each meal in advance by making a menu for every single break-fast, lunch and dinner," he said. "This is very important. So after we make the menus, we take what we need before going to the islands. After we are sure we have everything we need, we buy a few extras, just to make doub-ly sure we have enough."

In addition to the fishing, the Yates family likes island camp-ing better than setting up in a public camp ground because everything is much quieter.

"It's just so nice and quiet out there," he said. "This is especial-ly true at n i g h t. We just sit around and talk, and it is much more peaceful than in regular camping areas."

Yates is a collector of bottles, horseshoes and most any other unusual item, and the island camping has proved profitable for him in this respect. Walks on these islands have led the family to uncover an old well, arrowheads, one horseshoe that still had nails in it, and many unusual rocks.

"You see, before the lake was built all these lands were used for farming, and you can always find something if you'll just take the time to look around a bit," he said. "The kids started taking things home, and now we have a big collection of the different things they have found on the islands."

One unusual thing he found last summer was a large round spindle that had once been used for telephone cable. This spindle was put to good use as a table for their cooking and eating.

Yates insists on leaving an is-land as clean—or cleaner—than his family found it. For that rea-son, one of the first jobs on ar-rival is to dig a trash pit. On de-parture, the last job is to check the area for papers and cans, then fill in the pit.

So, if you are tired of being overcrowded in a public camp ground, you might do well to fol-low the example of the Yates clan. You know for sure that you will have the island all to your-self. What could make for a bet-ter family camping weekend? ♣

CRACKSHOTS and BACKLASHES by Rod Amundson

The human race has learned, the hard way, that all things that are feasible are not necessarily desirable. For example, the development of pesticides was entirely feasible, and at first seemed highly desirable, since the insects and diseases that attack plants threatened to destroy the world's food supply.

Now the pendulum of time and technology is swinging the other way. Food, world wide, has been so contaminated with DDT, Dieldren, etc., that our bodies have absorbed so much of this that if human flesh were a market commodity the Food and Drug Administration would declare it unfit for human consumption!

What about our wildlife? The introduction of coho salmon to Lake Michigan brought about a tremendous sport and food fishery. But recently the FDA confiscated several tons of salmon in Chicago because the fish contained so much accumulated pesticide poison their flesh was dangerous to eat. And these fish were headed for the dinner table!

Thousands of coho salmon died recently. The eggs hatched successfully, but when the tiny fish absorbed their yolk sacs they died. Lethal amounts of a pesticide had concentrated in the yolk sacs . . .

This real and growing problem is not confined to the United States. Following are some excerpts from the Conservation Foundation news letter. (The Foundation is located at 1250 Connecticut Ave., N.W., Washington, D. C. 20036)

One cannot help wondering how long it will be before bobwhite quail will eat enough insects killed or poisoned by pesticides to soften their egg shells to the point where parent birds crush the eggs, or die before they can lay eggs. How much insecticide-sprayed vegetation will rabbits or deer have to eat before they become sterile, or simply die from accumulated poisons?

North Carolina is still an agrarian state, and crop pests must be controlled. Some states have already banned the use of certain pesticides, others are soul-searching the problem. But isn't it up to the technology that developed present pesticides to develop equally effective ones that won't become concentrated in the organs and tissues of birds and mammals and humans?

THE ULTIMATE—NO SHELL

Scientific examination has shown that DDT residues cause a hormone induction in eagles and other birds which upsets calcium metabolism and produces egg shells too thin to protect embryos. Now, according to Alexander Sprunt IV, research director of the National Audubon Society, "the ultimate has been reached—no shell at all."

On April 13, Sprunt said, Audubon researchers found an eagle nest on the shores of Lake Superior in northern Michigan which contained the "ultimate"—no shell, just a membrane. The egg was apparently laid with only the membrane covering and, of course, did not survive. The discovery was made by Milwaukee ornithologist Daniel D. Berger and University of Wisconsin graduate student S. Postupalsky during research sponsored by the National Audubon Society.

Sprunt disclosed this latest finding from Audubon's eighth-year study of eagles at the society's annual meeting in St. Louis in late April. He said that "unless we ban DDT, the American eagle will become extinct." He also pointed out that "hard" pesticides such as DDT have caused similar eggshell problems in other species and have eliminated the peregrine falcon as a breeding bird in the eastern United States.

IT WORKS SLOWLY

Dr. Heinrich Mendelssohn of Tel Aviv University, describing one result of extensive use of the rodenticide thallium sulfate to prevent crop destruction by mice:

"It works slowly, causing paralysis, and causes the death of the mice after several hours or up to two days. As the poisoned mice move slowly on the surface of the ground, and have difficulty in reaching their burrows, they are easy prey to birds of prey . . . Beginning from the fifth day after the distribution of thallium bait, paralyzed and dead birds of prey were found in the fields . . . First the flight of the birds is labored and unsteady, then they are unable to fly but still are able to stand. Later they are unable to keep their wings in the normal posture and the wings droop, then the leg muscles become paralyzed, the bird is unabled to stand, it squats . . . leaning on the drooping wings and the tail. Soon it is unable to lift its head and eventually it lies prostrate on the ground and death soon follows . . . (This) may take between three to 10 days . . . Even partly paralyzed birds are unable to feed, (and) are unable to adopt the proper posture in case it rains; they become soaked, are unable to keep up thermoregulation and die of exposure." (13)

DILEMMA

Conflict over the use of pesticides is not always confined to agriculture. Authorities in Florida recently sought permission to spray DDT on patches of seaweed along the beaches, to control stable flies, a great nuisance to people in the area. But the In-

28

terior Department objected on grounds it would be extremely hazardous to the valuable Gulf shrimp population. The Department of Agriculture, says Harold G. Alford, assistant director of its Pesticides Regulation Division, denied permission for the DDT spraying. But the Florida Board of Health has been desperately urging that permission be granted because of the flies' effect on the valuable tourist business.

A MORAL HERE?

"In San Joaquin, Bolivia, a DDT malaria-control program aimed at mosquitoes had the side effect of killing off the numerous village cats. In the absence of the cats, there occurred an invasion of a wild small mouse-like mammal. This creature, unbeknownst to anyone, harbored the black typhus virus. Before this was discovered and the former chain could be restored, more than 300 villagers had lost their lives in plague . . . There is certainly a moral here for man who can no longer afford the single-minded innocence of his past when using dangerous chemicals."

—Stewart Udall in Scientific Aspects of Pest Control, National Academy of Science-National Research Council, 1969.

MAN'S FUTURE NOT SECURE

"We cannot say that the continued use of herbicides, insecticides and other biocides will lead to the eventual extermination of man. Neither, however, can we afford to rest easily. With uncontrolled use of poisons which have received little or no ecological testing, the future of man on earth cannot be considered secure."

—CF's Director of International Programs, Dr. Raymond F. Dasmann, "Vital Issues," April, 1969.

Bluebird Day?

Dear Sir:

Ref: May 1969 issue, page 28, "I Made A Bluebird Cry."

The apparent implications are:

1. Bluebirds will abandon a nest which has been visited by a human.

2. The Eastern Bluebird is extinct.

Both implications are incorrect. However, I am not referring to the presence or absence of the bluebird in North Carolina because I have not made such observations since spring of 1959, at which time bluebirds were being harassed by starlings in the vicinity of Charlotte.

Who are "they" who say "all bluebirds are gone?" Who are the "experts" who claim, "not a one could be found in all the land?" Bluebirds are not uncommon in north central Florida, and can be observed in groups of seven or more mature individuals. In that area they usually raise two broods each spring and with human help can raise a third brood.

I am not attempting to discount Mr. Carlton Morris' criticism of pollution of soil, water and air with permanent type insect poisons or with various industrial wastes. Doubtless the pollution problem is so critical in a long range view that we need not worry about any other problem if we are not going to solve the pollution problem. However, the struggle for survival is not yet a lost cause for humanity, or the bluebird.

My observation of bluebirds indicate that their most significant natural enemy is meat-eating ants. Obviously the supply of nest sites has been reduced by modern forestry practices and farm use of treated fence posts.

Some people in Tennessee who have made regular inspections of their personally-established route of bluebird houses have kept population records with aid of hinged roofs on the bird houses. These studies also indicated meat-eating ants to be a major killer of young bluebirds and have developed a bluebird aid program by dusting the eggs, young birds and nests with "Bee Brand Insect Powder." (Or at least that was the situation several years ago when that poison powder was not harmful to the birds. I do not know if any change has been made in that particular brand of poison in recent years.)

I solved the ant attack problem by nailing a small diameter rope around the post at base of bird house and soaking it with ant and roach poisons. I think the smear-on types are best for such outdoor use, such as Johnson's Ant and Roach poison.

The risk of snakes taking young birds can be reduced by keeping weeds around the nest cut down.

Instead of holding a funeral serv-

Turtle Nest

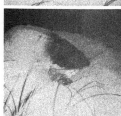

The nest building and egg laying of the giant sea turtle were captured on film by Malcolm Arey of Raleigh on a trip to the coast. The activity takes place at night above the high tide mark.

KNOW YOUR PROTECTOR

Jerry R. Rich

Wildlife Protector Jerry R. Rich, stationed at Lenoir in Caldwell County, was born July 30, 1940, in Mecklenburg County. He is the son of Mr. and Mrs. Robert G. Rich of Charlotte, North Carolina. Jerry graduated from Central High School, Charlotte, North Carolina, and attended N. C. State University for two years. Prior to employment with the N. C. Wildlife Resources Commission, Jerry served four years of active duty in SAC of USAF, stationed in Texas, Puerto Rico, and Arkansas.

Mr. Rich completed the Basic Recruit School for Wildlife Protectors at the Institute of Government in Chapel Hill, North Carolina. He was employed as a Wildlife Protector Trainee in November 1966, stationed in Roanoke Rapids. In October 1967, he was appointed Wildlife Protector and transferred to Southern Pines. Jerry has attended Pursuit Driving, Defense Tactics, Investigative Techniques, and First Aid Instructors' School. He is a member of the NRA.

Mr. Rich is married to the former Charlotte E. Osborn of Charlotte, N. C.

ice for bluebirds prematurely in North Carolina, why not dismiss Mr. Morris' "experts" and get busy helping the bluebird to increase its population. I think that can be accomplished with nest boxes which are properly constructed, positioned and guarded with insect poisons.

Sincerely,
J. D. Mac Gregor
604 Elm, Conway, S. C. 29526

Dear Sir:

I just read the story in the May issue by Carlton Morris, "I Made a Bluebird Cry."

He says there are no more bluebirds. I live on a farm just outside of Concord, and there are quite a few bluebirds here on the farm. I counted 7 at one time the other day and I can see one on a fence post several times a day when I look out the window towards the pasture. So please print this and let Mr. Morris know there are still bluebirds with us.

Very truly yours,
Clyde E. Carrigan
Concord

One of the 13 "Wildlife in North Carolina" TV programs is planned by host John R. Parker, Jr. (center), Duane Raver, left, and WTVD's George Phillips. The series is readied for this fall.

Of Tales and Tomes
by Jim Wood

BOOKS, one of man's most wondrous moldings, have changed little since their inception. Good ones come. Some bad ones follow. Always have. I could as easily get along without my gun, my tent, and even a few dove shoots as I could do without my books. I can't remember when I have camped without one. Maybe never. On the Chatooga River not long ago, not the smoothest river trip I know, I found room in the canoe for some reading and many the story I remember reading by a Coleman lantern pumped up so tight it was hissing like a mad possum.

Sometimes you don't get around to reading, there are immediate things that delay it. Things like a camp that has Taylor Crockett in it, one of the best hog hunters around. Taylor's reminiscing while he trims a section off a cured wild hog ham and slaps it onto a hot skillet will momentarily put the stops on any reading, and a lot of other things for that matter. Many good books show their covers each year, and at intervals longer than I like, a great one. New generations come to get acquainted with the world of outdoor writing, and a man that talks about books would be remiss in his task if he failed to mention the good new ones and to remember the old.

Great books are to be revered like great paintings. You will never find an outdoor book on the best seller lists, and that despite some of this country's great writing has been in the outdoor field. But I wonder often which books are the best loved. Any store handling old books has hundreds piled about, but you will dig all day turning over one book on hunting, nature, camping. A man keeps his outdoor books and when he's through with them he passes them on to someone who will love them as he did. To sell his treasures for a token sounds like a preposterous proposition to him indeed.

In the days of the Civil War a book was thrust on American outdoorsmen that they took to with gusto. And little wonder. "Game Fish of the Northern States of America" is the kind of book that causes such commotions. It gave them their money's worth certainly, it's knowledgable, readable, enough humor, a love for the woods and waters spills off all its pages. Robert Barnwell Roosevelt, his name for writing was Barnwell, was a pursuer of fish and a relentless one. But he did other things, a Democratic member of Congress, the Fish Commissioner in New York State, editor. If his talents at these things were as good as his fishing writing, then the country and New York fared well by his work.

The Abercrombie and Fitch library ferrets out these old and good books for reprint in their original form, and "Game Fish" is one of their late attempts. There is not much reason it shouldn't get as much reading as it once did, and with reward because it is good reading. Striped bass, the trouts, bluefish, haven't changed much in their ways since Barnwell's days. Only their wanderings have been diverted in many instances. His observations needn't be taken with a grain of salt because of their age. They are as valid and vital now as they ever were. Barnwell had a particular liking for the striper you soon gather. On using the lowly squid for striper bait, "The only bone in his body is in the middle of his stomach, and what it is put there for unless to give him an accurate idea of indigestion, no one knows".

Barnwell's one real dedication was to conservation, in a day when it was hard for most to see any use for it. He saw quickly even though fish were about thick enough to walk on, that undiminished careless use would beget tragedy to this nation's fisheries. He was never timid about spreading his thoughts on this subject. Barnwell pretty well summed up his feelings for fishing in not many words. "A tyro was once fishing in the same boat with me, using bait, when he struck his first trout. One can imagine how entirely misspent had been his previous existence, when it is said he had never taken a trout, no, nor any other fish before".

Some men's sheerest joy is tangling with an old bull bass, and amidst the flying of plugs and the accidental unloosing of a choice word, hoisting him from behind a stump for a fair fight in open water. The big game of fishdom? Ask the fellow who chases him, who would have written into the Constitution the pursuit of bass as an inalienable right of every man. The bass in most of its forms, especially black, is a revered word to him.

The perfect fish, that's what he is to Grits Gresham who wrote "The Complete Book of Bass Fishing" published by Harper and Row, and that's going way out on a limb with praise. But Grits Gresham is worrying little about it. There are too many fishermen standing back of him with some more bragging to do about the bass. Gresham pretty well pins down much of the lore of the bass in the book. There is more to know but "Bass Fishing" furnishes a good solid map of the bass' lair and ways to get him from it. The "Bass Fishing" chapter that intrigues me as much as any is the one that covers the artificial baits for the bass, the flies, streamers, the plugs and popping bugs, baits familiar to many of us who know them well, know what they do, but not much about how they got that way. Gresham has delved into some years long gone and come up with some interesting stuff, valuable to the bass man.

The famed Heddon lures, for instance, began under circumstances far more modest than present surroundings. Jim Heddon sat on a creek bank whittling one morning in the late 1800's. He absently threw a piece of stick into the water that he had cut off and was astonished to see a large bass try to gobble it. He carved more sticks, with some refinements, mounted hooks on them. Today—one of the greats in the lure making world.

All these bits of history, real gems for a man who wants to know all he can about bass fishing. No doubt Gresham is as bad to chase bass as most of us, and the real meat of this book is where and how to chase them and finally he touches on one of the most glorious positions for a bass, in a pan. Grits Gresham has some thoughts on bass worth listening to. ♦

THE GOLDEN RULE OF BOATING

Safety First

INSURES HAPPY DAYS AFLOAT

NATIONAL SAFE BOATING WEEK
June 29 - July 5, 1969

Raleigh N. C.
Doc.

Wildlife IN NORTH CAROLINA

25 CENTS / AUGUST 1969

Wildlife
IN NORTH CAROLINA ■

The official publication of the NORTH CAROLINA WILDLIFE
RESOURCES COMMISSION, Raleigh 27602. A monthly magazine
devoted to the protection and restoration of our wildlife resources
and to the improvement of hunting and fishing in North Carolina.

VOL. XXXIII, NO. 8   AUGUST, 1969

WILDLIFE IN NORTH CAROLINA recognizes the need
for close cooperation between State and Federal
conservation agencies and the people who hunt
and fish—to bring about a restoration of our renewable resources. The Editor gratefully receives
for publication news items, articles, and photographs dealing with the North Carolina out-of-
doors, but reserves the right to reject materials
submitted. Full credit is given for all materials
published.

* * *

WILDLIFE IN NORTH CAROLINA is published at the
Wildlife Resources Commission offices, Motor
Vehicles Building, 1100 New Bern Ave., Raleigh,
N. C. 27601.

* * *

Second class postage paid at Raleigh, North
Carolina 27602.

* * *

SUBSCRIPTION—One dollar per year, two dollars for two years. Make remittance payable to
WILDLIFE RESOURCES COMMISSION. Any
employee of the Wildlife Resources Commission
may accept subscriptions, or they may be forwarded to Post Office Box 2919, Raleigh, N. C.
27602. Stamps cannot be accepted.

Wildlife circulation this issue, 118,038.

IN THIS ISSUE

EDITORIAL STAFF

ROD AMUNDSON _ _ _ _ _ _ _ _ _ _ EDITOR
DUANE RAVER _ _ _ _ _ MANAGING EDITOR
LUTHER PARTIN _ _ WRITER-PHOTOGRAPHER
JOHN PARKER _ _ _ _ _ _ BOATING EDITOR
TOM JACKSON _ _ _ WRITER-PHOTOGRAPHER

The handsome sparrow hawk,
smallest of the American hawk
family, feeds largely on insects,
especially the lubber grasshopper. The sparrow hawk will
take a small bird occasionally,
but this little hawk certainly
poses not threat to game bird
populations. It, along with all
members of the hawk family,
is protected by North Carolina
law. Painting by Wade Walker.

PHOTO BY HUGH MORTON

Mildred

Mildred, Grandfather Mountain's somewhat tame "wild" bear, provides an interesting silhouette as she climbs one of the boulders beside the road leading to the top of Grandfather Mountain. Bears may be making a comeback here.

Deer Predation in North Carolina

and other

Southeastern States

Conclusion

by Frank B. Barick

Chief, Division of Game
North Carolina Wildlife Resources Commission
Presented at Southeastern Deer Symposium, Nacogdoches, Texas,
March 25, 1969.

PHOTO BY JACK DERMID

An uncontrolled bobcat population could increase to the point that it consumes half the annual deer reproduction on a given 15,000 acre area.

BOBCATS are the third most important predator on deer in the Southeast (after man and dogs). Thirteen "known" kills were reported for 1968 by North Carolina wildlife area managers and 151 "estimated" kills. Reports from ten of the eleven states responding to our questionnaire indicated an "estimated" 201 deer kills on 51 areas aggregating 2,906,985 acres. This indicates that the bobcat has been able to survive in good numbers in remote localities throughout the Southeast. It would appear that most "wild areas" of 10,000 acres or more have at least a few bobcats.

While some may question the ability of a 25-pound bobcat to kill a deer several times its own weight, there has been a sufficient amount of testimony to this effect from our own personnel to convince us that this does take place. Furthermore, review of the survey figures indicates that this has the potential of being a more serious problem than commonly suspected. While "known" bobcat kills of deer averaged only .4 per 15,000-acre area in western North Carolina, and this figure is only one-fourth the value derived for "known" dog kills, many of the dog kills were the result of races intercepted by the area manager. In contrast, cat kills are silent and usually in more remote localities than dog kills, and furthermore cats usually cover their kills thus making them even less likely to be discovered by man. Thus, it is not at all inconceivable that cat kills could approximate and even exceed dog kills on areas where the cat population is not kept under control.

The potential kill by bobcats may be further explored by considering that on those areas where cat control has been exercised the annual take of bobcats has ranged from one to 15, for an average of 4.5 per 15,000-acre area. On a few areas trapping has netted an average annual catch of six to ten cats per year. Thus, if annual reproduction of cats averages about 25 percent, the normal November population could average about 40 cats. The average of western North Carolina area managers' estimates of cat populations is a very reasonable 43 per 15,000-acre area.

We are thus led to the conclusion that an uncontrolled bobcat population *could* increase to the point that it consumes about half the annual reproduction of a 300-animal herd with a 25 percent reproductive rate on a 15,000-acre area. This level of drain, in addition to that due to stray dogs, would be capable of wiping out an established herd and certainly capable of preventing the establishment of a new herd.

In contrast to stray dogs, which are domesticated animals rather than a part of the native fauna, bobcats should be considered to have a rightful place on wildlife management areas. In addition to the interest they engender, they also serve a useful purpose in removing weak and diseased animals, thereby preventing disease outbreaks. Reasonable control could probably be exerted by classing them as game animals and restricting hunting to declared open seasons.

Predation by Other Predators

Predation on deer by panthers in the Southeast appears to be limited to the State of Florida. However, only one of the five Florida area reports showed the species present, with an estimated population of only five animals.

While bears are much more wide-spread, only a few North Carolina area managers listed them as potential predators. Only one "known" kill was reported and another report indicated fawn hooves in the spoor of a bear. The relatively low population of bears and the fact that their season of heavy feeding is in late summer leads us to discount the species as a serious predator of deer. In our opin-

this average value is not especially significant, individual values on some areas were very substantial. For example, 12 known car mortalities on a 7,000-acre area in Missouri made up 37 percent of the annual drain. In Arkansas, miscellaneous mortalities, mostly due to cars, accounted for 16 percent of the annual drain on eight reporting areas. On a 42,000-acre area in Tennessee, misceallaneous mortalities accounted for 26 percent of the annual drain. They accounted for 27 percent of the annual drain on a 100,000-acre area in Mississippi, and 30 percent on a 14,000-acre area in Oklahoma. Virginia data showed a statewide loss to vehicles of 1,502 deer in 1967.

Illegal Kills and Unretrieved Legal Kills

Deer hunting on North Carolina wildlife management areas covered by this report is by daily permit and hunters are required to submit their bag for examination when they leave the area. Hence a complete record is secured of all legal kills. The areas have well developed road and foot trail systems in which the overall objective of having no part of any area more than one-fourth mile from developed access has been brought to near accomplishment. Thus, it may be presumed that there are relatively few unretrieved kills.

Illegal hunting is held to a minimum by intensive patrolling, at the average rate of one wildlife protector per 15,000 acres. Boundaries are painted and posted with appropriate signs and large entrance signs are placed at major points of entry. Hunting and use restrictions are substantially more severe than those applying to adjoining "non-refuge" public lands. Enforcement of hunting regulations on "non-refuge" lands by "county" protectors averages about 200,000 acres per protector. Thus, intensity of protection on the management areas is about 13 times as great as throughout the state generally.

In spite of this intensive development and protection, there is a substantial loss to illegal hunting throughout the year and to illegal kills during the hunting season. In addition a substantial number of legally killed deer are not retrieved. On 23 manned areas in the western part of North Carolina averaging 15,000 acres each, an average of 4.3 people were arrested per year for hunting deer illegally. The "known" loss to illegal hunting other than during the hunting season averaged 2.0 and the "estimated" average loss was 8.0 deer per year. The "known" loss due to illegal deer kills during the hunting season averaged 3.4 per area and the "estimated" number was 14. The "known" loss due to unretrieved legal kills averaged 3.2 deer per area and the "estimated" loss averaged 9.1.

Thus the total drain due to illegal hunting and unretrieved kills was estimated to average 31.1 deer per 15,000 acres per year. This amounted to 40 percent of the checked out legal kills which averaged 77 per 15,000 acres. This is also three times the loss to stray dogs and five times the loss to bobcats. Thus, more deer are wasted by sloppy and

PHOTO BY JACK DERMID

Unretrieved legal kills accounted for over 250 deer on North Carolina Wildlife Management Areas during the period covered by this report.

ion, bear feeding on deer is probably limited to carrion consumption.

Foxes were listed as suspect by several North Carolina area managers but none reported any "known" kills. Similarly, coyotes were listed as predators by area managers in several other states but none reported any deer kills by them.

Six of eight Arkansas wildlife area managers reported substantial populations of wolves but only two of the six indicated predation on deer. In one case an estimated population of 170 wolves was shown as killing an estimated 20 deer on a 150,000-acre area. On another slightly smaller area the wolf population was estimated at 185 and their predation on deer at 12. There were no cases of "known" kills of deer by wolves reported.

Miscellaneous Mortality

Deer mortality by running into m o t o r.i z e d vehicles was reflected at significant levels in most states. It is felt that this type of mortality is probably more obvious than that due to other causes and it is likely that these mortalities are much higher on less remote deer range than that of wildlife management areas covered by this study. Of 994 deer mortalities due to miscellaneous causes in eleven southeastern states, 73 percent were attributed to cars, 12 percent to fences, five percent to trains, two percent each to falling off cliffs and tick bite, one percent each to drowning and disease and three percent due to unknown causes and a trace each to cold water shock and study collections.

The overall average of these deaths on all southeastern areas was 4.6 per 15,000 acres per year. In a herd of 300 animals reproducing at the rate of 25 percent per year this would amount to a little over six percent of the annual increment. While

illegal hunting than through both dog and bobcat predation combined. Man is not only the most effective predator but also the most wasteful.

Legal Harvest

Legal harvest of deer on southeastern wildlife management areas open to hunting accounts for only a little over half of the annual drain. On some areas it is estimated to be as low as 14 percent of the annual drain while on others it is estimated to be 98 percent. On about three-fourths of the areas it ranged between 40 and 80 percent of the annual drain.

We feel that one of the primary objectives of management is to insure that as much as possible of the annual drain be in the form of legal harvest. In examining the data from areas showing low percentage of legal harvest the major competing factors were cited as illegal hunting and stray dogs in all cases and, in addition, highway kills in some cases, and other predators in others.

In view of the fact that only a little over half the annual drain is consumed by legal hunting on these intensively protected areas, it is interesting to speculate what proportion is taken by legal hunting in less protected localities. In regions where hunting regulations are not sufficiently stringent and where the protection staff is inadequate, legal kills may constitute less than ten percent of the annual drain.

In our opinion an "ideal" ratio of legal kills to annual drain would be about 85 percent, with about ten percent going to unavoidable kills such as vehicle collisions and another five percent going to wild predators such as bobcats.

Components of Annual Drain

The primary predator, other than man, in North Carolina, is the uncontrolled dog. The only other predator listed by area managers was the bobcat but some also suspected the black bear and foxes.

Dogs and bobcats were listed as the primary predators in the other states responding to our questionnaire. Wolves were cited in a few western states of the southeast region and coyotes were suspected in several. It is interesting to note that only one state (Florida) listed panthers.

Other causes of mortality were cars, fences, trains, drowning, cliffs, ticks, cold water shock, and disease. No states listed starvation.

We find that hunting by man accounts for 85 percent of the annual drain but only 63 percent is legal harvest. The other 22 percent is taken illegally or lost in the woods. Predators account for an average of 8.5 percent of the annual drain with free-running dogs getting six percent and bobcats only two percent. Miscellaneous mortalities account for 6.3 percent with cars killing five percent and the remainder succumbing to a variety of causes.

Further examination of the percentage composition of annual drain indicates that the pattern in regard to predation is rather varied. Estimates of loss to dogs range from 0 to 30 percent of the annual drain. Estimated values for miscellaneous mortality ranged from 0 to 55 percent and their individual values averaged about the same as those of losses to dogs. Estimated losses to wild predators also ranged from 0 to 55 percent of the annual drain on individual areas but they averaged only about one-third of the magnitude of losses to dogs or miscellaneous kills.

A questionnaire survey of 79 wildlife management areas in 11 southeastern states indicates that predation on deer is largely limited to free-running

Magnolias, Mockingbirds and Moonlight

by Charlotte Hilton Green

IN my woodland are a couple of seedlings. I feel the dark, glossy leaves—and wonder. What a strange thing is a tree—especially this one, the great *Magnolia grandiflora*—and what it has meant to the South.

Magnolia and moonlight and mockingbirds that poets and romanticists h a v e rhapsodied over. Yet there is much more to claim our interests—if we have inquiring m i n d s. *Magnolias!* What a place in history, and not just the history of the South. As far as we know, so botanists claim, the *Magnolia* was the first of the flowering trees. Its large, perfect flowers, fragrant and white, are borne solitary on the ends of twigs, sometimes six to eight inches across, even larger.

Strange as it may seem to us, this delicate, fragrant, aristocratic-looking blossom is our most primitive flower. This, according to modern botanists, is based upon the fact that the flower is large, radial in symmetry, with all flower parts present and all distinct: separate sepals, separate petals, separate pistils, separate stamens.

And contrasts! Beneath my four-foot magnolia seedling is a small golden flower, common and abundant, that in childhood lore "buttons down the grass." Classed as a "weed" it is found in all continents, growing throughout the spring and summer. *Taraxacum officinale*—t h e common dandelion. Yet, according to Dr. B. W. Wells, in *The Natural Gardens of North Carolina*, "m o s t

botanists recognize the dandelion as the most highly specialized plant in the world. One of its peculiarities is that it has given up reproduction by pollination and fertilization, the seeds develop normally without these processes."

The most primitive and the most highly developed flowers growing together in my woodland. Romance indeed—a n d beauty—and history. Ancient history, indeed.

But that is not all that intrigues us about *Magnolia grandiflora*. Once upon a time, in the geologic long-ago, in what is known as the *Cenozoic Period*, *Magnolias* grew even beyond the Arctic C i r c l e. *Magnolias in Greenland!* We know they existed there by the story the rocks tell us. And the reason we have them—and many more kinds, or species of trees than has Europe, is because they learned to *migrate*, or retreat, before the advancing glaciers of the Ice Age. Once upon a time *Magnolias* grew not only in our own Arctic, but also over much of North America and the midcontinental plain of Europe. Fossil forests showing the trunk, leaves, even seed cones of these trees have been found in rocks.

What happened? Into the warm northern land came the searing, bitter cold. No one knows what brought this about, though there are many theories. What we DO know is that great ice sheets, sometimes nearly a mile high, formed and moved

slowly, relentlessly, southward. And as these sheet-like glaciers spread slowly, slowly, SLOWLY southward, all life, both plant and animal, was either destroyed —or forced to retreat before them.

Even before the approaching ice mass reached them, its chilling influence killed the trees on the northen side of the forest belt. Remember, though, this was a slow process—taking thousands of years for the great ice sheets to advance. And always, somewhat ahead of them, trees and other forms of plant life, as well as animal life, were retreating. Or dying out.

And so our magnolias—and many, many other kinds of trees and plants—grew, bore seeds, and scattered those seeds by various agencies: birds, animals, the winds and waters. Some that were scattered southward took root, grew to maturity, and in their turn bore seeds that were scattered—some, thanks being, southward. Thus generation after g e n e r a t i o n of these trees, through hundreds and thousands of years, gradually moved southward, or "migrated" ahead of the slowly advancing ice towards a life-giving chance in the warm Southlands.

But why magnolias here—and not in Europe? And WHY do we have more species of trees than has Europe, which once had many more than she has today? *Look at the maps.* Our great mountains systems, the Rockies and the Appalachians, *extend mainly north and south*, thus presenting no barrier to this southern migration of trees and other plant life. And Europe? Note *her* main mountain ranges —the Alps, the Pyrenees, the Carpathians—extended *a c r o s s* the path of the advancing ice. And the trees could not retreat before it. They grew as far up the mountains as they could—and there d i e d from cold. Thus Europe lost hundreds of her tree species.

And the South—to fully appreciate its Magnolias, moonlight, mockingbirds, and migration— must add "and mountains." ◆

Establishing Good, New Stands of Southern Hardwoods

By J. S. McKnight
Southern Forest Experiment Station
Forest Service
U. S. Department of Agriculture
Stoneville, Mississippi

This is the fourth of a series of five articles on hardwood management by Mr. J. S. Mc-Knight. We are reprinting these articles which first appeared in the **National Hardwood Magazine**, because of the importance of hardwoods to wildlife. Many of Mr. McKnight's findings and recommendations in regard to hardwood management are applicable in North Carolina. We invite the attention of landowners to profit from these articles since more emphasis on hardwood production in North Carolina would be highly beneficial to wildlife.

OVERCUTTING was not the major cause for the current shortages of high-quality hardwood logs. Failure to provide for good new stands when old ones were cut, and high-grading, which amounts to the same thing in the long run, were the real culprits, and they are still with us today. Landowners must learn to establish adequate new stands, if we are ever to balance growth and cut in our hardwood-supply b o o k s. Two approaches are necessary: silviculture that encourages the best possible young stands to develop naturally, and supplemental planting plus intensive care.

New Natural Stands

The four formal silvicultural systems that are adapted for reproducing southern hardwood are clearcutting, shelterwood cutting, group selection, and seed trees. Each system is designed for particular species and circumstances. It should be recognized, however, that these systems are not substitutes for management throughout the life of the stand. They are designed simply to establish young trees when old ones are harvested, and thereby assure a perpetual sustained yield of wood from the land. Where an adequate amount of desirable growing stock is present, there is no need for a new stand.

*Reprinted from NATIONAL HARDWOOD MAGAZINE, volume 42, number 5, pages 46-47. May 1968.

Good new stands of mixed hardwoods can be established by clear-cutting either the entire stand or large areas in it. For this method to succeed, however, either adequate seed must be present or assured, or seedlings or rootstocks must already be on the ground. In addition, competing vegetation must be eliminated to permit small trees to develop.

All too often, cull and weed trees occupying the understory of a mature hardwood stand are overlooked. This stand component must be totally removed, if desirable young trees are to get an adequate start. When one leaves this component, he is not practicing silviculture; he is doing a modern form of high-grading. Little valuable wood will be produced in the new stand until the weed trees grow old and die. Where vines grow lushly, they too must be reduced to get an adequate new stand.

Shelterwood cutting is often the best choice for heavy-seeded species such as oaks. In this method, all understory trees and many of those in the overstory are removed in the first cut to admit sufficient light for seedlings to establish themselves. After desirable young trees are established, the remaining overstory trees, which have been a source of seeds and shelter, are removed in one or more cuts. The shelterwood system is not recommended for species that re-

quire direct sunlight during the seedling stage.

The group-selection method is well adapted to mixed forests, particularly where patches of young trees are being nurtured to maturity and maximum value. Openings with a minimum size of about 1/5 acre are created for new young trees by removing groups of trees that are mature or undesirable. The minimum size of opening is dependent mainly upon the height of the surrounding trees. The immature trees in the rest of the stand are thinned and weeded. Thus, maximum growth and seeds for the new stand are obtained from desirable trees.

The seed-tree system is used primarily to establish light-seeded species over large areas. Generally, 8 to 12 well-spaced seed trees are left per acre. As with clear cutting, cull and weed trees must be eliminated. Since bare, mineral soil is usually required for prompt seed germination and seedling establishment, some form of site preparation is often necessary. To reproduce cottonwood, for example, the site may require trenching to retain moisture. To date, little success has been achieved in reestablishing stands of species other than cottonwood from seed trees, and the system is not generally recommended.

Planting or Seeding

Many landowners have open

fields, large cleared areas, places where attempts to establish natural stands have failed, or tracts that should be converted from one type of forest to another. In many such situations, planting is the answer.

Hardwood planting has not been encouraged in past years for two reasons. First, until recently, there was a surplus of small hardwoods; second, experimental successes were few. Rules of thumb, such as "Never plant hardwoods on open fields," have discouraged commercial-s c a l e planting.

Recently, however, a number of plantations of cottonwood and sycamore have been established in the South. In addition, yellow-poplar plantations and pilot-scale plantings of sweetgum and oaks are thriving on appropriate sites.

Domestic livestock often destroy young trees. Cattle and horses browse hardwoods heavily, and hogs gorge on acorns and dig up young seedlings to get at tender roots. Exclusion of domestic animals from areas that are being reforested, therefore, is almost always beneficial. Overpopulations of deer have also destroyed the young trees in many areas. A biological balance achieved by joint planning between wildlife and forest managers appears to be the b e s t solution to such a problem.

Although a great deal remains to be learned about hardwood planting, success hinges on five practices: (1) careful choice of sites, (2) good site preparation, (3) selection and care of planting stock, (4) tending of plantations to keep competition to a minimum, and (5) protection from animals. Much useful information has been presented in publications which are available on request from the Southern Forest Experiment Station, T-10210 Federal Building, 701 Loyola Avenue, New Orleans, Louisiana 70113. ◆

Commercial cutting of hardwood forests often leaves a jungle of useless vegetation that must be eliminated to establish good new stands of usable timber.

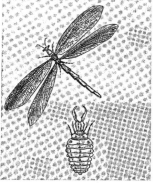

The Doodlebug

by Frank Mooney

THE awesome, sword-like jaws reached up through the sand to grasp its hapless victim in a death-like h o l d shaking and slamming it violently upon the ground. Locked in a death struggle, the opponent twisted in mid-air trying desperately to bite its tormentor, but the powerful vise-like jaws continued to bite and shake the dazed prey. The fight was much like an angry boxer and an unlucky tomcat. Slowly the life left the victim as it was pulled beneath the sand where the succulent fluid would be sucked from its body. The slight

The ant lion larva may take 1-3 years to develop into the relatively harmless flying adult. The photo shows the pits used to gather food during this time.

pulsation in the funnel-shaped trap was the only reminder of the death drama.

One would think of this savage battle taking place in an un-civilized jungle far removed from mankind; however, this mayhem took place beside a picnic table which was located only a few feet from a paved highway. These tooth and claw battles go on around us everyday and night in the animal world, yet at times it is hard to realize amid the usual tranquility of nature.

What I had witnessed was an everyday occurrence of life and death in nature's outdoor setting. An ant had tumbled into a sandy death trap made by an ant lion, or better known as the doodle-bug. These funnel-shaped sand traps go unnoticed by a lot of outsiders, but for ants and other small creatures this can be their doom. Most anywhere there is loose, sandy soil the ant lion makes these shallow depressions, that can quickly be a small creature's last mistake. A favorite place is among several ant cavities where the chances are good that some busy ant will stumble into the pit.

The ant lion is similar to a spider in appearance with a humped back and three legs on each side, with a small head equipped with two fierce looking jaws. This savage p r e d a t o r spends its life beneath the soil with only the jaws exposed for a quick meal. When making a death trap, this critter moves backward into the sand while flinging sand into the air with its head. Swiftly working in a circle while throwing out the sand with a toss of long jaws, a death trap has been cleverly excavated where the sand will shift when anything falls into the cavity. When a victim is in danger of escaping, the ant lion starts a sandstorm by throwing the sand from the bottom of the pit by slinging its head from side to side thus hurling the sand from the trap. This causes the prey to slide back into the funnel. One day I saw a beetle several times larger than an ant lion trapped in a sand pit by one of these pre-

dators that had one of its legs in a death-like grip.

One balmy, Spring day along the cypress studded banks of the Black River, I dropped off Cecil Reaves and Paul Council with one-man boats to bug the tur-bulent waters for robin that in-habit this scenic river, with a promise to pick them up about two miles downstream. Before reaching the car, I noticed some unusually large ant lion cavities. There were several among the ant nest that dotted the hillside. Fishing had been slow that day so I was in no hurry to start fish-ing again. With the solitude and tranquillity that comes only with close association with nature I ambled up the steep bank to where the busy ants were carry-ing on their private world.

After a long wait, a carpenter ant fell into a sand trap and was grabbed instantly by s h a r p, strong jaws. Now the carpenter ant is a large strong-jaw creature himself, and the struggle was on a more even scale. The doodlebug dragged the ant almost beneath the sand, but the ant finally suc-ceeded in locking its jaws into the doodlebug and broke free. Quickly it raced up the pit and almost made it, but the loose sand made treacherous footing with the ant lion making a sand-storm. The fight continued, but the large ant bit the predator again and the second try made a mad dash over the lip of the trap.

The ant lion is known most everywhere as doodlebug. Young children in their gay fashion have knelt beside these funnel-shaped cavities blowing gently into the pit and saying "doodle-bug, doodlebug, your house is on fire."

With a little observing and teaching, children can grow up living among and enjoying our bountiful nature. Like the old saying, "you can't see the forest for the trees" people go about their busy life with all of na-ture's wonders so close, yet it goes unnoticed. The next time that you are close to nature, stop and look around, there will be some life or death drama for you to witness . . .

Over 500 Lake Norman fish have been tagged by the Wildlife Commission using tiny plastic tags like this. Tag return stations are located at most marinas and access points around the lake. Envelopes are provided here.

ATTENTION FISHERMEN

it is an "official tag return station." Tags may also be returned by mailing them to: William D. Adair, Fishery Biologist, North Carolina Wildlife Resources Commission, Box 2919, Raleigh, N. C. 27602.

When the tag is returned, records of the tag number and date and place of capture should be supplied. Special envelopes can be obtained at tag return stations to record this information or a slip of paper can be included with the tags returned to Raleigh.

Knowing the place and date a fish was tagged and then recaptured, the biologist can determine how far that fish traveled and how long it took to get there. This information will help increase our knowledge of fish migration. And you can help. ✦

TROUT

Which Fork at the Crossroads?

by Dr. Frederic F. Fish
Assistant Chief,
Division of Inland Fisheries

ABOUT a year ago, *Wildlife** developed the thesis that economics, if nothing else, will soon force a decision in the dilemma between the increasing number of trout fishermen on one hand, and the skyrocketing costs of the current trout management program on the other. *Wildlife* then announced a joint interdivisional study of the Tarheel trout fishery and ended on the optimistic note: "hopefully, we will see the answer to trout fishing in the future more clearly one year hence than we do right now".

The first year of that programmed two-year study is now history and we do indeed see things in much better perspective—albeit still much remains to be learned.

One important facet of this study was the solicitation of spontaneous opinions from the trout fishermen themselves as to what *they* thought should be done. Almost 6,000 self-addressed, return-postage-paid postcards were mailed last Labor Day to individuals selected at random from the list of 1968 Special Trout License purchasers. An accompanying letter asked the recipient if, in the interest of improving his trout fishing, he would fill in on the postcard the total number of trout he brought home during the 1968 season, his estimate of the total time spent fishing for them, and any opinion he might care to voice about just what the Commission might do to improve trout fishing? About 1,200 of the recipients responded.

Some of the opinions received might prove a bit difficult to carry out—such as "fewer snakes", "just teach me how to fish", "find a way to stock trout streams, those we now have are too crowded", and "dissolve private ownership of streams." One fisherman apparently had concluded he was not receiving full value on his license investment when he wrote "do away with fishing licenses and return the natural resource of trout back to the people

*See "Trout at the Crossroads", Wildlife in North Carolina, April, 1968.

and stop selling the people what is theirs."

By and large, however, the suggestions offered much food for thought. Considering that the suggestions were completely spontaneous in origin, the facts that: so many as one fisherman out of every six responding wanted more fish stocked (apparently oblivious to the fact that the trout hatcheries now are operating at peak capacity and, until the trout fisherman will accept his full share of the production costs, the Commission cannot afford to build more capacity); one in twelve wanted the trout stocked in the fall "so they can adapt by spring" (a popular concept that refuses to die in spite of the fact it was proven fallacious many years ago); one in twelve wanted more patrolling of the trout streams (all the protectors the Commission can afford are now working some very long hours during the trout season); and one out of every twenty wanted the stocked fish "spread out" when liberated (the previous statement goes for the hatchery personnel as well)—all seem indicative of weaknesses either in the Commission's program of education or in its trout management.

Perhaps the most significant conclusion of all to be derived from the many suggestions received is that among the trout fishermen themselves there is no consensus concerning what effective trout management should be! Some respondents wanted more fingerlings stocked but others recommended stocking fewer, but larger, trout. A fair number wanted the use of treble hooks restored but just as many wanted only fly fishing. Many wanted the creel limit increased but, at the other extreme, a very sizeable group wanted it reduced. Several recommended more general use of live baits, but many more wanted live baits prohibited altogether.

From the wide diversity of opinions expressed, it became perfectly apparent that the only basis for the Commission's trout management program must be the welfare of the fish themselves and that universal approbation of the fishermen is hopeless of attainment. What is good for the fish will, in the long run, be best for the fisherman and, through education and experience, most of the fishermen themselves ultimately will come around to this point of view.

Two points, each of crucial significance in North Carolina's trout management program emerged from facts so far developed in this study: 1) the contribution made by hatchery-propagated yearling trout to the total annual trout harvest is minor at best; and 2) biologically, North Carolina's "Native Trout" philosophy of catch restriction is serving its intended function—at least within the limits of time and place of this study.

Concerning the first point, the estimated contribution to the total trout harvest made by hatchery-propagated yearling trout simply will not support a contention that hatchery fish of this size constitute essential protection against extermination of the wild trout. Wild trout are exterminated by destruction of their habitat and, while fishing suc-

The attempt at stocking designated trout waters five or more times a year overloads available hatchery equipment to the point where stocking the trout consists of dumping them into a very few pools close to the roads.

cess may be greatly reduced through intensive hook-and-line fishing, the fish themselves will not be exterminated. Hatchery-propagated yearling trout are just too expensive a commodity to be employed merely as insurance for the wild trout which are perfectly capable of fending for themselves.

Unquestionably, releasing prior to opening day approximately one-fourth of all the yearling trout to be stocked during the entire season is extremely wasteful. For the most part, these protected hatchery products are expected to remain near the site of their liberation—with neither food nor shelter—for as long as seven weeks waiting to be caught. Population pressure alone can be expected to force many of these newcomers to migrate downstream, for few of them can compete successfully against the more resourceful wild trout. At that time of the year, congenial trout habitat exists downstream all the way to salt water. With the onset of warm weather, however, any migrants forced downstream will be trapped as the upper temperature limits tolerated by trout advance upstream faster than the fish can return. The occasional trout authentically reported caught from Badin and Tillery Reservoirs on the Yadkin River, far below the normal limit of trout water, probably is a hatchery release forced into a downstream migration.

The attempt at stocking most designated trout waters at least five times a year—including some so remote that even the wildlife protectors will not get to them during the season—overloads available equipment and manpower to the point where stocking trout must consist merely of dumping all the fish into one, or at best a few, of the pools immediately adjacent to the highway. Here, the newly liberated fish are extremely vlunerable and the effects upon catch rates—which may reach a level of 10 trout per hour of fishing—are obvious. "Truck chasing" by predatory anglers offers a reasonable explanation for the atypically large number of anglers, as well as the undesirably high catch rates,

so apparent on the more popular trout streams most days they are stocked.

Stocking a stream, usually with a six-weeks ration of trout in one batch, inevitably results in an immediate, extremely temporary, and undesirably high catch rate which falls almost as rapidly as it increased. The word seems to get around for, where records are available, one can pick out the days when the stream was stocked merely by the peaks in the number of anglers present. All of these facts add up to the distasteful conclusion that the relatively infrequent and large trout releases which equipment and manpower limitations require be restricted to the immediately accessible stream reaches provide a piscatorial bonanza to the truck chaser but not much to the angler who arrives several days later.

Sound economics, as well as effective fish management, dictate that hatchery-propagated yearling trout be stocked in such manner, and only in such situations, where a maximum return to the angler is assured and adequate protection can be provided. However, even if these high-priced fish are stocked frequently and in relatively small numbers so as to maintain uniform catch rates, and the effort is applied only in accessible waters where laws can be adequately enforced, still the contribution of these fish to the total trout harvest will remain a fraction of the total number of yearling trout that the hatcheries can produce.

The maximum annual producing capacity of the Commission's trout hatcheries combined approaches 400,000 yearling trout. The Federal hatcheries have contributed an additional 350,000 yearling trout each year for stocking North Carolina trout waters. In other words, with luck and everything stretched to the limit, about 750,000 yearling trout can be produced and stocked each year. If these were liberated under the ideal conditions described above, probably not more than four-fifths of the number released would ever be caught. So, the trout hatcheries we now have possess a potential contribution of some 575,000 trout to the annual harvest. The study data of last year led to an estimate that the total number of trout caught in 1968 was somewhere between 2,160,000 and 3,326,000— with 2,743,355 being the most probable number. In other words, the most State and Federal hatcheries combined could contribute would be about one fish for every five caught.

Now the argument must be conceded that highly successful anglers tend to reply to questionaires whereas the less fortunate ones keep silent (a definite possibility that will be explored this year) and therefore this estimate is inflated. But, assuming that the harvest estimate quoted above does miss the true value by an extremely wide margin, still the conclusion seems inescapable that the *wild fish* are supplying the bulk of the trout harvest. If this conclusion is tenable, the effective protection of the wild trout resources is the obvious key to the future of trout fishing in North Carolina.

The second point of major significance apparent at this time in the study is the biological success of the "Native Trout" philosophy of catch restrictions. Within the time and place of the data recorded so far, the total catch rates on every "Native Trout" stream consistently remain at a satisfactory level between two and three fish per hour, with the concurrent "take-home" catch rate consistently being about one-tenth the total catch rate. How long these streams could sustain these catch rates, or how acceptable the entire philosophy may be to the general trout fisherman, cannot be answered with these data, but both questions are receiving continuing study. At the present time, however, all evidence points to the facts that North Carolina's "Native Trout" catch restrictions will sustain a high level of "fun-fishing", some take-home catch, and involve little risk to the wild trout resources.

Considering the ominous threat to the future of trout fishing arising from the constantly increasing number of trout fishermen, that is about the most security a fisheries administrator can hope to find.

P.S. In case anyone should be interested, there are still available a very few copies of the first-year report of the Commission's Trout Study.

The maximum annual production of the Wildlife Commission's trout hatcheries approaches 400,000 yearling fish like these (top to bottom, rainbow, brown and brook). Federal hatcheries contribute an additional 300,000 trout and it is estimated that no more than 80 percent of this total are ever caught. Hence of the almost 3 million trout caught last season from Tarheel waters, the hatcheries contributed about one trout for every five caught.

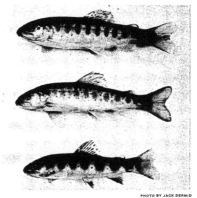

A Morsel in Disguise

by Jim Tyler

Division of Commercial and Sports Fisheries
Dept. of Conservation and Development
Photos by the Author

That sandpaper-skinned rascal that puffs itself up with air when taken from the water; that no-good, dumb looking fish that wastes your time, bait, and temper . . . but hold on a minute. You will not believe it until you try it, but there is some fine eating meat on the puffer (sometimes called blowfish or swelltoad).

"It's just like chicken breast right up next to the bone," says Bobby Dudley, a commercial fisherman and dealer at home in Beaufort.

"Trouble is," Bobby continued, "people don't know how to skin them." So he showed how. Workers in the Dudley Seafood Plant (owned by Bobby and his father, Roy) can get 70 to 100 pounds of meat an hour.

Put on gloves and hold fish by head, slipping knife through skin and meat behind head. Stop blade before it cuts through belly skin. Below, still holding onto head, lift fish up and use blade to tuck tail under, toward you. Then lower the jack-knifed carcass to the wooden surface and anchor meat with blade.

Pull the head; skin and viscera follow along. You might have to move the blade toward you a couple of times for a solid hold as you pull everything clear. You end up with a chunk of meat that is ready for cooking. Some people prefer to remove the backbone before cooking. Below, Dudley packages processed puffers for shipment.

Salty Rock

by Jim Tyler

*The striped bass or rockfish
leads a double life: he is important to both the sport and
the commercial fisherman. It is up
to us to see that he prospers long.*

Dept. of Conservation and Development Photos

A STRONG competitor and excellent eating, the striped bass (or rockfish) is fair game for both commercial and sport fishermen. In North Carolina this handsome fish, easily recognized by prominent black stripes and that bassy look, can be found year-round somewhere in Albemarle Sound and Pamlico Sound or their tributaries. A few call the Cape Fear River home, and you can even find some land-locked in select inland reservoirs. During winter months you can find stripers in the ocean along the beaches from Cape Lookout north to the Virginia line.

Sporters After Rock

Stripers are definitely one of the glamour fishes. When stripers are hitting, outdoor sections of newspapers seldom fail to carry photos and accounts of successful anglers and their prizes. And it doesn't take many trips to the newsstand to see that popular fishing magazines go strong on striper fishing.

From 1960 to 1965 the number of salt-water anglers in the continental United States catching striped bass increased by 26 percent to total 866,-000, according to a 1965 estimate by the U. S. Bureau of Sports Fisheries and Wildlife (the 1965 Salt Water Angling Survey) which is the latest conducted by the Bureau. Even with more fishermen trying for stripers, their success ratio showed a healthy increase with an estimated 18,251,000 caught in 1965.

Along the Atlantic coast, 79 percent of the stripers were caught in New England and New York, 17 percent from New Jersey to Cape Hatteras, and four percent from Cape Hatteras to and including Florida, according to the 1965 estimate.

Information on North Carolina striper anglers is sketchy. Dr. William Hassler, professor of zoology at North Carolina State University, who studies striped bass and fishermen who catch them in Albemarle Sound and its tributaries, reports an estimated 67,000 stripers caught by hook and line in Albemarle Sound during 1967, and 50,000 in 1968. The Roanoke River yielded some 10,000 stripers to sport fishermen in 1967, 50,000 in 1968.

A survey of North Carolina residents and their salt water fishing, conducted in 1966 by the Institute of Statistics, N. C. State University, asked the question: "What kind of fish did you catch the most?" The pollsters tallied their results and estimated .3 per cent of the Tarheel salt water anglers would say striped bass. Striped bass ranked 22nd down the list of preferences on this particular question. But a .3 per cent is not at all indicative of the actual enthusiasm for striped bass fishing. It does, however, show that many, many people catch many, many other not-so-glamorous fish.

Tarheel sport fishing for rock takes place in the sounds, estuaries, and fresh-water rivers and reservoirs. Until recently practically no one could hook a North Carolina ocean-going rock. And even now very few are being caught. Tarheel anglers, so the word goes, are just getting on to the methods of catching stripers in the ocean.

North Carolina Stripers For Market

When it comes to gear, commercial fishermen, like sport fishermen, use different rigs for different waters. In the sounds and tributaries, stripers are taken by gill nets, pound nets, long haul seines, purse seines, fyke nets, trot lines, hand lines, and bow nets. Most successful of the lot are gill nets. For the past five years gill nets have taken five times as many North Carolina rock as any other commercial gear, according to the U. S. Bureau of Commercial Fisheries. During 1968, 1,300,000 pounds were gilled. A gill net *gills* fish. Swimming fish come upon a

gill net set in the water and try to swim through the openings. They become entangled, usually behind the gill covers at first, and then as they twist and turn they become completely enmeshed. Gill nets can be fished in different ways and are named accordingly: anchor, drift, run-about.

Pound nets are the third best rock catcher. Pound nets are large traps set in sounds and rivers. Commercial fishermen set up lengths of net to lead fish into the traps. Once a striper swims inside the trap area, on its own accord, it is trapped. Fishermen check their pounds periodically and remove their catch. The 1968 striper catch from pound nets was 91,000 pounds.

Winter months bring the big stripers romping along northern North Carolina beaches. Watching a beach seine crew of commercial fishermen ply their trade in the winter surf is great spectator sport, and when the stripers are running well the hard-working commercial men can make good money. Beach seines are the second best rock catcher. When a school of rock is spotted just out from the beach, a small boat loaded with a seine is launched into the surf. As the net is payed out over the stern, the boat travels in a large arc until it reaches shore again thus encircling the fish with the seine. The net is pulled ashore, the fish are loaded in boxes and the net is loaded on the boat ready for another set. The 1968 beach seine catch was 435,000 pounds.

Trawlers (boats pulling trawl nets along the bottom) are also used successfully in the ocean to catch rock.

From 1887 to 1945 the annual commercial catch of striped bass in North Carolina, with the expected variations from year to year, averaged about 500,-000 pounds. From 1945 to 1966 the catch averaged about 700,000 pounds yearly with the exception of

1954 and 1958 when the catch exceeded 1,000,000 pounds.

The 1967 commercial catch of stripers was 1,800,-000 pounds, with the 1968 catch at 1,911,808 pounds, having a dockside value of $385,064.

Coastal Striper Life

The weight of evidence points to two large and distinct populations of stripers along the North Carolina coast. These two groups go about their business with little intermingling. The biggest group, as far as numbers, is the Albemarle Sound population. Stripers in this group can be found in different areas of the sound and its tributaries at various seasons. They average two to four pounds, and 15-20 pounders are uncommon. Dr. William Hassler and his N. C. State University students have been studying this population for 14 years.

In the spring and early summer months, mature Albemarle Sound stripers travel up fresh-water rivers to spawn, usually 100 miles or more from salt water. The Roanoke is the main striper spawning river in the State.

Males usually mature at the age of two, sometimes three years. Females, however, mature more slowly and it is usually four years before they are ready for the up-river jaunt. The bigger the female, the more eggs she has; several thousands for the smaller ones, several millions for the larger ones. There likely is a maximum number of eggs a fish can produce, however, no matter how large she becomes.

Dr. Hassler has found that at least one to one-and one-half billion eggs come down the Roanoke after the adults have completed their spawning in late April and May. The eggs hatch as the current carries them downstream. The young drift down to the west end of the Sound where the water is still fresh. They spend the summer months there and then move into the deeper waters in the fall and winter. Dr. Hassler has tagged thousands of rock in the Albemarle population and none of the tags

17

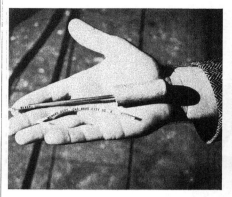

Biologists of the Department of Conservation and Development's Division of Commercial and Sports Fisheries have tagged many a striped bass with plastic tags like this (left) in a continuing study of the ocean populations along our coast. Trawlers (above)also take rockfish successfully.

has been returned from rock caught in the ocean. He does get a tag returned occasionally from Pamlico Sound.

A two-year old striper measures 11-14 inches and reaches about 20 inches by its fifth year. Stripers grow rapidly until their tenth year and then growth tapers off. A 125 pounder taken near Edenton, North Carolina, in 1891 seems to be the biggest caught.

Those huskies caught outside along the Outer Banks, in winter months, have a different story. They are cagey, though, and not all the questions about their existence have been answered. Stripers in the 40-60 pound class are not uncommon. Life evidently is not too bad for the big ones; but it takes several years for one to get that big. North Carolina commercial fishermen catch the stripers near or actually from the beach, from the Virginia line south to Ocracoke Island, and every now and then some show up as far south as Cape Lookout. This population travels north with warm months and south with cold ones. It is doubtful that the real big ones enter North Carolina fresh waters to spawn. There are always the oddballs, though, even with fish. Nothing is absolutely certain with fish and their habits. Biologists have to use their share of *generally, usually*, and *evidently*, to account for the wayward fish that always shows up where it "generally" is not found.

There are stripers in Pamlico Sound and its tributaries, and a small population can be found in Cape Fear River. But the Albemarle and ocean populations are by far the main stocks of coastal North Carolina rock.

Although the striper population fluctuates from year to year, statistics and experts say the stripers are doing fine and their numbers seem to have increased over the years. But if we do not take a

strong stand on intelligent management of our environment, especially our estuaries, the good life for Mr. Striper will sour.

Looking Closer

"It's a changing picture," said a State Biologist attempting to o b t a i n data for management of stripers. Quantities of smaller rock, one to three pounds, were taken along North Carolina beaches the winter of 1968-1969 by researchers and commercial fishermen. Usually the rock caught in the ocean are jumbos.

Biologists aboard the North Carolina Division of Commercial and Sports Fisheries exploratory fishing vessel, *Dan Moore,* have been studying for the past two seasons the winter ocean population found along the northern North Carolina beaches. This past winter on cruises from Cape Hatteras to the Virginia line they captured, tagged, and released stripers. So far they have had tags returned from stripers taken in Chesapeake Bay, in Rhode Island, and from the inside waters of Pamlico Sound. They will tag the ocean stripers at least one more season.

Dr. Hassler continues his studies on the Albemarle Sound population and he and his students also study spawning habits, survival of spawn, migration, and various other aspects of the stripers. They also keep tabs on the success of commercial and sport fishermen after Albemarle rock. In the near future, Dr. Hassler plans to enlarge his studies to include physiological changes of spawners, abundance of stripers in other areas, and to check more closely on enviornmental conditions. Dr. Hassler's research is sponsored by the North Carolina Department of Conservation and Development, the U. S. Bureau of Commercial Fisheries, Weyerhaeuser Company, and Albemarle Paper Company. ◆

It Costs More To Hunt And Fish

Your combination hunting-fishing license expired on July 31. To replace it you will have to pay your license dealer $7.50 instead of the $6.25 you paid last year. The 1969 General Assembly raised the price of North Carolina's hunting and fishing licenses an average of just less than $1.00 each. Funds therefrom are needed to meet rising costs of conducting the State's wildlife conservation program. Also increased are the prices of state resident county and state hunting licenses. There is also an increase in fishing license averaging less than $1.00. A complete schedule of new license costs will be published in the September issue. The increase in fishing license costs does not take effect until January 1, 1970.

Upland Migratory Game Bird Seasons Set

The hunting season on doves and rails this year will begin on September 1. Coincidentally, September 1 is Labor Day, and despite usual September hot weather, a record number of dove and rail hunters are expected to take to the fields and marshes. This year dove hunters will be allowed a daily bag of 18 birds with 36 permitted in possession. Bag limits on rails will be the same as last year—15 daily, 30 in possession. The unusually large allowable bag limit on doves is part of an experiment on the part of the U. S. Bureau of Sport Fisheries and Wildlife designed to determine whether a heavy hunter harvest of doves will affect next year's breeding population.

Safety Rules Still in Effect

Where fatal boating accidents are concerned, Tarheels enjoyed a reasonably safe summer. With the 1969-70 hunting season underway on September 1, the Wildlife Resources Commission reminds outdoorsmen of the need for using common sense and courtesy in the handling of firearms, pointing out that outdoor safety is a year-around proposition.

Angler's Widow

by
Jennie M. Barrett

RIDING down the highway one summer Friday evening after a full day of work in the office, the young lady rested back in the bucket seat of their cozy little T-Bird, loaded down with a tent, a bit of short-order food, bedrolls and what she thought to be a ridiculous accumulation of rod, reels and other fishing tackle. Having camped out and fished a number of times with her angler husband, she was wondering many things about the weekend ahead—where they would be camping, the type of people she would be meeting, what sort of eating they would do and what kind of fishing was in store for them. It was very difficult for her to adjust to this life of camping and fishing and being a helpmate to this dyed-in-the-wool fisherman, but she was enjoying, and looking forward to, each trip a little more than the last.

It had been a lovely week, weather-wise, and it seemed the weekend was going to be much the same mellow mood.

It was about a four-hour drive from home to camp that evening, and as they drove down the Tarheel coast, over the bridge crossing the sound and into the camping area, there was a peaceful breeze blowing and the air smelled of salt water and, wouldn't you know, FISH! They stopped their car and stood outside to inhale deep breaths of this refreshing air, becoming acquainted with the atmosphere that lay around them, seeping from the rippling, splashing waters. The first chore after picking out their camp site was the setting up of their small tent.

This took only about five minuets, including throwing in their bedrolls and meeting their new neighbors for the weekend.

By this time it was nearly 10:00 p.m. and you would think that after a full day of the general run-of-the-mill office procedures and the long drive down, she would be pretty tired out and ready for bed. Well, it didn't exactly turn out that way. Rather, she had her husband drive up to a small boat house next to the camping area to buy some shrimp for bait, picked up her rod and reel and struck out for the small fishing pier adjacent to the camping ground near the sound.

There she eagerly lined up the rod, baited the hooks and cast out into the dark, quiet sound. Now remember, I told you that her husband was the angler in this family, but it seems she is the one who instigated this hour of fishing rather than retiring so they could get up early the next morning, as he wanted to do. Of course he didn't resist the temptation and in a few minutes was along side his wife fishing.

SOMETHING kept picking at the bait, and after dragging the baitless, fishless line in several times, they learned it was only crabs snitching their bait. After an hour or so of pulling in those tough little pin fish and feeding the crabs, they prepared for bed, anxiously awaiting the beginning of a new day, which was only a few hours away for this angler and his wife.

After a good night's rest and a healthy breakfast in the cool and calm of the early mornin they set out for the big pier the ocean. The fishing was slo on the pier this morning, so the took off for the sound, fishin along the sand there below th bridge near camp. The day w hot, but the breeze coming fro the cooler waters was just rig! to keep them comfortable durir the 90-plus degree temperatur

The flounders seemed to ! hitting Mr. Angler's line prett well, so Mrs. Angler tried to col centrate on flounder. And—lo and behold—a big flounder latcl ed onto her bait like a duck on junebug. It gave a tug like horse pulling a heavy plow an boy!!—What a thrilling feelin; At last, she had hooked a floun er that felt like it might weig 3 or 4 pounds. She tugged ar tugged, very slowly easing th flounder toward her, trying n to pull the hook out of its mout (she had experienced before The flounder came closer and sk could see the mottled grey fis lying there on the sand beneat the clear water, so close but y(so far.

By now she was so excited an nervous she was getting weak and too anxious to get him i She pulled a little too hard on h line and "snap!"—right out that big flounder's mouth, fre ing the flat fish to return to h place in the living waters. Ho sick she was! She looked at h hook (bent somewhat from th struggle), then looked up at h husband who was almost as e: cited for her as she was. Tea filled her eyes because of disa pointment after all of the excit ment.

She started out again in a fe minutes, determined not to ! defeated. During this time th sun was baking her skin and sl began to feel a burny sting. D ciding she had almost too mu(sun, she settled back in th shadow of the bridge to find shady spot to fish—and to res For the life of her, she couldn pull in anything else but doze of pin fish and several hog fis Feeling defeated and getting little hungry, she sat down c the fish box, crossed her legs an decided to just "feed" those little fish out there while she waited for her husband to give in and eat lunch.

ALL of a sudden—WHAM! What was it this time? Felt like a mighty whale to her! Never before in all her fishing, including the freed flounder, had she ever felt anything pull quite so strongly just to get a little piece of shrimp off the hook! Well, this young lady didn't know what she had, but she knew she had something all right, and with all the determination she could muster, and the strength she had left on an empty stomach, she jumped from the fish box to her trembling feet and set that hook but good. She caused such a commotion that her husband stopped his fishing to see what was going on. "Whatcha got? Whatcha got?", he shouted. She was too weak to speak and the fish was having it pretty much its way with the inexperienced fisher woman. So, to her husband's amazement, the next thing he knew she started out running across the beach, holding firmly to that rod and pulling the line through the waters. And, would you believe she successfully landed the most beautiful fish she had ever seen—a beautiful three pound speckled trout—on her own without any coaching from hubby.

This time she did cry, but these were tears of happiness. With tears in her eyes, she flopped down on the sand from exhaustion of the excitement, (you know that feeling that runs a weak streak through you when you're about to land a big'un), plus the running and the heat of the day. Hunger was overtaken by this thrill and she just kept admiring it, this glistening catch, not allowing her husband to touch it except to remove the hook from the defeated trout's throat. "Just look at it! I ain't believing it! Can we take pictures of it, with me holding it? Can you mount it for me? And it's so heavy—so big and beautiful!" And on and on were the remarks that flowed from the beaming but sunburned face.

This called for a little celebration so they retreated into a cool restaurant to eat. Then back to the big pier to try again from the ocean. But there was nothing this little lady could do now to add to her weekend; she felt right then that it was complete. All it took to win her over to the wiles and woes of the angler's life, feeling this deep down in her system flowing into her blood, the thrill and excitement of this adventuresome hot sunny day at the coast was one three-pound speckled trout. What a beauty to behold and a momentous weekend for the angler's widow, but now no longer a widow. She, herself, had become an angler; I know, because I am this angler! ♠

Almost any type of fishing can be a woman's sport too, if the proper gear is supplied the fisherwoman. Trips can be arranged with the girls in mind. It does help to catch a nice big fish once in a while, too!

PHOTO BY TOM JACKSON

by
John R. Parker
Jr.

AS this column is being prepared for your August edification—June slowly slips away. This means, for one thing, that the boating season is in full swing. But you know that. Now stand by for something of which you may be unaware, the bad news: fatal boating accidents have doubled, as compared to the first half of 1968. That increase started in late March and continued through the third week of April. There was another increase during the first week of May (with four fatal accidents in one day, May 3) followed by a tapering off through late May and June. Total deaths to date, 32.

Since many of the accidents of which we speak occurred in the early part of the season, the fishing fraternity was most often involved.

Later in the season, accidents involving boats being used for skiing, cruising and miscellaneous activities also show in the reports.

About Life Saving Devices

Occasionally I receive promotional literature from manufacturers of life saving devices. The latest comes with an idea attached. Their pitch is: folks just don't utilize those orange, oversize, hot, clumsy looking life preservers or vests approved by the Coast Guard—so why not approve something that will be worn, something like this company, and others, manufacture.

But this is not just sales talk and the idea isn't new. Too often the drowning victim purchased the life saving devices and stowed them aboard, but never tried one on. He most likely stowed them where they were not accessible. The Coast Guard and the Wildlife Resources Commission are well aware that people simply don't use the things they approve, and the Coast Guard is looking into the problem. And to speed things up, the House Government Operations Committee has recommended that the Coast Guard take leadership in providing improved life saving devices that will be worn—devices like those described in the literature that comes across my desk.

Here's an idea—you can use those form fitting, plaid covered, stylish devices if you like. Vests, hunting coats, jackets, etc., are being manufactured which do a life saving job. And that's all that really matters. (A few are in fact approved by the U. S. Coast Guard). But hold on, I am not suggesting that these devices replace the standard U. S. Coast Guard approved material just yet; but if you and yours (especially nonswimmers and small children) will use the more stylish devices, then why not have both aboard.

Skiing Safety

The North Carolina boating accident records are certainly not absent of reports on ski boat accidents. Neither is the ski tow boat accident represented out of proportion. Why not shoot for complete elimination of skiing accidents? Idealistic? Perhaps. But an article in the *Water Skier* reports that in the past 30 years the American Water Ski Association has sanctioned over 1,000 tournaments, fatality free. The article goes on to say that the record was made possible by careful supervision and constant attention to safety rules.

Nothing is more valuable to the water skier—novice, skilled or competitive—than a capable driver at the controls of the tow boat. A competent boat handler can enhance the skill of a skier, just as errors in judgment by the driver can be damaging and dangerous.

The Evinrude News Service advises that it is just as important for the tow boat driver to be properly instructed as it is for the water skier. Successful water skiing at any level of skill depends upon the boat driver and the skier working together as a well-knit unit.

The skier's safety depends in a large measure on the boat driver. He should be alert to obey signals from the skier, and to obstructions in the path of the boat and skier; and always refrain from recklessness when pulling a skier.

The driver and skier should understand each other's signals before they start. An observer

Last month Gov. Scott signed North Carolina's Safe Boating Week Proclamation and discussed boating safety with these boating enthusiasts and Safety Week Chairman. Pictured are (left to right) H. A. Schmidt, Manager, Southport Small Craft Harbor; Charles H. Kimbrell, New Bern boat dealer; Dr. Dan A. McLaurin, Sect. 27, N. C.'s U. S. Power Squadron; Cmdr. Glasgow, U. S. Coast Guard, Elizabeth City; Fred M. McCutchen, Cmdr. U. S. C. G. Auxiliary Flotilla 91 (Raleigh); William T. Casey, Cmdr. Dis. 27, N. C.'s. U. S. Power Squadron; John Parker, Wildlife Commission; and Howard Braxton, Red Cross Representative, Elizabeth City.

should be along in the boat to relay signals between skier and
driver.

When starting, the driver
should maneuver the boat so that
he can start and continue in one
direction until the skier has gained his bearings after coming out
of the water or off the dock.

Keep the tow line taut until
the skier gives the "hit it" signal,
being careful to play the winds
and current so they do not force
you off course before you start.

When the skier is ready, pull
him out of the water quickly and
cleanly with steadily increased
speed. A sudden burst of the full
throttle may jerk the tow bar
from the skier's hands or pull
him off balance.

When underway, the driver
should avoid abrupt meaneuvers
of any kind. He should swing
wide on turns and especially
avoid tight turns when the skier
is on the inside of the curve. In
this case, the skier could lose
speed and sink. The d r i v e r
should not change course without signaling to the skier.

A tow boat driver should know
the water in which he is operating, and should never drive the
boat into shallow water where,
if a skier falls, he could be hurt.

Respect for the rights of others
is one sign of a competent boat
driver. He should give other
boats a wide berth and be careful
to stay away from canoes, sail-
b o a t s, fishermen, swimming
areas, and skin divers. He should
also avoid passing too close to
private or public piers and landings.

Don't clown at the wheel.
Avoid other skiers. Never should
a boat driver follow behind another skier or allow another boat
to follow the skier he has in tow.

If a skier s h o u l d fall, the
driver should always return immediately to pick him up. Don't
turn too quickly, however, because it may cause the tow line
to snag in the propeller. Never
leave a tow line dragging in the
water when not in use, and pick
up floating skis quickly if other
boats are operating in the area.

If the fallen skier wishes to

continue skiing, the d r i v e r
should circle around him at a
safe distance, and the tow rope
will come back into his hands.
Never bring the boat within ten
feet of a skier in the water.

If you wish to take the skier
aboard, always stop the motor
while he is getting into the boat.
Avoid boarding over the transom. A boarding ladder is safer
and more convenient than attempting to crawl over the side.

When landing a skier, keep
constant speed until he lets go.
Stay clear of piers, swimmers
and shores. Remember the skier
can swing in and land closer to
shore than you should get with
the boat.

Let the skier establish the
speed. Never tow him faster than
he wants to go and never keep
him out after he is exhausted.
Enjoyment of skiing is the reason for the sport.

If the driver also remembers
that others like to enjoy their
favorite sports, be it swimming,
canoeing, fishing or skin diving,
and does not drive so as to interfere with their enjoyment, he has
learned one of the most important lessons of the tow boat driver.

Eating Aboard

The old saying, "W a t e r !
Water, everywhere, but not a
drop to drink!" is a constant
companion for many boatmen.

Suprisingly, even many experienced boatmen put out in
their boats without taking along
drinking water, or some other
beverage to quench their thirst.

When that happens, all that
water seems to make those
aboard even more thirsty. It
sounds very basic, but it's surprising how often it happens.

More and more boatmen are
carrying small coolers aboard
their boats, whether they are
cruising or fishing. These coolers
serve the purpose both for drink
and food. It is natural that they
would keep beverages cool, but
they do more with food.

For instance, the most common snack aboard a boat is sandwiches. Unlike the soggy sandwiches in the school l u n c h
bucket, those from a cooler have
crisp lettuce and firm tomatoes.
Meats, cheeses, and other materials used to prepare snacks can
also be kept fresh and cold in the
cooler.

Breads, cakes, or c o o k i e s
should be kept in tight containers and then placed in the cooler
where they will stay fresh and
retain their flavor. But keep
them in a watertight container
so they don't absorb the moisture
of the cooler.

Common sense also dictates
the utensils to carry aboard a
small boat. There are plastic
glasses, plates, knives, and forks
that are shatterproof and easy to
clean. If paper cups and plates
are used, be sure to dispose of
them and all other refuse in proper waterfront receptacles. Litter turns waterways into eye-
sores.

Often forgotten but practically indispensable is the bottle
opener. A combined bottle-can
opener should be aboard always!

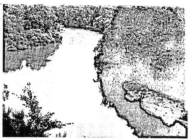

Cliffs of Neuse

by Duane Raver
Photos by the Author

Nature is on display at the Cliffs of Neuse State Park. These are but a few of the scenes that greet the visitor to this Wayne County site. Whether you're a serious student of geology or simply want a spot of relaxation, you will enjoy Cliffs of Neuse.

Y ELLOW jasmine spreads over the forest floor, mountain hardwoods luxuriantly cover the nearby slopes, a 98-foot sheer cliff dives to the river below, large cinnamon and regal ferns line the cool, damp trails . . . yet this is only a part of the 378-acre Cliffs of Neuse State Park. Located in the southeastern tip of Wayne County, very near the community of Seven Springs, the park offers everything from nature study to swimming, boating and fishing.

● It doesn't take the visitor long to discover where the Park's name comes from. The "cliffs" drop from the Sunderland plain almost a hundred feet to the meandering Neuse River below. A set of sturdy steps winds its way down the wall to the banks of the river. To the serious student of geology, the pages of history unfold with clarity. Layer upon layer of multicolored strata have been cut by water and wind. The carving process may have begun as much as 13 million years ago and still continues bit by bit today.

● Bands of sand, pebbles, sandy clay, limestone, bits of shells, and "basement rocks", each with a characteristic color, represent geologic deposits dating back as much as 100 million years.

● But to most visitors, the Park means a place to picnic, hike, or swim in an atmosphere that varies from the kind usually found in the highlands of North Carolina, to that associated with the cypress swamps of further east. Dr. B. W. Wells studied the plant communities represented here and found that no less than seven major plant associations were found in this rather limited geographical area. Although the erect poison oak is found here, Dr. Wells predicted before the Park was developed: "since it will be in the shady hardwood areas that the trails will be developed, it is most fortunate that the vine-like poison ivy is almost absent."

● Swimming is available at a protected bathing area, with boats also on hand for rent. Nature trails are numerous and bird study is a favorite pastime in the Park. Limited camping is permitted but no developed campgrounds are available.

● No matter when you go nor how long you stay, you'll enjoy Cliffs of Neuse State Park.

CRACKSHOTS and BACKLASHES
by Rod Amundson

Opossum	86
Rabbits	58
Squirrel	12
Raccoon	10
Quail	14
Grey Fox	6

Sincerely,
Bob O'Neal
Bath

First Aid Anyone?

You're one of the eight million owners of small boats in the United States—outboard and inboard motor boats, sailboats, rowboats, and canoes.

You are miles from the marina and an accident causing serious injury occurs aboard your craft. The victim may die before he can be brought to professional medical care. Will you know what to do if this happens?

The last few lines are not pleasant, but it does happen.

What can we say except why not take a few minutes from your busy boating season and think "first aid training," a Red Cross course, and first aid equipment. Is your boat equipped with a first aid kit? Something to think about.

Action Now!

Dear Sir:

My attention has been brought to the fact that the Corps of Engineers is planning to conduct snagging, clearing, and dredging operations on Six Runs Creek in Sampson and Pender Counties. This will take place for some fifteen miles upstream from Black River to Highway 421 and another eleven miles from this point upstream on Six Runs Creek and its tributaries.

As you well know, this will destroy the fish population, breeding grounds for future fish generations, and will drain the low lands lying along the stream. This drainage will destroy nesting areas for Wood Ducks and refuge areas for deer, raccoon, and other animals. It will have a very detrimental effect on all bird life, and especially the Pileated Woodpecker, who is hard pressed to find a haven safe from mankind. In

short, one of eastern North Carolina's most beautiful streams will be lost forever.

As an outdoorsman and conservationist, can you sit idly by and let this happen? I cannot, and I have found many others who cannot.

Can you see your way clear to support us in this matter through your fine magazine, and in the North Carolina Wildlife Resources Commission? If you have any information on this project, especially what agencies gave state approval, I would appreciate having it.

We will be corresponding with the Wildlife Resources Commission concerning this project.

Sincerely,
Charles T. Haigh, Jr.
Fayetteville

Dead Game

Dear Sir:

My work as a sanitarian with the Beaufort County Health Department carries me about 20,000 miles each year on the highways and secondary roads of Beaufort County. For my own information, I decided to make a count of all wild animals I saw killed on the roads. The following is a record of animals for exactly one year from May 8, 1968-May 8, 1969. I thought some other readers might be interested. I counted only the animals I saw in Beaufort County.

American motorists kill one million animals a day, according to a UPI story quoting the American Automobile Association. "We kill more game with our cars than our hunters do with guns," the association reported.

The recent AAA report said that in 1968 at least 365 million animals, most of them wildlife, were struck and killed by vehicles in the United States. As an example, Pennsylvania vehicles killed 22,610 deer and 37 bears in 1967.

Why?

Dear Sir:

Have you ever heard birds cry? I have. They cried all day long.

In the heart of the city was a small vacant lot. Maybe 50 feet wide. No more. Small trees grew there. Bushes, vines. Seeds and berries ripened there. No path crossed the lot. It just grew, as Nature intended. A refuge in summer and winter for song birds. Their feeding grounds and nesting places. Their hiding place in winter from the cold winds and ice. Robins, cardinals, blue jays, mockingbirds, brown thrashers, towhees, the tiny song sparrows. Last week a bulldozer roared and crashed down there. Ripping, tearing, uprooting, smashing. Laying waste the whole place. It is wrecked and ruined. To me an eyesore, a wasteland. Not for a "park" or playground. Not for a building; too small.

After all these years, why in May? When the birds are nesting. Many

These little stinkers, photographed by Robert A. Cathey of Asheville, better hurry or end up as statistics on the highway.

KNOW YOUR PROTECTOR

Larry T. Barnes

Wildlife Patrolman Larry T. Barnes stationed at Raleigh, North Carolina, was born in Johnston County on January 5, 1942. His parents are Mr. and Mrs. W. Lester Barnes of Four Oaks, North Carolina. He is a graduate of Four Oaks High School, Four Oaks, North Carolina and prior to his employment with the N. C. Wildlife Resources Commission, he was employed by Fieldcrest Mills, Inc.

After completing Pre-service Training School for Wildlife Protectors at the Institute of Government in Chapel Hill, North Carolina, in 1963, he was employed as Wildlife Protector Trainee in Ahoskie from December 1963 to October 1964. In October 1964, he was transferred to Plymouth as Wildlife Protector and in January 1968, he was promoted to Wildlife Patrolman and transferred to Manteo. Since his initial employment, Mr. Barnes has attended five In-service Training Schools and serves as an instructor in Defensive Tactics.

Patrolman Barnes is a member of the Southeastern Association of Game and Fish Commissioners, Law Enforcement Section, and the Dare County Peace Officers Association. He is married to the former Brenda Massengill of Four Oaks, North Carolina, and they have a daughter Susan, age 4. The Barnes' are members of St. Mary's Grove Free Will Baptist Church.

young out of the nests but still unable to fly? How many nests were destroyed? How many young birds died? Where will they shelter from the cold next winter?

Because someone wanted all vacant lots "cleaned up".

Have you ever heard birds cry? I have.

Name withheld on request

'Bye 'Bye Blackbird

Dear Sir:

First I would like to say that I enjoy reading WILDLIFE magazine very much. However, I would like to add a word or two in "Crackshots and Backlashes" in regard to the article *Just Plain Cuckoo* by William W. Williams, Raleigh; also the article by Floyd Sprouce, Marshall.

I wonder if Mr. Williams has ever seen the complete destruction that starlings and blackbirds—they usually ranged together in this section—can do to a patch of millet or sorghum—even before the doves get a chance at it? I think there should be an all-out effort made to eradicate them.

And a word to add to *Only Hunters Understand*, I would like to invite Mr. Sprouce down here squirrel hunting in some of our Robeson County swamps. I believe he would find—when one finds a good hollow to get into—that he can wait a good bit more than 20 minutes before the squirrel will move again.

I believe I should know as I have been doing it nearly 50 years.

An ardent reader of WILDLIFE,
Sincerely,
B. L. Tyner,
Lumberton

Lumber River

ONE day after an evening shower I decide to go for a boat ride on the beautiful Lumber River. I get in my boat and slowly drift down stream. The rain-cooled air fans' the dripping leaves of the trees. A thick haze resembling fleecy white clouds hangs over the water. As I slowly move along with the current, shafts of sunlight filter through the moss-draped limbs of the trees. I come to a bend in the river and the eddy swells rock the little boat like a crosswind over the bow. In its rhythmic flow, the river is kissed daily by golden sun rays and caressed by silent moon beams at night.

The branches hanging over the water seem intent on reflecting their mirrored beauty to the sky for all who ride its waters to see. The wind-swept sandbars jutting out at intervals along its shore, glisten like golden nuggets. The cooling, rippling swells from the rocking boat dance like fairies as they cast their reflection on the bosom of the river. The late evening shadows resemble little. elves as they race up and down the gently swaying tree limbs that line its banks.

From a distant field I hear the soft cooing of a dove; high up in a tree I hear the noise of a squirrel. As I drift nearer, he scampers down, chattering away as if to scold me for disturbing him. It is getting late and the darkness has a velvety softness as it begins to spread its mantle over the clear, crystal water. Still in a reflective mood, I think of the graceful deer, the feigning possum, the bushy ring-tailed raccoon, the silky mink and the sliding otter who satisfy their thirst by drinking from its limpid water; the bass and saucy panfish which have given untold pleasure to so many anglers in days of yore.

It is a beautiful stream and there is something about it that breathes a sweet freshness, and gives a cheerful contentment, and lifts one above the commonplace into the realm of natural beauty. ✦

The popularity of the big channel bass in Pamlico Sound could cause the fish some trouble, says Dr. Thomas Linton, Commissioner of Commercial and Sports Fisheries. Most of the schools (100-500 drum each) show up in Pamlico Sound in April and remain on or near a particular shoal until late September.

It is generally accepted that the supply of big ones is limited and unless anglers after them keep only their legal limit of two over 32 inches long, the number of Pamlico jumbos could diminish rapidly. Why not be a real sport fisherman and release your fish alive?

What may be a new inland record striped bass for North Carolina was caught by Ralph Nelson (Bill) Dula of Granite Falls. The 39¼-pound fish came from Lake Hickory, May 10, 1969, and fell to a live spring lizard. If you know of a bigger one, let us know.

The Nature Lover's Evening Psalm

By Charlotte Hilton Green

The Lord is the Creator of all Nature; my heart giveth thanks.

He maketh the new moon to shine through dark pine trees, and through the slender branches of willows.

He leadeth me beside still waters, wherein are reflected the glories of His Heavens.

He sendeth peace to my soul, in the calm of a purple twilight, with a thrush singing at the edge of a woodland.

Yea, I walk in a moonlit garden, and I know only peace, for He is beside me; His tall trees arch overhead, and the path my feet must trod is soft with pine needles.

The wind in the forest sings a Hymn of Praise to Him, and the white flowers of the dogwood hold the promise of His everlasting love and mercy.

The air is sweet with many odors, and my soul is attune to the murmur of soft flowing waters.

Surely this, His Handiwork, is a part of the Divine Plan. I shall accept with reverence, and strive to understand.

LITHO BY THE GRAPHIC PRESS, INC., RALEIGH, N. C.

Tiger Swallowtail

James H. Carmichael, Jr.

Wildlife IN NORTH CAROLINA

25 CENTS / SEPTEMBER 1969

WILDLIFE IN NORTH CAROLINA recognizes the need for close cooperation between State and Federal conservation agencies and the people who hunt and fish—to bring about a restoration of our renewable resources. The Editor gratefully receives for publication news items, articles, and photographs dealing with the North Carolina out-of-doors, but reserves the right to reject materials submitted. Full credit is given for all materials published.

• • •

WILDLIFE IN NORTH CAROLINA is published at the Wildlife Resources Commission offices, Motor Vehicles Building, 1100 New Bern Ave., Raleigh, N. C. 27601.

• • •

Second class postage paid at Raleigh, North Carolina 27602.

• • •

SUBSCRIPTION—One dollar per year, two dollars for two years. Make remittance payable to WILDLIFE RESOURCES COMMISSION. Any employee of the Wildlife Resources Commission may accept subscriptions, or they may be forwarded to Post Office Box 2919, Raleigh, N. C. 27602. Stamps cannot be accepted.

Wildlife circulation this issue, 119,123

IN NORTH CAROLINA ■

The official publication of the NORTH CAROLINA WILDLIFE RESOURCES COMMISSION, Raleigh 27602. A monthly magazine devoted to the protection and restoration of our wildlife resources and to the improvement of hunting and fishing in North Carolina.

VOL. XXXIII, NO 9   SEPTEMBER, 1969

IN THIS ISSUE

EDITORIAL STAFF

ROD AMUNDSON _ _ _ _ _ _ _ _ _ EDITOR
DUANE RAVER _ _ _ _ MANAGING EDITOR
LUTHER PARTIN _ _ _ WRITER-PHOTOGRAPHER
JOHN PARKER _ _ _ _ _ _ BOATING EDITOR
TOM JACKSON _ _ _ WRITER-PHOTOGRAPHER

The chances are many a marsh hen will get bypassed this season as they are every year. The clapper rail pictured has at least a temporary reprieve. Actually these game birds of the marsh are considered by most biologists to be underhunted, and the harvest could be substantially greater on September rails.

Painting by John W. Taylor

Marsh Hen

From a stable boat, this camouflaged hunter bags another marsh hen. The bag limit is liberal . . . 15 birds daily, 30 in possession. Pick a high tide and go hunting!

September Rails

Boats used for rail hunting vary a bit from 12-foot, wooden skiffs, to shallow draft fiberglass and metal craft up to 16 feet long. Be sure that yours is a stable one with room for hunters, gear and retriever.

Poling the boat through the marsh is hard work and requires a certain skill that is developed by practice. Usually a small outboard is used to get the hunters to the hunting areas but must not be used in pursuit of birds. Shooting from the boat looks a bit risky, but the craft is steadied by the poler, and the shot is usually almost directly ahead rather than from side.

*T*HEY'RE called rails by some people and marsh hens by others, but the experienced marsh hunter can identify them as either the sora, Virginia, or clapper rail.

All three of these migratory birds are legal game in our coastal marshes from September 1 through November 6. The bag limits are 15 daily and 30 in possession, an indication of the low hunting pressure rails get.

Although all of our coastal marshes are host to rails, most of the hunting is concentrated from Beaufort to Shallotte. This area has the highest tides along the North Carolina coast and high tides are necessary for good rail hunting. As long as they can hide, they are mighty slow to fly. But when the tide covers all but the tallest cordgrass, hunting for marsh hen compares well with upland game birds. A retriever can save cripples that might elude a man, and using a dog adds something to the sport as well.

The tides are predictable (see table on page 27) but the wind is not. A persistent blow can cause a difference of several inches in the water level, and this can really affect hunting. It can hurt or it may help, depending on the direction. The salt marshes of Smith Island may have higher than predicted tides with a northeast wind while the fresher marshes just across the inlet at Southport may be several inches lower than expected. If you have a choice of marshes, the relationship of each to the prevailing winds might be important, especially during lower tides.

Most people prefer a flat-bottomed, narrow-beamed boat that can be poled through the marsh vegetation. Usually one man poles while the other stays ready for the flush. Beating the water occasionally with the oar may help flush a rail that has submerged, leaving the tip of his beak sticking up like a short blade of grass.

Wading is popular with many during the early season when the air and water are warm, but stout footgear is a must. Shells and sharp pieces of stiff vegetation can inflict a nasty cut. Tidal creeks can be a threat to the inexperienced wader until he learns to recognize them in a marsh. ◆

Text by Luther Partin

Photos Courtesy Travel and Promotion Division
Department of Conservation & Development

There is little question that a retriever is a great help in finding downed rails in the heavy marsh grasses. A good duck dog usually adapts to marsh hen hunting. Even the best of them need a little help in scrambling back into the boat! At right is part of the result of a successful day's shoot in the marshes.

Cooners

Photos by the Author

by Roy Martin
Greensboro Daily News

"**L**OOK here, look here, this is a good 'un."
The fellow spoke quietly, hands working steadily over the Bluetick hound on the bench before him. His eyes followed the show judge.

"Ah," he breathed, when the class trophy was placed before his dog and the judge's hand came down on the hound's back, signaling the win. "That's the way."

The place was the Ellisboro Community Building near Madison in Rockingham County. The event was the September Bench Show and Wild Coon hunt, a semi-annual event staged by the Dan River Coon Hunters Club, Inc., of Madison.

"We carry on these events and are organized to promote the anatomy of the coon dog and to foster the conservation of the raccoon," said A. M. Icenhour of Winston-Salem, secretary of the Dan River Club. "We have a good time and we do what we can to create an atmosphere for better hunting and good sportsmanship."

The Dan River Coon Hunters Club, organized in 1961, now numbers about 50 members. The organization recently purchased seven acres of land near Madison and is in the process of establishing permanent club facilities. Until their headquarters is built, the group has been using the Ellisboro Community Building for monthly meeting and general activities.

The concept of the Dan River Club's activities and the function of similar clubs around the state and nation is competition—involving dogs. The semi-annual Dan River Club event is a three-phased affair, including a dog show, a treeing contest and a night coon hunt. Each of the three phases is designed to test coonhounds in varied methods of competition.

Icenhour explained that the United Kennel Club licenses the Dan River Club's show and hunt. The activity is carried out according to UKC regulations.

"The United Kennel Club is the coonhound's kennel club," said Icenhour. "It recognizes six breeds of coonhounds, including the American Black and Tan, Bluetick, Plott, English, Redbone and Treeing Walker."

The bench show, the initial phase of competition, pits hound against hound in terms of p h y s i c a l soundness and general performance while on display and appearance. Class winners and general show winners ase declared and trophies awarded.

The treeing contest, recently instituted as a phase of the Dan River Club's competition, is a spirited event for everyone, except for a caged raccoon, the bait. It works like this: the dogs are held at a starting point by handlers. The raccoon's cage is brought to the starting point to attract the hound's attention. Then the cage is drawn across an open circle and hoisted into a tree above the dog's reach. The hound, of course, charges the tree and is judged on treeing performance, including such points as the number of times it strikes the tree in jumping for the suspended raccoon. A dog leaving the circle drawn around the tree is disqualified. Each hound's performance is also limited by time.

The night hunt is the main event of the competition. No guns are allowed on the hunt. No raccoons are killed. Like the other events, the night hunt is based on competition between dogs. Ranging over four or five counties, the hunt involves dogs being broken up into "casts" of four dogs each. Each cast hunts for three hours.

"The reason we cover so much territory is that each of us likes to take his cast to a place where he's hunted before, a place where there are known to be a lot of coons," Icenhour explained.

"The dogs are graded by judges on such points as striking a trail, treeing and the proof of the pudding: the number of raccoons sighted as a result of trailing and treeing."

Emerging from the competition are the highest scoring dogs of each cast. The cast winners are then ranked in descending order according to the number of points scored. An over-all winner is then declared on the basis of points.

"We sometimes have 200 dogs in our hunts," said the club secretary. "We also have a number of out-of-state people who come to North Carolina especially for our hunts."

The most important figure in the night hunt is the "Master of Hounds."

"He is the last word on the hunt," said Wayne Baker of Pilot Mountain, who served as "Master of Hounds" for the September hunt. "He settles all disagreements that might arise from the hunt and his word is final."

G. E. Blake of Madison is president of the Dan River Coon Hunters Club. Ed Young, also of Madison, is treasurer and Robert Walker of Winston-Salem is the corresponding secretary. The organization also has a board of directors consisting of five members.

"None of us make a nickel out of it," Icenhour said of the Dan River Club. "We feel like we're doing something for hunting, we like to meet and compete. The only gain is fellowship and making your dog a champion."

The atmosphere of a coon dog event is a mixture of many flavors with the center of attraction, the cooner. It's a day when the dogs show off, and the owners swap yarns and enjoy good fellowship. It's a sport you must see to appreciate.

Snake Tales

PHOTO BY JACK DERMID

PHOTO BY JOEL ARRINGTON

by Luther Partin

Which is which? They're both poisonous "moccasins?" Well, the top photo at right shows a harmless water snake; the lower one is the poisonous cottonmouth. What do you know about snakes?

IT'S hard to find anything under the sun that is the source of as many exaggerations and superstitions as the snake. As an object of lowly comparison, it has no equal.

It's no wonder these members of the reptile family hang out under logs and rocks, or retreat to the seclusion of swamps and thickets. They're ashamed to be seen in public.

Just about every year you can hear the old story about someone who jumped in a pond or stream and was bitten to death on the spot by dozens, or maybe hundreds, of "water moccasins." But I defy you to get anyone to identify the victim. It's always somebody in a neighboring community, the next town, or somewhere. Nobody is quite sure of the locality or the name.

According to a newspaper item of several years ago, this story has been circulating since kids started swimming. It was invented by someone who wanted to keep their children from swimming in dangerous waters without supervision. The story had such an impact that it survived the centuries and is still going strong.

Even today, in sections where stumps reportedly produce an intoxicating "juice," you can hear stories from time to time about a dangerous bear prowling the woods. The bear story is different from the "water moccasin" story, but they both use a form of wildlife as the scapegoat. The idea is to keep children out of the water in one case and everybody out of the woods in the other.

A teenage boy at the 4-H Wildlife Camp last year told of a vicious snake that attacked his father. It seems the snake grabbed its sharp-pointed tail in its mouth and came rolling like a hoop. When it got within striking distance it lashed out with its tail, but missed the boy's father (who had taken evasive tactics) and struck a big white oak. The tree died, according to the boy, not in a few days, or hours or even minutes, but instantly. You have to admit that's pretty fast, approaching the speed of light, or maybe faster.

Of course, there's no snake known to science that can roll like a hoop, although several species have tails that seem to have a strong, sharp point, for example, the sting snake, more properly called the rainbow snake. The tail of the coachwhip appears to be braided and has a sharp-pointed appearance. But it would hardly roll around stabbing people with its tail when, according to more folklore, it can beat a man to death with the tail without working up a sweat.

The "hoop" snake was probably invented by someone who saw the contortions a snake can go through when being beaten to death. Unless a fatal blow is administrated in the beginning, they may twist, roll and grab anything in reach, including their own tail, particularly if the spinal cord has been broken near the tail and there is no additional pain when they latch on. Under these circumstances, the snake may seem to be trying to roll away—or at least this is one explanation for the legend.

The old paperback westerns often compared a man's character or quickness on the draw to rattlesnakes. A man could be "ornery as a rattler" (this was probably in reference to the big diamondback rattler's reluctance to give ground), shifty as a side-w i n d e r (self-explanatory) or

Kill 'em both! Yet the snake on the left is the completely harmless and even beneficial hognose. The one to watch out for is the copperhead, on the right. So much in the out-of-doors is misunderstood; take time to learn more about these elements we call nature.

"crooked as a rattler." None of these was intended to be complimentary. However, to say, "he's quicker'n a rattler on the draw," was definitely an admission of respect for a man's ability with a .44. The multitude of devices for accurately measuring speed today show while a rattler's strike is faster than the average human eye can see (action taking place in less than 1/10 second is a little fast for the average human eye), it's slow compared to a lot of things.

And there's the snake tale to end all snake tales, as far as I'm concerned. It's about a man who tried to kill a copperhead (the type of snake varies with the locality) with a hoe. He was aiming to cut off the snake's head, but missed, and the copperhead sunk his fangs in the hoe handle. The hoe handle started swelling and pretty soon it was as big as a saw log. The man opened a sawmill and started selling lumber. It swelled so much at night he had to cut it in half, lengthwise each morning to be able to handle it. By the time the effects of the snake's poison wore off, he had become a millionaire.

This is about as far out as Jack's overnight beanstalk to the clouds, but if you can tell it with a straight face, you'll get some believers. They may think the amount of lumber is exaggerated, but the rest is gospel.

Some snakes really put on a show when fronted with danger.

Take the hognose for example. It will hiss, blow, flatten its head like a cobra, and play dead. It is frequently called "puff adder," "blowing adder," "spreading adder" and even "ground rattler" in some places. These allusions to poisonous snakes testify to the effectiveness of the hognose's bluff and this accounts for much of the misinformation about snakes, the hognose is not poisonous—its bite is no more dangerous than any other animal that makes small puctures in the skin.

People with access to the information say that over 90 percent of our snakes are nonpoisonous. The poisonous varieties include rattlesnakes, cottonmouth, copperhead, and the secretive coral snake. The cottonmouth is the snake usually referred to as the "water moccasin." Any cottonmouths identified in the piedmont and mountain sections are highly questionable, since their western limit in this s t a t e is around the fall line. Rattlers are not common in the central part of the state. Pigmy and canebrake rattlers occur in the eastern part of the state, with timber rattlers found generally in the west.

Coral snakes have been found only in the southeastern corner of the state and in the lower Sandhills area. The copperhead is more adaptable and can be found in virtually. all parts of the state, but in nowhere near the quantity it is reported.

The rattler, cottonmouth, and

copperhead are all members of the pit viper group. They have triangular heads, a small neck, a short, thick body and a conspicuous "pit" or cavity between the eye and nostril on each side of the head. Their venom attacks the blood stream. It is injected into the victim through hollow, hinged fangs that swing into position when the mouth is opened.

Of course, rattlers have "rattles" on the ends of their tails. But several other snakes, when excited, may vibrate their tails and, in dry leaves, may sound like a rattler. So you need more than sound to identify a rattler.

The cottonmouth may expose the white inside of its mouth when agitated, hence the name. The tendency to call any water snake a "water moccasin" results in reports of cottonmouths being seen all over the state, while they are basically an eastern water snake, seldom venturing far west of the black water swamps.

Copperheads, as the name suggests, have copper-colored heads. But its over-all color p a t t e r n causes it to be confused with the corn snake, several water snakes, the hognose, the eastern kingsnake, and others. Probably over half of the "copperheads" killed are actually one of these other snakes. It's an unusual copperhead that exceeds three feet in length, and one this long would have a body so thick there would be no doubt in your mind that it was dangerous.

The coral snake is in a class by itself, belonging to the c o b r a group. It's venom attacks the nervous system and its fangs are erect and grooved. Positive identification of the coral snake has only been made in eight southeastern counties in sandy-pine-o a k areas. Their burrowing habits isolate them from most humans and greatly reduce the potential danger. The scarlet snake and the scarlet king snake may be mistaken for coral snakes. However, only the coral has a black snout and red, yellow and black rings encircling the body, with the red and yellow rings

PHOTOS BY JOEL ARRINGTON

Both the snakes pictured above are colorful, and display reds, yellows and black. The deadly coral snake, left, has the red and yellow bands touching. The beneficial scarlet kingsnake has black bands separating the reds and yellows. The little pigmy rattlesnake, at right, is seldom over a foot and a half long, but can inflict a poisonous bite.

meeting. The others have red snouts with black rings separating the red and yellow rings. A good rule of thumb is, "red touching yellow can hurt a fellow."

Just how dangerous are poisonous snakes? Well, the statistics show that your chances of being killed by lightning are much greater—maybe 10 to 20 times as much. Sunstroke, heat exhaustion, or venomous insects take a much greater toll of human life than do p o i s o n o u s snakes. Shoveling snow would have to be considered a greater danger, when fatalities are counted. Less than two percent of the people in the United States bitten by poisonous snakes die, according to Roger Conant, a national authority on reptiles.

North Carolina has the highest incidence of poison snakebites of any state east of the Mississippi, according to a survey conducted by Dr. Henry M. Parrish of the Public Health Service. (N. C. Medical Journal, Volume 25, No. 3, March 1964.) But he found the case-fatality rate to be one-tenth of one percent, much less than the national average, or three people during the 1950-59 period. Our record keeping only shows two snakebite fatalities since that time, for a total of five people in 19 years. More people than that have been killed by one bolt of lightning, one car wreck, or any one of a number of tragic events during the same period.

Dr. Parrish theorized that our extremely low death rate could be attributed to the low incidence of rattlesnake bite. The records would indicate some logic in this, since four of the five snakebite deaths in the past 19 years were caused by rattlers. The other fatality involved a copperhead and a child. His research showed over half the snakebite cases involved copperheads, while only seven percent involved rattlers and 15 percent were attributed to cottonmouths. The rest, well over a fourth, were assigned to "unidentified" poisonous snakes. His research also showed than in 50 percent of the cases studied, punctures assumed to be made by fangs were present, but there was no venemation, or signs of venom poisoning.

And this should make you furrow your brow and do a little head scratching. In view of the very limited ability of the majority of people to identify snakes, just how many of these cases actually involved p o i s o n o u s snakes.

The standard treatment for snakebite is the tourniquet-cut-suction (TCS) technique. This involves a constricting band around the limb just above the bite to restrict the spread of the poison but not arterial blood flow. Small cuts are made with a sterile instrument through the punctures and around the immediate area and suction applied to remove as much poison as possible. The patient should have professional medical help as soon as possible, keeping the patient quiet and loosening the tourniquet each 10-15 minutes for one to two minutes.

The most important points to remember probably are: try to restrict the spread of the poison with the tourniquet (shoestring, handkerchief, belt, etc.); get the victim to a doctor quickly, but calmy and safely. There's not even a chance in a thousand that the victim will become a fatality in this state if he receives medical treatment, according to the record.

If you are interested in a different and very controversial type of treatment for snakebite, write to the Poisonous Animals Research Laboratory, Arizona State College, Tempe, Arizona. For ten cents they'll send you a summary of the Ligature-cryo-therapy (L-C) method of treatment. This method is not generally accepted by physicians, in fact, all that we've talked to would not consider using it. The Journal of the American Medical Association has contained several references indicating that cryotherapy might cause needless amputation of limbs in snakebite cases. If you want a different opinion, write to the above address. ♦

Solo On Doves

by Frank Mooney
Hallsboro, N. C.

Don't let a big, empty field scare you away from dove hunting. If you have to solo on doves, here are a few ideas that should help make the afternoon more interesting.

I'M not antisocial in any way when it comes to dove hunting with a group; however, at times when I have some free time on my hands and my hunting compadres have their noses to the grindstone, I hunt alone. The other day I heard a dove hunter complaining about waiting all afternoon for his hunting partner to show up so he could go hunting. If your friends are busy, instead of holding your hands and moaning the blues, get out and hunt doves alone. It takes a little more work and strategy, but at times it's more gratifying to know you outsmarted the feathered missiles all by yourself. So many hunters think it's a waste of time to hunt doves alone when there is a large field to cover by one hunter.

It's easy to find a place to conceal yourself and wait for the birds to start flying when hunters have surrounded the field to keep the doves circling and looking for a place to eat, but the lone hunter with a few tricks can have fun and meat too. When possible I enjoy hunting with friends at a good dove shoot with competition keen among the best shots. Competition always adds spice to any sport; however, with hunters in all walks of life with varying free time and days off, it pays to be able to fill your limit under adverse conditions. Through the years of hunting alone, I have a few tricks that have helped fill the gamebag.

Today I went into new territory around three o'clock to ask a dairy farmer if I could hunt in his field where he had cut corn for silage. After getting permission to hunt, I drove the car to one end of the field. I observed the doves' flying patterns for several minutes—w h e r e they came into the field, what part of the field they were using, and what cover they flew over while circling the field for a better look. During dove activity it's easy to get an idea of their pattern in a few minutes of watching. This field was about 25 acres, and the larger the field, of course, the harder it is for one hunter to · cover it. The doves were flying over the pasture interspersed with small pines that adjoined the field on one side, and on the opposite side they were drifting in over some low pines and hardwoods.

These mourning doves were feeding almost in the middle of the field. Most of the time doves have a certain place in the field to feed and after picking one spot clean they shift to another. If you see doves feeding on a certain side of the field, you can bet most of the doves will be using that area. The doves were flying high over the pasture and the low pines, then dropping down as they reached the center of the field. I knew if I was to get much action I would have to be near the center. There was a clump of waist-high grass near the place the birds were using.

I crouched low and started for the birds, the clump of grass I hoped, would hide my stalk. Several birds flushed beyond range and I was beginning to think all the birds had left when 15 or 20 got up about 35 yards to my left. I managed to grass two before they got out of range. One hunter can often stalk doves successfully with a little cover and some knowledge of their habits. I found out that day that practically all the birds would flush back over my head rather than fly across the paved road that bordered the field on one side. When stalking I always get them toward the road before trying for a kill. When stalking doves and they fly up beyond shotgun range, continue on, because usually one or two will stick longer than the rest.

After retrieving the birds I settled down on my cushion to await the return of the main bunch that had flushed when I drove into the field. At times it pays bigger dividends not to shoot any birds as they leave the field especially if it's late in the afternoon when most of the birds have fed heavily. On this occasion as I stalked the birds, most had flushed out of the field before I fired a shot. When birds have fed unmolested for sometime, and you shoot as they leave the field, most often the birds will not return that day. I found this out the hard way by waiting in vain on several occasions for the smart birds that failed to remake the scene.

When hunting alone it helps to keep the birds moving by parking the car on the opposite end of the field. Often they flare off from the car and fly down one's gun barrel. When possible, get into a shaded spot to conceal yourself from the sharp eyes of the experienced dove. Just a little natural foliage does great wonders in disfiguring your silhouette. An old shirt tied to a bush or corn stalk and placed strategically often will turn the doves your way. When possible, sit with your back to the sun for two good reasons. First, the doves cannot see you as plainly because of the glare from the sun. Second, when a dove comes behind you its shadow often can be detected on the ground near you, and serves as a warning signal, like calm water mirrors incoming birds when you are duck hunting.

The smart doves like a dead tree to light in to check the area before commencing to eat. Decoys placed in the correct place will often help get the single hunter his limit. Be sure the facsimile is perched where the real McCoy would be, and remember to have the decoys facing the wind. Doves like to sit on the top limbs where it's the hardest to place the decoys, but it pays to set them right.

About 20 minutes later the birds started drifting back one and two to feed. I was stationed between the feeding area and the pasture. I was directly under one of the flying lanes. If you cannot get in the exact spot they are feeding, the next best is the flying lane, or the place where most of the birds leave the woods to enter the field. I had some fast shooting which was mostly pass shooting, and I stalked several birds successfully after they reached the feeding area. By five o'clock I had my limit of 12 birds with less than a box of shells. I was proud of my shooting, because my average doesn't hold up that well.

One day I was shooting with plenty of doves feeding in a picked milo field, but the doves were hard to get within gun range. They were using a certain spot in the field and no cover was near, the grass and milo stalks were only inches high. After trying to intercept them between the forest and the field with no luck, I sat in the field where the birds were feeding. I was spotted every time before the birds were in range and they would head for the woods. I was about ready to give up and admit defeat when an idea struck me.

After finding a small sunken place between two rows, I laid

There are many little things that will help the lone hunter (and the group guys, too) when it comes to fooling doves. For example, stay out of sight as much as possible, yet be in a position to see the birds as they head in. And be ready! You can't hit 'em if you can't see 'em.

down with my gun held in ready position, when the birds came in all I had to do was sit up and fire. I quickly grassed my limit, because the birds came in low without hesitation. It was rewarding to outwit the elusive targets

On several occasions when going to a field alone to hunt I have found other hunters in the same condition. Most gunners will welcome another hunter to help keep the doves flying. I have found nimrods in this situation that later turned out to be close friends. Some hunters that you run into want to be left alone, and usually within a couple of minutes you can tell if the hunter wishes company. Maybe the fellow has a problem he wants to work out alone, so politely bow out and continue to the other side of the field.

By keeping your gun in a ready position may mean the difference between getting off a shot or letting the bird slip past. The mourning dove is king of the road when it comes to slipping over the hunter from a blind side. I sit with my left hand on the forearm and right hand around the stock with my finger on the safety. When a bird reaches shooting range all I do is slip off the safety and place my finger

on the trigger as I bring the gun to my shoulder. After some practice one can sit in that position for a long time.

When downing a bird I quickly line it up with a tree or some stationary object, then I walk straight toward the marker. If I fail to find the bird where I think it should be, I place my hat or handkerchief to keep me from wandering too far off course. The polaroid glasses that are invaluable to the fisherman can also be great for the dove hunter on these bright, cloudless days.

When possible, select a clean field to shoot in. Looking for downed birds in tall g r a s s or weeds can be time consuming and thus cut your actual hunting time. Sometimes you have to sit in a high weedy place or tall g r a s s if you want some fast shooting. When downing a bird in this type of terrain, do not take your eye off the spot where the bird hit. If you walk straight to the spot it will save time and birds. Do not try to double in this fashion because usually it will take a lot of time to find both birds.

In damp cloudy weather when birds fly most of the day, the mosquitoes are often on the prowl too. A bottle of insect re-

pellent will be a welcome item should this occur. Without the repellent you may wave a lot of doves away during the afternoon. There are several other items that will make the ardent hunter's day more pleasant. A thermos of cold liquid and a sandwich or candy bar will refresh on a hot dry day. A low stool or cushion will make the sitting more comfortable and enjoyable. During hot days of the first segment of the season, it's usually around 1:30 or two o'clock before much dove activity can be noticed in the field, so don't be in any hurry during these periods. Most doves quit feeding around five o'clock to get gravel and water before going to roost.

If you're lucky enough to find a roost, the short span just before sundown can be fast and furious. Also when dry weather thins down the watering places, this can be a great climax to a bad day. I have seen old logging roads produce good action late in the afternoon where doves were using them to get gravel. Gunning pressure is light around the southeastern part of North Carolina, and I think a lot of hunters are unaware of the great sport the first segment of the season offers. Most outdoor enthusiasts have been fishing for six months with August and the first part of September usually a slow time for fishing.

The Piedmont section seems to offer more for the avid dove hunter than the rest of the state. The eastern part doesn't plant the grain like milo and millet or cut silage like other parts of the state, but if you can find the select spots, the shooting can be fantastic. However, doves can be found anywhere with a little checking. Feed lots, corn that hogs are fenced in, old gardens that weeds have taken over, old pea patches, and other places will often produce good dove hunting.

Most hunters have some trick of their own, so with my tips and your ideas even if your buddy has to work or maybe mow the lawn, you can help yourself to dove hunting alone with a good chance to bag your limit. ♦

PHOTO BY LUTHER PARTIN

The dove hunter can also help himself to better future hunting by returning bands he finds on downed birds. This bird being banded here may fly your way before long. And, even though the bag limit this year is a generous one, play the game according to the regulations.

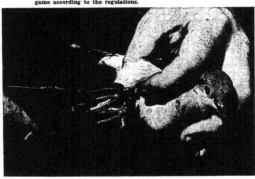

THE trout streams of western North Carolina constitute an unique and valuable resource. These trout streams are located at the extreme southern range of the normal trout habitat on the eastern seaboard. This habitat exists only by virtue of high elevation, thus cooler water temperatures and, because that habitat cannot be expanded, the ever-increasing pressure from fishermen on the streams can be satisfied only by intensive and critical trout management.

It requires only a small amount of habitat tampering to tip formerly productive trout waters into the non-productive class. Water temperatures, for example, in many North Carolina streams are near the lethal limits for year around survival. Any factor, such as destroying stream cover, altering stream flows, and the building of impoundments may increase the water temperatures to a point where trout cannot survive throughout the year.

Each year more and more of North Carolina's trout streams are being lost. With the building of small impoundments for flood control by the Soil Conservation Service and by the construction of large impoundments for flood control and/or electrical power by the U. S. Army Corp of Engineers, privately-owned power companies, and the Tennessee Valley Authority on trout streams several things may happen: (1) the stream habitat may be replaced by reservoir habitat; (2) the new impoundment may invite the invasion of warm-water fish which compete with trout for living space and food; (3) water temperatures may warm within the impoundment and below it, thus destroying downstream trout habitat; (4) silt loads may increase downstream during construction, which decrease the fish food supply and reduce egg survival during the incubation period; and (5) the upstream movement of trout may be blocked, most significantly, during the spawning season.

With the addition of new and better State and Federal highways throughout the mountains, the trout habitat is diminishing. New highways often (1) cause removal of stream bank vegetation where new roads parallel trout streams, thus increasing the water temperature beyond that tolerable to trout; (2) cause stream realignment, and thus the destruction of pools and riffles; (3) cause changes in natural flow regimens and reduction of normal stream depths; and (4) create increased siltation and turbidities downstream during and following construction.

Turbidity in the streams is also increased with farming activities, the construction of residential developments, golf courses, and the like. During periods of construction, the increased silt load in the stream can reach a proportion where trout eggs can be covered up and destroyed.

ANOTHER major loss of trout waters results from the posting of private lands. During 1969, 26 miles of trout streams were posted against trespass. With more money available to purchase summer resort property on streams, more posted signs are surely to occur. Ultimately, the State may approach the point where the only managed trout waters left are on publically held lands.

The above examples show that existing trout habitat has decreased and will continue to decrease. Fishermen utilization per acre of these existing waters is increasing yearly. The number of trout licenses sold in 1954 was 24,713 and in 1968, fourteen years later, 62,328. The 1968 figure does not include minors under sixteen years of age who, based on past wildlife management area data, account for 16.7 percent of the total fishermen. By combining the two, the total was 72,736 trout fishermen in 1968, about three times as many as in 1954.

This pattern of increasing rod pressure will continue because of increasing population, with increasing leisure time, because of the increasing mobility of the fisherman with his camper, and because the trout streams are becoming more accessible by new and better roads.

The crisis faced is an increasing fishing pressure on a limited and shrinking mileage of trout water. The problem is—can the North Carolina Wildlife Resources Commission preserve and even improve trout fishing in the face of these forces now at work?

The first decision must be which way to go—increase hatchery production and stock more trout

14

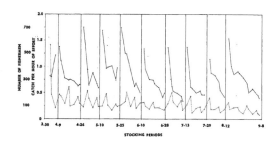

FIGURE 1. The solid line is the catch of trout from the Davidson River during the investigation period in 1965, while the broken line shows the fishing pressure in numbers of fishermen. Both of these figures are related to the times when trout were stocked.

in the streams, or go to a "catch and release" fishery. These, of course, are the two extremes and there are areas in between which appear to be the most economical and practical.

PRESENTLY, North Carolina is stocking 603,600 "catchable" size trout which can be subdivided into 175,700 brook, 292,100 rainbow, and 153,900 brown trout. Of these, the Federal Hatcheries are producing 211,000 trout and the four State Hatcheries 392,600 trout. Of the trout waters open to public fishing, about half are on Federally controlled lands. Stocking these waters is the first priority of the Federal Government, and they provide about half of all trout stocked in the State. The State and Federal stocking programs are integrated so that all waters open to the public receive equal consideration.

These 603,600 trout are presently being stocked into 253 trout streams open to the public, plus several trout lakes and reservoirs and the suitable streams in the wildlife management areas. Present trout stocking consists of one pre-season stocking and five in-season stockings in most streams. The number of current stream-stocking truck trips is about 1500 per year. With the number of existing distribution trucks and present manpower, this provides little time to distribute the trout throughout the streams. At best, only pools near the roads are stocked on each stream. This leaves the trout vulnerable to anglers, and the immediate effects on catch rates following stocking are obvious.

For example, consider the Davidson River data during 1965 to see how angling pressure, catch rate, and stocking are correlated. In 1965, 21,000 rainbow and brook trout were stocked into the stream during 10 stocking periods spaced at approximately two-week intervals (Figure 1). Throughout the ten stocking periods, on this stream, fishing pressure was greater immediately after the stocking, and then tapered off until the next stocking period. As can be seen in the Figure, a few exceptions did occur; those being when stocking occurred prior to Wednesday (the management area streams are open only on Wednesdays, Saturday, Sundays, and legal holidays during the season). In each case, the following Saturday, when anglers were not working, fishing pressure increased significantly. The catch per hour of effort immediately following stocking was exceptionally high. Throughout the ten stocking periods, the catch rate on the first Saturday after stocking was about 2 trout per hour. By the end of the stocking period, the catch rate had declined to about one-third trout per hour of effort. As can be seen, the catch rate was directly related to the stocking density.

The sharp increases in both catch rate and fishing pressure following each stocking occurred because more fish were available for harvest, with the bulk of the pressure coming from local fishermen who were familiar with the stocking schedules. As a result, the fishermen fished the stream heavily following stocking and harvesting a large percentage of the stocked trout.

Because of this, a large percentage of the hatchery trout released into the Davidson River were harvested immediately after stocking. The result was: (1) it provided a temporary buffer to the wild trout; (2) it produced a high harvest of the hatchery product, and (3) it attracted local fishermen to the stream for a limited time where they enjoyed a high catch rate per hour.

To obtain a more even catch rate than was obtained on the Davidson River, the number of stockings could be increased and the number of trout stocked per trip decreased. It should be pointed out that more frequent stockings of hatchery trout are not possible at the present time under existing finances with the existing manpower and distribution equipment.

From interviews with 36,126 North Carolina trout fishermen in 1964, it was learned that 71.3 percent traveled less than 35 miles one way to fish a given stream, whereas 13.5 percent traveled from 36-65 miles, 6.4 percent traveled between 66 and 100 miles and 4.3 percent traveled greater than 100 miles. From this data, it is evident that trout streams are fished primarily by local fishermen.

The ideal return of the hatchery product under the principles of "put and take" management should be 80, 80, and 60 percent, respectively, for brook, rainbow and brown trout. Under the existing trout stocking program, returns of the stocked trout are about 60-65 percent. These data are based on returns of hatchery trout on management areas, 1955-1964. On heavily fished streams, the returns may reach 80 percent, but on the many lightly fished streams, the returns are probably in the vicinity of 30-35 percent, a waste of hatchery trout.

THE economics of a "catchable" stocking program must be considered. At the present time, the "catchable" trout stocked into North Carolina's waters average about 3 fish per pound. At a cost of raising and delivering the trout to the stream for release presently at $1.25 per pound and with a harvest per trip of about 4 fish, the average cost to the State is $1.66 per fisherman trip. To go one step further, if we presently have a return of only 60 percent of our fish, then the cost to the State per fisherman trip is $2.66, or more than twice the price of a trout license.

In a recent survey published by the Colorado Game, Fish and Parks Division on trout licenses, North Carolina was shown to rank fourth highest, out of 13 states having trout licenses, in pounds of trout stocked per license holder. North Carolina stocked 3.74 pounds of trout per trout license in 1968, 1.26 pounds higher than the national average.

And why not stock fingerling trout? The cost of producing trout in the creel by stocking fingerlings versus "catchable" fish is significantly higher. Of a total of 238,000 marked "fingerlings" stocked in 21 experimental stockings in the United States, the mean rate of return was 2.4 percent with a range of 0 to 3.3 percent. Based on a return of 2.4 percent and a cost of 1.8 cents to raise one fingerling, it costs the State 75¢ to put a trout in the creel by stocking fingerlings. The cost of "catchable" trout stocked in the stream and creeled by the fisherman is only 41¢.

From a management basis, the actual increase in trout available to anglers, achieved by stocking fingerlings, is negligible if a wild-trout population is present.

If the trout fisherman were paying the total cost, then the existing stocking program might be justifiable. Presently, fishing license funds are being used to make trout fishing available to fishermen who are not utilizing the fishery. Therefore, stocking should be reduced to balance the expenses with the income and the trout stocked where they will be harvested.

Those who work with a "catchable" trout program recognize it for what it is: recreation pure and simple, largely unrelated to resources management. This type of program serves thousands of individual anglers and the many family groups who seek casual fishing on trips to the mountains. Without this type program, mass angling in most North Carolina roadside trout streams would collapse.

The antithesis of a "catchable" trout program is a "catch and release" program where all trout taken are released. This philosophy allows the angler to catch an unlimited number of trout but kill none.

This extreme for all waters is not practical because many of North Carolina trout fishermen prefer the use of bait rather than artificial lures. These fishermen consider "good fishing" in terms of the kill and not the total catch. There is also the fact that a great number of our streams have too much cover, thereby making fly fishing difficult.

At present, North Carolina is trying a middle of the road approach which appears to have promise. These ventures are the "Trophy Trout" streams and the "Native Trout" streams, both programs being located on the wildlife management areas.

The two "Trophy Trout" waters have restrictions of one trout per day with a minimum size of 16 inches for brown and rainbow and 12 inches for brook trout. A further restriction is that only artificial flies having one single hook are permitted. There is no stocking of trout of legal size in these streams.

"Native Trout" waters, of which there are 12, have a creel of 4 trout per day, a size limit of 10 inches for brown and rainbow and 6 inches for brook, and a restriction to artificial lures equipped with one single hook. These streams are stocked only with fingerling trout and then only when biological investigations reveal a shortage of naturally propagated trout.

A 1965-67 research study, which was carried out on four "Native Trout" streams: Steels, Harper, Curtis, and South Toe River, gives an idea of what these streams are producing. The ratio of retained to total catch ranged from 1:25 to 1:20.3 fish per trip. The take home harvest during this time ranged from 0.1 to 0.52 trout per hour of effort. All in all, the trout fishermen fishing the streams enjoyed catching, but not killing, all trout caught and yet being able to take home a few for supper. How long these streams will sustain the current catch rates, under this type program, or how acceptable the philosophy may be to a majority of trout fishermen, cannot be fully answered with the data collected to date. Further study is planned for 1969 in answering the two questions.

In a recent research study entitled "Trout Fishery Surveillance", Dr. Frederic F. Fish found that the 1968 trout catch approached the magnitude of about 2,750,000 fish of which the State stocked 750,000. Of the 750,000 trout stocked, approximately 575,000 were creeled. In other words, it appears that the hatcheries are producing only about one in five of the trout harvested. If the foregoing conclusion is valid, then the effective protection of the wild trout resource is an essential key to the future of trout fishing in North Carolina.

Which way the trout program is developed will have to depend on recognized principles: the wishes of the fishermen, the limits of the resource, now and in the future, present and future fishing pressure, and the economics of producing each form of management. ◆

RESOURCE-O-GRAM
A ROUNDUP OF THE LATEST WILDLIFE NEWS

Public Hearings for Fishing Regulations

The Wildlife Resources Commission will again hold three public hearings to give Tar Heel anglers a voice in setting the fresh water fishing regulations for the 1970 fishing season. The schedule:

October 7, Asheville Courthouse 7:30 p.m.
October 8, Salisbury Courthouse 7:30 p.m.
October 9, Washington Agriculture Auditorium 7:30 p.m.

Main topic of discussion at these meetings will be proposed changes in current regulations.

Dove, Marsh Hen Seasons Open September 1.

The fall hunting season opens half an hour before sunrise on Labor Day when shooting begins for marsh hens. A few hours later, at 12:00 noon, dove hunting begins. Shooting for both types of birds ends at sundown daily. Bag limit for marsh hens is 15 birds daily, 30 in possession after opening day. Dove limit is 18 birds daily (a record) and 36 in possession after opening day. The large dove limit is a federal experiment to determine whether more birds may be taken by hunters without cutting into the breeding stock. Biologists contend 80 per cent of doves are lost annually from natural mortality whether they are hunted or not.

"Estuarine Resources"—A New Book

Persons interested in reading the latest literature on the State's estuarine resources and their importance to the marine fishery may obtain a compilation of recent papers on the subject by writing to "Estuarine Resources," Wildlife Resources Commission, Box 2919, Raleigh 27602. Copies are free while the supply lasts.

The 1969 General Assembly set a record for longevity, and almost set a record for the number of wildlife-related bills. Altogether, a total of 45 bills pertaining to wildlife conservation and boating safety were introduced. Of these, 22 House bills and six Senate bills passed, while eleven House bills and six Senate bills were either killed or died in committee.

Following is a concise summary of this legislation in the order in which it was introduced:

Bill Number (Introducer)	Descriptive Title	Date Ratified
House Bills		
HB 19 (S. Johnson)	To make appropriations to provide capital improvements for state institutions, departments and agencies.	6-11-69
HB 169 (Moore & H. Johnson)	Hunting from public roads in Duplin and Pender counties. Permission needed from landowner onto whose land firearms will be discharged. Amended to delete Duplin and add New Hanover counties.	3-27-69
HB 220 (H. Johnson, Mohn, Moore, Ragsdale)	Establishes the hunting season for bear, deer, and squirrel in Duplin and Pender counties. Season to be open from October 1 to January 1.	4-22-69
HB 240 (Barr)	Regulates the use of firearms in field trials in training dogs. Prohibits the use of shotgun or rifle, and the taking of game birds or animals during closed season by reason thereof.	3-17-69
HB 241 (Barr)	Requires skin divers to display a warning flag as approved by the Underwater Society of America. Amended to exempt Pender and New Hanover counties. Amended so that a diver is not re-	3-19-69

	quired to surface within 25 feet of the warning flag.	
HB 242 (Barr)	Exempts boats operated on private ponds from Motorboat Law.	3-17-69
HB 254 (P. Godwin)	Closes the bear season in a portion of Gates County until 1973.	3-25-69
HB 263 (Barr)	Prohibits the taking of wildlife at night with the aid of any artificial light from or through the use of any conveyance. Does not prohibit the use of a conveyance in reaching the location of the hunt.	3-28-69
HB 292 (McFayden)	Amends Chapter 215 of the Public Local Laws of 1931 relating to fox hunting in Hoke and other counties so as to except Hoke County from the provisions of said Act. Allows fox hunting in Hoke County other than between Sept. 1 and March 15.	4-7-69
HB 299 (H. Johnson)	Prohibits hunting from public roads in Duplin County without permission from landowner onto whose land firearms will be discharged. Includes Durham and Stokes counties.	4-7-69
HB 325 (Burrus & Roberson)	Prohibits the hunting of game animals with dogs between March 1 and October 15 in Beaufort County.	4-22-69
HB 413 (Barr)	Allocates 1/8 of 1% of the net proceeds of the tax on gasoline to the Wildlife Resources Commission on a continuing basis.	7-1-69
HB 453 (Messer & L. Ramsey)	Prohibits the discharge of firearms on or across any highway in Haywood County.	4-22-69
HB 573 (Roberson & Burrus)	Prohibits the taking of bear in Tyrrell County until 1973.	6-9-69
HB 667 (R. Jones)	Permits the snagging of nongame fish in a portion of Polk County.	5-29-69
HB 941 (Harris)	Permits residents of the state who are blind to fish in Lake Norman, at Camp Dogwood, without a fishing license.	6-11-69
HB 1008 (Speros & Quinn)	Provides for a permanent hunting and fishing license for state residents over 65 years of age upon payment of $10 and proof of eligibility. Provides for a permanent hunting and fishing license for persons over 70 years of age for no charge.	6-25-69
HB 1101 (Bryan & Boshamer)	Directs the Division of Commercial and Sports Fisheries to make a comprehensive study of the estuaries of North Carolina.	6-30-69
HB 1225 (Baugh)	Establishes a North Carolina Water Safety Committee, empowers local governments to create and sponsor local water safety committees. Grants the Wildlife Resources Commission the power to make regulations over matters of water safety, and to implement the Uniform State Waterway Marking System.	6-30-69
HB 1258 (C. Taylor)	Protects wild or feral hogs in Jackson and Transylvania counties.	7-2-69
HB 1263 (Barr)	Adopts the gray squirrel as official State mammal.	7-1-69
HB 1324 (Leatherman)	Establishes the Lake Norman Marine Commission.	6-30-69

House Resolution

1431 (H. Johnson)	Directs the Legislative Research Commission to study the cost and feasibility of the propagation, processing, and marketing of quail.	Adopted 7-2-69

Senate Bills

SB 311 (Wood)	Amends Chapter 146 of the General Statutes of North Carolina to authorize the Department of Administration to issue permits to riparian owners adjoining navigable waters to dredge in navigable waters and to establish a schedule of charges for spoil taken from navigable waters and state-owned lakes.	6-11-69
SB 312 (Wood)	Amends Chapter 146 of the General Statutes of North Carolina to establish regulations to preserve the natural beauty of navigable waters within the State.	6-12-69
SB 425 (Patterson)	Prohibits the taking of game from public highways in Stanly County.	6-16-69
SB 428 (Robinson)	Authorizes commercial and sports fisheries inspectors and wildlife protectors to obtain and execute search warrants.	4-28-69
SB 613 (Moore)	*Amends the General Statutes relating to hunting, trapping, and fishing license fees (See below).	6-27-69
SB 683 (Moore)	Amends G.S. 105-294 to declare the policy of the State with respect to the advalorem taxation of marshlands.	6-19-69

—Compiled by Charles Fullwood.

* If you hunt deer, bear, wild boar or wild turkeys this fall, you will need to buy a separate big game hunting license. It will be available from your license dealer along with other licenses. Its cost: $1.75 ($.25 of this goes to your license dealer).

A tax-weary Legislature raised the price on all hunting, fishing, and trapping licenses except nonresident hunting licenses. The increase averages less than a dollar per license, and the added funds are absolutely necessary for the Wildlife Commission to carry on and improve its wildlife conservation program in the face of rising operational costs.

Without this increase, the Commission would not have been able to pay its employees salary increases granted by the Legislature to all other state employees, since the Commission is not supported by general taxation.

The new big game license is expected to yield about $150,000 in additional revenue. This will be used for acquisition and development of new big game restoration areas, improvement of current programs on existing wildlife management areas for big game, and expansion of programs for big game populations throughout the state. For only $1.75 you are sure of getting your money's worth.

Here are the new license price schedules:

Hunting and Trapping	Old Price	New Price	Date Effective
Resident County	$1.65	$2.50	Aug. 1, '69
Resident State	4.25	5.50	"
Resident State Trapping	3.25	4.25	"
Resident County Trapping	2.25	3.25	"
Controlled Shooting Preserve	5.25	6.50	"
Resident Combination Hunting and Fishing	6.25	7.50	"
Nonresident Landowner's County Hunting	5.25	5.50	"
Fishing			
Resident State Daily	.85	1.25	Jan. 1, '70
Resident County	1.65	2.50	"
Resident State	4.25	5.50	"
Nonresident State Daily	1.65	2.25	"
Nonresident State Five-Day	3.75	4.25	"
Nonresident State	8.25	9.50	"
Resident Special Trout	1.25	2.25	"
Nonresident Special Trout	3.25	4.25	"

Public Hunting Areas
1969-70

In its continuing program of providing Tarheel hunters with small game and dove hunting throughout the state, the Wildlife Resources Commission again this year has made available the areas shown on the accompanying map. The legend at far right indicates the days of the week on which hunting is permitted and other conditions of interest to the hunter. Those areas carrying a letter designation (A-E) are called Small and Migratory Game Public Hunting Areas, while those numbered (1-17) are labeled Dove Hunting Areas. All these areas require the $5.50 Season Game Lands Permit in addition to your hunting license.

The mourning dove season has been set in two segments, the first to open September 1, ending October 11. The second segment gets underway at 12 noon December 18, and ends January 15, 1970. The daily bag limit this year is 18, with 36 in possession after the first day's shooting.

A. Union County—Braswell and Covington land. Nine miles south of Monroe on US 601 to Secondary Road 1005, thence east 3 miles to Secondary Road 1919, thence south along Secondary Road 1919.

B. Davie and Davidson Counties—Cooleemee Plantation. Accessible from US 64 west of the Yadkin River in Davie County and from Secondary Roads 1176, 1178 and 1185 south of US 64 in Davidson County.

C. Granville C o u n t y—Corinth Community Farms. Five miles north of Wilton on NC 96. Area lies north of the Tar River and south of Secondary Road 1618.

D. Wake County—Perry and Poe Farms. South from New Hill 2.5 miles on Secondary Road 1135.

E. Robeson C o u n t y—King and Keith Farms. Two miles north of St. Pauls on US 301.

F. Sandhills Wildlife Management Area.

G. Caswell Wildlife Management Area.

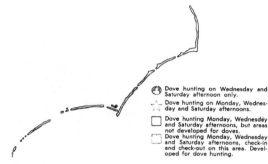

Dove hunting on Wednesday and Saturday afternoon only.

Dove hunting on Monday, Wednesday and Saturday afternoons.

Dove hunting Monday, Wednesday and Saturday afternoons, but areas not developed for doves.

Dove hunting Monday, Wednesday and Saturday afternoons, check-in and check-out on this area. Developed for dove hunting.

1. Buncombe County—Parks Farm. Seven miles south of Asheville on Highway NC 191.

2. Caldwell County—Wilson Farm. Two miles west of Granite Falls on Secondary Road 1122, thence .6 mile to Secondary Road 1123.

3. Catawba County—Sigmon Sons Farm. One mile west of Newton on NC 10 to Secondary Road 2013, thence two miles south.

4. Gaston County—Hallman Farm. Six miles south of Cherryville on NC 216 to Secondary Road 1401, thence east to farm.

5. Mecklenburg County—County land. Seven miles north of I-85 on US 21, between Secondary Roads 2116 and 2117.

6. Cabarrus County—Foil Land. Two miles northeast of Mt. Pleasant on Secondary Road 2604.

7. Union County—Marsh Farm. One and one-half miles south of Marshville on Secondary Road 1902.

8. Forsyth County—Davis Farm. Four and one-half miles south of Clemmons on Secondary Road 3000. Farm is on right approximately one mile after crossing railroad tracks.

9. Randolph County — Johnson Farm. West 2.5 miles from US 220 in Randleman to Secondary Road 1939, thence northeast one mile to Muddy Creek.

10. Guilford County — County Farm. Two miles north of Gibsonville on Secondary Road 2741 to Secondary Road 2240, thence east to farm.

11. Orange County—Perry Farm. One mile north of Hillsborough on NC 86 to Secondary Road 1332, thence northwest .7 mile to Secondary Road 1306, thence southwest to farm.

12. Vance County—Nutbush Peninsula. 4.7 miles northwest of Williamsboro on Secondary Road 1329, thence 1/4 mile north of the intersection of Secondary Roads 1329 and 1333.

13. Wake County—Fish Farm. Eight miles south of Raleigh on US 401 (.9 mile south of Middle Creek) to Secondary Road 2752, thence .8 mile to farm.

14. Nash County—Anderson Farm. Three miles west of Battleboro and 6 miles north of Rocky Mount on Highway NC 48.

15. Edgecombe County—Dail Farm. Four miles east of Leggett on NC 97 to Secondary Road 1500, thence one mile south to farm.

16. Jones County—Foy Farm. Four miles west of Trenton on Highway NC 58 and Secondary Road 1300.

17. Pasquotank County—Coppersmith Farm. Three miles southwest from Elizabeth City on US 17 to Secondary Road 1144, thence east on Secondary Road 1144 one mile to Secondary Road 1141, thence south on Secondary Road 1141 .6 mile to Secondary Road 1142, thence on Secondary Road 1142 1.5 miles to the area.

SNAKES ALIVE

by Patricia F. Ross
Wilson, N. C.

THERE are snakes in these woods of ours, and I was unprepared to meet them. We moved from New England to East Caroline and built among ing pines, dogwood and bay, not dreaming invading reptil

Soon after from a da encounter of talking

Mam dog got where w took film

He ha

A kno is big swelled up,

Come see

Mrs. Ross, us drawled

I looked and saw tion of the sod flug yard and the mutilated the snake. Enough was left identification purposes so I sent for the book on snakes. I could see two distinct hour glass markings. It was a poisonous copperhead for sure! I felt a quiver up my spine as I thought about the workman who weeks before killed two snakes and laid them out on a log.

"Are they poisonous?" I asked.

"Yes ma'am! They is poisonous all right," the workman replied.

ANXIOUS to welcome friends to our new home, I invited 30 girls to drop by for coffee one morning. Going to the door, I found one of my guests inching her way backward, slowly toward the street.

"What's the matter, Mabel?" I called.

Mabel's shaky voice answered, "There's a snake in your walkway and I'm afraid of snakes."

Jean, standing near me in the doorway, shouted, "Get a hoe or shovel—or something!"

22

I ran to fetch a tool while the snake, unattentive to the commotion of excited women, made his way slowly across the walk; but, with hoe in hand I managed to get him before he reached the hollow tree.

That night at dinner family about it thinking how pro be of me for it?"

was ligh

"Yo

he

ed across the yard to see black snake emerge from a in the base of a maple tree snake was so flabbergasted his dark forest flooded light and the alien sur that he didn't move and friends agreed be ficial and should not ed one of the child could be the family

Weeks passed end of summer playing in the excitedly, "Mo There's a big s creek."

Down by the c to be a cottonm veloper had warned about those poisonous moccasins in the low areas. I yelled for him to keep back and ran for the hoe. The snake opened his mouth as I approached and sure enough it was all white inside. Standing far back I made several licks for he was finished

A
c
sn
ex

Th
to
F
So

Skipper's Corner
by John R. Parker Jr.
SAFETY FIRST

THE General Assembly cruised out of the Capitol City a month or so back and in its wake there remained four ratified bills affecting boating. The new legislation ranges in magnitude from a bill to give added safety to an individual diver, to a money bill that will affect the boating program of the entire state. Notice I said "will affect" and not *could have affected*. So let us shove off on that happy note.

The new marine fuel tax bill, *H. B. 413*, allocates one eighth of one percent of the net proceeds of the tax on gasoline to the Wildlife Resources Commission on a continuing basis. Continuing, is the key word. The 1967 version was a two-year appropriations bill leaving future funding in doubt. The percentage will amount to approximately $200,000 a n n u a l l y, a fair sum of money indeed. However, those of you following this important legislation and the information published thereon may remember that every survey made, revealed that boaters annually pay more than *twice* that amount into the Highway Fund via gasoline tax. So, good boating buddies, keep that in mind in 1971.

House Bill 241, the skin diver flag bill, was ratified early in the session, March 19. This new law requires that skin and SCUBA divers display a diver's flag (red, not less than 12 inches square and with a d i a g o n a l white stripe). Boats underway are not to approach within 50 feet of such a flag unless the flag is positioned so as to "constitute an unreasonable obstruction to navigation." The law goes on to say that divers shall not dive where legitimate navigation is obstructed. The flag may be flown from a

buoy, or mast or other structure.

There is an interesting footnote to this piece of water safety legislation. The counties of Pender and New Hanover are exempt. Let us not forget also that New Hanover is among the nine counties that still remain exempt regarding life saving devices being required on boats of under ten horsepower. And further, it is this nine-county exemption that still, after many years, prevents North Carolina's boating law from being formally approved by the Federal Government in the form of the U. S. Coast Guard. And add to that the fact that this area (nine southeastern counties) accounts for its fair share of boating fatalities. A curious way to attack the water safety problem.

House Bill 1225, often referred to as the Water Safety Committee Bill was a voluminous piece of boating legislation that has undergone a little surgery since the 1967 version. This bill adds a new article, Article 2, to Chapter 75A, the Boat Law. Very briefly, this addition establishes a North Carolina Water Safety Committee "to function as a continuing advisory and coordinating body with respect to the activities of the various public and private agencies, organizations, corporations, a n d individuals with responsibilities or interest relevant to the maintenance of an effective program of water safety in North Carolina." Additional text, of course, describes how the Committee is to be set up and function.

Secondly the bill provides for the establishment of local water safety committees, their function, authority, etc.

Thirdly, in this bill, Section 15 of Article 1, dealing with local regulation was rewritten to expand the part played by the Wildlife Resources Commission in local water safety problems and to step up the implementation of the Uniform State Waterway Marker System.

In all of this the bill provides for coordination between State and Local Water Safety Committees, and the Wildlife Resources

Commission. Built-in safeguards such as public hearings, committee m e m b e r s representing a variety of organizations, etc., should make this a workable and significant step forward in boating safety.

House Bill 1324 establishes the Lake Norman Marine Commission, membership consisting of the four counties surrounding the lake. The b i l l provides for commissioner appointments, powers of the commission, financing its undertakings, etc. Regarding authority "the Commission, may make regulations applicable to Lake Norman and its shorelines area concerning all matters relating to or affecting public recreation and water safety. These regulations may not conflict with or supersede provisions of general or special acts or of regulations of State agencies promulgated under the authority of general law." In other words, any regulations passed by the Lake Norman Commission cannot conflict with or supersede the State Boat Act.

The establishment of a local Commission with powers over public boating is a first in North Carolina. I know some of the people interested in the passage of this legislation and they are enthusiastic boaters. This bill should promote water safety on Lake Norman. However, we would hope that all concerned keep in mind that Lake Norman is state or public water for all the people and not just a four-county lake. Any regulations promoted by the new Commission should be needed, should be uniform with others of the state, fair to the various user groups and based on fact, not emotion.

Boating Course

It is our policy to publicize courses in boating provided by the U. S. Power Squadron, Coast Guard Auxillary, etc. A letter from George A. Jones, Commander of the Asheville Squadron, informs us that his group is starting a free 11-week Piloting Class beginning September 9. We suggest those of you in the

● continued on page 27

PHOTO BY JACK DERMID

Wildlife
and Diverted Acreage

by Luther Partin

IT looks now like a pretty sure thing that the national administration ushered in last January will not make any major changes in Agriculture Stabilization at least for the remainder of 1969.

Many of the programs of the past have made a contribution to the restoration of wildlife habitat. The Soil Bank and Conservation Reserve, for example, have played an important role in the expansion of deer populations in Tarheelia during the past 20 years.

The present cropland diversion programs have great potential for increasing small game habitat, feeding areas for big game, and in the right location, for waterfowl. Cropland diverted from wheat or feed grain production must be designated as such and handled under approved conservation measures.

There is no problem here—approved conservation uses vary from letting the land grow in weeds to planting perennial sod plants such as fescue or sericea lespedeza. Cover crops are permitted and encouraged, but no harvesting is permitted and no grazing is permitted between April 30 and October 1, *except by wildlife.*

Small grains (wheat, oats, rye, barley) planted as a cover crop must be clipped or mowed and left on the land or destroyed by May 31. If these crops are cut high enough to leave a good small game cover and cut early enough to cause only a minimum amount of nesting disturbance, rabbits and quail will get a big helping hand.

Small grain plantings can be made specifically for wildlife on diverted land if approved in writing by the county ASCS committee before planting and, if no utilization other than by wildlife is permitted. In this category, no crop destruction is required and the full food and cover benefits are available for as long as the land manager desires. Of course, small grains are usually fall-planted in this state, so make plans for 1970.

Millet, corn, grain sorghums or soybeans can also be used for wildlife in the same manner on diverted land. These crops are spring-planted here and could be used in wildlife plantings for next year.

Conservation base acreage has the same potential for wildlife, except that the amount of land in this category is considerably less and there are no grazing restrictions except on plots designated as *wildlife food or habitat plantings.* Soybeans and feed grains may be used in these plantings approved by the county committee.

So it's up to the land manager. He can modify land use practices in handling diverted acreage and designate specific areas for wildlife. If he (or she) is a hunter, the dividends are tangible. The non-consuming wildlifer may have an even greater return.

Sportsman groups, or even people who just like to hunt or fish together but have limited access, are missing a good bet by not contacting landowners who have this type of idle land. Certainly they can reach mutually-beneficial agreements whereby legal requirements for diversion can be met, and wildlife production and approval land use can exist in harmony. Check with your local ASCS office for more details. ◆

24

CRACKSHOTS and BACKLASHES

by Rod Amundson

Saltwater Angling License

Bureau of Sport Fisheries and Wildlife Director John S. Gottschalk spoke on "The Pros and Cons of a Federal Fishing License" at a Fishermen's forum in Atlantic City, New Jersey, last February. After outlining the basis of need for substantially increased funding of marine game fish research, both on the part of the states and his own federal agency, he suggested that a Federal saltwater license might be in order.

It is true, as Dr. Gottschalk noted, that only a few states (actually, Alabama, Alaska, California, Louisiana, Oregon, Texas, Washington—plus a "land-and sell" license in North Carolina) presently have some sort of marine license. We do not at present agree, however, with his twin contentions that "the chances of others enacting provisions for saltwater licenses seem remote" and that "the only other alternative, then, is a Federal saltwater license." Contrary to this view, moves are known to be currently afoot in several states to propose enactment of saltwater angling licenses in the next year or two.

Be that as it may, Director Gottschalk's criteria for a possible federal saltwater sport fishing license, being of far more than casual interest, are as follows:

"1. The proceeds would be earmarked to be spent for research and development work related to the marine sport fisheries, with a limitation on the amount that could be spent for other activities.

"2. It would be universal for the states in each of three zones: Atlantic, Gulf, and Pacfic. All anglers except children 12 years of age and under would be required to have the license. Thus, in the Atlantic zone a license bought from a dealer in New York State would be good in any state along the Atlantic Coast, and similarly in the Gulf and Pacific zones.

"3. The income would be divided between the states and the Federal government in order to give the government funds needed to do basic research and to carry out studies of species which range up and down the coast. The state share would be divided among the states on a formula similar to that used in the Dingell-Johnson program, with primary weight being given to the number of fishermen in any state and a lesser amount being distributed according to the area of coastal waters in each state as compared with the total area of coastal waters.

"4. The cost of the l i c e n s e would be $5 annually. On the basis that there are upwards of 10 million saltwater anglers, such a proposal would solve the financing problem for the immediate future.

"5. In order to qualify, a state would have to have an equitable system of commercial licenses for commercial fishermen."

After outlining these basic criteria for a possible Federal license, the Sport Fisheries and Wildlife Bureau Director then reviewed various of the arguments for such a license as well as some of those against it. Our own considered view is that such a Federal license is only the third best solution—after state licenses carrying reciprocity between adjacent states and after still another alternative, that we have suggested previously. The Director also outlined it as a more promising alternative to all-out Federal licensing, viz:

"I suggest, therefore, that you consider still another alternative, the genesis of which I trace back to the boat registration act of several years ago. In outline, this other approach would give the states the opportunity to establish a saltwater license, to apply to the waters of neighboring states on a reciprocal basis, with all the revenue going to the state in which the license was sold.

"If a state failed to enact a saltwater license statute within a reasonable period, the federal government would be given the authority to do so for that state, the license to carry the same rights, privileges and limitations as though it were issued by the state. A portion of the income, however, would go to the Federal government for the conduct of its basic and interstate research.

"The approach broadly outlined above seems to have the considerable merit of being relatively more likely of adoption than a straight-out Federal licensing system. It recognizes the primary interest of the states and

A license to fish in saltwater? The idea isn't a new one. What do you think? Let us hear from you.

William Earl Lawrence

William Earl Lawrence is stationed at Swanquarter. He is the son of Mr. and Mrs. R. B. Lawrence of Route 2, Windsor, and was born in Bertie County on September 27, 1940. A 1959 graduate of Windsor High School, Bill served three years in the U. S. Army. He was employed by Thurston Motor Lines of Charlotte prior to his employment with the Wildlife Commission.

Mr. Lawrence atended the Basic Recruit School at the Institute of Government in Chapel Hill in June 1964. He was employed as a Wildlife Protector Trainee at Asheboro in December 1965, and was assigned as Protector at Troutman in May 1966. In September 1966, Mr. Lawrence was transferred to his present assignment in Swanquarter. Since his employment, he has completed all In-Service Training Schools.

Bill is married to the former Judy Phipps of Harmony, and they have one son, Jim, age two. The Lawrences attend Scranton Christian Church.

DIVISION ENFORCEMENT RECORD FOR JULY 1969

HUNTING & FISHING

Persons checked	31,425
Total prosecutions	801
Total convictions	779
Total cases not guilty ..	5
Total cases nol prossed ..	12
Total cases dismissed ...	5
Total fines collected	$ 2,645.80
Total costs collected	$10,030.05

BOATING

Persons checked	14,117
Total prosecutions	375
Total convictions	365
Total cases not guilty	3
Total cases nol prossed ..	7
Total cases dismissed	0
Total fines collected	$ 535.60
Total costs collected	$4,786.45

All fines and any arrest or witness fees are paid into the school funds of the counties in which the violation occurred, and no part of the fines or costs collected are paid to the North Carolina Wildlife Resources Commission or its personnel.

gives them the opportunity to decide whether they wish to exercise their inherent responsibilities. It would not solve the problem of financing the federal program immediately, but t h i s would tend to solve itself as the obvious gaps in data, and the fiscal responsibility of the states, became evident."

Director Gottschalk w i s e l y concluded his talk by noting that the present situation of inaction and inadequate funding in the face of increasing need prevents protecting the vital marine sport fishery resources. His closing words were: "What you do is up to you to decide. But I say: Do something!" It's good advice .

Sport Fishing Institute Bulletin, July 1969.

Right or Wrong?

DEAR SIR:

Our neighborhood, until recently, has been a haven for all kinds of small wildlife. They have been a pleasure and a treasure to all of the residents.

We have provided food when needed, and have built nesting places for these little ones. Our greatest favorite has been the gray squirrel. They have played among us so happily, and became our friends. A good number of these were eating out of our hands.

Now all of that has changed. One resident brought in a hunter to kill off our pets. Two Sundays in a row we were submitted to shot gun blasts during the daylight hours and three fourths of our squirrel population has departed this life. Apparently this was done with some authorization, inasmuch as it was done out of season, on Sunday, within the city limits and without any retaliation. Couldn't these small creatures be trapped and set free in their natural element?

I appreciate your magazine more than I can possibly tell you. I wish it would go into every home in North Carolina.

Yours truly,
Moir L. Clark
Mt. Airy

Protest Now

DEAR SIR:

I believe that most people are genuinely interested in preservation and conservation and become very disheartened when they read the articles in your magazine describing how the encroachment of man in his greed is destroying the coastal areas and breeding grounds of shrimp and crab, and too the wetlands needed by the waterfowl for survival. Most of us, however, do not really know how to go about protesting these things and one voice here and there is not sufficient. Could you print a special letter of protest with the address of the proper authority, which could be

clipped out, signed and mailed to the proper place where it would do the most good. It certainly would do no harm and it is sincerely hoped that it would do much good in stopping this devastation.

Sincerely yours,
Marilyn E. Stout
Charlotte

Net Problem

DEAR SIR:

My Father and myself truly love the great out-of-doors as much as anyone in this state. We have spent many wonderful days fishing in the rivers and creeks in eastern North Carolina for bass just for the sport and relaxation of it. In fact many of the fish we catch are released because we feel there is another day and if we want fish to eat we can always go to our freezer or our local fish market and get some.

In the past year we have run into a problem concerning our fishing in public waters. This problem concerns nets clogging our favorite coves in Black River here in Sampson County. I am not exaggerating when I use the term clogging. It is almost impossible to throw a plug anywhere near the bank for the nets. Hanging our plugs in nets is not enough to disturb us to the point of reaction, but when we find game fish tangled, dead and dying by the dozens in those nets, it is time to say something. I reported this problem to a local game warden and he said he would check into it for us. Three weeks later Dad and I returned to Black River to find the problem just as bad as before. I know there is a netting season and the people using them are in the law, but I ask you, is it fair to deprive tax paying citizens of this state, who love the sport of fishing, not meat getting, the enjoyment of a morning or afternoon of fishing? And the more important question is, how many game fish are destroyed by these nets in a year? Perhaps we need to look into our netting laws to see if we can't do something about this mistake. It's not right!

Sincerely,
Charles A. Northcutt
Clinton

SKIPPER

• continued from page 23
Asheville area interested in enrolling contact Commander Jones for further details.

Commander Jones also reminds us that information on each of the state's dozen or so Squadron's free courses can be obtained by calling Western Union Operator 25.

Boat News

Boaters across the nation will appreciate a move by the U. S. Coast Guard to halt a recent tide of bills in state legislatures, which condition boat registration on payment of personal property tax. They claim such a procedure distorts the purpose of the Federal Boating Act of 1958. We agree.

The Southeastern Association of State Boating Law Administrations (SESBLA) of which North Carolina is a member has resolved to support a strong Fed-

eral pre-emptive clause in vessel pollution control on navigable waters to eliminate current conflicts in state and local regulations. As you know, the present North Carolina boat sanitation device law does not include coastal waters. Such coverage is no doubt inevitable and when and if it comes, one thing is for sure, there must be national uniformity. Thus the reason for the resolution.

Southport Sunrise-Sunset

DATE	SUNRISE EDT	SUNSET EDT
Sept. 3	6:47	7:35
8	6:50	7:29
13	6:54	7:22
18	6:57	7:15
23	7:00	7:08
28	7:04	7:01
Oct. 3	7:08	6:53
8	7:12	6:47
13	7:16	6:40
18	7:19	6:35
23	7:24	6:29
	EST	EST
27	6:27	5:25
28	6:28	5:24
Nov. 2	6:33	5:19
7	6:37	5:14

HIGH TIDES
FOR SOUTHPORT, N. C.

DATE	TIDE (in feet)	TIME EDT
Sept. 15	4.8	10:54 AM
20	4.8	4:06 PM
22	5.2	6:12 PM
23	5.3	7:06 PM
24	4.9	7:24 PM
24	5.3	7:54 AM
25	5.2	9:00 AM
26	5.4	9:00 AM
27	5.4	9:48 AM
29	5.0	11:12 AM
Oct. 11	5.0	8:30 AM
13	5.2	9:54 AM
14	5.2	10:42 AM
15	5.1	11:30 AM
16	4.9	12:30 PM
17	4.8	1:36 PM
20	4.8	4:54 PM
21	4.9	5:48 PM
22	4.9	6:42 PM
23	5.1	7:06 AM
24	5.3	7:54 AM
25	5.4	8:36 AM
		EST
27	5.2	9:00 AM
28	4.9	9:24 AM
Nov. 8	4.9	6:18 AM

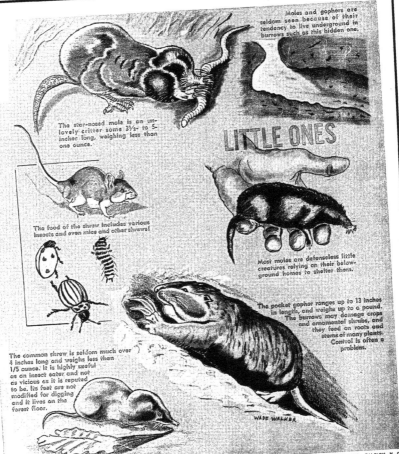

Moles and gophers are seldom seen because of their tendency to live underground in burrows such as this hidden one.

The star-nosed mole is an unlovely critter some 3½ to 5 inches long, weighing less than one ounce.

LITTLE ONES

The food of the shrew includes various insects and even mice and other shrews!

Most moles are defenseless little creatures relying on their below-ground homes to shelter them.

The common shrew is seldom much over 4 inches long and weighs less than 1/5 ounce. It is highly useful as an insect eater and not as vicious as it is reputed to be. Its feet are not modified for digging and it lives on the forest floor.

The pocket gopher ranges up to 13 inches in length, and weighs up to a pound. The burrows may damage crops and ornamental shrubs, and they feed on roots and stems of many plants. Control is often a problem.

WADE WALKER

LITHO BY THE GRAPHIC PRESS, INC., RALEIGH, N. C.

dlife IN NORTH CAROLINA

25 CENTS / OCTOBER 1969

IN NORTH CAROLINA ■

The official publication of the NORTH CAROLINA WILDLIFE
RESOURCES COMMISSION, Raleigh 27602. A monthly magazine
devoted to the protection and restoration of our wildlife resources
and to the improvement of hunting and fishing in North Carolina.

VOL. XXXIII, NO. 10   OCTOBER, 1969

IN THIS ISSUE

EDITORIAL STAFF

ROD AMUNDSON _ _ _ _ _ _ _ _ EDITOR
DUANE RAVER _ _ _ _ _ MANAGING EDITOR
LUTHER PARTIN _ _ WRITER-PHOTOGRAPHER
JOHN PARKER _ _ _ _ _ _ BOATING EDITOR

A slightly different cover format shows a sleek-coated black
bear foraging in the October
sunshine. The chances are that
he will not hibernate like some
of his northern cousins, but may
take a few naps lasting several
days when the weather really
gets cold. This fine game animal
needs c a r e f u l management.
Painting by Eldridge Hardie of
Denver, Colorado.

Financing Wildlife Conservation

and

Boating Safety

By Clyde P. Patton

Executive Director

PROFESSIONAL conservationists, and especially those concerned with wildlife, are riding on a rising tide of public awareness of and interest in total conservation. This is rapidly becoming a mass concern for human environment, its control and its betterment.

Unless they keep abreast of this tide, or a little ahead of it, they will be left stranded somewhere on a snag; and the public will make certain that their successors do not make such a mistake.

Beside the rising tide of public concern is the parallel tide of rising costs of operation: salaries and wages, supplies, materials, equipment, repairs, and alterations.

The 1969 North Carolina General Assembly, although weary and wary of new or increased taxes, recognized the Wildlife Resources Commission's need for adequate funds. It raised the price of all hunting and fishing licenses except nonresident hunting licenses, instituted a special big game hunting license, and provided for the continuing use of unreclaimed motorboat fuel taxes for boating safety purposes.

When word got out that the Commission was getting an increase in hunting and fishing license prices, a big game hunting license, and a fuel tax allocation, there were those who assumed that the Commission would be "swimming in money." Such assumption, of course, is far from the facts.

Let's take a close look at these facts. Funds from the hunting and fishing license increases are not expected to provide for any expansion in the general wildlife conservation program. They are expected to be sufficient, only for a time, to keep up with rising costs of operation, and to recoup losses in programs and services that had to be cut back during the past few years because of lack of money.

Until provisions for additional funds were made by the 1969 General Assembly, the Commission's wildlife protection and boating safety operations had been reduced by around 30 per cent, inland fisheries operations by some 15 per cent, game management by about 15 per cent, and all other operations by at least 15 per cent. In short, the Wildlife Resources Commission had been put in the unenviable position of not being able to keep up with rising costs of operation and an increasing public demand for a sound wildlife conservation program.

At least a year will be required to determine how much money will be received from the increase in the cost of hunting and fishing licenses. The estimate presented to the General Assembly was $669,000 annually. This estimate was made before a bill was passed allowing residents 70 years old or older to hunt and fish on a free license, and those 65 years old or older to buy a lifetime hunting and fishing license costing $10.00. The records thus far indicate that these will make a serious inroad on the estimated $669,000 from license cost increases.

Based on hunter surveys, the special big game hunting license is expected to produce an annual income of about $150,000. This has been earmarked for the acquisition and development of new big game management areas, improved programs on existing big game management areas, and expansion of programs for big game populations throughout the State.

Because motorboat operators generally do not reclaim refundable non-highway-use motorboat fuel tax money, the 1967 General Assembly allocated to the Commission one-eighth of one per cent of the net proceeds of the gasoline tax for boating safety law enforcement, boating safety education, and administration. This was only for a two-year period.

The 1969 General Assembly put this allocation on a continuing basis. This is not "new" money, but simply an extension on a continuing basis of funds urgently needed to serve the increasing number of boaters plying the waters of the State.

The 1967 motorboat fuel tax act brought about annual revenue of just under $158,000. With a 2¢ increase in gasoline taxes, it is estimated that annual receipts provided by 1969 legislation will be about $200,000.

In summary, the big game hunting license money is earmarked for big game management. The gasoline tax money may be used only for boating and water safety law enforcement, education, and administration. This leaves somewhere around $600,000 to restore reduced services and keep up with increasing costs of operation.

Yes, the tides are rising; and the Wildlife Resources Commission is making every effort to keep abreast of them, and hopefully, with the cooperation of our good sportsmen, a little ahead.

OCTOBER, 1969—WILDLIFE IN NORTH CAROLINA

Wildlife Commission Initiates

BLACK BEAR STUDY

by Frank B. Barick,
Chief, Division of Game

THE accelerating decline of the black bear in North Carolina has become an item of concern to both professional and sportsman conservationists. Informed estimates (as opposed to statistical surveys) indicate that only about 431 were taken by hunters during the 1968-69 hunting season. By using these figures statistically, we compute a total statewide bear population of only about 2,000 to 3,000. Since this is only about a fourth of the number 20 years ago there is obvious reason for concern.

Several factors appear to have contributed to this decline, some of them controllable and others not. In order to secure information on the nature and impact of these factors, the Wildlife Resources Commission has initiated an in-depth study during the next several months.

The study is designed to develop detailed information on distribution and abundance of the species in North Carolina, impact of changing land use on its habitat, effect of hunting on populations, and biological characteristics of the species that influence its survivability in the twentieth century. It will also test the validity of a series of tentative conclusions in regard to management.

The study is divided into four major segments, with each assigned to a different biologist. One biologist will conduct a study of the 34 black bears held in captivity in the state by various individuals and agencies, to secure basic biological data. While captive animals behave differently in some respects from their wild brethren, some facets of behavior, particularly those relating to reproduction, can best be determined by study of captive specimens.

The second segment of the study, assigned to another biologist, will be to review those research projects which have been conducted and to contact other states and agencies which are now investigating the black bear. His assignment is to abstract and compile information from these studies which will be helpful to us in sustaining, and restoring where possible, the black bear in North Carolina.

The third segment of the study will consist of a detailed inventory of bear habitat in North Carolina. We know that the black bear is a beast of the backwoods—a denizen of the wilderness. But how many acres does it take to make an acceptable wilderness for the black bear? Which such areas does he now occupy and are there other such areas that he could occupy under proper management?

The fourth segment of the study will explore current hunting methods and their effectiveness, as well as the capacity of the species to survive hunting. As a conservation agency our primary purpose is to develop a program that will insure the survival of the black bear in North Carolina. We owe this to future generations. But as an agency supported by hunting licenses we must have as our second priority the perpetuation of bear hunting as one of the most exciting of outdoor sports. We are particularly concerned about perpetuating bear hunting with dogs as it is now practiced, since still-hunting is generally considered nonproductive in our snowless southland.

THE study will stress investigation of those biological characteristics of the black bear which are unique to the bear and which influence his survivability in twentieth century North Carolina. Among these may be listed a very low reproductive rate, a very wide cruising radius and solitary nature, a feeding cycle which some investigators have characterized as six months of gluttony followed by six months of fasting, and hibernation.

Some investigators report that bears do not breed until they are three and a half years of age while others have found evidence of breeding at two and a half. Some studies indicate that the female bear in the wild breeds only every other year, apparently because she will not tolerate the approach of another bear while her newborn cubs are at her side. Other studies indicate a rather high mortality of newborn cubs. Each of these factors contributes to a very low reproductive capacity when compared with other wild animals. It can be demonstrated mathematically that two male and two female yearling bears will have increased to only 23 animals at the end of ten years, assuming start of breeding at two and one-half years and one cub per female in alternate years. And if we assume two cubs per birth the number at the end of ten years would be only 68. The same number of deer, in the same ten-year period, would increase to 123 at one fawn per doe per year and to 576 at two fawns per doe per year, since they start breeding at one and a half years and breed each year.

EXAMINATION of 20 years of hunting records of western North Carolina wildlife management areas indicates that it takes from about 3500 acres to 7500 acres to produce a kill. Assuming a 20 percent population turnover, i.e., that only 20 percent of the population was taken, the population density computes to 700-1500 acres per bear. (Most deer populations have a density of one per 50 acres or less, and on some areas we have one deer for less than 10 acres!)

Many bear hunt races are terminated in fewer than five miles but some cover a course exceeding 20 miles. If we can assume that the bear is familiar with the terrain over this course, it can be taken as further substantiation of a very extensive home range in comparison with other game animals. It also indicates that in the course of his normal foraging for food he is very likely to come in contact with civilization unless his home is a very extensive forested area.

It thus becomes apparent that extensive forested regions are required for sustaining bear populations. And if the bear population in a particular area is to be sufficiently large to produce an annual kill of five or six, the area must be still larger. For example, it can be mathematically demonstrated that to support this level of hunting would require a population of about two dozen bears containing animals up to about ten years of age. A smaller population harvested at this rate would be exterminated in a few years, even with mortalities resulting from legal hunting only.

If each bear requires, on the average, 1000 acres of elbow room, two dozen would require 24,000 acres. If they require 1500 acres each, then a minimum huntable population would require about 36,-000 acres. Furthermore, this acreage would have to be a relatively solid block. A long narrow area would not do since the bear's wide-ranging habits would tend to bring him in contact with a sometimes not so humane or tolerant humanity.

A very cursory examination of woodland distribution in North Carolina indicates that as of A.D. 1969 the black bear has dim prospects for survival in most parts of our state. The picture looks the blackest in the east where, until recently, most of our bears found sanctuary in extensive wooded swamp lands. These are being drained and converted to farming at such an accelerated rate that we can probably cross off all of the area north of Albemarle Sound. (Well-founded rumors indicate that even the Great Dismal Swamp has been scheduled for conversion to soybean production in the near future.)

AT this writing it appears that two areas in the east may yet be saved for the black bear. One of these is the Pamlico Peninsula including Dare, Tyrrell, Hyde and Washington counties and the northern part of Beaufort County. The other is the southern coastal plain from Carteret to Columbus County. Both of these sections contain extensive forested areas much of which is in large ownerships. If we can develop an effective program through statewide hunting regulations and establishment of Commission-managed game lands through purchase, lease, or cooperative agreement, the bear may perhaps be saved in these portions of the east.

In the west the situation is somewhat but not much better. It would appear that the Great Smoky Mountains National Park was established in the nick of time to save the black bear. Had it been postponed until 1960 there probably would be no black bears in western North Carolina today. But the fact that it e x i s t s—all 512,673 acres of it, astride the North Carolina-Tennessee line—will, we believe, insure the perpetuation of the black bear in its immediate vicinity for future generations of big game hunters.

The Park, together with several Commission-managed wildlife areas serving as satellite sanctuaries, sustain the bear in western North Carolina. A few other tracts of privately-owned land, together with some large blocks of U. S. Forest Service land, provide additional bear range. The type of management required to sustain the remaining bears in these sections will warrant very careful study.

This is the picture of the black bear in North Carolina as we see it today. Twelve months from now we hope to have a much more definitive report, with more specific recommendations for insuring his survival and even, in some places, his increase. ♣

PHOTO BY HUGH MORTON

Thoughts on Trout Regulations

by J. H. Cornell
Chief, Division of Inland Fisheries

FOR some twenty years, public hearings have been held annually by the Wildlife Resources Commission to receive recommendations from fishermen for changes they would like to see in the fishing regulations for the coming year. It has long since become evident that our fishing fraternity encompasses diametrically opposed views on many aspects of trout management and, consequently, of desirable fishing regulations.

The Commission always has budgeted a definite amount of money for trout production, and has raised a maximum number of fish per dollar by careful feeding and disease control. Trout have been stocked as impartially as possible in those waters which were suitable for trout survival and open to general public fishing.

The Federal Government, too, produced thousands of trout to help stock the public fishing waters. The State and Federal hatcheries stock the North Carolina trout streams in a coordinated program to assure equitable distribution. These hatchery trout, plus harvestable surplus of the wild trout, represent the total trout resource available to our fishermen, the taking of which is the subject of the fishing regulations.

A previous article discussed the two basic principles of trout management and the considerations involved.* If hatchery fish constitute most of the resource and there are hardly any wild trout, then we should have a year-round open season and no

*See Wildlife in North Carolina—September 1969
"Principles of Trout Management"—D. E. Louder

size limits. It would be desirable to catch every one of those expensive hatchery trout and make sure none was wasted.

But, on the other hand, if the trout resource is made up principally of wild trout and the total number of hatchery trout is relatively insiginificant, then we must have regulations designed primarily to protect and enhance the welfare of the wild trout populations. A closed season is necessary to protect the fish while they move up into the little spring runs to spawn. Size limits are needed to assure the maintenance of adequate brood stocks. And hatchery trout should be stocked in greatest proportion in the most heavily fished streams to act as a buffer in helping protect the wild brood stock from over-exploitation.

THIS year there is information never before available. In addition to the annual public hearings, in some years various types of personal interviews with the fishermen have been attempted during the fishing season. None produced information which could be considered dependable. In the fall of 1968, however, an inquiry sent to 10 percent of the trout license holders gave information which could only be guessed at before. A story on the result of that study included information on the annual take of trout.** It showed the number of trout killed annually to total approximately two and one-half million, consisting of about one-half million hatchery

**See Wildlife in North Carolina—August 1969
"Trout: Which way from the Crossroads"—F. F. Fish

fish (State and Federal combined) and about two million wild fish.

This ratio of four wild fish to each hatchery fish in the annual catch verifies the necessity of a suitable closed season, and the need for a general size limit on all streams to assure an adequate brood stock. It is unfortunate indeed that a trout caught on a worm usually is landed with the hook in its belly and cannot be released. It will be practical to have a size limit on all trout streams only when our fishermen use artificial lures so they can return the small fish to the water alive.

The census mentioned above included many gems of information. On the subject of live bait, the recommendations totaled in the proportion of 40 percent for its "more general use" and 60 percent to "prohibit live bait" altogether. An even greater number suggested a size limit on all waters.

Regulations, of course, are useless without enforcement. As long as many of our trout fishermen insist on using live bait, it will be impossible to establish a minimum size limit on trout in all waters. It would not be possible to employ enough Protectors to keep the "converted" fisherman, on a dull day, from "tipping his fly" with a bit of worm. The size limit will come when fishermen demand it —to improve their sport.

For the time being, it will be necessary to restrict the benefits of a size limit to publicly-owned lands. We have Native Trout and Trophy Trout regulations on them now. There it is practical to have special regulations and restrictions without having some private landowner feel that he is being imposed upon and, consequently, posting his land against trespass. Of course, the streams on the Management Areas represent only about one-fourth of our public trout streams—56 compared with 253 on the outside—or less than 500 miles compared with nearly 1500 miles on the outside. At any rate, the study shows an extensive demand for more "Native Trout" type regulations. They will have to go on the Management Areas.

Also on the Management Area streams the regulations can apply the concept of "Every Day an Opening Day". This is one type of fishing on Wednesdays, Saturdays, and Holidays—those days on which most people are not required to work— and have the streams closed at all other times. Although it may not make much difference to the trout, this concept makes a lot of difference to people. It probably does improve the rate of catch —and, hence, produces "better fishing".

Over the last 20 years there has been very little difference in stocking rates between streams *on* and *off* the Management Areas. Better protection has been provided on the Areas simply because the Commission has had more men per stream mile. But fishermen have continually demonstrated their interest in this type of management by paying extra daily fees to fish there. Although this was not mentioned in the study, the continuing willingness of fishermen to pay extra for a "lay-day" system

of protection demonstrates its acceptance and the demand for it.

The increasing popularity of the "Native Trout" streams is understandable. On the open streams, with no size limits, the angler averages three or four trout per day—if he keeps all he catches regardless of size. On the "Native Trout" streams, the average catch is between two and three trout *per hour.* This is a vast increase in the amount of fun he has in catching fish. Again, on the average, about one fish in ten is above the minimum size of 10 inches. Consequently, he takes home two or three trout exceeding the minimum size limit, and probably of greater weight than the 3 or 4 caught on the "no limit" stream. It is indeed unfortunate that small trout caught on live bait cannot be put back to grow up.

The suggestion very reasonably has been presented that since the "Native Trout" stream regulations protect the trout to spawning size, those streams should be open to fishing every day of the week. However, the important factor is the enforcement of the regulation. Regulation, supported by adequate enforcement, is required to protect the fish.

A fishing day, on the Management Areas is from one-half hour before sunrise to one-half hour after sunset. In most of the trout season, that is a fourteen-hour day. The enforcement officer who works three such days in a week has worked forty-two hours. He has exceeded the prescribed forty-hour work week, and no more can be expected from him. The Native Trout regulations are only as good as the enforcement supporting them. Since the Commission cannot afford to double the number of enforcement officers, we find a second compelling reason for restricting the use of the streams to three days per week.

O N the other hand, there are several camp grounds in the Management Areas and regulations might be designed for this fraction of the public. With exceptions, of course, the camper tends to be a casual fisherman. If there are fish nearby, he would like to catch some. So would Mama and the kids. But he is not usually the dedicated trout fisherman who wants to fight off deer flies and rattlesnakes during a three-hour hike in order to drop a dry fly over a wild trout that never saw a hatchery. For the camper, and for neighborhood fishermen, too, who wish to drive to the area, regulations could be designed to permit the development of catch-out ponds near each camp ground. Such ponds could be operated as an adjunct of the camp ground or they could be operated as a concession by the Forest Service.

It is probable that some one, or more, of the licensed catch-out pond operators in the State would be interested in leasing such a concession. Only commercial hatchery fish would be involved, and the campers could have a field day. There would be no size limits, no creel limits, no fishing

• continued on page 30

Small-Game Hunting on Western North Carolina Wildlife Management Areas

Part I

Characteristics of Hunters

by
*George A. James, Harold K.
Cordell, Frank B. Barick, and
Robert L. Downing

MALL-GAME hunting is big business! A recent comprehensive survey by the Bureau of Sport Fisheries and Wildlife on hunting and fishing revealed that nationally over 10½ million persons, 12 years of age and older, hunted small game during 1965. They spent over $600 million and traveled 4 billion automobile miles on approximately 128 million hunting trips. In North Carolina alone there are over 400,000 licensed hunters, most of whom hunt small game. During the 1964-65 season, a mail survey by Barick, Weber, and Wood (September 1965 issue of *Wildlife in North Carolina*) revealed that hunting for squirrels, rabbits, quail, and grouse accounted for 68 percent of North Carolina's hunters and for 74 percent of the hunting trips. Whether we can continue to satisfy such a huge demand will depend on our future supply of small game.

Two factors are of crucial importance in providing hunters the opportunity to hunt small game. One is maintaining habitat in suitable variety, size, and location to produce an adequate supply and variety of game. The

*George A. James and Harold K. Cordell are Principal Recreation Specialist and Associate Recreation Specialist, respectively, Southeastern Forest Experiment Station, USDA Forest Service, Asheville, N. C. Frank B. Barick is Chief, Division of Game, Wildlife Resources Commission, Raleigh, N. C. Robert L. Downing is Wildlife Research Biologst, USDI, Bureau of Sport Fisheries and Wildlife; he was formerly located in Asheville, N. C., and is now stationed at Blacksburg, Va.

other is making the game accessible so that the hunter receives a rewarding recreational experience and harvests enough surplus small game to prevent wasted resources.

Game harvest is often inadequate because hunting pressure is poorly distributed within an area. There is a tendency for hunting to be concentrated in the easily accessible areas, where overkill of game could result, and for the more remote areas to receive little or no hunting. At the 22nd North American Wildlife Conference, Hunter stated, "Unless special inducement is made . . . the more inaccessible areas suffer from lack of adequate harvest." The obvious inducement is to make such areas more accessible by developing roads and trails. Uhlig remarked at the 21st Conference that ". . . possibly the only way to increase harvest in extensive forests would be to develop roads and well-marked foot trails into areas where the average hunter is normally reluctant to venture."

In an effort to provide basic statistics about North Carolina hunters, a cooperative study was conducted during 1964 and 1965 on wildlife management areas in the western part of the State by the USDA Forest Service (Southeastern Forest Experiment Station and National Forests in North Carolina), the North Carolina Wildlife Resources Commission, and the U.S. Fish and Wildlife Service. The purpose was to learn about the characteristics of small-game hunters and to find

out how roads and trails affected their distribution over the management areas.

Information about small-game hunters was collected during the two-year period from five wildlife management areas, including Pisgah (North Mills), Standing Indian, Rich Laurel, Daniel Boone (Fox Camp), and Flat Top (Spivey Gap). These areas provided an excellent opportunity to document the distribution of hunting pressure resulting from a well-developed system of forest roads and trails. Approximately 65 percent of the total acreage within these areas is within 660 feet of a road or trail; 86 percent is within 1,320 feet; and 98 percent is within 2,640 feet. Such extensive road and trail development provides easy access to practically all of each area.

During 1964 and 1965, the early-opening seasons began in mid-October and included hunting of squirrels, raccoons, opossums, and ruffed grouse. The late-opening seasons began in early December and included rabbits, quail, and the other small-game species. The three-week intervening period was occupied with scheduled deer hunts.

As they left the management areas, hunters were systematically interviewed at the checking stations .Each hunter interviewed was asked several questions about his use of roads and trails and about personal characteristics such as place of residence, age, occupation, and education level. In addition, he was given a small-scale map of the compartment in which he hunted and asked to trace his day's walking activities. Four hundred and forty-five hunters were interviewed during the early-opening seasons and 108 during the late-opening seasons.

The first analytical step was to determine whether questionnaire data obtained for two years from the five wildlife management areas, during both the early- and late-opening seasons, could be combined for final analysis or whether separate analyses had to be made for each of the major strata. The analysis revealed that the relationships between years and between areas were not significantly different for the important variables and that these data could be combined. Variation between early- and late-season small-game hunters was significantly different, however, and separate analytical treatment was necessary. Results and discussions are therefore based on two separate populations: small-game hunters for the early-opening and late-opening seasons.

The findings of this study will be presented in two parts. Part I presents information concerning the socioeconomic characteristics of those who hunted small game on wildlife management areas in western North Carolina during 1964 and 1965. Part II will discuss the movement and distribution of these hunters in relation to developed access.

Part I
Characteristics of Small-Game Hunters

A close look at the socioeconomic characteristics of the 553 small-game hunters interviewed during the early- and late-opening seasons confirms what is already known: There is no "average" hunter. Yet enough similarity exists in most of the characteristics that an image, a composite, begins to form.

This composite small-game hunter is male, married, a resident of North Carolina, and lives in a rural area within 50 miles of the wildlife management area in which he hunts. He is about 40 years old, a high school graduate,

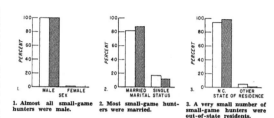

1. Almost all small-game hunters were male.

2. Most small-game hunters were married.

3. A very small number of small-game hunters were out-of-state residents.

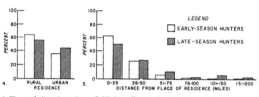

LEGEND
☐ EARLY-SEASON HUNTERS
▨ LATE-SEASON HUNTERS

4. The majority of small-game hunters were rural residents.

5. Most small-game hunters lived within 50 miles of the management area. The average was 28 miles for early-season and 41 miles for late-season hunters.

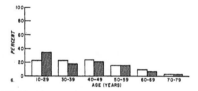

6. Most small-game hunters were under 50 years of age. The average age was 41 for early-season hunters and 39 for late-season hunters.

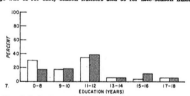

7. Few of the hunters had more than a high school education. The average was 10 years for early-season hunters and 11 years for late-season hunters.

and earns about $5,000 a year. He is a blue-collar worker, actively engaged in any one of a number of occupations. He is an enthusiastic hunter, walking about three miles on each small-game hunting trip. He hunts about 2.5 times each season on wildlife management areas and about 10.5 times per season off wildlife manage-

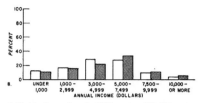

8. Most hunters made under $7,500 per year. The average was about $5,000 for both early-season and late-season hunters.

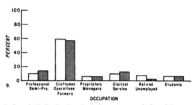

9. Over half the hunters in both seasons worked as laborers. Few were in occupational classes requiring advanced education.

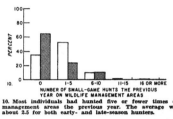

10. Most individuals had hunted five or fewer times on management areas the previous year. The average was about 2.5 for both early- and late-season hunters.

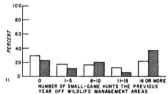

11. The majority of individuals had hunted more than five times off management areas the previous year. The average was 13.7 times for late and 9.7 for early-season hunters.

ment areas. He makes good use of roads and trails in the areas he hunts but prefers to h u n t away from access, penetrating about 1,100 feet into the forest.

The accompanying series of graphs presents several characteristics of small-game hunters in detail and shows some important and interesting differences between early- and late-season hunters.

Some of the differences between early- and late-season hunters are readily apparent. Generally, m o r e early-season hunters than late-season hunters were single, more of them were rural residents, and they lived closer to the management area in which they hunted. Early-season hunters were a little older and had slightly less formal education. Similarly, they had lower incomes and fewer of them were in occupational classes requiring advanced education. The number of small-game hunts on wildlife management areas was about the same for hunters in each season, averaging 2.5 trips a year. But late-season hunters hunted a great deal more off the management areas, averaging

13.7 trips a year as compared with only 9.7 for early-season hunters.

This study was not designed to explain the difference between early- and late-season small-game hunters or their hunting activities. We have dealt strictly with the problem of developing a complete picture of current conditions. However, through such re-

search efforts we learn a great deal about our society and its behavior. Such information is a necessary first step toward effective planning and development of projections of future use.

In next month's issue, we will discuss the movement and distribution of small-game hunters in relation to developed roads and trails. ◆

Grouse hunting can be a rugged sport, but this fine game bird represents a high point in the small-game hunter's experience. This scene is Mitchell County.

DEPT. OF CONSERVATION AND DEVELOPMENT PHOTO

10

What's Your O.D.Q.?

Outdoor Quiz

by Charlotte Hilton Green

And Nature spreads wide her book,
In a temple fair and free;
To all who may listen she cries, "Come look!
Come and learn at my knee.
Watch the change in the finch's vest,
Note how the highhole carves his nest,—
Come with light foot and loving breast,
And bury your ills with me!"
Doris Reade Goodale

What's your Out-Door Quotient? Name one relative of the common Spanish moss of our Coastal Plain.

TODAY the world in general seems to have far too many *ills* of all kinds. Never, perhaps, has there been such a need for folks to "bury their ills."

And how better than in the *out-of-doors* and through an awareness of all Nature has to offer—to you who would "look and listen, and love and learn".

How many today, the young people flooding our schools, the farmer in his fields, the very students in our colleges—many of them those "land grant colleges of yesteryear" that have burgeoned into so many great institutions today—even recognize the man Liberty Hyde Bailey? Yet he was one who fought, a few generations ago, for the land grant colleges—of which our great N. C. State University of today, is one.

A few years ago, at Cornell University, I was privileged to attend a 90th birthday celebration for him—at which scientists, land-lovers, conservationists, educationers from many parts of this country and many lands, attended. The next day I had a long conference with him.

Yet, on his *actual* 90th birthday he was in the tropics, flying, alone with a pilot, in a low plane, seeking new species of palm trees (of which he was an authority). And he discovered two new species!

Many years before, when the Nature Study movement was in its youth, he had helped develop it—and put it across to the school children of New York and other states. As he interpreted it: "Nature is ever our companion whether we will or not. Even though we shut ourselves in an office, nature sends her messengers. The light, the dark, the moon, the cloud, the rain, the wind, the fall of the leaf, the fly, the bouquet, the bird, the cockroach—they are all ours. If one is to be happy, he must be

Although author-naturalist, Charlotte Hilton Green, is no stranger to the readers of Wildlife, this month's article begins a continuing series of informative stories designed particularly for school use.

in sympathy with common things. He must live in harmony with his environment. One cannot be happy yonder or tomorrow, he is happy here and now, or never. Our stock of common things should be great."

And so, let us question ourselves! How much *do we know* of the dear common things about us? Let's try an *Outdoors'* Q. Instead of the common "I.Q'S" popular a while ago, let's create one of our own . . . an "O.D.Q." Get it? An *"Out-Doors Q."*

Let's try some quizzes—to find out! They might be "True and False;" or "Multiple Choice." In the first group, read each question or statement carefully, then underscore it as either *True* or *False*, whichever you decide is correct. In "Multiple Choice" there are also statements and questions. Underscore the one or more words you believe gives the correct answer. Look them up if you do not know them. Any answer or observation we make for ourselves is tenfold better than being told. Moreover, it gives one self-confidence.

True or False

1. Many more birds migrate by night, than by day. True or False?

2. There are more species of trees in our own State of North Carolina than in all of Europe. True or False?

3. The tulip tree, often called "yellow poplar," is not a poplar but belongs to the *Magnoliaceae*, and is thus related to the magnolia. True-False?

11

4. The yellow-breasted chat, the ovenbird, the redstart, the Louisiana water thrush, and the myrtle warbler, all belong to the *Compsothylpidae*. the wood warblers. True or false?

5. In all maples the fruit is a double samara. Each half falls away separately and is carried by the wind with a spinning motion. True, False?

6. The cardinal is the only all-red bird with a crest. True or False.

7. Snakes sometimes swallow their young to protect them. True or False?

8. The female red-headed woodpecker also has a red head. True or False?

9. All American red cedars (*Juniperus virginiana*) when mature, have berries. True or False?

10. A good way to remember to identify the snowy egret is that it has black bill and black legs, but yellow feet, or "golden slippers." True or False?

11. The acorns of all oak trees mature in a year. True or False?

12. The earthworm is a valuable "little plowman of the soil" who helps turn over, aerate, and fertilize the soil. True or False?

13. The mockingbird, the brown thrasher, and the catbird belong to the same family, the *Mimidae*. True or False?

14. Spanish moss is not a moss, but belongs to the same family as the pineapple, the *Bromeliaceae*, and is thus a flowering plant. True or False?

15. The pine warbler is apparently in the whole State at all seasons, but is much less numerous in the mountain regions. True or False?

Multiple Choice

(In the following statements or questions, underscore the one or more words that will give the correct answers.)

1. In the bird world, with few exceptions, it is the male—the female—who goes ahead and establishes territory.

2. Kingfishers carry their prey in their beaks; in their feet.

3. Of the following "Heavenly Bodies" pick out the planets: Sirius, Venus, Vega, Deneb, Pluto, Regulus, Saturn, Fomalhaut, Rigel, Mars, Jupiter.

4. The praying mantis is an animal, an insect, a bird, a flower.

5. The white pine has needles in clusters of threes; of twos, of fives.

6. Poults are the young of geese, of moose, of swans, of turkeys, of foxes.

7. The flowers of the pines are pollinated by insects; by the winds.

8. The wood thrush, our thrush of summer, is reddest on head; on the rump.

9. Mourning doves lay two white eggs; three-four eggs in a nest.

10. The chipmunk is closely related to the weasels; the squirrels; the beavers.

12. The young of woodpeckers are naked when hatched; are downy.

13. Vireos build flat nests, saddled on a limb, or branch; cup-shaped nests, suspended from a forked twig.

14. Yaupon belongs to the Holly Family; the Elm Family; the Oak Family.

15. A physical characteristic of the Family Accipitridae: Hawks, eagles and kites (as with the owls, also) is that the female is larger than the male, smaller than the male.

Correct answers, page 30

SOUTHERN HARDWOOD FORESTS OF THE FUTURE

by J. S. McKnight
Southern Forest Experiment Station
Forest Service
U. S. Department of Agriculture
Stoneville, Mississippi

BECAUSE his crops take so long to mature, a forester must be unusually concerned about the future. He cannot help but wonder what kinds of wood people will want 50 years from now, and how much forest land will be left on which to grow it. I think that, although the world may change much in 50 years, the people in it will change little. I think American consumers will continue to want the warmth and satisfaction of high-quality hardwood furniture, architectural trim, and flooring. Per-capita buying of such items may even increase as the purchasing power of individuals increases.

Were it not for research, there would be little hope of growing sufficient wood in our shrinking

Reprinted from NATIONAL HARDWOOD MAGAZINE, volume 42, number 6, pages 44, 48-49. June 1968.

southern hardwood forests. In very recent years, industries, public agencies, and universities have turned much research talent to improving the culture and management of hardwoods. Results are highly promising.

The rapid growth in experimental cottonwood plantations under intensive care has been well publicized, and commercial plantations as large as 10,-000 acres have been established. Trees averaging 52 feet tall and 6.5 inches in diameter have been grown in 5 years in experimental plantings. Keys to such rapid growth are proper choice of site and clean cultivation of competing vegetation.

Advances have been made recently in the identification of sites suitable for individual hardwood species, and ways to improve these sites through ditching, plowing, irrigation, and fertilizing are being sought. Fertilizer application may not be economically justifiable now, but it almost certainly will be justified in the crowded world of the future. Responses of trees to fertilizers have been impressive. In one study, nitrogen application in pole-size gum-oak stands improved d i a m e t e r growth by 65 percent, and NPK fertilizer increased height growth 44 percent. Pilot-scale trials are showing that control of water supply also increases growth.

Research geneticists are developing better trees for future plantations. Sycamore, cottonwood, sweet gum, tupelo, yellow-poplar, and the oaks are the southern hardwoods receiving the most attention. Experiences with agricultural crops indicate that great gains in productivity will result from breeding specifically for response to the intensive care that will be given in future plantations.

No one is surprised anymore to find researchers in the swamps, learning to manage the valuable tupelo. Thinning, water management, harvesting, protection, and regeneration are problem areas that require increased study.

Up to now, protection of hardwood forests from insects and disease has been largely a matter of prevention through removal of infested and high-risk trees. The same will not be true 50, or even 5, years from now. As an example, entomologists have isolated the substance that attracts male to female carpenterworms. These insects do $60 million worth of damage yearly by boring holes in oak tree trunks. We soon hope to find a synthetic capable of attracting the adult males to a centralized point in a forested area, where they can be destroyed or sterilized.

Seed researchers are now unraveling the chemistry that takes place from seed maturity to germi-

This is the last of a series of five articles on hardwood management by Mr. J. S. McKnight. We are reprinting these articles which first appeared in the **National Hardwood Magazine,** because of the importance of hardwoods to wildlife. Many of Mr. McKnight's findings and recommendations in regard to hardwood management are applicable in North Carolina. We invite the attention of landowners to profit from these articles since more emphasis on hardwood production in North Carolina would be highly beneficial to wildlife.

nation. Acorns, for example, germinate anywhere from a few days to a few years after they mature. Theoretically, we will some day be able to turn germination on and off with chemicals. Direct-seeding of new stands may then be feasible.

We are not neglecting the traditional silvicultural problem of proper tree spacing in managed stands. We are also concerned with the degrade of lumber during drying. Research is seeking to correlate loss in quality with the physical and chemical properties of the wood. It may be possible to enhance some of the key properties discovered through species choice and stand treatment.

The hardwood forests of tomorrow will differ from those of today as a field of hybrid corn differs from a back pasture. Much information that is not yet known will be required to manage these new forests. Scientists at the U. S. Forest Service Southern Hardwoods Laboratory and elsewhere are working hard to assure that the Nation is not found wanting in the necessary know-how. ◆

Modern research is not always done in a laboratory. This experimental sweetgum plantation is being cultivated during its first year of growth with a three-row harrow developed for this purpose.

Ready for Ducks?

Feature by John R. Parker, Jr.

Photos by Luther Partin

As ducks assemble for their flight south, why not assemble your equipment for check and repair. Start opening day with a bang . . . not a bust.

Reading what others have learned may improve your success. And remember, duck calling should be practiced at home; a call record will help. Personal gear should be carefully checked, especially those items that keep you warm and dry. Note the rubber gloves; these can be worn over others for decoy handling in icy weather.

Once you have gathered all the materials and have color patterns in mind, decoy painting is fun. Under heavy use, decoys may need painting every season, not so much for color, but to reduce glare. Whether you use a commercial paint mixture or mix your own, make certain that it dries flat. A water-resistant glue and plenty of pressure will put this mallard hen (left) back in the decoy flock.

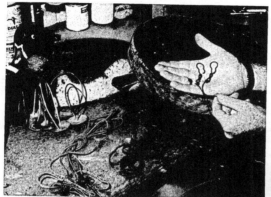

Anchor and lines are checked (left) on these homemade (heads are commercial bluebill) decoys. Double snap system permits ten-foot line to be quickly shortened to 5 feet. This heavy braided line wears well and does not tangle easily. The canvas blind (below) is convenient to handle and serves as a good windbreak. Inexpensive folding stools and plastic ground cloth add to comfort.

A new "stump" is added (above) to the blind. Only a small amount of native vegetation is required to make the blind "disappear" along with the hunter, well concealed inside. Boat, motor and trailer should be in top shape. Take along something to wrap the motor in. Sharp hatchet and machete plus extra camouflage net round out the blind building kit.

Fishing Coastal Plain Waters

by Joel Arrington
Outdoor Editor, Dept. of Conservation & Development
Conservation & Development Photos

WHERE Tarheel rivers flow off hard crystaline rock of the Piedmont onto softer sedimentary formations, there is a broad drop-off zone characterized by falls and rapids. An imaginary line connecting these falls and extending roughly northeast and southwest is called the "fall line" and marks the inner boundary of the North Carolina Coastal Plain.

This region, from the fall line to the Outer Banks, is largely made up of heavily-forested flood plains, peat pocosins interspersed with savannahs, dark swamps, tidal estuaries, and great reaches of inland sounds. The area takes in half North Carolina's land and water.

In the large, slow-flowing rivers here are practically all the freshwater game fish species of the southern United States and, during spring spawning runs, such anadramous species as shad and striped bass. The vast brackish sounds inside the Outer Banks harbor not only fresh-water species, but a host of salt-water denizens as well. A benign climate, coupled with an abundance and variety of fish, makes angling a year-around sport throughout the Coastal Plains.

While bank fishing is commonly practiced, particularly along black-water rivers, many of the best fishing spots can be reached only by boat, and the angler in a boat can range farther and fish more water in a day than the land-bound fisherman.

Fortunately, the public launching ramps which dot river and sound shores in all popular Coastal Plain fishing areas provide ample access to these coastal waters.

While the largest percentage of Coastal Plain fishing occurs in summer, practically everyone, except for the growing army of winter striped bass addicts, agrees that spring and fall generally offer better angling than other periods.

Stripers may be taken from sounds and river mouths during any month, but summer stripers are likely to be small and scattered. December and January probably produces more striped bass than other months, even though there are fewer anglers fishing during these cold months.

Striped Bass

Albemarle Sound, extending east and west in the northern part of the Coastal Plain, has the second largest striper population in the world, after Chesapeake Bay. Beginning usually in October and running through January, anglers fish the mouths of all Albemarle Sound tributaries and out into the center of the sound itself. Embayments such as East and South Lakes harbor large striper populations in winter.

A flotilla of charter boats based at Manns Harbor on the Dare County mainland fishes the eastern end of Albemarle Sound and Croatan Sound near the William B. Umstead bridge. During October and November 1967, these party boats averaged about 30 fish per trip while private craft averaged about 11. Roanoke Sound frequently is good for stripers and sometimes offers better protection from wind than Croatan. The mouth of the Alligator River was unusually good during the fall of 1968, and Currituck Sound, particularly in the channels off Poplar Branch, is a consistent producer during waterfowl season.

Although most striped bass are caught in the northern sector of the Coastal Plain, a significant number are taken each winter from river mouths as far south as the Cape Fear. During November and December 1967, a section of the Intracoastal Waterway near Carolina Beach called "Snow's Cut" gave up many stripers, some of them going to 25 pounds.

Spring striper fishing may be as productive as winter angling, and a great deal more comfortable. Tarheel stripers begin their spawning run "about

Striped bass range many of our coastal waters and provide some excellent angling particularly during fall and winter months. The scene here is East Lake near Manns Harbor.

the time the dogwood blooms." That usually means around the first of April. But for several weeks before the water warms to that magic temperature which triggers the run, stripers congregate in the mouths of such rivers as the Roanoke, Pasquotank, Little, Chowan, Neuse, Tar and Northeast Cape Fear.

Once the migration gets underway, however, anglers trolling bucktails, spoons and deep-running plugs favor waters upstream. The major spawning river is the Roanoke and when conditions are just right in the rocky stretch below Weldon, action is as frenzied as anywhere and anytime in the state.

Spring Shad Fishing

For the past several years, shad fishing has increased in popularity on several North Carolina rivers. This has been the result, partially, of state and federal agencies cooperating to operate locks on the Cape Fear during peak spawning runs. The practice opens over 60 miles of spawning water from which shad previously were blocked.

But the Cape Fear is only one good Tarheel shad river. The upper Neuse near Goldsboro is fine for American shad, even better for its smaller cousin, the hickory shad. The upper Tar within the Rocky Mount city limits is excellent for both American and hickory shad. The Black and the Northeast Cape Fear rivers have good spring runs of American shad, but neither is heavily fished.

April and May usually are the best months for shad fishing. Both bank and small boat fishing are practiced, although boat fishermen have the advantage of increased mobility.

The most popular tackle is light spinning gear with small spoons and tiny jigs called "shad darts." Frequently the lures are presented on a double rig, with the jig on a short dropper ahead of the spoon.

Practically all shad fishermen cast across the current and work their lures upstream. Frequently the strike comes just as the lures reach the farthest point of the swing. If the current is sufficiently swift, it may be possible, and productive, to hold the lures in one spot, working them in short jerks and slow pumps.

American shad are unusually sporty fish. The

These two lunker channel bass were wrestled from Pamlico Sound. This is now an important summer fishery.

species has been called the "poor man's tarpon" with justification for its savage strike and aerial battle make it a formidable game fish on light tackle.

Its reputation as a table fish is even more illustrious. Although shad are boney, they are delicious when baked at a low temperature for several hours while wrapped in oiled paper and lying in a shallow pan of water to dissolve or soften the bones. Fresh shad roe is thought by some to be superior to that of any fish, including sturgeon. When dredged in flour and fried in a small amount of bacon drippings, shad roe is a rare treat for a stream-side supper.

Big Drum

About the same time shad are moving up coastal rivers, channel bass, sometimes called red drum, are moving along Atlantic beaches and into Tarheel sounds through such inlets as Oregon, Hatteras, Ocracoke and Drum. For many years, anglers have come great distances to fish for drum from the beaches and from boats in inlets and sounds in spring, and again during the fall migration. Some of these fish weigh over 50 pounds.

Although channel bass fishing has never been considered a summer sport, in July of 1968, the State Department of Conservation and Development demonstrated that great schools of channel bass in Pamlico Sound could provide an important summer sport fishery.

Drum, it was learned, school each summer near certain shoals in Pamlico Sound, and feed over them regularly. Pilots in small planes have spotted the red giants on at least nine permanent shoals scattered from near Rodanthe southward to the mouth of the Neuse River. There is little doubt that additional schools are yet to be found.

Fishing from outboard-powered boats with surf rods and artificial lures, C & D men took channel bass going to 49 pounds on Piney Point Shoal off Broad Creek in the mouth of the Neuse River. Hopefully, North Carolina sportsmen will use information supplied by state researchers to aid them in catching summer channel bass. A small group of anglers based at Vandemere has for several years caught large drum between April and September from the shore. Baiting with squid, the fishermen have most success between Piney Point and Bay River.

Whether from boat or shore, the practical drum fisherman will not trifle with light tackle. Unless a line-test record is the object, at least 300 yards of 20-pound test monofilament on a heavy-duty spinning reel and a stout eight-to ten-foot rod is recommended. Conventional reels may carry 30- to 50-pound test squidding line.

The fishing method most likely to produce results is baiting fresh cut mullet, finger mullet or squid, attaching a three or four ounce lead pyramid, and casting out onto the shoal. It becomes a waiting game then, but fish are likely to forage over the sand bottom anytime during the day. However, the hours after 4 p.m. are best. Night fishing, although yet untried, could be productive since drum are nocturnal feeders.

Frequently red drum may be sighted from a boat. However, they are devilishly hard to approach within casting range. The noise of an outboard, or even of a hull scraping on the bottom, will send the fish dashing to deep water. If you sight a school, however, you may be in for some of the most exciting angling anywhere.

Maneuver your boat well upwind of the school, which may reveal itself by breaking the surface or by muddy water stirring up from rooting in the bottom. Shut off the motor, tilt the outboard or outdrive unit and drift toward the fish, being careful not to bang anything in the boat. With luck, you may get within casting r a n g e. Hammered spoons such as the Hopkins, MirroLures and other swimming and diving plugs with sufficient weight for casting will usually produce a strike. With stout hooks and a strong back, you may land a channel bass within a half-hour of the strike.

A Coast Guard chart of the mouth of the Neuse will show three shoals where drum were taken during July of 1968: Piney P o i n t Shoal, Gum Thicket Shoal, and Garbacon Shoal near Merrimon.

Fall Speckled Trout

Elsewhere, it may be called spotted weakfish, but most North Carolinians refer to it as speckled trout. Beginning around the first of October, large schools of these freckled beauties sally into the sounds and up coastal rivers from Calabash north to Albemarle Sound. Cold snaps seem to drive them up brackish creeks where they frequently congregate in surprising numbers.

A wide variety of baits and lures are productive on trout, but the MirroLure probably tops the list among artificial foolers. A bucktail jig tipped with a small bit of shrimp frequently produces when other lures fail. Although live shrimp are simply murder on specks, shrimp are difficult to find at coastal bait shops in winter.

Usually it's boom or bust with trout. They move in schools and may show up in an area where the day before you couldn't get a strike. Three consistent hot spots are Croatan and Roanoke Sounds, particularly off the south end of Roanoke Island, Pamlico Sound near Englehard, especially in the Gibbs Point vicinity, and the White Oak River from the mouth upstream to Stella.

Winter Jacks

More and more Tarheel anglers are taking their vacations in winter, not only because of excellent striped bass fishing, but because chain pickerel provide exciting cold weather action. The toothy "jack," as it is more commonly called, is not known as a table delight, but on suitable tackle, its fight rivals more reputable species.

Perhaps no game fish strikes a surface lure more readily than the chain pickerel. It doesn't seem to matter whether water temperature is 80 or 40. Flip a balsa or plastic minnow out between the cypress knees of almost any black-water stream or lake

along the Coastal Plain and you may expect a savage strike instantly. However, jacks sometime tantalize anxious anglers with their curious habit of following a lure to the boat. Perhaps such fish are glutted with a recent meal, but you may sometimes tease them into striking by suddenly increasing the lure's speed. Frequently, jack will take the lure just at the rod tip. Many a Tarheel angler has gotten wet from the violent gyrations that ensue.

The Meherrin River, from its mouth to the Virginia state line, is well known for its chain pickerel fishing, as is the Black River from its mouth to the confluence of Great Coharie and Six Runs Creeks. Another consistent producer is the White Oak River upstream from Stella.

Summer White Perch

White perch are closely related to striped bass, but life histories of the two species differ markedly. Salt- and fresh-water bodies may have perch populations, but in North Carolina they are most plentiful in brackish bays and streams. Among good fresh-water spots, Lake Waccamaw is widely known for white perch and it offers fine fishing during most months of the year. In summer, however, when much coastal fishing has slowed, Kitty Hawk Bay, lower Currituck Sound and Albemarle Sound produce thousands of perch. The mouths of the North, Chowan, and Roanoke Rivers are equally productive.

White perch are most often found over a firm mud buttom. Experienced fishermen have their favorite spots, but if the fish have moved away, as they will do, it's time to go prospecting. You should bait with a worm or small piece of shrimp or cut fish and bump the bottom while allowing the boat to drift. Once a school is located, action will be fast. It may cease suddenly as the school departs for more favorable feeding water.

A small spinner is the likeliest producer among artificials. Tip it with a worm or piece of shrimp for deadly combination. Nearly all strikes will be on or near the bottom.

Everyone agrees that white perch are among the best fish species on the platter. Filleted and dipped in an egg batter or dredged in meal and fried, they are hard to equal. The average white perch weighs a pound or less, so it takes several to make a meal. But when you find a school, usually there is no problem filling the stringer.

When you speak of panfish in reference to coastal North Carolina, you are using a generic term that applies to several species. These include crappie, bluegill, white and yellow perch, warmouth, redbreast, pumpkinseed, green sunfish and redfin pickerel. The abundance of these species within our fresh coastal waters practically guarantees fishing success every month of the year.

Experienced panfish anglers delight in bundling up in their warmest clothes, trailing a small juniper boat to such waters as the Alligator River and loading aboard a generous supply of hot coffee and at least a half-dozen cane poles. Spreading the poles fan-like over the gunwales, they drift or paddle

18

The bountiful white perch (left) is caught by the thousands from various coastal rivers. East Lake (above) provides some rugged scenery as well as a variety of good fishing. Casting Currituck Sound (below) usually means black bass.

along near the bank and bait with small live minnows, worms or cut bait. When action gets hot, there are not hands enough to tend the throbbing canes.

Virtually every coastal stream has an abundance of panfish, but a few favorites include the Chowan River from the Edenhouse bridge to the Meherrin River, the Meherrin from its mouth to the Virginia state line, the Tar River from the mouth to Rocky Mount, the South River from the mouth to its origin at Mingo Swamp, and the Lumber River from the South Carolina state line to the U. S. 15/501 bridge.

Largemouth Bass Year Around

A few years ago, there appeared in one of the outdoor magazines an article entitled, "Winter Bass R In Season." Although the story did not deal with coastal North Carolina bass fishing, it well could have. Except for the coldest winter days, our largemouth bass may prowl about at anytime in a feeding mood.

Sunny days in November and December, when the wind is not up, are particularly good for surface-feeding largemouths. The lipped balsa and plastic minnows sometimes are irresistible, as are Jitterbugs, popping plugs of several varieties, hair and cork fly-rod bugs, and the highly regarded Devil's Horse.

As the sun approaches the horizon and a chill creeps through your clothes, pour yourself a cup of hot coffee and switch to a rubber worm. Work it slowly on the bottom for a yard or two, then let it rest while you take a slow sip. When the line begins to run out, free-spool until the fish stops, count ten and set the hook. But don't forget to put down that hot coffee.

Good, cold weather bass rivers are the White Oak from Stella to a point four miles above Maysville, the Black River from its mouth to the confluence of the Great Coharie and Six Runs Creeks, and the Lumber River from the South Carolina state line to the U. S. 15/501 bridge. These rivers are good at any time, but success falls off during hot summer months.

Spring fishing on Currituck Sound for largemouth probably enjoys as good a national reputation as any water body in the eastern United States. Some anglers feel that the recent intrusion of grass has hurt fishing, but others continue to bring home admirable strings of fish. Probably fishing techniques must be changed to suit the new conditions. Plastic worms seem to be the favorite lures. Mattamuskeet, famed as a waterfowl lake, provides some good bass, bluegill and striped bass fishing too.

Kitty Hawk Bay is fished less than Currituck and has equally good fishing. Guides may be engaged in the communities of Colington, Kitty Hawk and Kill Devil Hills. Grass is not as great a problem in East and South Lakes, which are embayments off Albemarle Sound, and stripers are an added bonus for the bass angler. The Pasquotank River is excellent in fall and spring as is the Little River from its mouth to Halls Creek. The Tar River from its mouth to Chicod Creek has a good reputation for bass and is not heavily fished in winter.

Clearly, fishing on the Coastal Plain is a year-round sport. For the small boat owner, the problem of access is solved by numerous public and private ramps constructed on rivers, lakes and sounds. The dilemma for many of us is finding a free weekend for a little hunting too. ♦

An Audubon
Bird Study
Program

by Charlotte Hilton Green
Raleigh, N. C.

OCTOBER is a fine month to get under way with an AUDUBON BIRD STUDY PROGRAM. The complete KIT ($2.00)[1] includes the large BIRD CHART (26 by 40 inches) which makes an excellent wall piece. It has pictures of 38 American birds (in full color) all but three of which are in our own State, *in some section*, at *some time of the year*. In the center is a large picture of the Bald Eagle, our national bird, which is now becoming very rare.

"At one time it was abundant from the Arctic Circle to the Gulf of Mexico. Now you will find its picture everywhere—on the Great Seal of the United States, on many State Seals; on every dollar bill, half-dollar and quarter—in many magazines and papers. In fact, we see it everywhere—except in the sky. For today it is in serious plight."

Below the eagle's portrait and description is an interesting section, with outline drawings, depicting birds' bills, wings, feet, and tails, each part giving details as how the type is of primary importance to the bird's way of life. Thus, the many ways birds' bills are used; how birds' wings are the organs of flight, and the close relationship between shape of wing and style of flight—hence the wide variation.

Bird's feet and their importance, the different types, as is demonstrated in wading, perching, climbing, preying, scratching, are explained, as are birds' tails, their chief function as a "rudder in flight" and a "balancer" when perching; also the different types, as the forked tail, the spine-tipped tail, the rounded tail, and the well-rounded tail.

In using the CHART, with smaller children place it low enough on wall so they can read description (if reading) and note details. Also, in using this program, our own *BIRDS of NORTH CAROLINA* should be on hand for local references and checking. Too, it would be helpful to have a copy of the excellent LIFE Nature book, *The BIRDS*. And of course, Peterson's *FIELD GUIDE TO THE BIRDS*.)

1 National Audubon Society
1130 Fifth Avenue
New York, N.Y. 10028

2 Copies which are termed "imperfect" but still contain the same text as previous copies, are specially priced at $4.00. These are available from the State Museum of Natural History, Raleigh, N. C.

3 Available from Time-Life Books, 540 N. Michigan Ave., Chicago, Illinois, 60611, $4.95 plus postage and handling.

If you don't know this pleasant little bird of field and shore, perhaps it's time you brushed up on birds!

The Story of Birds

Included in the KIT is a fine leaflet "The Story of Birds" applicable to any study group; schools, 4-H, scouts, church, home, etc. The attractive cover has pictures, in color, of eight birds; it contains various helpful ideas for birders: as a "roadside silhouettes of birds," also of shore and water ones, each named by key and number. *Birds Are Fun* suggests many things to do, as making a *Bird Calendar*, tells the fascinating details of feathers, how birds fly, how to get acquainted with birds, how birds get a living, how to attract birds—as feeders, bird baths, water, plantings; how to build bird houses and what types for those birds that use them. And, very important, where to find birds: something of their habitats, as woodlands, open spaces, parks, wet places, seashores.

For the older scholar there is the interesting story, with details, of the history of birds; how, as far as scientists can tell from the study of fossils, the first birds appeared between 190,000,000 and 150,000,000 years ago. (In the British Museum, in London, I looked up the fossil remains of *Archaeopteryx*, which was discovered in a slate quarry in Germany in 1861. There is an illustration of this on page 8 of *THE BIRDS*.)

BIRD MIGRATION! "One of the greatest shows on earth is staged every autumn and spring, when billions of birds make their way between their winter and summer homes." This leaflet has a brief sketch on migration, touching on the highlights . . . also a map showing our continent's four main *flyways*. (Again check with our own state bird book, and some of our wintering sanctuaries —as Mattamuskeet and Swan Quarter.)

BIRD CONSERVATION with the need, even greater today where is far too widespread use of wrong insecticides (especially DDT); too much

BIRDS of NORTH CAROLINA and check the kill-deer here: "A well-known bird in the State . . . the *one plover* regularly found *inland* as well as on the coast . . . of great economical value on the farm . . . conspicuously shows up all over the State . . ." And much more interesting information.

Audubon Leaders' Guide

A third leaflet in the KIT is a 16-page one in black and white, dealing with all phases of making this BIRD PROGRAM a meaningful and enjoyable experience. It contains a variety of projects and activities for implementing the program, with specific suggestions for interpreting each section of the children's leaflets. "Do they want to form a club?" If so, here are all the procedures to follow. (Today over 11,000,000 children in various school classes and other youth groups—as 4-H, Boy and Girl Scouts, church groups, neighborhood groups, home groups, etc.—have been members of these Audubon Junior Clubs since this educational activity for children was inaugurated in 1910.)

A section in this GUIDE is devoted to various suggestions and ideas, including language arts, geography, elementary science, creative arts. All kinds of contests, quizzes, puzzles, etc. are mentioned, as "Yes . . . No." For example: "All birds have the same n u m b e r of feathers. Yes—No." "Birds have very heavy bones. Yes—No." "Birds use their bills to help build their nests. Yes—No." (Answers to all quizzes, puzzles, games, etc. are to be found somewhere in the KIT material.)

There are sections on how to attract birds, where to find birds, bird nests, bird migration, bird conservation; on flannel boards, bulletin boards, elec-

The woodcock, a migratory game bird of our wetlands, has a flexible probing bill just about unique in the bird world.

are three important things that mankind and birds need in order to live, but the ways each get these are very different. Peoples' hands are probably their most important tools. A bird has no hands, but its bill, its feet, its wing and tail—even its keen eyesight—all help to solve its living problems.

Let's look at the large BIRD CHART again and note the midlower section which discusses, with outline drawings, birds' bills, feet, wings, tails and how they function.

Bills

BILLS: Primarily, the bills of birds are important in food-getting, but the bill is also used as a "comb to dress the feathers, a weapon of defense and a tool in constructing the nest." (Here I'll add "and a tool in courtship, as the wave albatrosses of the Galapagos Islands use them.")

Each kind of bird has a bill especially adapted for getting its food. However, birds that ordinarily eat one kind of food eat another kind in emergencies: seed-eaters may eat berries, or fruit, etc.

1. *Seed-eaters.* The bill is short and thick for breaking seeds and obtaining the contents. Sparrows, cardinals, goldfinches are seed-eaters.

2. *Insect-eaters.* (a) Most insect-eating birds have slender, pointed bills. Examples: warblers, vireos, robins, orioles, bluebirds, meadowlarks, kinglets, redwings, killdeer, etc. (b) For catching insects on the wing the bills are usually small and the mouth wide open with bristles at the corners. Examples: barn swallows, kingbirds, purple martins. (c) For boring into trees in search of bugs, the bill is chisel-shaped, strong and sharp. Examples; woodpeckers.

3. *Birds of Prey.* Some birds have strong, sharp, hooked bills for carrying and tearing animal food. Examples: Hawks, eagles, owls.

4. *Ground Feeders.* Some birds that feed on the ground have very short, stout, horny bills for picking seeds and insects off the ground. Examples: Quails, pheasants, chickens, turkeys.

5. *Nectar-eaters.* Long, slender, tapering bills are fitted for probing into the deep tubes of flowers for insects and honey. Examples: the hummingbirds.

6. *Mud-feeders.* Some water birds have broad, flattened bills for pushing into the mud and straining out the food. Examples: Ducks and geese. (If your school has a copy of *THE BIRDS* available, look at marginal sketches pages 59-61, showing long, flexible tongue of woodpecker thrust far beyond the bill; the scissor-like bill of the crossbill which gets seeds out of evergreen cones; the oystercatcher's bill inserted like a chisel in partly-opened oyster shell, paralyzing occupant before able to snap shell shut. An anhinga (water turkey, or

snake-bird) impales a fish under water on its spear-like beak, and a flamingo—which lives on organic matter found in mud—their bent bills, fringed at the edge, filters out mud and water, retaining the minute plants and animals. (We have all these birds in the State, though only rare records of the flamingo.)

7. *Fish-eaters.* The long, sharp bills of some fish-eating birds are well adapted for catching fish. Examples: herons, egrets, kingfishers.

(If the teacher is artistic—or even better, a student is—how about having enlarged drawings on blackboard or flannel board, of these different types of feet, wings, tails, all of which will be covered in detail in following numbers of this magazine. Perhaps Museum Director William Hamnett could arrange a guided tour of such types.

Museum's "Traveling Exhibits"

These are small cases with bird mounted in natural position for display. (With this beginning study I would suggest asking for downy woodpecker, sparrow hawk and robin, noting especially their bills and feet.) They are sent free, the only charge the return postage. For further information and lists available, write:

N. C. State Museum Natural History
P. O. Box 2281
Raleigh, N. C. 27602

Next month: Bird's Feet and how they are used.

RESOURCE-O-GRAM
A ROUNDUP OF THE LATEST WILDLIFE NEWS

Don't Forget Those Public Hearings!

Fresh water anglers will get a chance to air their views on the 1970 inland fishing regulations at a series of three public hearings early this month. The Wildlife Resources Commission met in Raleigh September 22 to set up proposals for next year's fishing rules, and these will be discussed at the hearings:

    October 7, Asheville Courthouse, 7:30 p.m.
    October 8, Salisbury Courthouse, 7:30 p.m.
    October 9, Washington Agriculture Auditorium, 7:30 p.m.

Major changes will likely involve mountain trout fishing.

Another Trout Survey Under Way

The Division of Inland Fisheries of the Wildlife Resources Commission has sent questionnaires to about 5,000 licensed resident trout anglers, and urgently requests persons receiving them to respond promptly. Information from these will be extremely valuable in establishing trout management programs and setting trout fishing regulations.

Many anglers have already responded, but those who have not are requested to do so as soon as possible.

Special Big Game License Needed This Year

The 1969 Legislature passed a law requiring persons hunting deer, bear, wild boar and wild turkeys to purchase a special big game hunting license costing $1.75. Funds from the sale of this license are earmarked for use in establishing new big game management areas, and expanded programs of big game management. Deer, bear, and boar hunting begins October 13 in much of the state. The big game license is required in addition to regular hunting licenses.

First Segment of Dove Season Ends October 11

Dove hunters will cease their activity at sundown October 11, but may begin again December 18 and hunt afternoons only through January 15. Daily bag limit of 18 birds is expected to produce a record harvest of birds.

Wildlife Protector Burley Clark inspects Tar River log jams. Burley wants to help, but his county is "exempt" from regulating laws. "Once I informed a logger of the local concern," said Burley, "and he volunteered to remove the tree laps. But they aren't all like that."

It's The Law!

by John R. Parker, Jr.
Boating Editor

THE free flowing small stream, complete with natural surroundings that provide habitat for fin, fur, and feathers might well be considered one of our "endangered species." When channelization, pollution and littering are considered, prospects for survival seem dim.

Let us briefly consider littering which at first may appear less detrimental. Stream littering involves everything from paper bags to porky pigs and including the kitchen sink. Much of this is covered by health or stream pollution laws.

Another form of littering, perhaps the most noticeable on a given stretch of stream, is caused by careless logging operations. Felling tree tops into streams, either by plan or accident, leads to greater problems. The immediate and obvious effect is often the blocking of boat traffic. Then come the rains. The creek's natural flow is impaired and someone yells flood. Then up goes the cry for complete channelization and the end of another stream.

Snagging, in so many instances, will reduce or prevent lowland flooding because water is permitted to flow more freely. The Wildlife Resources Commission now has a full-time snagging crew.* This crew has opened many miles of small streams to boat traffic in the last year or so. However, the work of one careless logger can cause weeks of work for the crew. And at least indirectly cause

*See *Wildlife* February 1969, "New Fishing Water".

more tax dollars to be spent in harmful channelization. A citizen aware of this problem and the law can help reduce the paradox which often terminates in habitat destruction.

The law covering felling tree tops and depositing other products of logging into the state's streams is G. S. 77-14 of Chapter 524. It applies to all counties except Chatham, Forsyth, Franklin, Gaston, and Lee. The logic behind these exemptions is not clear to this writer.

"§ 77-14. If any person, firm or corporation shall fell any tree or put any slabs, stumpage, sawdust, shavings, lime, refuse or any other substances in any creek, stream, river or natural or artificial drainage ravine, ditch or other outlet which serves to remove water from lands whereby the natural and normal drainage of said land is impeded, delayed or prevented, the person, firm or corporation so offending shall remove such above-described obstruction or substance within seven calendar days and, upon failure to so remove, shall be guilty of a misdemeanor and fined or imprisoned in the discretion of the court: Provided, however, nothing herein shall prevent the construction of any dam not otherwise prohibited by any valid local or State statute or regulation.

"All sheriffs, wildlife protectors, highway patrolmen and township constables, or other persons knowing of such violations, shall report to the Board of County Commissioners, of the county in which such above-described obstruction of drainage takes place, the names of any persons, firms or corporations violating the provisions of this Section, and it shall be the duty of the chairman of the Board of County Commissioners to report to the county court solicitor, if there is one, and, if not, to the district solicitor, facts and circumstances showing the commission of any offense as defined herein, and it shall be the duty of the solicitor to prosecute such violators."

by
John R. Parker
Jr.

THERE often arises some confusion and misunderstanding as to why so many of those big, beautiful cruisers are not adorned with a registration number. For example, we occasionally hear someone remark that they passed a large and expensive-looking cruiser in the waterway and it was not numbered. Why? Good question. And the answer is, most likely, the boat was *documented*. Let us explain.

Of course if you are, as we say respectfully, an old salt, you may know more about documentation than we have room to w r i t e about it. But in case you have been a victim of that documentation, registration, numbering, and license word-game confusion, then maybe I can help. Generally small pleasure boats, outboards, smaller inboard cruisers, etc., are registered by the states, and larger boats, pleasure and most commercial, are documented by the U. S. Coast Guard. You will recall that in accordance with North Carolina law, boats of over ten horsepower must be registered and assigned a permanent number which is affixed to the forward half of the boat. You also may recall that the Motorboat Owner's Guide lists exceptions to numbering and one of these (there are six) reads "Vessels documented by t h e United States Bureau of Customs" (documentation is now administered by the U. S. Coast Guard).

With that background, let us now offer a definition. Documentation is the process of obtaining a marine document or paper for a vessel. These official documents are required by law for all United States vessels of over five net tons used for commercial purposes. Pleasure craft of over five net tons are *permitted* to be doc-

umented.

The five-ton limitation prevents documentation of your outboard runabout, for example. It takes about 30 or so feet of pleasure craft to reach five tons. For this reason you will see a number of small commercial boats, like inland shrimpers, etc., and pleasure cruisers with North Carolina registrations.

A documented boat carries its name on each side of the bow and name and port on the stern. A documented boat does carry a number but it is stamped on the main beam (very much out of sight).

Why documentation as opposed to registration for large pleasure boats? There are some practical advantages in favor of documentation. Examples are: a documented boat can be used in any state with no concern of reciprocity time limits; makes cruising out of and back into United States waters easier, (concerning customs, etc.); makes financing the boat easier and assures a complete record of ownership; financial liability, etc.; *legally* empowers you to fly the yacht ensign.

Documentation does not exempt the craft from applicable State or Federal taxes, it does not permit you to transport merchandise or carry passengers for pay; and it does not exempt the boat from safety and equipment regulations provided for in the State Boat Law.

Documentation is somewhat more complicated than registration, the first time at least, in that detailed description, sketches, measurements, tonnage, etc., are submitted for the craft. Various forms are involved and depending on what type of documentation you apply for, an appointment with a Coast Guard official may be required in order to "measure" your boat.

Docking

How you handle your boat at and around the dock or landing will do a great deal to impress spectators with your boatmanship—or lack of it. Of course, the important thing is how you handle the boat, not the impression you make; but the former will take care of the latter.

Docking, contrary to the boat operation of a few, is certainly a time for slow speed (no wake), alertness, and attention to details. Too much throttle at a crucial moment and you have tossed your lineman overboard or impaled your craft on a piling.

Approaching the dock is usually done at a shallow angle and heading into wind or current, which ever is stronger. Obviously, this is not always practical but it is a good rule of thumb. Docking lines and fenders should be ready. It is especially embarassing to attempt to toss a line to a marina attendent only to find there is a great glob of

• continued on page 30

An approach to a pier should always be made at slow speed, heading into tide, current or wind. When bow is close to the pier, toss out a line. One end of line is secured to the bow and the other end to the pier. Driver should then shift the motor into reverse, turn it toward pier and back in. A stern line can then be secured to pier.

Some Call Him Baldhead
Smith Island

by Wiley McKellar
Wilmington, N. C.

Abandoned Coast Guard shacks are framed by leaning sea oats and a proud egret surveys its ancestral home . . .

PHOTOS BY H. E KNICKERBOCKER

SMITH ISLAND is an exercise for the senses.

North Carolina's most isolated coastal area lies only a few miles from the urban humdrum of Wilmington. Yet in a time perspective, it could be a thousand years in the past. There is no motorized din, no foul exhaust fumes and almost no evidence of man's well-known tendency to commit assault and battery on his land and his environment.

This is Longfellow's f o r e s t primeval. It is Thoreau's Walden and Hudson's Green Mansions. Smith Island could be Nature's last stand on the Atlantic Coast.

Visitors to the island are occasional. Smith Island can be reached only by boat, either from the ocean or across the choppy mouth of the Cape Fear River from Southport. People have been visiting Smith Island on and off since prehistoric times, but significantly, they never stayed. Indians came and went. Hardy mariners and settlers stayed longer, but eventually they packed up and left. The Coast Guard dug in for a few years, but abandoned the island to the elements.

Now Nature has completely taken over. She decorates the abandoned shacks with tenuous vines and slowly obscures with green canopies the small roads which criss-cross the forested island.

Man's natural senses, dulled by the clamorous efforts of his fellow, are given a refreshing rejuvenation on Smith Island. He is able to see and hear Nature in her own element. The things he feels there and the things he smells may jolt the memory to bring back the way things were years ago.

He is struck by the initial quiet when he steps from the boat. There are no heavy trucks gulping diesel, no factories belching steam and hydrocarbons. Just silence.

Then, far away, there is the call of a small bird. He is answered in counterpoint by others. Perhaps a seagull files a vocal complaint. The forest comes alive with sound. The wind moves through the palmetto and oak groves with a sibilant voice of its own. Cicadas, crickets, mosquitoes and the myriad insect voices join the island chorus.

The visitor uses his eyes more keenly. There may be a painted bunting fluttering around in a thicket. The corner of his eye catches an osprey cutting an arc over the horizon or a larger-than-usual lizard sunning on a bleached cedar log.

He sees the vast stretches of lush marsh grass waving rhythmically in the breeze and the precise, almost dainty, tracks left by the predatory mink during his foray the night before. The graceful white ibis is a Schubert melody in flight. The million unknown creeping things startle with their covert scurrying in the underbrush. The sea is alone in its rolling majesty embracing the Smith Island shores the way it did millions of years ago, unjettied, unspoiled and untamed.

When a person touches something on Smith Island, it is almost a holy thing, as if he were touching something which had never been touched before, as if he were picking up a rock on the moon. He is drawn to touch a certain hidden wildflower, yet he hesitates to pluck it from the stem, as if it would bring down destruction.

On visiting the massive Baldhead lighthouse, the first thing the visitor does is place the flat of his hand against the concrete wall and look upward. He has seen the tower from a distance, and now he

All kinds of wildlife call this sub-tropical island home. But its value goes far beyond a dwelling place for such as this chicken snake and his myriad cousins.

Only wind and wave . . . and the screech of the sea bird, are heard on Baldhead. Fifty years from now? . . . ten? A rusty relic from the past, a plow share, used in a horticulture station once operated on Baldhead, stands silently.

...miliar landmark on Baldhead, the Coast Guard lighthouse ...s back to 1817. A view of much of the island is available ...t its weathered top.

...finally touch it. He can even climb up the ...den staircase inside if he is extremely careful ...unafraid of heights. But most people feel the ...t is accomplished if only they can place their ...ds on the tower, and marvel at the ingenuity of ...people who in 1817 raised this monument and ...gave it up more than hundred years later.

...ore abstract is the fleeting parade of smells ...the forest and the sea. At low tide, the smells ...he marsh creep upward—a conglomeration of ...ying vegetation, salt water and other com- ...ents that produce a distinctive aroma which can ...xperienced only along the coast.

...the spring and summer, honeysuckle, sweet ...wild plum—and even skunk cabbage contri- ...to the woodland smells. There are the well- ...bbed pine and cedar smells. The odors of gaso- ...fumes, wood pulp, cleaning fluid, ammonia ...asphalt are easily forgotten.

...ese sights, sounds, feelings and smells are ...ily disappearing. Sociologists, urbanologists ...anthropologists say that man will continue to ...ue the earth and remake it to his best ad- ...age. They say man right now needs more ...w room and will need even more in years to ...e. Biologists, ecologists and environmental ...tists warn that man only further endangers ...species by his program of despoilation, and ...unless present trends are reversed, he will ...nothing on earth but himself, and this asset ...for a short time until oblivion.

...ok quickly! Smith Island is still hanging on!

. . . Dedicated to the safety of every young hunter who goes afield with gun, youthful energy and high hopes. . . .

THE young hunter was as loaded with anticipation for his hunting solo as was the single barrel .410 scatter-gun atop his steadily broadening shoulders. For the next few hours, this anticipation, coupled with youthful energy—this urge to hunt— would carry him on a somewhat aimless trek along the east side of his uncle's farm. During this time he would feather one of a covey of quail that had surprised him down by the old barn; send a few crows on their way that had alighted in a dying persimmon tree and bag a squirrel that was feeding in a lone white oak which stood amidst a pine thicket.

As the morning's events unfolded the boy became just a little discouraged. The squirrel was not as highly rated as the quail which he had missed. But he remembered his uncle saying that most youngsters start their hunting with old bushy tail. And too, he guessed he was lucky to find this gray since most of the farm's woodlots had been converted to pine.

The November morn was not so chilled now; at least it seemed so to the youngster. He moved on with feet slightly dampened by frost that had given away to warming rays. Occasionally he halted in his rush toward maturity and booted clods of dirt down a corn row bowling alley. But what hunter hasn't, young and old alike. At any rate, the boy was mature enough to understand that he had many years of the good hunt ahead of him, many years of challenge and companionship. He had heard his dad talk about that. But still the missed quail on this particular morning stayed foremost in his mind.

He remembered hearing about another covey over by the tobacco patch. He'd have to backtrack a little but that would be ok. Check the gun, he thought. Loaded. Cocked. I won't shoot slow this time, he thought. This time I won't be late.

Shadows began to lengthen and further to the north, along the county line, the well-dusted patrol car of a wildlife protector eased to a stop at a junction station. The proprietor, named Sam, had just put the gasoline hose back on the pump and had bid farewell to a customer.

"Hi ya Sam!" the protector called. "Why aren't you out popping quail?"

"Got two limits yesterday", Sam replied, jokingly. "Besides that, I knew you rabbit sheriffs would be on the north side today. Say, did you hear about the boy?", Sam continued in a more serious tone.

He hadn't given the protector a chance to reply to his standard tale of two limits, rabbit sheriff and all, and now the jovial conversation was about to end before it really started.

"What about a boy?"

"A youngster was killed west of here a bit on the Smith Farm. Believe it was his nephew."

"Hunting?" the protector asked.

"Yep, first time out alone. Seems he was late for dinner so they started looking. Strange thing, seems as if . . ."

The protector didn't hear the last of Sam's words. He was now heading to the patrol car saying something about stopping by on the next round. He thought as he buckled the seat belt . . . might as well get this over.

He knew it would come sooner or later, but it had been three years since the last one in his area. The bad news just didn't fit the bright November afternoon.

He was more disturbed about this than he thought he would be. Perhaps it was because he had just finished teaching a hunter safety course in another part of the county. He liked to work with the young ones.

The protector would head toward the farm but he wasn't sure what he would find, what with the confusion and grief that accompanies any such tragedy. Perhaps he would see someone he knew. Some might wonder why he was there, as certainly everyone isn't aware that his department keeps records on such accidents.

The drive took about 10 minutes and as the protector pulled to a stop in front he began thinking again that this wasn't the time to question the family. There would be too much going on. However, the farm place was quieter than he expected. The uncle, who was in the back, explained that he was about to leave—to be with the family in town as soon as he checked around the place. The protector quickly offered to return for a report, but the uncle agreed to tell him what he knew and show him the accident site.

THE protector went to his patrol car and returned with a faded Hunter Safety Casualty Form—the form he had hoped never to use. He quickly filled in location information, date, etc. The uncle knew most of the personal information about the boy. But he was not sure if the boy had been exposed to any formal hunter safety training.

"Probably not," he said, "but we all talked to him."

The uncle also was not sure about the game being hunted. "Just hunting," he said. 'But then he did get a quail and a squirrel."

The uncle went on to tell the protector how the quail was near the boy's hand. And how the family was puzzled about how the single barrel gun had delivered the fatal shot after the boy had downed the quail.

But as they talked and visited the site it became clear that the boy, like any good hunter, had reloaded prior to approaching downed game. But where he failed was when he again cocked the .410. Under the broad heading of "Unintentional Discharge," the protector checked "Trigger caught on bush or other object." The gun had no doubt discharged when the boy leaned over to pick up the bird which had fallen in a thicket.

As he pulled onto the country road the protector thought . . . Did the boy fail or did someone fail the boy? Had the practical side of the gun safety been repeated many times? Had the boy been exposed to a little of the philosophy of it all . . . things like, self-discipline, and how that bagging game was not worth the risk of injury. Hunting, after all, is a form of recreation, to many . . . the greatest. It should never be treated as a form of combat.

And the protector thought, as he radioed a location check and skillfully headed the patrol car into the November sun, it would have been a good day except for the report.

CRACKSHOTS and BACKLASHES
by Rod Amundson

From time to time the Wildlife Resources Commission receives letters from irate citizens who want to know what the Commission is doing about water pollution, air pollution, and littering. These letters describe the deplorable condition of many of our polluted waters where pollution is concerned, the air near pulp mills, and the litter that is strewn along lakes, rivers, and trout streams.

While it is, in a sense, flattering to be expected to do something about such matters, the best we can do is deplore the conditions. The Commission has no legal jurisdiction whatever of air pollution. Where water pollution is concerned, it can only monitor our lakes and streams to detect pollution sufficient to have an adverse effect on fish.

Littering is a matter of public attitude. You can be fined as much as $50.00 for littering along a highway, but this comes under the jurisdiction of the highway patrol.

The Commission furnishes free boating access areas, nearly 100 of them across the state, and provides them with litter receptacles. Judging from the amount of litter scattered around these areas, and the cost of cleaning them up, people really are not as appreciative of these facilities as they might be.

Hunters and fishermen rank at the bottom of the scale of people who habitually litter the countryside. But only a few careless hunters and fishermen leaving a few cans, bottles, paper, and other trash, can get a lot of private land closed out to hunting and fishing.

Humans are the only animals that litter the countryside, streets and highways, pollute the atmosphere and the water. Maybe something ought to be done about people.

Dog-Napper

Dear Sir:

Last year while deer hunting, our hunting club had five dogs stolen. Other clubs in our area lost dogs also. Our club borders the Sandhills Wildlife Management Area on the northeastern side. From the information we have gathered, we seem to think that the persons connected with the theft of these dogs belong, in some way, to a dognapping outfit with the headquarters based in Charleston, South Carolina. These men would drive along the road on the reserve and call up our dogs while we were still in the woods. By the time we could drive across to the reserve, we would find no one and no dogs. The men on the reserve have cooperated with us fully, but they have so much to do themselves.

Gentlemen, would you please see if you can put additional men in this area during deer season to protect our dogs or find some way to stop this. There are not many clubs in this area that can afford to lose dogs, some valued at $200 or $300. I am afraid that if one of these men is found to be stealing dogs by someone from a club in this area, there is liable to be serious trouble.

I have talked to a member of a club in South Carolina. He stated that this dog stealing ring had bothered their dogs until they filled one of these men's pants full of buckshot. I sincerely hope that such drastic action will not be necessary. What

● continued from page 7
license, and they could fish every day and take all the fish they could pay for.

A final thought on trout regulations is that they should be simplified, especially so far as the Management Areas are concerned. At present, we have streams restricted to "only artificial lures", others to "only artificial flies", and still others to "no fish as bait", and all of these with no other restrictions. Then we have the "Native Trout" and "Trophy Trout" regulations which require artificial *lures* and artificial *flies* respectively, and which also have minimum size limits and reduced creel limits.

The obvious thought is to discard the regulations which have been outmoded and to settle on the three in general use. We might have two or three Trophy Trout streams and a considerable number of Native Trout streams on the Management Areas. As was pointed out, special regulations must be confined to lands in public ownership. Some three-fourths of our trout streams then would have basic regulations consisting of a 7 fish limit, no size limit, and any bait. The special restriction streams would be under Native or Trophy trout regulations and would be open three days a week plus holidays. All streams could be brought under one of these three concepts.

The 1968 survey showed numerous fishermen who wanted more fish stocked. We cannot afford to raise more, but these regulations would provide more fish in the streams not restricted to finger-ling stockings. The effect would be the same.

The 1969 survey of fishermen's opinions will be a matter of record before the regulations are established for 1970. New data from that survey may indicate different attitudes on the part of the fishermen. And in any case, take time to think over the needs for changes in the 1970 regulations. Then come to Room 207 at the Buncombe County Courthouse at 7:30 on the evening of October 7, 1969 and give us *your* opinion. We want it!

Our first responsibility is to have regulations that protect our fish from over-exploitation, yet permit a maximum harvest. Beyond that, we try to have some of the type of fishing that each angler may want. We don't please everybody—but we try!

PHOTO BY JOHN R. PARKER, JR.

Ted Dossett, Wildlife Commission motion picture photographer, zooms in on Duane Raver's field sketch of the sheepshead. This is the closing scene of TV program number 10 in the current Wildlife series. It is a combination salt water fishing and boating safety program. An autographed reproduction of the sheepshead sketch will be offered the viewers. The series is currently seen over the WUNC-TV network and WFMY-TV, Greensboro.

ANSWERS TO OUTDOOR QUIZ

Page 11

1. True 2. True 3. True 4. True 5. True 6. True
7. False 8. True 9. False 10. True 11. False
12. True 13. True 14. True 15. True

Multiple Choice

1. male 2. beaks 3. Venus, Pluto, Saturn, Mars, Jupiter 4. insect 5. fives 6. turkeys 7. winds 8. reddest on head 9. rounded lobes 10. two white eggs 11. squirrels 12. naked 13. cup-shaped 14. Holly Family 15. larger

---

we need is helicopter pilots patrolling these roads with orders to search any trucks on the wildlife area for dogs. Your help will be appreciated.

Sincerely yours,
Mike Hogan
Norman

Your Job?

Dear Sir:

A number of us who hunt deer have been concerned for some years about the scarcity of bucks in our hunting areas. We are trying to do something about it by trying to increase the available food for deer—and other species of wildlife.

Mr. Patton had the nearest game biologist call on us to advise suitable plants for our location, and we are loaded with seed of everything that deer and grouse might eat.

We put out persimmon, mulberry and wild cherry, and hope to get grapes, muscadines, locust and anything we can seed or transplant this fall and now on.

If Pennsylvania can bring the deer back to the point that a single county has an annual buck kill of 2500 it is proof that North Carolina has done very little indeed to seriously increase our deer population.

At the age of 69, I am just realizing that each hunter must do anything and everything he can to ensure a food supply for wildlife. We are so accustomed to depending upon officials to do a job that we forget what a prodigious amount of work even a dozen individuals can do in this effort.

Sincerely,
Glen S. Ballard
Huntersville

SKIPPER

● continued from page 25
an anchor attached. Prepare two or three lines to use especially for docking.

If approaching the windward or weather side of a pier, the boat, after positioning parallel to

Wildlife at the Fair

You might have to stand in line for the wildlife exhibit at the North Carolina State Fair this year. But it will be worth it — especially if you have the children along.

As a showcase for wild animals native to North Carolina, the wildlife exhibit at the fair is in a league of its own. And last year, during the busiest hours, hundreds of fairgoers waited as long as 30 minutes to get in. Some even waited in the rain.

And rain it did last year, on four of the six days of the fair. Attendance was way below normal. Less than half a million people came. Still there were lines at the wildlife exhibit.

This year, though, the fair will run for nine full days—from Friday, October 17 through Saturday, October 25. It will be the longest ever held. If the weather is good, fair manager Art Pitzer expects close to a million people to attend.

Children under 12 will be admitted to the fair free this year. All others will pay $1.00 admission. Admission to the fair includes admission to the wildlife exhibit at no additional charge.

Darrell Louder, who arranges the wildlife exhibit, says attractions this year may include a black bear and some black vultures, commonly known as buzzards.

Louder, a member of the Division of Inland Fisheries staff of the Wildlife Resources Commission, sets up and operates the wildlife exhibit on his own time. He gets a helping hand from Duane Raver of the Division of Education, who also donates his time and talents.

Louder says experience has shown that children always enjoy a fawn better than anything else, so he plans to have a new one this year. Also a great horned owl, a red-tailed hawk, and a pelican from the coast.

He'll also have flathead and blue catfish weighing from 20-to-25-pounds, six species of snakes, and Canadian geese. And there'll be skunks, squirrels, rabbits, woodchucks, raccoons, and opossums.

Many of the animals will be appearing for the second time and third time. Louder keeps several of them in captivity and he has friends around the State who keep others.

"We'd never get an exhibit ready on time if we had to go out and catch all the animals every year," he says.

Improvements in the exhibit come slowly. For the first time, all animals will be housed in steel cages—except the fawn, which will be in a wire enclosure. Ultimately, hopes are to have a permanent building.

The fair continues to grow and expand each year. Every year it promises to be "the biggest and best yet." And usually it delivers.

The gray squirrel has been officially designated as our State Mammal. They are hunted statewide, and reach a length of 16 to 21 inches, and a maximum weight of 1½ pounds.

The chipmunk lives on the ground and is not considered a game species. They are quite small, reaching a length of 9 to 11 inches and a weight of only 3 to 5 ounces.

A creature of the night, the flying squirrel glides softly from tree to tree. Their soft fur makes them look larger than their 2- to 5-ounce weight.

Compared to our other squirrels, the fox squirrel looks almost ponderous. Some individuals reach a length of 28 inches, and weigh up to three pounds.

Tarheel SQUIRRELS

Known locally as "boomers," the red squirrel of the mountains is a noisy critter. They are considerably smaller than the gray squirrel and reach a maximum length of 14 inches and a weight of 5 to 11 ounces.

Wade Weeber

LITHO BY THE GRAPHIC PRESS, INC, RALEIGH, N. C.

Wildlife

IN NORTH CAROLINA

25 CENTS / NOVEMBER 1969

WILDLIFE IN NORTH CAROLINA recognizes the need
for close cooperation between State and Federal
conservation agencies and the people who hunt
and fish—to bring about a restoration of our renewable resources. The Editor gratefully receives
for publication news items, articles, and photographs dealing with the North Carolina out-of-
doors, but reserves the right to reject materials
submitted. Full credit is given for all materials
published.

• • •

WILDLIFE IN NORTH CAROLINA is published at the
Wildlife Resources Commission offices, Motor
Vehicles Building, 1100 New Bern Ave., Raleigh,
N. C. 27601.

• • •

Second class postage paid at Raleigh, North
Carolina 27602.

• • •

SUBSCRIPTION—One dollar per year, two dollars for two years. Make remittance payable to
WILDLIFE RESOURCES COMMISSION. Any
employee of the Wildlife Resources Commission
may accept subscriptions, or they may be forwarded to Post Office Box 2919, Raleigh, N. C.
27602. Stamps cannot be accepted.

Wildlife circulation this issue, 118,654.

EDITORIAL STAFF

ROD AMUNDSON _ _ _ _ _ _ _ _ EDITOR
DUANE RAVER _ _ _ _ _ MANAGING EDITOR
LUTHER PARTIN _ _ WRITER-PHOTOGRAPHER
JOHN PARKER _ _ _ _ _ _ BOATING EDITOR

The Frame House Gallery of
Wildlife Art, Louisville, Ky.,
makes available to us this striking painting of a cardinal pair.
The artist, Guy Coheleach, is a
precise workman yet he catches
the spark of life and warmth of
the birds. This is one of the
prints featured in the offer
described on page 31 of this
month's magazine. Read it for
further details.

Be smarter than a fox—

give subscriptions to *Wildlife*
IN NORTH CAROLINA

SMART AS THEY ARE, FOXES DON'T DO THEIR CHRISTMAS SHOPPING EARLY. BUT YOU CAN. FOR ONLY $1.00 A YEAR YOU CAN REMEMBER YOUR FRIENDS WITH A GIFT THAT WILL REMIND THEM OF YOUR THOUGHTFULNESS THROUGHOUT THE YEAR.

IF YOU GIVE SUBSCRIPTIONS TO 25 OR MORE FRIENDS, THE PRICE IS ONLY 80¢ A YEAR . . . AND IF YOU HURRY THEY WILL GET THE CHRISTMAS ISSUE. WE WILL SEND THEM A CARD NOTIFYING THEM OF YOUR GIFT.

Send *Wildlife* in north carolina to

- Your farmer friends on whose land you hunt
- Your farmer friends on whose land you would like to hunt
- Your children's teachers and scout leaders
- Your hunting, fishing, and boating pals

Only **$1.00 a year**

PHOTO BY DON ABOOD, JACKSONVILLE

Left Face!

A chill, off-shore breeze scuds low clouds toward this formation of seagulls on a Swansboro pier. Soon they will be up and away in search of food.

submitted. Full credit is given for all materials published.

• • •

WILDLIFE IN NORTH CAROLINA is published at the Wildlife Resources Commission offices, Motor Vehicles Building, 1100 New Bern Ave., Raleigh, N. C. 27601.

• • •

Second class postage paid at Raleigh, North Carolina 27602.

• • •

SUBSCRIPTION—One dollar per year, two dollars for two years. Make remittance payable to WILDLIFE RESOURCES COMMISSION. Any employee of the Wildlife Resources Commission may accept subscriptions, or they may be forwarded to Post Office Box 2919, Raleigh, N. C. 27602. Stamps cannot be accepted.

Wildlife circulation this issue, 118,654.

EDITORIAL STAFF

ROD AMUNDSON _ _ _ _ _ _ _ _ _ EDITOR
DUANE RAVER _ _ _ _ _ MANAGING EDITOR
LUTHER PARTIN _ _ WRITER-PHOTOGRAPHER
JOHN PARKER _ _ _ _ _ _ BOATING EDITOR

The Frame House Gallery of Wildlife Art, Louisville, Ky., makes available to us this striking painting of a cardinal pair. The artist, Guy Coheleach, is a precise workman yet he catches the spark of life and warmth of the birds. This is one of the prints featured in the offer described on page 31 of this month's magazine. Read it for further details.

Left Face!

A chill, off-shore breeze scuds low clouds toward this formation of seagulls on a Swansboro pier. Soon they will be up and away in search of food.

Rifleman's Small Game

by Bob Gooch
Troy, Virginia
Photos by the Author

ALERT, elusive and reasonably abundant throughout North Carolina, the squirrel is a worthy quarry for any hunter. Many won't admit it though. They agree bushytail is excellent game "for young hunters to train on", but for some reason seem to feel that squirrel hunting is beneath their dignity.

Admittedly, a squirrel perched in the crotch of a tree is not much of a challenge for a shotgunner at close range, but try swinging on him as he swishes through the swaying branches of a tall oak. Or try to nail him scampering pell mell over the leaf littered floor of a tree studded forest. The bowhunter will swap a quiver of blunt tipped arrows for every bite of tasty squirrel meat he puts in the pot, but many archers enjoy the challenge. But for the best in squirrel hunting, go after him with the small-bore .22 rifle. For many hunters there is no finer sport than bagging a mess of squirrels with the little .22. Success demands crack shooting, but it can come quickly for the rifleman who keeps his shooting eye sharp. The squirrel is the rifleman's small game, and the only North Carolina game truly appropriate for the small-bore rifle.

Hunter surveys show the squirrel rates high in the esteem of the sportsmen in a number of states.

Three squirrels make up the North Carolina hunting population, the gray s q u i r r e l, the fox squirrel and the red squirrel. Scientifically, they are called *Sciurus carolinensis*, *Sciurus niger*, and *Tamiasciurus hudsonicus*, Latin tags of scant interest to the average hunter. A fourth member of the tree squirrel family, the little flying squirrel is on the protected list. The gray is the most popular among hunters because of its abundance and wide distribution.

The average gray weighs a pound and measures 19 inches from its nose to the tip of its constantly flicking tail. The bushy tail consumes 9 of the 19 inches. Its rich coat is usually salt-and-pepper gray except for a white belly. The solid white extends to the underside of its bushy tail. The gray is extremely agile and moves rapidly—either on the ground or through the tree tops.

Bushytail's habits are pretty regular, and the hunter quickly learns to rely upon him. He is up and moving by daylight, and headed for an early breakfast in a rich nut grove. He feeds and rustles about for a couple of hours, and then either returns to his den tree or naps in the sun until late afternoon. He then feeds again before bedding down for the night.

The big fox squirrel is somewhat larger than the gray, but slower and more cumbersome. He is also less industrious, stores less food, and consequently may suffer from hunger late in the winter. In appearance, he is redder in color and more hairy.

The little red squirrel is the smallest of the three, and as its common name indicates, it is reddish in color. Like the gray, its underside is white.

The fox squirrel's feeding habits reflect its laziness. He arises later, feeds more toward the middle of the day and returns to his nest or den earlier than do the gray and red squirrels.

The squirrels are great harvesters, storing as many nuts as they eat. Some authorities say they never find many of their caches, and thus make a substantial contribution to posterity as the buried nuts sprout and form new trees.

The grey squirrel is found in dense forests and woodlands throughout North Carolina, and will thrive wherever it is given a reasonable break. This means leaving him several den trees per acre of forest, and a few nut-bearing hickories, oaks and beechnuts. Unfortunately, good squirrel range has been drastically reduced by extensive logging operations. Loss of habitat, not hunting, has been the

---

The grey squirrel (and other species of small game) is most often the quarry of the Tarheel hunting accident victim. Squirrel hunting accidents usually lead the list due, for one thing, to the popularity of this species.

One squirrel hunter shot another when the victim's head or cap was mistaken for a squirrel on a tree trunk. Another hunter received a self-inflicted, fatal wound when he attempted to kill a wounded squirrel by clubbing it with his gun stock. In another situation, two hunters approached a tree from different directions. One hunter fired at a squirrel, the slug from his .22 rifle missed the target, hit a limb and ricocheted downward, striking the other hunter.

Moral—don't reserve basic gun handling, safety rules and common sense for big game hunts only.

John R. Parker, Jr.

real culprit in the reduction of a once thriving North Carolina squirrel population. However, there is still good squirrel territory in the state and the outlook for the future of the sport is encouraging.

Grays love the wooded areas along the streams of the Coastal Plain and the hardwoods of the Piedmont and the mountains. The big fox squirrel prefers the Sandhills and the woodlands of the lower Coastal Plain. He frequents the edges instead of the deep woods and swamps, and is usually found where there are mixed stands of pine and hardwoods. The noisy litle red squirrel is an inhabitant of the coniferous forests; and so is much more common in Canada and the northern United States than he is in North Carolina. However, he can be found at the higher elevations of the mountainous western part of the state. Red squirrels are rarely considered game animals—even in sections of the country where they are abundant. They receive very little attention from North Carolina hunters, because of their small size and limited range.

The squirrel is a vegetarian, feeding primarily on nuts during the fall and winter when the hunting season is open. Scouting pays off in squirrel hunting. The hunter should look for hickory, oak and beech trees and search the forest floor for "cuttings"—cracked nuts left there by feeding squirrels. If nuts are plentiful, squirrels will be also. Corn, both standing and in shocks, will attract squirrels—much to the dismay of the farmer who so carefully cultivated it. Fox squirrels, particularly, like to feed on corn. During the spring and summer, both the fox and gray as well as the little red, feed on buds and fruits of various kinds. However, nuts are the key to successful fall and winter hunting trips.

Breeding activity occurs twice a year—first in

mid-winter and again late in June. The gestation period runs for about 45 days, so most litters are born in March and August. They average 3 to 5 blind, hairless, nub-eared young. Squirrels reach adulthood in one year, but continue to grow until they are two years old.

The August offspring are rather small when the hunting starts in October, and even the March squirrels are not fully grown. Of necessity hunting seasons must be wedged between these breeding periods, giving the August youngsters time to grow a bit, but ending before the winter breeding activity starts. The 1969 North Carolina season extends from October 13 through January 1, 1970.

The squirrel hunter's rifle need not be an expensive one. It should be fitted with a 4-power telescopic sight, though peep sights are adequate if the hunter is blessed with good vision. Open sights are crude and difficult to adjust. Bolt actions, automatics, lever actions, repeaters—all find their way into squirrel woods. All are satisfactory squirrel pieces.

If the rifleman is marksman enough to consistently make head shots, solid point bullets are fine, but they don't pack enough shock effect for body shots. Too many squirrels, shot in the body, make it to dens to die a slow death. For all except the most skilled shooters, hollow point bullets are recommended. The long rifle size is a better hunting bullet than either the long or short.

Camouflage clothing, so popular among turkey and dove hunters, and useful in other forms of hunting requiring concealment, improves the squirrel hunter's chances. In cold weather it can be worn over warmer clothing.

The squirrel hunter has to overcome his quarry's sensitive ears, alert eyes and remarkable agility.

The most effective form of squirrel hunting is undoubtedly the stand method. The hunter scouts an area, locates a good nut tree, and gets on his stand before dawn. If his scouting job has been thorough, he has dressed properly and selected a good stand, the success of his hunt is assured—if his shooting eye is sharp.

An advantage the rifleman has over the shotgunner is the subdued report of his rifle. While the bark of a scattergun will send game scurrying, the

It takes a sharp eye to spot a grey amidst the fall foliage. The scampering squirrel at the top of the page is in high gear and presents a tough shot.

very early dawn and late afternoon as the squirrels leave and return to their dens. Active dens are usually well worn and easy to spot.

Some hunters refuse to sit still very long. For them, stalking or still hunting is the only answer. This calls for moving as quietly as possible through good squirrel woods, and stopping every 10 or 15 feet to search the area for game. It can be a very interesting kind of hunting, calling for good woodsmanship. Stalking is recommended for strange territory when the hunter has not had the advantage of a pre-hunting scouting trip. The still hunter may locate a good nut tree, and then switch to stand hunting. Disturbed squirrels will usually resume feeding after 10 or 15 minutes if the hunter will remain quiet and concealed.

R ifles and squirrel hunting are by no means new to the American hunting scene. The bushytail was

Some days you may come home with one, other times, the limit . . . some days none. That's squirrel hunting, and it's real fine sport for the rifleman.

Eastern Lowland Squirrels

by William E. Chauncey
New Bern, N. C.

T HE best squirrel hunting in Eastern North Carolina is usually to be found near water. This is not to say that the squirrel cannot be found where there isn't water nearby, but they do seem much more plentiful in the swamps or lowlands accented by rivers and streams. These areas must also include the types of trees in which the squirrels feed and nest such as oak and hickory trees. One of these locations, a favorite of local hunters, is a place called "Tickbite." It is located in northern Lenoir County about three miles south of Grifton and from that point, two miles east of Highway 11.

Tickbite is a maze of oak, hickory, and cypress trees just to mention the most numerous types of trees, and the ground beneath them is usually wet. It is almost at waterlevel and good stands to hunt can be found ranging from just at the edge of Contentnea Creek up to five or six hundred yards inland.

Because the ground is wet and matted, with very few dry, crisp leaves on the surface, it is not difficult to walk quietly when approaching the area you wish to hunt or to move closer to a tree in which squirrels have been spotted. Once in a chosen location when the normal quiet of the woods has

returned completely, the hunter should remain as still as possible. The squirrel has extremely sensitive ears. He can detect the slightest noise a man might make.

He also has keen sight, however; he will watch you move slowly, before he will stay around to listen to you at all! Youngsters just learning to hunt these animals should keep in mind, remaining quiet above all. At times, it may be necessary to move short distances, but this should be done very slowly. Fifteen feet in ten minutes might be within reason. Quick, jerky movements will "spook" a squirrel as quickly as noise, provided of course, he sees you.

The best hunting stand will be a place where the squirrels have been feeding. This may be immediately under a feed-tree, or on the open ground between several trees, but it will be near those trees bearing the nuts the squirrels most often feed from. Some of the oak and hickory trees I have mentioned in Tickbite are so tall the tops of them are almost out of range of a shotgun. At the beginning of the season, as many as eight to ten nests can be seen in the branches. These are the trees to look for, those in which the squirrels have nested. Here, they will invariably be feeding and storing food for the coming season.

As you walk through the woods looking for these "nest-trees", keep checking the ground. When you are in the right place, a feeding area, there will be nutshells and partially cracked and eaten nuts scattered over the ground. They can also be seen on logs and in clear pools of standing water. When you walk into one of these areas, find a good vantage point from which two or three of the huge trees can be seen and from which you cen see a reasonable portion of the ground beneath.

If there are any tall weeds or small saplings nearby, one can take a stand in them or sit on a log to wait for feeding time; very early morning or late afternoon. There will, of course, still be a goodly amount of greenery on the trees and foliage on the ground at the beginning of the season, and this makes good camouflage. Don't however, become overly camouflaged. The squirrels may not be able to see you if you are covered in greenery, but neither will you be able to get a good shot at them!

About the only clearly visible shot at a squirrel this time of year, will be on the trunk of a tree. When making such a shot, caution should be taken because you are shooting "on the level." You will probably have known where your fellow hunters were at the beginning of the stand, but they may have been the ones to move that fifteen feet— fifteen feet which could prove very dangerous! Also, while mentioning safety, it is not a bad idea to wear bright red or some other bright color in the woods. This gives each hunter the great advantage of knowing whether anyone is within his line of fire when shooting on the level or when making ground shots.

The gun's safety catch should always be left *on* until immediately before shooting at a squirrel.

Most safeties are operated by thumb or forefinger. It is not difficult to disengage the safety after the gun is on your shoulder. This is important because accidental discharges are always possible with a loaded weapon.

Never shoot the first squirrel you see! Give the others time to approach the feeding area and to come well within the area. Once there are several squirrels in the trees and on the ground, a shot may be taken. Those on the ground will make for a tree in a hurry, but those in the trees will either crouch on the limb they're on, lying very still, or dash for a hole in the limb, but none of them will be in hiding long.

If you make a kill, mark it down and let the animal lie where it falls. Do not move! The squirrels that did not happen to see you will not know where you are or even if you are still there. Their reaction will be to the sudden, shattering noise of the gun; not necessarily to the sight of the hunter. When the normal quiet of the woods returns, they will resume their activities. If you are using a gun which requires action on your part to reload, such as a single-shot or a pumpgun, reload it immediately after firing, so that silence may be reattained almost at once. Again, the less noise, the sooner the squirrels will be back out "in force."

Next season use your spare time in late September or early October to go into the woods and look for the feeding areas. Perfect enjoyment can be yours—almost as perfect as a good day's hunt itself.

Dressed appropriately for a lot of moving around in the woods, choose your place of entry. Foot-high marsh grass or other wet undergrowth makes a good entry point. This is readily available at Tickbite and other swampy areas and is usually some distance from the best hunting stands. It provides an easy but quiet way into the woods. Plan to spend a day. A lot of ground can be covered and more than one stand found. A lunch of sandwiches is always good out-of-doors and a small thermos will keep liquid easily.

It is also a good idea to take along a small pistol since snakes are still out at this time of year. Tickbite has its share of Cottonmouth Moccasins, Copperheads, and Whiteoaks but—it also has the squirrels! A rifle or shotgun should be left at home before the season opens. A wildlife protector might too easily assume you were hunting before opening day should he hear a gun fire, then if you couldn't produce that snake, you would not long have a gun! A pistol will suffice.

If you are coming to the eastern lowlands for the first time, good hunting can easily be had by checking the woods before opening day and finding this year's feeding areas. Then, at your first opportunity to hunt after opening day, you will know where to go and what stand you want to use. You won't be disappointed. The possibility of bagging the limit will be topped only by the aura and excitement of another squirrel season opening, and the lowlands provide that excitement every time you hunt! ♦

"Gosh, but there sure is

Fun, Fellowship and Forestry

by George E. Dainty
Special Audience-Education Manager
Southern Forest Institute
Atlanta, Ga.

OSH, but there sure is a lot to this forestry business. We had to learn about a lot of trees and then learn a lot about each of them. You know, trees are an awful lot like people."

That's the way one boy from the coast talked after attending the recently completed North Carolina Forestry Camp. And he was just one of more than 90 who felt the same way after spending an action-packed week in North Carolina's mountains.

Held at Camp Schaub near Waynesville, the camp program was designed to educate boys on the part trees play in their lives and to give them basic information that they can use in managing and developing the trees on their woodlots at home.

Now in its 23rd year, the camp program stands as a tribute to the cooperative spirit exhibited between the pulp and paper industry of the State and the North Carolina Forest Service. Both groups, working together, have provided this week of fun, fellowship, and forestry at no expense to more than 1,600 North Carolina boys since the program started back in 1947. Over the years the camp location has alternated from mountain to coastal sites so boys from all sections of the state can attend at convenient locations.

This year's camp was conducted by the North Carolina Forest Service, with Tom Rhyne, Senior Staff Forester from the Raleigh headquarters, acting as Camp Director. It was sponsored by Southern Forest Institute and financed entirely by contributions from member pulp and paper companies of the Association: International Paper Company, Wilmington; The Mead Corporation, Sylva; U. S. Plywood-Champion Papers Inc., Canton; Westvaco Corporation, Manteo; and Weyerhaeuser Company, Plymouth.

Camp Director Rhyne said, "I didn't believe it possible that these kids could get so enthusiastic about trees and forestry, but

The "Cradle of Forestry" visitor center near Brevard is one stop on the Camp tour. The boys were also given opportunities to see modern forestry management equipment in action on the job (below).

Classroom studies provided opportunities to learn the details of this fascinating profession of forestry management. From groups like this will come the forest managers of tomorrow.

they did. I guess some of the enthusiasm our forester instructors have for their profession kind of rubbed off on the boys."

Foresters from the North Carolina Forest Service and the sponsoring pulp and paper companies were the instructors, while North Carolina Forest Service Rangers served as cabin counselors. In recent years the Agricultural Education Division of the North Carolina Department of Public Instruction has been cooperating with the two groups in the selection of the boys and by providing teachers to serve as curriculum coordinators at camp. The campers for the most part were students active in the Future Farmers of America organization.

Instruction in forestry came in tree identification (You don't know how to manage the trees if you don't know what kind they are.); forest management (It won't grow if you don't treat it right.); fire control (You can't have your trees for use if they burn up in a forest fire.); pest control (You can't have good grade or quantity if insects and disease play havoc with your woods.); and forest measurement (You don't know what your trees are worth if you don't know what volume you own.). During instruction periods, insight into all of these concerns was provided and although the boys didn't leave camp as professional foresters they did obtain a workable knowledge of forestry that will help them with home woodlots.

Although the boys did have a pretty full instruction schedule, there still was plenty of time for recreation, fun, fellowship and lots of real honest-to-goodness food. Sports have a place in any camping p r o g r a m, everyone makes at least one life-long friend at camp, and we all know how much food a growing, active teenage boy can consume in one day. Although classified as fringe benefits, they still help make the camping program complete. And as a special reward, prizes of radios, cameras, knives, axes, and fishing equipment were awarded the top boys for superiority in the various forestry exams and camping activities.

Because each sponsoring group has a special concern for the timber resource of the State, each looked upon this camp as one way of providing for that resource in the future. With about 75 percent of the wood used by the pulp and paper industry coming from the forests of private landowners, leaders from this industry see the camp as a vital tool in educating future timberland owners and informing them of the vast potential for growth their lands hold.

With concern for the woods expressed by i n d u s t r y and agency personnel and with projects in operation such as this, forestry leaders are optimistic about the future of the timberlands of North Carolina. They feel the private landowner will supply his share of wood to meet the ever-increasing demands of a wood hungry nation. ◆

The importance of fish and game management was stressed, and this visit to the Wildlife Commission's Waynesville Fish Hatchery gave the boys a look at fish culture activities. And of course, there were always plenty of chances for wholesome recreation (below).

by
*George A. James, Harold K.
Cordell, Frank B. Barick, and
Robert L. Downing

and Trails

THIS is Part II of a two-part series concerning small-game hunting on five wildlife management areas in western North Carolina. Part I (*October* issue of *Wildlife in North Carolina*) discussed the characteristics of hunters who hunted these areas during 1964 and 1965. Readers are referred to Part I for details and discussion of the study.

Scientific management of game has two primary goals: (1) To produce and to sustain an adequate supply of game, and (2) to make this game available for hunting in an enjoyable and safe manner. One is not complete without the other. Yet, surprising as it may seem, more is apparently known about game production than is known about game harvest. Though it is generally assumed that developed access (roads and trails) is important in making game available, little is known of its value in the distribution of hunting pressure.

Managing for small-game hunting presents different problems from those of managing for big game. In deer hunting, for example, several hundred hunters may congregate on a single area at the time. But during a small-game hunt on the same area, the number of hunters is likely to be fewer than 1 or 2 dozen. Without the pressure of large numbers, small-game hunters are usually not forced to move out and away from other hunters. Under these conditions, what role do roads and trails play in distributing hunting activity and small-game harvest? The few published articles on the subject do not answer this question.

Wildlife management areas in North Carolina provided an excellent opportunity to study and document the distribution of small-game hunters in areas having excellent networks of roads and trails. The average amount of access on each of the five study areas was 44.5 miles of roads and 67 miles of trails. Approximately 65 percent of the total acreage within each area lies within 660 feet of a road or trail, 86 percent within 1,320 feet, and 98 percent within 2,640 feet.

* Harold K. Cordell and George A. James are Associate Recreation Specialist and Principal Recreation Specialist, respectively, Southeastern Forest Experiment Station, USDA Forest Service, Asheville, N. C. Frank B. Barick is Chief, Division of Game, Wildlife Resources Commission, Raleigh, N. C. Robert L. Downing is Wildlife Research Biologist, USDI, Bureau of Sport Fisheries and Wildlife; he was formerly located in Asheville, N. C., and is now stationed at Blacksburg, Va.

DEPT. OF CONSERVATION AND DEVELOPMENT

The success of the small-game hunter is often determined by the access available. Forest roads and trails are vital to any game management program.

Five hundred and fifty-three small-game hunters (about one out of every six) were interviewed during the early- and late-opening seasons as they left the management areas after a day's hunt. Hunters were asked how they used roads and trails while hunting, and they were then requested to trace the route they had walked on a small-scale map of the area they had hunted. We were thus able to study and compare what hunters said about access and how they actually used it in their hunting activities.

Importance of Access

The two principal questions asked about access were:

1) Are well-marked forest roads and trails important to you in planning your hunt?
2) Do you prefer to hunt primarily along forest roads and trails, or away from roads and trails? What are your reasons for this preference?

Eighty-six percent of the hunters interviewed during both the early and late season responded that well-marked roads and trails were important in planning their hunts.[1] About two-thirds, however, said they preferred not to hunt along forest roads and trails but used them only for access into the forest. Of those hunters who preferred to get away from access, 61 percent in the early season and 71 percent in the late season said they liked to hunt within one-half mile of access. Twenty-three percent of early-season hunters and 13 percent of late-season hunters preferred to hunt between one-half mile and 1 mile of the nearest road or trail, and 16 percent during both seasons preferred to hunt beyond 1 mile.

The hunters who preferred to hunt primarily along forest roads and trails (about one-third of the interviewed hunters) gave one of three principal reasons for their preference. The majority said that "hunting along roads and trails was less hazardous." The breakdown of the various reasons given is shown in figure 1.

Hunters who said they preferred to hunt primarily away from roads and trails gave several reasons for their preference. The principal one was "to get away from other hunters." The breakdown of the various reasons given is shown in figure 2.

Before we asked hunters to trace their day's walking on the maps, we asked them how far they thought they had walked during the hunt. Early-season hunters estimated an average distance of 3.4 miles, ranging from 500 feet to well over 5 miles. Late-season hunters indicated they had walked an average of 3.7 miles.

Responses to all questions indicated that hunters made excellent use of available access, walked considerable distances, and dispersed themselves quite well over each of the wildlife management areas in quest of game. Our next step was to study the maps on which hunters had traced the route they walked so that we could determine how access was actually used and the extent to which roads and trails dispersed hunting pressure.

Use of Access

Hunters, indeed, walked considerable distances and made good use of roads and trails. The map tracings showed that early-season hunters walked an average of 2.8 miles and that late-season hunters walked an average of 3.2 miles. The distribution of hunters by the distance they walked is shown in figure 3.

The fact that hunters walked considerable distances and made good use of roads and trails tells only part of the story, however. If hunting activity were limited to road and trail zones, only a small portion of each area would be hunted. To attain the best distribution of hunting pressure, hunters must use available roads and trails to disperse themselves, but they must then move cross country to interior areas away from access. Hunters did just this.

Though it was evident from the map tracings that much of the walking was on roads and trails, the abundance of access did not produce a group of

1/ Early- and late-season hunters differed significantly in a number of important socioeconomic characteristics, and separate analytical treatment of the data was necessary. These differences were discussed in Part I

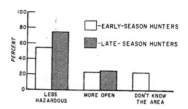

Figure 1. Percentage breakdown of reason given by hunters preferring to hunt mainly along roads and trails.

Figure 2. Percentage breakdown of reason given by hunters preferring to hunt away from roads and trails.

Figure 3. Percentage breakdown of total distances walked by small-game hunters.

Figure 4. Furthest zone penetrated by small-game hunters. Percentages of total area are in parentheses.

"road hunters." Most hunters were willing to leave developed access and penetrate the forest. The average distances penetrated were 1,050 feet in early season and about 1,200 feet in late season. Only 9 percent in early season and 6 percent in late season hunted solely along access. Fifty-two percent of early-season hunters and 67 percent of late-season hunters penetrated distances greater than 660 feet. Twenty-five percent of the early-season hunters and 39 percent of the late-season hunters hunted in the zone between 1,321 and 2,640 feet from nearest access. These relationships are shown in figure 4.

Distribution of Hunting Pressure

We had yet to demonstrate that the considerable amount of walking on and off developed access represented good distribution of hunters—that is, that hunters spread into new areas and did not merely cover the same general terrain each day of the season.

The maps on which hunters traced their walking were used to construct a single master composite map for each area showing the routes of all hunters during the entire small-game season. A transparent grid of squares, each square representing approximately 10 acres, was superimposed on each composite map. Each 10-acre block of the respective management area was considered hunted if one or more hunters had walked through it at any time during the season. The number of squares through which hunters passed, divided by the total number of squares within the entire area, represented the approximate total percentage of area hunted.

By this method, we calculated that an average of 45 percent, ranging from 22 to 67 percent, of the total area within each of the five study areas had been hunted. Though these values may not necessarily represent optimum utilization of game, they do indicate good distribution of hunting pressure. Distribution appeared good for three reasons: (1) Percentages were based on responses of 553 hunters, who represented only 15 percent of all hunters during the 2-year period; (2) 100 percent coverage of each area by hunters can likely never be attained because of rough, steep terrain and limited access in certain sections; and (3) parts of each management area are unsuitable for certain small-game species and are avoided by hunters.

Distribution of Game Harvest

Hunters using the five wildlife management areas harvested a considerable amount of small game during the 1964 and 1965 hunting seasons. Almost 1,100 animals (primarily squirrels) were taken by interviewed hunters, who represented only 15 percent of all hunters using the areas. During each season, 62 percent of the interviewed hunters were successful and bagged an average of 3.6 animals on each hunting trip. The largest daily bag for any interviewed hunter was nine animals. Forty-one percent of late-season hunters were successful and averaged 2.8 animals per hunter.

The average number of animals killed per hunt-er within the four penetration zones appeared quite uniform within either season. During both seasons, the largest kill was made by hunters who moved the farthest from access, as shown in the following tabulation:

Distance penetrated from access (feet)	Mean harvest per hunter per trip	
	(early season)	(late season)
0-660	2.0	1.4
661-1,320	2.5	1.1
1,321-2,640	2.1	0.9
More than 2,640	2.9	2.0

Actual distribution of game harvest could not be determined because the location of kill was not plotted on maps. It appeared, however, that the distribution of hunters was directly related to the distribution of kill. During early season, the 48 percent who stayed within 660 feet of access killed 34 percent of the total animals taken; the 24 percent who went beyond 660 feet but stayed within 1,320 feet killed 39 percent; the 25 percent who moved out to 2,640 feet killed 23 percent; and the 3 percent who went beyond 2,640 feet killed 4 percent. Late-season hunters had a similar harvest record. Thirty-four percent of kills was made by the 33 percent who stayed within 660 feet of nearest access; a 32-percent kill was made by the 26 percent who moved out to between 661 and 1,320 feet; a 31-percent kill was made by the 39 percent who moved out to between 1,321 and 2,640 feet; and a 3-percent kill was made by the 2 percent who went beyond 2,640 feet. This pattern of harvest is very similar to the distribution of hunters shown in figure 4.

In summary, we can say that most small-game hunting was closely tied to access. The excellent network of well-spaced roads and trails permitted ready access to most sections of each management area by vehicle and by foot. Most hunters indicated by word and action that access was important. They made good use of roads and trails. Although most of them did not hunt primarily along developed access, they used this access to gain entry into the forest, where they covered considerable cross-country distance. Hunting pressure was well dispersed; the hunters covered an average of 45 percent of each management area. Finally, there was strong evidence that game harvest was well dispersed on each of the five study areas. ✦

These grouse hunters know the importance of forest roads and trails to hunting ease and success.

DEPT. OF CONSERVATION AND DEVELOPMENT

An Audubon
Bird Study

 Part 2 Program

by Charlotte Hilton Green
Raleigh, N. C.

NOVEMBER is also a good month to get under way with that AUDUBON BIRD STUDY PROGRAM, *if* you missed it in the October number of our magazine. However, by now we hope many of you may be under way with the complete KIT.*

If you did miss it, look up the October *WILD-LIFE in North Carolina* in your library — school, public, or home—for details. Briefly, last month we discussed this program, with its fine BIRD CHART, picturing (in color) 38 American birds all but three of which, *at some time of the year,* and *in some section,* are found in our own state—in the coastal regions, inland, or the mountains. (See how fortunate we are in a wide variety of habitat!)

Some of these birds might be permanent residents, as the cardinal, blue jay, white-breasted nuthatch, robin, field sparrow, pine warbler; or summer residents, as the wood thrush, the chimney swift, the purple martin, the ruby-throated hummingbird, yellow warbler; or winter residents, as the white-throated sparrow, fox sparrow, hermit thrush, slate-colored junco, myrtle warbler, purple finch; or just transients, passing through on migrations as the bobolink, yellow-bellied flycatcher, many of the warblers, as the black-throated blue, black-poll, baby-breasted.

By now we hope many schools, and especially individual schoolrooms, (as well as homes, scout and 4-H headquarters) have this program, with its fine CHART hanging on its walls.

(Also, by now we hope many of you have access to our state *BIRDS of North Carolina,* and of course, every bird watcher should have Roger Tory Peterson's *FIELD GUIDE TO BIRDS.* I also hope some of you have ordered the Life NATURE LIBRARY book *THE BIRDS.*†)

Last month we dealt mainly with a resumé of the important part different types of birds' *bills, feet, tails, wings* have played in their way of life—wonderful examples of nature's amazing ingenuity in evolving the problems of survival. We featured especially, birds' *bills.*

It is also helpful and interesting, as well as aiding in bird identification, to note, in Peterson's *FIELD GUIDE,* the brief paragraphs *before* each *family* of birds. There are 27 *ORDERS* of birds in

* AUDUBON BIRD STUDY PROGRAM, National Audubon Society, 1120 Fifth Ave., N.Y., N.Y. 10028 ($2.00)

the world; names of all *Orders* end in *es as GAVIL-FORMES* for loons; all *family* names end in *ae,* as *Gaviidae,* for loons. "The sharp-pointed *bill* is a characteristic feature . . . in flight the outline is hunch-backed and gangly with a slight downward sweep in the neck and the big *feet* projecting beyond the *tail.*" Thus in that one paragraph we learn something about these birds' *bills* and *tails.*

Now let's skip to *Terns. Sterninae* "Gull-like seabirds, more slender in build, narrower of *wing,* and more graceful in flight than gulls. The *bill* is slenderer and more sharp-pointed, usually pointed downward toward the water. The *tail* is usually forked . . ."

(In this one paragraph you learn something about *bills, wings, tails.*)

Let's consider one more. *Nuthatches: Sittidae* Small, chubby tree-climbers, smaller than a sparrow, with a long *bill* and a stubby *tail* that is *never* braced against the tree woodpecker-like as an aid in climbing. No other tree climbers attempt to go down tree-trunks *headfirst,* as these little birds habitually do." Here you learn four important things: something about the bill and tail, that it is never braced against the trunk . . . and that these birds habitually go down tree-trunks *headfirst.*

Do some of you beginners wonder how and where they get on the tree trunk? They land on it higher up, and work downwards. By now you should be interested enough to realize how easy these birds are to identify—and be curious enough to look up how many *kinds* or species of nuthatches we have in our own state—and when and where. For all that check the Peterson *FIELD GUIDE* and our own *BIRDS OF NORTH CAROLINA.*

(Getting interested, and curious? Good, then you are well on the way to becoming a bird-watcher.)

Birds' Feet

"They share with wings the responsibility of locomotion." And there is as much diversity in their feet as in their bills. How many functions they perform: running, hopping, wading, swimming, perching, climbing, seizing their prey . . . even fighting and courting. And in some queer cases even incubating a lone egg!

Now let's note the different types of legs, feet, toes, etc. and their adaptations. Study the outline drawings of the different types on the CHART, too.

Wading. The long legs and slender toes of wading birds are adapted for life along the shores and in marshes. Examples: herons and egrets, gallinules, sandpipers. (Can you name and identify all the herons and egrets we have in our state? Two of them are pictured on the CHART.)

Herons' toes are slender and widely spaced, which keeps them from sinking too deeply in the soft muck where they may be standing, alert but still, for long moments, watching for their prey. "Herons have a 'toothed' comb on the center toes with which to scratch themselves." (If you have

† THE BIRDS—TIME-LIFE BOOKS, Dept. 7101, Time & Life Bldg., Chicago, Ill. 60611. Price $4.25.

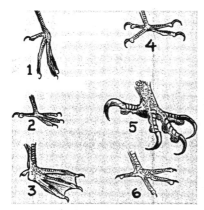

The types of feet illustrated here are, number 1, wading; number 2, perching; number 3, swimming; number 4, climbing; number 5, grasping; number 6, scratching. For examples of each, see text.

The BIRDS note the marginal sketch on page 29.)

Perching. The feet of perching birds, with three toes in front and one behind, are so specialized that by automatic action of certain tendons the birds are locked to their perches while sleeping. The majority of our land birds are perchers and they spend much time in trees, and on the ground, and usually move in a series of hops. Examples: sparrows, chickadees, blue birds, robins.

Swimming. The feet of some birds that swim are webbed (although *not all* water birds have webbed feet). Examples: geese, ducks, gulls, loons, cormorants, gannets and albatrosses are web-footed, while some, such as coots and phalaropes have flaps or lobes along the sides of their toes. With grebes (also called hell-divers) even the shanks and toe nails are "flattened to form sort of propellor blades."

Climbing. The feet of climbing birds have muscular, spreading toes, each provided with a strong, curved claw. Woodpeckers, which have been called "the tree trunk patrol" have two toes in front, two in back, which act as braces. (We have seven kinds, or species, of woodpeckers in the state. Can you name them—and better yet—identify them?)

Grasping. Birds of prey have powerful feet and legs bearing strong, curved talons for grasping and tearing their prey; Examples: hawks, owls, eagles. (We will feature our birds of prey in a later issue.)

Scratching. Many ground-feeding birds use their feet in scratching for food. The three forward pointing toes are fairly long and each bears a short, blunt claw. The hind toe is small and raised above the level of those in front. Examples: quail, grouse, chickens, pheasants.

There are other ways in which birds use their feet, some using them as hands. Ever watch a tufted titmouse or chickadee holding a sunflower seed with its feet, while it hacks it open with its bill? (Having a Bird Shelf by a window helps you observe a lot of interesting things.) In certain species birds' feet are also used as attack or defense—as the spurs on domestic fowl—notable in "cockfights." When we were in Africa, stopping at an ostrich farm, our guide warned us, "Don't get too close; an ostrich has a powerful kick." And later, at a party the university gave our group, the ornithologist prof told me, "If you ladies would only make ostrich plumes fashionable again, it would help our economy."

Too, in Africa, the weaverbirds—rated as the world's best nest builders—have learned how to hold down a strand of grass with one foot while weaving and fastening the other end with its bill. Surely, that is foot and bill cooperation!

An even weirder use of feet is when "Papa Gannet" places a big webbed foot on the single egg, like a warming pad (gannets winter off our coast) . . . and a still stranger use of feet is what Papa Emperor Penguin (address, the Antarctic) does. The female lays one egg in May (just as the long antarctic night is setting in) and Papa takes over, placing the egg on top of his feet where the warm skin and feathers of his belly form a protective mantle—and there he broods it . . . but all the penguins have a deep parental urge and almost any will take over . . . it's an interesting tale . . . again you might read more about them in *The BIRDS*, or in *OCEANIC BIRDS of SOUTH AMERICA* (Published for American Museum of Natural History).

Tails

Yes, *feet* are important to a bird's way of life. And so are *tails!* The chief function of the tail is to act as a rudder in flight and a "balancer" when perching and flying. The shape of the tail is largely governed by the character of the bird's flight. Short-tailed birds generally fly in a straight course and cannot make short turns, while long-tailed birds can pursue an erratic course with marvelous ease and grace.

Forked tail. The erratic, graceful skimming flight of birds in pursuit of flying insects is made possible by the forked tail. Example: swallow. (Though having different food habits, terns, frigate-birds, swallow-tailed kite, everglade kite, and swallow-tailed gull have forked tails and are graceful in flight.)

Spine-tipped tail. Among tree-creeping birds, which always climb upwards, the tail is used as a brace, or prop. Example: Woodpeckers. (Yes, Downy may be seen creeping downwards, but it isn't actually creeping; he does it by a series of hops, as when trying to reach suet on tree trunk below.) The brown creeper's tail-feathers are long, narrow, and sharply pointed, and the tail is also used as a brace, as are the tail-feathers of the chimney swift.

The chimney swift also has a spine-tipped tail. Its

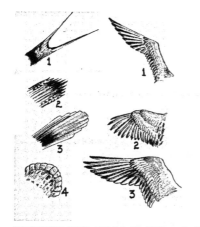

Tail illustrations include, number 1, forked tail; number 2, spine-tipped tail; number 3, long-rounded tail; number 4, wide-rounded tail. Wings, number 1, long, pointed; number 2, short-rounded; number 3, broad-long.

feet are weak and it cannot perch, but clings to the inner side of a chimney, bracing its weight with the stiff tail-feathers. (A good illustration of a swift's foot and tail is on page 223 of *BIRDS of NORTH CAROLINA*.) An interesting feature about this bird—one of our common summer residents—is that until the white man came, and built chimneys, it had roosted and nested in hollow trees, and must revert to that custom in the wilds of its winter range. For a long time it was not known where they wintered, but a few years ago banded bird returns came from Peru.

Long-rounded tail. Such tails are necessary for birds that dart in and out of foliage. Examples: mockingbirds, sparrows.

Wide-rounded tail. Rapid escapes from the ground and swift flight over short distances are possible when a bird has wide, rounded tail and short-rounded wings. Examples: quail, woodcock, grouse.

With some birds tails also play a part in courtship display, as with the wild turkey and the peacock.

Wings

Birds are not the only animals that fly . . . most insects do . . . and there is also a flying mammal—the bat. Man himself who, almost as soon as he stood upright, and began noticing a bird in flight—must have longed for wings. Only lately has he reached the moon—on man-made wings.

The wings of birds are the organs of flight, with a close relationship between shape of wing and

style of flight, which means a wide range in variation.

Long, pointed wings. Such make possible the speedy, easy, skimming flight of birds that spend much time in the air in pursuit of flying insects. Examples: swallows and purple martins. (The purple martin is in the whole state in summer; the barn swallow is mainly transient in the central part, but breeds in our mountains and along the coast.)

Short-rounded wings. Many ground birds take wing only when danger is so near that they must fly quickly. Short, rounded wings provided for quick, easy take-offs and rapid flight over short distances. Examples: quail and pheasants, woodcock, grouse.

Broad, long wings. Most birds of prey have broad, long wings for strong, soaring, easy flight. Examples: hawks and eagles.

Wings, too, are sometimes used in the rituals of courtship. The male wandering albatross starts wooing his lady by flapping his wings—she may ignore him at first, then becomes interested, when both stretch their wings and shriek loudly. These great birds—with a wing span of ten feet—are some of the world of birds' best fliers. Watching them far out at sea, one feels they are riding the air currents with no effort. More familiar to us, however, is the soaring of the turkey vulture, seemingly also with little effort.

Another "wing courtship" is the drumming of the male ruffed grouse, which is resident in our mountain regions. During the breeding season the male makes a practice of drumming, by rapidly beating his wings while he stands on a log or stump. This is also to announce to other males (ruffed grouse): "This is *my* territory. You keep out—or . . .!"

Flight and Feathers

Ah, the feather! Only the bird has feathers—one of nature's marvelous and beautiful creations, extremely light, nearly weightless, yet structurally strong. (And here I hope some of you have access to *"The BIRDS"* p. 34). "Feathers contribute more than the gift of flight to birds. As an extremely light, tough, durable padding they also protect the bird's thin and sensitive skin and act as an efficient air conditioner, trapping body heat in the spaces between the fluffed feathers when the temperature is cold, transmitting it through flatly pressed feathers to the outside when it is warm."

Nor should we forget how much feathers add to beauty in color, texture, crests, beards, plumes and such.

But—beautiful, strong, wonderful as a feather is —it is subject to wear. And so wise Nature has seen to it that "every grown bird must renew its cloak completely at least once a year, usually in late summer after the nesting season." Many birds also have a second complete or partial molt in spring when some males come out in colorful courtship attire— as the goldfinch.

Next Month: Hawks and Owls.

Wildlife Photography Contest-1969

Here are the winners and those receiving honorable mention in the 1969 Wildlife Photography Contest. Our thanks to those who submitted photos but did not score this year. The decision of the judges, Fuller Rice, proprietor of Raleigh's Capital Camera Store, and Joel Arrington, Outdoor Editor for the Department of Conservation and Development, wasn't easy. Remember next year because the contest starts all over again right now. Rules will be published in a subsequent issue of **Wildlife in North Carolina**.

FIRST PRIZE: SALAMANDER
DAVID T. JOHN. CHAPEL HILL

THIRD PRIZE: GREY SQ
JAN BUFFKIN. WILMING

SECOND PRIZE: GARDEN SPIDER
MURRAY CRAGIN. FORT BRAGG

BOX TURTLE
S. DUNCAN HERON, JR., DURHAM

GARTER SNAKE
GEORGE RORRER, MADISON

NOCTUID.MOTH
DAVID T. JOHN, CHAPEL HILL

CHIPMUNK
S. DUNCAN HERON, JR., DURHAM

Wildlife Management in Action

Great Lake

by Grady L. Barnes,
Management Area Supervisor

EACH year as the machines of "progress" bite deeper and deeper into the remaining marshes, swamps and woodlands of this country, sportsmen—from bird-watchers to goose hunters—become increasingly pessimistic about the presence of any kind of machine in their favorite corner of the outdoors. Most of them see the coming of a machine as the mark of doom on another stretch of wildlife habitat.

However, with care and forethought, man can sometimes alter a wildlife habitat to improve it rather than to destroy it. This is the kind of alteration which is taking place at Great Lake in Craven County.

Great Lake is a 3000-acre depression of dark, acid water. It is nearly inaccessible because of surrounding swamps and pocosin, too shallow for safe boating, too stained and turbid to support much more than stunted catfish and a meager growth of aquatic plants.

The origin of this rather strange lake is a mystery. Was it plowed out of the soft eastern North Carolina soil by a large meteorite, as some people believe, or was it formed when ancient fires burned a depression into the peat soil? Nobody knows for sure. However, the large stumps which show on the lake bottom from 50 to 100 yards from shore indicate that a substantial part of the lake was once covered by a forest.

As these stumps are worn down, the steady swirl of the waves keeps small fragments of wood, decayed leaves, twigs and other debris in suspension in the water. Since no streams enter or leave the lake, except during periods of extremely high water, the suspended particles create water so turbid that only the toughest aquatic plants can survive in it. Such lakes become aquatic deserts, offering little food or shelter for fish, waterfowl or other wildlife.

Great Lake's location within the Croatan Wildlife Management Area and its particular conditions indicated to Wildlife Commission biologists that a number of specialized management techniques might renovate this lake, making it more hospitable to several wildlife species and more productive for man. They were especially interested in providing a more suitable habitat for the three thousand Canada geese and the two to five thousand ducks that use the area as a resting place during winter months. Since no food was available along the shoreline the waterfowl kept mostly in the center of the lake, leaving from time to time to feed in surrounding fields, swamps and smaller lakes. Management area regulations did not permit hunting on the lake.

The biologists decided that a renovation program for this lake should aid toward providing the aquatic growth conducive to good waterfowl management and clearer water necessary for fish survival.

The general procedure in managing shallow lakes for waterfowl is to draw off water during the summer months, seed the exposed shores to provide waterfowl foods and then to reflood the lake during the fall and winter.

This is the way that Great Lake looked at maximum drawdown. The soggy peat soil shows evidence of water-soaked logs and debris. These flats were planted with waterfowl food plants in hopes of making the area attractive to waterfowl.

The United States Forest Service, owners of most of the surrounding land, readily agreed to cooperate in controlling the water level on Great Lake and work was started on an outlet canal. This canal was cut two miles through the pocosin from the lake to Hunter Creek.

Meanwhile, other agencies concerned with water sanitation and shellfish development were contacted and asked to cooperate in the project. Since the original plan called for lowering Great Lake 3.6 feet o v e r a 63-day period, removing 7,560 acre-feet of water (2.46 billion gallons), would mean that 39 million gallons of water per day (or 450 gallons per second) would be emptied into White Oak River via Hunter Creek. Data were not available to indicate the effects of this much fresh, acid water on the shellfish in White Oak River, so work on the canal was stopped 75 feet short of Hunter Creek and studies were undertaken to determine the rate of fresh water release which could be tolerated by these shellfish.

In cooperation with the research division of the Department of Sports and Commercial Fisheries, twelve water sampling stations were set up in the White Oak Sound eastward from Stella, N. C. Each week measurements of water salinity, temperature, and acidity were recorded. These studies were continued until a yearly record could be made.

The year's accumulation of information indicated that the White Oak River salinity levels varied, at many stations, from no salinity to sea strength, depending on the amount of rainfall on the White Oak watershed.

Supported by this information relative to the characteristics of the White Oak River, biologists resumed work on the Great Lake project by installing a 48-inch culvert with dropboard gates at the lake and completing the channel to Hunter Creek.

In February of 1967 the gates were opened and Great Lake began to drain. As further insurance against damage to shellfish and other resources in the river, biologists sampled and analyzed the river water each day, but could discern no significant change in the river water. As a final insurance policy against upsetting the balance of the river, trays of live oysters were planted at check points in White Oak Sound. There was no observable evidence to indicate the fresh water being released constituted a threat to the oysters' survival.

Two additional precautions were taken to reduce any possible dangers to shellfish in the area. First, the water was removed during the winter months when the oysters were dormant and able to withstand more fresh water. Second, the proposed 3.6-foot drawdown was reduced to less than two feet and the drawdown time was extended over a longer period to reduce the daily volume of water discharged.

During the late winter and early spring of 1967, 19 inches of water were removed from Great Lake to expose approximately 250 acres suitable for seeding with waterfowl foods. Since the area was inaccessible by either land or water, the 1,000 pounds of brown-top millet planted there in August of 1967 had to be seeded with a cropdusting airplane.

In late August of 1967, just when it seemed the Great Lake project was at last ready to show results, another problem arose: rain. The unusually heavy August rains raised the level of Great Lake so fast that the 48-inch drainage pipe could no longer maintain the low water level and most of the millet crop was lost to reflooding before it matured. Then, in 1968 summer drought prevented the development of a stand.

However, these setbacks did not defeat the project. An additional 48-inch drainage culvert was installed; Great Lake was again drained and seeded and this year is providing both food and shelter for waterfowl. The project has been so successful that the Wildlife Resources Commission will open the lake to hunting this fall. Hunters will be allowed to use the area under the same season permit required on the mosquito control impoundments at Pamlico Point and White Oak River. ◆

Water control gates were constructed on the outlet canal and the lake was lowered some 2½ feet. At right, author Grady Barnes observes drainage canal.

How's Your Shucking?

by Jim Tyler
Division of Commercial and Sports Fisheries
Dept. of Conservation and Development
Photos by the Author

If you happen to be a frustrated shell shucker or want to try shucking, here are a few pointers on the right way to get inside and carry off the treasure intact. These are not the only ways to do the job; individuality is everywhere. But Dr. Al Chestnut, THE shellfish authority of the North Carolina coast and Director of North Carolina University's Institute of Marine Sciences at Morehead City, was willing to show how he suggests going about the job.

You can buy a scallop, oyster, or clam shucking knife in many coastal hardware and seafood stores. A stout pocket knife will work until you happen upon such a store.

Examine the oyster and place the rounded side on the bottom so that you will be loosening the flatter shell. A rap with something solid will break off the edge of the shell (called the bill). Smaller oysters, like the one shown below, are more easily attacked from the rear.

But the general method calls for inserting knife blade as shown above. Work it along the upper shell until the muscle is severed. Keep knife close to upper shell as you slide it along entire surface. After muscle is cut free, slip blade under oyster, cutting other side.

Clams call for about the same general procedure as oysters, but with a bit of variation. Scratch the bill of clam back and forth on a rough surface as shown until an opening is found. Using the same knife, insert and run it along the entire surface of the top shell.

With oysters and clams you eat the whole critter. Not so with the scallop; only the large, white muscle is eaten. Find the natural opening just below the "ears" of the scallop. Insert knife blade at this point and cut, keeping blade along the upper shell, toward bill. Only one adductor muscle is present.

Clams have two muscles which must be cut through; position of these will be learned with practice. After cut has been made, part the shells, slip knife underneath and cut loose the other sides of the muscles. Removal of meat is then an easy matter.

Using your thumb and knife as grippers, pull viscera free from the white meat. Dispose of viscera. Then run knife along shell and cut the meat free.

I'll Take Dogs Everytime

by Hal S. Atkinson, Jr.
District Game Biologist

THE alarm clock shatters the predawn darkness as I grope for the button to restore quiet to the house before *everyone* is awakened. With a hurried glance, I realize that I have only twenty minutes to dress in warm clothing and meet the boys down at the cafe for our usual prehunt breakfast and planning session. After scraping the frost from the windshield and assuring myself that all necessary equipment is in its proper place, I start the short trip to the cafe wondering if all this is really worth the trouble in the cold and darkness of an early November morning.

This thought doesn't last long as I meet the smiling faces of hunters who are already enjoying a hot meal, and I soon involve myself with planning the deer hunt which has caused many other hunters to rise early in order that they might be included in our day's activities. After a filling meal, we journey to the dog lot where we are greeted by about twenty-five anxious deer hounds. Their barking reminds me of the many fine races I have enjoyed with these dogs and also of the many long hours and miles I have spent in search of them after a day's hunt was completed.

My trance is broken by the cold chain on the dog pen gate; and after mumbling under my breath, I remind my hunting partner to include several puppies with the old dogs in order that they might start to learn what this game is all about. With a dog box full of hounds, we drive to the area selected for the first hunt of the day.

The morning sun has just cleared the horizon as the hunt master dumps the numbered discs into his hat and passes them among the hunters who have been designated as standers. These individuals draw a number which gives the location or stand number that they will occupy during the first hunt of the morning. As usual, I have been designated a driver by the hunt master since I own a pack of deer dogs. With a rush of excitement, the standers mount trucks which will take them to their stands; and the drivers gather to decide where each will release his pack of hounds.

As I fumble with the catch on the dog box, I cannot help but remember the first time I ever released a pack of deer dogs back in my home state of Virginia; and the excitement and anticipation now is almost as great as it was then. After loading my shotgun, I follow the hounds into the woods and shout encouragement to them in their search for a deer. I'm not surprised when one of my best jump dogs, Major, opens in a thicket of young pines where he is soon joined by the rest of the pack. With the dogs at full voice, several deer bound out of the thicket showing me only a glimpse of white in the far distance.

During the course of the day, several hunters are lucky enough to bag nice bucks, while others are not so fortunate and have to surrender part of a shirt tail to the hunt master. The air is full of talk about old Whistle-Tail, the big buck who slipped by an unwary stander once again. And several of the drivers tell of deer who just outsmarted the dogs in the brambles and water of the hardwood swamps. All of this talk is helping to light the fire for another hunt next week.

After the deer are dressed, the meat divided, and the shirt tails

RESOURCE-O-GRAM
A ROUNDUP OF THE LATEST WILDLIFE NEWS

1970 Fishing Regulations Set By Commission

At its October 20 meeting in Raleigh the Wildlife Resources Commission set the regulations for the 1970 fishing season. These include all inland waters, and in printed booklets will include general regulations and those pertaining to game lands.

Major changes include banning the possession, transportation, sale, purchase, or release to the waters of the state, any Asian walking catfish or piranha. The Commission placed a daily creel limit of 25 and a possession limit of 75 on catfish in inland waters. Catfish are not classed as game fish, and may be sold on the market.

Waterfowl Hunting Begins November 20

With the opening of the waterfowl hunting season Nov. 20, the outlook for shooting is a little better than last year despite a reduction in the bag limit on Canada geese from two daily to one, and from four in possession to two. This reduction may reduce the number at Mattamuskeet, but last year was the best there for ducks in ten years and should be even better this year. Many of the 18 blinds available on the refuge are vacant during the latter part of the season. For first come, first served reservations, write Blind Reservation Committee, New Holland, N. C.

There will again be a bonus allowance of two scaup on certain coastal waters.

Rabbit, Quail, Woodcock, Snipe Seasons

The season on rabbits and quail opens November 15 with a good supply of both expected to be on hand in most of the state. Hunting for woodcock begins November 28, while the Wilson's snipe season opens December 13. Hunting for rails and gallinules (marsh hens) ends November 8.

What Town, Please?

Mr. Richard Parrish, 110 East Lynch St., paid $2.00 for two year's renewal subscription to WILDLIFE magazine at the State Fair. We forgot, however, to write down the name of the town. Can somebody help? We don't want him to miss a single issue!

Safety Instructional Kit

A limited number of safety training kits are available for the asking. Hunting, boating and camping safety tips are depicted in a 20-sketch series. Included with the series is a quiz. The kit is especially helpful in working with youth groups. Write: Safety Kit, Box 2919, Raleigh, N. C. 27602.

by J. R. Parker, Jr.
Boating Editor

THE scene is a duck blind somewhere on the North Carolina coast. The morning is still and hazy. Three hunters stare out over motionless decoys and wait. Periodically they discuss the large raft of diving ducks located some 500 yards out from their decoy spread. After a brief wait one hunter nods to another and the two step out of the blind, guns in hand. They wade to a runabout that is beached and partially camouflaged some 100 yards from the blind.

In a matter of moments the flock of divers is up and the runabout is in hot pursuit. The "hunters" try desperately to drive the flock to the blind. But the birds soon tire of this "sport" and head down river out of sight.

Elsewhere in the state a youth maneuvers his small skiff at idling speed along the edge of an island reservoir. Approximately fifty yards ahead, three black ducks swim from behind some shore vegetation into the open. Necks become erect as the puddlers catch sight of the boat. The lad reaches for his shotgun, opens the throttle of the small outboard and closes the distance. He fires and one duck falls.

On an inland river a fast outboard races upstream. As the boat rounds a bend, six startled wood ducks scramble from beneath a willow tree and take flight, squealing. A standing occupant fires three shots; two ducks stay behind. The retrieve is made and the boat continues the upstream race.

In all three of these true-to-life situations, those involved set out to hunt the ducks—a type of hunt second to none in tradition, excitement and companionship.

But in all three situations those involved violated federal or state laws or both. They risked the chance, and a good chance, of heavy fine or having equipment confiscated.

In all three situations those involved lessened the opportunity for legal, traditional duck hunting. **Because waterfowl will leave an area if boat traffic is heavy, they will abandon an area, especially if chased by power boats.** Temptation had changed sportsmen into spoilers.

Briefly and simply—it is illegal to concentrate, drive, rally, stir up or take waterfowl with the aid of, or by means of any power boat.

There is of course an exception to the above. Waterfowl may be taken from a motorboat if the motor is completely shut off and the boat's "progress therefrom has been ceased" and if the boat is drifting, beached, moored, resting at anchor, or is being paddled, rowed or poled.

The above explanation also applies to retrieving of cripples with the use of a boat. This may seem somewhat restrictive but it is easy to see how anything less would allow too many violation cases to end up as loophole dismissals.

Approximately 25,000 North Carolinians set out on one or more duck hunting trips annually. Many use boats. The boat, be it outboard or inboard powered, or manually propelled is certainly useful and often necessary to the waterfowler. The motorboat can be legally and sportingly used in planning or scouting, transporting, decoy work, as a blind, and retrieving as specified — but not while under power, in the actual taking of waterfowl.

North Carolina has vast water areas to receive the migrants, but it is not all ideal habitat. And even if it were, the migrating flocks would keep right on migrating if exposed to heavy boat pressure.

Planning, skill and patience, not horsepower, are the tools of a real duck hunter.

SKIPPER'S CORNER
by John R. Parker Jr.

THE month that we are cruising through may simply be a repeat of October for many Tarheel boaters. That is to say, more fall fishing or a cool-weather cruise. The majority of the small craft however, may have already been settled down into winter storage.

Two thoughts, then, lead off Skipper's Corner this month. One, simply consider letting some cold water slip beneath the hull in the weeks ahead. Thousands of pleasure craft are "owned" jointly by the skipper and the finance company thus involving a monthly payment. Since you are paying for the boat twelve months a year, I suggest that you use her a little longer.

Our second suggestion is somewhat contradictory to the first. If it *is* storage time around your place, there are a few basics to remember. I will not belabor the subject, but here are a few reminders: use mild detergent and wash down entire rig, make certain bilge is dry, put blocks under axle to get tires off of ground (or remove wheels and store in boat), cover for entire boat or store in garage, there a dust cloth may be desirable, check motor manual for winterizing procedure, repack wheel bearings (layup time is when the rust forms), check and wash down equipment such as lines, anchor and life saving devices, give special security and inside storage consideration to expensive electronic equipment. Finally, in our partial listing, make a repair schedule and use the winter months to put boat and equipment in ship shape for spring.

New Division

In a move that is certain to provide you, the North Carolina boater, with efficient administration, coordination and over-all progress in the State's boating program, the Wildlife Resources Commission has established the Division of Motorboats and Water Safety. At the helm of the new Division is Charles R. Fullwood, Jr. Charles, formerly an administrative officer for the Commission, is a native of Jacksonville, N. C., and he knows boats, boating, and fishing from boats, among other things.

Small Craft Warning

The Weather Bureau feels there is a misunderstanding as to the real meaning of small craft warnings. These warnings are to alert the boater, says the Bureau, and not necessarily make him stay at dock.

As all boatmen should know one RED pennant displayed by day and a RED light at night indicates winds and seas, or sea conditions alone, considered hazardous to small craft operations are forecast. Winds may range as high as 33 knots.

Many yachtsmen and boating enthusiasts have mistaken ideas as to the true meaning of the small craft warning. Many seem to feel that the display of the small craft warning means that they must head immediately for shelter or spend the day on the beach. The small craft pennant was never intended for this type of signal, says the Bureau. It signifies only one thing:

BE ALERT TO THE FORECAST OF HAZARDOUS WEATHER THAT COULD AFFECT NAVIGATION OR SAFETY OF SMALL CRAFT: A change in the present weather condition is occurring or will occur in the next 6 to 12 hours. Find out what that change is and how it will affect you.

It is the *responsibility of the skipper* to use his radio, telephone or whatever means of communication he has found most suitable to inform himself about the details of the impending change, evaluate them and then make his decision. This decision will vary with the type of boat and the seamanship of the skipper. The definition of "small boat" or "small craft" *cannot be based on a given size.* A 30-foot U. S. Coast Guard surf boat can safely perform rescue operations in turbulent inlets or waters that will broach and sink a 60-foot yacht. The capability of a particular boat and the skill and knowledge of the skipper are equally as important as the size of the craft when determining the effect of weather in a given situation.

If severe afternoon thunder squalls are forecast for an otherwise bright and sunny day, the Weather Bureau might hoist the small craft pennant during the morning hours. A boatman thus alerted would investigate and upon finding out the reason for the small craft warning, could safely cruise through the morning and into the afternoon, providing he keeps a "Weather Eye" on the western horizon and stays within a reasonable distance of a safe anchorage. Similarly, the Weather Bureau has hoisted small craft warnings because of rough surf and high waves at inlet entrances caused by a storm far at sea. However, this would not prevent a boatman from fishing and relaxing in a 12-foot rowboat on protected inland waters. Unfortunately, in the past, many have seen the small craft pennant displayed under these conditions and cancelled their day's outings.

Wet Suits for Boaters

Referring to a boating accident of last year in which two duck hunters "drowned", the Coast Guard has suggested that those who are frequently on the water in the dead of winter may wish to consider the wearing of a SCUBA diver's wet suit.

A Coast Guard official said that of three duck hunters thrown into frigid waters when their boat capsized, only one survived. "He was found in good shape probably because he wore a wet suit beneath his clothing."

According to life expectancy charts based on long experience, the unprotected capsizing victim will become unconscious in 30 to 60 minutes in 40 to 50°F. water. Death follows in about 1 to 3 hours.

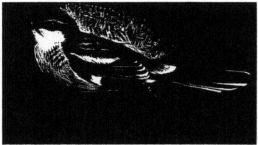

In Defense of the Loggerhead Shrike

by Mrs. Grace S. Draper
Pleasant Grove, N. C.

ONE November morning, as I casually walked past the little red cherry trees planted near my garden the year before, I noted a large grasshopper impaled on a sharp twig. This was definite evidence that that interesting bird, the loggerhead shrike, had been visiting in the yard and had thoughtfully saved an extra insect for some cold, and hungry, day in the future. I had seen him fly across the yard many times, and had often heard his quaint, flat "que-ank" echo in the walnut grove. In the two weeks following, the grasshopper began to disappear, bit by bit, until it was gone. Later, another grasshopper and a large caterpillar were also found impaled on twigs at other places around the farm. Birds have been known to even use barbed wire fences for such storage, too.

The shrike is the only one of our songbirds that became a predator, such as our hawks and owls, and this has earned him a questionable reputation. The bird, not having sharp talons, anchors its prey on a sharp twig or thorn in order to tear it apart, and is, therefore, called a "butcher bird". It is felt that it generally catches small birds and mice in winter, when other prey is scarce. Its favorite food consists of large insects, such as grasshoppers, dragonflies, locusts, and crickets; a shrike can spot a moving insect from as far away as 70 yards.

The loggerhead shrike is a year-round resident in our area. He is a meticulously groomed grey and white bird, slightly smaller than a robin, often mistaken for the familiar mockingbird. However, he is shorter-tailed and heavier, with a large head and hooked beak. His grey and white coloration differs considerably in color tone and placement, especially on the wings. The shrike has a wide white band on the top of his charcoal-colored wings; the mockingbird has small white wing bars across the upper part of its wings. The shrike also has the distinguishing feature of a black raccoon-like mask across his eyes, and this same mask is duplicated in many species of shrikes around the world. There are 67 species of this particular family *Lanidae*, with only two being found in our country, the loggerhead and northern shrike. The northern shrike is a larger bird, but a carbon copy in coloration. He is well-known for his habit of catching small birds and mice, and impaling them on thorns!

The shrike will sit perched upon a tree branch, immobile, scanning the ground below for any movement there, suddenly darting down and expertly plucking a hapless insect from some spot. He is usually working alone, as is characteristic of predators, and will fight fiercely to defend his territory when other shrikes appear on the scene. One winter day I watched with binoculars as a large loggerhead shrike carefully worked his way completely across an open field, perching on first one tall brown weed stalk, then another, alternately flying down to the ground to lift a leaf or fallen stalk as he perhaps sighted some i n s e c t movement there.

This bird is also, surprisingly, a mimic in song. On another winter day I glanced out the window to see what bird was pouring forth such a medley in song, and I was quite surprised to see a loggerhead shrike sitting on a low branch of the oak tree, turning first this way and that, as he kept close watch for any possible movement on the ground below, gayly singing a lovely collection of trills and tunes, not unlike some of the mockingbird's song, punctuated by his familiar "que-ank".

It constructs a sturdy, deeply hollowed nest of twigs and grass or rootlets in thickets or scrubby trees, in which four to seven buff-colored, mottled, eggs are laid. The incubation period is 14 to 16 days, and the young are ready to leave the nest in about three weeks.

Because of its reputation, interesting stories about shrikes may be found in bird books. "Land Birds of America", by Robert C. Murphy and Dean Amadon (both with the American Museum of Natural History), tells of residents of a community in North Carolina who found a locust tree on which no fewer than 21 small snakes were ● continued on page 30

Poplar Branch Access Area

This is Poplar Branch from the air. Work on boat mooring berths is continuing. Other improvements are planned.

by Rod Amundson

LESS than a century ago Van Slack's Landing at Poplar Branch was a busy place, as Currituck Sound landings go. Barges from Norfolk put in there to unload cargos of supplies, fertilizer, lumber and hardware, and loaded up with potatoes, yams, and other products of the rich, black Currituck County soil.

Then came highways and trucks. Barge traffic was reduced almost to zero. Fishing boats used the landing, and a fish house was set up to handle commercial fish netted from the Sound.

A few years ago the landing consisted only of a couple of ramshackle buildings and a forest of piling rotted off almost to the surface of the water. But this, too, has changed.

The Wildlife Resources Commission has acquired and developed a tract of land at the water's edge, just where N. C. Highway No. 3 ends at the brink of Currituck Sound. This road also serves as Main Street of Poplar Branch, a deceptively quiet little fishing village consisting of a general store, a gas station, a post office and a few neat little white houses.

On this waterside tract the Wildlife Commission has constructed a launching ramp for small boats. Fill from channel dredging was used to create ample parking space and a 300-foot causeway that forms a snug harbor for larger, inboard boats.

Boating is a year-round activity at Poplar Branch. From early spring to late fall, fresh-water anglers go out into the sound for some of the finest largemouth bass fishing in the entire country. Then, in late fall, the waterfowl season opens and dozens of boats and their guide-owners are needed to take duck and goose hunters out to their blinds for some of the finest waterfowl hunting along the east coast.

Outboard-driven skiffs don't do very well during the waterfowl season, especially when there is real "duck" weather. Water gets too rough for anything but larger, inboard boats, and this is where some 300 yards of bulkheads and mooring berths come into the picture.

These berths will be assigned to licensed guides on proper application for use permits. Each guide must construct his own berth of creosoted four-by-four piling according to Wildlife Commission specifications.

Thirty guides have already applied for these berths, and there is room for at least thirty more, plus tie-up space for casual users.

As far as actual operation is concerned, the Poplar Branch public marina is raring to go. A little more filling and grass planting are needed, and plans call for construction of a windbreak shelter and a toilet.

It is safe to predict that Poplar Branch, in the vernacular of bass fishermen and wildfowlers, will be dubbed "Popular Branch."

CRACKSHOTS and BACKLASHES by Rod Amundson

Ladybugs, those active and colorful little red and black beetles known to millions of school children, have reached a peak of popularity in north-central Kansas, according to the Wildlife Management Institute. Many gallons of the busy predators have been loosed by farmers to dine on aphids, greenbugs, and other insect pests of young milo plants. Most agree that the ladybugs did the job.

The ladybug love-in began when an employee of the Kansas Forestry, Fish and Game Commission and a farmer friend decided to import a supply from California to test their effectiveness in controlling insects harmful to young milo. Others joined in, the ladybugs were obtained and released, and after six weeks, most farmers agreed that the experiment was a success.

One farmer, after releasing two gallons of ladybugs in a 50-acre milo field badly infested with greenbugs, reported his plants were nearly free of pests three days later. A second, who did not take part, watched ladybugs move in from an adjoining farm and rid his milo of greenbugs.

One of the largest users of ladybugs distributed the beetles at the rate of one gallon per 15 acres at a cost of about 75 cents an acre. After viewing his successful reduction of plant pests, he asked "Why pay $2.50 per acre to have milo sprayed when you can accomplish the job with 75 cents worth of ladybugs?" Most users also noted that the ladybug is superior to chemical pesticides in that the latter, while

killing the target insect, also eliminates all of its natural enemies.

Duck Stamp Contest Under Way.

Artists wishing to compete in the 1970 Duck Stamp Contest have until December 1 to submit their entries, the Wildlife Management Institute reports. The winner will be reproduced on the 1970-71 Migratory Bird Hunting Stamp.

This year designs may be submitted in black and white or full color. Any American waterfowl, except the old squaw, canvasback, hooded merganser, white-winged scoter, and whistling swan—winners in the past five years—will be acceptable. Contest information is available from the Office of Conservation Education, Bureau of Sport Fisheries and Wildlife, Washington, D. C. 20240.

Bad Reputation?

Dear Sir:
With regards to the current North Carolina laws governing nonresident fishermen, North Carolina gets a rather bad reputation when game wardens give citations to out-of-state persons who want to fish for perch and other small fish for only a couple hours. I think it is a little absurd to take an out-of-state fisherman from the boat in which he is fishing and take him to the county seat until bond is posted.

Why not initiate a complimentary warning ticket with the second such ticket being the same as citations now being issued? North Carolina is doing a fine job of public relations in many other fields, why not in recreation laws too?

When traveling through other areas of the state I see a number of North Carolina Wildlife Public Ac-

cess Areas. Yet Beaufort County, which is completely divided by navigable waters and has quite a large number of both resident and nonresident fishermen, has no such provision. As far as I know, there are no plans in the making to provide this area with N. C. Wildlife Access Areas. Where do we start efforts to get such provisions?
Sincerely,
Miss Lynda G. Oden
Pinetown

Dear Miss Oden:
As much as we would like to issue complimentary warning tickets, this act has been ruled unconstitutional by the Supreme Court. North Carolina has very specific laws regarding license requirements, and persons found fishing without a license must be cited to court.

Once we start winking at the law we would soon be in a position of having to close both eyes to it. Does fair, courteous and impartial law enforcement really give us a bad reputation?
Yours very truly,
Rod Amundson, Chief
Division of Education

Good Reputation?

Dear Sir:
On Saturday September 6, 1969, I had the misfortune of being charged with hunting doves over a baited area. The area was new to myself and I never suspected the area of being baited.

North Carolina has fine game laws and outstanding game protectors. During the whole proceeding, the North Carolina game protectors were respectful and very considerate. The wildlife protectors took the time and consideration to show me and others the area and what to look for in a baited area.

The citizens and sportsmen of North Carolina should feel proud and thankful to have such men working for the protection of their wildlife.

Again, I would like to thank wildlife Supervisor Mr. Caine, and wildlife protectors Mr. Register and Mr. Clark for the consideration shown.
Robert Burger
Franklinton

Family Affair?

Dear Sir:
We used to feed birds only in the winter. Some five years ago we be-

28

gan feeling sorry for the hard-working parents and now keep feed in our window feeder on through the summer.

Four years ago we were watching a family of cardinals feeding and being fed. This was when they were off the nest and the young were full-feathered and as large as their parents. It came to our attention that the beautiful young male in all his color was being fed by his mother while his sister was fed by the father.

Since that time we have observed about eight families of nearly-grown cardinals and have yet to see the father feeding a son or a mother feeding a daughter.

While we admit that the habits of the birds keep the young from coming close to the feeder and thereby permitting us to see the feeding of more than a half dozen times to the family, it seems singular that the pattern of feeding the opposite sex has remained unchanged.

Is this a rare coincidence or is it a standard procedure?

Sincerely,
T. A. Fuller, Col.,
USAF (Ret.)
Sylva

Let Us Spray

Dear Sir:

I have observed Bluebird nests numerous times without disturbing them—but mocking birds will "Dive-bomb" them until the Bluebirds will leave their eggs; and, the nests were built using *Wildlife in N. C.* plans.

Sometime ago I requested information on how to get rid of the mocking birds—but you had nothing to offer that I had not done. However, we did find, accidently, that a little house and garden (Raid) spray will make the mocker leave his nest before it is lined. If they cannot nest, they leave.

Very truly yours,
W. O. Couch
Clover, S. C.

Kind Words

Dear Sir:

I teach Remedial Reading in the country near my home in Columbia. My children, being rural and being so sweet and unsophisticated love the outdoors and your magazine. I think some of the High School ones subscribed to it.

I am thankful to be reminded of good old North Carolina. Even your envelope (expiration notice) seems just right, I love the state and your magazine is typical of the good sort

of thing our state produces; the real thing and no kind of sham about it—beautiful for the sake of the pure beauty. I like the pictures and the writings and thank you for your magazine.

I grew up in Elon College, North Carolina. My heart is still in the flat and rising lands of the good old North State, and I guess because of the people who sing of their modest living in the State Song (by the way print it someday in your magazine).

Sincerely,
Mrs. Maedell Rice
Columbia, Mo.

Fish Dish

Dear Sir:

I have a question in reference to an article in your August issue.

The article, "A Morsel in Disguise," calls the puffer a "sandpaper-skinned rascal" that presents fine eating.

In my August-September issue of "National Wildlife" on page 52 there is a picture of a puffer fish. The article states that it can be lethal if eaten. My question is, is this true? Also the picture shows many spines present while your photo is different. Are there different species, some of which may be lethal?

Maybe your other readers might be interested in this question.

Yours truly,
Warren A. Williams
Raleigh

Dear Mr. Williams:

Thanks for your interesting letter about puffer fishes.

There are several species of puffer fishes. The poisonous varieties are usually found in tropical waters. Those along our coast are not poisonous and lack the bony spine usually present on the poisonous species.

Rod Amundson, Chief
Division of Education

Gunning the Atlantic Coast

The November issue of *Field & Stream* magazine contains an article entitled "Gunning the Atlantic Coast" by Stephen M. Miver which should be of great help to the waterfowl hunter looking for duck and goose shooting. The piece covers each state of the Atlantic coast, and the section on North Carolina certainly hits the high spots for Tar Heel gunning. It looks like a well researched story and makes good reading and it is a valuable guide to the waterfowler.

Salt Water Fishing License

Dear Sir:

I would like to comment on the salt water fishing license. The license itself represents only one facet of the salt water fishing problem. We need to place the license issue in its proper perspective. The ocean and its environs represent the last free fishery in our society. There is competition for its resources between commercial and sports fishermen, to a lesser extent between various sports fishing groups, and between the states for migratory species. Some seven or eight years ago, the American Littoral Society reported on the marked decrease in some 18 species of fish, amounting to as much as 50% in some species over a five year period. Industrial pollution and use of the hard pesticides, dredging, and filling procedures, trash fishing, and perhaps even the foreign fisheries which are exploiting the deep sea billfish and salmon populations; all of these factors are responsible for the steady diminution in our marine resources.

As far as remedies are concerned, pollution must be controlled by a combination of Federal and State laws, and I might add that all of these need urgent action. More and more states are taking action against the chlorinated hydrocarbons such as DDT, and it is regrettable that our own state has declined to take similar action. A study of estuarine areas is nearly complete and will be presented to the President by the Secretary of the Interior on or by January 30, 1970. Pending completion of this study and the applications of recommended solutions, emergency regulations should be enacted, and indeed have been enacted in some northern states.

Trash fishing, a poorly defined and poorly measured industry, plays a definite role in the destruction of sport species such as gray trout, flounder, spot, croaker, etc. No one in the field of marine biology seems to doubt that this is a harmful practice; but, on the other hand, few feel that we know enough about it to take the necessary steps. The problem needs immediate and accurate definition and control. The role of foreign fisheries is an international problem and lies with both the State Department and advisories from the Department of the Interior.

So, what role would a salt water license play in harvesting of the marine resource? The answer to that lies in the competitive elements using the free fishery. Primarily, the com-

Scott L. Beasley

Mr. Scott L. Beasley was born November 30, 1930 in Hoke County. He has been employed by the Wildlife Resources Com-

mission for fifteen years. Six years of this time he was employed in the Division of Inland Fisheries, stationed at Waynesville and Morganton. He is presently stationed at Elizabethtown as a wildlife protector.

Mr. Beasley attended Recruit School in 1960 at the Institute of Government in Chapel Hill, and since that time he has attended in-service schools every year. He is a member of the Bladen County Peace Officers Association, Southeastern Association of Game and Fish Commissioners (Law Enforcement Section), N. C. State Employees Association, N. C. Police Voluntary Benefit Association.

Scott is a member of the Elizabethtown Baptist Church. He is married to the former Minerva L. Matthews, and they have three children, Howard, Terry and Sandra. Scott likes camping, hunting, fishing, and reloading ammunition.

DIVISION ENFORCEMENT RECORD FOR SEPT. 1969

HUNTING & FISHING

Persons checked	30,332
Total prosecutions	1,016
Total convictions	986
Total cases not guilty	4
Total cases nol prossed	19
Total cases dismissed	7
Total fines collected	$ 5,735.65
Total costs collected	$11,734.65

BOATING

Persons checked	3,481
Total prosecutions	256
Total convictions	242
Total cases not guilty	5
Total cases nol prossed	7
Total cases dismissed	2
Total fines collected	$ 340.95
Total costs collected	$ 3,186.10

All fines and any arrest or witness fees are paid into the school funds of the counties in which the violation occurred, and no part of the fines or costs collected are paid to the North Carolina Wildlife Resources Commission or its personnel.

---

petition lies between the commercial fishermen and the sportsmen and between the various states utilizing the migratory species. The big question is who is responsible for these studies. In the case of certain migratory species such as fluke which are spawned in the north, and spend the next year or two in southern waters, and in the case of gray trout which are spawned in southern waters and subsequently migrate to northern waters, the issue is compounded by the crossing of lines of state jurisdiction (I do not wish to oversimplify the problem. As Dr. Daiber of the University of Delaware has shown, gray trout populations are probably divided into two major overlapping groups. More definition is needed). There are two and possibly three groups who might pay for this research. The commercial and the sports fishermen are the most likely ones, and possibly some of the cost will be passed along to the consumer. Everyone who takes from this particular resource should be licensed in some form. If this were controlled by the states, tagging studies, studies of spawning areas, and other methods of value could be carried out by state biologists, although it would only have great value when related to similar studies in the adjacent and nearby states. On the other hand, if this were carried out under Federal jurisdiction, it would primarily be

Outdoor Quiz

If you're a bit confused about the mis-match of questions and answers in last month's article "Outdoor Quiz", straighten it out this way: multiple choice question 9 should read, "The white oak's leaves have rounded lobes; are bristle-tipped." Question 10 then becomes, "Mourning doves lay two white eggs; three-four eggs in a nest." Now you've got the right questions for the correct answers. Sorry 'bout that.

---

studied as a migratory resource. The funds could be split between State and Federal, as suggested in the article. Perhaps the "Federal" end of the research could be carried out under the auspices of the Atlantic States Marine Fisheries Commission. A law would have to be enacted to allow this.

Seen in this perspective, the eventual enactment of some form of salt water license seems inevitable. A splitting of the fee also seems inevitable. The question of safeguards to insure proper use of these funds and subsequent regulation seems less clear at this time.

Sincerely yours,
R. Wharton Gaul, M.D.
Charlotte

• continued from page 26

impaled upon thorns! At least one child's story has been written using this "snake tree" as theme. The fascinating book, "Birds of the World", by Oliver L. Austin, Jr. (Florida State Museum), relates that "Back in the latter part of the 19th century, shortly after the European house sparrow was introduced in this country, northern shrikes became so numerous on Boston Common one winter that men were hired to shoot them to protect the sparrows. Little did our forefathers realize that the house sparrow would soon become far too plentiful for man himself, much less for shrikes, to control!"

Mr. Austin points out also that we must realize that this predator is a useful biological regulator of lesser, and perhaps weaker, species (of small birds, etc.) and is therefore an essential part of Nature's overall scheme. As we better understand the bird and its habits, we can learn to properly appreciate it, for it *is* a very beautiful and interesting member of our wonderful world of birds. ◆

30

Circulation Manager

Wildlife in North Carolina

Box 2919, Raleigh, N.C. 27602

From _____

Address _____

Please send my friends below the magazine for a whole year, and send them a card in my name

NEW ☐   RENEWAL ☐   NEW ☐   RENEWAL ☐

Name_____   Name_____

Street_____   Street_____

City_____   City_____

State_____ Zip Code_____   State_____ Zip Code_____

NEW ☐   RENEWAL ☐   NEW ☐   RENEWAL ☐

Name_____   Name_____

Street_____   Street_____

City_____   City_____

State_____ Zip Code_____   State_____ Zip Code_____

NEW ☐   RENEWAL ☐   NEW ☐   RENEWAL ☐

Name_____   Name_____

Street_____   Street_____

City_____   City_____

State_____ Zip Code_____   State_____ Zip Code_____

NEW ☐   RENEWAL ☐   NEW ☐   RENEWAL ☐

Name_____   Name_____

Street_____   Street_____

City_____   City_____

State_____ Zip Code_____   State_____ Zip Code_____

NEW ☐   RENEWAL ☐   NEW ☐   RENEWAL ☐

Name_____   Name_____

Street_____   Street_____

City_____   City_____

State_____ Zip Code_____   State_____ Zip Code_____

Frame House Gallery dealers in North Carolina:

ASHEVILLE
Bell's Gatehouse
11 Lodge Street

BLOWING ROCK
House of Creative Crafts
Route 1, Box 101C

CHAPEL HILL
The Intimate Bookshop
119 East Franklin Street

CHARLOTTE
Carson McKenna Galleries
523 Fenton Place

GREENSBORO
Colonial Furniture House
3819 High Point Road

RALEIGH
Little Art Gallery
North Hills Shopping Center

ROBBINSVILLE
Inez Devore
Thunderbird Mtn. Resort

WINSTON-SALEM
Trotman's
615 Walnut Street

Applications with remittance may be submitted to your nearest Frame House Gallery Dealer, or mailed to:

National Audubon Society
P. O. Box 65054
Charlotte, N. C. 28201

Please make checks payable to: NATIONAL AUDUBON SOCIETY.

NAME (Please print) _____

ADDRESS _____

CITY _____ STATE _____ ZIP _____

IMPORTANT: This Collector Print offer is for **new members only.** Present Audubon members may receive the free print of their choice when their **renewal** is accompanied by two new membership applications.

Please indicate whether this is a new membership or a renewal by checking the proper box.

    NEW ☐   RENEWAL ☐

My choice of free print is (check one):

    State Bird ☐ "Cardinals" by Guy Coheleach
    State Flower ☐ "Dogwood" by Anne Ophelia Dowden

Please make checks payable to:
    National Audubon Society.

There are two and possibly three groups who might pay for this research. The commercial and the sports fishermen are the most likely ones, and possibly some of the cost will be passed along to the consumer. Everyone who takes from this particular resource should be licensed in some form. If this were controlled by the states, tagging studies, studies of spawning areas, and other methods of value could be carried out by state biologists, although it would only have great value when related to similar studies in the adjacent and nearby states. On the other hand, if this were carried out under Federal jurisdiction, it would primarily be and Federal, as suggested in the article. Perhaps the "Federal" end of the research could be carried out under the auspices of the Atlantic States Marine Fisheries Commission. A law would have to be enacted to allow this.

Seen in this perspective, the eventual enactment of some form of salt water license seems inevitable. A splitting of the fee also seems inevitable. The question of safeguards to insure proper use of these funds and subsequent regulation seems less clear at this time.

Sincerely yours,
R. Wharton Gaul, M.D.
Charlotte

too plentiful for man himself, much less for shrikes, to control!"

Mr. Austin points out also that we must realize that this predator is a useful biological regulator of lesser, and perhaps weaker, species (of small birds, etc.) and is therefore an essential part of Nature's overall scheme. As we better understand the bird and its habits, we can learn to properly appreciate it, for it *is* a very beautiful and interesting member of our wonderful world of birds. ♦

30

Audubon Society Drive

THE question has been asked, "Why is an organization in Louisville, Kentucky, lending total support to a campaign in the State of North Carolina, the purpose of which is to add at least 3-thousand new members to the National Audubon Society within the state?"

The answer is simple. The Frame House Gallery of Louisville was formed for the sole purpose of developing an ever-widening appreciation of wildlife, wildlife art and conservation organizations which protect wildlife for the enjoyment and edification of all of us.

Two years ago membership in the National Audubon Society in Kentucky totaled 217—obviously not much support for proposed conservation programs. With the full cooperation of National Audubon, Frame House undertook the expansion of the Society in Kentucky, with the result that in 12 months time Kentucky jumped from 47th to 1st place in National Audubon membership with 9,000 new members.

During the winter of 1968-69 the Gallery undertook to help broaden Audubon membership in Florida, following the same pattern used so successfully in Kentucky. Two Frame House Gallery artists—Guy Coheleach and Don Richard Eckelberry—each did a painting especially for the campaign, from which high quality lithographs were produced. To each person or family that became a member of the Society during the campaign in the $12.50 class or higher, two prints were given free. Since the prints themselves were worth more than the cost of membership, the Florida drive was a repeat of what happened in

Kentucky. Audubon membership was doubled—from 7,500 to over 15-thousand in three months.

November has been officially proclaimed "National Audubon Month in North Carolina" by Governor Scott. A statewide membership campaign will take place in North Carolina during that month. It will be well publicized in all news media—television, radio, newspaper and other publications. It will receive the active support of the many important groups and individuals in North Carolina interested in the cause of conservation—members of the State Legislature, the North Carolina bankers, leading businessmen and industrialists.

Two Frame House Gallery artists—Anne Ophelia Dowden and Guy Coheleach—have each done paintings for the North Carolina drive. Mrs. Dowden, who is probably America's leading botanical artist—has painted the State Flower, the Flowering Dogwood. Mr. Coheleach's contribution is the State Bird, the Cardinal, as pictured on this month's cover. New members will be offered their choice of **one print** with each $12.50 membership.

The State of North Carolina has an abundance of wildlife—not only its own resident birds, but a great many migratory species. Protection for the birds and the other wild creatures in some respects becomes protection for the people themselves. And further, protection of the yet unspoiled wilderness in North Carolina adds much to the daily pleasure of living for both residents and visitors, and thus becomes something that all of us need to protect. There is no better way that anyone's contribution to such a cause can better be implemented than by joining the Audubon Society.

This is why the Frame House Gallery and its artists are working to increase Audubon membership in the State of North Carolina in the forthcoming campaign.

N. C.
Doc.

IN NORTH CAROLINA

25 CENTS / DECEMBER 1969

WILDLIFE IN NORTH CAROLINA recognizes the need for close cooperation between State and Federal conservation agencies and the people who hunt and fish—to bring about a restoration of our renewable resources. The Editor gratefully receives for publication news items, articles, and photographs dealing with the North Carolina out-of-doors, but reserves the right to reject materials submitted. Full credit is given for all materials published.

WILDLIFE IN NORTH CAROLINA is published at the Wildlife Resources Commission offices, Motor Vehicles Building, 1100 New Bern Ave., Raleigh, N. C. 27601.

Second class postage paid at Raleigh, North Carolina 27602.

SUBSCRIPTION—One dollar per year, two dollars for two years. Make remittance payable to WILDLIFE RESOURCES COMMISSION. Any employee of the Wildlife Resources Commission may accept subscriptions, or they may be forwarded to Post Office Box 2919, Raleigh, N. C. 27602. Stamps cannot be accepted.

Wildlife circulation this issue, 118,194.

IN NORTH CAROLINA ■

The official publication of the NORTH CAROLINA WILDLIFE RESOURCES COMMISSION, Raleigh 27602. A monthly magazine devoted to the protection and restoration of our wildlife resources and to the improvement of hunting and fishing in North Carolina.

VOL. XXXIII, NO. 12   DECEMBER, 1969

IN THIS ISSUE

EDITORIAL STAFF

ROD AMUNDSON _ _ _ _ _ _ _ _ EDITOR
DUANE RAVER _ _ _ _ _ MANAGING EDITOR
LUTHER PARTIN _ _ WRITER-PHOTOGRAPHER
JOHN PARKER _ _ _ _ _ _ BOATING EDITOR

Artist George Werth, Jr., of Raleigh, has captured the several moods of the "little bear with a mask," the raccoon. The ring-tailed rascal always has an inquisitive look about his shoe-button eyes, and seems ready to poke its shiny nose into most anything. The coon furnishes many a good chase for the hunter with a pack of hounds on a frosty evening.

Mistletoe

by Charlotte Hilton Green
Raleigh, N. C.

The mistletoe hung in the castle hall,
The holly branch shone on the old oak wall.
Thomas Haynes Bailey

MANY of our Christmas legends, traditions, folklore and use of decorations came from northern Europe. "Actually," says Hal Borland, outdoors writer, "traditional Christmas as we know it is a composite festival with elements that come from such far-apart places as Persia and Scandinavia and such disparate non-Christian sources as the early Greeks, the Germans, and the Druids of Britain."

Native of Europe, the mistletoe of legend (*Viscum album*) derives its name from the Greek words meaning "thief" and "tree," as it is a parasite deriving its nourishment from the tree on which it grows. Usually a small evergreen shrub, it has oval, greenish-yellow leaves and tiny yellow flowers; the fruit is small, pearly-white berries with a sticky juice and is eaten by many birds, thus being propagated by birds wiping their bills to which the berries cling, on the branches of trees. If not dislodged, the seed may germinate, and small suckers gain a foothold.

Growing in the air, and thus not earth-bound, mistletoe became a symbol of the spiritual, and was gathered by white-robed Druid priest with a golden sickle, and must be caught in a white cloth, before it touched the ground. At the year's end—the time of the winter solstice—two white bulls were slain beneath the sacred oak on which it grew.

By the ancient Britons it was held in highest esteem for its supposed magical virtues, as a charm against witchcraft, and also as a medicine. It was considered sacred to Frigga, the Saxon goddess of love, and the custom of kissing under the mistletoe at Christmas time is of very ancient origin among the English and Germans. A kiss could be claimed from anyone caught under the mistletoe as long as the berries last—but, for every kiss a berry must be gathered from the bough.

Another northern legend is that the young sun God, Baldur, was slain with an arrow of mistletoe shot, in play, by his young brother, and dying, he became an emblem of purity and innocence.

In time, because of its pagan history, the Christian church forbade mistletoe's use in Christmas ceremonies or decorations . . . but people continued to use it in secret. The common people hung it over their doors, believing it protected them from fits, apoplexy, poison, lung fever . . . even from witches. Some mistletoe branches were even used as a "divining rod" somewhat as witchhazel is even used today, in some regions.

Today in Europe mistletoe is held in high esteem as a Christmas decoration used with holly. At one time large quantities were gathered from the famed apple orchards of Normandy and shipped to England each year.

In the early years of our own country's ways and traditions, many of the customs, legends of the old country were adopted here, applying them to our native

mistletoe, *Phoradendron flavescens*, a close kin to the European form. Growing in the South, in the coastal regions in time it gives way to Spanish moss. In Oklahoma it is treasured and honored as the State Flower.

In Appalachia there is a constant demand for it. Growing plentifully on many of the trees, the problem is—collecting, or harvesting, as it usually grows near the tips of branches on mature trees. Climbing is not possible, limbs will not support such weight. Southern sharpshooters "who can hit a squirrel in the left eye" are adept at shooting down clumps of mistletoe with a rifle. However, a local friend, also a "mighty Nimrod" says that is dangerous . . . one never knows where a rifle shot will hit. Instead, he advocates, "find a clump growing low enough to get with a shot-gun—AFTER asking permission from the landowner."

Unfortunately, in our mountains, where it is part of the local economy, and is shipped north by tons, that may not be possible. The problem remains.

In Edwin Way Teale's third "Book of the Seasons", entitled *Wandering Through Winter*, we meet the western form of America's mistletoe (*Phoradendron californica*) in a California desert. It produces berries that range from white through pink to red. Although this desert semi-parasite manufactures its own food, it drains water and obtains minerals from the host and, in time, may cause its death.

On that Christmas day, in the desert, a fine gift of the Teales was "collecting" a new bird for their "life-list" the silky flycatcher, known as phainopepla. (Here I had to stop and look it up in my Peterson's Western Field Guide.) EWT suggests it might well be called "Mistletoe Bird" as, "throughout the deserts of the Southwest, whenever we encountered concentrations of mistletoe, we looked for and almost always found this bird."

The bird is also of particular interest as it is the only representative of this family in North America—and "the male does most of the work of nesting and incubation." Good for you, Mistletoe bird!

And now, soon it will be time to "Hang the mistletoe in our own castle halls—and may its message be a modern hope of "Good will to all men."

The American Wildlife Scene

During 1968, a Wildlife Conservation Fellowship was awarded by the Winston Churchill Memorial Trust to W. A. Newlands, Information Officer at Fordingbridge, Hampshire, England. The object of his three-month tour was to examine the relationship between shooting men and wildlife conservation in the USA. This is his personal report.

THE game management lessons to be learned in America are political rather than practical. The contrasts between state management of game and our own system are so fundamental, both in concept and scale, that the visitor from Britain is inclined to find all of it interesting and none of it applicable.

The first and most basic lesson to be learned is that idealistic, eighteenth-century theories of hunting as "free for all", established by settlers fleeing from persecution in Europe, are becoming unworkable in the crowded conditions of the twentieth century. (The term "hunting" is used in its transatlantic sense: the pursuit of game, whether by shotgun, rifle, bow or dogs.)

The American hunter expects to have free access to enormous tracts of land in exchange for a licence fee. He is unlikely to have any land under ownership or lease, but probably has favourite spots for grouse or quail, waterfowl or pheasants. The typical hunter lives in a city or small town and has little or no direct connection with the land over which he shoots. At the most, he will pay a courtesy call on the owner of private land before going shooting. He is unlikely to share the bag with the landowner, since this is quite likely to be limited to one or two birds per day.

The essence of his sport is that it must be "rugged." He professes less interest in the bag than in the pursuit of his quarry and enjoyment of the surroundings in which he finds it.

It is a remarkable tribute to the success of public relations work—and some strict laws—that the average American, so competitive in other ways, seems to have submerged nearly all his urges to go out and kill a big bag, under a warm feeling of "backwoodsmanship" and a delight in the equipment and techniques of hunting.

His concept of hunting has little to do with shooting prowess. He wants to move, to see new country and new sights, to stalk his quarry and pit his wits against it on more or less equal terms.

Sport fishing and hunting, to use the local terms, are Mass Entertainment in America. One person in four takes part in field sports. This proportion greatly outnumbers birdwatchers, for example, of whom there are reckoned to be about 8 million, compared with 13½ million hunters and 28½ million fishermen. These figures* consider only those who have been active and taken out licenses during that particular year. The total number of hunt-

* National Survey of Fishing and Hunting, 1965, published by the Department of the Interior.

ers, past and present, is probably nearer 20,000,000.

Short seasons and a wide variety of quarry make the American an allrounder. He is likely to own as many rifles as shotguns—probably two or three of each, if he is anything of an enthusiast at all. In Utah, the average household (not just those interested in hunting) is reckoned to have four guns: large and small calibre rifles, a shotgun and a handgun.

To make generalisations about any country as vast as America obviously leads to pitfalls. The problems which are being tackled on the Alaskan tundra or the peaks of the Rockies are very different from those in the subtopia around New York. A keen hunter can—if he is rich enough—shoot whitewinged doves and javelina (wild pigs) one week in the semi-desert, and follow it up the next with moose and ruffed grouse in the northern forests.

However, as a generalisation, it can be said that the American system of State-managed game suits the city-based, weekend shooter. It is, on the other hand, frustrating and unrewarding for the man who personally wants to "put something back" on his land. For this reason, the farmer is by no means the backbone of shooting as he is in this country. He will almost certainly kill a few cottontail rabbits or "varmints" on the farm, but he has to be quick on opening day if he is to beat outsiders to his pheasant or quail.

In these circumstances, under which the man who maintains the habitat fails to get the reward, it is not surprising that farmers in the more prosperous agricultural areas make almost no effort to conserve game. There are many State-subsidised schemes for planting cover, hedges and food plants, but they seem to have very little effect.

Farmers near large urban centers could not be blamed if they were entirely against game. The only noticeable result of a high game population is an annual invasion by scores of hunters. Even where these remember to close gates, avoid disturbing livestock and damaging crops, the constant presence of uninvited guests must be annoying. Very few British farmers would relish the prospect of this type of public-park agriculture.

Near American cities it is now common to see "no hunting" notices along the roadside. Regulations and laws vary from one State to another, but these "posted" areas are becoming more common and they are putting much traditional hunting land out of reach of the average shooter.

This comes as a hard blow to the American hunt-

The American big-game hunter spends upwards of $250 to bag a buck, and maybe even more to bring home a bear, yet he will have paid only a relatively few dollars for license and permit fees.

er, who has been accustomed to enjoying the wilderness as his own. Today more and more land is in private ownership, particularly in the Eastern States, and the posted zones extend deeper into the countryside.

The basic concept that game belongs to the people, not to any one individual, would have to be changed before American game management could come into line with British practice. And the intensity of our management is almost puzzling to them. Many feel that it would be splendid to kill a pheasant to the acre, but the cost of employing a gamekeeper, feeding, rearing, controlling serious predators and so on, is looked upon as exorbitant.

The American hunter may take a week's vacation, drive 2,000 miles and spend $250 in bagging just one buck. However, he will have paid only a few dollars for the licence. The total expenditure will be high; the proportion devoted to game management very low.

The systems of management used by State bodies must be extensive, and the picture is painted with a very broad brush. There is no place for efforts which can have only local or short-term effect. For this reason, the most interesting techniques to British eyes are flooding, burning and mowing.

Our foresters would cringe if they heard an Arkansas waterfowl reserve manager talking about putting 12 in. of water throughout a complete 1,000-acre stand of oaks, or watched a Georgia plantation-hand setting a pine wood ablaze (at ground level, at least) in order to encourage bobwhite quail.

And yet these systems work—and work well—if used at the right time and place.

It is no exaggeration to say that quarter of a million mallard may sometimes be found on less than 1,000 acres of flooded pin-oak woodland in Arkansas. This compares well with European concentrations, since the highest numbers achieved on this side of the Atlantic are also about 250,000, but on areas up to 25 miles square rather than 2 square miles.

The density of duck is exciting for the waterfowl hunter. Unfortunately, it largely represents a shortage of good wintering habitat rather than a super-

abundance of ducks. North American waterfowl populations, according to the Federal census graph, are on a gradually declining switchback—showing much the same inability to pull out of the troughs as our own grey partridge in recent years.

Flooding, pothole blasting and the burning of dense reedbeds have done much to create valuable duck feeding grounds, mainly on Federal or State-owned land in the main migration flyways.

Until now, it has been worthwhile for wealthy duck clubs to buy land in some States and improve the habitat for wintering ducks by growing grain crops and flooding them just as the migrating waterfowl begin to arrive. One large club, with a total of 25,000 acres devoted entirely to ducks, can flood 15,000 acres of cultivated fields and woodland.

However, low production of wildfowl in the major breeding region—the "prairie pothole" district of central Canada—forced the Federal Government to declare a 28-day season in 1968/69 and the bag limit in the Central Flyway was one mallard per day, plus two wood ducks (the Carolina of our ornamental ponds) and two of any other species. So the 18 members of this particular club, with 30,000 mallard on their flooded fields, could hardly take the reward they had earned.

It will be sad if the restricted bag limit forces wealthy men like the members of this syndicate to give up their duck hunting. Such men are obviously putting in much more than they take out, and yet they have to share the results of their outlay and labours with millions of hunters who contribute nothing but a few dollars towards a duck-shooting licence.

The main spur behind most successful human enterprises is self-interest. Game habitat can be saved only if the people who do the work are allowed to take the rewards. The acreage and expenditure on State or Federal refuges is enormous. But it is only a drop in the bucket compared with the area of privately-owned land where game is being neglected through apathy.

In the plantation country of the Deep South, there is still some remnant of the gracious living of pre-Civil War days. Here the State laws are kinder to private enterprise in the field of game management, with the result that there are traditionally long seasons on bobwhite quail and landowners are able to harvest their own birds.

Among the most satisfactory quail habitat is open longleaf pine forest, interspersed with small fields. In the climate of Georgia or Florida, however, the woodland would soon become choked with underbrush, even in mature stands, so efforts have to be made to control ground herbage. The most speedy and economical way to do this is by burning.

When conditions are right—with rainfall, dew, temperature and windspeed all taken into account —a fire can be run quickly beneath the tall timber, destroying unwanted scrub without damaging the main stand or setting the litter ablaze. The longleaf pine is a remarkably fireproof species and natural

Quail hunting is about the only type of field sport in America that can be directly compared with British conditions. Techniques in other types of hunting are quite different.

regeneration can be maintained if there is a slight break in the burning rotation to allow seedling growth.

In the open woodlands, the quail thrive and give excellent shooting. The explosion of a flushed covey of bobwhites is startling and exciting for even the most steady-nerved of hunters. The birds usually burst in a "bouquet", whirring away in all directions.

They are shot over pointers, the brace of dogs being allowed to run for 15-20 minutes in hot weather before they are given a drink and a rest. Large-scale shoots will use hunting buggies, which may be either mule-drawn traps or converted Jeeps, complete with high seats for watching the dogs working ,and boxes for the pointers not actually running. When a covey is located, the hunters dismount and walk in on the point. After the birds are flushed, singles may be followed up.

This is much less rugged than shooting as enjoyed by the average American, and it has the qualities of a more leisured era. In many ways, plantation quail shooting is the only field sport in North America which can be directly compared with British conditions, although a bag limit of about 10 birds per day does intervene.

That mainstay of British shooting, the pheasant, is also extremely popular. The range of wild pheasants extends from coast to coast, northwards into the fringe of the conifer forest and south to a very sharply defined line which leaves the southern States without any wild populations, despite many years of attempted introductions. In the heart of this range, pheasants are quite common, but the bag limit is usually two or three cocks per day and the season is never long. The intensity of the harvest is very high and it has been calculated that more than three-quarters of the available cockbirds will be killed on any given area during the season.

Pheasants are also used to take the pressure off other upland gamebirds, on shooting preserves. Some of these are run by the State, but most by private enterprise. Basically, a shooting preserve is a place where pheasants are released an hour or so before shooting parties go over the land. A set price is paid—either for each bird released or each bird harvested.

The shooting is carried out over dogs and where the farmland is suitably maintained for this purpose, with strips of grain crops interspersed with mowed openings, very good shooting can be had. This is in direct contrast with wild game shooting, upon which Americans place such high values, but it can be made available within easy driving distance of the major cities and certainly helps to provide recreation for many thousands of hunters.

The economics of preserve shooting are rather complex, and few make a profit unless combined with some farm enterprise. The average area of successful preserves is about 600 acres and the price charged per pheasant shot is around £2. ($5.40)

Under British legislation, direct release of pheasants for shooting would be illegal. It was not possible in America until the State laws had been changed, in many cases, but this has now been done in almost all parts of the country.

Providing pheasants for preserve shooting at the age of 16 to 18 weeks is the main market for gamefarmers. The farms therefore concentrate on adult birds kept in large flight pens. Many labour-saving systems are to be seen. For example, a typical gamefarm would feed its pheasants only once every nine weeks—direct from the feed company's truck into large hoppers—and all water is piped. By using these methods, one or two men can handle enormous numbers of birds. On a typical farm, two men rear and sell 30,000 adult pheasants each year, using only a little seasonal help from schoolboys.

On a quail and chukar farm, the owner, with the help of two men and his family, produces 50,000 adult birds each year. The scale of this operation can be judged from the fact that the quail alone eat 10 tons of watermelons during the summer!

Other wild gamebirds suffer from the problems known in Britain. Modern farming takes its toll and habitat changes have been enormous within living memory. The virgin grasslands of the western tallgrass prairies are now entirely under cultivation. The prairie chicken (described in our Annual Review 1965/66) is now a protected species almost everywhere, although it was once the most abundant upland gamebird the world has ever seen.

On the other hand, introductions like the chukar partridge from the Middle East, now found in many inter-mountain States, have been extremely successful. This gamebird, closely related to our redlegged partridge, occupies land which had no native gamebirds at all and is so well adapted to this arid, rocky country that game biologists claim it can never be over-harvested.

The grey partridge of Europe has also been moderately successful and is found mainly in the small-grain growing districts of the prairies and the inter-mountain States. Again, it does well in cool, dry areas which do not support much in the way of native game. After a surge of numbers following introduction, the grey partridge seems to be doing well on a rather reduced range. These birds are shot over pointers and are popular with hunters. In these surroundings, one of the main limitations on their numbers seems to be the depth of snow during the winter. In some areas they thrive only where exposure to the prevailing wind blows snow off the fields and gives the birds access to their food.

One of the gamebirds which is really thriving today is the wild turkey. Its range was formerly restricted, following over-hunting, but it has been re-introduced in many States. This King of North American gamebirds is dependent upon large forest tracts. Settlement and agricultural clearances almost sounded the death knell of the species, but it has come back strongly under good management, and selective hunting of gobblers during the spring prevents any harmful reduction in numbers.

The secret of re-introduction has proved to be the use of wild-trapped adults. Semi-domesticated gamefarm turkeys have invariably failed and true wild turkeys are most unwilling to breed in captivity. Where the correct techniques are used, these streamlined, fast-flying relatives of our domestic turkey will quickly settle down in any woodland habitat—from dry scrubland in Texas to hardwood forests in New York.

The other success story among North American game is the white-tailed deer. There are said to be more deer now than when the Pilgrim Fathers landed. Their history parallels that of British deer, since they became uncommon and local in the face of agricultural pressure, but seem to have come to terms with people and now occupy all possible sites, from dense mountain forests to brushwood thickets in the suburbs. The growth rate and intensity of the harvest of hunters is quite staggering. In good mixed country, with woods and crops, a young white-tailed buck will have a six-point head. Very few see their second winter, since the harvest rate of bucks in good years may top 80 per cent, half of them killed on the opening day.

The main management for deer consists of opening "skylights" in the forest to encourage growth and regrowth of woody species which give browse in winters. The animals need closed canopy softwood stands for snow shelter, surrounded by mixed hardwoods, with a dense shrub layer. Trophy antlers seem to be comparatively unimportant to the majority of U.S. hunters. They want to kill something—whether buck, doe or fawn—and they place great value on the meat. Most hunters—not all—want the primitive satisfaction of killing the first animal they see and eating it, rather than the sophisticated pleasure of undertaking a season's stalking in order to achieve one really good trophy.

Most other species of big game seem to be in a very healthy state in North America, and this is a direct result of their game studies. Public hunting is much more favorable to big game, since extensive management systems and the purchase of wilderness areas can be effective in maintaining their numbers. A good example is the prong-horned antelope, once a rare and endangered species, which is now quite common over a large range in the drier western States—particularly the inter-mountain area. Antelope hunting is now legal in many of these States, and a high licence fee helps to buy land which will protect the herds and prevent poaching.

The police have very few powers as far as poaching and other game law violations are concerned. This is the province of the Game Department, which employs Law Enforcement Officers. The complexity of the laws is quite astounding. The laws of one State, not including the Federal regulations, run to 114 pages of closely spaced print. Americans find it hard to believe that we have maintained the same game seasons for so many years and that we genuinely have no interest in shortening them or declaring bag limits. The problems of North American wildlife populations emphasise that laws cannot enforce conservation: this has to be in the hearts of those who actually live on the land.

Despite the monolithic structures of State conservation, there is still a place for private enterprise in some fields. The number of professional "wildlifers" is enormous. The Wildlife Society alone has more than 7,000 members, all of whom are professionals engaged in wildlife management or conservation, but this number is far exceeded by the membership of the National Wildlife Federation, for example, with 2½ million subscribers.

Private money is also poured into research. One wealthy Texas family made a single donation of 1½ million dollars for a particular conservation study, while another rancher donated half of his land and the income from several oil-wells to set up a foundation. Either of these gestures—neither of which is considered remarkable by local standards —would be enough to pay for all game management research in this country for several years.

The scale of expense is enormous. The Missouri Conservation Commission's postage bill alone is £32,000 ($86,400.00) a year, which must be equal to about one-half of the entire game research budget in this country.

Much money from game shooting sources goes into general conservation work, and it was encouraging to see the efforts being made to save such birds as the whooping crane. The total population of this American bird is now about 50, and many thousands of dollars are being spent in rescuing eggs which would otherwise be unproductive, and raising the progeny in captivity in an effort to establish a breeding flock. If dollars save the whooping crane, it will certainly not go the way of the great auk or the dodo.

The game shooter's America in a nutshell? England has 850 people per square mile, while North America has only 26, so the game shooter does not have to look far for contrasts. There is space and solitude in plenty for the true outdoorsman, but frustration for the hunter who wants to conserve his own game. In the land of private enterprise, the game conservationist is the odd man out. ♦

THIS subject might not seem appropriate for an article in "WILDLIFE IN NORTH CAROLINA"—a magazine designed primarily for light reading by our wildlife-minded public. Perhaps it would be more appropriate for a scientific journal. But the purpose of this article is to give our public an idea of how we are gaining information and insight into one facet of the apparently quite complex problem of restoring wild turkeys in North Carolina.

Small, remnant flocks of wild turkeys now inhabit many areas of seemingly excellent turkey habitat across North Carolina. It would seem that some of these areas should support flourishing turkey populations, yet only a few turkeys persist. Or worse yet, in some areas they have become extinct. Why? We don't really know. The decline is understandable in areas where the habitat has been destroyed, or in areas which are hunted too heavily. But what about the areas where conditions seem optimum but the turkey populations still don't increase or even hold their own?

We know that wild turkeys once flourished t h r o u g h o u t North Carolina, and that after the early settlers came, turkeys were persecuted almost to extinction by habitat destruction and overhunting. Yet the re-attainment of good habitat in certain areas and the development of intensive protection have failed to stimulate increases in remnant turkey flocks. With the settlers, came their chickens and other domestic fowl—and their diseases and parasites. These have remained present in many areas while the habitat and other factors improved. Perhaps pathological factors *are* seriously limiting the comeback of our wild turkeys. Little is know about this.

The information we have gained thus far about the parasites of North Carolina's wild turkeys has been the result of a cooperative effort. The parasite study was originated by former turkey

Internal Parasites of North Carolina Wild Turkeys

by Thad Cherry
Wildlife Biologist

project leader Sam Gooden, who left North Carolina in 1966. During the 1964-66 and 1966-67 wild turkey hunting seasons, cooperating turkey hunters collected and submitted entrails from their turkey kills. These entrails were taken to the Zoology Department of North Carolina State University, where Dr. Reinard Harkema supervised and assisted graduate students in removing and identifying parasites. Dr. Harkema and his students worked long and hard on the parasite study, and did an outstanding job. The final removal and identification work was completed in the spring of 1968.

In the study, 94 specimens of wild turkey entrails were carefully examined for parasites. Seven of the specimens were found to be free of obvious parasites. The entrails were collected mostly during the winter hunting season in the central and northeastern sections of the state, although a few specimens came from the mountains as a result of spring gobbler hunts on wildlife

management areas. Because of our specimen collection method, our study was limited to the parasites of the intestinal tract— from the crop to the c l o a c a. Crops, livers, and/or gizzards were missing from some of the specimens.

Parasites of the Class Nematoda, roundworms, were most abundant in the entrail specimens. This class includes the hookworms which are sometimes a serious parasite in dogs. (See Table I) One species, *Heterakis gallinae*, was found in 57 percent of the birds examined. The next most common nematode was the species *Ascaridia dissimilis*, which was present in 39 percent of the birds. Nematodes, or roundworms, have long been recognized as one of the most numerically represented forms of life, existing in both free-living and parasitic forms. To begin their life cycle, most parasitic nematodes enter the host—wild turkeys in this case—orally, as eggs attached to foods taken by the birds. As they hatch and de-

Dr. Reinard Harkema of North Carolina State University examines a slide prepared from turkey entrails. Parasites are identified and recorded.

INTERNAL PARASITES FOUND IN NORTH CAROLINA WILD TURKEYS—

Table I CLASS NEMATODA

Parasite	Organ	No. of Turkeys Infested	Least Found in one Specimen	Most Found in one Specimen	Average
Heterakis gallinae	Small Intestine Large Intestine Diverticulum Cloaca	54	1	141	24.4
Heterakis spp.	Large Intestine Diverticulum	3	1	32	13
Ascaridia dissimilis	Small Intestine Large Intestine Liver Gizzard	37	1	59	11
Ascaridia spp.*	Small Intestine Large Intestine Diverticulum	12	1	5	2.7
Capillaria caudinflata	Small Intestine Large Intestine	2	1	10	
Capillaria spp.	Small Intestine Large Intestine Diverticulum	3	1	8	*
Cyrnea spp.	Crop, Gizzard	5	2	4	
Trichostrongylus tenuis	Diverticulum	1	3	3	
Unidentifiable nematode	Small Intestine Crop	2	1	4	2.5

*Probably mostly female *A. dissimilis*—hard to identify.

Table II CLASS CESTODA

Parasite	Organ	No. of Turkeys Infested
Raillietina williamsi	Small Intestine Large Intestine	3
Raillietina cesticillus	Small Intestine	4
Raillietina ransomi	Small Intestine	2
Raillietina carioca	Small Intestine	1
Raillietina spp.	Small Intestine Large Intestine Diverticulum	20
Metroliasthes lucida	Small Intestine	2
Hymenolepis spp.	Small Intestine	2
Unidentifiable Cestode	Small Intestine	2

Table III CLASS TREMATODA

Parasite	Organ	Number Found	No. of Turkeys Infested
Brachylaema virginiana	Viscera around intestines	200	1

velop, they travel throughout the host in the blood stream before returning to the intestinal tract for their adulthood. Eggs are passed back to the soil with the feces to complete the cycle. The role of parasitic nematodes as a possible limiting factor in wild turkey populations is still quite uncertain, although they are generally thought to be significant in effect.

Parasites of the Class Cestoda, or tapeworms, were the next most abundant in the turkey entrails. (See Table II) The tapeworms in the entrail specimens were broken up into segments and were uncountable. Tapeworms unidentifiable beyond the genus *Raillietina* were found in 21 percent of the entrail specimens. No positively identified single species of tapeworm was found in over 4.2 percent of the specimens. As far as wild turkeys are concerned, tapeworms are generally accepted to be serious as parasites mainly in young birds, but there is little known about their relative importance as a possible limiting factor. Their life cycle is complex, and may involve several intermediate hosts.

Only one parasite species was found to represent the Class Trematoda, or flukes, and only one entrail specimen was infested with it. The viscera outside the intestines of one specimen was found to contain the species *Brachylaema v i r g i n i a n a*—a fluke. Flukes are small, flattened worms—somewhat similar in appearance to leeches. Trematodes, like the nematodes and cestodes, have a complex life cycle, and often involve aquatic snails as intermediate hosts.

A review of all available literature on internal parasites of wild turkeys and their effects as limiting factors indicates that much remains to be learned. Continuing study will shed more light on the subject, and some day biologists will be able to put the pieces together to gain a clearer picture of the relative importance of the role of parasites in wild turkey populations.

Story From the Morning Mail
Hunting Accidents 1968-69

by J. R. Parker, Jr.
Boating Editor

PHOTO COURTESY OF GUN WEEK MAGAZINE

Approximately half of each season's hunting accidents involve youngsters. But younger hunters don't have to be accident prone. Instruction in safe gun handling, advancing into trap or skeet shooting, will provide dad with a safe partner.

IT is the type of mail that all of us in the Wildlife Resources Commission would rather not receive. The message inside the envelope always contains a much too familiar story—someone has been hurt. And hurt, or perhaps even killed, while participating in a wonderful form of outdoor recreation.

Hunting accident reports in the morning mail serve as an unwelcome type of reminder to this writer that it's again time to inform you of the hunting accident story in North Carolina.

In the October 1968 issue, I reported on the hunter safety program in general, how it was admistered in other states and some suggestions for improving the North Carolina program.

In contrast we will now take a look at some basic statistics of the 1968-69 season. Incidentally, as this is being prepared (late October) accident totals to date are below that of last hunting season. A good start that can finish good, if we all help.

The *when* of the 1968-69 hunting accident situation serves to remind us that most of the accidents occur in early to mid-morning, 7:00 A.M. to 10:00 A.M., and from mid-afternoon to sunset, 3:30 P.M. to 6:00 P.M. Time of sunset varies of course with season. Remember, sunset is the legal time to end

the day's hunt for most game. There are a few exceptions.

What is the injury like? I don't believe I have to describe the scene when one hunter steps in front of his partner's 12 gauge gun at zero distance. Or, what happens to a man's walking ability when a 30-30 rifle he is carrying in his belt, as he climbs down a tree, discharges into his leg. As this magazine has often reported to you, amputation, loss of an eye, disfigurement and painful, if not serious pellet burns, are too often the results of a moment's carelessness.

Slightly less than half of last season's 55 accidents were self-inflicted. This means that the victim was injured by his careless act. Fence climbing, muzzle on toe, dropping gun, and climbing trees are examples of the self-inflicted injury.

Thirty-two of last season's accidents were not self-inflicted. That is, there was a shooter and a victim involved. Mistaking another hunter for game, horse-play, and victim moving in line of fire are examples of this accident type. Some occur at close range, and a few at medium range as we shall see later.

Ages of those involved is always a subject of debate. Without first seeing the record, many citi-

10—

c

8

7

6

5

4

3

2

1

Number of Hunters

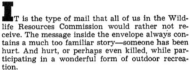

| | NON FATAL
| FATAL

Accident reports began coming in with the opening of the September dove season and reached a high point in mid- to late October when additional hunting becomes available. Another high point comes during the Thanksgiving period with additional game and holidays. Afterward there is a slow tapering off with few if any accidents reported from preserve shooting, still open in March.

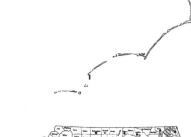

zens might guess that 80-90% of those involved are youthful hunters. The statistics reveal this to be untrue. However since there are certainly many times more adults than youth hunting, there is then, a disproportionate share of youthful hunters involved. Last season, exactly half of those injuring themselves or someone else were 12-19 years of age (total included one 9 and one 10 year old). Others involved in the accident story ranged in age from 9-67 years of age.

There are two other pertinent pieces of information about the shooters and victims. Briefly this: not any of the shooters claimed having been exposed to any formal gun handling training. And only a small percentage of those hunters being shot by someone else wore a safe or bright color.

What species of game was being hunted at the time of the accident? Usually we can say small game and leave it at that. Last season, however, there was an increase in deer hunting accidents. The breakdown: deer—12, rabbit—12, squirrel—10, dove—6, quail—4, and duck—4. Crows and "unknown" made up the remainder.

In several areas of the state, use of the rifle for deer hunting is restricted or prohibited. This type of local legislation appears on the increase. It would seem that there is an inherent fear of rifles. And this is a tempting subject for editoralizing, but let us simply turn again to the facts. Forty-six of last season's accidents involved the old scatter-gun; six involved rifles. In two cases an arrow was the projectile, and in one case a handgun caused injury. Of the six rifle accidents reported, three involved deer hunting and two of those were self-inflicted. Is the rifle realy more dangerous than the shot gun?

Range? Close! Because the shotgun is the weapon primarily involved in hunting accidents in North Carolina, the range is close. In 31 cases the range was from 0-10 yards. In 15 cases the range was from 11-50 yards. In two cases the range was from 51-100 yards. And in three cases the range was 101 or more yards. In the few remaining, the distance was reported as being unknown. (Three, 101-yard cases were with shotguns and for the most part were not serious even though buck shot was the load.)

Cause of the casualty is divided into two categories on the accident report form. "Intentional Discharge" means just that, the shooter intended to fire. Of the four types of intentional discharge accidents, "Victim moved in line of fire" and "Victim mistaken for game" were each listed three times.

"Unintentional Discharge" is the larger of the two casualty categories. The miscellaneous listing had 10 entries during the 1968-69 hunting season. These entries or causes ranged from dropping the gun to using the gun as a crutch. Among the standard listings, "Shooter stumbled and fell" was listed six times, "Horseplay—Didn't know it was loaded" was next with four, "Weapon fell from insecure rest" and "Clubbing cover or game" were listed three times each. The remaining accidents involved one of the following causes: trigger caught on brush or other object, removing loaded weapon or placing same in car, crossing fence with loaded gun, loading, unloading, defective gun and unknown.

Of the 16 accidents listed under Intentional Discharge, nine reportedly took place in dense cover. Remember here that only five of those shot by others, out of a total of thirty-five, were wearing a bright protective color. In dense cover, on deer, rabbit and quail hunting, as an example, a protective safety color is certainly recommended.

Here then is how it was last hunting season across Tarheelia. The picture is very similar to the seasons past and, like the story of seasons past, it is one that can be improved upon. Just how the story will shape up this season as the season peaks and closes out will depend on how courteous and thoughful all of us are as we go afield with the gun.

... Because He Passed This Way

R. Floyd Crouse

Few natives of North Carolina's mountain area ever graduate from the Harvard University School of Law. Even fewer return to their native county to practice law. R. Floyd Crouse did both of these, and much, much more.

Sportsmen, conservationists, politicians and just plain "folks" were saddened to learn of his death last October 22. He was a young, balding, 77-year-old whose hair refused to turn gray, and whose influence will be felt for a long time and far beyond the boundaries of his native Alleghany County and his native state.

Besides his law practice in Sparta, Crouse had a life-long interest in hunting and fishing, conservation, public education, and politics. Once asked which he liked best, hunting, fishing, or politics, the answer was typical of the man: "That depends on the time of year!"

He served on the state Board of Conservation and Development from 1944 to 1946, and was one of the strongest leaders in bringing about the creation in 1947 of the Wildlife Resources Commission to replace the former Division of Game and Inland Fisheries. He was one of the original members of the Commission, on which he served until 1962. He retired from the Commission that year, and was named "Conservationist of the Year" by the North Carolina Wildlife Federation.

His was a cool head and a strong guiding hand during the first struggling years of the Commission, which continues to benefit from his foresight and wisdom.

North Carolina is a much better place in which to live because he passed this way.

—Editor.

RESOURCE-O-GRAM
A ROUNDUP OF THE LATEST WILDLIFE NEWS

Dove Shooting Again—December 18 - January 15

Tarheel dove hunters who failed to get their 18-per-day limit on doves during the fall segment of a split season will have another chance to try again from noon to sunset December 18 to January 15. Odds are in favor of the birds, however, since there won't be as many around as there were last September 1.

Tarheel Oldsters Are Active

Records are not complete, but Tarheels who have passed the 70-year mark still plan to do some hunting and fishing. By Veterans Day, November 11, 17,300 people in this age group had received lifetime free combination hunting and fishing licenses from the Wildlife Resources Commission as a result of legislation passed by the 1969 General Assembly. Meanwhile, 5,300 persons 65 years old or older had bought similar licenses at $10.00 each. Totally disabled war veterans had been issued 325 lifetime combination hunting and fishing licenses.

Which Is Most Dangerous?

Out of a total of 55 hunting accidents reported to the Wildlife Resources Commission last season (September 1, 1968 - March 31, 1969), 6 involved rifles. Three of these 6 involved deer hunting and 2 of the 3 were self-inflicted. This leaves 1 accident where 1 hunter shot another with a rifle on a deer hunt. The accident was fatal.

On the other hand, shotguns were involved in 5 deer hunting accidents where 1 hunter shot another. One of these 5 was fatal.

Write Your Autobiography?

Currently, to buy a box of shotgun or rifle shells you have to put down your name, address, age, and condition of servitude. This is a result of federal legislation intended to reduce crime. Hopefully, a bill now in the Congressional Mill will eliminate sportsmen from this bothersome and useless detail.

December a "Wide Open" Month

During December the hunting seasons are open in most parts of the state for all types of game except rails and gallinules. Counting both migratory and nonmigratory game, this totals nearly 30 different species. Check your 1969-70 Hunting and Trapping Regulations for details.

Skipper's Corner
by John R. Parker Jr.
SAFETY FIRST

IT'S a safe bet that one or more of the people on your Christmas shopping list is a boater. And I'll venture another bet that you have not planned to buy him or her a nautically-flavored gift. With gift buying in mind, Skipper's Corner offers the following gift suggestions, any one of which might well please the small-craft owner on your list.

Some of the specialty type gifts such as jewelry, lamps, desk sets, etc. may be offered only by specialty gift shops. If your marine dealer does not stock the fancy items, he will most likely have catalogs from which to order.

* Boating book * Nautical tie pin or other similar accessories * Boating shoes * Subscription to boating magazine * Foul weather suit * Form-fitting life preserver * First aid kit * Compass * Barometer * Waterproof lantern * Distress signal kit * Nautical desk lamp * Glass or cup set with nautical motif.

Talk the purchase over carefully with a marine dealer. Be certain the items to be used on a boat are just that and not of indoor quality that might rust, leak or in some way detract from the gift.

How We Have Grown

In 1913, according to the Outboard Boating Club of America, there were some 400,000 recreational boats plying the waters of these United States. By 1968 that figure had risen to 8,440,000.

The dollar value of retail boating rose from $680,000,000 in 1959 to $3,150,000,000 in 1968 (yes, 3 *billion*).

And here in Tarheelia registrations will likely rise to 71,000 before the books are closed for 1969. As you may recall, 1960 was the first year of boat registration in North Carolina; the total was approximately 37,000. At this writing, the 1969 total is just over 70,000 which is, regardless of final total, the highest increase for any year since 1960. Miss Nell Barker, who skippers the Registration Section, says that approximately 10,000 new boats were registered this year. Of course, a goodly number were dropped from the books (not re-registered) for one reason or another so the grand total has not actually increased by 10,000.

Boating Course Starts

* Raleigh—USPS course starts on Thursday, January 2, 8:00 P.M., Harrelson Hall, N. C. State University.

* Winston-Salem—USPS course starts Thursday, February 27. Contact Thomas F. O'Brien, Jr., Squadron Educational Officer, for location and time.

* Fayetteville—USPS course starts January 27 at Fayetteville Technical Institute. Contact John C. Ellsworth, Squadron Educational Officer, for time and confirmation.

Maintenance Tip

If your motor has an electric starter, remove the battery for winter storage. Clean the top and terminals with a baking soda solution and rinse with fresh water. Fill the cells to the recommended level and charge the battery. Store in a cool, dry place.

Barometer Tells Story

Weather is unpredictable as most boatmen know all too well. A sunny day can turn into a torrential downpour without much notice.

And despite our advanced technology, weather forecasting is still a chancy business. Some boatmen would prefer to go by their own theories about the red sky at night than take the word of the weatherman.

Besides theories, the boating enthusiast should look to the barometer reading before he packs up his gear for a day's outing. If the barometer reading is falling or rising, chances are there will be c h a n g e in the weather within 12 to 24 hours. A change in the wind direction or movement of a front will also affect the weather conditions.

Here are a few barometer facts which should be common knowledge among boatmen:

1. If the wind is in the easterly quadrant and barometer is falling, bad weather is on the way.
2. If the wind is shifting to the westward and the barometer is rising, clearing and fair weather is in store.
3. A steady but slowly rising barometer means the weather has settled.
4. Unsettled or wet weather is indicated by a steady but slowly falling barometer.
5. When the barometer rises rapidly, it usually means clear but windy weather.
6. If the barometer falls rapidly, head for shore. Chances are a storm is approaching.

Life Preserver Reminder

Whichever type lifesaving device you choose, follow the Coast Guard's 4 A's: Have APPROVED devices; ASSIGN one per person on board; ACQUAINT each person with their location and proper method of wearing; and keep them readily AVAILABLE.

"Greatest little rig I've ever had!"

The New Conibear Trap

A Humane Trap for Taking Furbearers

by Kenneth A. Wilson
Wildlife Area Supervisor
PHOTOS BY THE AUTHOR

THE new conibear trap currently being used by many trappers in North Carolina was invented in 1929 by Frank Conibear, a professional Canadian trapper. Its invention marks the first successful attempt by man to produce an efficient, humane steel trap since the production of the conventional leg-hold steel trap made by Sewell Newhouse at Oneida Castle, New York, in 1823.

Frank Conibear, a professional trapper, lived in the mountainous wilderness of northwestern Canada. For years he had set hundreds of leg-hold steel traps in the snow covered spruce-fir forests along the slopes and valleys of the high Sierras for

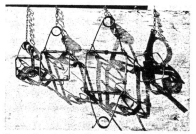

Here are three sizes of conibear traps (sprung) and one conventional, leg-holding trap, shown set. Below, Mr. Q. J. Stephenson is shown with a fine catch of four beaver and one otter (on ground at right). These were taken with conibear traps set under water.

sable, fox, lynx, wolf, otter, mink and wolverine. He had seen the suffering of animals in traps and he did not like what he saw.

For many years on his periodic wanderings to Hudson Bay outposts of civiliation with his catch of fur, he had read about the complaints of humane societies and individuals whose main objective was to prohibit by law the trapping of all furbearing animals in steel traps. He, too, was concerned and sympathetic with many of their complaints. Where possible he would always make drowning sets for otter and mink. But the heavily-furred land animals like wolverine, wolf and lynx seldom froze to death and often suffered for days as captives in the traps. This distressed Conibear. There must be a better way, he thought. The vision of the trap he wanted came through precise and clear. Early models failed. But after years of dogged effort, he finally succeeded in making a humane trap that worked.

Nearly twenty-five years and a depression passed before mass production of the trap was seriously considered. That was in 1953 when a humane group called the Association for the Protection of Furbearing Animals met with several professional trappers in Western Canada. Following extensive tests of the trap by many Canadian trappers in 1954, 1955 and 1956, mass production of the trap was started in 1957 by the Animal Trap Company of America in Lititz, Pennsylvania.

Acceptance of the trap in North Carolina was slow. Most trappers were dubious. They set them but didn't catch anything. Many said in disgust, "The trap doesn't work! It's not any good!" Q. J. Stephenson, a professional trapper from Nothampton County was one of these trappers. "I bought two dozen No. 11 conibears for muskrats and was about to give them away. I was discouraged; I couldn't catch a thing. But when I thought of the money spent, I started experimenting with them. Today I do most of my trapping for muskrats with conibears. They are the best. No more feet in traps, no more animals escaping from traps. Its scissor-like jaws kill muskrats almost instantly. The trapped victim doesn't suffer. It's a humane trap!"

Subsequently, Stephenson bought the large No. 33 conibear trap size for beaver and otter. But he warns: "Take great care in setting them. They pack a lot of power. One slip and you've got a broken finger or arm. And another point: Never set these traps on land. They are deadly to dogs." Robert Rice, another excellent trapper who lives near Lumberton, N. C., also gives the conibear trap high marks. He prefers the No. 22 size for raccoon. But he, too, warns, "Don't set any conibears on land! They'll catch fur animals all right but they'll also take anything else that comes along, small game, pets and dogs."

The Wildlife Commission agrees with trappers Rice and Stephenson. For humane and "dollar bill" reasons dispose of your leg-hold steel traps and stock up on conibears. We also echo their advice. DON'T USE COINBEAR TRAPS ON LAND. They are lethal to game animals and dogs. ♦

Rosebay Rhododendron–
Boon or Bane to Resource Managers

by Robert M. Romancier*
U. S. Forest Service
Southeastern Forest Experiment Station
Asheville, North Carolina

U. S. FOREST SERVICE PHOTOS

Rosebay rhododendron flowers dot the rich green foliage of the sturdy plant. Often entire hillsides are a mass of white, pink or pale red.

ROSEBAY rhododendron poses an interesting paradox for land and resource managers in the Southern Appalachians. On the one hand, it is an attractive shrub prized for its aesthetic appeal and for the protection it offers wildlife and watersheds. On the other hand, it is a forest weed that prevents the regeneration and growth of valuable timber species on many thousands of forest acres. In this age of forest management for multiple-use, with intensive timber management, widespread recreational use of forest land, and with much concern being given to watershed and soil protection, rosebay rhododendron is both a boon and a bane to the resource manager.

Also called great rhododendron or even great laurel, rosebay rhododendron (*Rhododendron maximum* L.) may reach 40 feet in height and can possess a trunk 12 inches in diameter. It ranges from Nova Scotia southward to Georgia and Alabama. While it thrives best in the coves and along the streams of the Southern Appalachians, it can survive on drier, poorer, and higher sites, and is even found in raised areas in bogs and swamps.

Rosebay rhododendron tends to grow in dense thickets that exclude almost all sunlight from the forest floor, creating a perennial gloom in the maze of twisted, tangled stems. Mountaineers have labeled these all but impenetrable snarls of vegetation "hells" or "slicks." This dense growth habit is the reason many foresters want to limit rosebay rhododendron to areas where high value is placed on aethetics.

Estimates vary, but there are at least 3 million acres of forest land in the Southern Apalachians that are covered by dense thickets of rhododendron and the related mountain-laurel. Landowners, foresters, and most land managers agree that this is too much productive land to devote to rhododendron.

But rhododendron can be aggressive when it comes to seizing and keeping control of land. This plant is exceedingly fruitful—each of the insect-pollinated flowers turns into a capsule containing 300 or 400 or more seeds, usually with high germinative capacities. The seeds are small and light (5,000,000 to the pound) and can be carried by the wind for considerable distances. When mature plants are damaged, they frequently layer or sprout in profusion, often replacing a single stem by a colony of 15 or 20 stems.

It is in winter that one of rosebay rhododendron's unusual habits may be seen. At below-freezing temperatures the leaves droop and curl up. The lower the temperature, the tighter the curl and more acute the droop, providing the viewer with a sort of "phyto-thermometer." This phenomenon may be a natural mechanism to retard water loss or to shed snow.

Rosebay rhododendron is unquestionably a scenic asset to any mountain road or overlook. The dense clusters of blooms, coming after the flowering time of many neighboring plants are large and appealing. The evergreen leaves, which generally live about 3 years, also add aesthetic appeal.

The evergreen appearance and the general ruggedness of the plant make rhododendron well suited for utility purposes, such as screening campsites. It would also make an excellent plant for highway median strips, where an added benefit would be the cushioning effect of the dense growth. A driver would be hard put to crash an automobile through a rhododendron stand even a few yards wide. It

*Robert M. Romancier holds a B.S. in forestry from the University of Massachusetts, a Master's Degree in Forestry from Yale, and is currently a Ph.D. candidate at Duke. He has served with the Southeastern Forest Experiment Station, Asheville, N. C., since 1957, and is currently assistant chief, Branch of Timber Culture and Ecology, Division of Timber Management Research, U. F. Forest Service, Washington, D. C.

dromedotoxin, was isolated at the end of the 19th century. However, in cataloging its harmful effects, scientists noted that even small doses caused a profound depression of blood pressure. Andromedotoxin is now being studied for the relief of high blood pressure and may become a valuable medical aid to mankind.

The wood, too, has had its uses. Rhododendron is in the same botanical family as mountain-laurel, sourwood, madrone, manzanita, huckleberry, blueberry. cranberry, and briar. The traditional material for tobacco pipes is briar (*Erica arborea*), a plant of southern Europe. During World War II, when briar was unavailable, huge root burls of rosebay rhododendron were dug up and used by pipe makers as a substitute. The hard, close-grained wood has also been used for tool handles.

In broad terms, all the rhododendrons require acid, well-drained soils in organic matter. They abhor dry conditions. Rosebay rhododendron is primarily a mountain species. It can resist extreme cold, but it prefers shaded locations and protection from winds. Under these conditions, trees thrive for 100 years or more. Moss carpets or bare mineral soils are preferred seed beds; few or no seedlings are found in the litter under mature plants.

This general knowledge is not enough, however. Foresters, recreation specialists, watershed managers, wildlife biologists, and landscape architects must gain a better understanding of the rosebay rhododendron's tolerances and needs before they can intelligently set out to restrict or to favor the plant in any given place.

Here then is a plant valued in some places and undesirable in others. Until much more is known of the particular requirements of rosebay rhododendron, students, researchers, and resource managers will find the species an appealing yet troublesome plant that will provide both challenge and potential.

Canine World

PHOTOS BY FRANK MOONEY

by Frank Mooney
Hallsboro, N. C.

I shudder to think what our complicated world would be like, and how many joyful hours we would miss without man's best friend, the dog. This beneficial animal has played a major role in man's world by affording pleasant hours afield, as companions for the blind and old, saving of lives during World War II and even now at work in muddy swamps and grassy savannahs of Viet Nam. The scout dogs being used in Viet Nam can detect buried ammunition, tunnels, trip wires, mines, food caches, booby traps and other items that might be of value to the military.

The Army and Marines utilize German Shepherds of about 50 to 60 pounds, due to better movement through heavy underbrush, and better stamina. These German Shepherds are sent through a 12-week training course at Fort Benning, Georgia. Then these scout dogs will "alert" the handler when something is amiss. Each dog alerts in a different way, however; they are trained not to whine or growl, but to alert with their body. A dog's body will tense up as its head pulls sharply in the direction of the object or smell.

It's rewarding to see the warmth in the little eyes of a child when it first sees a puppy or hugs it tightly as it cuddles in the child's loving arms. How well

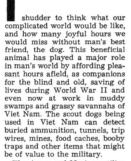

I remember the happy hours I spent as a child playing with a puppy or romping the hillsides with an older dog. Having dogs as pets seems to give most people a better look at nature, and they appreciate more fully the wonders of its strange ways.

The American Kennel Club recognizes 115 different breeds. They are divided into six groups, sporting dogs, hounds, working dogs, terriers, toy and nonsporting dogs. There are an estimated 25,000,000 dogs in the United States. Man's best friend inhabits most of the globe, from the hot rain forests of the jungle villages to the cold arctic North with the Eskimos.

The dog will spend his day happily with its master and never say an unkind word, while working its heart out with no complaint, trying to point a covey of quail or flush a rabbit. A dog will quickly and without remorse give its life to save its master. Cattle and sheep dogs work tirelessly for their masters to keep the animals going and herded together. Avalanche shepherd dogs have been known to smell a hapless man buried under 20 feet of snow. The nomadic Indian once used dogs to carry large packs on their backs when moving their household goods.

Our canine friends rank fifth in intelligence with other animals, and have done much to help man in the medical profession when used in experiments for testing drugs which later would be used on humans. Recently, the dog played an important part when testing better treatments for snake bite. The seeing eye dog has virtually given life back to the blind who are lucky enough to own one. The blind are able to enjoy a much better and more fulfilling life because of these dogs. Until the last few years, the sled dog in some remote parts of the North was the only means of transportation. Without them the Eskimo would have lived a very restricted life.

The Dachshund, which means "badger dog" in German, was bred to fight animals underground and ferret them out. This dog, which sometimes is described as a half a dog high and a dog and a half long, is a determined, hard fighter at close quarters. The dachshund is supposedly the national dog of Germany, but actually originated in France. At one time this low-slung critter was used frequently to fight badgers in some countries, but now is mostly a house pet and a good one.

Dogs are most popular animals, and very understandably

18

Here are four "working dogs" including the popular beagle (upper left); a setter pup (upper right); bloodhound (above); and German shorthair,

so with all the major roles played in our modern world. Toy dogs such as the Chihuahua are popular breeds among dog fanciers, and add fun to many a household. Once the greyhound was used exclusively for running down and catching rabbits, foxes, etc., but now greyhound racing is a nationally known sport.

Retrievers are a rugged breed, such as the Labrador, that braves the icy cold water of the North to retrieve ducks and geese. Even turbulent currents and ice-clogged streams do not stop these hardy dogs. Springer spaniels and other spaniels are great versatile hunting dogs that hunt close to flush game within gun range, then to "fetch" on command.

The Germans have a wire-haired pointer, the Drahthaar, that is growing in popularity in the United States. This pointer has recently been recognized in the American Kennel Club. This dog was bred to be a versatile animal that could do anything such as pointing, retrieving in water

or on land—then track fur or feather and even be an easy dog to handle.

English sportsmen bred the bulldog for a sport known as baiting or fighting bulls. The Chow is a good watch dog; poultry and animal raisers think highly of this dog for protecting their stock and killing predators. The terriers also are aggressive and handle this job efficiently.

The most fascinating hunting dog is the Catahoula Leopard Hound or Leopard Cur. Myth mingled with legend d o w n through the years about the ancestry of the Catahoula until the truth is unknown. However, most dog fanciers agree that the Spaniard DeSoto had some vicious, man-killing dogs during the gold hunting expeditions. Later, the Natchez Indians captured some of the brutes and crossed these with their own dogs. In the deep South, the Catahoula Cur is used mostly as a hog and cattle dog, but will run about anything that puts its feet on the ground.

Ben Lilly, the famous bear and mountain lion hunter, had a motley, glass-eyed, battle-scarred

pack of these dogs that helped to make him a legend in his own time. I once read where President Teddy Roosevelt wanted Ben Lilly to find him a large bear for a trophy, and after Ben found the bear the President was too busy with his work to come and told Ben to watch the bear for him. Now I wouldn't think the President stayed busy that long, but Ben was said to have kept track of that bear for four years!

The faithful bloodhound has saved many lost children who wandered into forbidden swamps or lonely forests. Many escaped convicts and would-be criminals have been captured by the cold nose of the relentless bloodhound. German shepherds have served well as security dogs for many different organizations, plus the added enforcement of the law officers.

The canine world has not been covered completely here, but perhaps with some of this information and the knowledge of your own combined, this will give you a broader insight into one of Nature's great phenomenons, our friend, the dog. ◆

Index for Wildlife in North Carolina, 1969

20

"Keep the Hawks and Owls Flying!"

by Charlotte Hilton Green
Raleigh, N. C.

THUS pleads Roger Tory Peterson in his Foreword to *NORTH AMERICAN BIRDS OF PREY*, by Alexander Sprunt, Jr. (A South Carolinian, one of the authors of *SOUTH CAROLINA BIRD LIFE*, and member of our Carolina Bird Club.)

An article in NATURE Magazine, some years ago, by E. Lawrence Palmer, of Cornell University, is titled, "LET'S PRAY FOR THE BIRDS OF PREY." Throughout the years they have needed our prayers and thoughtful consideration, though in the last decade there has been a great change in attitude. In our own state I proudly record that, with the exception of buzzards, all birds of prey are protected by law, and all other birds except crows, jays, starlings, English sparrows and blackbirds. But, more than that is needed: *enforcement of the law*—and interest, education, understanding and appreciation of the part they play in the balance of nature.

AUDUBON Magazine (Jan. '69) states: "Twenty-two states now have laws that protect their birds of prey; twenty protect all but a few species; only three states protect none of their birds of prey."

Birds of prey, some 400 species strong, "divide all nature into two parts—day and night. Two-thirds of their number are hawks, eagles, kites, falcons and vultures which are diurnal—between sunrise and sunset. The other one-third, the owls, are mainly night hunters."

What a role hawks and eagles have played in history! In his introduction to his book, Sprunt states: "Throughout history man has been keenly aware of the admirable qualities of the birds of prey. Imperial Rome set the eagle upon the standards of its legions; the Vikings adorned their helmets with the wings of hawks, while from the eastern mountains to western plains and canyons, Cherokee, Sioux and Apache selected flawless plumage of hawk and eagle for headdress. In our day the caracara dominates the State Seal of Mexico while the bald eagle is the emblem of the United States." (An emblem that is becoming far too rare in life.)

Sprunt also adds a plea for *"Grass Roots Education."* "Enlist the interest of your friends and neighbors in better protection for the raptores, try to see that the facts and viewpoints in this and other books and articles are spread widely in schools, youth groups, farmers' and sportsmens' organizations. *The future of the birds of prey is in your hands."*

Some years ago the Conservation Department of the North Carolina Federation of Women's Clubs and the Carolina Bird Club had a joint project, "Protect Our Hawks and Owls" in which we endeavored to place on bulletin boards in every schoolroom the National Audubon Circular 25 "EATERN HAWKS, WHAT THEY LOOK LIKE IN THE AIR on one side; on the other side a diagram of WHAT HAWKS EAT (based on the studies by the U. S. Department of Agriculture of 5,185 hawk stomachs). With this was a U.S. Fish and Wildlife Service bulletin by Harold S. Peters, "Protect Our Hawks and Owls."

Such a program is needed again. How about considering it? What organizations could you work through . . . Bird Clubs, Garden Clubs, Woman's Clubs, Scouts, 4-H, PTA, church groups, civic groups, Audubon Jr. Clubs.

Never forget that when we destroy the birds of prey through ignorance (or just for a target) we release an army of other creatures like rodents and insects. (Here let's stop for some "Mouse Arithmetic.")

Biologists state that a 25-day old meadow mouse is old enough to breed, one pair being capable of having 17 litters a year, each averaging five young. Thus in a year's time, the offspring from that *one pair* theoretically could be over a million mice! . . . if, of course, they all lived and thrived. Because of natural controls, disease, AND the birds of prey and other enemies, thankfully they would not. Unfortunately, however, far too many of them do live and breed.

Think of the amount of food they consume! Seeds, grass, corn, hay, vegetables, girdling young trees. Statistics state that: "20% of grain fields in the U.S. are at times destroyed by mice and other rodents. Yet in the past, and too often today, farmers and others have warred on hawks and owls—"their own best friends."

We need to do more than protect hawks for the good they do. We should recognize and gain enjoyment from their grace, beauty, and the ability of these magnificent flyers and soarers—learn something of their life histories.

Hawk Mountain Sanctuary

Read the dramatic story of Hawk Mountain Sanctuary, established in 1934, near Allentown, eastern Pennsylvania. It had long been known that a high percentage of birds from widely scattered areas are funneled into fairly narrow flight lanes during fall migration. One of the greatest is in this area. In the past it had been a great shooting region—those hawks made magnificent and challenging targets for proud Nimrods! Even after bird watchers had established the sanctuary, "within a 30-mile radius of it there were more than 100 hawk-shooting stands." According to Maurice Brown, curator of the sanctuary and author of *HAWKS ALOFT*, upwards of 1,500 hawks a day had been shot outside the protected area. There was resentment by the shooters when part of the region

It is doubtful that anyone could justify needless slaughter like this. Hawks have always been the target of uninformed or misguided "hunters" who seldom realize the value of these majestic birds. Please don't shoot!

This defiant Cooper's hawk doesn't stand much of a chance of carrying out his mission in Nature's scheme of things. His reputation is often far worse than his actual life story. Education is one key to the protection of these birds.

Have you named them? To help out, 1. is the screech owl; 2. is the saw-whet owl, a winter visitor to North Carolina; 3. the barred owl; 4. is the long-eared owl, another uncommon winter visitor; 5. is the barn owl, a real flying mouse trap; 6. is the majestic great horned owl.

was set aside as sanctuary . . . the first one to protect migrating hawks during autumn passage.

Here, each fall hawk enthusiasts and other bird watchers gather from far points, and from strategic Lookout Rocks, thrill to the winged drama. Hawks are fascinating to watch . . . "they exhibit every technique . . . soar like gliders, hover like helicopters, and can launch attacks in the form of strafing, dive-bombing, and dog-fighting." Or, which you are more likely to see, the soaring "mouse-catchers" wheeling in circles over woodlands and meadows, note how well they understand and use various air currents.

Hawks are credited with mating for life, and many return to the same nests year after year. They are usually crude affairs, largely of sticks, with a few more added each year. They are also said to be devoted parents.

Among birds of prey, both the hawks and owls, the females are larger than the males. The young, born naked are soon covered with a white, fuzzy down . . . and since incubation begins when the first egg is laid, the young are usually in different stages of development.

North Carolina has (not counting subspecies) as residents, winter or summer visitors, transients, including rare records, 19 of the hawks, eagles, vultures, kites, falcons.

These birds of p r e y belong to the Order Falconiformes, which is divided into three families: Cathartidae — American Vultures; Accipitridae, hawks, eagles and kites; Falconcidae, falcons.

Owls, though not closely related to the hawks, are also classed as birds of prey and they function much alike. They have similar adaptations for preying: the heavy curved beak, powerful, grasping talons, keen eyesight, strong flight muscles. . .

Hawks and owls counterpart each other; between them they help keep the good earth clean, the hawks hunting by day, while most owls are on duty at night.

A label of "all good" or "all bad" seldom fits much of anything. This red-tailed hawk will take a bird or small game animal, but the good he does far outweighs his potential harm. State law protects all hawks, owls.

Owls belong to the Order Strigiformes, of two families: *Tytonidae*, barn owls, and *Strigidae*, typical owls.

Owls have large, rounded heads and definite facial disks, appear neckless; and plumage being soft and fluffy, they have a noiseless, ghost-like flight. Some species have conspicuous feather-tufts, called "horns", others lack them. Their large eyes are directed forward, necessitating them to turn the head when looking sidewise. They have keen eyesight and keen hearing.

Though principally inhabitants of woodlands, some species are found in open country and one, the burrowing owl (of the West) nests underground.

Their eerie, quavering "hooting" sounds coming from a dark woodland remind some frightened or superstitious folks — especially children — of "haunts" and ghosts. But show a child a picture of that owl (a barred owl lives in our Crabtree woodland), tell him something of its life history, and he becomes interested.

Unfortunately, history, tradition, and folk-lore have been unfair to the owls. Ignorance and superstition have leagued them with witches and evil repute and misfortune, but when we actually learn something about owls we realize that most of them are beneficial to mankind. Science—in the form of research—especially in the contents of their *pellets*, has come to their rescue, one scientist claiming: "Owls are the most beneficial of all birds, inflicting little damage and conferring vast benefits to the farmer and orchardist, in particular, as they feed largely on insects and rodents—though granted, an occasional chicken or bird falls prey.

Like other raptorial birds of prey, owls capture theirs with their feet. If the victim is not too large, it is swallowed whole; if too large, the upper mandible of the bill is long and curved like a hook, for tearing flesh. The indigestible part—fur, bones, teeth, hair, feathers—is regurgitated in tightly packed *pellets*—which are clean and odorless. These are usually found beneath trees where owls perch and are easy to take apart for study. And there is the actual proof of the owl's diet.

The Audubon Nature Bulletin "Story of Owls" states there are 18 species in North America. Of these North Carolina has eight species. (See *Birds of North Carolina* if you want to deal with subspecies.)

These are: barn owl, resident; screech owl, resident in State especially west of Raleigh; great horned owl, whole state at all seasons; snowy owl, irregular winter visitor; barred owl, throughout State all seasons; long-eared owl, uncommon winter visitor; short-eared owl, scarce winter visitor; saw-whet owl, casual winter visitor.

All owls' eggs are white.

Barn Owl: 15-20 inches. Long-legged, with white heart-shaped face. In U.S. south through Mexico to Nicaragua. Resident in N.C. Nest—may be in hollow tree, or stump, in barn, old buildings, tower, church. Eggs, 4-9 laid at intervals, so eggs and young different sizes in nest. Food, mainly mice. Great economic value.

Screech Owl: 9 inches. Eastern N.A. south to N. Ga. In N.C. resident (The *only* small owl with ear-tufts.) Two color phases, red and gray. Range, eastern N.A. from Ontario southward to N. Ga. Nests—hole in tree or tall stump. Eggs 3-5. Food, mice, insects, caterpillars, occasional birds.

Great Horned Owl: Nearly 2 ft. (The only *large* owl with ear tufts.) Range: Resident from Labrador and Hudson Bay s. to Florida, Texas, and Mexico. N.C. Whole state all seasons. Nests— usually old ones of hawks, ospreys, crows. Eggs, 2-4. Food, rats, mice, rabbits, squirrels, etc. also birds, chickens.

Snowy Owl: N. part of N. hemisphere, straggling south in winter. In N.C. irregular winter visitor.

Barred Owl: 19 inches. Olive-brown, breast barred. Range: Eastern N.A. In N.C. common resident throughout much of State. Nest—generally in hollow trees, been found in old hawk's nest. Usually two. Food, mainly rats, mice, frogs, some birds, chickens.

Long-eared owl: 14 inches long, ear-tufts. Uncommon winter visitor N.C.

Short-eared owl: 15 inches. Range, nearly whole world, except Australia. In N.C. scarce winter visitor.

Saw-whet owl: 8 inches Northern N. America, winters sparingly south to Carolinas and Louisiana. In N.C. casual winter visitor.

Today, with a wider knowledge of a balance of nature, and the important part predators play in that role, we realize there are no "good" or "bad" hawks and owls. Each has its place in the long plan. There may be a definite need for the weak, the unalert, to be weeded out—that one role of predators is to develop alertness and speed in game birds.

Next month: Eagles and Ospreys

Keep Clear!

Read White Jugs—Save Time—Maybe Life

by Jim Tyler
Division of Commercial and Sports Fisheries
Dept. of Conservation and Development
Photos by the Author

WHEN a sport fisherman in coastal waters of the northern sector of North Carolina comes upon a long line of white floats bobbing in the water, he knows that there are commercial fishermen's nets or crab pots in the water. He then has three choices. He can take a couple of minutes to figure out the pattern of the devices and choose the closest place to motor through safely; or he can say to heck with it, rev up and go flying through (he might make it through with no trouble, he might tear a big hole in the net, or he might get hung up and end up drowning himself); or he might (with disgust, surely) go clear around a line of nets that may run more than a mile in length.

By law, gill nets in Albemarle, Roanoke, and Croatan Sounds and their tributaries, and in Pamlico River are marked for the protection of boat operators. Prior to this year the required marking of gill net floats was confusing and it was difficult to find the spaces to get through. This year, however, the spaces between gill nets set in a line are easy to spot. Each end of an individual net is marked with a white floating object, usually a jug.

Getting around gill nets is not a problem when there are only a couple of nets linked together, but a line can contain up to 20 nets (60-100 yards each) strung in a line.

Do not let your eyes fool you. The net could be set a few inches below the surface and you will not be able to see it. You will only see the floats on each end.

Take a minute and study the sketches below. You will surely save some aggravation and time, and you might even save your life.

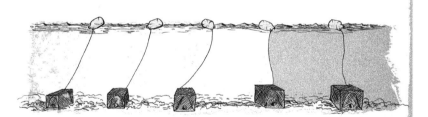

CRAB POTS (above), are usually set evenly spaced, and the white floats, several in a row, indicate what's below. Pass to either side of these evenly spaced floats.

ANCHOR GILL NETS (below), are usually set in long lines of individual nets fastened together in series. They are anchored to the bottom at either end, and the end floats are comparatively close together.

PASS THROUGH HERE   PASS THROUGH HERE

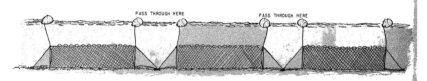

CRACKSHOTS and BACKLASHES

by Rod Amundson

Last September we published an excerpt from the Sport Fishing Institute Bulletin that reported some comments made by John S. Gottschalk, Director of the U. S. Bureau of Sport Fisheries and Wildlife, regarding the possibility of establishing a salt-water sport fishing license.

We believe that most of our readers are aware that the Wildlife Resources Commission does not have any jurisdiction over salt-water fishing—sport or commercial. None the less, response to Mr. Gottschalk's proposal was almost overwhelming. Letters were about ten to one in opposition to the proposal, the concensus of opposition being, "Let's keep at least one of our outdoor recreation activities untaxed!"

Space will not permit printing all the letters we received. It is gratifying to know that our readers are alert—and k e e p i n g abreast of the times and trends.

Just as a reminder, however, here are some exemptions from fishing license requirements pertaining to inland waters:

Persons fishing on their own property; in private ponds; in county of residence with use of natural bait; under 16 years of age, or 70 years old or older. The latter must have a license granted by the Wildlife Resources Commission upon satisfactory proof of age. There is no charge for this, but special fishing licenses and permits apply.

Dear Sir:

I am not in favor of a salt-water license, especially if it applies to all salt water. It is worse than the Old Worm bill that hit our Legislature in the '50's.

I would not object to license for surf fishing which I do occasionally; the salt-water sounds, bays and creeks should be omitted. The license would be a nuisance and deprive many people of their natural habits or relaxation.

Joe Williams
Swan Quarter

A Case for the Puffer

Dear Sir:

For sometime now I have been an ardent reader of your enjoyable articles. WILDLIFE rates with the finest of outdoor magazines.

I just read the story in the August 1969 issue by Jim Tyler, "A Morsel in Disguise." However, in regard to the article, I would like to add a few words concerning the cleaning and eating of puffers.

A native of Wanchese, N.C., I have often cleaned as high as 1,000 pounds of these hoghedge skinned fish in a day's time to help finance college expenses. To begin with, an individual has very little invested in the puffer skinning business since many seine fishermen are only too glad to make you a gift of their day's catch of these oddly streamlined sea creatures. So with special knife and fork in hand, you are ready to prepare this tender, white-meated fish for the table—and a different kind of knife and fork. I say this because after having cleaned a number of these fish for several weeks, I discovered that one can skin them much faster with an every day table fork! After the cut has been made behind the head, the meat can be easily snatched from the tough skin, into whatever container is being used, with a somewhat modified fork. Simply bend the prongs of an old fork until they curl, build up the handle with two sticks of wood and layers of masking tape, and you have a fireball implement for puffer skinning. This handy tool keeps you from having to hold the meat with your knife blade. This method has a two-fold effect: A) it keeps the skinner from cutting the flesh of this tender fish, and B) it prevents worry about having a solid hold on the fish.

I readily admit that the above described method works much better if there are two of you working together—one man cutting and the other skinning. It seems worth noting here that the skinning partner can often keep apace with the cutter!

In conclusion, I agree whole heartedly with Jim Tyler about "the fine eating meat on the puffer." Often called "chicken of the sea," the puffer affords some excellent eating and is considered a delicacy in many Northern restaurants. It seems to support the adage that "beauty is only skin deep," doesn't it? Why don't more people eat them, you ask? Perhaps they confuse the swelltoad with the toadfish that is often poisonous when eaten. Or maybe, as Tyler's article suggested, many people do not realize that swelltoads or puffers are delicious. Glamourous looking? No. Easy cleaning and good eating? Yes. And I can only feel sympathy for those people who are missing out on some of the best fish eating available because they continue to "judge a fish by its cover." A case for the puffer? I think so.

Sincerely,
R. Wayne Gray
Wanchese

Deep Sleep

Dear Sir:

I am a very new resident of North Carolina, having come to this State from New York State. I have very recently come across your publication "Wildlife." I wish to subscribe to this excellent magazine.

I enjoy your articles which I have read thus far, except to say that bears do not hibernate. They do go into a short and temporary sleep, not in hibernation.

Sincerely yours,
Benjamin R. Coonfield
Professor Emeritus
Brooklyn College of New York

Professor Coonfield makes a good point about the term "hibernation" which was r a t h e r loosely if not down right incorrectly used in connection with the October "Wildlife" cover illustration. Hibernation is actually a biologic condition in which the animal's respiration and circulation are barely perceptible,

E. R. Jarrett

Wildlife Patrolman E. R. Jarrett, a thirteen year veteran officer with the N. C. Wildlife Resources Commission has served both in eastern and piedmont North Carolina as a wildlife officer.

Mr. Jarrett is a native of Alapublic school and business college. Prior to his joining the Wildlife Commission he served with the U.S. Navy. He is married to the former Judith Taylor of Burlington and they now make their home at Haw River with their five children.

Mr. Jarrett has attended the many special training schools for wildlife officers conducted at the Institute of Government at Chapel Hill since 1955, aside from special training in various other fields of law enforcement and wildlife related activities.

In addition to his law enforcement duties he has done extensive work with young people as well as adults in the fields of water, boating and firearms safety; and has been recognized for his work by various national as well as state and local organizations.

Mr. Jarrett is recognized by the National Rifle Association as a certified firearms instructor, holding various ratings as a qualified instructor and has been

awarded with their Instructors Training Award for his outstanding work in firearms training. He has also been recognied by the N.C. Outdoor Safety Council with their Service To Safety Award for his extensive work relating to outdoor safety.

As further recognition for his work over the years he has received four Conservation Awards from the N.C. Wildlife Federation in addition to the Governors Award as Protector of the Year in 1967 and also their Outdoor Safety Award in 1968 for leading a Wildlife Commission Water Safety team that appeared before more than 25,000 persons throughout North Carolina and many thousands more through similar T.V. programs.

Aside from Wildlife related activities he is also active in various civic organiations and community projects. Mr. Jarrett and his wife Judith are members of the Haw River Baptist Church where they attend with their children; Dee, Jeffrey, Laurie, Jody and John.

---

and the animal feels cold to the touch. These things don't happen when a bear takes his winter naps. Woodchucks and ground squirrels hibernate; bears, raccoons, skunks and badgers sleep varying lengths of time during cold weather. Yet the temperature may not be the factor that influences their sleep, since even in Florida the black bear naps for days at a time during the mild winter months. At any rate, it is just a "deep sleep", and not hibernation with ole bruin.

Estuarine Study Could Have Far Reaching Effects

A use plan for every acre of North Carolina's 2,300,000 acres of estuarines will be included in a report handed to the Governor on November 1, 1973.

So, fishermen, both commercial and sport, have a lot riding on this report.

While fisheries figure strongly in coastal use recommendations,

other users, such as industry, ports, navigation, recreation other than fishing, real estate development, cities, and communities will most certainly be considered.

The first phase of the study will be an inventory to see what is actually in our estuaries. Division [of Commercial and Sports Fisheries] biologists will do some of the inventory; how many fish and what kind, for example. Other State agencies will inventory resources under their care, such as water, air, wildlife, and minerals. This inventory will cover the waters, bottoms, and fringe lands (marshlands) of the estuaries.

While an inventory of the natural resources goes on, a detailed inventory of the coastal people (residents and visitors) and industries will take place. This will include meetings with county and local officials and industry representatives.

Varying needs and problems of coastal people, industry, and

natural resources of the respective estuarine regions will then be considered. The pot will really boil when the needs of our natural coastal resources (such as sections of unaltered marshland, pollution-free water, closed nursery areas) are mixed with the needs and WANTS of humans.

Nevertheless, decisions will have to be made.

The resulting report should contain, according to the 1969 act directing the Fisheries Commissioner to study the estuaries, "a comprehensive and enforceable plan for the conservation (wise-use) of the resources of the estuaries, the development of their shorelines and the use of the coastal zone of North Carolina."

Anyone with an interest in the coastal area should follow the progress of this report.

> Division of Commercial and Sports Fisheries
> Department of Conservation and Development

Dr. Fish Receives Award

The much-coveted Clarence W. Watson Award was established in 1964 by Southeastern Section of the Wildlife Society, which meets annually concurrently with the Southeastern Association of Game and Fish Commissioners. The award honors the man for whom it was named. Watson is one of America's outstanding conservationists, and the award is presented to individuals for distinguished service in the field of wildlife conservation.

This year at the Southeastern meeting in Mobile, Alabama last October, the award was presented to the Wildlife Resources Commission's own Dr. Frederic F. Fish, who has been with the Commission's Division of Inland Fisheries for ten years.

Following are remarks made when the award was presented.

"The C. W. Watson Award is honoring tonight a man that has had experience in many areas of his field.

He is not a native of the South, but all of us that have known him for many years, have accepted him to the point that we no longer use the normal prefix to "Yankee" when referring to him.

In reality, his assignments have carried him to so many sections of this great country of ours that he probably is not sure of his origin. The northeast, the midwest, far west, southwest and the southeast have all reaped the benefits of his knowledge. The trail left by his travels has resulted in forward progress.

This forward progress in the prevention and control of fish diseases resulted in treatments that are still widely used today.

It also resulted in an expanded knowledge of the effects of pollution upon fishes through his organizing and coordinating various pollutions studies.

Ten years ago he joined a state organization and since then has contributed his talents to aid in the advancement of his chosen field, fish, in that state.

If you have not guessed by now through my use of his name several times in this introduction, I would like to now introduce the man we are honoring by the presentation of this award established to honor not only an outstanding man or woman in conservation each year, but to honor Dr. C. W. Watson in whose name the award is made, Dr. Frederic Forward Fish".

by Sarah L. Sheffield

Now who ever heard of using frogs to make ammunition? Warts, yes, ammunition, no.

Well, in Central and South America a group of tiny tree frogs, the Dendrobatidae or "Arrow-poison" frogs are used by the Indians of the rain forest to kill game.

The little animals are easily caught. For one thing, they move about the forest floor during the daytime, and their brightly-colored backs can be quickly spotted. And even though they aren't more than one inch long, these frogs fear no enemies. They just hop around the jungle, flashing their vivid colors and daring other animals to come after them.

Whenever a frog is injured or even touched, the poison glands become active. The glands are in the skin side-by-side with the mucus-making glands responsible for keeping frogs "slick."

Before "frog poison" can be used in hunting, though, it must be collected in large quantities. The Latin American Indians gather many resident "Arrow-poison" frogs, impale the tiny creatures on sticks, and hold them over a fire. As the thick, milky fluid comes from the skin, the needle-sharp tips of bamboo blow-gun darts are rolled over the bodies of the frogs and dowsed with venom.

Poisoned darts can kill birds, monkeys, and sloths; the animals are paralyzed instantly and die from heart and respiratory failure in just a few seconds.

The poisons made by these frogs are similar in chemical structure to steriod hormones, and a small amount in the blood stream affects the nervous and muscular systems. Some people break out with a rash similar to poison ivy when the venom touches the skin. A species found in Colombia, the kokoa frog, secretes the most deadly poison, one having no known antidote.

The poisons made by these bold little frogs are being studied for their possible uses as beneficial drugs, but the jungle Indians have found one good use for them already—free ammunition! ♣